Risk Management Handbook for Churches and Schools

James F. Cobble, Jr.
and Richard R. Hammar

Risk Management Handbook for Churches and Schools

ISBN 1-880562-43-X

Christian Ministry Resources
PO Box 1098
Matthews, NC 28106
704-821-3845
704-821-3872 (fax)
icl@wans.net
www.iclonline.com

This publication is designed to provide accurate and authoritative information in regard to the subject matter covered. It is sold with the understanding that the publisher is not engaged in rendering legal, accounting, or other professional service. If legal advice or other expert assistance is required, the services of a competent professional person should be sought. "From a declaration of Principles jointly adopted by a Committee of the American Bar Association and a Committee of Publishers and Associations."

Table of Contents

INTRODUCTION: RISK MANAGEMENT FOR CHURCHES AND SCHOOLS AND THE CAMBRIDGE CERTIFICATE PROGRAM

Risk management, from a theological perspective, is more than protecting buildings, preventing lawsuits, or lowering costs. It's primary purpose is not to remove risk from ministry. Rather, risk management embodies *caregiving leadership*. The goal is to empower congregations and schools through acts of leadership and caring to differentiate good risks from bad risks, and to the extent possible, eliminate those things that harm people and ministry. In the biblical image of the good shepherd, risk management is not self-serving, but self-sacrificing.

The purpose of this book is to help churches and schools create and maintain safe and caring environments.

This volume is part of a comprehensive set of risk management resources for churches and schools that also includes an extensive series of safety and liability checklists.

The *Risk Management Handbook* describes the risk management process, and provides comprehensive reference material on the most common risks that affect churches and schools. The *Checklists* provide detailed forms to inspect and identify the risks discussed in the *Risk Management Handbook*. When used together, these resources provide churches and schools with both the strategy and the means to engage in effective risk management.

What makes this program unique, however, is the opportunity for learners to complete a self-directed study program leading to a certificate in risk management for churches and church sponsored schools from the University of Cambridge Local Examinations Syndicate. Completing the certificate program can elevate the practice of risk management to an even higher level, providing the church or school with more highly qualified staff, and rewarding those who complete the program of study.

The Cambridge Certificate Program in Risk Management

The Cambridge Program involves self-directed study with Internet support. The *Risk Management Handbook* serves as the textbook for the program. Individuals complete the program at their own pace. Once a participant is ready, he or she takes a final examination. Those who pass the examination receive a certificate in risk management from the University of Cambridge Local Examinations Syndicate.

What are the benefits of the program

The Cambridge Program provides several important benefits.

First, it creates a structured approach to learning leading to advanced knowledge in risk management for churches and schools. Since participants are tested on their knowledge, the program enhances both motivation and accountability. It provides assurance to both churches and schools that their staff members are involved in a serious learning program.

5

Second, learners are recognized and rewarded for their efforts. The Cambridge Certificate provides those who complete the program with enhanced status and formal recognition for their accomplishment from one of the world's most prestigious universities. Those who complete the program can be proud of their accomplishment. Completing the program provides a high level of personal satisfaction for both paid and volunteer workers.

Who should enroll

Many individuals will benefit from the Cambridge Program including both paid and volunteer workers. Almost every leader or staff member in a church or school has risk management responsibilities. The Certificate Program is highly recommended for the following individuals:

- Pastors
- Associate Pastors
- Church Business Administrators
- Office Managers
- Youth Ministers and Lay Leaders
- Christian Education Directors
- Church Board Members, Elders, Deacons
- Day Care Directors
- Preschool Directors
- School Principals and Administrators
- Denominational Leaders
- Insurance Agents
- Attorneys
- CPAs

How to enroll

For additional information, or to enroll in the program contact Christian Ministry Resources at 1-800-222-1840 between 8 A.M. and 4:30 P.M. eastern time, visit us online at www.iclonline.com/cambridge.htm, or write:

Christian Ministry Resources
PO Box 1098
Matthews, NC 28106

You may also email your request for information to: icl@wans.net.

CHAPTER 1. RISK AND MINISTRY

Risk has always been a part of ministry. In fact, risk taking is an essential part of ministry. Yet, not all risks are good ones. A need exists to differentiate good risks from bad risks, and to develop some basis for distinguishing those risks that enhance ministry from those that harm it.

From a faith perspective, risk taking emerges from a different set of assumptions and values than are found in the business community or even in many nonprofit organizations. The driving force behind risk taking is ministry that expresses the love of God and neighbor.

Risk taking and ministry are integrally related. Jesus called his followers to take up their cross and follow him. He warned his disciples of the risks associated with following him and admonished them to count the cost. Following Jesus involves risk, both personally and corporately. Risk taking, however, is only half of the story. Caring and thoughtful service to God is also manifested in avoiding certain risks and attempting to reduce others.

Holistic ministry involves engaging in certain risks that require self-sacrifice as well as reducing other risks that endanger those that are vulnerable. While Jesus made his way to Jerusalem knowing that he would suffer and die, he did so on his own terms. When necessary, he took steps to protect both himself and his disciples. His motivation, though, was to fulfill the will of his father. He engaged in self-sacrificing love. Similarly, Paul faced physical and spiritual hardships in his apostolic service. Yet, when arrested, he made full use of his Roman citizenship to defend himself, again motivated by his mission and calling. Perhaps no better biblical image exists for this exercise in risk management than that of shepherd. Risk management requires both caring and leadership.

The shepherd cares for the flock. This caring involves both risk taking and risk management. Jesus warned that the thief comes to steal, kill, and destroy (John 10:10). The good shepherd, alert to these dangers, guards the flock. Providing this care requires knowledge and understanding of what the risks are and of the steps necessary to protect the sheep and the shepherd. The good shepherd is prepared to make the ultimate sacrifice to guard the flock. The shepherd is both a risk taker and a risk manager. Ministry always contains both of these dimensions of risk.

1.1 The Nature of Risk

From a theological perspective, little has been written about the art and science of risk management. As an applied discipline, risk management is perceived as being more central to the insurance industry than to faith communities. That is reflected in the literature that is available as well as in the language of risk management. While the concepts have direct application to churches, the terminology is somewhat foreign. For example, most books on risk management differentiate between *pure risks* and *speculative risks*. These two concepts are not commonly used with respect to ministry, yet they do have significance. Pure risks have no upside. If they occur, the best you can hope for is that nothing bad happens. Speculative risks can generate losses or gains as well as breaking even. For the purpose of this book, which focuses on churches and church sponsored schools, two additional categories of risk are identified: *faith risks* and *ministry risks*. The nature of these four categories of risk is discussed below.

Faith risks

Churches and Christians have always faced perils. Persecution, for example, is to be expected as an outcome of being faithful to God. At times this has resulted in imprisonment, exile, and even martyrdom for those who would follow Christ. The prophets and the saints create their own risks through obedience to their calling. For the purpose of this book, we call these *faith risks*. Faith risks are inherent in one's relationship with God. They arise first from who we are and the core values we hold, and second from what we do based on those values.

Pure risks

While faith risks are uniquely tied to our relationship with God, pure risks describe any form of risk that has two possible outcomes: loss or no loss. For example, if lightning strikes a church building, a fire may start. Then again, it may not. There will either be a loss or no loss. That is a *pure risk*. When such losses do occur, we generally think of them as being the result of an accident. From a theological perspective, an argument can be made that even pure risks have an upside. We can learn from our losses, grow in our relationship with God, and both receive and share God's grace in new and important ways. With Paul we can proclaim, "We know that in everything God works for good with those that love him, and are called according to his purpose" (Romans 8:28). So even in the midst of loss, good can happen.

Speculative risks

As noted above, a *speculative risk* can have a loss or a profit, or neither. A church that invests money in a piece of land, for example, may sell it for a profit, a loss, or may break even. That is a speculative risk. For many people, the most common form of a speculative risk is investing in the stock market. The value of the stock may increase or decrease. Generally, the goal of a speculative risk is profit, although it need not be financial.

Ministry risks

While church leaders generally understand the nature of speculative risks with respect to financial investments, they rarely if ever use such language when talking about ministry risks. The focus of ministry is not on profit or financial gain. Yet church leaders understand that ministry requires an investment of time, money, and resources, and that ministry goals may or may not be achieved. For example, a church may make a considerable effort to establish a program for senior citizens. The program may or may not be successful. The time, money, and effort going into the project may be lost. Rather than calling this a speculative risk, for the purposes of this book we call it a *ministry risk*. While faith risks are inherent in one's relationship with God, ministry risks arise out of a deliberative process. Ministry is driven by faith, but also depends upon values, vision, decision making, circumstances, and the knowledge and skills of many people. The results are not guaranteed. Risks are involved. Furthermore, the occurrence of a pure risk can devastate a ministry and cause severe harm and suffering for many people. Ask any congregation that has experienced a case of sexual molestation of children. The purpose of risk management is to reduce and, to the extent possible, eliminate *pure risks* from ministry. That is the goal of this book.

Examples

The following two examples illustrate these concepts of risk as applied to local churches and church sponsored schools in two quite different settings and circumstances.

Example 1

The risk of faith: calling and service

John is a middle management executive in a company where he earns a better than average salary, and has considerable opportunity for advancement. His wife Erin serves as a counselor at a local high school. After considerable prayer and reflection, John and Erin decide to resign from their positions and to pursue a calling to the ministry to begin a new church and work with troubled inner city youth. They do so out of obedience to their faith, and in response to a deep feeling of who they are in their relationship to God. The decision emanates from their faith, and they accept the risks.

The speculative risk: investing funds

John and Erin have some savings and they face an uncertain financial future. To help underwrite the cost of their ministry, they invest a portion of their money in money market funds.

The ministry risk: establishing the new church

With the help of supporting churches, facilities and office space are rented, equipment is purchased, literature is printed, and John and Erin, with the help of considerable volunteers, launch their new ministry. Extensive time, effort, planning, and expense have gone into establishing the new inner city church. Church leaders supporting the project understand that the burnout rate for inner city workers is high. The ministry is difficult. Together, they work hard with John and Erin to develop a strategy that will work.

The pure risks: problems of safety and security

The church facilities are located in an area with a high crime rate. Vandalism and theft are common. Violence occurs within the neighborhood. The building the church uses is old and in poor repair. Fires are not uncommon in the neighborhood.

Example 2

The corporate risk of faith: calling and service

Several years ago, as part of their sense of calling as a congregation, First Church made a commitment to care for all members of the congregation, from birth to death, through every stage of life, and to reach out to their community with concrete acts of compassion. For this congregation, caring is not simply a mission, it is a fundamental expression of who they are collectively as the people of God. They understand the cost can be high in being obedient and faithful to that calling.

The ministry risk: starting a preschool and an elementary school

Five years ago, in partial response to their calling, First Church began a preschool for children ages 2 to 4 and an elementary school for grades K through 5. Both the preschool and the elementary school grew faster than anyone expected. While the church was thrilled by the initial response, leaders and teachers experienced high levels of stress due to space and equipment shortages, and also due to a planning process that always appeared to be one step behind the needs. The first principal resigned after the first year, and the next one also lasted only a year. At that point the school was at a point of crisis. The third principal, though, helped turn the situation around, and through a lot of effort and prayer from many people, both programs are moving forward.

The speculative risk

Since tuition to the school is prepaid in advance, a decision had to be made on how to handle the funds until they were used. The board determined that stocks were too risky, but that an appropriate investment would be to put the tuition payments in government insured certificates of deposit.

The pure risk: a playground injury

Volunteers from the church built a playground for the school and preschool. One afternoon during recess, a girl, age 7, fell from a platform and hit her head on the ground causing serious injuries. The parents of the girl sued the church and the school for negligent supervision and for maintaining unsafe playground equipment. The playground did not have an adequate protective surface under the platform, nor was the platform built according to standard safety specifications. The accident was aired on the local news and the lawsuit was reported in the local newspaper.

The above two examples illustrate, in a simplified manner, different aspects of risk. This book, and risk management in general, focuses on *pure risks*. In the first example, John and Erin faced not only the challenge of ministry, but crime, vandalism, theft, violence, and hazards associated with an old building including fire. In the second example, a playground accident hurt a young girl and endangered the ministry of the church and school. Churches and schools face similar problems on a daily basis. The main purpose of this book is to assist church leaders to understand and reduce the risk of accidental losses through a planned program of risk management. Fundamentally, it is a program of caring through acts that promote safety and security. The other three categories of risk are important, but fall outside the scope of this book. That is not to say, however, that an interrelationship does not exist between all four levels of risk. Clearly one does, and at times those connections will be made.

1.2 Pure Risk and Ministry

Risk management is a relatively new discipline. While people have always engaged in acts to promote safety, it is only within the last 50 years that managing risks has emerged as a specific skill of the managerial process. Risk management is now common within the business community, yet churches are still less likely to engage in systematic and intentional risk management processes, or to be familiar with the language of risk management. To a large degree, with the exception of buying insurance, churches practice risk management today much like churches have done over the centuries. It is embodied in the actions of individuals who spot a problem and who take the initiative to correct it. Many of the same perils that exist today have existed since the church began. We face the same forces of nature—hurricanes, floods, winds and storms. Church buildings face threats from fire, vandalism, and theft. From the very beginning people have been injured participating in church activities. One thing is different today, however, than at any other time in the history of the church. In a single word it's *litigation*.

In the past, when accidents occurred within church programs, little thought was given to litigation. Shortly after World War II, a church was having a picnic at the farm of one of its members. It was an annual event and much celebrated for the food, games and fun associated with it. However, in a single moment, what had been a time of joy turned into sorrow. A young boy drowned while swimming with others in a pond located on the farm. Everyone felt the loss and sadness. As a church community, the people drew together to support the grieving family. They experienced the loss together as a church, and as a church they cared for one another as they coped with the pain. No one turned to an attorney for advice or threatened a lawsuit. At that moment in time, such actions were not part of the culture. People thought of what happened as an accident—there was no corporate blame even though there was a widespread feeling of loss and guilt. Yet there was also love and compassion.

Today, such events tend to be handled quite differently than they were just a few generations ago. Churches are sued just like any other organization. A number of factors contribute to the increased level of litigation that churches experience today. First, litigation has evolved into a frequent and acceptable form of settling conflicts. Over 20 million civil lawsuits occur annually in the United States. Taking someone to court has become popularized through television programs as a form of personal entertainment. Second, society is becoming saturated with attorneys. Compare the number of physicians in the yellow pages of any phone book to the number of attorneys and you'll quickly see the lopsided ratio. To earn a living these lawyers need clients. When lawsuits do occur, generally multiple defendants are named. The court system becomes clogged with individual cases involving many different people and organizations. Third, our legal system continues to evolve, adding new theories of liability, and becoming increasingly complex in the application of law to any professional practice, including ministry. Fourth, getting people into court has become so expensive that it often becomes cost effective to settle out of court. The threat of litigation becomes the first stage of financial negotiations. And finally, large settlements receive broad media coverage. Winning some lawsuits is like holding the winning lottery ticket for a multi-million dollar jackpot. All of these factors fuel litigation.

11

1.3 Risk Management and the Response of Churches

Our research indicates that church leaders place little emphasis upon risk management. Findings from a study of over 1,100 churches revealed that only 1 church in 5 had any risk management plan, and only 1 church in 10 even conducted a risk management audit within the past year. This was true even though 45 percent of these churches claimed to have someone on their staff responsible for risk management. Among this same group, 1 church in 50 had been sued the previous year and 40 percent had filed an insurance claim during the same period.

Why don't churches engage in risk management? The two most common responses to this question are: (1) we leave it to the insurance agent; and (2) we do not feel the need to do risk management. Both of these responses cause concern. First, insurance and risk management are not the same thing. Insurance is a form of risk financing. It provides funds to cope with a loss after it has already occurred. Risk management is concerned with not only controlling losses, but with preventing them from occurring in the first place. Second, insurance agents are in the business of selling insurance, not in managing risks. While some insurance agents are experts in risk management, many are not. While an insurance agent can be helpful with respect to many risk management concerns that confront churches, risk management should be viewed as a process that is internal to the church. Third, church leaders do not fully appreciate the risks that their congregations face. Often, they do not understand that some risks they face are not even covered by insurance. Our research on churches revealed the following:

- 3 percent reported that a minor had been sexually molested by a paid or volunteer staff member or while participating in a church program

- 8 percent reported that sexual misconduct had occurred between a staff member and an adult member of the church

- 52 percent reported that an accident requiring medical attention had occurred at a church program within the previous three years

- 12 percent reported that they have a sexual harassment policy

- 11 percent reported that they have a church handbook that has been reviewed by an attorney

Although the typical church faces many pure risks (risks that can have a negative outcome, but not a positive one), too often nothing is done to prevent them. In addition to the two reasons noted above, other theological, organizational, and legal factors contribute to this problem.

1.4 Factors that Impact a Risk Management Response

Theological factors

Some theological perspectives, grounded in the experience of the church as a community of faith and mission, can lead to a feeling of false security or to a willingness to embrace any risk without making any attempt to differentiate between good risks and bad risks. In both cases, these perspectives arise out of commitments of faith, but they present one-dimensional perspectives on a problem that is far more complex. Some common expressions of these perspectives are noted below:

- *A holy place.* No place is safer than a church or a church affiliated organization. Churches are holy places; sanctuaries embody the very essence of protection. *The problem:* people are hurt in sanctuaries and in church programs.

- *Trust and obey.* Churches are communities of trust and faith. No one can be more trusted than those who engage in ministry and service to others. We can trust such individuals to do what is right. *The problem:* church leaders and members cannot always be trusted. A few do things that harm people.

- *Lack of faith.* Risk is inherent within ministry. Trying to lower risk goes against the grain of faithful service. We must trust God to protect us. Risk management shows a lack of faith. *The problem:* faith and ministry risks are different from pure risks; we embrace the former but try to minimize the latter following the model of the good shepherd.

Organizational factors

In many respects, churches are no different than other organizations in their assessment and response to risk. Risks often seem to be remote and responding to them seems to produce more burdens than benefits. Common expressions of these attitudes include the following:

- *It can't happen here.* A mentality exists that losses and accidents will not happen at "our church." These are things you read about in the paper or see on television that happen to others. *The problem:* no church is immune from loss.

- *Passive acceptance.* An acknowledgement exists that risks may occur, but no felt need is present to do anything about it. The risk is viewed as remote and unimportant. *The problem:* accidents and losses can strike without warning.

- *Fear of alienation.* Some leaders believe that risk management can create fear and scare volunteer workers away. *The problem:* when developed properly, risk management enhances confidence and attracts volunteers and new members. Severe losses, on the other hand, can hurt the ministry of a church or school.

- *Too cumbersome.* Risk management requires too much time and energy. It creates too many burdens and we don't have the time or resources to do it. *The problem:* properly organized, risk management is manageable in any congregation or school. Losses always create even more stress and drain resources away from ministry.

Legal factors

Today, legal factors have a profound impact on both risks and risk management. On some occasions, fear of litigation drives the risk management process. When legal concerns dominate, the expression of risk management in the life of a church can be counter-productive. People may view it as harsh or uncaring in light of faith commitments and values. On the other hand, ignorance of legal concerns or failure to take them seriously can put a congregation in jeopardy. Legal factors that affect the risk management process in congregations and schools include the following:

- *Ignorance.* Few religious leaders fully know or understand the current legal realities or trends involving religious organizations and the resulting implications. As a result, congregations retain many risks without any idea that the risks are even present. *The problem:* church leaders do not know where to go to get help. Few resources exist.

- *Litigation.* Church litigation is increasing and jury awards are unpredictable. Awards can exceed the insurance coverage. Punitive damages are being accessed against churches and church leaders. Attorneys are receiving training on how to sue churches. Church litigation is becoming a niche market for some attorneys. *The problem:* churches are unprepared for possible litigation. Often they have done nothing to reduce their legal risks.

The need is present today, more than ever before, for church leaders to engage in risk management. In the next chapter, attention is given to the basic foundations of a risk management plan that can be used within a church or church affiliated ministry such as a school.

Summary

Risk is a natural part of ministry. The purpose of risk management in churches is not to eliminate risk, but to differentiate good risks from bad ones, and then through a process of caring and leadership to reduce or control bad risks. Jesus' image of the "good shepherd" captures the spirit of risk management in the life of the church.

Risks occur in many ways. Most textbooks on risk management differentiate between pure risks and speculative risks. Pure risks have no upside potential, while speculative risks can have a loss, no loss, or a gain. In applying the principles of risk management to churches and church sponsored schools it is also helpful to differentiate between faith risks and ministry risks. Faith risks arise out of our calling and relationship with God. Ministry risks surface in the programs we create to express our faith in acts of mission. The goal of risk management in churches and schools is to prevent or control *pure risks* (accidental losses) that impact ministry.

Currently few churches engage in intentional or systematic risk management. For the most part, they either do not see the need for it, or they leave it to their insurance agent. Insurance, however, is not designed to prevent risks. Rather, insurance helps to recover from losses after they occur. Furthermore, churches face greater risks today than in the past due to litigation. More churches are being sued today than ever before, and the litigation process is costly and stressful.

Many factors affect how churches respond to risk management. A risk management strategy must address theological, organizational, and legal concerns. In the chapter that follows, attention is given to developing a strategy for risk management in the life of the church.

CHAPTER 2. DEVELOPING A RISK MANAGEMENT STRATEGY

Most churches and many church sponsored schools follow no risk management *strategy*. That is not to say, however, that no risk management occurs. While it may be haphazard and done at the level of intuition and common sense, most churches and schools engage in some risk management practices including the purchase of insurance. Other than insurance, though, many risk management practices are often done by individuals on their own initiative. Frequently, risk management emerges out of a *collection of activities* rather than a *coherent integrated strategy*.

This chapter explores three important issues:

    (1) the significance of risk management strategy;

    (2) the relationship between motivation, language, and the practice of risk management; and,

    (3) establishing a risk management planning model for communities of faith.

How church and leaders respond to these concerns has a critical impact on both the nature and effectiveness of a church's risk management strategy.

2.1 Risk Management Strategy

What is the best way for a church or school to engage in the practice of risk management? Risk management strategy must address this question. Until recently, little thought has been given to the practice of risk management within church settings. Insurance companies, more so than any other group, care about this issue and have made attempts to help churches and schools. Yet not even the insurance industry has come to grips with this question in a meaningful way.

The "checklist" strategy

Currently, the most common strategy to help churches is to give brochures, video tapes, and booklets on a range of risk management issues. The heart of the strategy is to provide checklists to guide inspections of potential problem areas. While this approach may provide some limited help to those who already care deeply about such concerns, and while the resources do contain important information, for the most part this strategy is ineffective. The checklist strategy lacks any transformative power to bring about change in the life of a church or school.

At the heart of the checklist strategy is the assumption that churches and schools will engage in risk management if they *know what to do*. Risk management is then reduced to a series of steps. Each step requires some mitigating action. Furthermore, if the risks are segmented too finely—which often happens—the process can appear trivial. Consider the following safety list about driving in the rain:

- Be cautious, wet roads are slippery.
- Make sure the tires have adequate tread.
- Turn on your wipers once the windshield is adequately wet.
- Have an extra fuse in the vehicle if the wiper fuse should blow.

- Keep a safe distance between yourself and the car in front of you.
- Reduce your speed.

From a strategic planning point of view, such a list has minimal value in planning. People might agree with every point on that list, but what are they to do with it? Are they suppose to carry the list around with them and pull it out when it begins to rain? Do most people need to be told to turn on their windshield wipers? Who gets into their car and asks if they have an extra fuse before they take off? Even if every item on that list is important, something critical is missing. The checklist strategy has an implicit assumption that if people are given enough information a synthesis will occur that unifies content and practice into a comprehensive and coherent risk management effort. The strategy is to provide as many checklists as possible, on every area of risk. The problem is not with the checklists, which may be quite good, but with the strategy. The strategy fails to address important issues of *motivation* and *implementation*.

What motivates church or school leaders to engage in risk management? Once motivated, how does motivation become transformed into practice? One challenging aspects of risk management strategy is to come to grips with these questions. The value based strategy described below responds to these concerns.

2.2 A Value Based Strategy

Within churches and schools, motivation regarding risk management tends to revolve around four primary issues: fear of litigation, financial concerns, a desire to have an effective and ongoing ministry or school, and caring for others. Leaders, employees, volunteers, and members respond to these factors in very different and often unpredictable ways. Some leaders develop an almost instant motivation to develop an aggressive risk management program, while others wonder what all the fuss is about. Understanding the motivational dynamics helps in framing the discussion and laying the groundwork for a risk management plan.

Motivation and litigation

In recent years the driving force behind risk management in many congregations has been the fear of litigation. Church leaders become concerned that either they or the church could become the target of a costly lawsuit. In response they often implement a top down strategy of risk management, frequently based upon a new set of policies and procedures that congregational members may view as foreign and out-of-sync with the faith based values of the church. The new procedures may seem rigid and even offensive to some people. This has been particularly true with respect to conducting criminal background checks on volunteers who work with youth or children. Church leaders are often surprised by the negative reaction and don't know whether to try and enforce the new rules or to do something different. Confusion can result and in these circumstances the attempt at risk management dies on the vine. Fear of litigation does motivate some church leaders, but it is not a major concern to most church members.

Motivation and money

Business leaders often view risk management on the basis of a cost-benefit analysis. Financial factors, including the survivability of the business following a catastrophe, become primary considerations. Within many churches, finances play only a minor role with respect to risk management. For the most part, church leaders generally feel that insurance covers the majority of their financial risks. Financial issues, though, do motivate some leaders, especially once they understand the potential scope of some risks.

Motivation and the desire to have an effective and ongoing ministry

People who invest time, money, and energy into any effort hope that it succeeds. When threats occur that jeopardize those efforts, people want to do whatever is in their power to mitigate those threats. The same is true for church and school leaders. Leaders and staff members who invest themselves into the work and ministry of the church or school, and who care deeply about that work, want it to continue and prosper. Such feelings can provide motivation for risk management. Part of the problem, however, was addressed in chapter 1. Many leaders simply do not see or appreciate some risks as being significant. As a result, the motivation to engage in risk management may be low.

Motivation and caring

While important, concerns related to *litigation, finances*, and *continued success* generally do not provide the underpinnings to establish and sustain an effective risk management program in a church. Risk management programs are more likely to succeed when churches place primary emphasis upon creating *caring* and *safe* environments for children, youth, and all other people who attend church programs or use church facilities. When a strong connection is made between risk management and the core values and beliefs of church members, the foundation for success has been established. These values often include acts of caring and love—values closely associated with the biblical image of the good shepherd. They are present in every congregation and become manifest in many different ways through prayers, liturgies, the eucharist, sermons, classes, outreach ministries, fellowship, and music. An effective risk management strategy within a church should flow out of these core values and expressions of faith. The exploration and identification of those values will provide answers to the question of why engage in risk management. While no two churches will have the exact same experience in the identification of those values, most churches will come to a similar conclusion: that churches need to care for their members, for the weak and the vulnerable, and for those with special needs. The church should be a good steward of all that God has entrusted to its care. Theologically, these concerns are at the heart of risk management. Risk management is an outgrowth of caregiving leadership. Unfortunately, a disconnection often exists between risk management and caring.

The problem of language

Part of the problem facing many churches in establishing a risk management program is language. The very phrase *risk management* creates difficulties. For some people the phrase itself is offensive. It conjures up images of lawyers and insurance people taking over and stifling ministry. It's like spiritual managed care. For others, the idea of "managing risks" is contrary to their understanding of the gospel itself. We addressed this concern in chapter 1 in the discussion about risk taking and risk management as two different dimensions of ministry. The goal is not to diminish ministry, but to reduce or eliminate pure risks (the accidental losses that can do significant harm). Yet, for some this distinction is either rejected or not considered. Finally, some people simply find the phrase "risk management" too commercial or secular. It seems to speak far more to the pocketbook than it does to the spirit. It comes across as self-serving, putting one's own interests first, of being spiritually dead and lifeless. The language of risk management should surface from the ordinary conversations of people about the ministry of the church or school. This occurs through dialogue.

Facilitating a value based strategy

The starting point in a value based strategy is to facilitate dialogue, story telling, and reflection. The key first questions are not "*How should we do risk management,*" or "*Why should we do risk management,*" but "*As God's people, what should we care about? . . . what do we care about?*" A discussion that revolves around these issues can help values to surface that open the door for acts of caring and safety. In turn, that provides the foundation for risk management.

Consider how the following questions might facilitate a dialogue on managing risks:

- Share a story of how being a part of this congregation (or school) has inspired you?

- When, as part of our work and ministry together, have you felt closest to God?

- When you look around at what God has done in our midst together, what gives you the greatest sense of joy? As a leader, how do God's blessings shape your feelings and attitudes about your responsibilities to this congregation (or school)?

- As you look to the future, what can we do together as a group to multiply God's blessings, to express His care, and to fulfill our duties as good shepherds to His people?

- In what ways can we use and maintain the facilities, equipment, and resources we have to further glorify God and to provide for the future needs of this ministry (or school)?

These questions, and similar ones, provide a different point of departure for establishing a risk management program. They enable leaders to see the practice of risk management through a different lens—one that emerges from the values they most cherish. One theological concept that helps to bridge the gap between the language and practice of risk management within the church is *stewardship*. What does it mean for God's people to be good stewards of that which has been entrusted to their care? How do we care for church finances, facilities, property, and for people from the youngest to the oldest? Looking at risk management through the lens of stewardship helps to ground our discussion in more conventional language and ideas that many church members already understand and support. Using such language, and grounding the discussion both biblically and theologically in the traditions, worship, and life of the church are critical factors in the practice of risk management within congregations and church sponsored schools. Unless risk management is part of the fabric of congregational life, it will not be sustained over time. On the other hand, if church members embrace the underpinning values and understand the reasons and goals of the risk management program, the likelihood of establishing and sustaining an effective program increases.

The strategy proposed here embraces this approach. It begins with building a base of support among congregational or school leaders. All four motivational factors should be used in the course of those discussions. Ultimately, that dialogue must move into all levels of the congregation or school. Then comes the formulation of deliberate plans and additional training. Functionally, the program must be part of the organizational life of the church or school, but emotionally, the practice of risk management arises out of the faith commitments of the people. At this point, the resources that were at the core of the "checklist strategy" take on a new meaning and power. Rather than collecting dust on a shelf, or being used out of robotic obedience, they become a ministry tool to express acts of caring to help fulfill the mission of the church.

2.3 A Risk Management Planning Model

Once dialogue begins and leaders develop a commitment to risk management, a deliberate plan is needed. Our focus in the remainder of this chapter is to describe a simple, but effective plan for conducting a risk management program in your church or school (how the plan is implemented is discussed in the next chapter). The plan outlined below is based on a traditional and widely used five-step risk management process. The five steps include the following:

1. Identify your church's or school's exposure to loss. What risks do you face?

2. Analyze the potential impact and scope of the identified risks on the church or school.

3. Select the best risk management techniques that your church or school can use to reduce the identified risks.

4. Implement the appropriate risk management techniques and training to reduce risks.

5. Evaluate the effectiveness of your risk management program, provide feedback to leaders and members, and make changes as needed.

2.4 Step 1: Risk Identification

Risk identification should be a systematic process that takes into account specific risks that are associated with *people, property,* and *liability*. With respect to churches and church sponsored schools, this handbook focuses on the following areas of pure risk, which are divided into three categories.

1. *Risks to People (chapters 5-12)*

● Church nurseries and equipment for infants and toddlers

● Playgrounds

19

- Recreational programs and fellowship activities
- Transportation
- Slips, falls and other accidents
- Construction projects
- Ergonomic concerns
- Acts of violence

2. Risks to People and Property (chapters 13-17)

- Fire
- Cold weather
- Natural disasters and severe weather
- Crime and vandalism
- Embezzlement

3. Liability Risks (chapters 18-33)

- Defamation
- Undue influence
- Invasion of privacy
- Counseling
- Contracts
- Failure to report child abuse
- Sexual misconduct
- Clergy malpractice
- Common forms of liability
- Immunity statutes
- Copyright law violations
- Securities law violations
- Premises liability
- Employment discrimination
- Negligent selection and retention of volunteers and employees
- Negligent supervision of volunteers, employees, and activities

As can be seen from the above three categories, identifying risks can be a demanding and complex task. Some risks may be obvious, but identifying others may require special knowledge or skill. Typically, certain techniques are used to identify risks including conducting inspections, reviewing records and documents, getting appraisals, analyzing environmental factors, and reviewing insurance.

Methods to identify risks

At first glance, church leaders may feel overwhelmed at the process of identifying risks. However, it is not as bad as it appears. Several key points should be kept in mind. First, resources are available to assist in the risk identification process. Inspection protocols and checklists are available from Christian Ministry Resources for each area discussed in this book.[1] Second, while the process involves a certain amount of start-up energy, once going it is far less difficult to maintain. Third, the methods of identifying risks can be broken down into smaller, manageable tasks. The whole process does not have to occur at once. And finally, with proper training and encouragement, congregational members can provide extensive feedback to correct problems as they occur. The more people that are involved, the easier the process becomes.

While the methods to identify risks vary somewhat depending on the nature of the risk, the following approaches are the most common.

1. *Inspections.* One of the best ways to identify many risks is through visual inspections. About half of churches claim to conduct a visual inspection of their property on an annual basis. However, only about 25 percent use a written checklist. Here are some tips to keep in mind when doing a visual inspection of church property.

(a) *Solicit the input of professionals.* In establishing a protocol to conduct a visual inspection of church or school property solicit the help of several key professionals. Invite someone from your local fire department to assist you in identifying fire hazards. Contact your local police department to assist you with crime prevention and security. Many communities have public service departments to assist community organizations with these tasks. Have a qualified electrician check church wiring. This is particularly important if you have old wiring. Heating and air conditioning units should be properly maintained and serviced at least twice a year (once before the cooling season and once before the heating season).

(b) *Be thorough and systematic.* Examine every room within every building. Do a complete inspection of the outside of each building as well as the property and grounds including parking lots, sidewalks, playgrounds, driveways, utility poles, landscaping, and athletic fields. If the church owns property at more than one location, be sure that each location is inspected. Normally, it is recommended that the visual walk through involve at least two people, and be done twice—at least in areas representing the biggest hazards. It is easy to miss items the first time through, and a second go around can assist in spotting needs that were overlooked the first time.

(c) *Use a written checklist.* Do not leave your inspection protocol to memory. Prepare written guidelines that conform to the order in which the property is inspected. That will assist those doing the inspection to be thorough, and will enable the protocol to be passed on to others who may be unfamiliar with the inspection process. Note: companion resources to this handbook are available that contain extensive inspection protocols and checklists that churches and schools may adapt for their own use. See footnote 2 below.

(d) *Prepare a written list of needed corrections.* Again, do not leave things to memory. Once a problem is recognized, write it down on your list. The best approach is to use a standardized form to list problems and needed corrections.

---

[1] To order, contact Christian Ministry Resources at 800-222-1840 between 8 AM and 4:30 PM, eastern time, Monday-Friday.

(e) Devote extra attention to hazard areas. Some areas, such as a furnace room or kitchen, normally reflect higher levels of risk. Do not rush through these areas. Generally it is a good idea to go over these areas twice. Problems can easily be missed the first time through.

2. *Appraisals.* A second important technique in assessing risk is to have your property appraised periodically. Unless you know what your buildings, furnishings, and equipment are worth, you cannot make an informed decision regarding risk financing. Your insurance agent can assist you with this process. Also, some items may require special attention. For example, appraising a pipe organ or a piece of art may require professional input.

3. *Financial records and other documents.* Receipts and other financial records can assist in several ways. First, records can help determine the value of some church property. Second, financial statements help leaders to assess how much money is available to fund risks that may be retained, or how much the church or school may be able to borrow if the need should arise.

4. *Environmental trends and changes.* Monitor environmental developments around your church. Property values, for example, can change as the result of neighborhood developments. Leaders should understand legal trends with respect to liability claims and judgments.

5. *Insurance audit.* An annual insurance review should occur with the church's or school's agent. Make sure the coverage is what you want and need based on your ongoing analysis of risk.

2.5 Step 2: Analyze the Impact and Scope of the Identified Risks

Once risks have been identified, the next consideration is to assess their scope and potential impact. One approach to assessment is to consider two separate risk factors: *frequency* and *severity*. Examining the relationship between frequency and severity, as illustrated in the Table 1 below, can help church leaders to respond appropriately to risks.

Table 1: Assessing Losses Based On Frequency and Severity

High frequency	3	6	9
Moderate frequency	2	5	8
Low frequency	1	4	7
	Low severity	Moderate severity	High severity

Using the above table, risk categories can be assigned a risk rating from 1 to 9 based on the relationship between frequency and severity. Frequency indicates how often a particular risk is likely to occur. Severity describes the degree of the loss. Thus a rating of 3 indicates high frequency, but low severity.

The key starting point for analysis is severity. The above table classifies severity into three broad categories: low, moderate and high. Part of the dilemma facing church and school leaders is to determine what *severe* really means. One approach is to classify severity based on a church's or school's ability to pay for losses. For example, losses that can be paid out of cash flow may be classified as low severity. Losses that can be paid out of cash reserves may be classified as moderate severity. Losses that require a church or school to look for outside financing, or that jeopardize normal operations may be classified as high severity. The following examples illustrate this threefold classification:

- *Low severity.* The church van has a tire go flat when it hits a pothole in the road. The treasurer writes a check for $180 for a new tire.

- *Moderate severity.* Vandals spray paint slogans on the side of a school building. The clean up cost is $2,700. The school pays for the loss out of savings or cash reserves.

- *High severity.* A tornado destroys the church's sanctuary. Replacement cost is $1,700,000. Insurance pays all but a $1,000 deductible.

Frequency, however, also affects the total impact of a particular risk. As the frequency increases, the accumulative impact may become significant. For example, a church that replaces a flat tire once a year may pay for it out of cash flow. If it begins to replace flat tires every week, the impact changes. A different response strategy may be needed.

When severity is based strictly upon money, financial capabilities shape the impact of the loss. What is a low risk for one church or school may be a moderate or high risk for another. A dollar amount, though, is only one dimension of severity. Other dimensions are personal pain and suffering, plus the perception and reaction of the church or school family and the broader community to the loss. These cannot be easily quantified and they have a profound and lasting impact. Consider the following examples:

- *A boy age 9 has both legs amputated after he falls off a wagon at a church hayride and is run over by the wagon.*

- *A youth minister molests a girl age 13 while on a church ski trip. The trial is covered extensively by the local media. The youth minister is found guilty and sent to prison.*

- *A boy age 5 drowns on a school swimming trip to a community lake. The parents sue the school for 10 million dollars.*

- *The single mother of three children slips on icy stairs at the church. She falls, hitting her head, and becomes paralyzed from the waist up.*

In each case, most churches and schools would need insurance to cope with such losses. While insurance can help cover the financial risks associated with specific losses it cannot restore legs that have been lost, the innocence of childhood that has been stolen, the laughter of a child that is forever gone, or the lost sensation of hugging a child or shaking a hand. In addition, accidents can dramatically impact the public image of the church or school in the community. When that image suddenly turns negative, the survival of the institution may be in question.

Drawing from the two sets of above examples, one way to think about risk is to separate *property losses* from those that involve *personal injury* and then to assess frequency. The severity of a property loss can be quantified. If fire destroys a building, a fairly accurate estimate can be made of the replacement cost. The church or school can assess in advance how it will finance the loss. Severity, though, is not so easy to determine with respect to personal injuries and liability claims. Until the loss occurs, there is no way to measure its severity in terms of human pain, financial impact, or the public's perception and response. Thus, to be adequately prepared, leaders should consider all personal injuries, regardless of frequency, as *potential* high severity losses requiring insurance coverage and a crisis management plan.

Examples

The following examples illustrate the relationship between frequency and severity. Attention is given to low, moderate, and high severity losses with different frequencies.

Low severity

> *Low severity/Low frequency.* These losses occur occasionally, if at all, and when they do happen, they are either insignificant or manageable. As a result they require little attention or concern. If finances are involved, losses are paid out of cash flow.
>
> ● *Supplies turn up missing from the office supply cabinet. Estimated annual cost: $12.*
>
> ● *A tire on a vehicle is punctured, on average, about once every four years. Estimated cost: $145.*
>
> *Low severity/Moderate frequency.* When a loss is minor, but begins to occur on a more frequent basis, it becomes a source of irritation or frustration. Normally, we try to find some way to reduce the frequency, not because the loss is a threat to our well-being, but simply to avoid the irritation it creates. Such risks test our patience and the accumulative impact can take a toll. When financial losses, occur, they normally are paid out of cash flow or cash reserves.
>
> ● *Pencils are stolen from the church supply cabinet nearly every month.*
>
> ● *A secretary feels neck tension after working at the computer all week.*

Moderate severity

> *Moderate severity/Low frequency.* These losses do not occur often, but when they do happen they exact some financial toll or personal pain. They may cause a person to lose work, or force the church or school to use savings or file an insurance claim to pay for the loss. They do not, though, jeopardize the church or school.
>
> ● *Vandals spray paint slogans on the side of a school building. The clean-up cost of $1,200 is paid out of savings.*

- *A custodian strains his back while lifting a box. He misses work for 3 days.*

- *A strong wind blows a tree over which hits the roof of the church. The repair is $2,200. The insurance coverage has a $1,000 deductible. The expense is paid out of savings.*

- *Lightning strikes a church and starts a small fire which results in $7,500 of damage. An electrical surge from the strike also damages the church organ and telephone system resulting in another $20,000 of losses. Insurance pays for the loss, except for a $500 deductible.*

Moderate severity/Moderate frequency. When a loss increases in frequency and severity it begins to have a more direct and serious impact financially, physically, and emotionally. We try to find ways to reduce both the frequency and the severity. When financial losses, occur, they may be paid out of cash flow, savings, or insurance, depending on the financial capabilities of the church or school, and the frequency and severity of the loss.

- *Supplies are stolen from the church supply cabinet nearly every week.*

- *A secretary feels neck and shoulder pain several days a week after working at the computer all day.*

- *During heavy thunderstorms, the roof leaks and drips into the kitchen.*

High severity

High severity/Low frequency. Serious and catastrophic risks fall into this category. They do not happen very often, but when they do they can seriously harm people as well as the ministry of a church or school. They may even jeopardize the church's or school's survival. Normally, when these risks occur they trigger an insurance claim. The church or school pays the deductible and the insurance covers the rest. Two important issues surface here. The first is whether the deductible is set at the proper level. If it is set too low, the church or school may be paying for insurance coverage it does not need. On the other hand, if the deductible is set too high, the church or school may face a financial burden if the loss should occur. The deductible amount should reflect a balance between what a church or school can afford financially and its willingness to bear risk. Some leaders sleep better at night knowing that certain risks have been transferred to the insurance company even if it means paying a higher premium.

The second issue is whether the insurance limits are adequate. Most church and school leaders do not want to be unprotected if a catastrophe should strike. But they may not have a good idea of what the true cost might be in a worse case scenario, or even be aware of all the risks they face. When the severity of a risk reaches the level of a catastrophe, not only does it trigger the need for insurance, it also indicates a need for a crisis management plan (see Chapter 4). Crises pose a serious threat, in part, because they are not taken seriously. Few people believe these risks will happen to them. Generally, since frequency is low, no sense of urgency exists to respond to them and as a result, often nothing is done. One important goal of a risk management program is to identify, assess, and respond directly to these risks. Often insurance coverage will be limited, precisely because the insurance industry recognizes the true threat these risks pose. Thus it becomes even more important for churches and schools to implement loss prevention and loss control strategies for catastrophic risks, including the development of a crisis management plan (see chapter 4).

- *A tornado strikes church facilities and destroys the sanctuary and educational building. It turns out the buildings were underinsured by over $200,000 and the congregation will be without facilities for months with no alternative plan in place. The congregation has $7,000 in a savings account.*

- *A child is molested while attending an overnight activity for youth at the church. Insurance is needed to pay for the legal defense and possible judgment against the church. The church has a $1,000 deductible and $100,000 of coverage for sexual misconduct. The plaintiff is suing for $3,000,000 in damages.*

- *A pastor is disabled when he slips and falls while leading a men's retreat. As a result of his injury he is paralyzed in one arm and has slurred speech. The pastor does not have disability insurance and opted out of social security coverage. The church does not carry workers compensation insurance.*

High severity/High frequency. Over time, no organization can maintain an exposure to a risk that results in both high severity and high frequency. The toll is simply too great. One or both of the dimensions of severity and frequency must be reduced. For that reason, few real life examples of churches or schools facing high severity, high frequency risks will exist.

- *A school in a high crime area is continuously burglarized. The staff members are assaulted and robbed again and again.*

- *A church outreach clinic treats people with highly contagious diseases. Volunteers who assist the staff members continuously become infected.*

- *A church building is located in a flood plain, which on average floods once a year. No adequate insurance is available.*

2.6 Step 3: Select the Best Risk Management Technique

Once risks have been identified and assessed, the next step is to select the best available technique to manage the risk. For many churches and schools, this process is done without a great deal of reflection. Understandably, not much thought is given to risks that are low frequency and low severity. They tend to be ignored. Many other risks are treated somewhat on an *ad hoc* basis. To be effective the selection of risk management techniques should be an intentional and systematic process. Consideration should be given to the following five approaches to manage risks:

- Avoid the risk
- Retain the risk
- Share the risk
- Transfer the risk
- Reduce the risk

Avoid the risk

Key point. Some youth activities pose especially high risks and are not recommended for churches or schools. These include sky diving, hang gliding, rock climbing, the use of trampolines, or the use of all-terrain vehicles.

Church leaders may decide that some risks are simply not worth the potential loss. Consider the following example:

Example. Youth members from First Church volunteer for a summer mission's project helping poor, elderly homeowners in a rural community. Nearby the project is a bridge where a company operates a bungee jump over a river. The drop from the bridge to the river is 175 feet. Several members of the youth group want to bungee jump off the bridge. The youth leader prohibits any member of the group from jumping saying, "It's simply not worth the risk. This is one activity that our church will not sponsor. If you want to bungee jump, you will have to do that at another time when you are with your own family."

While the avoidance of some risks may seem obvious, making a decision to avoid other risks may be difficult and controversial. This is especially true when the odds of a loss are high, but come into direct conflict with the church's vision and mission. In essence, ministry risks may come into conflict with pure risks. For example, an inner city ministry may establish boundaries concerning ministry activities. Perhaps certain areas of the city are to be avoided after dark. Some church members may feel that if such boundaries are enforced, the ministry will suffer. Yet on the other hand, they may also feel that one serious incident could damage the ministry and that such risks should be avoided. The competing values lead to tension on how much of the risk to retain, and in what manner.

After identifying and assessing the risks, church leaders should determine if any specific risk should be avoided. Most people agree with the proposition that we should not risk a lot for a little. That is one factor to consider in assessing whether or not to avoid a specific risk. For example, a report comes back that a piece of playground equipment poses a risk to preschoolers, but that it is okay for older children. Leaders may decide simply to remove the piece of equipment and completely avoid the risk. The feeling may be that removing the equipment does not significantly reduce the quality of the playground. On the other hand, if a small child was injured, that loss could be great both in terms of human suffering as well as potential liability. Of course, other risk management techniques are also available such as retaining the risk, but controlling access to the equipment. At times retaining a risk can be the best option for a church.

Retain the risk

Churches and schools retain risks for many different risks. Some risks are retained intentionally while others are retained either unwittingly or because the church or school has no other option. Churches or schools that retain a risk that could be severe, yet have no idea that the risk even exists are in a particularly vulnerable position.

Intentional retention. Leaders may decide to retain certain risks for financial reasons. For example, increasing the deductible on the property insurance may result in substantial savings. The deductible amount represents a retained risk. The rationale to do so may arise from a financial analysis that shows the church or school can pay for the increased exposure directly out of its cash flow. In such situations, leaders may agree that the decision to retain risks through a higher deductible makes financial sense. Insurance may be used primarily to cover large or catastrophic losses, rather than smaller losses that the church or school can finance in more cost effective ways.

The lack of money can also lead leaders to retain certain risks, often unwisely. For example, leaders may face competing demands for limited financial resources. They may intentionally underinsure church property in order to save money for other needs. The rationale may be that the odds of a major property loss are small. While they retain the risk, they may not be in a position to handle the loss if it should occur. In such circumstances, it becomes critical for the church to take steps to reduce the potential for loss. If the loss should occur, the ministry of the church may be greatly harmed, and the leaders will have to account for their actions.

In addition to financial factors, ministry also plays an important role in the decision to retain certain risks. Faith convictions and ministry goals often compel church leaders to retain some risks. Leaders recognize the risks but accept them as part of the cost of doing ministry. Again, the church may or may not be able to handle some losses if they should occur. That concern, however, is viewed as secondary. Risks are retained as part of the cost of ministry. Loss prevention and loss control are important to help such churches reduce accidental losses that can harm individuals and hurt ministry.

Unwitting retention. While some risks are consciously retained for the reasons noted above, other risks may be present, but unknown to church or school leaders. For example, no one may know that several serious hazards are present on the property because inspections are never done. Or perhaps they know that the hazards exist, but they take no action to correct them without realizing that failure to act may result in a claim of gross negligence if an injury occurs followed by a civil lawsuit. Furthermore, they may be unaware that the insurance policy does not cover punitive damages based on gross negligence.

While every action has an element of risk associated with it, we tend to discount and ignore many risks, especially those without much consequence. Church leaders, however, often are unaware of severe risks that the church has unwittingly retained. A case in point is the sexual molestation of children. For example, a church may assume that it has insurance coverage for such acts under its general liability coverage. However, such coverage may have been excluded. Or the church may have coverage but the insurance is very limited. Leaders may not understand that the church may be retaining a risk that can greatly exceed the value of the insurance coverage. Furthermore, they may have no idea that child molestation poses a threat to their own congregation, and that their own church programs promote easy access to potential victims. The conditions for molestation may be present, and yet no one is even aware of the danger to potential victims or to the church.

Churches that unwittingly retain severe risks generally face a crisis if the loss actually occurs. They are caught completely off guard and are not prepared to respond. This is quite different from a church that knowingly retains a risk. Once church leaders know that a risk is present, they can take steps to prevent it and to control it if it should occur. Informed leaders can reduce risks; uninformed leaders face full exposure.

Forced retention. In some circumstances a church or school may have no option but to retain a risk. Insurance may not be available or may be limited. No other organization may be available to share the risk. The fact that a risk cannot be transferred or shared may indicate that it poses too great a threat. In such circumstances, leaders should proceed with caution, placing significant emphasis upon loss prevention and loss control.

Share the risk

Risk sharing can occur in a variety of ways. Some church groups pool their risks. They may do so out of the belief that it is more cost effective than buying insurance. Operating such a pool, however, is a complex process requiring special knowledge and expertise. A number of denominational groups have formed pools only to disband them at a later date. Others have employed professional companies to provide underwriting and claims administration and have achieved some level of success.

On a smaller scale, most churches and schools permit outside groups to use their facilities. Often this is done without the recognition that the host may be liable for the negligent actions of the outside group while it uses the facilities. Some churches and schools knowingly bear this risk while others retain it unwittingly. In some situations contractual arrangements are made between both groups to share risks. In others, the host church or school requires the outside group to provide a certificate of insurance that provides evidence of insurance coverage. In most cases, both the property owner and the outside user will share some risks.

Transfer the risk

The most common method to transfer risk is through the purchase of insurance coverage. Insurance is a form of risk financing and not primarily a means of loss prevention (although it may prevent or mitigate further losses following payment of a claim). The topic of insurance is covered more fully in chapter 34.

Risks can also be transferred in ways other than through insurance. For example, some churches use *hold harmless agreements* or *indemnity agreements* as a means of risk transfer.

Hold harmless agreements. A church or school may use a hold harmless agreement to protect itself from a potential lawsuit. For example, adult participants on a foreign mission's trip may sign a hold harmless agreement whereby, while on the trip, they assume certain risks that are detailed in the agreement. In essence they agree not to bring any legal claims against the church based on the nature of the contract. Courts often view hold harmless agreements with a high degrees of skepticism, but they do have value when used appropriately. Hold harmless agreements should be used only with adults and not with minors. A church or school that plans to use a hold harmless agreement should seek the assistance of an attorney.

Indemnity agreements. An indemnity agreement has two contractual parties, an *indemnitor* and an *indemnitee*. The indemnitor agrees to pay the indemnitee if a specific loss should occur. For example, an outside group may borrow church or school equipment and sign a contractual agreement to pay the cost of replacing the equipment if it should become damaged. Obviously, the value of an indemnity agreement depends upon the capacity of the indemnitor to fulfill the contractual obligation if a loss should occur.

Churches and schools often use hold harmless and indemnity agreements when working with contractors and subcontractors during construction projects. Churches and schools can also transfer risks through incorporation, leases, waivers, and contracts.

Reduce the risk

Regardless of the risk management techniques used, an associated goal is to manage risks through *both loss prevention* and *loss control*.

Loss prevention. Loss prevention focuses on the steps that a church or school can take to reduce the *frequency* of a loss. For example, while a church or school cannot control the frequency of hurricanes, it may be able through the use of shutters to control the frequency of broken windows from a hurricane. The goal of loss prevention is to intervene *before* the loss occurs to reduce the likelihood that it will occur in the first place. Loss prevention is dependent upon identifying potential risks as noted in Step 1 above, and to the extent possible, to take appropriate action to prevent them.

Loss control. Loss control focuses on the steps that a church or school can take to reduce the *severity* of a loss. For example, using a fire extinguisher to put out a fire is a form of loss control. The goal of loss control is to intervene *after* the peril has occurred to limit its impact and to prevent additional losses from occurring. One peril can often generate others. A fire that destroys a building can impact church attendance, ministry efforts, finances, and the physical and emotional well-being of church staff members and others. Having a proper response strategy in place to control losses is a critical component of risk management. Loss control is dependent both upon advance planning as well as upon training people on how to respond to specific types of loss.

2.7 Step 4: Implement the Appropriate Technique

Overall, the implementation of risk management is not a job for one person, but for the entire congregation. That is not to say, however, that certain individuals will not play key roles. Success is dependent upon committed leadership who oversee an implementation strategy that is intentional, systematic, and sustained.

Leadership. Leadership plays a critical role in the implementation of any risk management program. Without the support and input of leaders, a program is not likely to last long. The nature of leadership will vary with congregational size and complexity. Clearly, the church board must be behind the effort. Most congregations will also benefit by forming a risk management or a safety committee to design and oversee the implementation of the program. One person can be designated as the church safety officer, who serves as the spokesperson for the congregation on safety issues. These individuals provide formal oversight to the risk management program. Normally, their responsibilities will include identifying needs, selecting risk management techniques, implementing congregational wide efforts including conducting inspections, leading training events, monitoring the process, and making reports to congregational leaders. Chapter 3 is fully devoted to the issue of leadership.

Intentional. Most congregations have a limited approach to risk management that includes the purchase of insurance, implementing selected safety precautions, and attempting to correct some hazards. This is in contrast to an intentional strategy that reflects a broad base of knowledge and a clear sense of purpose that become transformed into a well-designed and led risk management program that is both systematic and sustained.

Systematic. A systematic program is both thorough and regular. No part of congregational life is left out. A systematic program addresses the needs of *people*, of *property*, and of *liability*. It takes time and effort to implement a systematic program. One person cannot do it alone. Establishing an intentional, systematic approach to risk management will take the typical congregation 12-18 months. First, it takes considerable time to recruit and train leaders and then to educate and train congregational members. Then, once a plan is in place, it takes at least 12 months just to work through the process once since some risk management tasks are seasonal. A risk management plan is always emergent in nature, adapting to new issues and changes in congregational life. Once a base program is established, the next task is to see that it is sustained over time.

Sustained. Risk management exists in some congregations because of the vision and efforts of one person. If that person leaves, the whole program collapses. In other cases a turnover in church staff or leadership can cause a program to die. While church leaders may care enough to take action at one point, over time those leaders are replaced and the institutional memory concerning the need for the program may not live on. Sustaining the program over time also requires an intentional strategy. Several factors can be helpful to keep a program meaningful and alive. First, the program needs a strong start that includes the support of key opinion leaders, the endorsement of the church board, visibility among the members, and a solid plan. Second, the program should be institutionalized into the leadership structure of the church. One of the best ways to do that is to create a standing committee, team, or task force to provide leadership and direction. Third, accountability is needed between the risk management team, congregational leaders, and congregational members. In part this can be achieved through the establishment of annual activity standards that spell out the specific tasks that the risk management team must complete including reports to the leadership and to the congregation. Fourth, ongoing training is needed at all levels of congregational life. That involves communication and education that explains the purpose and importance of risk management, and how congregational members can be involved. The goal is to establish a program that becomes part of the very fabric of congregational life. That is most likely to happen if the program reflects the values and concerns of congregational members. An ongoing program will constantly evolve and change.

2.8 Step 5: Evaluation and Feedback

A risk management program needs to be monitored on an ongoing basis. That involves staying informed on what is being done, evaluating the outcomes, and providing feedback so that improvements can occur.

Staying informed. Activity reports on risk management should be provided to church leaders on a regular basis. The number and frequency of reports will vary from one church and school to another. Minimally, the risk management or safety committee (see Chapter 3) should provide an annual written report that summarizes the risk management activities of the preceding year and identifies current needs. Oral and shorter written reports should also be presented several times a year. The frequency of and audience for these latter reports depends to a large degree on the scope of the risk management program. For example, a small rural church may have a report once a quarter at a board meeting. A larger church may have a monthly report for the board. Still in other situations, reports may be more frequent and given to department heads or pastoral staff members. For example, the Director of a preschool program may meet with teachers on a monthly basis to review risk management concerns. Churches may encourage members to provide immediate feedback on any concern. While no single approach will work for every church, a formal structure should exist to collect feedback and information on both risk management concerns and practices. The scope and nature of the feedback should be proportional to the risks that a particular congregation faces. As congregations increase in size, the frequency of reports, and the number of people involved in the monitoring process should increase.

> *Example. Prairie Church, with a Sunday morning attendance of 75 people, is located in a rural setting. The church's property committee also oversees risk management concerns. Once each quarter a member of the committee makes a brief report to the church board on the activities of the committee. If a special need arises, they meet with the board or pastor as needed. Once a year they review the church insurance, and prepare a report for the church's annual business meeting.*

> *Example. Community Church has an average Sunday attendance of 340 people. The church maintains a risk management committee with a member of the church board appointed to the committee. The risk management committee meets monthly and conducts ongoing inspections and training. Risk management is also a standing agenda item for the monthly meeting of the church board. The board representative to the risk management committee provides a brief report at each monthly board meeting.*

> *Example. First Church operates a day care program, preschool and elementary school through grade five. Over 500 children participate in these programs. The church has over 2,000 members and 75 full-time employees. One staff member is the church business administrator whose responsibilities include risk management and chairing a risk management committee that meets monthly. A member of the church board is assigned to that committee. The committee provides training, oversees insurance, and conducts regular inspections. All department heads within the church meet weekly for a regular staff meeting. One agenda item is risk management. In addition the department heads also meets regularly with paid and volunteer staff members that work in their respective departments. Risk management is also discussed in those*

meetings. All paid and volunteer workers are trained to monitor risk management needs in their area of responsibility. A system is in place to report concerns, and to facilitate corrective action as needed. The business administrator provides the church board with a monthly risk management report at the regularly scheduled board meeting. An annual report is provided to the entire congregation.

Evaluation. Risk management is not always easy to evaluate, in part because chance impacts every church. For example, no losses may occur at a particular church in a given year. That does not mean, however, that the church has a good risk management program. The church may have done little or nothing. It simply is the beneficiary of chance—in that year no losses occurred. Yet the church may face many hazards. On the other hand, a church may work hard at risk management and still have a considerable loss. Even the best efforts cannot prevent every peril from occurring.

Often, two approaches are used to evaluate risk management.[2] One is based on *activity standards* and the other is based on *outcomes.* Activity standards provide an objective, quantitative basis for evaluating the risk management practices of a particular church. For example, one standard may be to conduct a criminal background check on each paid employee as part of the hiring process. Leaders can determine through an inspection of documents if that procedure was followed in every case. An insurance company may require such a standard in exchange for providing higher limits of liability coverage. On the other hand, an evaluation of outcomes focuses on losses rather than on the practice of risk management. For example, suppose a church is sued for negligent selection of an employee who molests a child. Then a jury determines that the church is not liable, largely due to the fact that it conducted a criminal records check prior to hiring the employee, and no evidence was found that raised any concerns. In that case the outcome of the risk management practice can be evaluated over against the claim of liability. In many situations, however, it is impossible to know with certainty that a particular risk management practice prevented a risk from occurring. For example, does the practice of conducting a criminal records check protect children from child molesters? While in general the answer may be in the affirmative, no one can know with certainty that it has worked that way in a specific church. Thus two churches, one with no risk management program and one with an extensive risk management program, may experience the same results in a particular year. Based on an outcome evaluation, they may be the same. Based on an activity standards, however, one is evaluated much better than the other. One may face significant retained risks while the other has lowered those risks through preventive measures. In either case, the factor of chance also affects the evaluation of outcomes. Church leaders should focus on both areas—outcomes and activity standards—to obtain a more complete and accurate picture of risk management practice within the church.

Providing feedback. At its best, risk management is part of the life and fabric of a congregation. It is both a process and expression of caring. Feedback is needed if that process is to improve. Feedback is needed at all levels of congregational life.

---

[2] See *Essentials of Risk Control, Volume II*, edited by George L. Head (Malvern, PA: Insurance Institute of America, 1995), p. 261f.

Otherwise, the practice of risk management will become more narrowly defined over time, involving fewer and fewer people until it reaches the point of being lost in the consciousness of congregational members. While the process of providing feedback will vary from one congregation to another, depending upon factors such as congregational size and how the congregation practices risk management, a structured approach to feedback is needed. Pulpit and bulletin announcements, articles in newsletters, posters, oral and written reports, and training sessions all provide opportunities to share information that can keep people up-to-date on ways and means to enhance safety throughout the church.

Sample announcements in church bulletins

> *Example. Please make sure you use the handrails when you use the outdoor, back stairway to enter the fellowship hall. The stairs can be slippery this time of year.*

> *Example. Last week, several cars were broken into during the Wednesday evening church service. Make sure you keep your car locked and do not leave valuables visible inside the car. Please report any helpful information on this problem to the church office.*

> *Example. Thanks to Bill and Patty Wilson for inspecting our church playground last weekend. As a result of their quarterly inspection we are adding more wood chips to improve the protective surface under the equipment. We encourage all parents to report any problems of playground equipment to the church office. If you notice something that needs attention, please let us know.*

Summary

Risk management is not a priority with many congregations. Some congregations develop programs out of fear of litigation, but most simply rely on insurance as their main risk management strategy. Part of the problem is the very language of risk management does not connect to the most important values of congregational life. Church leaders should work at grounding risk management biblically and theologically so that it makes a better connection with congregational life. Using theological concepts such as stewardship and conducting Bible studies on issues of risk and caring can help accomplish that goal. Dialogue that emerges out of congregational values and concerns provides the best environment to establish a risk management plan.

Many congregations can use a five-step planning model to establish a risk management program. The five steps include:

(1) identifying exposures to loss;

(2) analyzing the potential impact and scope of the identified risks on the church by assessing the relationship between frequency and severity;

(3) selecting the best risk management techniques including avoiding the risk, retaining the risk, sharing the risk, transferring the risk, and reducing the risk;

(4) implementing the selected risk management techniques in an intentional, systematic, and sustained way under the leadership of a safety officer and a risk management committee; and,

(5) evaluating the effort based on both outcomes and activity standards, and providing feedback to all levels of congregational life.

In the next chapter attention turns to implementing the risk management strategy.

CHAPTER 3. IMPLEMENTING THE RISK MANAGEMENT STRATEGY

In the previous chapter a planning model was presented that a church or school can use to develop a risk management program. This chapter focuses on the implementation of that strategy. Several factors impact the implementation process. One critical factor is church or school size. As size increases, so does the complexity of implementation. Another important factor is location. A rural or small town setting creates a different environment and set of perspectives than an urban or suburban setting. Ethnicity and culture also impact the implementation process. For example, a Hispanic or Vietnamese congregation may respond very differently than an Anglo congregation to a variety of risk management issues. Another important factor is congregational structure and governance. The implementation process may be quite different for a church with a hierarchical form of governance compared to one which is congregational in nature. Finally, and perhaps the most important factor of all, is the availability, skill, knowledge, and commitment of the people responsible for implementing the program. No single blueprint will work for everyone. Yet, a basic model, such as the one proposed below, can serve as a point of departure for any congregation or school. The model is based upon two components:

(1) the formation of a team, committee, or task force to oversee the risk management process; and

(2) the appointment of a safety officer (or coordinator) who provides leadership to the committee and who embodies the essence of the program to the church or school.

In many churches, these individuals most likely will be volunteers. In larger churches they may include paid staff members. In a school, these roles are likely to be filled by both paid staff members and volunteers. This is true because schools have more employees to draw from than do churches. Parents of students may also desire to volunteer.

The two components above emerge from several considerations:

● The task of risk management in a church or school is too large a job for one person. The scope is both extensive and diverse, as reflected in the multiple chapters of this handbook.

● Risk management requires a broad range of expertise and input. A team approach draws upon the knowledge and skills of a number of people. One purpose of the committee is to create a division of labor to make the process of risk management more manageable and effective.

● The team approach integrates risk management more deeply into the life of the church or school. Rather than being a top down administrative approach, it arises out of the shared interests and concerns of the congregation or school.

● The appointment of a safety officer provides leadership and symbolism. The role of the safety officer can vary widely depending upon the individual's knowledge, expertise, and time available to devote to the position. One purpose of the role is to personalize the issue of safety within the church or school. The person becomes both a spokesperson and a symbol of safety. In a school, the safety officer is likely to be a paid staff member. Students can also fill safety roles. In a church, the safety officer is likely to be a congregational member.

3.1 The Risk Management Committee

Establishing a risk management committee helps to move away from an informal approach to risk management to one that is more structured, organized, and, in the end, more effective. For example, about half of churches claim to do some kind of building inspection. Yet most of these churches use no written guidelines, are unable to identify who is in charge of the inspection, and have no schedule for conducting it. If an inspection does occur, it tends to be haphazard and sporadic. A risk management committee can bring structure and substance to improve such efforts. The goal is to establish a team of qualified individuals who, following clear policies and procedures, engage in regular and thorough risk management practices. For this to occur, attention must be given to authorizing the work of the committee, clarifying its tasks, getting it staffed, and equipping it for action.

3.2 Authorizing and Overseeing the Work of the Committee

The risk management committee should be formally established and empowered by action of the governing board as a standing committee of the church or school. In turn, the committee should also report to the board. This is important because without board support the committee's work will often be hampered and perhaps even thwarted. A board member may be appointed to serve on the committee to facilitate communication. While support of the board does not guarantee a successful outcome, lack of support almost guarantees limited effectiveness.

Even when a risk management committee is formed, the board will always bear responsibility for the ultimate oversight of risk management practice. That is part of their fiduciary duty. In one sense, a risk management committee becomes an extension of the board's caretaking role in the life of the church or school.

The church or school board, more so than the risk management committee, must take leadership concerning liability issues. This is true for several reasons. First, the basis for liability often flows out of the actions and decisions of board members. Second, the board is responsible for the general formulation and oversight of policy. Often only the board has the power and authority to establish, implement, and enforce policies that impact potential liability. The risk management committee is more likely to make recommendations concerning policies and procedures than to create policies and procedures. This means that board members need training in risk management concerning their legal duties and fiduciary responsibilities.

The risk management committee, more so than the board, must take leadership to correct unsafe property conditions. Unsafe conditions may need immediate correction. Time may be of the essence. In such circumstances, the risk management team needs the authority and the power (often money) to follow through. The board retains accountability for the work of the committee.

In a few churches and schools, the initial motivation for establishing a risk management program arises within the board itself. On those occasions, establishment of a risk management committee is not a difficult task. Most churches, though, give little if any thought to risk management. If concerns do exist, they often come from a single individual who cares deeply about one issue. For example, in recent years the single most powerful issue that has motivated churches to engage in screening employees has been the sexual molestation of children. While an individual member of a congregation or a paid staff member can care deeply about that issue, it does not automatically follow that church leaders will share the concern. Even if they do share the concern it may be years before action is taken to implement a risk reduction program. While it may seem obvious to some that a church should have a comprehensive risk management program, church leaders do not always share that perspective. Gaining authorization is not an automatic process. It involves motivating church and school leaders and gaining the support of congregational members or the school family. This concern was addressed in the previous chapter.

3.3 Tasks of the Committee

Once the committee is authorized, its mission should be clarified. This model proposes that the risk management committee should complete the following tasks:

1. Prepare a written risk management plan;

2. Establish a protocol for safety inspections;

3. Establish and maintain a regular schedule for inspections;

4. Recruit inspectors;

5. Review insurance coverage to see that it is adequate;

6. Provide training to staff, members, and students about risk management practices;

7. Motivate congregational members or students with respect to the risk management goals;

8. Provide feedback to leaders and members concerning risk management needs and developments; and,

9. Develop contingency plans for crisis management.

How these tasks are carried out will vary from one church or school to another. A general overview of each task is provided below.

1. *Prepare a written risk management plan.* The plan should briefly touch upon each of the eight tasks described below for which the committee is responsible. In addition the plan should describe how the committee fits into the overall organizational structure of the church or school, including the

relationship between the committee and the board. In addition, the plan should clarify who is responsible for overseeing the risk management process including lines of authority, scope of authority, and communication between the committee and the board. The plan should also include a list of organizations and individuals who can provide assistance in completing the inspection protocols listed in point 2 below.

2. Establish a protocol for conducting safety inspections and selecting risk management techniques. Many churches and schools will become bogged down in completing this task if they attempt to create their own inspection checklists. Checklists are available from Christian Ministry Resources (800-222-1840) that have been prepared as companion resources to this handbook. In addition, most insurance companies also have checklists that can be helpful.

3. Establish and maintain a regular schedule for inspections and other tasks. To develop effective loss prevention and loss control measures, a congregation or school must engage in regular and thorough inspections. The committee should establish an inspection schedule for each area listed in point 2. Certain inspections, such as preparing for cold weather, should be synchronized with seasonal risks. The frequency of inspections will depend upon the nature of the risk. For example, a vehicle that will be used on an out of town trip should be inspected prior to each trip. Once a risk management program is in place, church staff members and congregational members can be trained and motivated to conduct their own informal inspections and to provide ongoing feedback to the committee on a continual basis.

4. Recruit inspectors. To the extent possible, members of the risk management committee should be capable of conducting the needed inspections. However, outside assistance may be required. A list of support organizations and consultants should be maintained in the written risk management plan. This issue is addressed later in this chapter regarding the recruitment of committee members.

5. Review the church's insurance coverage to see that it is adequate. Purchasing church insurance can be challenging and somewhat confusing. One important task of the risk management committee should be to examine the church's existing coverage including policy limits, deductibles, exclusions, riders and any excess coverage that might exist. Attention should also be given to the service and support that the insurance company and agent provide. This topic is covered in more detail in chapter 34.

6. Provide training to church staff and members about risk management practices. Training plays an important role in any congregation's risk management program. One goal is to equip both paid staff members, congregational members and students in schools to identify and report potential problems that pose a safety risk. A little training can greatly enhance the early identification of problems and provides the church or school with the opportunity to engage in prevention before losses occur.

7. Motivate congregational members with respect to the risk management goals of the church. As noted earlier in this book, roadblocks often exist within congregations that impede and even thwart risk management efforts. Yet when risk management goals and strategies are properly formed and integrated into the life and values of the congregation, support tends to be high. Church members value programs that provide safe environments for children and adults. Often, though, the emphasis within churches tends to be upon avoiding litigation or grounding risk management in legal or insurance concerns. That approach often turns people off. Proper motivation is dependent upon involving congregational members in the early stages of forming risk management strategies, and then providing training and ongoing communication about the church's efforts. This process is discussed more fully later in this chapter.

8. Provide feedback to church leaders concerning risk management needs. Church leaders need to stay informed concerning the activities and findings of the risk management committee. Each new board member should receive an orientation concerning the role of the risk management committee in the life of the church. While it is not necessary or even desirable to report every development, leaders should be updated at least monthly or quarterly. These reports help church leaders to maintain appreciation for the importance and role of risk management within the life of the church. When important issues emerge, the board should be notified immediately and prompt action should follow.

9. Develop contingency plans for crisis management. Crises strike quickly and create serious problems and confusion. Contingency planning can help a church or school reduce confusion, clarify roles, and control losses. One task of the risk management committee is to identify potential crises that might impact the church or school and to develop a contingency plan for each one. Chapter 4 is fully devoted to this important task.

As can be seen from the above description of tasks, the risk management committee has an important and challenging role to play in the life of a congregation and school. Once the specific tasks of the committee are clarified, recruitment can begin to staff the committee.

3.4 Staffing the Committee and Selecting the Safety Officer

Once the committee is authorized and its mission is clarified, the next task is to recruit qualified members to serve on it. As noted earlier, the makeup and functioning of the committee will vary from one church or school to another based on factors such as size, location, available funds, and the people involved. In addition, the process will be slightly different in schools than in churches. Schools will probably use faculty and staff members on the committee. Church committees will probably include mostly volunteer workers. The typical committee will have anywhere from 3-8 members, depending upon the size of the church or school and upon the qualifications of individuals available to serve on the committee. One key appointment is the selection a Safety Officer.

The Safety Officer

The Safety Officer (or Safety Coordinator) should be a member of the risk management committee. Perhaps the most important criterion in recruiting a

Safety Officer is to find someone who cares deeply about providing safe environments for both children and adults and who is willing to champion the cause of risk management. This individual needs the motivation and drive to help organize and sustain the church's risk management efforts. The Safety Officer takes on not only a leadership role for the committee, but also becomes a symbol for safety within the church or school. As such, the Safety Officer should feel comfortable speaking to groups of children and adults about safety issues and concerns. Once selected, the Safety Officer should be formally commissioned or recognized at a service or assembly. That elevates the importance of the position and provides an opportunity to educate congregational members or students on the safety efforts of the church or school.

Use of a title such as Safety Officer or Safety Coordinator helps the congregation more easily understand the role of this individual, and reinforces the objectives of the committee. The term also suggests some level of authority with respect to issues of safety within the congregation. A church or school should use whatever title that works best for them.

The Safety Office may serve as the chairperson of the risk management committee. Some responsibilities that might be included as part of the role include the following:

- Speaking to classes of children and adults about safety.

- Addressing the congregation or school assembly about safety issues.

- Writing articles for bulletins and newsletters.

- Having his or her picture used as part of a safety campaign.

- Possibly serving as chairperson of the risk management (or safety) committee.

- Taking the initiative to motivate others concerning safety.

- Being a symbol of safety to the congregation or school.

- Recruiting members for the risk management committee.

Selecting the committee members

In addition to the Safety Officer, attention should be given to recruiting the other members of the committee. If already appointed, the Safety Officer can play an important role in that process since he or she will be the leading spokesperson on safety issues.

If available, recruit committee members who are acquainted with the broad range of safety issues that are addressed in this handbook. The ideal situation is to find people with backgrounds in insurance, fire fighting, law enforcement, transportation, building security, law, child care, and the building trades (carpenters, electricians, plumbers, roofers, heating/ac). Other important qualifications include people who enjoy learning, care about the church or school, and are willing to devote some time to safety issues. Don't be concerned if they have limited knowledge about risk management. Training can be provided. Also, outside experts from the fire or police department are usually available to provide help. Outside consultants can also be used to provide additional training if needed. If necessary, the church or school should provide funds for training and consultants to get the committee established.

Most churches will find individuals within the congregation who can do some if not all of the inspection checklists. Some churches or schools may have to recruit outside help to get going, but often these resource people can train someone from within the congregation or school to carry out the inspection tasks for the future.

3.5 Equipping the Committee

When a committee is first established, it will often flounder if it is not provided with direct support and resources. A committee is more likely to get off to a good start if it receives a sample risk management plan and inspection checklists. The committee then has something to respond to which they can modify and adapt to meet the specific needs of the congregation or school. When such samples are not present, often the whole process quickly grinds to a halt. The church should establish a library of risk management resources. Most insurance companies will provide free pamphlets and other resources to assist their policyholders reduce risks. Contact several different companies that specialize in church insurance and request such literature. Invite experts from your community to speak to your committee members. Often, both the police and fire departments have public service offices that provide speakers and training on a range of issues. Have your committee meet with your insurance agent to discuss risk management concerns. Your committee will function best when members receive outside support, training, and adequate resources to get them off to a good start. Extensive resources that accompany this handbook are available from Christian Ministry Resources, (800-222-1840).

One of the key tasks in equipping committee members is providing an adequate orientation at the time a person joins the committee. The orientation should help the new member understand the purpose and role of the committee, clarify expectations concerning his or her specific duties, review the schedule of activities, examine the various checklists, clarify lines and scope of authority, and respond to any questions that the new member may have. Once a committee has been functioning for a while, it is also helpful to have the new member examine existing reports and findings from earlier inspections and reviews. That provides the new member with a sense of where problems have occurred and gives some insight on what to watch closely in the future.

3.6 Communication Issues

Communication plays a vital role in every group. Sustained and clear communication will help the committee perform better and stay motivated. The same is true for the congregation. A number of communication mediums can assist this process including the following: (1) written agendas, (2) inspection forms and checklists, (3) newsletter and bulletin articles, (4) posters, signs, and symbols, (5) activity reports, and (6) an annual report.

Written agendas. Prepare a written agenda for each meeting of the committee. A written agenda can help your committee stay focused when you meet and can help you accomplish more in less time. Invite members to propose agenda items. Make sure that each member of the committee receives the agenda prior to the meeting.

Inspection forms and checklists. Every inspection protocol should be in writing. A checklist format is best because it facilitates a thorough inspection with a simple way to identify problems or needs. Always provide space for written comments. Once completed the form or checklist should be used to make the needed corrections and then it should be filed and retained for future use. Maintaining historical records provides important data that can be used for future planning as well as evidence that the church has engaged in reasonable care if that should ever become an issue. Checklists are available from Christian Ministry Resources (800-222-1840).

Newsletter and bulletin articles. The church bulletin and newsletter provide an excellent way to inform and educate congregational members and to reinforce messages and behaviors that are important if the church is to maintain a safe environment. The more important the message, the greater the need to repeat it on a frequent basis. Key seasonal messages should be repeated on an annual basis.

Posters, signs, and symbols. Posters, signs and symbols are effective tools to communicate messages about safety. Use signs to warn people of hazards and to guide behavior. Posters can remind people of important safety tips. Increasingly, symbols are used to convey many different messages with respect to safety and risk management. Such symbols are available on many different and inexpensive clip art programs, are universally understood, and can be used to reinforce safety inside church or school facilities. Warning signs and posters can be used in nurseries, kitchens, furnace rooms, science labs, locker rooms, and other locations in which potential hazards exist.

Activity reports. Activity reports are used to document the activities of the risk management committee. They help church board members understand what committee members have done, and they also provide an historical record of the church's efforts with respect to risk management. Such reports can be important if the church is ever charged with negligence. A standardized form can be used to complete the report. A report should include the date, the persons involved, and a brief summary of the risk management task that was completed. It should be signed, preferably by two people involved in the project or by one person if only one person was involved. A copy of each report should be forwarded to the church board, and also distributed at the next meeting of the risk management committee. The original should be retained as part of the records of the committee.

An annual report. Most churches have an annual business meeting, which often includes reports from various departments and ministries within the church. The risk management committee should prepare an annual report which includes (1) a summary of the committee's work during the previous year, (2) plans for the coming year, and (3) any other safety message that is important for the church or school.

3.7 Sustaining the Committee

One key to sustaining any committee that is composed of volunteers is to show appreciation for the time and effort that they contribute on behalf of the church or school. Find tangibles ways of thanking the members of the risk management committee for their efforts including recognition from the pulpit, thank you cards, and notices in church or school publications such as your newsletter and bulletin. Like all positions in the church or school, turnover will occur and a need will exist to find new volunteers. It may be helpful to ask volunteers to serve a specific term such as three years with one-third of the committee rotating off each year. However, it may be difficult to find replacements for some individuals with key skills and knowledge. If possible, enlist these individuals to serve as long as they are willing, at least to assist with inspections.

3.8 Factors that Affect Attitudes and Responses

As noted in the introduction to this chapter, factors such as congregational or school size, location, culture, and organizational structure affect attitudes and responses concerning risk management. These and other factors shape the environment out of which a risk management plan emerges. While every congregation and school is unique, some generalizations can be made about each factor and its impact on the risk management process. Understanding these factors can help in the formation, orientation, and training of a risk management team.

Size

The size of a church or school affects the risk management process in several important ways. It becomes manifest in the number of people needed for the risk management team, the division of labor among team members and others, the frequency of risk management activities, and the level of concern for property and liability risks.

- *Team size.* As church size increases, the number of people involved in risk management also needs to increase. More people with a broad range of expertise will be needed to respond to numerous and diverse church programs. Large churches are more likely to have a full-time business administrator and other paid staff members who spend time on these issues and recognize their importance. Large congregations are also more likely to have members who can provide expert assistance with a broad range of risk management concerns. Small churches are often dependent upon a few people to do many things. Often, conflicts arise concerning competing priorities and limited time. In such situations, risk management may not be a high priority, in part because no sense of urgency exists regarding many risks, even though they may have high severity. While a small church may have a smaller team or committee, the goal should be to use as many volunteers as possible to get the job done.

- *Division of labor.* As just noted, in small churches a few people tend to do many different tasks. However, even in a small church it is possible to involve larger numbers of people in a variety of risk management duties. The issue becomes more one of the expertise that is available within the congregation, than of the size of the church. In large churches, a division of labor should occur reflecting higher levels of specialization and expertise. As congregations increase in size, the tasks associated with risk management tend to flow into various departments increasing the number of people involved in the risk management process. This requires extensive and ongoing training and education of staff members and congregational members. Our research also indicates that insurance agents devote more attention and time to large churches than to smaller ones. Not only do large churches have more help from members and staff, they also get more help from outside the church as well. They tend to develop extensive networks of individual and organizational relationships. The goal of every congregation, regardless of size, should be to make safety part of the fabric of congregational life. Everybody has something to contribute and the congregation benefits when everyone plays an active role, even if it is a small one.

- *Frequency of activities.* The number and frequency of church or school activities and programs affects the scope and timing of risk management tasks. As churches and schools increase in size, they tend to have more frequent and diverse programs. In turn, that impacts the risk management process. In a small church, it may be sufficient for a risk management committee to meet on a quarterly basis. The committee may be composed of three or four people who do all the inspections, planning, and handle the insurance. In a large church, the formal risk management process may involve many different groups. Risk management may be a standing agenda item for weekly staff meetings, departmental meetings, and board meetings. The risk management committee may meet monthly and use the services of outside consultants to conduct some inspections. Programs, such as a preschool, may require a daily playground inspection by one of the teachers. In part, the scope and nature of church or school activities affects the timing and agenda of risk management tasks.

- *Liability and property concerns.* Typically, leaders in small churches are less concerned about liability issues than are leaders in large churches. High levels of trust exist within small congregations because people know one another. Members do not believe that anyone would molest a child or embezzle funds. As a result, they are unlikely to initiate a screening program or do background checks. In addition, fewer accidents occur. Often, for small churches and schools, the main risk management focus is to obtain the insurance necessary to provide property and liability coverage. Additional loss prevention or loss control efforts may be given a low priority. Leaders in large churches tend to reflect a broader range of risk management concerns that include both property and liability issues. Often they are concerned about their own personal liability. In large congregations, relationships are quite different. Members do not all know one another. As a result, the rationale for screening volunteer workers may be more easily accepted. Churches, both large and small, often do not know how to address risk management concerns in a formal, organized way. Size may impact the breadth of concern, but not the quality of the response. Most churches, regardless of size, do not have a formal risk management plan.

Location

Our research and experience indicate that geographical location has an impact on how churches and schools approach risk management. The main differences are seen between churches and schools located in rural settings or small towns and those located in more cosmopolitan settings.

- *Rural settings and small towns.* Rural churches and schools focus more on property and safety concerns than on liability concerns. Generally, they do not feel a strong need to engage in risk management practices such as screening volunteer workers to reduce liability exposure. In part this is true because people often know and trust one another. If conflict does arise, litigation is less likely than in urban or suburban settings. While these churches and schools are less likely to face a lawsuit, they are also less likely to have taken action to reduce liability risks if a lawsuit should occur. Churches and schools located in rural settings and small towns often feel vulnerable to fire, accidents, crime or vandalism because of their isolated location. Property insurance is important, but often finances are limited. Loss prevention and control take on increased significance in these areas because medical help or fire fighters are not always nearby. Students in rural schools experience about the same level of theft as do students in other locations, but are less likely to experience acts of violence.

- *Other settings.* Churches and schools in suburbs, urban settings, and medium size towns face a higher frequency of litigation and more severe judgments than do churches in small towns or rural settings. These churches and schools are also more willing to engage in practices such as conducting criminal background checks on paid and volunteer staff members. Liability risk becomes a key motivational factor for board members. Violence is higher in urban schools than in other locations.

Culture and ethnicity

Culture and ethnicity have an impact on risk management practice, especially on liability concerns. Our experience indicates that non-English speaking congregations often reflect a high level of community and camaraderie among the members. Litigation is less likely to occur. In part this may be true because of the cohesion that exists within the congregation, but also because some individuals are suspicious of the legal system and want to avoid contact with it. For example, in working with some Hispanic congregations in the southwest, fears existed that conducting criminal background checks on volunteers who work with children might impact families who have illegal immigrant relatives living with them. Risk management must be approached in a way that reinforces community and diminishes fear, especially of potential legal entanglements.

Congregational structure

Congregational structure impacts the decision-making process within a congregation. Some congregations can make decisions quickly and adapt to changing circumstances. In others, the decision-making process is slow, and even simple decisions take time. Congregational governance affects the power and authority of a risk management team. A team needs sufficient authority to correct unsafe conditions. Often that involves some expense so budgetary considerations must be taken into account. The working relationship between the church board and the risk management team requires careful clarification. Some issues include the following:

- *Unsafe property conditions.* It must be clear who takes the initiative, and under what conditions, to correct unsafe conditions. Does the risk management committee have the authority to act, or does it refer the problem to the board for action?

- *Reporting.* One important issue is how the committee reports to the board for both oversight and decision-making. How often are reports made? What is the purpose of a report?

- *Accountability.* Committee members should know in advance how their work will be evaluated. Who sets the standards for the committee—the board or the committee itself? Who evaluates the work?

- *Crisis management.* During a crisis decisions must be made quickly. Roles, authority and power must be clarified between the board and the committee. For example, during a crisis, how does information flow—who receives priority notification first, and under what circumstances? Who is the spokesperson for the church or school?

The factors of size, location, ethnicity, and organizational structure all interact with one another. Their impact will vary from one congregation or school to another. Thus, the risk management process described in this chapter will also vary based upon the needs and perspectives of individual congregations or schools. In some cases the felt need concerning liability risks may be lower. More emphasis may be placed on property than liability. Some committees will be small; others will be large. In some a few people will do most of the work; in others many people will be involved including outside experts and consulatnts. This challenges boards and committees to be flexible, to implement policies and procedures that reduce risk, and retain the support of congregational members. As noted in chapter 2, this is more likely to happen when the risk management practice are grounded in biblical and theological foundations, and make a direct connection to the deeply held values of the congregation or school family.

Summary

Churches and schools need a formal structure to implement and sustain a risk management strategy. One model is to create a risk management committee and appoint a safety officer. Factors such as size, location, ethnicity, and organizational structure will impact how the committee and safety officer function.

To establish its authority and power, the church or school board should authorize the establishment of the risk management committee. While tasks may vary slightly from one committee to another, some that deserve attention include the following:

(1) Preparing a written risk management plan;

(2) Establishing a protocol for safety inspections;

(3) Establishing and maintaining a regular schedule for inspections;

(4) Recruiting inspectors;

(5) Reviewing the insurance coverage;

(6) Providing training to staff, members, and students about risk management practices;

(7) Motivating congregational members and students with respect to the risk management goals;

(8) Providing feedback to leaders and members concerning risk management needs and developments;

(9) Developing contingency plans for crisis management.

The committee should be composed of members who can assist with the planning, inspection process, and training responsibilities of the committee. Sometimes outside experts may be needed to assist the committee with its work.

The committee is more likely to succeed if it gets off to a good start. It needs an adequate budget and resources such as a sample risk management plan and inspection checklists. As it performs its work, communication is important between the committee and the board, and also with church members or students. The use of written agendas, inspection forms, checklists, newsletter and bulletin articles, posters, signs, symbols, and activity reports can enhance the communication process.

Tangibles expressions of appreciation can help sustain any group of volunteers. Turnover should be planned for by rotating members on a periodic basis. Individuals with special expertise should be retained as long as they are willing to serve.

In addition to routine risk management tasks, a church or school should also be prepared for a crisis. That requires a different planning model. Crisis management is discussed in the next chapter.

CHAPTER 4. CRISIS MANAGEMENT FOR CHURCHES AND SCHOOLS

Crisis management is one dimension of risk management. In general crises do not occur frequently, but when they do happen the loss is often severe. One popular definition of a crisis is big trouble that arises suddenly.[1] Since crises are infrequent, many churches and schools do not prepare for them. No sense of urgency exists, and no one really expects to be hit by one.

What may be a crisis for one church or school may not be for another. Factors such as size, organizational skill, and the circumstances surrounding the event all affect the degree of trouble a church or school may experience. Leaders that can spot trouble early and intervene in ways to dispel it can avoid a potential crisis. Some crises, such as a hurricane, provide advance warning. Others, such as the moral failure of a pastor, may present red flags. Sometimes they just strike without notice and it is not possible to prevent them. What happens afterwards, however, is a different story. A planned response is possible to any crisis.

Crises affect churches and schools in many, and often unpredictable ways. Facilities can be destroyed or damaged, and programs can become interrupted or terminated. Giving and attendance may decline. The image of the church or school in the community may be harmed. Division may occur concerning the support of staff members. Sometimes a crisis pulls a congregation or school family together. Other times they can be pulled apart. To a large degree the outcomes are affected by the leadership that emerges during the crisis.

Churches and schools can be prepared in advance for a crisis. While a church or school may not know in advance that a crisis will strike, they can identify potential crises for which they should be prepared. Several of the most common crises that affect churches and schools include the following:

- Natural disasters
- Fires
- The accidental death of a member or student while participating in a church or school program
- The criminal behavior of a pastor, principal, staff member, volunteer, or student
- The moral failure of a pastor, principal, or staff member
- The suicide of a pastor, principal, staff member, congregational member, or student
- The disability of a pastor or principal
- Lawsuits brought against the church or school
- An act of violence

Confusion often accompanies a crisis. Church and school leaders may feel overwhelmed and uncertain of what to do. Since crises tend to be infrequent, most people have little experience in responding to them. Developing a crisis

---

[1] Otto Lerbinger, *The Crisis Manager* (Mahwah, New Jersey: Lawrence Erlbaum Associates, 1997), p.4

management strategy can prepare a church or school to reduce confusion, clarify responsibilities, and help to control losses. A key component of crisis management is to develop contingency plans. One of the purposes of a contingency plan is to remove ambiguity during a time of crisis. This is accomplished by establishing procedures that people can follow if a particular crisis should occur.

In order to establish a crisis management strategy, the contingency plans for a church and school should clarify the following concerns:

- Areas of vulnerability. *Key question: what are the most likely crises for which planning should occur?*

- Crisis management responsibilities. *Key question: who should do what if the crisis occurs?*

- Crisis Communications. *Key questions: what should be communicated, how should it be communicated, when should it be communicated; and to whom should it be communicated?*

- Facility, Staffing and Program Concerns. *Key questions: how will the church or school respond if facilities are unusable, if staff members are no longer present, or if ministry or school activities are suspended?*

- Financial Concerns. *Key questions: what steps should be taken to safeguard the church or school financially if a crisis should occur; where will funds come from to cope with losses that may occur?*

4.1 Developing Contingency Plans

Developing a crisis contingency plan is similar to making a capital investment. A contingency plan is an asset that can serve the church or school for many years. Furthermore, crisis planning can be approached somewhat on a modular basis. For example, the effort to establish a crisis communication plan can have multiple uses. Once a plan is created for one crisis, it can be used for other purposes as well.

Crisis planning should be one of the tasks of the church's safety or risk management committee. The committee may invite other individuals to help prepare a plan. The planning process should include a *normative* and *comparative* needs assessment. The purpose of the normative assessment is to solicit information and input from *recognized experts* such as the Red Cross, insurance companies, and federal agencies on specific crises. The comparative assessment should obtain *sample crisis plans* from other organizations such as the public school district, the local YMCA, scouting organizations and others that can provide assistance in the preparation of your own plan.

When complete, the crisis management plan should be in writing. The plan should be streamlined and easy to follow. It does not need to be lengthy. Often, the use of a flowchart format to identify tasks and steps that can be easily followed is the best approach.

Those responsible for carrying out the plan should receive training on an annual basis. For example, the hurricane season begins each summer and lasts until the fall. Churches in hurricane zones should review the crisis plans annually just as the hurricane season begins. Church board members should review contingency planning procedures once a year, perhaps when new members join the board. Teachers generally receive in-service training prior to the beginning of the school year. That is a good time to provide training for them. The idea is to establish periodic, routine patterns for training. Failure to do this will diminish the value of the contingency plans. They will end up collecting dust on a shelf. Crises occur unexpectedly, and often without warning. To respond effectively, those responsible must stay informed both on duties and procedures that can reduce harm to human life and to the ministry of the church or school. The goal is to reduce ambiguity during a crisis by clarifying roles, policies and procedures that should be followed during the crisis period.

4.2 Step 1: Identifying Areas of Vulnerability

A number of factors including geographical location, size, programs, governance, and legal status impact the vulnerability of a congregation or school. Some churches are located in a hurricane zone; others are not. Rural churches are less likely to be sued than suburban or urban churches. Large congregations are more likely to have serious personal injuries on church property than smaller congregations. An unincorporated church or school, for example, faces different risks than one that is incorporated.

While every congregation and school is unique, certain similarities also exist concerning vulnerabilities that can lead to a crisis. While the following list is not exhaustive, most congregations and schools should have contingency plans that address the following areas:

Natural disasters. Each natural disaster that might impact the church or school should be identified (see chapter 15). Most leaders know if the church or school is located in a tornado, flood, or hurricane zone. They may not know, however, if they are located along an earthquake fault. So much attention is given to California, for example, that people fail to understand that serious earthquakes can occur in several regions of the United States. The local Red Cross can identify natural disasters that pose a local threat. A contingency plan should be developed for each identified disaster (see the appendices at the end of this chapter).

Fire. Fire is a risk to every church and school. A contingency plan is clearly needed to protect human life, safeguard property, and respond to the aftermath of a fire (see chapter 13).

Sexual molestation of children. Every congregation should be prepared to respond to an allegation of child sexual molestation. Few events shake a congregation to the degree that child sexual molestation does. It creates a crisis of the highest degree. Our research indicates that in a typical year, 3 percent of congregations respond to an allegation of child sexual molestation. The likelihood of an allegation increases with congregational size, and lawsuits are more likely in urban and suburban churches, or when multiple victims are present. Congregational leaders need to know how to respond to the victim, to the alleged perpetrator, to congregational members, and to the media.

Moral failure. The moral failure of a pastor or principal can create a crisis for a congregation or school. The most common problem is sexual misconduct. Church members are generally in a state of disbelief and lay leaders generally have no idea of how to respond or what to say. The potential for this problem can be reduced through establishing proper boundaries (see chapter 24).

Embezzlement. Embezzlement occurs far more frequently than churches know. Most embezzlement in churches goes undetected. On some occasions, often after large amounts of money have been stolen, the embezzler is caught. Suddenly the church is embroiled in legal and criminal proceedings with members feeling betrayed and shocked. Leaders often feel confused and guilty, and a crisis of confidence can spread throughout the congregation. This problem can be avoided through proper internal controls (see chapter 17).

Conflict and Lawsuits. Historically, lawsuits have not been a major source of concern to churches and schools. That is no longer true. Today churches face civil lawsuits similar to other organizations with claims ranging into the millions of dollars, often in excess of insurance coverage. These lawsuits often create division within the congregation resulting in high levels of stress and tension, as well as financial problems. Leaders should develop contingency plans to respond to lawsuits and conflict in ways that promote peace and reconciliation.

Violence. Schools should have a contingency plan for acts of violence (see chapter 12). While mass shootings, for example, are rare, no school can afford to be unprepared if one should occur. Mass shootings in two religious organizations in 1999 raised the level of concern among church leaders on how to respond to such threats. A more fundamental concern for churches, however, is to have a plan in place that responds to threats from transients or homeless people that come to a church seeking help. Often, the only person present at the church to respond to such needs is a church secretary. Churches should provide secretaries and other employees training in responding to such situations (see chapter 16).

4.3 Step 2: Defining Roles and Responsibilities

Most churches have few paid staff members and rely heavily on volunteers. Leadership during a crisis will involve both paid staff members as well as volunteer workers. To a large degree, the nature of the crisis shapes the roles that are needed. Some of the more important tasks include the following:

- *Emergency communication.* Someone must be responsible for emergency communication. This may include contacting 911, setting off an alarm, or contacting other people and organizations that fall under emergency notification. This is addressed below as part of Step 3, the crisis communication strategy (also, see appendix 4G at the end of this chapter).

- *Evacuation procedures.* Staff members, teachers, paid employees, and volunteer workers should know how to evacuate the building during an emergency. That may include leading others of different age groups and mobility to a safe location (see appendix 4C at the end of this chapter).

- *Moving to a safe place.* Staff members, teachers, paid employees, and volunteer workers should know where to go in the facilities to find safety during a tornado, hurricane, or severe weather. That may include leading others of different age groups and mobility to a safe location.

- *Building shutdown.* A building shutdown helps limit losses during a fire or natural disaster. The shutdown includes turning off the appropriate utilities such as gas and power, and taking all other necessary precautions to protect the property as time and safety permit (see appendix 4D at the end of this chapter).

- *Using fire extinguishers.* Quick intervention can prevent serious fire damage. Staff members need training and practice in using a fire extinguisher. They must know when intervention is safe and sensible and when they should evacuate.

- *Building inspection.* A building must be inspected for safety following any natural disaster. This requires following safety and inspection protocols (see appendix 4E at the end of this chapter).

- *Caregivers.* Natural disasters often require evacuations. Churches need a plan to help vulnerable members such as the elderly or disabled to evacuate, and also to check on them following a natural disaster to see that they are okay. Churches and schools also need a plan to provide support and care to those who are victims of violence, as well as to their family members (see appendix 4F at the end of this chapter).

- *Spokesperson.* During a crisis, a church or school needs a designated spokesperson that is trained and prepared to respond to the media (see appendix 4G at the end of this chapter).

- *Legal decisions.* Some crises require immediate legal input to avoid potential liability or to minimize a loss that has occurred. Churches and schools need to have a good working relationship with a legal counsel that they know and trust.

- *Making key contacts.* A church or school may need to contact a list of key people such as an insurance agent, denominational leaders, a building contractor, and others. The list should be kept current and should be accessible in more than one location during a crisis.

4.4 Step 3: Developing a Crisis Communication Strategy

Communication is a vital component of a crisis contingency plan. When a crisis occurs, individuals generally find themselves in an ill-defined situation. People are not sure what to do. Often they lack the experience and the knowledge needed to respond effectively. As a result confusion levels are high. The ability to communicate rapidly, factually, and helpfully are vitally important. A crisis contingency plan should provide guidance in conducting emergency communication, communicating with congregational members or the school family, and responding to the media.

Emergency communication

Emergency communication has several dimensions to it, which differ depending on the scope and nature of the crisis. The emergency communication plan should clarify communication roles and identify and prioritize each individual or group with which to communicate.

At the top of the list is the issue of reporting a crisis or seeking assistance in the midst of a crisis. The first contact should always be those who safeguard life and property. When human life or property are at risk, the proper response is to call 911. This has become a well known fact for most people, but it should not be taken for granted. Individuals should be taught to do this. Other phone numbers and individuals may also be listed, such as poison control, the police, or the fire department. Crisis phone numbers should be posted next to each office phone.

Other forms of emergency communication can be used in addition to phones or personal communication. Sounding alarms is another common form of emergency communication. The use of fire alarms, for example, can signal that a building should be evacuated. A direct alarm to the fire station may facilitate immediate help. A bell or buzzer that sounds in the pastor's office or in other locations in the church may indicate an emergency need in the church office, such as help in responding to a transient or street person. The secretary may simply push a button located under the desk to signal for help.

In order to contact a large number of people quickly, a system must be in place. One approach is to use a phone tree. A phone tree is an effective means to notify key leaders of the crisis so that an emergency response team can respond quickly. Each person called must know whom to call and what to do in such circumstances. The information and the plan flow quickly from one person to the entire crisis leadership network. For example, a phone tree may be used to assemble a team to initiate a building shutdown prior to a hurricane or following an earthquake.

Once the primary emergency contacts have been made, others should be promptly notified. That may include the insurance company, denominational leaders, building contractors, or an attorney depending on the nature of the crisis. Some individuals on the contact list do not need to be notified as quickly as others. In addition to a phone tree, churches can also use bulk e-mail programs, a web site, and fax distribution systems to disseminate information quickly to large numbers of people. When using these systems, however, the sender does not know with certainty when the message will be read. These approaches work well when information is being disseminated to those with a lower communication priority. In short, the contingency plan should use at least two systems: one that enables quick communication to key leaders, and one that facilitates speedy, congregational or school wide communication.

Communicating with congregational members or to the school family

The ability to communicate effectively with congregational members or to the school family during a period of crisis is critical. Rumors and partial information flow quickly during a crisis. One task of leadership is to keep individuals informed in a timely way concerning information in which there is a shared and common interest. The timing, audience, and content of information depends largely on the nature of a crisis.

When time is of the utmost importance, a phone tree is often used. The phone tree may be limited to key leaders or extended throughout the entire congregation. For a phone tree to be effective, each person must know whom he or she is to call and have access to the list and phone numbers. The list must be kept current with accurate phone numbers. That can be a challenging task and one that should be coordinated with the church or school secretary.

Communicating sensitive information

Confidential information, on the other hand, must be disseminated with high levels of care and discretion. The focus is not on speed but on maintaining privacy. For example, church leaders that respond to a crisis of moral failure or to the sexual molestation of a child must ensure that they communicate only to other individuals with a need to know. Often this will include congregational members, but not the general public. Precautions must be taken to maintain confidentiality such as mailing the information in a letter marked "privileged and confidential" that goes only to church members, and which notifies them that the information must remain confidential. Whenever confidential information must be shared to the congregation or school family, the assistance of legal counsel should be sought concerning the content of and the manner in which the information is presented. Finally, leaders should differentiate between factual information and opinion or commentary. During periods of a crisis, speculation and opinion should be avoided. Leaders should stick to the facts of what is known.

Communicating with vulnerable members

One paramount concern immediately prior to and following a natural disaster is communicating with vulnerable members of the congregation. Some members may need special assistance to evacuate their home, or may have medical or physical needs that require assistance. Once a threshold level is reached in the crisis, the contingency plan should initiate a communication strategy to collect or disseminate information to vulnerable members so that the church can provide the support that is needed during the crisis period. Since hurricanes provide advance warning, help can be provided before hand. With many natural disasters, however, the communication will automatically follow the event.

Responding to allegations

Communication is also vital in responding to allegations of misconduct or to a lawsuit. Unfortunately, many church leaders respond to victims in ways that deepen their pain and alienate them from the church. This has been especially true regarding church members who are victims of sexual molestation. The tendency has been for church leaders to engage in a threefold pattern of denial, minimization, and blame. The victim brings an allegation to a church leader against someone else in the church and the leader just cannot believe it. The leader may deny the allegation by saying something like, "This just cannot be true. I know that person. He would never do such a thing." Or the leader minimizes the importance of the allegation by saying something similar to, "It doesn't sound like it was that bad," or "But it only happened once." Finally, the leader may say something that removes the responsibility for the act from the offender and places it on the victim. A comment may be made such as, "Why didn't you stop him?" or "You should have told someone earlier." In all three cases the victim begins to feel re-victimized. This drives the person away from the church, and to someone who will listen—often an attorney. On the other hand, church leaders that take allegations seriously, that reach out and communicate a genuine sense of caring and compassion, and who take steps to see that such actions will not be repeated, help the victim and reduce the potential for an adversarial relationship.

Communicating with the media

In recent years, scandals involving churches have made front page and even national news. The media is especially attracted to sexual misconduct, lawsuits, violence, and financial mismanagement within churches or schools. These events bring the local television reporters, along with their minicams, directly to the church or school and to the homes of church leaders. The reporting can do great damage to the public image of the church or school. Churches and schools should have clear procedures on communicating with the media if such a situation should occur. One person should be designated as spokesperson and all calls and inquiries should go to that individual. The spokesperson should be provided with guidelines on what to say, and the content should be reviewed in advance with legal counsel if the crisis involves potential litigation. In the midst of a crisis, leaders should all speak with one voice. Information should be timely and accurate.

A scandal can tarnish the image of a church or school, and in some cases the media reporting can be devastating. How the church or school is viewed depends in part on whether it is a victim of a devious scheme or some malevolent action, or whether it is reaping the fruit of its own negligence. If it is the former, the public may express sympathy and support. However, if it is the latter, individuals are likely to develop a negative and perhaps even hostile attitude toward the church or school. The problem is that in the early stages of a crisis the facts are often difficult to sort through and portray accurately. When a crisis occurs, church leaders should not remain passive with respect to the media.

Often, the first image the public gets is from a newspaper or television report that provides the details of the scandalous action, but generally in a limited context. The church, for example, may be portrayed in a very negative light. Talking with the media as early as possible provides the church with an opportunity to provide the reporter and the public a more complete picture. For this to be done well, however, a planned response is needed. The spokesperson can emphasize that the church takes such allegations seriously and is taking steps to respond according to church procedures, and is cooperating with any law enforcement agencies that are involved. Secondly, the spokesperson should also emphasize the church's determination to respond to the needs of victims as well as to the alleged offender. Thirdly, the spokesperson can help place the events in some context, describing the precautions that the church has taken and will continue to take to prevent such actions. A church that has taken risk management seriously, and can communicate that to the public, can improve its public image and diminish negative fallout. Churches or schools that say nothing give an impression of hiding something. The first image that is portrayed is a lasting one for many people. Furthermore, what is front page news on the first few days of a story may not be later on. The church or school wants to respond quickly and early to help provide a balanced perspective to the reporting when it gets its widest exposure.

Church leaders should be prepared to respond quickly to negative stories. To facilitate this process, the church should maintain a database of media contacts, including e-mail addresses, fax numbers, and phone numbers (the database can also be used for routine press releases). Leaders should correct inaccuracies in reported stories and provide additional information when helpful. The capacity to respond quickly and accurately is important during a time of crisis when the image of the church or school is under assault.

4.5 Step 4: Responding to Facility, Staffing, and Program Concerns

Some crises, such as a natural disaster or a fire, can leave a church or school without useable facilities. Suddenly there is no place to gather. Often in such situations, other congregations or organizations within the community reach out to help. The best approach, though, is to have alternative arrangements already in place before the crisis occurs. The contingency plan should identify possible meeting sites such as schools, park facilities, recreational centers and other congregations that have facilities that could be used in the case of an emergency. Each potential site should be contacted to determine if its facilities would be available during emergency circumstances. In order to sustain church or school programs, modifications may necessary. Times, locations, and dates may need to be changed on short notice. Again, effectiveness becomes dependent upon having a good communication network in place.

In some crises, such as the moral failing of a pastor, an interim pastor may be needed until a resolution of the crisis occurs. Some denominational groups make arrangements for interim pastors, but many churches are left on their own to work out such arrangements. Church leaders should review how this process would work if the need for it should ever arise. A church is far better off having advance guidelines for such circumstances than flying by the seat of the pants in the midst of turbulence and chaos.

4.6 Step 5: Organizing Emergency Funding

All crises, regardless of the nature, take some toll on finances. While most churches and schools rely upon insurance to provide funds to recover from losses, insurance is generally insufficient to cover every expense. Factors such as deductibles, co-insurance, policy limits, and exclusions from coverage affect the level of funds available from insurance. Church attendance and giving patterns may also decline. Suddenly church members may face their own personal losses if they too are victims of a natural disaster. They may have less money to give to the church. Or if the crisis is attached to a scandal, contributions may be withheld until trust is re-established. Often, during lawsuits, members may decide to withhold contributions if they feel their money is being used to pay large attorney fees or settlements. As a result, church and school leaders should have a risk financing plan in place to address the financial needs that surface during a period of crisis. That may mean establishing a reserve or contingency fund for emergency use, or developing a line of credit with a local lending institution. If the plan is to use a line of credit, it should be established as part of the overall contingency plan rather than waiting and trying to do it under crisis conditions.

Summary

A crisis can occur without warning, striking fast, and leave a church or school facing big trouble. When a crisis occurs, confusion often makes the situation even worse. Having a contingency plan helps to respond both to the threat and to the aftermath of a crisis. It can reduce losses and minimize the amount of time and expense needed for a full recovery.

Contingency planning is built around a five-step process:

1. Identify areas of vulnerability. For most churches and schools this list includes natural disasters, fire, sexual molestation of children, moral failure of leaders, embezzlement or other crimes, conflict, lawsuits, and acts of violence.

2. Define roles and responsibilities of both paid and volunteer staff members.

3. Develop a crisis communication strategy including emergency communication, communicating with congregational members or the school family, and communicating with the media.

4. Respond to needs related to facility damage, staffing, and program concerns.

5. Organize emergency funding.

In part two of this handbook, which follows after the appendices at the end of this chapter, risk management strategies are applied to risks that endanger people in church and school programs. Topics include nurseries, playgrounds, recreational programs, transportation, ergonomics, construction projects, slips and falls, and acts of violence.

APPENDIX 4A:
DEVELOPING A CRISIS MANAGEMENT PLAN

As noted in chapter 4 on crisis management, a crisis creates serious trouble that appears quickly and often without warning. A crisis management plan provides church and school leaders with one tool to minimize the turbulence and losses that result from the crisis. Yet, because most crises are rare, few leaders develop a crisis management plan. One task of the safety committee should be to prepare a crisis management plan for each potential crisis that could impact the church or school. This appendix provides practical assistance in completing that task.

The Modular Approach

The strategy used in the following appendices is a modular one. The idea is to create "building blocks" that can be used to construct a variety of crisis management plans. To accomplish this, attention is given to the following concerns:

❑   Appendix 4B: Identifying Areas of Vulnerability

❑   Appendix 4C: Evacuation Plans

❑   Appendix 4D: Emergency Plans for Building Shutdown

❑   Appendix 4E: Emergency Plans for Damaged Facilities

❑   Appendix 4F: Emergency Plans to Assist the Injured

❑   Appendix 4G: Emergency Communication Plans

❑   Appendix 4H: Emergency Financial Plans

❑   Appendix 4I: Training Plans

Each church and school will have to complete planning for all of the modules for one basic reason—the risk of fire. Being prepared for a fire requires a plan for each individual module. The same is true for all natural disasters. Planning for other crises, such as the moral failure of a leader, requires the use of only selected modules. Once the planning has been completed for each module, detailed plans can be implemented for almost any crisis.

To begin the planning process, work through one module at a time. Complete each action step. Some modules incorporate checklists to be completed if and when the crisis occurs. Once you have completed working through each module, the foundation will be in place for a broad-based crisis management strategy.

For checklists on specific crises, see the companion inspection checklists to this handbook that are available from Christian Ministry Resources (800-222-1840).

APPENDIX 4B:
IDENTIFYING AREAS OF VULNERABILITY

The first step is to identify your areas of vulnerability. For purposes of planning, these areas have been divided into two sections: natural disasters and other crises. Since not all natural disasters affect every geographical area, a church or school only needs to plan for those disasters that impact their region. On the other hand, many other crises, such as those listed below, can strike any church or school. As a result, a plan is needed for each crisis in this second category.

Natural Disasters

Key point. Check with your local chapter of the Red Cross to identify the natural disasters that could strike in your area. For more information on each natural disaster, see chapter 15.

Place a check next to each natural disaster that could impact your church or school:

❑ Hurricane/Typhoon

❑ Tornado

❑ Earthquake

❑ Flood

❑ Mudslide/Landslide

❑ Volcano

❑ Other _____

Each natural disaster requires completing work on all of the planning modules.

Other Crises

The following crises can strike any organization, regardless of location. While planning for a fire requires the use of all of the planning modules, the remaining organizational crises vary in which modules they use. All churches and schools should have a plan in place for each of the following:

Crisis	Modules Possibly Needed for Crisis Planning
❑ Fire	All modules
❑ Moral failure of a leader	Training, communication, assisting the injured, financial plans
❑ Criminal conduct	Training, communication, assisting the injured, financial plans
❑ Acts of violence or suicide	Training, communication, assisting the injured, financial plans
❑ Death or disability of a leader	Training, communication, financial plans
❑ Personal injuries	Training, communication, assisting the injured, financial plans
❑ Litigation	Training, communication, financial plans

APPENDIX 4C: EVACUATION PLANS

Some evacuations, such as with a fire, require an immediate and speedy response. Others, such as with a hurricane, may occur with advance notice. In either case, having a plan and a trained staff can minimize personal injury and property loss.

Evacuation plans can be divided into four parts: (1) evacuation of buildings; (2) evacuation of a building and the need to relocate to a different location in the same city; (3) responding to a mandatory evacuation of a city or area; and (4) assisting with the evacuation of individuals with special needs.

1. Evacuation of buildings

Emergency planning factors for evacuating a building

❑   1.01   Obtain floor plans for each building

❑   1.02   Using the floor plans, identify two escape routes for each room designating a primary and a secondary route (note: use staircases—do not use elevators unless directed to do so by a uniformed firefighter or other safety officer).

Key point. If a window is used for evacuation purposes, make sure that it is not painted or nailed shut.

❑   1.03   Post a copy of the evacuation plan in each room.

❑   1.04   Establish an alarm system or signal to evacuate and contact 911.

Key point. If individuals who are hearing impaired use your facility, install a warning system such as a flashing light to indicate the need to evacuate.

❑   1.05   Instruct staff to close doors when exiting rooms.

❑   1.06   Have all exits clearly marked.

❑   1.07   Install emergency lighting and test on a regular basis.

❑   1.08   Establish a list of people in the building who may need special assistance in evacuating and designate a specific trained individual (or individuals) to assist them.

❑   1.09   Establish a list of vital documents or items that should be removed from the building and designate a specific trained individual (or individuals) to remove them as long as time permits and it is safe to do so.

Key point. Maintain an evacuation box that contains an extra supply of checks, a list of key individuals and phone numbers, computer back-up data, and key ID numbers or account numbers.

Key point. Keep all vital documents in a security box at a bank or as a second choice, in a fireproof safe.

Key point. Do not jeopardize any person's safety to retrieve documents.

❑   1.10   Designate a specific trained individual to shut off utilities as long as time permits and it is safe to do so.

Key point. Do not jeopardize any person's safety to shut off utilities.

Key point. If natural gas is shut off, only a licensed professional should turn it back on. Check with your gas company in advance to obtain their recommendation for emergency procedures whether or not to shut off the gas supply.

❑   1.11   Using the site map, identify safe gathering points at least 150 feet away from the building for those who evacuate.

❑   1.12   Develop a plan for leaders and staff members to conduct a head count to account for all people in the building.

❑   1.13   Instruct staff and leaders to keep people away from any downed power lines, or broken electrical lines.

❑   1.14   Instruct staff not to allow occupants to re-enter the building until directed to do so by an authorized person.

Key point. Some safety officers or firefighters may not be in uniform. Seeing individuals in plain clothes entering an evacuated building does not mean that it is safe to re-enter.

❑   1.15   Include emergency response information in the church directory or in a student handbook. Designate a backup phone number where people can call to get information.

Action steps for remaining in the building, but relocating to a safe location

❑   1.16   Using the floor plans, identify the safest locations within each building for occupants to remain until the crisis passes.

❑   1.17   Train staff members on the location and use of safe areas.

2. Evacuation to a different location in the same city

Key point. If you must evacuate a building and leave the property, it is important that you have a site selected in advance to which you may go.

❑   2.01   Identify a specific gathering point such as another church or school in another part of the city.

❑   2.02   Using a map, identify evacuation routes to the point of rendezvous.

❑   2.03   Include emergency response information in the church directory or in a student handbook. Designate a backup phone number where people can call to get information.

3. Responding to a mandatory evacuation of a city

Key point. Some communities have evacuation plans in place. Check with your local Red Cross or city government to obtain copies of such plans.

If your local government mandates an evacuation:

❏ 3.01 Identify a specific gathering point such as another church or school in a different city.

❏ 3.02 Using a map, identify main and secondary evacuation routes out of the city to the point of rendezvous.

❏ 3.03 Fuel all vehicles as soon as the possibility of an evacuation exists.

❏ 3.04 Establish a list of individuals with special needs within the congregation who would need help to evacuate and an action plan to assist them (see section 4.)

❏ 3.05 Initiate a building shutdown (see Appendix 4D).

❏ 3.06 Drivers of church or school vehicles should have clear and unequivocal instructions never to drive across roads with moving water during flood conditions.

❏ 3.07 Include emergency response information in the church directory or in a student handbook. Designate a backup phone number where people can call to get information.

4. Evacuation of individuals with special needs

Key point. If a citywide evacuation becomes necessary, some individuals may require special assistance to evacuate. This may include elderly, individuals with mobility problems, the blind, and other individuals with physical or mental impairments.

❏ 4.01 Maintain a list of members who will require special assistance.

❏ 4.02 Designate trained individuals to assist with the evacuation of specific individuals, including babies in a nursery.

❏ 4.03 Have all vulnerable individuals complete an emergency health information card that includes the following: insurance information, list of physicians, medications, allergies, emergency contact list and phone numbers, and other special needs. Retain copies of the cards. In addition, those assisting with the evacuation should have a copy of the card.

❏ 4.04 Train those who will assist with the evacuation to collect emergency documents (e.g., checks, credit cards, bank books, prescriptions, medical instructions, family records,), and special equipment, medical devices and supplies, eyeglasses, dentures, medications (in their original container), diapers, and keys.

❏ 4.05 Create emergency kits that contain non-prescription drugs including aspirin or nonasprin pain relievers such as acetaminophen or ibuprofen, anti-diarrhea medication, laxatives, and antacids.

APPENDIX 4D:
EMERGENCY PLANS FOR BUILDING SHUTDOWN

Key point. A building shutdown helps control losses during a fire or natural disaster.

❏ 1.01 Establish a team to shutdown the building if an emergency should occur.

❏ 1.02 Create a diagram that identifies the main shutoff switches and valves for electrical power, water, and natural gas. Post the diagram in a designated location.

❏ 1.03 Establish an action plan to shut off utilities.

Key point. If natural gas is shut off, only a licensed professional should turn it back on. Check with your gas company in advance to obtain their recommendation for emergency procedures whether or not to shut off the gas supply.

❏ 1.04 Establish an action plan to prevent water from backing up into the building through drains.

Key point. Install check values to prevent water backup. If check valves have not been install, use corks or rubber stoppers.

❏ 1.05 Prepare and install shutters over windows.

Key point. If detachable shutters are used, number or label both windows and shutters to speed up and coordinate the installation process.

Key point. Tape will not prevent windows from breaking.

❏ 1.06 Prepare and install plywood covers for glass doors.

❏ 1.07 Close doors and windows.

❏ 1.08 Secure backup copies of all computer data.

❏ 1.09 Collect vital documents that are stored at the church (e.g., deeds, checks, bank documents, and insurance policies).

APPENDIX 4E:
EMERGENCY PLANS FOR DAMAGED FACILITIES

Key point. Use the following checklist if facilities are damaged.

❑ 1.01 Provide immediate assistance to trapped or injured persons. Call 911 for help. Do not move seriously injured people unless other risks pose greater harm to them. Apply whatever first aid you can.

❑ 1.02 Implement the church's or school's building shutdown procedures. Have someone designated to shut off utilities until a proper inspection of gas lines and electrical wiring occurs. A gas leak or electrical problems pose risks of fires and explosions.

❑ 1.03 Post signs and install barriers to keep people away from damaged buildings.

❑ 1.04 Do not enter any building that has standing water around it. The combination of standing water and electricity can be deadly.

❑ 1.05 Do not use a lantern, blow torch or matches when returning to inspect or repair any flooded building until you know it is safe to enter. When you do enter, use a battery-powered flashlight.

❑ 1.06 If you smell the odor of gas, turn off the gas value if possible and leave immediately. Call the gas company from a nearby residence or business. Do not re-enter the building until you have received clearance from the gas company.

❑ 1.07 Examine the structure of the church or school building including the foundation, walls, floors, and windows. Look for cracks or other signs that damage has occurred.

❑ 1.08 If the building has been flooded, keep an eye open for animals and snakes that may have entered the building during the flood. Do not use bare hands to sort through debris. Use a stick, shovel or rake.

❑ 1.10 Watch your step to avoid exposed nails and other sharp objects. Wear shoes with thick soles.

❑ 1.11 Cleanup any spills of flammable liquids, but stay out of any building in which you smell fumes of gases.

❑ 1.12 Be careful when opening cabinets, closets, and cupboards since items may fall out when the doors are opened.

❑ 1.13 Inspect all chimneys before igniting any fires. Any structural damage could result in a fire.

❑ 1.14 Begin the clean-up process as soon as it is safe and feasible to do so.

❑ 1.15 Initiate whatever salvage operations are possible and document all of your losses in writing and with photographs.

❑ 1.16 Throw away all food from the church or school kitchen that has become contaminated.

❑ 1.17 If flooding has occurred and the church or school has a well, have the water tested before it is used. Also, do not drink city tap water until you receive notice that it is safe to do so.

❑ 1.18 If you vacuum water from the floor using a wet-dry cleaner, carefully read the manufacturer's instructions. Make sure that it is properly grounded and use a vacuum with a ground-fault circuit-interrupter (portable GFCIs are available which you can plug directly into an outlet).

❑ 1.19 Any furnishing that has been covered with water is a possible source of bacterial contamination. Such items, including carpeting, must either be thrown out or steam cleaned, sanitized, and dried.

❑ 1.20 Water damaged furnishings from a church nursery should be replaced to avoid any risk to children. In addition, wet insulation must also be replaced since it can harbor biological pollutants.

❑ 1.21 If flooding has occurred, make sure that electrical equipment such as furnaces, freezers, refrigerators and other appliances get a chance to dry thoroughly before they are used.

❑ 1.22 All electrical appliances that have been exposed to water should be inspected and tested by a qualified technician.

❑ 1.23 Check to see that smoke and carbon monoxide detectors are working properly.

❑ 1.24 Permit only experienced individuals to use chain saws on church or school property while assisting with the cleanup. The use of chain saws can be extremely hazardous.

❑ 1.25 Locate alternative facilities that can be used.

APPENDIX 4F:
EMERGENCY PLANS TO ASSIST THE INJURED

❑　　1.01　　See that all church vehicles are equipped with an adequately supplied first aid kit.

❑　　1.02　　See that an adequately supplied first aid kit is located in the church office.

❑　　1.03　　Require a first aid kit at all church construction projects.

❑　　1.04　　Have at least one staff member certified to do CPR.

Key point. Contact the American Heart Association for locations of CPR classes. Classes can generally be completed in one day.

❑　　1.05　　Complete planning for Appendix 4C, Section 4 (evacuation of individuals with special needs).

APPENDIX 4G:
EMERGENCY COMMUNICATION PLANS

Key point. A crisis contingency plan should provide guidance in conducting emergency communication, communicating with congregational members or the school family, and responding to the media.

1. Emergency communication

❑ 1.01 Post crisis phone numbers next to each office phone including poison control, the police, and the fire department.

Key point. All staff members should be trained to dial 911 if an emergency occurs.

❑ 1.02 Install alarm systems to notify building occupants of an emergency. Train staff on the use of the system.

❑ 1.03 Install a direct alarm to the fire department.

❑ 1.04 Install a bell or buzzer that sounds in the pastor's office or in other locations in the church to indicate an emergency need in the church office, such as help in responding to a transient or street person.

❑ 1.05 Establish a phone tree to contact a large number of people quickly during an emergency.

❑ 1.06 Install a bulk e-mail program to transmit e-mail quickly to designated individuals or groups.

❑ 1.07 If church facilities must be evacuated, establish a backup phone number that parents and others can call to get information. Publish the information in the church directory or in a student handbook.

2. Communicating emergency information with congregational members or to the school family

❑ 2.01 Create a phone tree to disseminate information to designated groups within the congregation.

❑ 2.02 Maintain a backup set of mailing labels for congregational members.

❑ 2.03 Collect e-mail addresses of congregational members and use a bulk- e-mail program to transmit messages.

❑ 2.04 Install and use voice mail messages.

3. Communicating sensitive information

❑   3.01   Communicate sensitive information on a need to know basis only following the guidance of legal counsel.

❑   3.02   If sensitive information is mailed to congregational members, mark the envelope "privileged and confidential."

❑   3.03   If confidential information is communicated to the congregation during a church service, do so only with congregational members present. Have all visitors and nonmembers leave.

❑   3.04   When communicating confidential information, report only facts known to be true and avoid personal opinion.

4. Responding to allegations of misconduct

❑   4.01   Train staff and leaders to take all allegations seriously.

❑   4.02   Train staff and leaders not to minimize the nature of an allegation in the eyes of a complainant or alleged victim.

❑   4.03   Train staff and leaders not to place blame on a complainant (or alleged victim) for making an allegation.

❑   4.04   Seek appropriate professional assistance (attorney, denominational leaders, insurance agent) to respond to an allegation of misconduct that has legal or ethical implications.

5. Communicating with the media

❑   5.01   Designate a specific individual to handle media requests.

❑   5.02   Train staff and members to refer media to the designated spokesperson.

❑   5.03   Provide training and guidelines to the designated spokesperson.

❑   5.04   Have an attorney review press releases and all other forms of communication that have legal implications.

❑   5.05   Provide timely and accurate information.

❑   5.06   Compile a list of media addresses, phone numbers, fax numbers and e-mail addresses.

❑   5.07   Take the initiative in communicating with the media during a crisis that can portray the church or school in a negative or hostile way.

❑   6.08   Respond immediately to negative stories.

APPENDIX 4H:
EMERGENCY FINANCIAL PLANS

❑   1.01   Identify the amount of funds available to pay for losses out of cash flow.

❑   1.02   Establish a cash reserve to be used for emergency funding.

❑   1.03   Review insurance coverage for disaster planning, including co-insurance, deductible amounts, debris removal, how property will be valued (replacement cost is preferred over actual cash value), and the need for special coverage for floods or earthquakes.

❑   1.04   Establish a line of credit with a bank.

APPENDIX 4I:
EMERGENCY TRAINING PLANS

❏ 1.01 Train staff members and church leaders regarding each crisis planning module found in the appendices of chapter 4.

❏ 1.02 Update training on an annual basis

❏ 1.03 Train each worker or volunteer who has a specific crisis management role regarding the following:

    ❏ (a) building shutdown including shutting off utilities

    ❏ (b) assisting individuals with special needs

    ❏ (c) administering first aid

    ❏ (d) evacuating a building

    ❏ (e) using a fire extinguisher

    ❏ (f) responding to an earthquake

    ❏ (g) responding to a tornado

    ❏ (h) inspecting for damage

    ❏ (I) responding to the media

    ❏ (j) communicating sensitive information

CHAPTER 5. SAFEGUARDING FACILITIES
FOR INFANTS AND TODDLERS

5.1 The Significance of Safeguarding Your Facilities

The number of children in childcare settings continues to grow. Currently 13 million of the 21 million children under the age of 6 are in a childcare program for part of the day. Nearly 100,000 licensed childcare facilities operate in the United States. Surprisingly, according to the Consumer Product Safety Commission, many of the most common hazards affecting children are not addressed through licensing requirements at the state level. In addition, many church programs are not licensed at all. Every week, hundreds of thousands of infants and small children receive care in church nurseries. Most of the care is provided through the services of volunteer workers. Recruiting those volunteer workers is no easy task. For the typical church, staffing the nursery is a never-ending process. Since church nurseries rely on the support of many different volunteers, it often means that the volunteers themselves have only a limited knowledge of the overall nursery operations. They may serve only a few hours each year and often are not thoroughly familiar with the nursery and its supplies. In addition, they may have only a limited understanding of church nursery procedures and policies. In addition to nurseries, churches also oversee extensive programs for preschoolers including the operation of childcare facilities, mother morning out programs, Sunday School classes, Vacation Bible Schools, and preschool programs. As one of the leading providers of programs for small children in the United States, churches need to give special attention to providing safe environments for infants and preschoolers.

The need to train both paid and volunteer workers concerning child safety is heightened by a recent study of 220 licensed child care settings nationwide conducted by the Consumer Product Safety Commission.[1] The Commission targeted eight product areas with potential safety hazards and found that two-thirds of the child care settings had a hazard in at least one or more of the areas. The areas under study included cribs, soft bedding, playground surfacing maintenance, child safety gates, window blind cords, drawstrings in children's clothing, and recalled children's products. The findings revealed the following:

- 38 percent of childcare settings had children wearing clothing with drawstrings at the neck.
- 27 percent did not adequately maintain the protective playground surface.
- 24 percent did not have safe playground surfacing.
- 26 percent had loops on window blind cords.
- 19 percent had cribs containing soft bedding.
- 13 percent did not use child safety gates where they were needed.
- 8 percent had cribs that did not meet current safety standards.
- 5 percent had unsafe products that had been recalled.

---

[1] "Safety at Child Care Settings," *Consumer Product Safety Review*, Spring 1999, p. 3.

During the past nine years, at least 56 children have died in childcare settings with at least half of those deaths associated with nursery equipment or soft bedding. These accidents can be prevented through proper supervision and routine maintenance. It all begins, however, with having the proper knowledge necessary to identify hazards and to take corrective action.

Nursery Product Related Injuries and Deaths to Children Under Age Five[2]

Product Category	Estimated Injuries 1996	Average Annual Deaths 1990-1994
Total	77,600	62.8
Baby Walkers or Jumpers	18,600	.2
Strollers and Carriages	14,000	2.4
Infant Carriers and Car Seats	12,700	5.4 (excludes motor vehicle incidents)
Cribs, Bassinets and Cradles	9,400	45.4
High Chairs	9,200	2.4
Changing Tables	2,100	.2
Baby Gates or Barriers	1,600	0
Playpens	1,500	4.4
Other	8,400	2.4

The Consumer Product Safety Commission provides extensive resources on safety. Their booklet, *The Safe Nursery,* is available on the Internet at http://www.cpsc.gov/cpscpub/pubs/202.html. The following information summarizes key points of relevance to churches and schools.

5.2 Major Hazards in Church and School Nurseries

Cribs

Cribs pose the single greatest hazard to infants in the church nursery. Each year thousands of infants are treated in emergency rooms for crib-related injuries, and cribs account for more infant fatalities than any other nursery product. In recent years, the number of crib fatalities has been reduced dramatically due to new safety regulations, but still nearly one child dies every week in a crib related incident. Many cribs are old and do not meet current safety standards. Furthermore, cribs have extended use as they are passed on from one person to the next. It is estimated that a crib has a useful life of 25 years. When buying a crib, look for a certification safety seal. Each crib located in your nursery should be inspected for the following:

---

[2] *Consumer Product Safety Review,* Winter 1998, p. 3.

1. The mattress and bedding. The mattress should fit snugly in place. Use the two-finger test. If the space between the side of the mattress and the crib is large enough to slide more than two fingers between, the mattress is too small. Suffocation is possible if an infant gets his or her head wedged between the crib and the mattress. The label on the mattress should indicate that it meets safety requirements. Do not cover a mattress with a plastic bag. The bag may stick to a child's face and cause suffocation. Children who can stand should be placed in cribs where the mattress is located at the lowest position. Soft bedding such as comforters, quilts, pillows, sheepskins, and pillow-like toys should not be used in cribs at church or for any child under **12 months.** Research findings indicate that babies are at higher risk for sudden infant death syndrome (SIDS) if their heads get covered by soft bedding while sleeping.[3] The risk is present even if babies sleep on their backs. The new research indicates that many deaths that have been attributed to SIDS may actually have been caused by suffocation when babies were placed stomach down on soft bedding. Babies should always be put to bed on their backs on a firm mattress that fits snugly in the crib. Rather than using blankets, the recommendation from the Infant Suffocation Project is to put the baby in a warm sleeper. If a blanket is used, it should be thin, and tucked around the mattress and extend only up to the baby's chest. The baby should be positioned with his or her feet at the foot of the crib.

2. Bumper pads. Bumper pads should only be used with infants who cannot move to a standing position in a crib. Otherwise they may use the bumper pad as a step and attempt to climb up the side of the crib. Since the typical volunteer nursery attendant at a church will generally not know this information, it is best not to use bumper pads in church nurseries. If bumper pads are used, they should go around the entire mattress and be tightly secured at six locations, including all four corners, with ties, straps, or snaps. If ties or straps are used, any excess material should be cut off so that a child does not become entangled in it.

3. Crib Hardware. Check all of the hardware on each crib. Replace any missing or broken parts. All bolts and screws should be tight and secure. The mattress supports should be bolted tightly or secured by closed hooks. Some mattress supports use hangers. Hangers must be checked prior to each use to ensure they have not become disconnected.

4. Headboards and footboards. Older cribs may contain openings in the headboard or footboard, or between a corner post and the top rail that may allow an infant's head to become caught. This can lead to strangulation. Do not use these cribs.

5. Corner posts. The corner posts should be no more than **1/16 of an inch** higher than the headboard or footboard. Remove any decorative knobs from corner posts and sand them so they are smooth and flush with the headboard or footboard. Clothes and other items can become caught on a corner post or a knob and pose a risk of strangulation.

6. Slats. No slats should be missing, broken, or cracked, and all slats should be secure. Slat problems are not restricted to older cribs. Since 1991 approximately 680,000 cribs with slat problems have been recalled or have required some corrective action. Of those where the age of the crib was known, about 85 percent

---

[3] *Consumer Product Safety Review,* Spring 1999, p. 5.

were less than 3 years old. The main problem is slats becoming dislodged from the side of the crib. The resulting opening can create an entrapment hazard. Of 138 incidents where crib slats have become disengaged, 12 children have died—nearly 1 in 12. The gap width between slats is also a critical safety factor. The gap between the slats should be less than **2-3/8 inches** (60mm). Larger spacing poses a danger of head entrapment and strangulation.

7. *Paint.* Use only lead-free paint to refinish a crib.

8. *Side rails.* When in the raised position, the top rail of the crib should be at least **26 inches** above the top of the mattress support. The child should not be capable of releasing the latch or lock to lower the side rail.

9. *Used cribs.* The church should purchase only new cribs. While churches are often dependent upon gifts, used cribs should be avoided. When buying a new crib, inspect it based upon the above criteria.

Other safety precautions for cribs

1. *Strings and cords.* Cribs should not be located near window blinds or drapes. All cords and pull-strings should be out of reach (not only for infants in cribs, but for all children staying in the nursery). These items pose strangulation risks. In addition, do not put toys or diaper bags in the crib (or hang them on the crib) that have strings or pull cords. Do not hang a mobile or any other object above the crib where a child could become caught in it. Strings on toys should be removed before small children play with them.

2. *Items around the neck.* Do not tie pacifiers around a child's neck, or place a child in a crib with a bib or necklace or any other item that is around the child's neck. These items pose strangulation risks.

3. *Climbing.* Do not place toys or any other item in a crib that a child can use as a step. The child may use them in an attempt to climb out of the crib. Nothing should be in the crib that the child can climb on.

4. *The side rail.* Whenever a child is in a crib, the side rail should be raised and locked in place.

5. *Size of child.* Children should not be placed in a crib once they are **35 inches** tall, or once the height of the top rail is less than **three-fourths** the height of the child.

6. *Crib toys.* Avoid any toy that can catch on a child's clothing, that has strings or cords, or that can be used to climb on.

Changing tables

Every year children are injured when they fall off a changing table. The accidents occur quickly—in the amount of time the caretaker turns away from the child to reach for a diaper. Churches and schools should use tables with safety straps. The straps should be used when the table is being used. A child on a changing table should never be left unattended. Changing tables should be cleaned before and after use with an anti-bacterial disinfectant. Latex gloves should be used when changing diapers.

Water hazards

Infants and toddlers can quickly drown in a few inches of water at the bottom of a bucket, in a sink, or in a toilet. Buckets and pails, even with a small amount of water, should never be left in an area occupied by small children. Nor should open buckets be used as diaper pails. According to the Consumer Safety Product Commission, about 50 children drown each year in buckets. Most victims are between 8 and 14 months old. Five-gallon buckets pose the greatest hazard. If the nursery has a bathroom, keep the door closed. Children should not have access to the toilet without proper supervision. On average, about two children drown in toilets each year. If children are bathed or cleaned in a tub or sink, use the least amount of water necessary, and they should NEVER be left unattended. Turning away, even for the briefest amount of time, can provide an opportunity for drowning to occur. Children are naturally attracted to water and enjoy playing in it. When water is present, adult supervision is always required.

Baby gates

Anyone who has worked in a church nursery knows that children are excellent escape artists. They'll do their best to find ways into places and areas they do not belong. Often baby gates are used at doorways to "corral" children or at stairways to prevent access. Baby gates, though, can pose their own dangers. The accordion-style baby gates with large V-shaped openings along the top and diamond shaped opening between the slats create entrapment and strangulation hazards. Children have died trying to crawl through or over these gates. These gates were discontinued in 1985 but thousands are still in use. New accordion-style baby gates have V-shaped openings that are no more than **1-1/2 inches** in width. Anything larger than that should not be used. If your church owns the older, larger accordion-style baby gate, see that they are properly discarded. Other alternatives today are gates that use mesh screen or ones with a straight top with rigid bars.

High chairs

Like cribs, high chairs are associated with significant injuries to children. Special attention must be given to preventing tips, falls, entrapment and strangulation. Thousands of children are injured annually while in high chairs and some die. The most common cause of death is when a child slips underneath the tray and becomes strangled. Both death and injury can be prevented through simple preventive care.

The proper use of straps is critical in the prevention of serious injuries associated with high chairs. Two straps are needed. First, the high chair should have a waist strap. A tray should never be used as a substitute for a waist strap in an attempt to wedge the child in place. Second, and this is vital, the high chair should have a strap that goes between the legs and prevents the child from slipping under the tray (some high chairs use a post between the child's legs and that achieves the same purpose). When used together, these two straps prevent the child from standing in the chair or sliding under the tray. Each high chair that the church owns should be inspected to ensure that they all have both straps and that they are in good working order. If a strap is missing the chair should not be used until the strap has been replaced.

High chairs should also be stable. Injuries occur when chairs tip over. Children will rock while seated in a high chair and can cause it to tip over. Use chairs with a wide base and never permit children to stand up in a chair. Some high chairs fold-up to conserve space. These chairs can collapse if the locking devices do not work properly or are not secured in place before using the chair. They also have pinch points that can cause injuries. These chairs must always be checked before a child is seated to make sure they are properly locked in place.

High chairs should not be located where a child can tip the high chair over by pushing on a wall, table, or counter. In addition, children should never be allowed to climb on a high chair or get into it by themselves.

Hook-on chairs

Hook-on chairs are a popular substitute for high chairs because of their compact size. The same precautions apply to hook-on chairs as to high chairs. Most injuries arise from falling out of the chair or dislodging it from the table. The hook-on chair should have a clamp that locks onto the table. Check to see that the chair is firmly in place and that the child cannot push on any items with his or her feet to dislodge the chair from the table. Do not use a hook-on chair on a table that has a single pedestal or that is unstable. Always use two restraining straps—one around the waist and one between the legs. Often, a hook-on chair has small rubber or plastic caps that cover the ends of metal tubing. Children should not be able to remove those caps, which if removed, may be swallowed and cause a child to choke.

Playpens

Mesh playpens pose a risk to children when the drop-sides are left down. Young infants can get their heads caught in the loose mesh and suffocate. Newer models of these playpens contain warning labels indicating that an infant should never be left in the playpen when the sides are down. Older models do not contain these warning labels. A church should ensure that a warning label is present on all mesh playpens, and the sides should remain up at all times, even when the playpen is not in use. When buying new playpens, purchase ones with tight woven mesh with openings smaller than the buttons found on infant clothing—**1/4 inch** or less. Regularly check the mesh on a playpen for tears, fraying, loose threads, or to see if it is coming loose. If any of these conditions are present, the playpen should not be used. Also, check to see if staples were used in the construction of the playpen. If so, make sure no protrusions exist.

Some playpens (and travel cribs) contain a rotating hinge in the center of each top rail that enables the playpen to be folded up for storage and mobility. Children have died when the hinges on these playpens were not securely locked in place, and then the playpen collapsed and trapped the child's neck. The Consumer Product Safety Commission has recalled several brands of playpens with rotating latches in the center of the top rails. Churches should not use these playpens. Note: Some playpens have a hinge located in the center of the top rail that has an automatic locking device that activates when the rails are lifted for normal use. These hinges generally use a button or some release mechanism to release the latch. The automatic locking hinges have not been associated with any fatal entrapment injuries. The problem is with the rotating hinges that require being "turned" to lock in place.

Several other hazards are associated with playpens. Some older wooden playpens use slats. The space between slats should be no more than **2-3/8 inches** wide. Larger openings create an entrapment hazard. Also, do not tie anything across the corner or top of a playpen. Such items are strangulation hazards. Similarly, do not tie toys, diaper bags, or anything else to the side of the playpen that a child may catch his or her neck on. Do not put large toys, bumper pads, or other items into the playpen that a child will use as a step to climb out of the playpen. Finally, like a crib, the mattress in a playpen should fit snugly. If it is too small, a child can become entrapped between the side of the playpen and the mattress and suffocate. Children can also become trapped between two mattresses and suffocate.

Rattles, squeeze toys and teethers

Small children and infants chew on toys. As a result, choking deaths have been associated with some toys such as rattles. Since 1978, a regulation has existed that requires rattles to be large enough so they will not get lodged in a child's throat. The Consumer Product Safety Commission notes that rattles the size of a golf ball or smaller have caused choking deaths. Special care must also be given to the handles of rattles, squeeze toys, and teethers. Some small handles can go far back in a child's mouth and obstruct the windpipe. Such toys should be thrown away. Some key safety tips include the following: (1) do not use small toys with ball shaped ends; (2) do not leave any toys or small objects in a crib or playpen while a baby is sleeping; and (3) never tie a teether, pacifier, or small toy around a baby's neck.

Toys

Almost half of all toy-related injuries are to children under the age of 5 (80 percent are under age 15). In one recent year, over 140,000 children were treated in emergency rooms for toy-related injuries. The most common injuries were lacerations, contusions, and abrasions, and a majority of the injuries involved the head and face. In this study, boys were more likely to be injured than girls. Riding toys such as wagons and tricycles accounted for the largest single group of injuries. Choking on a balloon was the most common cause of death.[4] The selection and use of toys should be age related. What is appropriate and safe for older children may not be for younger ones. Childcare workers in churches should remove any small toy or pieces of a game that could be a choking hazard. This includes small balls (less than **1-3/4 inches** in diameter), marbles, and balloons (inflated or not). Some older toys have small pieces that can become loose and come off such as eyes on dolls or squeekers on squeeze toys. Do not leave toys in a crib or playpen that a child could use as a stair to climb out of the crib or playpen. No crib toys should contain cords or strings. Do not use plastic climbing equipment indoors on a hard floor. Such equipment places children at risk for serious head injuries and even death from falls. Monitor closely the use of all riding toys. All toys should be checked periodically to see if they are in good shape. Discard or repair any toy that is damaged or is dangerous. Look for sharp edges, splinters, rusted parts, hinges that can pinch, tears, protrusions, broken glass or plastic, and exposed wires that may be used, for example, in a stuffed toy to give it shape. Cap guns should not be used. Some caps can damage hearing. Some toys that propel objects can be turned into weapons. Electric toys should be

---

[4] *Consumer Product Safety Review,* Winter 1998, p. 4.

age appropriate and only used with adult supervision. With so many excellent toys from which to choose, avoid those that pose risk.

Toy chests

Toy chests present two main concerns. First, children can be seriously injured if the lid of an open toy chest falls on them. Brain, damage, head injuries, and neck injuries can occur. The most vulnerable children are those **under two years of age.** Lids that will not remain open, such as those without a spring-loaded lid support, should be removed. A spring-loaded lid device is inexpensive and should be installed if the lid is kept. Second, another serious, but less frequent hazard is when children climb into a toy chest to hide or sleep. On some occasions, suffocation has occurred. This can be prevented by drilling ventilation holes in the chest, or by removing the lid.

Diaper pails

Do not leave a diaper pail where a child can gain access to it. Thirty children have drowned in diaper pails since 1977.

Electrical outlets

Cover electrical outlets with safety plugs.

Carbon monoxide

Small children can be injured more quickly from carbon monoxide poisoning than adults. If your church uses gas heat or any other form of fossil fuel, install a carbon monoxide detector in the church nursery. Do not use kerosene heaters in church nurseries.

Pacifiers

Almost every infant uses a pacifier. Pacifiers must never be tied around the neck of a child and today it is illegal to sell a pacifier with a ribbon, cord, string, or yarn attached to it. The risk of strangulation is too great. Pacifiers come with a shield that should be too large to fit into a baby's mouth. The shield must have air holes to allow the baby to breathe while sucking on the pacifier. Pacifiers wear out with use and can get holes or tears. Old ones should be discarded.

Walkers

Walkers result in the most frequent injuries of all nursery products. In 1993 an attempt was made to ban baby walkers, but it failed. However, the following year the Consumer Product Safety Commission began a process to implement mandatory safety rules regarding walkers. While the mandatory rules are still pending, during the past several years new, stronger voluntary standards have evolved. The need for increased safety is evident. In 1997, over 14,000 children were treated in hospital emergency rooms for injuries associated with a walker. The most likely victim is a child under 15 months of age. The accidents can occur quickly, and most of the time, the accident occurs in the presence of a caretaker. When a child uses a walker, he or she must always remain in the visible presence of an adult and special precautions must be taken. Three of the more common accidents include falling down stairs, tipping over, and getting burned. When a child falls down stairs it is usually because the caretaker has forgotten to close a door or a safety gate. Most falls occur at home, and nearly half are falling down basement stairs. New designs are now in progress to prevent walkers from falling down stairs, and some models are now available for retail sale. Look for labels that contain wording such as "Meets New Safety Standards." Tips occur when walkers go across uneven surfaces such as the threshold of a door or the edge of a carpet. As a result, walkers should only be used in areas with smooth surfaces. Burns are associated with touching hot radiators, heaters, ranges, and fireplaces. Walkers should not be used in a room with hot surfaces that a child can touch. Some walkers contain coil springs. These springs should be covered to avoid pinching fingers. Some older walkers have an x-frame design that collapses to make the walker more compact for storage or transporting. These walkers can amputate or pinch fingers and are not recommended for use. One alternative to a walker is an activity center that is stationary or has limited mobility.

Strollers and carriages

Strollers and carriages should not be used as a substitute for a crib. Infants, left to sleep, have died as their bodies have slipped out of a stroller feet first with their head becoming entrapped between the handrest (grab bar) and the front edge of the seat. The handrest should be able to be closed when the stroller is used in a reclined position as a carriage. The brakes should be secure and not allow the stroller to roll. Like high chairs, a stroller should have both a seat belt and a crotch strap. Keep children away from a stroller when it is being folded or unfolded. The folding mechanisms can crush small fingers and some children have had fingers amputated in these devices. To avoid suffocation, do not use pillows or blankets as a mattress in a carriage. Finally, some strollers have baskets to store items. These baskets should be located in the rear over or in front of the back wheels. If the basket is loaded, it should not cause the stroller to tip.

Bassinets and cradles

The mattresses for a bassinet or cradle should fit snugly and be smooth without folds or wrinkles. This is to avoid suffocation. For the same reason, pillows should never be used in either a bassinet or a cradle. The most common injury, however, results from a bassinet or cradle tipping over, or from the bottom falling out. Bassinets and cradles should have a wide base and all bolts and screws should be checked periodically to make sure they are tight and that none protrude (check for staples that may protrude as well). Remove all strings, cords, ribbons, or other items that could catch around a child's neck and cause strangulation.

Safety latches and locks

Keep the bottom drawer on cabinets locked. Children will pull out the bottom drawer and use it as a step. Cabinets have fallen over on children creating serious injuries. Never store medications, cleaning supplies, or any other poisonous materials in reach of a child. Use safety latches or locks to keep such items away from inquisitive little hands and mouths.

Window blinds

On average, a child dies every month from strangulation associated with a window cord. Most of these children are under age 4. Of this group, children between 8 and

23 months old are often in a crib that has been placed next to a window. The slightly older children are frequently standing on a toy when they loose their balance and slip, and become strangled in the cord. Any window cord that is looped poses a threat. Check all mini-blinds and venetian blinds for a looped cord. If a looped cord exists, cut the cord in two and make a safety tassel at the end of each cord. If a blind or drapery uses a continuous looped cord, the cord should have a non-detachable cord tension device that is secured to the wall or floor and that holds the cord tightly in place. The cord should not be able to loop back upon itself.

Clothing drawstrings

Drawstrings around the neck can get caught on playground equipment and furnishings inside, and pose a strangulation hazard. Over 20 deaths have occurred since 1985.[5] Instruct parents not to use jackets and hooded sweatshirts that use drawstrings. Rather, use clothing with snaps, Velcro, or zippers.

Rocking chairs and gliders

Rocking chairs or gliders are often used in a church nursery to rock children. A danger exists that a child may put his or her fingers or limbs under a rocker while the chair is in use. This can occur quickly with an adult not being aware that a child is behind or under the chair. Some gliders have open sides and present an amputation risk to children. The gliding mechanism is exposed to small fingers and limbs. These chairs should not be used. Use only gliders that fully enclose the gliding mechanism along the sides and in the front and back.

Audiovisual carts

Audiovisual carts are often top heavy and can crush a small child if they tip over and fall on the child. Do not store audiovisual carts in areas that small children use. Make sure the carts are stable before using them with children present. Do not let children play around a cart. Also, never ask children of any age to move an audiovisual cart, or to assist by guiding the cart. Only adults should move an audiovisual cart.

Walk-in freezers, refrigerators, and coolers

Children like to play hide-and-seek and sometimes they choose dangerous places to hide. Walk-in-freezers, refrigerators, and coolers all pose dangers to children. Do not store an old refrigerator at the church unless the door has been removed. If the door will not come off, disable the latch or secure the door with a chain and lock so that it cannot be opened. Walk-in freezers should be able to be opened from the inside and should contain an alarm to signal for help. Store coolers in safe locations where children cannot gain access.

Poisons

Several thousand children under the age of 5 are treated on an annual basis in hospital emergency rooms with poison-related injuries from ordinary products such as cleaning solvents and lubricants. Products that are petroleum distillates, such as gasoline, kerosene, mineral spirits, furniture polishes, pine oil, paraffin wax, and adhesives can cause serious injuries to children following aspiration of

---

5 *Consumer Product Safety Review,* Winter 1998, p. 6.

the substance into the lungs. These products are not required to be in child-resistant containers. Poisoning from these products occurs equally to boys and girls. The children usually locate the product in its original container and in its normal storage place. In nearly 70 percent of cases, the child reaches the product without climbing. Most of the time, the children get the product from under a sink, on a counter, or in a trash can. All poisons need to be stored out of the reach in children. No poisons should be stored under sinks, on counter tops or disposed of in trash cans that children have access to.

Summary

Over half of all children under the age of 6 spend part of the day in childcare, many in church programs. In addition, churches operate many programs for toddlers and routinely provide childcare in the church nursery for those attending services. Many potential hazards are present in the care of children. A nationwide study by the Consumer Product Safety Commission found hazards in two-thirds of the programs that were examined. Since most nursery workers in churches are volunteers, and few churches conduct regular safety inspections, the potential for hazards in churches is high.

Church leaders can reduce hazards that affect infants and toddlers through a systematic program of inspection, and training both paid and volunteer staff members to recognize unsafe conditions and correct them, and to follow safe procedures in the care of children.

In the next chapter, risk management procedures are applied to church and school playgrounds.

Additional Resources on the Internet

For additional information on making your facilities and programs safe for infants and preschoolers, review the material found on the following web sites. These resources were used in the preparation of this chapter. Also, some articles and books are listed that can be of further assistance.

"Baby Product Safety Tips: Safety Alert CPSC Document #5082." Consumer Product Safety Commission. <http://www.cpsc.gov/cpscpub/pubs/5082.html>.

"Childproofing Your Home - 12 Safety Devices to Protect Your Children." Consumer Product Safety Commission. <http://www.cpsc.gov/cpscpub/pubs/grand/12steps/12steps html>.

"CPSC Issues Warning That Choking On Small Balls Can Be Fatal To Young Children: Safety Alert CPSC Document #5076." Consumer Product Safety Commission. <http://www.cpsc.gov/cpscpub/pubs/5076.html>.

"CPSC Learns of More Injuries, Teachers Should Not Let Children Move or Play Near TV or Audiovisual Carts CPSC Document #5102." Consumer Product Safety Commission. <http://www.cpsc.gov/cpscpub/pubs/5102.html>.

"CPSC Warns About Child Entrapment in Household Appliances and Picnic Coolers: Safety Alert CPSC Document #5073." Consumer Product Safety Commission. <http://www.cpsc.gov/cpscpub/pubs/5073.html>.

"CPSC Warns Parents About Child Accidents in Recliner Chairs: Safety Alert CPSC Document #5071." Consumer Product Safety Commission. <http://www.cpsc.gov/cpscpub/pubs/5071.html>.

"Crib Safety Tips." National Safety Council. <http://www.nsc.org/lrs/lib/fs/cribtips.htm>.

"For Kids' Sake: Think Toy Safety: Safety Alert CPSC Document #4281." Consumer Product Safety Commission. <http://www.cpsc.gov/cpscpub/pubs/4281.html>.

"Hidden Hazard In The Home: Infants & Toddlers Can Drown in 5-Gallon Buckets: Safety Alert CPSC Document #5006." Consumer Product Safety Commission. <http://www.cpsc.gov/cpscpub/pubs/5006.html>.

"Improving Playgrounds." *Consumer Product Safety Review*. Fall 1997.

"Law Requires Review and Labeling of Art Materials Including Children's Art and Drawing Products: Safety Alert CPSC Document #5016." Consumer Product Safety Commission. <http://www.cpsc.gov/cpscpub/pubs/5016.html>.

"Making Cribs Safer." *Consumer Product Safety Review*. Winter 1997 Vol. 1, No. 3.

"Mattress and Bedding Fires." *Consumer Product Safety Review*. Spring 1998.

"Prevent Child Drownings In The Home: Safety Alert CPSC Document #5013." Consumer Product Safety Commission. <http://www.cpsc.gov/cpscpub/pubs/5013.html>.

"Preventing Children's Injuries." *Consumer Product Safety Review*. Winter 1998. Vol. 2, No. 3.

"Reducing Poisonings to Children." *Consumer Product Safety Review*. Spring 1997 Vol. 1, No. 4.

"Safe Nursery." Consumer Product Safety Commission. <http://www.cpsc.gov/cpscpub/pubs/202.html>.

"Safer Baby Walkers." *Consumer Product Safety Review*. Summer 1998 Vol. 3, No. 1.

"Safety at Child Care Settings." Consumer Product Safety Review. Spring 1999.

"Save A Child - Use Child-Resistant Containers: Safety Alert CPSC Document #5018." Consumer Product Safety Commission. <http://www.cpsc.gov/cpscpub/pubs/5018.html>.

"Tips For Your Baby's Safety: Safety Alert CPSC Document #4200." Consumer Product Safety Commission. <http://www.cpsc.gov/cpscpub/pubs/shower/images/cklsbk.html>.

"Window Covering Pull-Cords." *Consumer Product Safety Review*. Spring 1997.

CHAPTER 6. KEEPING CHURCH AND SCHOOL PLAYGROUNDS SAFE

6.1 The Significance of Maintaining a Safe Playground

According to the Consumer Product Safety Commission (CPSC) over 200,000 children, equally divided between boys and girls, are treated annually in hospital emergency rooms from injuries sustained on playgrounds. About 70 percent of the time the injury occurred away from home at a public playground. The single biggest problem is falling off equipment onto the ground, which accounts for about 75 percent of the injuries. Approximately one-third of playground injuries are fractures. Other problems include collisions with moving and stationary equipment, and contact with sharp edges, protrusions, pinch points, hot surfaces, and debris left on the ground. Children also become entangled or entrapped in ropes and openings; clothing can catch on slides; and equipment can tip over. Each year approximately 15 children die as a result of playground injuries, mostly to the head, and in almost every case, these accidents could be prevented.

The problem of playground safety is particularly relevant to churches. A majority of churches maintain a playground for children, yet many church playgrounds are not well maintained or inspected with any regularity. Also, supervision is often lacking as children make their way to the playground before, between, and after church services and engage in unsupervised and unstructured play. The lack of regular inspections, poorly maintained equipment, and unsupervised activities creates higher levels of risks for children. The good news is that many injuries can be prevented by implementing simple and inexpensive measures.

The Consumer Product Safety Commission's *Handbook for Public Playground Safety* provides safety specifications that are used by communities across the United States. The *Handbook*, which is available on the Internet (http://www.cpsc.gov/cpscpub/pubs/325.pdf), is one of the best sources of information available to promote playground safety for children between the ages of 2 through 12 years. Every church should obtain a copy and use it to evaluate its own playground. This chapter summarizes key points from the handbook on four areas that deserve special attention: (1) the surface under and around playground equipment; (2) the overall design and installation of the playground; (3) the safety of each individual piece of playground equipment; and (4) the inspection and maintenance of the equipment.

6.2 The Surface Under and Around Playground Equipment

No topic is more important concerning playground safety than playground surfaces. Falls off the equipment onto the surface of the playground are the number one cause of injury. Some are fatal. The nature of the surface affects the degree of the injury. Head injuries pose the most serious risk to children. A hard surface is more likely than a shock-absorbing surface to contribute to a serious injury that results from a fall. While no surface can totally prevent an injury, some surfaces are clearly more desirable than others.

Selecting the proper surface for playgrounds

Concrete, asphalt, dirt, and grass surfaces are not recommended for use under and around any playground equipment. This comes as quite a shock to many church leaders, especially concerning grass. All four surfaces, however, have poor shock absorbing qualities. Yet many churches use these surfaces on their playgrounds. In addition, many adults grew up playing on these surfaces while they were children. There is an implicit sense that they are okay since they have been in use for so long—*that sense is wrong.*

The CPSC recommends two types of surfaces for playgrounds: (1) those that use unitary materials made of some form of rubber or something similar to rubber, and (2) those that use loose-fill materials such as sand, gravel, shredded wood products, and shredded tires.

A number of different rubber mats or "rubber-like" materials are available for unitary playground surfaces. Some products are liquefied and poured in place. A key factor in evaluating a unitary material is to know its "Critical Height." Critical Height is defined as "the fall height below which a life-threatening head injury would not be expected to occur." To make a proper evaluation, you must also know on what surface the unitary material will be installed. While unitary materials are sometimes installed over a hard surface, loose-fill materials should never be installed over concrete or asphalt. Also, since loose fill material is generally sold as landscaping supplies, Critical Height information is usually not available. The CPSC has conducted its own studies and has produced the following table that lists the critical height for a number of loose-fill materials.

Critical Heights (in feet) of Tested Materials

Uncompressed Depth of Materials			Compressed Depth
	6 inches	9 inches	12 inches	12 inches
Material	Critical Height in feet		Critical Height
Wood Chips*	7 feet	10 feet	11 feet	10 feet
Double Shredded Bark Mulch	6 feet	10 feet	11 feet	7 feet
Engineered Wood Fibers**	6 feet	7 feet	>12 feet	6 feet
Fine Sand	5 feet	5 feet	9 feet	5 feet
Coarse Sand	5 feet	5 feet	6 feet	4 feet
Fine gravel	6 feet	7 feet	10 feet	6 feet
Medium gravel	5 feet	5 feet	6 feet	5 feet
Shredded Tires***	10-12 feet	N/A	N/A	N/A

* This product was referred to as Wood Mulch in previous versions of CPSC handbook on playground safety.

** This product was referred to as Uniform Wood Chips in previous versions of CPSC handbook on playground safety. In the playground industry, the product is commonly known as Engineered Wood Fibers.

*** This data is from tests conducted by independent testing laboratories on a 6 inch depth of uncompressed shredded tire samples produced by four manufacturers. The tests report critical heights which varied from 10 feet to greater than 12 feet. It is recommended that persons seeking to install shredded tires as a protective surface request test data from the supplier showing the critical height of the material when it is tested in accordance with ASTM F1292.

Two variables that affect critical height are the depth of the loose-fill material and the compression of the material. The deeper the material, the greater the critical height. However, as the material becomes more compressed, critical height declines. Compression is affected by several factors including frequency of use, weather conditions, maintenance, and depth of the material. The best safety occurs when loose-fill materials are kept loose and that may require frequent maintenance to stir up the materials. One recommendation for all playgrounds is to mark the legs or support posts of each piece of equipment to indicate the correct level for loose-fill surfacing material under and around the equipment. That way a quick glance can indicate if more material needs to be added or if the material is becoming too condensed. A margin of safety should always be added in when selecting the depth and type of material to use. Loose-fill material also requires some form of containment around each safety zone to hold the material in place.

6.3 Use Zones

Each piece of playground equipment has its own use zone that includes an area under and around the equipment. The entire use zone requires a protective surface that should be completely free from obstacles. The use zone varies for different types of playground equipment.

Stationary equipment excluding slides

The recommended use zone of stationary equipment is a minimum of **6 feet** completely around the perimeter. Often two pieces of stationary equipment are located next to each other. How close they should be depends on how high above the ground the respective play surfaces are located for each piece of equipment. If the play surface for both pieces of equipment is **30 inches or less** above the protective surface, the recommended distance between the two pieces of equipment is a minimum of **6 feet.** If the play surface of either piece of equipment is **over 30 inches high,** the minimum distance between the two structures should be extended to **9 feet.**

Slides

The use zone of a slide is divided into two areas. The first area is directly in front of the slide's exit. The second area is everywhere else around the perimeter of the slide. The second area requires a minimum of **6 feet** of protective surface (except for an embankment slide which follows the contour of the ground and at no point is the bottom of the chute—the inclined sliding surface—more than **12 inches** above the ground). The use zone in front of the exit of all slides, including embankment slides, is a minimum distance of **H + 4 feet** where H is the vertical distance from the protective surface at the slide's exit to the highest point of the chute. No matter what H is, the use zone should never be less than 6 feet but does not need to be more than 14 feet. For example, a slide on a level surface that is 8 feet high at the highest point of the chute, should have a protective surface that extends 12 feet away from the end of the chute and 6 feet away from the remaining perimeter of the slide. The use zone in front of the slide's exit should never overlap with any other piece of equipment.

Single-axis swings (to and fro swings)

Children like to get a swing in motion and then jump off. As a result, the use zone has to be larger both in front of and behind the swing than on the sides. To determine the use zone in front and back of the swing, measure the height from the connecting pivot point on the support structure to the protective surface directly below. The use zone both in front and behind the swing should be **twice** that distance. For example, if that height is 8 feet, the use zone should be 16 feet in front and 16 feet in back. The use zone in front and behind the swing should not overlap any other use zone. The use zone for the other areas of the swing should be a minimum of 6 feet from the perimeter of the swing structure and that area may overlap with an adjacent swing structure or other appropriate piece of equipment.

The use zone for tot swings is measured slightly differently. Rather than measuring from the connecting pivot point to the protective surface, measure down only to the lowest point of the swing's seating surface. Then use twice that height for in front of and behind the swing. The perimeter areas remain 6 feet.

Multi-axis swings (e.g., tire swings)

To determine the use zone of tire swings, start by measuring the length (L) of the suspending members (for example, the chain length that supports the swing). The use zone is the area that extends out in any direction from a point on the protective surface directly below the pivot point for a distance of **L + 6 feet.** This zone should not overlap any other use zone. In addition, the use zone around the swing structure extends out 6 feet in all directions from the perimeter. That 6 feet area may overlap with an adjacent piece of appropriate playground equipment

Merry-go-rounds

The use zone is a minimum of 6 feet away from the perimeter of the platform. The use zone should not overlap the use zone of any other equipment.

Spring rockers

The use zone is a minimum of 6 feet away from the "at rest" perimeter of the equipment.

Composite play structures

A composite play structure is when two or more play structures are combined as an integral unit that provides more than one play activity. The CPSC recommends that swings not be included in composite play structures due to the risk of impact injuries. To determine the use zone of a composite play structure, follow the same guidelines for each individual piece of equipment that is used in the structure. In addition, a supplemental circulation area is recommended.

6.4 The Design and Layout of the Playground

Four factors should be taken into account in the design and layout of a playground: (1) the site of the playground; (2) the location of playground equipment; (3) separation of equipment based on the ages of the children who will use the playground; and (4) playground supervision.

The site of the playground

In selecting a site for a playground attention should be given to hazards or obstacles and to slope and drainage. Remove any hazards or obstacles from the playground site. Examine the pathway to the playground for potential hazards. If the playground is located near a street, it should be enclosed by a fence or some other barrier to prevent children from running into traffic. At the same time, the fence or barrier should not obstruct the vision of those providing supervision. If the playground slopes, it should not be so steep that loose-fill materials used to create protective surfaces wash away during a rainstorm. If necessary, grade the site to prevent drainage problems. Locate the playground at least 30 feet away from electrical transformers and air conditioning units. The maximum number of users for the playground at one time should be based on a calculation of 75 square feet per child.

The location of playground equipment

Some playground equipment, such as a merry-go-round or a swing, promote high levels of physical activity, running and movement. Other activities, such as playing in a sandbox, tend to involve less movement. One of the first steps in selecting locations for playground equipment is to separate active areas from open and passive areas. The most popular activities should be separated from each other to disperse the children over the playground area and to avoid crowding. A clear line of sight should exist across the playground so supervisors can monitor the entire site. The CPSC recommends that moving equipment such as swings or merry-go-rounds should be located toward a side or corner of the playground (and maintain the necessary perimeters for protective surfaces). Slides should be in uncongested areas.

Separation of equipment based on the ages of the children who will use the playground

Playground equipment should be age appropriate. Children at different ages represent a range of physical skills, judgment, and abilities. The organization and selection of playground equipment should reflect these differences. Young children need smaller equipment. Pre-school age children (2-5) should have their own playground area which is clearly separated by some barrier (e.g., fence, low shrubs, benches). Signs can be used to provide guidelines on what ages should use what equipment. The CPSC recommends that the following equipment NOT be used for preschool-age children (2-5 years):

- Chain or Cable Walks
- Free Standing Arch Climbers
- Free Standing Climbing Events with Flexible Components
- Fulcrum Seesaws/Teeter Totters
- Log Rolls
- Long Spiral Slides (more than one 360-degree turn)

- Overhead Rings
- Parallel Bars
- Swinging Gates
- Track Rides
- Vertical Sliding Poles

6.5 Playground Supervision

Individuals who supervise playground activities should receive training on playground safety. They should understand the proper use of each piece of equipment and the ages for which it is designed. Supervisors should inspect the equipment for potential hazards and instruct children on what is appropriate and inappropriate play. Smaller children require more direct supervision than do older children—however, children of all ages need supervision. According to the National Program for Playground Safety at the University of Northern Iowa, it is estimated that 40 percent of playground injuries are related to inadequate supervision.[1] Supervisors need to be able to administer first aid if an injury occurs, and simply to be present to oversee and facilitate safe play activities.

6.6 The Inspection and Maintenance of Playground Equipment

Each piece of playground equipment is unique and as a result, installation procedures and manufacturer's specifications will vary from one piece of equipment to the next. Those installing the equipment should follow precise instructions on depth of footings and anchoring the equipment. When installed, the equipment should be completely secure and stable.

Churches should develop a comprehensive, systematic, and regular protocol for inspecting the playground and all equipment. All equipment should be inspected for potential hazards that can be caused by corrosion, rot, insects, weathering, wear and tear, or vandalism. Parents and supervisors should be trained to look for hazards each time they take children to the playground. More formal, detailed inspections should also examine moving parts. Nuts and bolts should be checked for tightness. Repairs should be made promptly once a problem is discovered. The ground should also be inspected for broken glass, anthills, and other debris that could cause an injury or an accident. During winter months, inspect for ice that could cause children to slip and fall. Remove all trash on the ground. Keep trash cans covered and empty them regularly. Some of the more common problem areas are noted below.

Lead paint

Lead paint poses a problem in many playgrounds, especially in those with older equipment. The CPSC conducted a study of 26 playgrounds located in 13 cities and found 20 of the playgrounds had lead levels over the maximum allowable levels. In a larger study of 223 playgrounds, more than half exceeded the allowable rate. Those at highest risk are children under seven years of age. Young children may ingest paint chips and dust. Often, they get it on their hands and from there

---

[1] See http://www.uni.edu/playground/safety_information.html.

it may go to the mouth. Parents and church leaders, however, should not be alarmed if children have played a few times on equipment with deteriorating paint and have put their fingers in their mouths. The paint, however, should be tested for lead and if a problem exists corrective measures should be taken. In addition to lead paint, some wood is treated with chemicals that may pose some risk to children. Before purchasing any playground equipment, obtain documentation from the manufacturer that the equipment does not contain any treatments that pose a health risk to the users. Finally, before establishing a new playground, have the soil tested for environmental hazards including lead.

Burns

Hot surfaces on metal playground equipment are a risk to children, especially the very young. Serious burns can occur upon contact in a matter of seconds. The CPSC reports incidents where children have received second and third degree burns to their hands, legs, and buttocks when they have sat on metal stairs, decks, and slides. Such surfaces exposed to the direct sun should always be tested prior to allowing children to come in contact with them. When possible, metal slides should be located in the shade.

Sharp points, corners, and edges

Special attention must be given when inspecting equipment to identify sharp points, corners, or edges that could cut or puncture a child's skin. The exposed end of tubing should have caps or plugs that can only be removed with a tool. Look for sharp edges on the sides and exit of slides. All metal edges should be rolled or have rounded capping. Wood equipment should be free of splinters. Corners should be rounded for both wood and metal equipment.

Protrusions and projections

Clothing, especially sweatshirts and jackets with hoods and drawstrings, have become entangled on protrusions or projections on slides with fatal results. Parents of small children should be instructed to avoid the use of clothing with drawstrings. In addition protruding parts can create contusions or lacerations. Bolts or screws that stick out on playground equipment, especially swings, present serious hazards.

Pinch, crush, and shearing points

The moving parts of playground equipment should be shielded or enclosed. Fingers can be pinched and, in some larger pieces of equipment, body parts can become crushed. Clothing such as drawstrings and scarves can also become caught.

Connecting parts

All bolts, hooks, rungs and other connecting devices should be tight and secure. They should not be able to be loosened or removed by hand.

Entrapment

Head entrapment is a common problem that can seriously injure children. Head entrapment can occur both by headfirst entry as well as feet first entry. The torso on a small child is smaller than his or her head. Openings should not exist that are between **3.5 to 9 inches in diameter.** A child that becomes entrapped can become scared and may face the risk of strangulation. Crawl spaces, such as in pipes or tunnels, should be large enough for adults to gain access. The CPSC provides extensive guidelines for the evaluation of entrapment risks that go beyond the scope of this text. Churches can obtain the guidelines, which are printed as Appendix B of the CPSC Handbook, on the Internet at http://www.cpsc.gov/cpscpub/pubs/325.pdf.

Tripping and suspended hazards

The retaining walls or forms that are used to contain loose-fill protective surfaces can create a tripping hazard. These walls and containers should be highly visible. Bright colors of paint can be used to set them apart. Footings and anchoring devices should be completely below the protective surface. Similarly, cables, wires, and ropes should be highly visible and should not be used in areas of high traffic. Sidewalks and pathways should be smooth without sudden, irregular surfaces. The playground area should be free of holes.

Climbing and platform hazards

Children love to climb and special attention should be given to a number of hazards associated with the use of ladders and platforms. Falls account for a substantial number of injuries. Steps and rungs should be evenly spaced. The space between rungs, however, should not be between 3.5 and 9 inches since the opening within those dimensions creates an entrapment hazard. The cross section of a rung should be between .95 and 1.55 inches, with a diameter of 1.25 inches being optimal for both foot and hand support (the same dimensions apply to handrails). Rungs should be secure and not turn.

Guardrails for preschool children

Guardrails or full protective barriers should be used to prevent falls off elevated platforms. When guardrails are used, however, special care must be taken not to create openings that pose a risk of entrapment. A full protective barrier is best for preschool children and should be used on any platform that is **over 30 inches** above the protective surface. Guardrails can be used for platforms under 30 inches. The top surface of a guardrail or protective barrier for children under six years of age should be at least **29 inches** high. If a series of platforms exist, the maximum difference in height from one platform to another for preschool-age children is 12 inches. If an opening exists between the platforms, it must not create an entrapment hazard.

Guardrails for school-age children

Different specifications apply to school-age children. For this age group, platforms **above 48 inches** should use full protective barriers while guardrails are appropriate for lower platforms. For this age group, the top surface of the protective barrier of guardrail should be at least **38 inches** high. The maximum height difference between stepped platforms is 18 inches, and once again, entrapment hazards between the platforms must be avoided.

Horizontal crosspieces should not be used below the top rail of a guardrail since they can be used as rungs to climb on. If solid panels are used, some visual space should be maintained that enables supervisors to monitor activity on the platform. Vertical spacers must be spaced properly to avoid entrapment.

6.7 The Safety of Each Individual Piece of Playground Equipment

Rope, chain, and tire climbers

These climbers are not appropriate for preschool-age children. Anchoring devices for climbers should be installed completely below the ground (the base of the protective surface). All openings should be checked to see that they do not present an entrapment hazard.

Arch climbers

These climbers may be made of wood or metal and have a series of rungs attached to convex side supports. Rungs should be at least 9 inches apart to avoid an entrapment hazard. If the arch climber connects to another piece of playground equipment, a second less challenging form of access should also be available. Preschool children should not use freestanding arch climbers.

Horizontal ladders and overhead rings

Ladders and rings require a level of upper body strength that normally is not found in children under four years of age. The rungs of an overhead ladder should be between 9 and 12 inches apart for preschool-age children and between 9 and 15 inches for older children. The initial rung should not be directly over the mounting platform, thus reducing the potential impact if a fall should occur. The maximum height of a horizontal ladder or rings above the protective surface should be **60 inches** for preschool age children and **84 inches** for school-age children. Chains that are used to suspend rings should not be longer than 12 inches.

Sliding poles

Sliding poles are not recommended for preschool age children. Poles should be smooth without any protrusions, welds, or seams. The horizontal distance between a sliding pole and the mounting platform, should be at least **18 inches.** That spacing between the pole and the rest of the structure should continue all the way down the pole. However, the pole should not be more than **20 inches** away from the structure at the point of access. In addition, the pole should extend 5 feet above the level of the platform from which it is accessed. The diameter of the pole should not exceed 1.9 inches.

Climbing ropes

A climbing rope should be secured at both ends and be taut enough so that it cannot be looped back on itself creating a loop of more than 1.5 inches in diameter.

Balance beams

Balance beans should be no higher than 12 inches for preschool-age children and no more than 16 inches for school children.

Sand boxes

Sandboxes should be covered when not in use. An uncovered sandbox will attract animals that will defecate and urinate in the sand. Inspect sandboxes prior to use for animal feces and insects.

Merry-go-rounds

Children like to jump on and off a merry-go-round while it is moving. Small children should always be supervised when using a merry-go-round. The underside of the merry-go-round should be at least 9 inches above the protective surface to avoid entrapment. No parts of the merry-go-round should extend past the perimeter of the platform. No opening should exist between the axis of the merry-go-round and the periphery that permits a rod with a diameter of 5/16 inch to penetrate completely through the surface. A merry-go-round should not go more than 13 feet per second and should not oscillate up and down. Since merry-go-rounds create substantial movement and running, they should be located in a corner or along the edge of a playground.

Seesaws/teeter totters

Anyone who has ever played on a seesaw knows the age-old trick of hopping off and letting the other person plunge to the ground. What children view as a joke, however, can crush hands and limbs. Some shock absorbing material, such as part of an old tire, should be secured on the underside of the seats or embedded in the ground to cushion the impact. Today, an increasing number of seesaws use a spring-centering device, rather than a fulcrum, which prevents abrupt contact with the ground. A spring-centered seesaw only requires one child to play, and does not depend upon the coordinated actions of two children. If one child should dismount, it does not cause the other child to fall to the ground. Fulcrum seesaws are not recommended for small children. In addition to abrupt ground contact, fulcrum seesaws can also present a pinch hazard. The maximum angle for a fulcrum seesaw should be 25 degrees. The handholds on a seesaw should not extend past the sides of the seat.

Slides

Slides are one of the most popular pieces of playground equipment attracting all age groups. While slides may be designed for children to go down feet first, they will actually go down in every imaginable position including headfirst. Children also like to run up slides and will also try to walk down slides. Slides can either be free standing or part of a composite playground structure. A freestanding slide should have a platform that is at least **22 inches** long and at least as wide as the slide. The platform should have either a guardrail or a protective barrier, including handholds at the chute entrance. No space should exist between the platform and the chute. The CPSC recommends that the average slope of a slide should be 30 degrees, but in no case should it exceed 50 degrees. The sides of the slide along the chute should have a minimum height of 4 inches. The final 11 inches of the chute leading to the exit should be flat and parallel to the ground. If the slide is no more than 4 feet high, the exit should be no more than **11 inches** above the protective surface. If the slide is over 4 feet, the distance should be at least **7 inches** but no more than **15 inches.** Embankment slides, which follow the contour of the ground, should not be more than **12 inches** off the ground. The edge of the slide exit should be rounded or curve. Metal slides can become very hot when exposed to the full sun. Children can burn quickly when bare skin comes in contact with a hot slide. Slides should be located in shaded areas. Children should not be permitted to climb on the top of tube slides. Since tube slides are fully enclosed, supervisors may not be able to observe children who are inside the slide. More attention may be required when supervising children using tube slides. Finally, some slides spiral in circles. Small children should not use spiral slides that have more than one 360-degree turn.

Swings

Swings are perhaps the most popular piece of playground equipment. They can be divided into two categories: those that swing back and forth along a single axis (to-fro swings), and those that move in multiple directions such as a tire swing. Children play on swings in many ways. They like to jump off while the swing is in motion, stand and swing, and lie face down on the seat and swing on their stomachs. Since children like to twist and twirl while in a to-fro swing, the swing hangers should be spaced no less than 20 inches apart to reduce side-to-side motion.

Swings should be located away from other playground equipment to reduce the risk that a child will run in front of a moving swing. A safety zone should exist around the perimeter of the swing and it should never overlap the use zone of any adjacent piece of playground equipment. While it is not uncommon to find three swings on a support structure, the CPSC recommends using only two swings. Swing supports should be secured in concrete footings that are below the base of the protective surface.

Swing seats should hold only one person at a time. Hard seats such as wood or metal increase the severity of impact injuries and are not recommended. A soft, lightweight, flexible seat made of rubber or plastic is the best choice. The edge of the seat should be rounded or smooth. The seat should located at least **1 foot** above the protect surface for preschool-age children and at least **16 inches** for school-age children. Tot swings, which are especially designed for children under four years of age, should be at least **2 feet** above the protective surface to reduce the risk that an unsupervised child will become stuck in one. Tot swings should provide full support around the child, but careful attention must be given to the openings in the seat to make sure they do not present an entrapment and possible strangulation risk.

Tire swings are popular with children. Normally, multi-axis swings use three suspension cables connected to a swivel mechanism. Since they can move in any direction, these swings should stand alone apart from other swings or equipment. Large heavy tires, such as from semis, should not be used because they generate a lot of force while they are in motion and can create more serious impact injuries.

Steel belted radial tires must be carefully inspected and continuously monitored to make sure that the steel belts do not become exposed. Drainage holes should be made on the underside of the tire. Multi-axis swings require more maintenance than to-fro swings. Pinch points can occur in the hanger mechanisms.

Certain swings are not recommended for use. These include the following: (1) Animal figure swings that have a rigid metal framework and pose a risk of impact injuries; (2) Multiple occupancy swings that are intended for more than one user (with the exception of tire swings); (3) Free swinging ropes which present a strangulation risk; and (4) Swinging exercise rings and trapeze bars on long chains which are considered athletic equipment rather than public playground equipment.

Trampolines

Trampolines are never recommended for use as part of a church playground. In 1996 alone, over 83,000 injuries requiring emergency room treatment occurred with the use of trampolines. The vast majority of victims were under 15 years old. For more information on the use of trampolines, see section 7.18 in chapter 7.

Summary

Over 200,000 children are treated annually in hospital emergency rooms for playground-related injuries. Of that group, on average 15 die. The most common injuries result from falls, collisions with equipment, contact with sharp edges, protrusions, pinch points, hot surfaces, and debris left on the playground.

The most important safety issue is the protective surface of the playground. The best protective surfaces use either a unitary material such as rubber or a loose-fill material such as sand or wood chips. The amount of loose-fill material that is needed depends on its "critical height" rating. Critical height is defined as "the fall height below which a life-threatening head injury would not be expected to occur."

Each piece of playground equipment must be positioned to take into account its use zone, which includes an area around the equipment. The protective surface must extend throughout the entire use zone. The size of the use zone varies depending on whether the equipment is stationary or not.

In designing the playground, four factors should be taken into account: (1) the site of the playground; (2) the location of the playground equipment; (3) separation of the equipment based on the ages of the users; and (4) playground supervision.

Regular inspections are needed for each piece of equipment. Safety factors differ depending on the design and use of the equipment.

In the next chapter, the focus is on recreational programs and risk management techniques to promote safety.

Additional Resources on the Internet

For additional information on making your playground safe, review the material found on the following web sites. These resources were used in the preparation of this chapter.

"5.3 Playground and Outdoor Areas of the Facility (FA219 thru FA262)." National Health and Safety Performance Standards. <http://nrc.uchsc.edu/national/5-3.html>.

"CPSC Staff Recommendations for Identifying and Controlling Lead Paint on Public Playground Equipment." Consumer Product Safety Commission. <http://www.cpsc.gov/lead/lead/html>.

"Fall Injury Interventions Playgrounds." <http://depts.washington.edu/hiprc/childinjury/topic/falls/playground.html>.

"Handbook for Public Playground Safety." National Program for Playground Safety. <http://www.uni.edu/playground/safety_information.html>.

"Handbook For Public Playground Safety: Safety Alert CPSC Document #325." Consumer Product Safety Commission. <http://www.cpsc.gov/cpscpub/pubs/325.pdf>.

"Prevent Burns on Hot Metal Playground Equipment: Safety Alert CPSC Document #5036." Consumer Product Safety Commission. <http://www.cpsc.gov/cpscpub/pubs/5036.html>.

"Questions and Answers: Lead Paint on Public Playground Equipment." Consumer Product Safety Commission. <http://www.cpsc.gov/lead/leadqa.html>.

"Trampoline Safety Alert." Consumer Product Safety Commission. <http://www.cpsc.gov/>.

CHAPTER 7. SAFEGUARDING CHURCH AND SCHOOL RECREATIONAL ACTIVITIES

7.1 The Significance of Safeguarding Recreational Activities

Fellowship and recreation play an important role in the life of every church and school. Sharing together, interacting, and having fun contribute to nurturing and sustaining community. Recess, gym classes, and athletic programs are common within schools. Many congregations also sponsor recreational and athletic activities as part of the fellowship ministry of the church. Such events may be a planned part of outreach programs and church growth. Thus, a growing number of churches plan activities for every age group from preschoolers to senior citizens. It is no longer unusual to find an aerobics class, soccer schedule, or beach trip listed along with a Bible study or prayer group in the weekly schedule printed in the church bulletin.

Certain risks and hazards are associated with a number of recreational activities that churches and schools sponsor. The following table highlights data from the Consumer Product Safety Commission on injuries associated with recreational activities for 1994. Data is presented on 18 separate activities.

Injuries Associated with Selected Sports and Recreation Equipment
Treated in Hospital Emergency Departments—Calendar Year 1994[1]

1.	Basketball	716,114
2.	Bicycles & Accessories	604,455
3.	Football	424,622
4.	Baseball/Softball	404,364
5.	Playground equipment	266,810
6.	Soccer	162,115
7.	Exercise & Exercise Equipment	155,231
8.	Skating (ex. In-line)	146,082
9.	ATVs, Mopeds, Minibikes	125,136
10.	Swimming, pool equipment	115,139
11.	Volleyball	97,523
12.	Lacrosse, Rugby, etc	90,252
13.	Hockey	81,885
14.	In-line skating	75,994
15.	Horseback riding	71,162
16.	Trampolines	52,892
17.	Skateboards	25,486
18.	Track and Field	18, 774

---

[1] National Electronic Surveillance System, U.S. CPSC, *Consumer Product Safety Review,* Summer 1996.

The study found that males had higher rates of injury in every category except horseback riding, skating, and volleyball. The injury rate was about the same for males and females regarding trampolines and track and field activities.

Churches and schools sponsor many of the above activities. Some general guidelines exist that can reduce the frequency and severity of many accidents associated with recreational programs. For example, churches and schools can significantly reduce risks by promoting the use of proper gear and equipment, by routinely inspecting equipment, facilities and grounds, by using an adequate number of trained supervisors, and by understanding the risks associated with specific activities and taking the proper steps to reduce them. Often, the steps required to reduce risks are simple and inexpensive. Two reasons they are not done are (1) that church and school leaders are not familiar with the true nature of the risks, and (2) safety is sometimes viewed as a burden. Rather than viewing safety procedures in a negative way as instilling anxiety or as imposing burdens on what is intended to be a fun activity, safety procedures should be portrayed in a positive light arising out of the caring values of the church or school. Several of the more important and common areas of risk associated with church and school sponsorship are discussed below. Particular attention is given to water safety, baseball and softball, soccer, bicycling, skiing and snowboarding, basketball, football, golf, volleyball, aerobics and exercise classes, skating, games, church carnivals, hayrides, camping trips, fireworks, and recreational programs for older adults.

7.2 Water Safety

Swimming

While few churches own a swimming pool, they regularly sponsor activities that include swimming. It may be a pool party for the youth at the home of a church member, a beach or lake trip, the use of a hotel swimming pool, or participating in a camping program with swimming in a lake or a pool. Some schools own their own pools. Reducing risks associated with swimming are critical because of the risk of drowning or severe brain damage. Slippery surfaces also contribute to slips and falls resulting in head injuries and fractures. In addition, drainage ditches and fish ponds also present water hazards that require proper barriers.

Swimming guidelines

Have a signed parental permission slip that authorizes minors to participate in swimming activities. Test each child for his or her swimming ability. Only experienced swimmers should be permitted in the deep end of a pool or other swimming area. Diving should never be permitted in shallow water. Periodically clear the pool to give swimmers a chance to rest.

Fences and barriers

Pools and other water hazards should be enclosed by a fence, a wall, or some other barrier at least **5 feet** high with the bottom no more than **3-1/2 inches** off the ground (heights vary with local zoning ordinances). The barrier should have no footholds that would permit a child to climb over it. If a fence with vertical slats is used, the spacing between the slats should be less than **3-1/2 inches.** A child should not be able to slip through the slats. If a chain link fence is used the diamond shaped openings should be less than **1-3/4 inches** across. Fence gates should be self-closing and self-latching. The doorknob or latch on the gate should be positioned higher than normal—at least **54 inches** above the bottom of the gate. If that is not possible, the latch should be located inside the gate (the pool side) and positioned 3 inches below the top of the gate. A gate should never be left propped open. A properly working gate is critical since it provides access to the pool. If the latch does not work properly, it does not matter how good the fence or barrier is.

Pool drains

No person should ever sit on a pool or spa drain due to the risk of disembowelment. The primary victims are children between the ages of 2 and 6 who sit on an uncovered drain in a wading pool. Drains should be equipped with a dome shaped cover. Sometimes the cover becomes broken, loose, or is missing. In such cases, the pool should be drained and not used until the cover is replaced. A similar risk is body entrapment. On average, during the past seven years one child has died per year in a swimming pool due to body entrapment. Drains create powerful suction. Any open or flat drain that the body can completely cover presents a hazard. Even more common are deaths that occur as the result of hair entrapment. The typical victim is a girl with long hair. While the head is underwater the hair becomes entangled in the small holes of the drain cover. Most accidents occur in spas. Avoid games in spas such as trying to see who can hold their breath the longest with their head under water.

Several steps can be taken to reduce the risk of entrapment hazards and injuries in pools and spas. First, two drains should exist for each pump. Second, always keep both the drain and the skimmer in the open position. If possible, lock them in place so there is more than one source of suction. Third, install a safety switch that shuts off the pump if blockage is detected. Fourth, install anti-vortex (dome shaped) rather than flat drain covers. The drain cover should have markings that indicate that it has been tested to the ASME/ANSI voluntary standards. Fifth, immediately replace any cracked or broken drain covers. Make sure they are securely in place. Do not use a pool with an inadequate or missing drain cover. Sixth, regularly check the skimmer for blockage. Seventh, have warning signs and safety rules in place around the pool with clear instructions for both swimmers and supervisors that also include emergency phone numbers. Adult supervisors should fully understand all rules and know how to shut off the pump. If an entrapment should occur, the pump should be turned off as quickly as possible. Eighth, make sure that all life saving equipment is in place including a ring buoy and rope, or a throwing line and shepherd's hook.

Ocean swimming

Beach trips are popular with church youth groups. Three safety precautions should be followed when swimming in the ocean. First, never swim in unsafe surf conditions. Rip currents can carry swimmers out to sea. Shore break (large waves that break on the beach with little water beneath them) can slam a swimmer down causing back, neck, and shoulder injuries. Avoid these unsafe conditions. Second, always use a buddy system. No person should swim alone. Third, never dive in shallow water or water of unknown depth. Ocean depths can be deceptive and swimmers have become paralyzed from neck injuries sustained while diving in the ocean. Individuals can easily overestimate their ability to swim in the ocean. Cold water reduces a person's strength. The ocean provides a wonderful experience when properly respected.

Boating, water skiing, and swimming

Boating and sailing are great fun and a few safety precautions should be followed to keep them that way. Always make sure that an adequate number of life vests are on the boat, including a throw line and a life preserver. The boat should be fueled before leaving the dock and it's a good idea to carry extra fuel on board. All boats should be equipped with a working fire extinguisher. Never dive off a boat into shallow water, or into any location where hazards may exists such as rocks or trees below the surface. While some states do not have an age limit or require a license to drive a boat, use only adult, experienced drivers. If water skiing or tubing is taking place, the boat needs both a driver and a spotter. Those skiing or tubing should wear life vests. Hand signals can be used to communicate between the spotter and those being pulled in case a problem should occur. A clinched fist, for example, can mean "stop the boat immediately." Provide safety instructions before departing the dock. In case of a capsize, individuals should stay together and cling to the boat until help arrives.

Supervision

Adults must closely supervise water and swimming activities. One adult should be designated to be the "watcher." The "watcher" stays completely focused on watching the children in the pool. When several adult supervisors are together, it is easy for them to begin to visit with one another and to lose eye contact with what is going on in the pool. Adults should rotate with each person taking a turn being the watcher. Each swimmer should have a "buddy" to help keep track of one another. Youth leaders should learn CPR (cardiopulmonary resuscitation). Emergency equipment, including a telephone, should be available by the pool. Supervisors should know how to shut off the pump in an emergency.

7.3 Baseball and Softball

Church softball leagues exist throughout the United States. Perhaps no other sport is as common in churches as softball. Softball attracts both males and females and members of all age groups. From a risk standpoint, baseball and softball rank right behind basketball and football as causing the most sport-related injuries to children on an annual basis. Three preventive measures, however, can greatly reduce the number of injuries associated with baseball and softball. They include using helmets with a face guard, substituting softer baseballs and softballs for the standard ones, and using modified safety bases.

Face guards

Facial injuries account for more than one-third of all baseball-related injuries to children between the ages of 5-14. According to a study conducted by the Consumer Product Safety Commission, in 1995, out of 162,000 baseball-related injuries treated in hospital emergency rooms, nearly 60,000 were facial. Furthermore, the younger the child, the more likely the injury was facial. For example, for the age group 5 to 7, facial injuries accounted for 84% of all injuries. What caused the facial injury? In most cases it was being hit by a ball. Most facial injuries occur when a child is playing in the field (49%). Batters, pitchers, and base runners account for 20% of the injuries. About one-third of the time the injuries occur during practice or while warming up for a game. This indicates the need for safety measures not only during a game, but also during the warm up and in practice sessions. The good news is that facial injuries to batters and runners can be all but eliminated by using helmets with face guards. While batting helmets are commonly used, it is not common for them to have a face guard. A face guard adds about $10 to the cost of the helmet, but is estimated that each face guard saves 10 to 11 times its cost over 10 years in eliminated injury expenses. Face guards should meet the ASTM F910 Standard Specification for Face Guards for Youth Baseball.

Softer-than standard balls

The number one cause of injuries in the CPSC study was being hit by a ball, which accounted for 55% of all injuries. Of that total, pitchers caused 20%, followed by being hit by a batted ball (18%), a thrown ball (14%), or hit while trying to catch a fly ball (3%). Hits to the head and chest created the most serious injuries. They were also the most frequent. Between 1973 and 1995 fifty-nine children died from being hit in the head (21) or chest (38). Nineteen other children died from other injuries. Using softer baseballs and softballs can reduce these injuries. Currently, the harder balls control 90% of the market and are involved in 97% of the injuries. Most importantly, no serious injuries have been reported with the use of softer balls. A study funded by CPSC found that the softer balls can reduce head injuries. Churches should use the Softer-than-Standard Baseballs and Softballs to reduce the hazards associated with being hit by a ball.

Safety bases

Sliding injuries are more common in softball than in baseball. The most common injuries are strains and sprains that result from sliding into a base. Girls between the ages of 10-14 appear to be the highest risk group for injury. Safety bases can reduce the frequency and severity of injuries. A safety base releases from ground upon impact and leaves a smooth area on the ground where it was located.

7.4 Soccer

Soccer continues to increase in popularity, both for boys and girls, and now more children participate in soccer than baseball. Only basketball, volleyball, and softball rank ahead of soccer. Nearly three-fourths of those playing soccer are under the age of 18. Many churches participate in organized soccer programs or play soccer as part of youth fellowship activities.

During a recent 15 year period, at least 21 deaths have been associated with moveable soccer goals. Each year, children are treated in emergency rooms for goal-related injuries. The problem is that some moveable goals tip over and cause injuries to the head, neck, chest, and limbs of victims. These goals often weigh between 150-500 pounds. Most problems have occurred with "homemade" goals rather than professionally manufactured ones. When not properly secured or constructed, the goal can tip over when children climb on the net or hang from the crossbar. Few accidents occur during soccer games. Rather, the accidents tend to happen during times when children are playing on their own, and often are not even playing soccer. Climbing on the goal or hanging from the crossbar present the greatest risk of a tip over injury. Other tip over injuries have occurred when one side of the goal has been lifted, or blown over by the wind. Since injuries often occur when the goals are left unattended, it is important to store moveable soccer goals properly when they are not in use. Goals can be stored in a variety of ways. They can be locked to a fence, stored in a building, locked face-to-face to another goal, disassembled and stored, or locked face down to the ground. Always remove the net when storing the goals for any extended time. Place warning labels on each crossbar that climbing or hanging is prohibited. Teach children the dangers associated with the goals and never permit anyone to climb on a goal or to hang from the crossbar. Goals should only be located on a flat, level field. Since moveable soccer goals require careful counterbalancing, churches should only use professionally designed and constructed goals. The goals should be anchored according to the manufacturer's instructions. Only trained adults should move the goals.

7.5 Bicycling

Many churches sponsor bike trips as part of their youth fellowship activities. Bikes are also used at church camp programs. Students may ride a bike to school. What most church and school leaders do not know, though, is that bike injuries rank second among all injuries associated with recreational activities. In 1996, for example, more than 350,000 children under age 14 were treated in hospital emergency rooms for bicycle-related injuries. Furthermore, the risk of a bike injury to someone under the age of 15 is more than five times higher than to those who are older. Furthermore, in 80 percent of the accidents, the behavior of the child is the main cause of the accident. Some of the main problems include the following:

- Not stopping at a stop sign or traffic signal
- Turning left into oncoming traffic
- Swerving into traffic that is approaching the rider from behind
- Riding against the flow of traffic

While head injuries account for 20 percent of all injuries to those over 10 years of age, they represent about 50 percent to the younger riders. This is significant because 60 percent of all bike-related deaths are connected to head injuries. Most bicycling deaths that involve children are in an accident with a motor vehicle. Perhaps one reason that younger children have more head injuries is that they are less likely to wear a helmet. It is estimated that only 5 percent of victims under 15 years of age had a helmet on at the time of their accident. Only about 18 percent of all riders wear a helmet, although it is the law in many states and localities. How important is wearing a bike helmet? One study reports that wearing a bike helmet reduces head injury by 85 percent and brain damage by 88 percent.[2] For this reason, in March 1999, the Consumer Product Safety Commission implemented a new, uniform, mandatory federal safety standard for bicycle helmets. Prior to then, several different voluntary standards were in place. Churches and schools that

---

[2] Robert S. Thompson, Frederick P. Rivera, and Diane C. Thomson. "A Case-control Study of the Effectiveness of Bicycle Helmets." *New England Journal of Medicine* 1989:320:1361-1367.

sponsor bicycle trips or use bicycles as part of any activity should require all participants to wear a helmet that meets this standard. Older helmets that meet earlier standards from the Snell Memorial Foundation, the American Society for Testing Materials, the American National Standards Institute, and the Canadian Standards Association also provide good protection. Helmets should be appropriate for the age of the rider and contain a label indicating they meet the CPSC standard. When worn, the helmets should be secure, but comfortable, and should not move around on the head. When worn properly, the helmet is positioned near the eyebrows and does not expose the forehead. Other safety considerations include the following:

- Fluorescent and brightly colored clothing can make riders more visible.

- All bikes should have a reflector.

- Bikes used at night should have both a headlight and a taillight.

- Have riders check to see that nuts and bolts are tight before beginning a trip; also inspect tires and brakes.

- Ride with the traffic, not against traffic. Stay in a single file to the far right of the road maintaining a safe distance between each bike.

- Obey the same laws for motorized vehicles.

- Never assume that a driver of a car sees you; stay alert and be on guard for a car turning into your path.

- Warn pedestrians before you pass them.

- Be especially careful when descending hills and be prepared to stop if there is an intersection at the bottom of the hill.

- When stopping for a break, move to a safe location away from the road.

- Keep bikes locked when not in use. Lock the back wheel to an immovable object.

7.6 Skiing, Sledding and Snowboarding

In recent years, the number of total injuries to skiers has declined, but the number of head injuries has stayed about the same. However, for snowboarders both numbers have significantly increased. The overall accident rate has tripled and head injuries have increased by a factor of five. One important factor is that children are more likely to experience a head injury and are participating in snowboarding in increasing numbers, especially for those between 7 and 11 years of age. During the 1990s about 24 deaths occurred per year with head injury often the cause. A collision with a tree was frequently involved. As might be expected, falls were the leading cause of head and neck injuries. The Consumer Product Safety Commission has estimated that a helmet would have prevented or lessened the severity of two-thirds of the injuries associated with a fall. Yet, few skiers or snowboarders wear helmets. Current usage is estimated only to be 2-3 percent. That, however, is likely to change. Helmets are the fastest growing area of sales related to skiing and snowboarding.

More professionals are wearing helmets as well as young children. Ski schools now regularly use helmets. However, no laws exist that require helmets. Adult supervisors who lead church youth groups on ski trips should wear helmets. Modeling safe behavior is important. Skiers should also be encouraged to wear wrist bands. Wrist injuries often occur as individuals stretch out their arms to break a fall. Sledding also requires careful supervision. Each year, serious accidents occur as the result of collisions with obstacles such as trees and with other children. Sleds can achieve high speeds and sleds with runners can cause particularly bad injuries. Makes sure that sled runs are clear and avoid the use of sleds that have runner blades.

7.7 Basketball

Many churches and schools have either indoor or outdoor basketball facilities. They sponsor organized play for children and adults, as well as provide opportunities for children to use the courts on their own without supervision. The demand for basketball facilities is high. Basketball has become the most popular sport among young people in the United States, and correspondingly has the most injuries on an annual basis. The number of boys that play basketball on a regular basis still far outnumbers the number of girls that play. This is reflected in findings that show boys sustaining injuries at a factor five times that as girls.[3] The age groups with the greatest number of injuries are those between 15 to 24 years of age and 5 to 14 years of age. Many injuries are minor ones including sprains, blisters, and jammed fingers. Eye injuries, damage to permanent teeth, and impact injuries also occur. Some basic safety procedures can be used to reduce injuries associated with basketball. [4] Often baskets are located near a wall. Secure padded mats on the wall under each basket to cushion collisions with the wall. Use breakaway rims. A breakaway rim helps prevent a glass backboard from shattering and it also allows those players who can dunk a basketball to hold onto the rim and negotiate dropping back to the floor in a controlled manner. A rim restrainer should also be used with glass backboards which keeps the rim attached to the backboard if the glass does shatter. Nets should be maintained in good repair. In the past, chain nets were often used on outdoor basketball hoops. If your church or school has any hoops with chain nets they should be replaced with a soft net. Chain nets can cut hands, wrists, and fingers. For outdoor courts, the pole support for the backboard should be located outside the playing area, including distance for a safety buffer. This can be accomplished by using either a gooseneck support or a double poled backstop. Weatherproof padding should also be put around the pole. When dividing up teams, try to maintain a balance between skill and size. Have children remove any jewelry such as rings, bracelets, or watches that could cut another player. Participants should wear shoes designed for basketball to reduce sprains and foot injuries. For organized basketball activities, protective eye gear and mouth guards are recommended to lower eye and teeth injuries. Headbands should be used to hold eyeglasses to the head. Any water spills or perspiration that gets on the court should be immediately dried to prevent slips and falls. Keep loose balls and other items off the court. Inspect outdoor courts and the area surrounding the court before play or practice begins. Outdoor courts should be kept free of debris including dirt and gravel. Always keep the court and

---

[3] *Consumer Product Safety Review*, Summer 1996, p. 5.
[4] See James E. Bryant, "Basketball," pp. 97-104, in Neil J. Dougherty IV, editor, *Principles of Safety in Physical Education and Sport*, (Reston, VA: American Alliance for Health, Physical Education, Recreation and Dance, 1993) p. 102f.

area surrounding it free from broken glass and other dangerous objects.

7.8 Football

Flag football and touch football are popular events at schools, church youth activities and at picnics. In organized contact football programs, extensive padding and safety equipment are used. Virtually no safety equipment is used for flag or touch football. Yet, participants in flag and touch football can still experience high levels of contact, both intentionally and unintentionally. Often a game gets started simply because someone shows up with a football. Rather than playing on an athletic field, the game may be played using someone's yard or on church property. Often trees, tree roots, wires, sprinklers, hoses, holes, signs and other hazards are present. A game should not be played unless a clear playing area exists without any hazards (including no debris on the ground). The playing area should be inspected, clearly marked and should include a buffer zone. Teams should be divided to reflect equal skills and physical size. All players should understand the rules of the game including what is acceptable and unacceptable behavior. The participants should warm up before play begins. Remove jewelry, watches and other items that could cut someone. No metal cleats should be permitted. The game should be supervised and inappropriate behavior should be immediately corrected.

7.9 Golf

Sponsoring an annual golf outing is a common activity for many churches. From a risk standpoint, it represents a good choice, although some risks are present. Many who participate in such events are experienced golfers, but others may have very limited or even no golfing experience. The motivation to participate may be less the golf experience, and more the fellowship that surrounds the activity. While many view golf as having far less physical exertion than many sports, nevertheless more injuries treated in emergency rooms are associated with it than with swimming, field hockey, tennis, volleyball or ice hockey.[5] Simply put, a lot of people play golf and they are swinging a club very fast while hitting a hard ball that goes, often, in unplanned directions. In actuality, most injuries in golf are minor, but some, such as blisters, have a very high frequency. Other injuries, though, such as being hit by a club or a ball can be serious. In almost every case, observing simple rules of safety can prevent serious injuries. When churches sponsor a golf outing, it should not be assumed that each player knows the basic rules of safe play. One way to communicate safety rules is to ask each player to read and sign a safety card or risk form. This is standard practice in many golf clubs and school programs. Common instructions include the following:

● Stay alert and completely clear of someone preparing to hit a ball. Do not assume that they can see you or that they know where you are standing.

● Do not swing a club unless a clear safety zone exists around you. Look around you before you hit the ball. Always direct your swing and follow-through to a clear area.

---

[5] See the chapter on golf in Neil J. Dougherty IV, editor, *Principles of Safety in Physical Education and Sport*, (Reston, VA: American Alliance for Health, Physical Education, Recreation and Dance, 1993).

- If other golfers are playing ahead of you, or there are grounds keepers at work, do not hit until they are out of your range. If you hit a ball and it heads for someone, shout "FORE" loudly to warn the endangered person. If you hear "FORE" being shouted, quickly squat down and cover your head.

- Do not retrieve balls or tees while hitting from the practice range tee.

- If a thunderstorm occurs, leave the course as quickly as possible. If you are caught in a storm go to a low lying place to seek shelter. Do not carry or stand by your clubs. Do not stand under trees.

In addition to these guidelines, remind inexperienced players to use a golf glove and to carry some band aids for possible blisters. Blisters can contribute to a club slipping out of someone's hands.

7.10 Volleyball

Volleyball is popular both among girls and boys and is regularly played at youth functions, camps, the beach, and picnics. It's played both indoors and outdoors and by all age groups. Volleyball represents a very low risk of serious injury, and from a risk standpoint is a good choice for a church or school recreational activity. The most common injuries are sprains and muscle strains. When played outside, the same precautions should be taken for other outside sports activities that use a playing field. Often a game may be set up in someone's back yard. Check for hazards before playing such as holes, sprinklers, tree roots and other items that could cause someone to trip or twist an ankle. Remove all debris from the playing area. A safe buffer zone of 10 feet should exist completely around the playing area. Control play that becomes too aggressive along the net. Spiking the ball is part of the excitement of playing volleyball, but players should be equally matched if more physical play is permitted. Individuals with back problems should not play. Often church groups purchase equipment designed for home use and stakes and cords are needed to hold up the poles. The stakes should not protrude from the ground. Higher quality equipment designed for indoor use requires special attention. The standards (or poles) that hold the volleyball net in place should be secure and not tip over. They should be positioned at least three feet outside the playing area. The top of the net should be covered with a protective surface and checked regularly for tears and wear. No wire should ever be exposed. A clear space of at least 6-1/2 feet should exist around the court. Similar to other sports, jewelry, watches, and rings should be removed before play. Knee pads can help reduce bruises and cushion falls to the ground or floor.

7.11 Aerobic Classes and Exercise Programs

Aerobic classes and exercise programs are becoming increasingly popular at churches and schools. Some congregations have fully equipped workout rooms with tread mills, stair stepping equipment, stationary bicycles, weight machines, dance classes, and other equipment. The demand for such programs continues to grow and churches view such efforts as ways to serve their members and to reach out to their community. One reason that people participate in these programs is to lower health risks. Regular exercise plays an important role in developing and maintaining a healthy life style. At the same time exercise poses certain risks. For some people, participation in these programs can aggravate pre-existing health problems. For example, it is important to know if a person is a diabetic, has asthma or cardiac problems, or experiences hypertension. Pre-existing conditions affect the entire exercise strategy. Exercising can also create new health problems. Some individuals may experience strains or injuries to muscles or joints. Orthopedic problems are not uncommon. Since every person is different, an activity that is beneficial to one person can cause problems to someone else. Thus, every person should develop an individual exercise program based upon his or her age, health, and personal goals. The starting point should always be to consult with one's physician as to the level and type of exercise that is wise and beneficial.

Church and school leaders need to understand that sponsoring or hosting an aerobic class or exercise program represents a different level of commitment and risk than a more traditional program. Churches and schools that sponsor such activities should do so only under the supervision of certified individuals. Not only are professional, certified leaders needed, the facilities must be properly equipped with safe equipment that is routinely inspected and properly stored. Attention must be given to layout, maintenance, lighting, ventilation, temperature controls, spacing, and emergency procedures in case of an accident or a health problem. Each participant should fully understand the risks involved, and should sign a legally valid release form that has been prepared by the church's or school's legal counsel. While aerobic and exercise programs are noble efforts, too often churches proceed with such programs without doing the proper groundwork or fully understanding the complete nature of what they are doing or the risks associated with it, both for themselves or for the participants. Once those hurdles have been cleared, a valuable service can be rendered. Before starting a program, church and school leaders should consult with their insurance agent and make certain that they have the necessary insurance coverage to continue.

7.12 Skating

In-line skating

In-line skating is popular with many age groups, from youth to adults. Some simple steps can greatly reduce injuries to in-line skaters. First, wearing wrist guards and elbow pads provides dramatic protection for those parts of the body, reducing injuries by up to 80 percent. This is important since wrist injuries are common among new skaters. Knee injuries can be reduced up to one-third by wearing knee pads. It is also known that helmets provide increased protection for bicycle riders, reducing the risk of head injuries by up to 85 percent, and are likely to provide significant protection for in-line skaters.

Ice skating or roller skating

Today, most skating occurs in indoor rinks. Inexperienced skaters and small children need close supervision to prevent falls and head injuries. Helmets provide the best head protection. For outdoor skating, use public rinks or areas that are certified as safe. Ice should be at least 4 inches thick.

7.13 Games

According to Neil Dougherty, with respect to recreational activities, games are the second most frequent cause of litigation brought against schools.[6] While other programs such as football and basketball have more injuries, games generate more lawsuits. The reasons for the lawsuits are not surprising: inadequate supervision, unsafe conditions, and improper activities. These same concerns apply directly to churches and schools. Church youth groups are more likely to engage in a game than in a formal, well-planned sporting activity. The same may be true for recess activities at schools. Often games are not sufficiently planned. Just a few rowdy people can cause them to degenerate quickly into rough play. Boys have a need to show-off for the girls. Environmental factors such as a safe area may not receive adequate attention. Often, there are too few adult supervisors, and the adults themselves often are playing and cannot supervise adequately. Youth and children want to have a good time at these activities. While too many restrictions can dampen the atmosphere, this can be avoided with proper planning and supervision. First, use a play area that is inspected for hazards and that always has a buffer zone around its perimeter. Do not use areas that are next to roads unless they have adequate barriers. Do not include tree climbing as a part of any game. Second, provide clear instructions about the rules for playing the game. Explain any safety concerns that are present. If necessary, have participants remove potential hazards such as jewelry or rings. Third, adults should supervise and not play. Supervisors should be able to see all the participants all the time. Fourth, balance the teams with respect to size and skill. Make sure the activity is appropriate for the age and skill level of those involved. Fifth, correct inappropriate behavior immediately. Use a whistle to gain immediate attention from the participants. Six, use time-outs to control the level of play. Seventh, do not force children to participate who are uncomfortable with the activity. Eighth, be prepared to respond to an emergency. A phone should be available if help is needed. Church leaders should keep a medical treatment consent form on file for each child that participates in youth activities. A good time to collect these forms from parents is in the fall when church activities get into full swing along with the school schedule.

7.14 Carnivals

Many churches and schools sponsor a carnival in the Spring or Fall. These festive occasions often include many fun activities for children and adults with a lot of games and food. The risk management issues associated with many of the activities that occur at these carnivals have been discussed elsewhere in this chapter and will not be repeated here. However, a few additional concerns deserve attention. One is slips and falls. Clean up any spills immediately. Keep a mop handy. Have plenty of garbage cans available and keep debris picked up off the ground. Have a fire extinguisher available for outdoor booths. Often, these carnivals have pony rides. A pony ride is an unusual opportunity for most children, and one that is very enjoyable and exciting. On several occasions, however, pony rides at a church or school carnival have resulted in serious accidents. Children should not be permitted

---

[6] "Games", pp 143-146 in *Principles of Safety in Physical Education and Sport*, (Reston, VA: American Alliance for Health, Physical Education, Recreation and Dance, 1993) p. 143. Gymnastics is the number one source of litigation.

to walk behind a horse. It may kick. All riders should wear riding helmets. Parents or organizers should hold on to small children and walk beside them during the ride. The pony should be led and the pace should be kept to a walk. A second concern is the use of an outside company to operate a ride. Before hiring any company make sure the equipment it uses meets all safety standards and has been properly inspected. Collect and check references before hiring the company. Get a certificate of insurance from each outside vendor. The church should also monitor the rides and require through a contract that the owner of the ride exercise reasonable care in the operation of the ride. Church leaders should be familiar with these circumstances and take steps to prevent accidents at their own church.

7.15 Hayrides

Many churches sponsor hayrides during the fall. The occasion may be a preschool class visiting a farm or a church youth group having a fellowship activity. What is intended as a fun activity can quickly turn into a tragedy. Hayride accidents can kill or seriously injury participants. The accidents tend to follow several patterns. Major concerns include falling off the wagon and sustaining injuries directly from the fall or being run over by the wagon or a vehicle that is following the wagon. Accidents also occur that crush participants who sit on the sides or back of the wagon with their legs hanging over the side. Several scenarios occur. Sometimes the wagon turns a corner next to a building (or some other physical object such as a bridge or a post) and the driver cuts the corner short. A person setting with his or her legs dangling over the side can be crushed as the wagon slams into the side or corner of the building. Or the wagon may clear the building, but the rider is literally scraped off the wagon by the corner of the building. On other occasions two wagons may be hitched together. Individuals sitting on the back of the first wagon get pinched between the two wagons during a turn. Sometimes they fall off the first wagon and are run over by the second wagon. Wagon rides can be very bumpy. Riders can be bounced right out of the wagon. Often hayrides occur at night and visibility is poor. Usually there is a lot of noise and the driver may be completely unaware that an accident has occurred or that a problem may exist.

Many risk management experts do not recommend hayrides. Few companies specialize in providing hayrides. As a result, hayrides are often one-time events without careful planning or awareness of the safety issues. If a church or school sponsors a hayride the following points should be taken into consideration.

1. *Equipment.* The tractor and the wagon should be in good repair. The wagon should be clean and equipped with side walls. Loose hay should not be used. Two wagons should not be hitched together. In addition, occasionally a wagon will become unhitched from the tractor during the hayride. It is best to use a chain as a secondary backup to connect the wagon to the tractor to avoid that problem.

> **Example.** *Two dozen people were injured when they rolled down a hill when a wagon became unhitched during a hayride. One individual had medical bills exceeding $50,000.*

2. *Driver.* The driver should be fully trained and experienced in driving the tractor while pulling a wagon. The driver should have a written checklist of all safety precautions and review them prior to beginning the hayride.

3. Route. The route should be selected in advance and fully inspected for hazards. The driver should practice driving the route with the wagon prior to the hayride. Avoid the use of busy roads or roads that are too bumpy.

4. Seating. No rider should be seated in such a manner than any part of the body can extend past the side, back, or front of the wagon. Riders should remain seated inside the wagon at all times. Arms, head, and legs should be kept inside the wagon. Trips sponsored for small children should only use wagons equipped with proper seat belts and safety equipment. Small children can bounce right out of a wagon.

5. Trailing car. A car can follow the wagon at a safe distance with the headlights on the wagon. The car should have on its hazard lights. This car provides additional protection for the wagon from a rear collision, and serves as a form of back-up transportation if the tractor should have mechanical problems. The driver can also serve as a rear spotter to monitor the back of the wagon. The trailing driver must maintain a safe distance between the wagon at all times.

6. Lighting and visibility. Lighting is a critical safety factor for hayrides that occur at night. The tractor pulling the wagon should have the headlights on, the warning hazard lights on, and lights on the back that illuminate the wagon. As noted above, the car following the wagon should have its headlights on the wagon. Supervisors riding on the wagon should have flashlights ready for use if needed.

7. Supervision. An adequate number of supervisors should be present on the wagon. Riders should be given clear safety instructions prior to the hayride. Rowdy conduct should be corrected immediately.

8. Speed. The speed should be kept low. This may pose a problem if a main road is used and cars are backing up behind the wagon, and then try to pass quickly. For this reason main roads should be avoided.

9. Communication. The driver, a supervisor on the wagon, and the driver of the car following the wagon should use walkie-talkies to stay in communication with one another. The driver should have a spotter that can rely information as warranted, such as the need to stop. A cell phone should be available in case a need arises for emergency assistance.

10. Emergency procedures. A first aid kit should be present in case an injury should occur. Supervisors should have an emergency plan in place with phone numbers that may be needed.

7.16 Camping Trips

Camping trips pose a diverse range of risks. One risk is carbon monoxide poisoning that can occur through the use of grills, portable heaters, lanterns, or stoves that use fossil fuels such as kerosene charcoal, wood, or propane. These appliances should only be used with adequate ventilation. When these items are used inside of tents, campers, or vehicles the risk for CO poisoning is present. As a general rule do not use portable heaters while sleeping inside of tents or campers, or inside of a vehicle. Flu symptoms such as headaches, nausea, dizziness, or fatigue are also signs of CO poisoning. If such symptoms occur, seek immediate medical attention. Rock climbing is dangerous and should not be permitted. Keep food properly stored away from tents and sleeping areas. Food can attract bears, raccoons, rodents, and other animals. Food should be kept in a vehicle or hung from a tree away from campers. All trash should be properly disposed of. Have hikers stay on trails and make sure campers can identify poisonous plants such as poison ivy. Never permit campers to wander off by themselves, or to get ahead of the group or lag behind the group while on a hike. People can become disoriented very quickly and get lost. In addition, an isolated child is at risk for attack from some wide animals, especially in those regions that have mountain lions or bears. Other wild animals such as a moose or elk can be extremely dangerous if startled. Others may be rabid. Some campers may be allergic to insect stings. If an allergic reaction occurs, seek immediate medical help. Use insect repellents and be aware that some tick bites can cause serious health problems. Avoid brush piles that may harbor snakes. Instruct campers to avoid contact with any wild animal.

7.17 Fireworks

While discouraged by insurance companies, some churches and schools sponsor firework displays over the Fourth of July or for special activities. Fireworks related hazards are less connected to organized and professional displays of fireworks than to individuals purchasing and using fireworks on their own. Males experience nearly 75 percent of the injuries. Children, though, are very vulnerable. Forty percent of the injuries reported in 1998 were to children under age 15. Most injuries involve burns and affect the hands, eyes, heads, and face. Churches that sponsor fireworks should make it clear than no individuals are permitted to bring their own fireworks. Sometimes youth obtain illegal fireworks such as a cherry bomb or an M-80, and have no idea of the danger associated with these devices. They may even light them and throw them at bystanders. The improper use of fireworks can result in death, amputations, and blindness. Children should never be allowed to use fireworks. For years, sparklers have been thought of as a firework device for children, but sparklers burn at high temperatures and can cause clothes to catch on fire. The improper use of fireworks leads to injuries. Launchers must be stable to prevent tipping over and engaging in a horizontal discharge. New requirements went into place in 1997 that govern the stability of launchers. Spectators should be positioned out of the range of fireworks. Fireworks can engage in erratic flight paths. Fireworks that do not function after being ignited should never be re-ignited. They should be dosed and properly discarded. Notify the fire department of your plans and take the necessary safety precautions to respond if a fire should occur.

7.18 Trampolines

The Consumer Product Safety Commission has reported a sharp increase in trampoline injuries. Furthermore, since trampoline gymnastics has been introduced as an Olympic sport, the popularity of "bouncing" will continue to increase. According to the CPSC, during the decade of the 90s, the number of hospital emergency room-treated trampoline injuries almost tripled from an estimated 37,500 in 1991 to almost 100,000 in 1999. Nearly two-thirds of the victims were children 6 to 14 years of age. About 15 percent of injuries involved young children under 6 years old. During the 1990s, the CPSC received reports of 11 deaths related to trampoline use.

The popularity of trampolines continues to increase and trampoline gymnastics was introduced as a featured sport at the Olympic Games in Sydney, Australia. Why should churches be concerned about trampolines? In 1998 alone, an estimated 640,000 backyard trampolines were sold in the United States. Many church youth programs sponsor activities at the homes of members and some will have trampolines in their backyards. With over 100,000 injuries now occurring annually, the use of trampolines poses a serious liability risk to churches.

How do injuries occur? The CPSC reports that most trips to the emergency room are the result of jumpers colliding with one another, falling on the trampoline springs or frame, falling or jumping off the trampoline, or attempting somersaults and stunts.

To reduce injuries, CPSC has worked with the industry to develop a new standard for trampolines, which went into effect in 1999. Four new requirements were added to make trampolines safer and alert consumers to potential dangers:

- Padding must completely cover the metal frame, hooks, and all springs.

- There must be a label on the trampoline box stating, trampolines over 20 inches tall are not recommended for children under 6 years of age.

- Ladders cannot be sold with trampolines to prevent access by young children.

- The warning label on the trampoline bed must alert consumers not to allow more than one person to jump at a time and to warn against somersaults that can cause paralysis and death.

Church insurance companies do not recommend the use of trampolines for any age group. If a trampoline is used, the CPSC recommends the following safety tips:

- Always supervise children who use a trampoline.

- Allow only one person on the trampoline at a time.

- Do not allow somersaults.

- Do not allow the trampoline to be used without padding that completely covers the springs, hooks, and the frame.

- Place the trampoline away from structures and other play areas.

- Do not use a ladder with the trampoline because it provides unsupervised access by small children.

- Trampoline net enclosures can prevent injuries from falling off the trampoline.

7.19 Recreational Programs for Older Adults

As the population ages, churches are increasingly sponsoring activities for older adults. Some of these activities are recreational in nature. According to the Consumer Product Safety Commission, sports-related injuries to persons over 65 years of age are increasing at a higher rate than to any other age group. One reason may be that more older adults are engaging in sports activities than ever before. The top five activities in which injuries occur include bicycling, exercising, golf, snow skiing, and fishing. These are all activities that churches may sponsor. Older adults, especially those who do not engage in regular physical activity, may overestimate their stamina. Most injuries are due to falls, tripping, and strains. Church programs should adapt activities to the development capabilities of this age group. Older adults should not engage in physical activities without first consulting with their physician. Then each activity should conform to the appropriate safety measures for that event. The proper use of helmets and proper safety gear, warm-up activities, and occasional breaks to rest can help reduce accidents. Individuals should stop if they experience pain, swelling, or feel tired or ill.

7.20 Hazardous Activities to Avoid

Some recreational activities pose especially high risks and are not recommended for church or school programs. These activities include rock climbing, sky diving, hang gliding, rodeo activities, the use of trampolines (see section 7.18 above) , and the use of all-terrain vehicles. Never use a car or other motorized vehicle to pull a child on a sled or inner tube across snow or ice. Do not sponsor scavenger hunts where cars must be used to go from one location to another (the competition causes drivers to speed and to drive in an unsafe manner). Some youth groups have sponsored "bus pulls" where teams compete to see how far they can pull a bus or other vehicle. Individuals have been crushed under the wheels of buses in these events. They should be avoided.

Summary

Churches and schools sponsor many recreational activities. While all recreational activities pose certain risks to the participants, they differ greatly in the frequency and severity of accidents. Some activities such as golf or volleyball pose only small risks. Bicycling on the other hand, has a much higher level of frequency and severity. A church or school is more likely to be sued for an injury in an informal game than in an organized sport. Church and school leaders should review all recreational and fellowship activities that they sponsor, and take steps to reduce potential hazards associated with each activity.

In the next chapter, attention is given to reducing risks associated with church and school transportation.

Additional Resources on the Internet

For additional information on making recreational activities safe, review the material found on the following web sites. Also, several publications are listed that are available from the Consumer Safety Product Commission. These resources were used in the preparation of this chapter.

"5.4 Swimming, Wading, and Water (FA263 thru FA284)." National Health and Safety Performance Standards. <http://nrc.uchsc.edu/national/5-4.html>.

"Baseball Safety." Consumer Product Safety Commission. Pub. No. 329.

"Children Drown and More Are Injured From Hair Entrapment In Drain Covers For Spas, Hot Tubs, and Whirlpool Bathtubs: Safety Alert CPSC Document #5067" Consumer Product Safety Commission. <http://www.cpsc.gov/cpscpub/pubs/5067.html>.

"Fireworks Safety." Consumer Product Safety Review. Spring 1999. Vol. 3, No. 4.

"Fireworks: Safety Alert CPSC Document #12." Consumer Product Safety Commission. <http://www.cpsc.gov/cpscpub/pubs/12.html>.

"Guide to Safe Ocean Swimming." Stormfax. <http://stormfax.com/safeswim.htm>.

"Guidelines for Entrapment Hazards: Making Pools and Spas Safer." Consumer Product Safety Commission. Pub. No. 363.

"Guidelines For Movable Soccer Goal Safety." Consumer Product Safety Commission.

"How to Plan For the Unexpected: Preventing Child Drownings: Safety Alert CPSC Document #359." Consumer Product Safety Commission. <http://www.cpsc.gov/cpscpub/pubs/359.html>.

"Improving Fireworks Safety." Consumer Product Safety Review. Summer 1996.

"Playing Ball Safely: Kids and Face Guards." Consumer Product Safety Review. Spring 1997.

"Sports and Older Americans." Consumer Product Safety Review. Summer 1998.

CHAPTER 8. TRANSPORTATION SAFETY FOR CHURCHES AND SCHOOLS

8.1 The Significance of Transportation Safety

Most people are conscious that an accident can happen anytime they ride in a vehicle, but a taken-for-granted attitude generally prevails that our trips will be safe. Most of us are willing to get into a car even though we have no idea of the skill or driving record of the person behind the wheel. Many people value safety measures such as using seat-belts or buying a car with an air bag, but when we get into the vehicle, we don't expect to be in an accident even though we may take some precautions. When it comes to safety regarding church or school transportation we transfer our trust to others. We assume drivers are qualified and that vehicles are well-maintained. If a problem should occur, we expect it will be handled properly and thoughtfully with a high regard for safety. Often we recognize that risk is present, but we view it as low and unlikely. As a result, with respect to church or school transportation, we are willing to entrust ourselves and the safety of our children to the care of others. We are willing to be both passengers and drivers. We trust others and others trust us.

Effective risk management is not based upon trust. Risk management involves an intentional, systematic, and sustained effort at the leadership level to eliminate, reduce, or transfer risks through a process of comprehensive planning and oversight. That is quite different than recruiting an adult to drive a car, asking the children to buckle up, and checking that the tires are in good shape.

Many factors affect transportation safety and some are out of the control of the church or school and the individuals who drive or maintain the vehicles. Yet much can be done to improve safety and lower the risk of a serious or fatal accident. Over 80 percent of all crashes occur with 25 miles of a person's home. Nearly 60 percent of fatal accidents and crashes resulting in injuries occur on roads with a speed limit of 40 mph or less. In a recent year, for example, nearly 3 out of 4 people who died in traffic accidents were passengers. Over 60 percent of those who died were not wearing a seat belt, the single most important safety device. Accidents tend to be local events and occur in places that are part of our normal, everyday world. In part, that is why they are so shocking. Out of the midst of our routine patterns tragedy can strike.

Alcohol-impaired driving is another major problem and a contributing factor in many accidents. Over 40 percent of all traffic-related deaths involve alcohol. Drug-impaired driving is also a serious problem. Some drivers have inadequate skills and poor judgment. Excess speed, road rage, and risky decision making all contribute to accidents. One out of every three traffic fatalities involves excess speed. Often the injured are innocent victims. That, however, does not mean that we are powerless to reduce risk. Church and school leaders can and should take steps to enhance transportation safety. A transportation safety program should focus on three broad categories: (1) vehicles, (2) drivers, and (3) occupant safety. Training and education plays an important role in all three categories.

8.2 Vehicles

An effective risk management strategy should address four issues with respect to church or school vehicles: (1) the selection and approved use of vehicles; (2) the maintenance of vehicles; (3) the inspection of vehicles; and, (4) responding to problems.

The selection and approved use of vehicles

Churches and schools depend upon transportation for many different programs. Finding vehicles and drivers can be a problem. Vehicle selection often boils down to what is available. Many churches and schools own a van, a bus, or a car, but these vehicles are often insufficient to meet all of their transportation needs. Often volunteers are recruited who use their own vehicles. Other times rental cars or vans are used to meet temporary demands. Sometimes vehicles are borrowed. On some occasions a specialized vehicle is needed, such as a tractor. A vehicle that may be safe and appropriate for one use may not be for another. Some vehicles may not be safe for any purpose. Selecting and approving a vehicle for church or school use has both safety and legal implications.

Church and school leaders need to understand that they have an obligation to use reasonable care in the selection and approval of any vehicle that is used for one of their programs. For example, if youth leaders recruit teenage drivers to use their own cars to transport members of the youth group for a church activity, the church assumes certain risks if the leaders fail to act reasonably in evaluating the safety of the cars that will be used. If a car is unsafe because it has a clear and obvious safety hazard, such as not having seat belts, then it should not be used. If it is used and an accident occurs and passengers are injured, the church or school may be found liable of negligence. This same principle applies to the use of all vehicles. Before using any vehicle, whether it is owned not, it should be inspected. If the church or school does not own it, a certificate of insurance or a copy of an insurance card should be obtained from the owner. Always check with the insurance agent before renting or using any vehicle that the church or school does not own to determine what additional insurance coverage may be needed. A first aid kit should be kept on all vehicles.

The maintenance of vehicles

All church and school owned vehicles should have regular cleaning and maintenance. The maintenance records should be retained. They may be needed if an accident should occur and the church or school is charged with negligent maintenance. Care should also be taken to reduce the likelihood of vandalism of theft.

- Vehicles should be locked when not in use with all the windows up. Make sure the trunks are locked on cars.

- Park vehicles in areas that have plenty of light.

- Do not leave any valuable items in the vehicle.

- Keep a copy of the vehicle's Vehicle Identification Number at the church or school. That number will be reported if a vehicle is stolen.

The inspection of church or school-owned vehicles

First, churches and schools should comply with all applicable laws regarding vehicle licenses and inspections. These laws may vary regarding the type of vehicle involved. Vehicles should always display up-to-date license plates and inspection certificates. Second, a professional, mechanical inspection should occur as part of the routine maintenance of the vehicle. Third, drivers should regularly monitor the vehicle's fluid levels (oil, coolant, washer, brake fluid), tire pressure and wear, headlights, taillights, turn signals, dashboard gauges or warning lights, mirrors, and seat belt use to see that they are in good working order. It's a good idea to maintain a vehicle log that is filled-in each trip. The log should indicate date, driver, purpose of trip, and any problems that occur with the vehicle. A repair form should be completed and turned into the office if a problem is noted. Corrective actions should be taken when the need arises. A written inspection checklist should be used prior to any trip out-of-town.

The inspection of non-church or non-school-owned vehicles

The safety of non-owned vehicles is just as important as the safety of those that the church or school owns. A tendency often exists to recruit volunteer drivers and to pay little or no attention to the vehicle they drive. Minimally, leaders should only permit the use of vehicles that have current license plates and an inspection certificate (if required by law). The driver should read and sign a form that indicates the vehicle meets the minimum requirements for church or school use (adequate fluid levels, tire pressure and wear; working headlights, taillights, turn signals, dashboard gauges or warning lights, mirrors, and seat belts). Vehicles that are rented or borrowed should be inspected in a similar fashion prior to use. These forms should be given out and collected in advance of a trip. If they are given at the last minute, problems can occur that can be embarrassing both to the volunteer driver and the church or school leader. If the vehicle is to be used for a trip out-of-town, a written inspection checklist should be used.

Responding to problems

Church and school leaders need to plan for the unexpected. Vehicles have problems and it is never convenient when they occur. Churches and schools should consider maintaining a roadside service plan for all of their vehicles in case a breakdown should occur. In addition, contingency plans should exist to obtain a back-up vehicle if the need should arise. Drivers should know whom to contact if problems occur and should have access to a cell phone while driving for church or school-related events.

8.3 Drivers

An effective transportation strategy should address two issues with respect to drivers: (1) the selection and screening of drivers; and, (2) driver training.

The selection and screening of drivers

Key point. Drivers who transport children must also be screened to reduce the risk of child sexual molestation.

117

Leaders should not assume that anyone who drives or owns a car is suitable to drive for the church or school. Rather, leaders should use only qualified drivers who are properly insured, and who have safe driving records. For purposes of screening, drivers can be classified into two groups: regular and occasional drivers. The first group consists of individuals who drive church or school vehicles, or who drive their own vehicle for the church or school on a frequent basis. The second group includes individuals who drive their own vehicle for the church or school, but only infrequently. First, it should be noted that both groups represent the church or school and that the church or school potentially can be held liable for the actions of both groups while driving on their behalf. For this reason, reasonable care must be exercised in the selection and screening of drivers for both groups.

Establishing standards for selecting drivers

A starting point in the screening process is to establish threshold standards that all drivers must meet. Minimally, all drivers should have a valid driver's license for the type of driving they perform, and they should have insurance. A church or school should extend the threshold standards to exclude certain drivers with bad driving records. Establishing these standards can be a challenging task, since not all leaders may share the same values or perspectives on this issue. One approach to this problem is for church and school leaders to consult other community organizations as part of a comparative needs assessment. For example, leaders should check with the local public school district concerning their standards for school bus drivers, and for any other driver, paid or volunteer, who drives for school-related activities. The public school's policy may serve as a good baseline for local churches and church sponsored schools in establishing their own standard of reasonable care. Conforming to the public school's standard provides the church with a rationale that could be important if an accident were to occur and the church had to defend itself in a court of law. Other organizations may also be checked such as AAA, taxi companies, or bus companies. The church's or school's insurance company may also provide guidelines.

The screening form

Once standards have been established, both regular and occasional drivers should complete a screening form (obtain a copy and review the form the public school district uses). Most screening forms (a) collect background information (name, address, driver's license number and status, and insurance company); (b) ask specific questions concerning the individual's driving history (number and type of tickets, accidents, suspensions, revocations); (c) state organizational policies and procedures for drivers; and (d) provide a place for the driver to sign indicating that he or she has truthfully completed the form, has current auto insurance, and agrees to abide by the organization's policies and procedures. The church or school can raise the standard of care to an even higher level by having the driver list two references, which are then contacted.

The question often arises if the standard of care in screening the drivers should be the same for both regular drivers and occasional volunteer drivers. An argument can be made that the standard of care should be higher for those who drive frequently or who drive church or school vehicles. The church or school can achieve a higher standard of care by conducting a background check on individuals concerning their driving history. These checks are relatively inexpensive and can be arranged through the church's or school's insurance company. Often, the insurance carrier will do these checks for each driver listed on the policy, which generally includes each person who drives a church or school insured vehicle. Leader's should discuss the use and need for background checks with their insurance agent. Note: driver's who work with children need additional screening to reduce the risk of child sexual abuse.

Teenage drivers

Another common question is about using teenagers as drivers for church or school activities. Studies indicate that teenagers have the highest accident rates. Drivers who are 16 years of age pose the greatest risk. The risk declines as they become older. Insurance rates are higher for these young drivers, and are higher for boys than for girls. Churches and schools who use teenage drivers retain significant liability risks. It is common, for example, for members of a youth group to serve as drivers for other members of the group. When leaders recruit these drivers, and have them drive a church or school vehicle or use their own cars, the church or school assumes a higher than normal risk. That factor should be taken into account, along with the unique factors that are present in every situation, in making a decision of who can drive on behalf of the church or school. In general, leaders should avoid using young and inexperienced drivers whenever possible. The argument in favor of their use is that the state has licensed them as qualified to drive. The argument against using them is the widespread and consistent finding that their accident rates are high.

Implementation of a screening program

Finally, and perhaps the most challenging of all concerns, is how can a church or school successfully implement a screening program. Often church leaders recognize the rationale for screening drivers, but feel that they cannot do it within their own congregations. School leaders may feel uncomfortable screening volunteer drivers. The two most common arguments against screening drivers are as follows: (1) screening is offensive and will repel potential volunteers; and (2) screening is too burdensome—the church or school cannot administer the program effectively. Both concerns are legitimate, but effective solutions exist.

Four key factors affect the viability of a screening program: (1) support of leadership; (2) establishment of a workable screening process; (3) education and training; and (4) accountability.

1. Support of leadership. Gaining the support of leaders is necessary both to initiate a program and to sustain it over time. Church and school leaders generally want to maintain balance. On the one hand, they recognize the need for safety. On the other hand, they do not want safety issues to overshadow or impede ministry. In gaining the support of leaders, it is important to allow safety to emerge out of the ministry values of the congregation itself. This issue was addressed in chapter 2. A second powerful factor that attracts the attention of leaders is potential liability— both personally and corporate. No church, school, or leader wants to become involved in litigation. Once leaders recognize that screening is consistent with the ministry values of the church or school, and serves the interests of the entire community, a basis exists to proceed. Without the support of leaders, a program will be difficult to establish and maintain. Key steps in gaining their support include developing a rational for the program, reducing fears about screening, and building support among key opinion leaders.

(*a*) *Develop a rationale for the program.* While a rationale is insufficient in and of itself, it is necessary to build support for screening. The following factors can help strengthen your rationale:

- Providing safety arises out of biblical concepts such as being a good shepherd and being good stewards. Jesus elevates in importance the need to care for children. Screening is consistent with the church's mission.

- Like all organizations within the community, churches and schools have a legal obligation to provide for the safety and welfare of members and visitors.

- Screening is a standard practice in other organizations, such as public schools and day care centers that transport youth and children. The church or school will be held to the same standard of care as these other organizations.

- Failure to engage in reasonable care can result in potential charges of negligence if an accident should occur. The penalties can be substantial.

- Parents want the best possible care for their children. A church or school that promotes safety is appealing to an important value that most people share in common. It attracts people and instills confidence.

(*b*) *Reduce fears that leaders may have about screening.* The biggest fears are that the program will repel volunteers or cannot be managed. Both of these issues must be addressed. When done poorly, a screening program can repel people. It may be viewed as intrusive and heavy handed, even going against the spirit and nature of the church. But when done well, just the opposite occurs. People feel good knowing that a church or school cares deeply about providing safe environments for members and visitors, especially for children and youth. A well-designed screening program does not need to be offensive or embarrassing to anyone, including those for whom it is designed to screen out. It becomes a question of the nature of the program, and of education and training. These issues are addressed in sections below.

(*c*) *Build support among opinion leaders.* The goal is to create a critical mass of support among those individuals within the congregation or school that others look to for leadership and guidance. That may include elected leaders or employees, but it also may include members in no current leadership position. Support can be built in a variety of ways. It may begin with individual conversations and extend to leading group discussions, writing articles, or making both formal and informal presentations.

(*d*) *Involve leaders and congregational members in establishing procedures and policies.* It is well known that individuals bring a higher commitment to things in which they have a personal investment. Involving both leaders and members in shaping a screening process heightens levels of commitment and also legitimizes the process. The congregation or school family owns the screening program rather than having it imposed upon them.

2. Establishment of a workable screening process. The second key component in establishing a successful screening program is to create a proper structure for the screening process. This will make or break a program. Three important structural factors include (1) the actual screening form, (2) the manner in which the form is distributed and collected, and (3) maintaining confidentiality. In establishing a workable screening process, a good starting point is to conduct a comparative needs assessment of other organizations that screen drivers. Some organizations to consider might include the local public school district, the city government, other churches and schools, and perhaps a bus transportation or taxi company. Find out what each organization does. Collect copies of their screening forms, policies, and procedures. A comparative needs assessment provides the church with ideas and can jump-start the process. A critical component is designing a screening form.

(a) The screening form. Often churches make a decision to engage in screening and then become paralyzed in creating a form. Sometimes no one is certain what questions should be asked. Disagreements may surface on wording. The process can become stalled and then die on the vine. A form should only collect information that is useful and necessary. A good starting point is to examine forms collected through the comparative needs assessment. Often, one or more of those forms can serve as a template for the church or school. One option is to obtain permission to use or modify those forms. Sample forms are also found in the inspection protocols that serve as companion resources to this handbook. Another option is ask your insurance company to provide a form, or to work with a local attorney to design a form. An attorney should review any form that your church or school uses to make sure that it takes into account local and state issues. Also, consult with your insurance company before you begin to use the form to make sure it is consistent with your insurance coverage.

(b) Distributing and collecting screening forms. How and when individuals receive a form is critical in shaping how they will respond to the screening process. This process, more than the form itself, is what often alienates people. Consider the following three examples.

> **Example 1.** *The church youth minister asks a father of one the youth group members if he can help drive the kids to a bowling alley on Saturday afternoon. The parent arrives at the church on Saturday shortly before it is time to leave. "Oh, by the way," the youth minister says. "I need you to fill out this driving form before we go. The church board now requires all drivers to complete this form. It's just a formality."*

This first example illustrates several problems. First, the form is "sprung" on the driver after he has already been asked to drive and has agreed to do so. No prior knowledge or understanding of the screening process exists. The youth minister treats the form as being unimportant. A very awkward situation could develop. Suppose the parent refuses to sign the form, or does not meet the qualifications required on the form. The parent, the youth minister, and the children all face the potential for embarrassment. The parent may feel angry and betrayed. The youth minister may feel the whole screening program is a burden. The example portrays a screening process that is not well understood, poorly implemented, and counter-productive.

121

Example 2. Pastor Smith announces to the congregation that beginning immediately all individuals who drive for church activities will be required to fill out a form. Forms are included in the Sunday Bulletin. Church members who drive are asked to fill them out and return them to the church office.

This example illustrates a top-down approach to implementation. Screening is treated as an administrative problem. The solution is to tell people what to do and then give them a form. No rationale is provided. No input is solicited. An administrative approach to screening may work with paid employees who are required to comply with church or school policies to obtain employment or keep their job. It usually does not work as well with volunteers. To endure over time, a screening program must become part of the church culture. For that to occur, it must be firmly interwoven into the values and commitments of the people, and not just a few leaders.

Example 3. Bill and Sally attend a class at the church for new members. They are parents of three children ages 8, 10, and 13. The class instructor makes the following comments about church transportation:

Our church works hard at providing the best possible experience for all age groups. One aspect of that is promoting a safe environment, especially for our children and youth. Several years ago our congregation went through a planning process on how we can implement safety at all levels within our church. Out of that process we developed a transportation policy that is very similar to that of our local school district. We require all individuals who drive on behalf of the church to complete this driving form which I am now passing around for you to look at. You'll notice that it collects some basic background information and asks several questions about a driver's personal driving history. We want you to know these things in advance. If you are ever asked to drive for the church you will first need to complete this form. Every paid worker in our church must complete this form as well as have a background check. Three times each year we have a church-wide campaign to recruit volunteer drivers. We go over the whole program, including this form. Occasionally parents are needed to help with transportation for our youth and children. We are looking for individuals who are willing to serve as a driver, and who also feel comfortable completing this form. For those of you who are parents, we want you to know that we are going to do everything possible to provide for the safety of your children when they participate in church programs. And for those who do complete the driving form, we are sensitive about their privacy as well. All information is maintained in a locked file cabinet and is reviewed only by our safety committee. Confidentiality is strictly enforced. I hope you understand the goals and purpose of this screening process. It embodies our commitment of being good shepherds and good stewards of all that God has entrusted to our care. Are there any questions I can answer?

This example illustrates an approach to screening that has become embedded into the very fabric of the church. It arises out of the shared values and commitments of the congregation. It appeals to strongly shared concerns that all parents have about the safety of their children. It is legitimized through connections with the school district and with a congregation-wide planning endeavor. The program is sensitive both to the needs of those who agree to participate as well as to those who do not want to for whatever reason. The whole process of sharing information in advance with new members, of having ongoing congregational training, and of keeping the screening process focused as an act of caring creates a strong contrast with the first two examples.

(c) Confidentiality. The last example above refers to keeping the information on the screening forms confidential. Once the church or school begins to collect personal and private information it has a duty to protect that information and to use it only for its intended purpose. The indiscriminate dissemination of confidential information or using that information to harm someone may create liability, both for the church or school and for the individuals who share the information. For that reason, all screening forms should contain a warning against sharing confidential information. All individuals who have access to the forms should understand that the information is strictly confidential. The forms themselves should be kept in a locked container.

3. Education and training. Screening programs evoke a wide range of responses. Some people quickly embrace them and others reject them. As noted above, how the program is introduced to the congregation or school family impacts how it is received. A thoughtfully planned and executed education and training program increases the likelihood of developing a successful screening process. We have already discussed the need to enlist the support of congregational leaders and members in formulating the program. Once the program is established, a similar process is needed for the entire congregation. While each congregation is unique, attention should be given to educating new members and visitors, and in providing ongoing training at all levels within the congregation.

(a) Educate new members and visitors. Example 3 above illustrates one approach to educating new members and visitors. Many churches sponsor a new members or visitors class. Such classes provide the perfect opportunity to explain the church's rationale and process for screening, and to respond to personal questions and concerns. Schools often have similar meetings for new students and their parents. Having this information in advance of being asked to drive is very important. People know what the church or school expects and if they do not want to complete a form—for whatever reason—it avoids potential embarrassment.

> **Example.** *John is a new member of the church and during the past several years has had several DWI convictions. After reading the form he understands that based on his recent driving history he should not volunteer to drive. John does not need to disclose to anyone his reasons for not volunteering if he should be asked to do so in the future.*

It's a good idea to prepare a brochure that explains the church's or school's transportation policy. The brochure can be given to visitors and new members, and can also be used for ongoing training. Promoting transportation safety gives the church or school a very positive image within the community, and will be a point of attraction for families with children.

(b) Ongoing training. To sustain the program over time, a need exists to keep congregational members or the school family informed concerning the program's policies and procedures. Every opportunity should be taken to accomplish this goal. Newsletter articles, pulpit announcements, training at teacher orientation events for Sunday School or Vacation Bible School, parent-youth programs, and leadership

training events should all be used to promote the goals of the program. Doing so will help integrate the promotion safety into the fabric of congregational life.

4. Accountability. Finally, for screening to be effective, accountability must exist. Leaders must know if screening is in fact occurring with consistency and regularity. Accountability is easier with paid employees since their screening can be controlled at the point of employment. It is more difficult with volunteers who may be called upon at the last moment to drive, or who take a relaxed approach to the need for screening. Part of the solution rests with recruiting a pool of drivers well in advance of the need. If a church or school waits until the last moment to recruit drivers and then tries to get individuals to fill out a form, it will not work well. A better approach is to maintain a large list of screened drivers. Most drivers will volunteer for specific needs, such as parents driving for activities in which their children participate. The master list of screened drivers should include that information so that specific individuals can be contacted when a need arises for which they have a vested interest. All drivers should update their form on an annual basis, or more frequently if needed. Driver recruitment should be an ongoing process. Then when drivers are needed, they should be recruited from the active list of screened drivers. That way the focus is not upon the need to screen, but upon finding available people. Accountability is built into the process. Furthermore, churches and schools that use such a process will probably find it easier to recruit drivers than those who do no screening at all, and recruit drivers on an *ad hoc* basis. In short, the screening program not only enhances safety, but improves the recruitment of drivers at the same time.

Driver training

Once drivers have been selected, they should receive training. The primary focus of the training should be on three areas: (1) operating the vehicle, (2) driving policies and procedures; and (3) occupant safety.

1. Vehicle operation. Those who drive church or school-owned vehicles should receive an orientation on the operation of each vehicle. Drivers should be familiar with the following:

- how to operate all vehicle controls (ignition, lights, wipers, radio, etc.)
- how to interpret all dashboard instrumentation
- how to adjust mirrors to eliminate blind spots
- how to back the vehicle up safely
- how to make a right turn if driving a bus
- how to fill the vehicle with gas
- how to open the hood and trunk
- how to check engine fluid levels
- how to change a fuse
- how to change a flat tire
- how to lock and unlock the vehicle
- any other routine maintenance issues

An operational manual should be kept in the vehicle.

2. *Policies and Procedures.* As part of their orientation and training, individuals should receive a complete review of all driving policies and procedures before they begin to drive. The policies and procedures should be in writing. The policies should clarify who can drive and under what conditions, the conduct and authority of drivers, and the responsibility of drivers. Attention should be given to the use of alcohol and drugs, including prescription drugs and over the counter drugs. No driver should be impaired in any way, including using medication that could make the driver sleepy. Procedures should clarify how to drive, including the use of driving checklists, and how to respond to a variety of specific situations including bad weather, an accident, an emergency, a mechanical problem or flat tire, getting lost, or running out of gas. Drivers should never back up without clear visibility of what is behind them or wear headphones while driving. Both policies and procedures have a direct impact on occupant safety.

3. *Occupant Safety.* Occupant safety is at the heart of a transportation program. The goal is to keep both the driver and the passengers safe as well as to prevent harm to others outside the vehicle whether they are pedestrians or travelers. Occupant safety involves many different dimensions ranging from the knowledge, experience, and judgment of the driver to the external hazards of the trip and the state of the vehicle and the passengers. A drunk driver, a poorly maintained vehicle, a slippery road, a rowdy passenger, or a tired driver are just a few of many factors that affect safety. Drivers should receive specific training that will enable them to take proactive steps in promoting safety and reducing risks. The topic of occupant safety is discussed in more detail in the following sections.

8.4 Occupant Safety

Traffic safety is a significant concern both to individuals and to the government. As a result, significant research has been conducted on human attitudes, behaviors, and failures.[1] Churches and schools can improve transportation safety through a coordinated strategy that encompasses vehicle maintenance, driver selection, training and education, and policy enforcement. The topics of vehicle maintenance and driver selection were addressed earlier in this chapter. Our attention now turns to research findings and strategies with respect to training, education and policy enforcement in the following specific areas:

- Seat belts and cars
- Air bags
- Transporting infants and toddlers
- Transporting children and youth
- Selecting routes
- Buses and safety
- Railroad crossings
- The use of vans
- Mechanical problems
- Weather problems

[1] See *Compendium of Traffic Safety Research Projects, 1987-1997,*
www.nhtsa.dot.gov/people/injury/research/COMPEND2.HTM

- Health problems
- Accidents
- Pedestrian safety

8.5 Seat Belts and Cars

According to the National Highway Traffic Safety Administration (NHTSA), "seat belts are the single most effective safety device in preventing serious injuries and reducing fatalities in motor vehicle crashes. Seat belts reduce the risk of fatal injury by 45 percent and reduce the risk of serious injury by 50 percent."[2] Seat belts have been required on cars since 1968. Currently, 49 states require that seat belts be worn in passenger cars and light trucks. While seat belt use has continued to increase, only about 69 percent of the population use a seat belt. Passengers are less likely to use seat belts than drivers. Plus, individuals who ride in the back seat are less likely to buckle up. Drivers are far less likely to check the seat belt use of passengers in the back seat compared to those riding in the front seat. While riding in the back seat is the safest place in the vehicle, failure to use a seat belt puts the rider at a serious risk if an accident occurs. The NHTSA reports that "in 1997, 38 percent of drivers and 58 percent of occupants killed in motor vehicle crashes were not restrained."[3]

Seat belts should include both a lap belt and a shoulder belt. The lap belt should be worn low across the hips and not across the abdomen. The shoulder strap should cross the collar bone and go over the breast bone. It should not be next to the neck. There should be no excess slack in the seat belt.

Safety seats and small children

The good news is that over 90 percent of infants and toddlers use car safety seats. The bad news is that many of these car seats are not installed properly. In recent years, new research has been done that has left many parents and individuals confused concerning child passenger safety. This concern is addressed in more detail in section 8.7 below on transporting infants and toddlers.

8.6 Air Bags

Air bags for front-seat passengers are now commonly found in most cars. Since 1998 all new passenger cars must have air bags for both the driver and the front-side passenger. The same is also true for new light trucks since 1999. Many vehicles with air bags have the letters "SRS," "IRS,", "SIR" or the words "air bags" on the passenger dashboard or on the steering wheel. There may also be a warning sticker on the visor. Some models also have side air bags as well as inflatable "curtains" that activate to protect the head from a side collision.

Safety precautions for children

Air bags have been proven to save lives for most passengers, but they present a risk to children who ride in the front seat. An air bag deploys at about 200 mph. The

---

[2] *Occupant Protection Program Update*, Fall 1999 Issue, p.2,
www.nhtsa.dot.gov/people/injury/enforce/opupdate/december.htm
[3] Ibid., p.2

force it carries can kill or seriously injury a child. That's why it is important for children age 12 and under always to ride, properly restrained, in the back seat. Under no circumstances should an infant ever be placed in the front seat in a rear facing safety seat. Research indicates that college educated women are the most likely to know this information. On the other hand, young adults, often in their prime parenting years with young children at home, are less likely to be aware of the need for children 12 and under to ride in the back seat. Other groups that are less well informed include individuals with a high school education or less, non college-educated men, individuals who do not have air bags in their cars, individuals earning less than $20,000, and Generation X men.[4] Church leaders should be aware of these demographic differences. Some people have asked how the age 12 was selected as the cut-off point for riding in the front seat. According to the NHTSA, it is not possible at this time to make recommendations strictly based on height or weight. Vehicles are equipped with unique air bags that deploy with different levels of force. The age 12 was selected after reviewing the current data based on actual crash findings involving children.

Occasions arise when a child under 12 must sit in the front seat. In those situations, secure the child in an age appropriate restraint based on his or her size and weight. There should be as little slack as possible in the belt. Children should not wear a shoulder strap behind their back, or sit on the edge of the seat. Remember that an infant should NEVER ride in the front seat using a rear facing safety seat. Once the child has been secured, move the passenger seat back as far as possible. Transporting infants, toddlers, and older children is addressed more fully later in this chapter.

Safety precautions for adults

Adults also need to take care when riding in vehicles equipped with air bags. Seat belts, including both lap and shoulder belts, should always be used (low on the hips and across the breast bone). The front seats should be moved back as far as practical to reduce the impact of the air bag if it should deploy. This is particularly important for smaller adults. The NHTSA recommends that the distance between the breastbone of the driver and the center of the steering wheel should be at least **10 inches,** assuming the driver can maintain full control at that distance (that distance includes a safety buffer). When measured, if that distance is less than 10 inches, the driver may be a candidate for an on-off switch. Based on its research, the NHTSA notes that almost all women over 4 feet, 8 inches in height are able to get back 10 inches. Serious injuries can occur if an adult is within 2-3 inches of a deploying air bag. If a vehicle has a tilt steering wheel, it is best to tilt it down so it will deploy toward the chest and not toward the head. Telescoping steering wheels should be extended no further than is necessary in order to maintain maximum distance between the air bag and the driver. Most adults, including pregnant women and teenagers, will be safer with the use of an air bag. The key is to wear a seat belt, and to maximize the distance between the rider and the air bag. Pregnant women should also tilt the wheel towards the chest rather than at the head or abdomen. Those individuals with special medical conditions should consult with their physician about the use of an air bag. The same guidelines that apply to adult drivers in general, also apply to older adults.

---

[4] *Attitudes and Awareness of Air Bag Safety and Seat Belt Use*, NHTSA, www.nhtsa.dot.gov/people/outreach/safesobr/15qp/web/opatt.html

Deactivation guidelines

When should an air bag be deactivated? According to the NHTSA guidelines, the following circumstances can lead to the deactivation of an air bag:[5]

- A rear-facing restraint must be placed in the front seat of a vehicle because there is no back seat or the back seat is too small for the child restraint.

- A child of age 12 or younger must ride in the front seat because the child has a condition that requires frequent medical monitoring.

- An individual who drives (or rides in the front seat of) the vehicle has a medical condition that, on balance, makes it safer to have the air bag(s) turned off (a letter from a physician is required).

- Drivers who must sit within a few inches of the air bag.

To obtain authority to turn an air bag off, contact the NHTSA at NHTSA, 400 7th Street, SW, Washington, DC 20590-1000. Letters must include the name and address of the vehicle owner or lessee, the reason for the request, and any supporting documentation (e.g., letter from a physician). Passenger side air bags may have an on-off switch in new vehicles if they do not have rear seats, or if the rear seat is too small to accommodate a rear-facing child safety seat. In all but these limited circumstances the NHTSA discourages turning off air bags. Based on their research, air bags reduce the risk of death from a frontal crash by about 30 percent. Smart air bags are now being developed that activate at different levels of force based on the weight of the driver or rider.

Finally, if a church or school sells any vehicles that have had air bags turned off, it is imperative that the buyer know that information. It should be provided on the bill of sale. Churches and schools should consult with an attorney to obtain a release of liability concerning such sales.

8.7 Transporting Infants and Toddlers

What is safe?

Part of the problem in transporting infants and toddlers has been the confusion on what is safe and what is not. Three areas require clarification. One is on the proper use of child safety seats, or in government language, child safety restraint systems. The second is on the relationship between safety and air bags. The third safety issue focuses on where children should sit. All three of these concerns are interrelated and are discussed below.

Universal child safety seats

In early 1999, a new federal standard was announced for a universal child safety seat system. While over 90 percent of children and toddlers use a safety seat, the problem has been that many seats are not properly installed in the car. The new standard addresses this concern and will make it easier to properly install a child

---

[5] *Air Bag On-Off Switches: Questions and Answers*, NHTSA, November 1997, www.nhtsa.dot.gov/air bags/airbgQandA.html.

safety seat. The new system requires the safety seat to be anchored in three locations, two lower anchors and one upper anchor. The new standard requires that 100 percent of all cars and light trucks manufactured after September 1, 2000 have the upper anchor tether installed in the car. The final phase-in for the lower anchor tethers occurs two years later. All safety seats manufactured after September 1, 1999 must comply with the new standard for the upper tether attachment. Full compliance for all three anchors must occur by September 1, 2002.

Booster seats

Once a child outgrows the safety seat, the child should use a booster seat in order to achieve a correct fit with the vehicle lap/shoulder belt. If only a lap belt is used, it can cause spinal and abdominal injuries due to belts lying across the abdomen rather than the thighs. Booster seats should be used when the child is about 40 lbs. and should continue to be used until the seat/lap belt fits properly, generally when the child is between 60-80 lbs. Children should never wear a shoulder belt behind their back or under their arms. Serious injury can result.

Air bags and child safety

The introduction of air bags as a safety measure in automobiles has also contributed to confusion. Air bags illustrate the reality that safety designs continually change, research is ongoing, and information that may have been accurate a few years ago may no longer be valid. While air bags enhance safety for adults, they pose risks to children 12 and under. In 1997, the National Highway Traffic Safety Administration provided seating guidelines which are described in the sections that follow.

Seating arrangements

Infants should always ride in the back seat in a rear-facing restraint. The safety seat should be positioned so the infant reclines at a 45 degree angle to keep the baby's head from dropping forward. The rear-facing position protects the baby's head, and protects the neck and back from spinal injury. Children should not face forward while riding in the back seat until they are at least one year old *and* at least 20 lbs. Both factors must be present. Once the child is large enough and old enough to face forward, he or she should ride in an upright position. Infants should never he held in someone's lap while riding. A safety seat should always be used. Children should not ride in the front seat until they are age 13. Air bags can cause death or serious injury to a child riding in the front seat. Riding in the back seat provides greater protection to all passengers. Understandably, many parents feel uncomfortable having an infant riding in the back seat facing toward the rear. The American Academy of Pediatrics notes that the risk of injury from a crash is much greater than a child having a serious health problem while riding in a car. The Academy notes that if the baby is buckled in correctly, riding in the back seat of the car is as safe for the baby as resting in a crib. For long trips, periodically stop and check the child or have a second adult ride in the back seat.

Temperature and safety

Finally, church or school vehicles that are used to transport children should be equipped with air conditioning. The National Health and Safety Standards for child care programs indicate that vehicles should be air conditioned when the outside temperature exceeds 75 degrees F. They should be heated when the outside temperature falls below 50 degrees F.[6]

8.8 Transporting Children and Youth

Children and seat belts

According to the National Highway Traffic Safety Administration, 40 percent of children do not wear seat belts.[7] It is estimated that child fatalities could be cut in half through the simple act of using age appropriate safety restraints. Children who weigh between 40 and 80 lbs. and who are under 4' 9" tall pose special problems with respect to the use of seat belts. These children, often between the ages of 4 and 8, are too large to use car seats designed for infants and toddlers. On the other hand, seat belts designed for adults often do not fit properly until a child has reached 60-80 lbs. When an adult seat belt does not fit properly it can cause injuries to the child. As a result, these children often ride with no protection or with a seat belt that could cause them harm. New initiatives are now underway to encourage the use of booster seats among this age group. Currently, only about 6 percent of children use booster seats. Simultaneously, an emphasis is being placed on getting children between the ages of 8 to 15 to use seat belts. Children between the ages of 5 through 15 are more likely to die from a traffic accident than from any other cause. Those in their early teen years (13-15) are the least likely to use seat belts among this age group. The problem is even worse for males between the ages of 16 and 25. Of all groups, they are the least likely to use a seat belt and they are also represent the highest risk of all drivers. They are more likely to drive while drunk, speed, and to be in a crash. Furthermore, education has not worked with this age group. They see themselves as invincible and discount the possibility of an accident. They have responded only to law enforcement. Finally, adults serve as powerful role models concerning the use of seat belts. When the driver does not use a seat belt, research indicates that 70 percent of the time children riding as passengers will not buckle up either.[8] Children tend to model behavior, and in this case, the unbuckled adult is sending the children a deadly message. On the other hand, when a driver buckles up, 94 percent of the time the children in the vehicle will too.

Children should wear the lap belt low on their waist so it goes across their thighs. It should never cross the abdomen. The shoulder strap should cross the chest, and not be close to the neck. Sometimes children will place the shoulder strap behind them. That should not be done. The shoulder strap should be adjusted to make it fit properly. If the child is too small, then a booster seat should be used.

In an attempt to increase public awareness and promote safety for children, the NHTSA has established a standardized training program for individuals aspiring to lead child safety clinics. Individuals who complete the training are eligible for national technician certification offered through the American Automobile Association (AAA).

---

[6] "Guidelines for Out-of Home Child Care Programs," *National Health and Safety Performance Standards*, http://nrc.uchsc.edu/national/5-7.html.

[7] *Youth & Generation X Planner, Sample Press Release*, NHTSA, p. 1.

[8] *Youth & Generation X Planner, Traffic Safety Outlook Occupant Protection*,. p. 4, www.nhtsa.dot.gov/people/outreach/safesobr/15qp/web/optraffic.html.

Safety restraints and older children ages 4-15

Churches and schools sponsor many programs that require transportation for children between the ages of 4 through 15. As noted above, the age group from 4 through 8 poses special problems with respect to the use of safety restraints. The NHTSA recommends the use of booster seats, yet few parents own or use them. Churches and schools should purchase and use booster seats when transporting children who are too large for car seats and too small to wear an adult seat belt so that it fits properly. Drivers should always check that each passenger is using an appropriate safety restraint device, and that it fits properly and is secured. Do not assume that older children will buckle-up. Nearly a third of those between the ages of 5 to 15 do not routinely wear seat belts, and teenagers are among the lowest of all users.

8.9 Selecting Routes

Selecting a safe route is fundamental to transportation safety. All routes should be planned in advance of a trip. Safety should be a higher priority than time. Some routes may save time, but pose greater risks. When travelling out of town, all drivers should have written instructions concerning the route and a map. It's a good idea to identify rest stops in advance, as well as to know how to obtain help along a specific route in case a problem should occur. Any hazards that are encountered on a trip should be noted so they can be taken into account for the future. In selecting a route, attention should be given to the following factors:[9]

- Road conditions
- Traffic congestion
- One-way streets
- Hills and curves
- Sunlight
- High crash locations
- Road construction and detours
- Railroad crossings
- Wildlife
- Trees and shrubs that block visibility
- Weather conditions
- Pedestrians
- Traffic patterns including speed
- Parking areas
- Loading and unloading areas
- Fueling
- Rest stops
- Food stops

---

[9] *Knowing Your Route*, NHTSA,
www.nhtsa.dot.gov/people/injury/buses/schbus/schoolbus_drivers/topic_5/index.html.

- Low clearances
- Weight limits
- Help if a break down occurs
- Tolls

Always begin the trip with a full tank of gas. Have money for tolls if necessary. If travelling in a caravan, designate a lead vehicle, and maintain a safe distance between each vehicle. Keep a cell phone handy in case a problem should surface and assistance is needed.

8.10 Buses and Safety

Public schools are one of the largest users of buses in the United States. Churches and church-related schools can learn from the experience of the public schools concerning bus safety. According to the NHTSA, school buses are the safest form of highway transportation. School buses log about 5 billion miles each year. In 1996, for example, 8 passengers were killed in school bus accidents. That compares to 5,495 children that died as passengers or drivers in other vehicles. Most school bus-related deaths occur outside of the bus. Between 1987 to 1997, 1,458 people died in school bus-related crashes. Of that group, 8 percent were passengers, 2 percent were bus drivers, 27 percent were pedestrians or individuals outside the bus (such as a bicyclist), and 63 percent were occupants in another vehicle that was part of the crash.[10] During that same time period 54 people died in school buses providing transportation for churches and civic organizations. Half of those individuals died in one crash.

Loading and unloading passengers

The loading and unloading zone of a bus represents an area of risk to school age children. Children are more likely to be killed or injured in the loading and unloading zone than while riding on the bus. Two-thirds of the pedestrian accidents involve the school bus and one-third involve motorists who illegally pass a stopped school bus. Furthermore, half of those who are killed are between the ages of 5 and 7. They tend to be killed by their own bus. The fatal accidents are more likely to occur in the afternoon than in the morning with 43 percent of the fatalities occurring between 3:00 and 4:00 PM as the children return home from school. Weather is not a significant contributing factor. Most of the time it is clear. The greatest risk occurs in the school bus loading zone and the primary point of impact is the front of the bus.

The danger zone around a bus is **10 feet** in any direction (front, back, or sides). The two most dangerous areas are the front of the bus and the back right side of the bus. Small children represent the greatest risk since they are hard to see, have little experience in riding a bus, and act in impulsive and unpredictable ways. The afternoon is more dangerous than the morning because the children have been cooped up all day and are anxious to get home. They are ready to release some of that pent up energy from sitting still all day.

---

[10] *School Buses Traffic Safety Facts 1997*, NHTSA,
www.nhtsa.dot.gov/people/ncsa/schbus97.html.

Church and school leaders need to take special precautions to establish safe behaviors for getting on and off vehicles. The driver is critical in training children on the proper procedure for stepping on and off the bus. The NHTSA has developed a comprehensive educational program for elementary age children called *Walk, Ride, Walk—Getting to School Safely*. The NHTSA also makes resources available to children on the Internet at www.nhtsa.dot.gov/kids/bussafety. Many churches own or periodically use buses. Certain precautions, such as those recommended below by the NHTSA, should be followed to enhance bus safety.[11] Furthermore, these lessons must be taught to children repeatedly:

- Riders who are waiting to be picked up by a bus should stand back at least 10 feet away from the edge of the bus. Children should be told to wait "five giant steps" away from the road. This distance should be increased in foggy weather.

- Train riders not to approach the bus until the bus stops, the door is opened, and the driver gives permission to get on.

- Stop slightly before you get to the waiting riders. Make them walk to you. Never pull into a group of children waiting at the curb.

- Secure the bus while the children load. Put on the parking brake.

- Stay to the right side of the roadway while loading and unloading.

- Watch for children who may be stragglers.

- Drawstrings on hoods and jackets, and straps on book bags and backpacks, can get caught on the handrail or door of a bus. Train riders to be on the alert to avoid this problem.

- Children should load the back of the bus first and sit down facing the front of the bus. Children should sit more toward the front if the bus will not be filled to capacity.

- Children should stay seated until the bus comes to a complete stop.

- Before stepping off, children should be taught to look toward the outside rear of the bus to make sure that nothing is coming such as a car or bicycle.

- Once riders exit the bus, they should immediately take five giant steps (go 10 feet) before turning left or right.

The bus driver should know where each rider is heading as they exit the bus. If riders must cross the street after exiting the bus, they should first go the sidewalk or side of the road and walk 10 feet ahead of the bus (5 giant steps). They should carefully check traffic left, right, and left before crossing. They should be able to make eye contact with the driver at all times. They should not cross the road in front of the bus until the driver signals that it is safe to do so. The signal should be a clear one that is not confused as a wave, or one that a waiting motorist might

---

[11] *Loading and Unloading*, NHTSA,
www.nhtsa.dot.gov/people/injury/buses/schbus/ schoolbus_drivers/topic_6/index.html

misinterpret as a signal that it is now okay to pass the bus (an external PA system is best). A warning signal such as using the horn should also be used to tell the child to stop and return to the curb. The driver must constantly monitor traffic and must never assume that an approaching vehicle will stop.

If the driver loses track of a child, it is best to check outside the bus before proceeding. Count the children as they exit the bus and then as they go away.

Train individuals never to stand behind the bus. This can be a problem when the bus is departing following a church service or at the end of a school day, or is getting ready to leave on a trip where parents are seeing their children off. Often, people will be milling around without regard for the bus. The 10 foot danger zone around the bus must be kept clear at all times. The driver should never move the bus if anyone is within the danger zone. A second person should always assist as a lookout when the bus is backing up. The horn should be used.

If a problem occurs on the bus while loading and unloading is going on, do not deal with it until the loading or unloading is finished. Stay focused on what is happening outside the bus since that represents the single greatest danger zone to children.

Managing children while on the bus

While on the bus, children should always keep the aisles clear of any tripping hazard. Children should know and follow three basic rules:

(1) stay seated while the bus is moving;

(2) face forward and keep arms and head inside the bus; and

(3) talk in a quiet voice so the driver is not distracted.

However, these rules are not going to be followed all of the time. Often, the driver is the only adult on the bus. If the driver is distracted, everyone's safety becomes endangered. Since drivers are different, some flexibility can be exercised on levels of noise. Noise levels that impact one driver may not affect someone else. The driver must be clear with the children on what is appropriate. While children should always remain seated and keep their heads and arms within the bus, it is unlikely that they will always face forward. However, facing forward provides the greatest degree of safety. Drivers should expect children to be more active in the afternoon after getting out of school. Maintaining control requires both tolerance and continual supervision. Children may push, shove, use abusive language, or engage in vandalism or lewd behavior. How can discipline be maintained? Here are suggestions from the NHTSA:

- At the top of the list, drivers must always maintain their own self-control. A driver should never hit or touch a child (unless, according to the NHTSA, a danger exists to the driver or to another student).

- Don't become a nitpicker. Focus on the important safety concerns. Don't feel a need to respond to everything that is said or done.

- Don't argue with students.

- Don't threaten something you cannot do.

- Don't threaten something unless you plan to follow through.

- Don't discipline a whole group. Focus on the ringleader.
- Maintain control.

Maintaining control is not always easy. If a situation appears to be getting out of control consider the following:

- Stop the bus by parking it off the road in a safe location, such as a parking lot.
- Secure the bus by removing the ignition key.
- Stand up and speak directly to the offenders. Be courteous but firm. Don't let your anger get the best of you. Tell the students exactly what behavior they are engaging in that is inappropriate and what the appropriate behavior is that they are expected to follow.
- If necessary relocate the offending student close to you near the front of the bus.
- Never ask a student to get off the bus except at his or her appropriate bus stop.
- If you feel that continuing to drive would be unsafe, call the school, the church, or the student's parent for assistance.
- Follow the church's or school's policy on preparing a discipline report. Maintain records of each incident.
- The church or the school should handle any additional discipline.

Other ideas to promote good behavior include the following:

- Welcome the students with a greeting and a smile when they load the bus. Get to know the name of each student.
- Use a reward program to promote good behavior.
- Reinforce good behavior with positive comments.
- Solicit feedback from the students. Invite suggestions.
- Focus on the positive. Tell a student what to do rather than what not to do.
- Be prepared to give a reason for your actions. Stay focused upon safety concerns.

Final inspection at the end of the trip

Once the trip is over, the driver should make a final inspection of the vehicle. Each seat should be inspected to make sure that no child has fallen asleep and is still on the bus. All windows and doors should be closed and any articles left on the bus should be removed. Any damage or vandalism should be reported. Make sure the key has been removed from the ignition. Leave the bus in good shape for the next trip. In the winter it may be necessary to spray the steps with a deicer.

Seat belts and buses

Many people wonder why school buses do not use seat belts. School buses must meet specific federal safety standards with respect to rollover protection, body joint strength, passenger seating, brakes, tires, fuel system integrity, lamps and reflective devices, emergency exits, window retention and releases, plus more. School buses rely upon "compartmentalization" to provide occupant safety. Compartmentalization utilizes closely-spaced seats that have high backs and that are well padded. The seats are securely anchored and are designed to absorb energy. Buses are larger, heavier, and safer than most other vehicles. As a result, children are more safe in a school bus than in a car with a parent or guardian. Even so, the NTHSA is engaged in research that is testing new and innovative ways to provide even more protection to children in buses. Currently, small school buses with a gross vehicle weight rating of under 10,000 pounds must be equipped with lap or lap/shoulder belts for all seats in the vehicle.[12]

Buses and the transportation of preschool age children

It is estimated that up to one million preschool age children now ride school buses or vans on a daily basis. Transporting this age group provides many challenges. First, the children are too small to get on and off the bus alone. The bus seats are not designed for this age group. They cannot climb onto the seat. While on the bus they will not sit still. Generally, they cannot sit alone. As a result, these children face a variety of safety risks.

In February, 1999, the NHTSA released guidelines for the safe transportation of preschool age children in school buses. The report was in response to the growing demand for information on this subject. More and more preschool age children are attending school programs and are being transported in buses. To analyze this issue, the NHTSA conducted crash testing of preschool age size dummies in school bus seats. Based on the findings from that study, the NHTSA concluded that preschool age children are the safest when they are transported in child safety restraint systems (safety seat) that are correctly attached to the seats. Federal Motor Vehicle Safety Standards (FMVSS) exist both for the child safety restraint system (FMVSS 213) and for how the system is attached to the seat (FMVSS 225). These findings mean that buses must be equipped with either a seat belt or some other means to secure the child safety restraint system to the seat. The seat belt should only be used to secure the restraint system, and should not be worn by a preschool age child. This recommendation involves some complexity in the actual execution of a safe transportation system since each passenger needs a child safety restraint system that is appropriate for the child's weight, height, and age. Perhaps the best solution to this need is to have the child's guardian provide an individualized restraint system that meets all applicable standards.

What happens if a church or school must transport a child and no safety seat is available? The NHTSA recommends that such children not be transported based on both safety and liability risks. Either get a safety seat or make alternative transportation arrangements.

Any church or school that transports preschool age children should be familiar with these guidelines. Attention must be given to loading and unloading procedures, developing a written emergency evacuation procedure, practicing an emergency evacuation, maintenance and inspection of the safety restraint systems, and the overall physical handling of young children including the potential

---

[12] *Seat belts on School Buses*, NHTSA,
www.nhtsa.dot.gov/people/injury/buses/pub/seatbelt.hmp.html.

exposure of communicable diseases. Small children have very unique and individualized needs, which must be taken into account.

Churches and schools that provide bus transportation to preschoolers should seek professional assistance in the development and evaluation of their transportation system.

Railroad crossings

Any vehicle that collides with a train comes out the loser. To avoid this outcome, all school buses follow strict safety guidelines concerning crossing rails. Similarly, church buses should take special precautions when crossing tracks. Trains always have the right of way and accidents occur more frequently than people may realize. An accident occurs every 100 minutes. More people die each year in highway-train accidents than are killed in commercial aviation crashes. A loaded train cannot stop quickly, and drivers often underestimate the speed of a train. Here are some general guidelines from the NHTSA that drivers should know about railroad crossings:[13]

- Always obey the crossing signals. Never try to go around gates.

- Never try to beat a train. People tend to underestimate the train's speed and overestimate how far it is away. It is a deadly combination.

- If two sets of tracks are side by side, always check both sets. If a train passes on one set, don't proceed until the second set has been checked.

- School buses should stop no closer that **15 feet** and no farther away than **50 feet** from the tracks. If the bus stops further away, visibility down the tracks is diminished. Stay on the right of the roadway.

- Keep the brake applied when checking the tracks. The driver's window should be opened, and the service door on the bus should also be opened when checking the tracks. Radios should be turned off and the passengers should be quiet while the tracks are being checked. The radio should not be turned on until the vehicle completely clears the tracks.

- Look and listen for a train when checking tracks.

- Before crossing the tracks, close the driver's window and the service door.

- A driver should never stop on the tracks or try to back up once the vehicle is on the tracks.

- The driver should always use a low gear while crossing the tracks and should not shift gears while on the tracks.

- If a gate closes while the vehicle is crossing the tracks, the driver should continue even if it means that the gate will break.

---

[13] *Highway-Rail Grade Crossing Safety*, NHTSA,
www.nhtsa.dot.gov/people/injury/buses/schbus/schoolbus_drivers/topic_3/index.html

- If a vehicle stalls on the tracks, evacuate everyone from the vehicle. Have them stand far away from the tracks and from the vehicle and out of the path of the vehicle if it a train should hit it.

- While waiting at an intersection while a train is crossing, the parking brake should be applied and the foot should remain on the brake so the vehicle cannot be pushed into the path of the train.

The use of vans

New vans that carry **11 or more passengers** and that are used to transport children to school or school-related events must meet the same Federal Motor Vehicle Safety Standards as school buses. This applies to private parochial schools as well as public schools.

8.11 Mechanical Problems

All drivers on out-of-town trips should know what to do in case the vehicle has mechanical problems. Some problems may completely disable the vehicle, while others may require a repair at the earliest convenience. In either case, the driver should have a planned response.

Preparation includes carrying emergency supplies in the vehicle. That includes roadside warning signs and flags, flares, flashlight, emergency phone numbers, and a cell phone or other means of communication, in addition to the standard tools and equipment needed to change a flat tire.

Disabled vehicles

If the vehicle becomes disabled two factors require attention. The first, and most important, is to maintain the safety of the passengers. The second is to obtain roadside assistance.

1. *Maintaining safety.* The vehicle should be parked in the safest location that is available. If the vehicle is parked on the shoulder of a road, or is in the lane of a road, the emergency flashers should be immediately turned on. Three warning signs designed for emergency roadside use should be posted behind the vehicle at intervals of 10 feet, 100 feet and 200 feet. The warning hazards should be positioned in such a way to direct traffic away from the disabled vehicle. The police should be notified and contact should be made for roadside assistance. The hood of the vehicle should be raised to indicate mechanical problems and a red or white flag or handkerchief should be tied to the door handle or antenna. If a public facility or waiting area is available within safe walking distance, the occupants should wait there until help arrives. If no such facility is available, they should stay together in the vehicle until help arrives. If weather permits and a safe location is available outside of the vehicle and away from the road, they may wait together there. The key concern is to protect occupants from oncoming traffic. Under no conditions should children be left unsupervised while an adult seeks help. If a vehicle becomes disabled in cold weather and help is not immediately available other factors should be taken into account (see chapter 14, section 14.5).

2. *Roadside assistance.* In preparing for this emergency, all vehicles should be equipped with either a cell phone or other means to summons help and drivers must know whom to contact for assistance. First, they should make immediate contact with the highway state patrol. The police can provide roadside protection for the vehicle and occupants until help arrives. Second, the church or school should maintain a 24-hour roadside service contract for such occasions with a reliable organization such as AAA. The phone numbers should be kept on the vehicle at all times, preferably as a sticker on the window so they do not get lost.

Vehicle repairs

If a warning light comes on or some other indication of a mechanical problem occurs, but the vehicle is not disabled, the driver must determine what to do. All vehicles should be equipped with a service manual that provides information to the driver to make informed decisions in such cases. In some cases it will be safe to complete the trip and then obtain mechanical assistance. In other cases, a repair will be needed to continue the trip. Some repairs may be simple such as changing a fuse. All vehicles should be equipped with extra fuses, and the driver should know how to change them. In addition, drivers should carry a list of emergency phone numbers to use in such situations. That may include toll free numbers for the vehicle manufacturer, a dealer, or for roadside service. A roadside service contract should be maintained on all church vehicles. Finally, drivers must be prepared to pay for repairs that may be needed. Perhaps the best approach is for the driver to carry an authorized church or school credit card, which can be used to pay for repairs.

8.12 Weather Problems

Two of the common weather related problems are slippery pavement and poor visibility. Once these conditions occur, the risk of an accident increases. People do not like to be delayed and often will continue to drive in unsafe conditions. Churches and schools should establish policies that provide guidance to drivers on how to respond to weather conditions. The guidelines, such as those presented below, should be in writing and each driver should be provided a copy.

Delaying trips

1. *Collecting information before the trip begins.* In many situations, some level of bad weather already exists before the trip begins and the question is whether to wait or go. The driver may be uncertain of how bad the road conditions are. The state highway patrol provides weather advisories to warn drivers of unsafe conditions. Before beginning a trip when where the weather is bad or is turning bad, drivers of church or school vehicles should contact the state police and obtain a road advisory. The most common causes of problems will be snow, ice, or fog.

2. *Deciding to stop in the midst of a trip.* Sometimes bad weather can occur suddenly part way into the trip. When visibility becomes poor as the result of fog, heavy rain, or blowing snow the driver should pull off the road at a safe location and wait for the conditions to improve. Most delays are brief.

General safety precautions

When bad weather strikes, drivers should move to a higher level of alert and take extra precautions. Some general safety precautions include the following.

- Stay in the flow of traffic, but maintain a larger than normal following distance
- Reduce speed based on traffic conditions
- Use the center line as a reference point
- Keep the headlights on
- Be alert for slippery pavement

Winter driving poses additional risks. This topic is covered in more detail in chapter 14.

8.13 Health Problems

Drivers must be prepared to obtain emergency health care for an occupant if the need should arise. If the occupants are minors, then parental permission slips will be required. Such slips should always be obtained in advance and carried on the vehicle. Vehicles should be equipped with a cell phone or other form of communication to contact 911 for an emergency health-related problem.

8.14 Accidents

Drivers should know how to respond if an accident should occur. The first concern is to provide for the care of any injured person. A second concern is to collect information concerning the accident. Third, notify other appropriate individuals.

Care for the injured

If someone in the vehicle is injured, immediately contact 911. One person should stay on the phone to provide as much information as needed. Do not hang up until the 911 operator is finished collecting information. WARNING: DO NOT MOVE PEOPLE WITH HEAD, NECK OR BACK INJURIES.

All vehicles should carry first aid kits that include bandages, gauze, cold packs, tape, protective gloves, and antibacterial crème. If a person receives a cut or a wound and is bleeding, while wearing protective gloves, apply fingertip pressure directly over the wound. If that does not stop the bleeding apply direct pressure to the wound for at least 10 minutes using a gauze pad or some other clean material.[14] If the wound is to a limb, elevate the limb above the heart. For example, if the wound is to a leg, have the person lay down and prop up the leg. Remember, do not move a person with a head, neck, or back injury. Do not attempt first aid for which you are not trained.

Collect information about the accident

Once the injured are attended to, information should be collected and recorded in writing about the accident. Accidents create a state of confusion and people are likely to forget what information to collect. A form and pen should be kept in the

---

[14] Goold, p. 65

glove compartment or elsewhere in the vehicle that the driver or someone else can use to collect all relevant information such as the following:

- The date, time, and location of the accident

- The names and phone numbers of witnesses to the accident

- The state and license plate number of the involved vehicles

- If available the names, driver's license numbers, and insurance companies of other drivers involved in the accident

In addition to collecting your own information, cooperate fully with the police.

Notify others

Part of the advanced planning of a trip is to have a prioritized list of contacts and phone numbers in case an accident or emergency should occur. Contact the persons on that list, such as a pastor or principal or other leader. They then can notify others on a need to know basis such as parents, family members, and the insurance company.

8.15 Pedestrian Safety

Tragic accidents have occurred at churches and schools where children have been killed crossing the street next to the building or parking lot. On other occasions, children have been killed crossing busy roads while participating in a youth activity. The reality is that pedestrians are twice as likely to be killed by a stranger with a car than a stranger with a gun. In a typical year, a pedestrian is injured in a traffic crash every six minutes and killed in a traffic crash every 97 minutes. Almost half of those under the age 16 were killed during the period from 4:00 to 8:00 PM. Older adults over age 70 also represent a vulnerable group accounting for 18 percent of pedestrian fatalities. Church and school leaders can take some simple but important steps to reduce the likelihood of injuries for activities that involve walking in traffic. Here are some basic guidelines:

- Teach children the proper way to cross a street: stop at the curb and look left, right, left. Continue to look as you cross the street.[15]

- Teach children, including elementary age children, that a green light does not mean that it is safe to cross the street. It is only safe if no cars are coming. Always look for cars that are making turns.

- Walk on the sidewalk. If there is no sidewalk, walk facing traffic.

- Always cross at an intersection. Most injuries occur when people cross roads at places other than the intersection. Stay inside the crosswalk and obey the traffic signal. Do not dart into the intersection.

- When crossing at an intersection, watch out for drivers across the street who get a green arrow to turn early. Maintain eye contact with drivers.

- Do not assume a driver sees you or members of your group. At night wear reflective clothing and use a flashlight.

---

[15] In countries that drive on the left side of the road, reverse the pattern: look right, left, right.

● Always supervise children when they cross a street, or walk along a street. Have children hold hands so that no one bolts unexpectedly into traffic. Have everyone stay together.

Summary

A church or school transportation safety program should focus on three board categories: (1) vehicles, (2) drivers, and (3) occupant safety. While inspections and vehicle maintenance are an important part of the safety program, education and training play a central role in creating a safe transportation program.

All church and school vehicles should be properly maintained and inspected on a regular basis. Only vehicles that meet designated safety standards should be used, including vehicles that the church or school does not own.

Drivers, both paid and volunteer, should complete a written screening form and receive training and instructions concerning policies and procedures. This requires that the church or school establish baseline standards for drivers, and that they implement an effective recruitment, screening, and training program. An effective program is one in which potential drivers understand, support, and can participate in with minimal inconvenience. In part, success depends upon having a good orientation program for new members to the church or school family, enlisting their support for the program, and using forms to collect information in advance, that is confidentially stored and maintained. Drivers should then receive training on vehicle operation, policies and procedures, and occupant safety.

Occupant safety is at the heart of the transportation safety program. Drivers should understand the importance and proper use of restraint systems including, seat belts, child safety seats, and booster seats. Children age 12 or younger should always ride in the back seat of a vehicle. A front seat air bag can cause serious injury or death to a child. While in the back seat, infants should ride in a safety seat that faces backward until they are at least one year old *and* weigh at least 20 lbs. Booster seats should be used once the child is about 40 lbs., and should continue to be used until the seat belt fits properly. The seat belt should fit low across the hips and the shoulder strap should go across the breastbone. The belt should not go across the abdomen or be near the neck.

Bus drivers need special training. While riding in a school bus is safer than riding in a car, accidents do occur. One of the most important safety concerns is the loading and unloading of passengers. A clear safety zone must be maintained around the bus and children need clear instructions on how to safely enter and exit the bus. Federal and state laws apply to bus transportation with which drivers must comply. Buses that transport infants and toddlers require appropriate age and weight related safety seats.

Transportation hazards can occur suddenly and without warning. Drivers must be prepared in advance to respond to mechanical problems, bad weather, passengers with health problems, or an accident. Responses should not be left to chance: drivers should receive training and understand how to enhance safety when emergency situations arise.

Finally, pedestrian safety is part of a safe transportation program. Church and school leaders can follow simple, but effective steps that can reduce the likelihood of accidents while children walk in traffic to and from vehicles or activities.

In the next chapter, risk management techniques are applied to reduce common accidents such as slips and falls that occur at church and school facilities and property.

Additional Resources on the Internet

For additional information on transportation safety, review the material found on the following web sites. Also, several publications are listed that are available from the Consumer Safety Product Commission. These resources were used in the preparation of this chapter.

"5.7 Transportation (FA303 thru FA323)." National Health and Safety Performance Standards. <http://nrc.uchsc.edu/national/5-7.html>.

"ABC's of Air Bags." National Highway Traffic Safety Administration. <http://www.nhtsa.dot.gov/people/injury/air bags/AirBagFlr/Abgaflr.htm>.

"Administrator Guide." National Highway Traffic Safety Administration. <http://www.nhtsa.dot.gov/people/injury/buses/schbus/schoolbus_drivers/admin/index.html>.

"Air Bag On-Off Switches: Questions and Answers." National Highway Traffic Safety Administration. <http://www.nhtsa.dot.gov/air bags/airbgQandA.html>.

"Attitudes and Awareness of Air Bag Safety and Seat Belt Use." National Highway Traffic Safety Administration. <http://www.nhtsa.dot.gov/people/outreach/ safesobr/15qp/web/opatt.html>.

"Buckle Up America." National Highway Traffic Safety Administration. <http://www.nhtsa.dot.gov/people/outreach.safesobr/15qp/web/bukeymess.html>.

"Buckle Up America! Week 1998." National Highway Traffic Safety Administration. <http://www.nhtsa.dot.gov/people/outreach/safesobr/15qp/ web/bupress.html>.

"Compendium of Traffic Safety Research Projects, 1987 - 1997." National Highway Traffic Safety Administration. <http://www.nhtsa.dot.gov/people/injury/research/ COMPEND2.HTM>.

"Driver Attitude." National Highway Traffic Safety Administration. <http://www.nhtsa.dot.gov/people/injury/buses/schbus/schoolbus_drivers/topic_1/index.html>.

"Guide to the School Bus Driver In-Service Safety Series." National Highway Traffic Safety Administration. <http://www.nhtsa.dot.gov/people/injury/buses/schbus/schoolbus_drivers/pupil/page1.html>.

"Highway-Rail Grade Crossing Safety." National Highway Traffic Safety Administration. <http://www.nhtsa.dot.gov/people/injury/buses/schbus/schoolbus_drivers/topic_3/index.html>.

"Is This Child on the Road to Danger?" National Highway Traffic Safety Administration. <http://www.nhtsa.dot.gov/people/outreach/safesobr/15qp/web/ danger.html>.

"Knowing Your Route." National Highway Traffic Safety Administration. <http://www.nhtsa.dot.gov/people/injury/buses/schbus/schoolbus_drivers/topic_5 /index.html>.

"Loading And Unloading." National Highway Traffic Safety Administration. <http://www.nhtsa.dot.gov/people/injury/buses/schbus/schoolbus_drivers/topic_6 /index.html>.

"Pedestrian Safety Talking Points." National Highway Traffic Safety Administration. <http://www.nhtsa.dot.gov/people/outreach/safesobr/15qp/web/ sbpeds.html>.

"Prevent Pedestrian Crashes: Preschool/Elementary School Children." National Highway Traffic Safety Administration. <http://www.nhtsa.dot.gov/people/ outreach/safesobr/15qp/web/sbprevent.html>.

"Reduce the Risk of Having your Vehicle Stolen." NewsNet5. <http://www.newsnet5.com/yoursafety-980504-100347.html>.

"School Bus Safety Rules." National Safety Council. <http://www.nsc.org/lrs/lib/fs/home/schlbus.htm>.

"School Bus Safety Talking Points." National Highway Traffic Safety Administration. <http://www.nhtsa.dot.gov/people/outreach/safesobr/15qp/web/sbsb.html>.

"School Buses, Traffic Safety Facts 1997." National Highway Traffic Safety Administration. <http://www.nhtsa.dot.gov/people/ncsa/schbus97/html>.

"Student Management." National Highway Traffic Safety Administration. <http://www.nhtsa.dot.gov/people/injury/buses/schbus/schoolbus_drivers/topic_2 /index.html>.

"Transporting Infants and Toddlers." National Highway Traffic Safety Administration. <http://www.nhtsa.dot.gov/people/injury/buses/schbus/ schoolbus_drivers/topic_7/index.html>.

"Vehicle Training." National Highway Traffic Safety Administration. <http://www.nhtsa.dot.gov/people/injury/buses/schbus/schoolbus_drivers/topic_4 /index.html>.

"Youth Fatalities Overheads." National Highway Traffic Safety Administration. <http://www.nhtsa.dot.gov/people/outreach/safesobr/15qp/web/mpmyouth.html>.

CHAPTER 9. REDUCING SLIPS AND FALLS AND OTHER ACCIDENTS ON CHURCH OR SCHOOL PROPERTY

Accidents resulting in personal injuries occur far more often on church and school property and in programs than most leaders realize. In a study of 641 churches that we conducted in 1995, over 50 percent reported that one or more accidents occurred within the past three years that required medical attention. The percentage of churches reporting such accidents increased with church size. Churches in urban, suburban, and medium size cities had about the same rate of accidents, while churches in small towns and rural settings had lower accident rates as noted in the table below.

CATEGORIES	ALL	CHURCH SIZE					
Size (number)	All (641)	0-100 (116)	101-250 (214)	251-500 (154)	501-750 (68)	751-1,000 (26)	> 1,000
Accident requiring medical attention within past 3 years	52%	26%	42%	68%	68%	68%	84%

CATEGORIES	ALL	CHURCH SETTING				
Setting (number)	All (641)	Urban (80)	Suburban (212)	Medium Size City (137)	Small Town (151)	Rural (49)
Accident requiring medical attention within past 3 years	52%	56%	54%	56%	47%	33%

9.1 Slips and Falls

Slips and falls are the most common accidents and they can result in serious injuries. They also prompt more church lawsuits than any other single cause. They represent a risk both to those who may fall and, as a result of potential litigation, to the entire congregation or school. The most common problem areas include the following:

- Playgrounds
- Ice, snow, and rain
- Uneven pavement or holes in parking lots
- Loose carpeting or runners
- Wet floors
- Waxed floors
- Dark stairways or uneven steps
- Obstructed walkways

- Unsafe use of ladders
- Cords across floors
- Falling out of windows

The single most important risk management strategy is the regular inspection, care, and maintenance of facilities and property with specific attention given to the elimination of hazards that contribute to slips and falls. In addition, church or school leaders should understand several important legal principles that affect whether or not negligence may be present with respect to such an accident. Both areas of concern are addressed below.

9.2 Common Problem Areas

Playgrounds

For children, slips and falls are most likely to occur on playgrounds. Many playground activities involve climbing and running, and falls, resulting in fractures and head injuries, are the most common cause of emergency room treatment.

Reducing the risk

The most important step churches and schools can take to reduce playground injuries is to maintain an adequate protective surface under and around the use zone of all playground equipment. Second, protective barriers and guardrails should be used on platforms. Adequate supervision is also needed. Reducing the risk of playground injuries is covered more fully in chapter 6.

Examples that have prompted lawsuits

> **Example.** *An Illinois court ruled that a charitable organization could be held responsible for injuries sustained by a child who fell off a slide. The slide was over six feet high, had no handrail going up the steps, and had a loose and slippery handrail around the platform at the top. Metal and concrete footings at the base of the slide were exposed. A child fell from the slide and was severely injured. The state appeals court ruled that the charitable organization that owned the slide could be found liable for both negligence and willful and wanton misconduct, if, as the lawsuit alleged, on prior occasions other children had fallen from the slide due to its defective and dangerous condition, and that the charity was aware of the slide's condition and of the prior accidents, but took no corrective action. Scarano v. Town of Ela, 520 N.E.2d 62 (Ill. App. 1988).*

> **Example.** *A 4-year-old child at a church day care center broke his leg when he fell while running. The parents claimed that the church was negligent in its supervision. The court ruled in favor of the church. Ward v. Mount Calvary Lutheran Church, 873 P.2d 688 (Ariz. App. Div. 1 1994).*

Older adults

Older adults have a high risk of falling. According to the Mayo Clinic, about 40 percent of people over age 65 fall annually.[1] As individuals age, both their reaction

---

[1] *Falls, You Can Reduce Your Risk*, Mayo Clinic Health Oasis, <http://www.mayohealth.org/mayo/9709/htm/falls.htm>.

time and sense of balance declines. Many medical disorders can impact falls. Medication, cataracts, cardiovascular disease, arthritis, emphysema, and balance disorders such as Parkinson's disease are just a few medical conditions that impact older adults and that can contribute to falls. As the Mayo Clinic notes, falls are particularly debilitating to older adults. A broken bone or other injury can affect the overall quality of life. Mobility may become reduced and isolation may increase.

Reducing the risk

Older adults can improve their balance through exercise and training. However, to reduce slips and falls by older adults, churches and schools need to be proactive in reducing hazards that contribute to falls such as those discussed below. In addition, an escort can assist older adults who have balance problems, especially in bad weather or under conditions that pose a higher risk of falling.

Slippery weather-related conditions

Snow, ice, and rain create slippery conditions that significantly increase the risk of slips and falls. Outdoor stairways are particularly dangerous when they become slippery.

Reducing the risk

Keep walkways and handrails clear of ice and snow. Use salt to keep ice from forming. Post warning signs in any area that poses a hazard. Make sure that all outdoor stairways have handrails on both sides of the stairs. Use nonskid strips on stairs. The removal of ice and snow is a demanding job. Keep adequate salt and sand on hand during the winter months. If a patchy spot remains after cleaning the walkways, place a barrier around it to prevent people from walking over it and cover it with sand.

Examples that have prompted lawsuits

> **Example.** *A woman was injured when she slipped and fell on an icy church sidewalk. A church custodian had shoveled the sidewalk removing several inches of snow. Normally he applied salt after shoveling to prevent ice from forming, but this time he did not. The women, seeing that the sidewalk was shoveled, used it to exit the church, but slipped on a section of the sidewalk that had a steep slope and seriously injured her cervical spine. The woman sued the church which defended itself by claiming that the danger was clearly apparent to any reasonable person. The jury ruled in favor of the woman and awarded her more than $400,000 in damages. The Montana Supreme Court upheld the award noting that the janitor created a new hazard by leaving a sidewalk with a sheen of ice that was different from the accumulation of snow. The ice, in conjunction with the steep slope without a handrail, created a hazard that constituted negligence on the part of the church. Davis v. Church of Jesus Christ of Latter Day Saints, 796 P.2d 181 (Mont. 1990).*

> **Example.** *A woman slipped on a patch of ice in the church parking lot while she was attending a community group that met at the church. The court ruled that the church was not responsible since no one from the church was present and aware of the condition, which had just developed within two hours of the meeting. The court concluded that the church did not have a reasonable amount of time to remove the snow*

and ice. On the other hand, if the church would have known of the condition and had a reasonable amount of time to correct the situation, the outcome may have been different. *Byrd v. Church of Christ, 597 N.Y.S.2d 211 (A.D. 3 Dept. 1993).*

Example. A woman attending a church event slipped and fell in the icy parking lot. She claimed the parking lot was covered with a sheet of ice and 5 inches of new snow. She sued the church alleging that it had been negligent in failing to "implement some remedial measure (placing salt or ashes, warning visitors of the presence of ice, or barricading the icy area)." After a trial court ruled in favor of the church, the woman appealed. A state appeals court agreed that the church was not responsible for the woman's injuries. The court observed:

[A]n owner or occupier of land is not liable for general slippery conditions, for to require that one's walks be always free of ice and snow would be to impose an impossible burden in view of the climatic conditions in this hemisphere. Snow and ice upon a pavement create merely a transient danger, and the only duty upon the property owner or tenant is to act within a reasonable time after notice to remove it when it is in a dangerous condition. . . . [I]n order to recover for a fall on an ice or snow covered sidewalk, a plaintiff must prove (1) that snow and ice had accumulated on the sidewalk in ridges or elevations of such size and character as to unreasonably obstruct travel and constitute a danger to pedestrians traveling thereon; (2) that the property owner had notice, either actual or constructive, of the existence of such a condition; (3) that it was the dangerous accumulation of snow and ice which caused the plaintiff to fall.

The court ruled that the woman had failed to satisfy this test, and accordingly the church was not responsible for the injuries. *Harmotta v. Bender, 601 A.2d 837 (Pa. Super. 1992).*

Example. An Illinois appeals court ruled that a church could be sued for injuries sustained by a member who fell down snow and ice covered stairs on church premises. The victim went to her church at around 6:30 P.M. on a January evening to practice with her rock band, Romantic Fever, in the church basement. A member of the church board served as the band's manager. The building is reached by a number of wooden stairs. The stairs have a handrail down the middle, but not on the sides. The victim left the church at 10 P.M. following the band rehearsal. As she faced the bottom of the stairs looking down, she could see a mixture of ice and snow on the right side of the steps to a depth of between one-half inch and three inches. Snow had been thrown to the left side of the stairs over the handrail and this side was impassable. The victim proceeded down the stairs and slipped on the first or second step. She fell down the rest of the stairs, injuring her back. She did not know the source of the snow on which she slipped, and did not know who had partially removed the snow from the steps. When asked whether anything about the stairs themselves contributed to her fall, she stated that there was no handrail down the right side and that the steps were warped. The board member noticed snow on the church steps on several occasions during the day of the accident. He discussed the problem with the pastor who was "very perturbed" that the snow was not being cleared within a reasonable time and was not being cleared to his satisfaction. The pastor expected complete snow removal, meaning edge to edge on the steps. Before the accident, the board member had talked with the church custodians (a husband and wife) about this problem and conveyed the minister's feelings about complete snow removal. It was the custodians' duty to remove snow from the stairs. The board member said following the accident that "had the snow removal been taken care of, this wouldn't have occurred." One the custodians stated that she had moved snow on the church stairs from one side to another on the day of the accident, but did not clear it completely. The woman sued the church, and a trial court threw the case out on the basis of the church's motion for summary judgment. The woman appealed, and a state appeals court reversed the trial court's decision and ordered the case to proceed to trial. The court observed that "there is generally no duty to remove natural accumulations of ice and snow" and that "[t]he mere removal of snow leaving a natural ice formation underneath does not constitute negligence." However, a church or other property owner can be legally responsible for injuries in two situations: (1) snow is removed in a negligent manner, or (2) "an injury occurred as the result of snow or ice produced or accumulated by artificial causes or in an unnatural way, or by the defendant's use of the premises." The court continued:

Here, there is sufficient evidence in the record from which a trier of fact could conclude that [the church] created or permitted to exist an unnatural accumulation of snow and ice on the steps. [The victim] testified that the snow had been removed from one side of the stairs and thrown over the handrail onto the other side. A jury could thus conclude that the ice on which [the victim] fell was caused by runoff from the snow piled on the other side of the stairs. . . . [The church] contends that [the victim] failed to show affirmatively that there was a "nexus" between the snow on the left side of the stairs and the ice on which [she] fell. . . . [T]he snow was piled on the left side of the stairs, separated from the opposite side by only a double handrail. It is reasonable to conclude that the ice on which [the victim] slipped came from the snow piled on the other side of the stairs.

The court rejected the church's claim that there was no evidence that it was responsible for the accumulation of snow on the left side of the stairs. The court noted that "there was ample evidence from which a jury could conclude that [the church's] agents were responsible for the unnatural accumulation of snow on the stairs." It referred to the fact that the board member testified that the custodians were primarily responsible for snow removal at the church, and that volunteer groups at the church or church members themselves would occasionally remove some snow. There was no evidence that anyone not connected with the church ever removed snow from the church steps. Moreover, the court concluded, "even if we accepted the tenuous conclusion that some unknown person completely unconnected with the church gratuitously undertook to remove the snow from the steps, a question of fact would still exist concerning whether the church was chargeable with knowledge of the unnatural accumulation on the steps and would thus be liable on this basis." The board member testified that he was aware of the situation prior to the date of the accident and had brought it to the attention of other church officials. Even if the church or its agents did not create the condition, "a jury could still find that it had knowledge of the condition and failed to correct it." The court also ruled that the trial court erred in not considering the victim's assertion that the church had been negligent in not constructing handrails on the sides of the stairway and in failing to correct the warped condition of the stairs. *Graff v. St. Luke's Evangelical Lutheran Church*, 625 N.E.2d 851 (Ill. App. 2 Dist. 1993).

Example. The New Jersey Supreme Court ruled that a church-operated school located on church property could be sued by a pedestrian who suffered permanent injuries when she slipped on a sidewalk abutting the school that had not been cleared of snow and ice. Such a result, concluded the court, was "less harsh than imposing the entire loss on a pedestrian injured by the negligent maintenance of a sidewalk," and "would in no way interfere with the exercise of religion" by the church. Further, requiring church schools to clear abutting sidewalks of snow and ice "would not greatly add to the type of maintenance tasks [such schools] routinely undertake." Finally, the court rejected the church's claim that the state "charitable immunity law" (which prevents charitable and religious organizations from being sued in some cases by their "beneficiaries") prevented it from being sued—since the injured pedestrian was not a beneficiary of the church. While acknowledging "the good works performed by religious and charitable organizations," the court concluded that "religious institutions do not enjoy an absolute immunity from worldly burdens." Brown v. St. Venantius School, 544 A.2d 842 (N.J. 1988).

Example. The Indiana Supreme Court ruled that members of an unincorporated church can sue their church for injuries they suffer on church property or in the course of church activities. The court reversed previous rulings in which it had applied the traditional rule that members of an unincorporated church cannot sue their church. The facts of the case can be quickly stated. A church member (the "victim") attended a meeting of a local "Toastmasters" chapter that had rented a portion of the church for the evening. Both members and non-members of the church attended the function. Over the course of the evening, some snow and ice accumulated in the parking lot of the church. After spending about two hours inside, the victim left the church and walked toward her automobile. As she neared her car, she slipped and fell. An associate pastor saw her fall and immediately drove her to the hospital, where she received treatment for a broken arm. The associate pastor later commented to the church's business manager that the parking lot had been slick on his way into the church earlier that evening and was still slippery on his way out when he saw the victim fall. The victim later sued her church and its 9-member board of trustees for her personal injuries, alleging negligence for failure to properly maintain the parking lot, failure to inspect the parking lot for dangerous conditions, failure to remove the snow and ice from the parking lot, and failure to warn her of the dangerous conditions. The trustees and church pointed out that the church was unincorporated, and as a result the victim could not sue them. A trial court agreed, applying the traditional rule that a member of an unincorporated association cannot sue the association for the negligence of another member. The victim appealed. A state appeals court agreed that the victim could not sue the trustees, but it concluded that she could sue her church. The church appealed to the state supreme court. The court concluded that the traditional rule had to be abolished, and that members should be allowed "to bring tort actions against the unincorporated associations of which they are part." The court sent the case back to the trial court for trial. Hanson v. Saint Luke's United Methodist Church, 1998 WL 904830 (Ind. 1998).

Example. A Georgia court ruled that a church was not responsible for injuries suffered by a woman who slipped and fell on church property. The woman had taken her daughter up a wooden ramp to the entrance of a church school, and was injured when she slipped and fell on the way down. It was raining at the time of the accident and the ramp was wet. Immediately after she fell the woman told the church's pastor that "it's not your fault . . . it was just raining and I was in a hurry and slipped and fell." The woman had slipped before on the same ramp, and was aware that it was slippery even under dry conditions. She sued the church as a result of her injuries. A *trial court ruled in favor of the church and the woman appealed. A state appeals court upheld the trial court's ruling. In sensible language that will be of use to churches in similar cases, the court observed:*

Everyone knows that any wet surface may be slippery. [The woman] has slipped on the ramp when it was dry. She had knowledge of its danger equal and perhaps superior knowledge to [that of the church], and she fell either because she was hurrying or because she chose to negotiate the ramp despite the danger which was obvious to her.

The mere fact that a dangerous condition exists, whether caused by a building code violation or otherwise, does not impose liability on the [property owner]. For a plaintiff to recover for injury from a fall, two elements must exist: (1) fault on the part of the owner, and (2) ignorance of the danger on the part of the [victim]. The basis of the [property owner's] liability is his superior knowledge; if [the victim] knows of the hazard, there is no duty to warn her, and no liability for injury because [she] has as much knowledge as the [property owner] and by voluntarily acting despite her knowledge, she assumes risks and dangers incident to the known condition. The evidence shows undisputedly that [the victim] was aware that a hazard existed; if the hazard was such that it could not safely be traversed, she should have exercised ordinary care to avoid it.

It is when the perilous instrumentality is known to the owner . . . and not known to the person injured that a recovery is permitted. Even where a [land owner] acts negligently, to recover in a slip and fall resulting from a foreign substance, such as water on a ramp, not only must the plaintiff show the [property owner] had knowledge of the foreign substance, but the plaintiff must show she was without knowledge of it. She must exercise ordinary care for her own safety to avoid the effect of the [property owner's] negligence after it becomes apparent to her or in the exercise of ordinary care she should have learned of it. She must make use of all her senses in a reasonable measure amounting to ordinary care in discovering and avoiding those things that might cause hurt to her.

In other words, adults must take some responsibility for their own actions. According to the Georgia court, persons who choose to use a ramp on church premises that is wet and slippery cannot blame the church for injuries they sustain when they fall as a result of the condition. Patterson v. First Assembly of God, 440 S.E.2d 492 (Ga. App. 1994).

Uneven pavement or holes in parking lots

Overtime, sidewalks settle, crack, and shift. A sidewalk with uneven payment can become a tripping hazard. Parking lots can develop potholes. People step in them and lose their balance.

Reducing the risk

Repair all uneven pavement and fill in holes. Use signs to warn people of the hazard until it can be fixed. Failure to take corrective action may result in a liability claim against the church or school if someone trips and becomes injured. Often, uneven payment can be around for years and nobody does anything about it. People who use the facilities on a regular basis may take it for granted. The same is not true for a visitor. Uneven pavement poses a risk of falling that may be infrequent, but which can be severe. As the case below illustrates, however, borders around flower beds and trees are not likely to be considered a tripping hazard, even if they are uneven.

Examples that have prompted lawsuits

> **Example.** *A child was injured on church property when he tripped on one of several bricks surrounding the base of a large tree. While it was dark outside, there was sufficient light from outdoor floodlights to permit the victim and other children to play football. A Florida appeals court ruled in favor of the church, on the ground that "we do not think that a tree with a surrounding brick border constitutes a dangerous condition or concealed peril," and accordingly "there was no duty on the part of the church to warn or take other precautionary measures, such as installing better lighting." Grajeda v. Winter Springs Community Evangelical Congregational Church, 509 So.2d 384 (Fl. App. 1987).*

Loose carpeting or runners

Carpeting can cause slips and falls in a number of ways. Throw rugs on a wood or tile floor often slide unless they are positioned on a nonskid mat. Carpeting can curl around the edges and not lie flat on the floor. As a result people can catch their shoe on the edge and trip and fall. Similarly, tears, holes, or cuts in a carpet can also cause a person to trip and fall.

Reducing the risk

Do not use throw rugs unless absolutely necessary. If they are used, make sure they do not slip or pose a tripping hazard. Inspect all carpeting and runners for loose edges, tears, or holes. Make sure all carpeting is properly tacked or glued down and repair tears or holes, or replace the carpet.

Examples that have prompted lawsuits

> **Example.** *An Indiana appeals court ruled that a synagogue can be legally responsible for injuries suffered by a member who tripped over a plastic runner covering an aisle. The court noted that the liability of landowners (including churches and synagogues) for injuries suffered on their premises depends on whether the victim was a "licensee" or an "invitee." One who enters premises for his or her own "convenience, curiosity, or entertainment" is a licensee and cannot recover for injuries caused by negligent maintenance of the premises. On the other hand, persons who are invited to enter upon premises for a purpose for which the premises are held open to the public or for business dealings with the owner of the premises are "invitees" who may recover for such injuries. The court concluded that members who attend activities at a church or synagogue are invitees under this test, since they are invited to enter the premises for the purposes for which they are held open to the public. Accordingly, a church or synagogue has a duty to protect them against negligent conditions on the premises, including improperly maintained runners. Fleischer v. Hebrew Orthodox Congregation, 504 N.E.2d 320 (Ind. App. 1987).*

Wet floors

Puddles around sinks, stools, drinking fountains or an ice machine can cause people to slip and fall. Wet floors that have just been mopped can cause people to slip and fall.

Reducing the risk

Use nonskid mats around areas that collect water. Once spotted, clean up water spills immediately. Use signs to warn people of wet floors. Use grab rails by toilets.

Examples that have prompted lawsuits

Example. *A New York court ruled that a church was not legally responsible for injuries sustained by a member who slipped on a puddle of water in a church hallway near a water fountain. The member acknowledged that the church would be legally responsible only if the risk of slipping on water in the hallway was a reasonably foreseeable hazard. However, she insisted that this hazard was foreseeable because the church had placed a stool under the water fountain to allow children to access it. She alleged that it is common knowledge that children who use water fountains cause spills and puddles on the surrounding floor. As a result, the risk of an adult slipping on a puddle of water near the water fountain was foreseeable. The court disagreed. It concluded:*

> *[T]o hold that [the church] created a reasonably foreseeable hazard by providing an unsecured step stool for children to access a hallway water fountain would be to stretch the concept of foreseeability beyond acceptable limits. Certainly there is no evidence that [the church] had actual notice of the water that had spilled in front of the fountain, or that the water was present for a sufficient length of time before the accident to permit [church] employees to discover and remedy it, or that [it] had actual knowledge of any prior spillage of water in front of the fountain, or that spillage was an ongoing and recurring condition that was routinely left unaddressed. Nor is an issue of fact as to [the church's] notice of a recurring condition raised by [the victim's] unsupported assertion that it is common knowledge that children are careless and that water will splash from fountains. A mere general awareness that some dangerous condition may be present is legally insufficient to constitute notice of a particular condition. Chaney v. Abyssinian Baptist Church, 667 N.Y.S.2d 737 (A.D. 1998).*

Example. *A mother, who was a member of the church, was taking her son to the church child-care program. As she entered the building she slipped and fell and injured her back. She sued the church alleging that it had been negligent in allowing the tile floor to become slippery from moisture. In addition to being a member of the church for 4 years, she was also a member of the church's administrative board. The church was unincorporated at the time of the accident. Both a trial court and a state appeals court dismissed the lawsuit concluding that an unincorporated church could not be sued by one of its members. The Texas Supreme Court ruled otherwise stating that a member of an unincorporated church who is injured because of the negligence of other members can sue the church for money damages. Cox v. The Evergreen Church, 1992 WL 14116 (Tex. 1992).*

Waxed floors

Freshly waxed floors can be slippery and cause people to fall. They are a significant cause of injury and have led to a number of lawsuits.

Reducing the risk

Use only nonskid wax and warning signs to indicate that floors have been waxed. Do not wax floors immediately prior to events attracting large numbers of people.

Examples that have prompted lawsuits

> **Example.** *A charity permitted an outside group to use its facility for a Christmas party. During the party, a woman suffered serious injuries when she fell on a slippery floor. As a result of her injuries the woman underwent surgery for a complete hip replacement. She later sued the charity, claiming that the floor was unreasonably slippery, and this dangerous condition caused her to fall. One witness testified, "It was obvious that floor was slippery. It was just waxed or something. I mean it wasn't dirty. It was clean. Probably too clean." The charity asked the court to dismiss the case, but its request was denied. On appeal, a state appeals court suggested that there was sufficient evidence that the charity retained control over its premises during the party to send the case to a jury. The court began its opinion by acknowledging that a property owner may be legally responsible for injuries that occur on its premises when they are under its custody or control. The court suggested that the charity had retained control over its premises during the Christmas party on the basis of the following factors: (1) the charity was responsible for setting up tables for the party; (2) the charity provided a custodian during the entire party; and (3) the charity was responsible for opening the premises at the beginning of the party and locking the premises at the conclusion of the party. The charity's custodian admitted that he had cleaned the floor prior to the party and that he was on duty and responsible for cleaning the floor during the party. Aufrichtig v. Progressive Men's Club, 634 So.2d 947 (La. App. 2 Cir. 1994).*

> **Example.** *An Indiana court ruled that a church member who was injured when she fell on church premises could not sue her unincorporated church, but could sue the church janitor who was not a member of the church and who she claimed negligently waxed the floor. The court observed that*

>> the general common law rule in Indiana is that members of an unincorporated association cannot sue the association for the [negligence] of one or more of its members. Because [the victim] is a member of [the church] she is barred, pursuant to this rule, from suing the church. Thus [her] sole remedy is to sue [the defendant], a non-member, part-time janitor . . . . Although the rule protecting an unincorporated association from a suit by its own members was originally adopted in an attempt to prevent collusive lawsuits between the members of an association, we find it hard to believe that the rule was also intended to allow a part-time employee of an association to shoulder the sole responsibility for a member's accident. Because we find it hard to accept that a non-member employee of an unincorporated association should be exposed to such liability of that an injured plaintiff could only look to the pockets of a non-member employee, we believe that it may be time to take another look at the rule and

particularly the rule's impact on the employees of unincorporated associations and injured plaintiffs.

The court concluded that the janitor may have been negligent in improperly waxing the church floor, and it permitted the victim to proceed with her lawsuit against him. *MacDonald v. Maxwell, 655 N.E.2 1249 (Ind. App. 1995).*

Example. The Mississippi Supreme Court ruled that an unincorporated church and its board of trustees could be sued by a member who was injured when she slipped and fell on a waxed floor while leaving a Sunday School class. The member argued that she was an "invitee" and accordingly that the church owed her a high degree of care which it breached. The church maintained that the member was merely a "licensee" to whom it owed a minimal duty of care. Under Mississippi law (as is true in many states) a property owner owes licensees only the minimal duty of refraining from willfully and wantonly injuring them through active negligence. A much higher duty applies to invitees—a property owner owes such persons a duty of keeping the premises reasonably safe and to warn them about (or correct) dangerous conditions of which it is aware (or should have been aware). A trial court ruled that the member was a licensee, and that her injury had not been caused by any active negligence on the part of the church. The member appealed, and the state supreme court ruled that the member was in fact an invitee at the time of her injury. The court observed that the term invitee includes both "public invitees" and "business visitors." A public invitee is "a person who is invited to enter or remain on land as a member of the public for a purpose for which the land is held open to the public," while a business visitor is "a person who is invited to enter or remain on land for a purpose directly or indirectly connected with business dealings with the possessor of the land." On the other hand, a licensee is one "who enters upon the property of another for his own convenience, pleasure or benefit pursuant to the license or implied permission of the owner." In applying these definitions to church members, the court concluded: "Members of religious associations, in general . . . fall within the category of 'public invitees.' Religious bodies do expressly and impliedly invite members to come and attend their services and functions. They hold their doors open to the public. While they do not charge admission fees . . . churches do depend on contributions . . . in order that they may continue to be open to the public. Therefore, a church member who does not exceed the scope of the church's invitation, is an invitee while attending a church for church services or related functions." Accordingly, the member who slipped and fell on the waxed floor was an invitee to whom the church owed a high degree of care, rather than a mere licensee to whom the church owed only a minimal duty of care. *Clark v. Moore Memorial United Methodist Church, 538 So.2d 760 (Miss. 1989).*

Dark stairways or uneven steps

People frequently trip and fall on stairways. Sometimes the stairway is too dark and they cannot see the correct number of steps. Sometimes one or two steps may appear unexpectedly, such as in a doorway between two sections of a building. People may lose their balance and fall. Also, in some stairwells the railing does not extend all the way to the last step. This can cause people to stumble and lose their balance. Make sure that railings are present for every step.

Reducing the risk

Install adequate lighting in all stairways. Use glow-in-the-dark light switches in dark areas. Have handrails on both sides of the steps along the complete stairwell. Use warning signs to notify people of steps that are not obvious. Use colored tape or bright paint to highlight stairs that may be difficult to see. Use nonskid surfaces or strips on all steps. In addition, make sure that handrails and the top rails of the stairrail system are not loose. The top railings should be able to withstand at least 200 pounds of weight applied 2 inches of the top of the edge in any downward or outward direction at any point along the top edge.[2]

Examples that have prompted lawsuits

Example. A member left a Sunday morning worship service to use the restroom, which was located in the church basement. To reach the restroom, the member had to go the church basement, cross the fellowship hall, ascend three uneven stairs, and walk down a hall. When the member went to the basement, the lights were on and she had no difficulty reaching the restroom. However, when she left the restroom, all the basement lights were off and the basement was completely dark. The member attempted to find her way back upstairs. Although there was a light switch in the hall leading to the restroom, the member could not find it because of the darkness. When she reached the three uneven stairs that led to the fellowship hall, she tripped and sustained serious injuries. The member later sued the church, alleging that her injuries were caused by the church's negligence. A jury agreed that the church was responsible for the woman's injuries, and the church appealed. A state appeals court reversed the trial court's decision. The court noted that "evidence of the church's negligence was minimal. [The member] did not establish that the lights were turned off by a person for whose negligence the church could be held vicariously liable." As a result, the court reversed the trial court's decision, and ordered a new trial. Thies v. St. Paul's Evangelical Lutheran Church, 489 N.W.2d 277 (Minn. App. 1992).

Example. A Louisiana state appeals court upheld a trial court's dismissal of a lawsuit filed against a church by a member who was injured when she fell on a church stairway. On the day of the accident, the member and a friend were preparing breakfast in the church kitchen for a youth recreational event. In the kitchen was a doorway leading to an outside staircase consisting of three steps to the ground. The member picked up an ice chest with the intention of standing in the doorway and emptying the contents to the side of the staircase. When the member stepped through the doorway she fell forward down the staircase and landed on the ground. She sued the church, arguing that the staircase violated city code since the top step was allegedly more narrow than the bottom two steps and the staircase did not have a handrail. The court concluded that even if the church had violated the city code, the member "loses because she was contributorily negligent. [T]he fact is she stepped through a doorway, with her vision at least partially obscured by the ice chest she carried, missed her step, and fell. Reasonable prudence required her to be more careful. . . . She had no right to assume that there was a place to land her foot because she could not see where she was going." The absence of a handrail, and the width of the top step, in no way contributed to the member's injuries, the court concluded. Richard v. Church Insurance Company, 538 So.2d 658 (La. App. 1989).

---

[2] *Stairways and Ladders*, U.S. Department of Labor Occupational Safety and Health Administration, <http://www.osha-slc.gov/Publications/OSHA3124/osha3124.html>.

Ladders

Falls from ladders during routine maintenance, clean-up days, or construction project are common and can create serious injuries. The problem may be that the ladder is in poor repair, but many accidents result from the improper use of the ladder. It may not be positioned safely, or the user climbs too high, tries to carry too much while climbing, or reaches too far and loses his or her balance. Similar problems occur while working on roofs or while climbing on rafters.

Reducing the risk

Be especially alert on jobs that require the use of ladders such as painting, cleaning gutters, washing windows, changing light bulbs, or getting or replacing items from high shelves. Use only ladders that are in good repair. Provide instructions on the proper use of ladders and monitor workers. See chapter 10 for more information.

Examples that have prompted lawsuits

> *Example. A church board member fell off a ladder while installing a ceiling fan and sued both the pastor and the church after sustaining permanent injuries. The court rejected the claim of negligent supervision since the board member sustained injuries that resulted from an open and obvious danger, and were not recoverable under the Premises Liability Act. However, the court concluded the board member could sue the church for a violation of the state "Structural Work Act," which provides protection for those engaged on a ladder while undertaking building repairs. Coates v. W.W. Babcock Co., 560 N.E.2d 1099 (Ill. App. 1990).*

> *Example. A Wisconsin appeals court ruled that a church can be legally responsible for injuries sustained by a volunteer worker who was injured severely while helping to paint a church's fellowship hall. The volunteer was painting a steam pipe using a stepladder that was owned by the church and that had been placed on a drop cloth. Following the accident, the victim was taken to a hospital where he was diagnosed as comatose and partially paralyzed, and was placed on a life support system. Several weeks later, he had "regressed to a very primitive, vegetative level." A lawsuit was brought against the church, and a jury determined that the victim and the church had each been 50 percent negligent, and awarded damages accordingly. The church appealed from this decision, arguing that the evidence had not conclusively established that the victim had fallen from the stepladder, and, even if he had, that the fall was due to a defect in the ladder and drop cloth. On appeal, the state appeals court disagreed with the church: "[E]xpert medical testimony indicated that injuries of the type . . . sustained could not usually be caused by someone falling on level ground . . . . Evidence also indicated that the ladder and drop cloth were a substantial factor in causing the fall. . . . [T]wo experts testified that the ladder [was unsafe] because it was warped and twisted, with bowed treads, loose joints and other defects, with the result that 'the ladder becomes rickety, teetery, when you get on it,' and could move suddenly, surprising someone on it . . . [and] that 'the front legs slipped and will slide on the drop cloth.'" Another expert witness testified that "the ladder and drop cloth combination would be a substantial factor in someone falling off." In light of this testimony, the court ruled that the jury had properly concluded that the church was negligent "in the materials it provided to [the victim]." Kluever v. Evangelical Reformed Immanuels Congregation, 422 N.W.2d 874 (Wisc. App. 1988).*

Cords

Telephone cords and electrical cords lying across the floor become a tripping hazard.

Reducing the risk

The best solution is to remove the cords. That is not always possible. If the cords are temporary, tape them to the floor using duct tape. If they are permanent, have a professional cover the cords with a secure casing that is designed for that purpose.

Windows

Children can fall out of windows. Particular attention should be given to rooms that are second story or above and that children use on a regular basis.

Reducing the risk

Train adults to adequately supervise children. Keep windows locked and closed. Use window guards or bars, in accordance with local zoning provisions, to prevent children from falling.

Obstructions

Debris, clutter, or other items are left lying in areas where people walk and become a tripping hazard. Often this happens following a meeting or social activity.

Reducing the risk

Make arrangements to have rooms cleaned immediately after social activities. Keep all walkways clear of items that can cause people to trip. Block off areas, redirect people to use alternative walkways, and use warning signs to notify people of potential hazards.

Examples that have prompted lawsuits

> **Example.** *A church permitted an outside group to use church facilities for an annual one-day celebration that included a religious ceremony and a reception. After the ceremony, guests were ushered into another room for refreshments. While the refreshments were being served, volunteers disassembled the tables and chairs in the room where the ceremony occurred. Some guests remained behind to socialize. Several minutes later, as one of the guests proceeded to the reception area, she tripped and fell over some of the disassembled tables. Later she sued the church. Both a trial court and an appeals court refused to dismiss the suit. St. Casimer Church v. Frankiewics, 563 N.E.2d 1331 (Ind. App. 1990).*

9.3 Other Common Accidents

In addition to slips and falls, churches and schools should take precautions to avoid accidents in the following common problem areas:

The kitchen

Kitchens can be very busy places in both churches and schools. Following a few simple guidelines can reduce accidents:

● Overcrowding and noise can lead to distractions, which in turn can lead to accidents. Limit the number of workers in the kitchen at any given time.

● Do not use power equipment such as a meat slicer while wearing clothes or jewelry that can get caught in the machine.

● Be careful that liquids such as coffee or water for tea are not scalding hot. Dispensers should be placed in areas away from children.

● Clean-up all spills immediately. Keep a mop handy.

● Make hot pads and mitts available to avoid burns. When removing food from a hot oven, have a designated place to set it. Keep the oven doors closed.

● Do not store cleaners or other chemicals under sinks or anywhere else where children may have access to them.

● Some frozen foods such as lasagna or chicken pies use an aluminum foil "pan." Once those foods are cooked and removed from the oven, transport them on a solid tray such as a cookie sheet so that the bottom of the "pan" does not collapse.

● Keep a first aid kit in the kitchen.

Industrial and vocational arts areas

Many schools and some churches provide courses or training programs in the industrial arts. Special safety precautions, including the use of personal protective equipment, must be used in such settings. See chapter 10.

School science labs

A primary concern in science labs is the use of hazardous chemicals, glassware, and fire. The Occupational Safety and Health Administration (OSHA) estimates that as many as 1,000 different hazardous chemicals, products, or materials are commonly found in elementary and secondary schools Over 2,000 hazardous chemical accidents occur each year in schools and colleges. Multimillion dollar lawsuits have been filed against school districts for chemical accidents. Safety goggles, aprons, and protective gloves should made available to students. Science teachers should meet with custodians to review the safe storage of science equipment and hazardous chemicals.

Art rooms

Most churches and schools maintain supplies of art equipment. Some art supplies include toxic materials that must be stored in a safe place away from children.

Swimming pool chemicals

Chlorine, acid, and other chemicals pose risks to adults and children. Swimming pool chemicals should be stored in a secure area, away from fire hazards and children.

9.4 Legal Principles that Impact Liability

As the above examples illustrate, when a person is injured from an accident, often a slip or fall , the potential for a lawsuit follows. The question is whether or not the church or school was negligent for the cause of the accident. This concern is related to the concept of *premises liability*. The issue of premises liability is covered in chapter 30 and should be reviewed in conjunction with this chapter on accidents.

Summary

Accidents requiring medical attention are common in both churches and schools. Our research indicates that the accident rate increases significantly with church size, but stays about the same for all geographical locations, except for rural areas which reported lower incidents.

Among accidents, slips and falls are the number one cause of injuries and lawsuits in churches. While they affect every age group and all geographical areas, churches and schools located in areas with ice and snow face greater risks. Slippery conditions contribute to many slip and fall injuries. Slips and falls pose a significant risk, both to those who are injured and also to a church or school due to the potential for a lawsuit.

Reducing the frequency of slips and falls requires the regular inspection and maintenance of buildings and grounds. Common problem areas include playgrounds, slippery pavement due to ice, snow, and rain, uneven payment or holes in parking lots, loose carpeting or runners, wet floors, waxed floors, dark stairways or uneven steps, obstructed walkways, the unsafe use of ladders, cords across floors, and falling out of windows.

In the next chapter, attention is given to maintaining safety in building maintenance and construction projects.

CHAPTER 10. REDUCING ACCIDENTS IN MAINTENANCE AND CONSTRUCTION PROJECTS

Churches and schools have ongoing maintenance needs and also engage in a wide range of construction projects. Whether it's a clean-up day, building new facilities, remodeling old ones, working on a house for Habitat for Humanity, or repairing homes for the poor, church members and school volunteers are active in maintenance and construction. Some custodians and members who work on these projects are expert carpenters, plumbers, and electricians. Many, though, are amateurs who rarely use circular saws, air powered nail guns, or other power equipment. The mix of inexperience, limited supervision, and power equipment poses real hazards. As a result serious accidents regularly occur in maintenance and construction projects. Many injuries, though, can be prevented by following a simple, but effective program that provides training for custodians and use of a safety supervisor for clean-up days and construction projects. In addition, churches and schools should require outside contractors to comply with all Occupational Safety and Health Administration (OHSA) requirements.

10.1 Custodians and Work Supervisors

Custodial training

Most churches and schools have a paid custodian on staff. Often this person works alone and does many maintenance jobs that include the use of hand tools, power tools, ladders, and hazardous chemicals. Training in the safe use of equipment should be part of the orientation and continuing education program for custodians and maintenance workers. Such employees should be familiar with the information provided in this chapter.

The safety supervisor

To minimize the risk of accidents during construction and clean-up days, churches and schools should appoint a competent person to serve as the safety supervisor. Every maintenance or construction project should have someone fill this position. The role of the safety supervisor is twofold: first, the supervisor monitors the work site and the workers for hazards, and corrects them when they are found; and second, the supervisor provides training and instruction to workers to minimize accidents and injuries. The supervisor must have the authority to dictate safety measures. Every worker should understand the role and authority of the safety supervisor. To help communicate that role and authority, each worker should sign-in at the work site and agree to a provision such as the following sample work agreement:

> Sample work agreement: To promote a safe work environment, First Church has designated (name of safety supervisor) to be the safety supervisor on this work project. The safety supervisor has full authority to dictate safety measures, and workers must comply with all safety precautions. I agree to abide by all safety rules for this project.

_____
Name and date

10.2 Monitoring the Work Site

One role of the safety supervisor is to inspect the site and monitor the work for hazards. Custodians or maintenance personnel should also keep their own work areas safe. Attention should be given to the work area, tools, safe work practices, and personal protective equipment.

The work area

The work area should be clear of materials that can cause workers to trip or fall, or that could fall from above. Pipes or beams that are at work level should be flagged. Any pits or holes should be blocked off. Lighting and ventilation should be adequate. All electrical or environmental hazards should be identified. Jobs should be identified that require personal protective equipment.

Tools

All tools should be inspected to make sure they are in good repair. Defective tools should be removed and marked "Do Not Use." Workers should be given clear instructions on the proper use of tools with which they are not familiar. Tools should be used only for the job for which they were designed.

Safe work practices

All workers should wear personal protective equipment for hazardous jobs they perform (see below). Workers should not wear clothing or jewelry that could get caught in a machine. No person should work in an unbalanced position that could result in a fall. Workers should be given clear instructions on lifting and handling materials that can result in physical stress and back injuries.

Personal protective equipment

Custodians and maintenance personnel should wear proper protective clothing for their work including shoes with nonskid soles. When a construction project or clean-up day is taking place, the safety supervisor should identify jobs that require personal protective equipment such as those noted below:

Guidelines for Personal Protective Equipment[1]

Key questions	Typical job at church or school construction site	Personal Exposure	Personal Protective Equipment
Do workers perform tasks that might produce airborne dust or flying particles? Do workers handle hazardous liquids or chemicals?	Sawing, cutting, drilling, sanding, grinding, hammering, chopping, compressed air operations, pouring, mixing	Eyes	Goggles, Safety glasses Note: eyeglasses designed for ordinary wear do not provide the level of protection necessary to protect against construction hazards.

---

[1] Adapted from, *Assessing the Need for Personal Protective Equipment: A Guide for Small Business Employers,* Safety Management Series U.S. Department of Labor Occupational Safety and Health Administration OSHA 3151, 1997.

Key questions	Typical job at church or school construction site	Personal Exposure	Personal Protective Equipment
Are workers exposed to extreme heat, hazardous chemicals, extreme light, or potential irritants?	Welding, cutting, spray painting, grinding	Face	Face shields
Might tools or other objects fall from above and strike a worker on the head? When workers stand or bend, are their heads near exposed beams, machine parts, or pipes?	Work stations or traffic routes located under catwalks, construction.	Head	Hard hat
Could tools, heavy equipment, or other objects roll, fall onto, or strike a worker's feet? Are workers near exposed electrical wiring or components?	Construction, plumbing, trenching, grass cutting, spray painting, working with flammable materials.	Feet	Safety shoes
Do workers' hands come into contact with tools or materials that might scrape, bruise, or cut? Do workers handle chemicals that might irritate the skin or come into contact with blood? Do workers place their hands and arms near extreme heat?	Grinding, sawing, hammering, material handling, pouring, mixing, cleaning, welding, drying.	Hands	Gloves
Are workers' hands and arms placed near exposed electrical wiring? Are workers' bodies exposed to irritating dust, chemicals, sharp edges, rough surfaces, acids or other hazardous substances?	Pouring, mixing, cleaning, sawing, installing fiberglass, compressed air operations, cutting, grinding, sanding, sawing, material handling, painting.	Body	Vests, coveralls, jackets, aprons
Are workers' exposed to loud noise from machines or tools?	Grinding, sanding, pneumatic equipment, generators, fans, motors.	Ears	Ear plugs, ear muffs

10.3 Training and Safety Instructions for Workers

A second role of the safety supervisor is to provide training and instruction to workers to minimize accidents and injuries. Custodians and maintenance personnel should apply these guidelines to their own work. Attention should be given to the use of hand tools, power tools, and ladders, all of which play an important role in every church or school construction project.

Hand tools and power tools

The Occupational Safety and Health Administration recommends five basic rules when using hand and power tools:

1. Keep tools in good working condition.

2. Use the right tool for the job.

3. Examine tools prior to use for damage and if damaged do not use them.

4. Follow the manufacturer's instructions when using a tool.

5. Always use the proper protective equipment.

When followed these five simple rules can reduce injuries. The church or school, though, is responsible to see that such rules are understood and followed. If an accident should occur, the church or school may be held liable.

Hand tools

Hand tools pose the greatest threat when they are misused, and are not properly maintained. For example, the head of a hammer may fly off if the wooden handle is cracked. Or if the head of a chisel has mushroomed, it might shatter on impact sending fragments into the air. The use of knifes, axes, or saw blades can result in injuries when people work close together and the tool is being directed toward another person, or where a person may suddenly walk by. Iron and steel tools can create sparks and ignite flammable gases or volatile liquids. At church or school projects, workers generally bring their own tools. Special emphasis should be placed on not using any damaged tool and not to improvise with tools. Following those rules can reduce hand tool injuries.

Power tools

Power tools are more dangerous than hand tools. The first basic rule is to use protective equipment including goggles and gloves. Many power tools are portable. Slipping and falling while using a power tool can result in serious injuries. Work floors should be kept dry and clean. Workers should not get in positions that cause them to lose their balance. OSHA recommends the following safety precautions concerning the use of power tools:

- Never carry a tool by the cord or hose.

- Never yank the cord or hose to disconnect it from the receptacle.

- Keep cords and hoses away from heat, oil, and sharp edges.

- Disconnect tools when not using them, before servicing and cleaning them, and when changing accessories such as blades, bits, and cutters.

- Keep all people not involved in the work at a safe distance from the work area.

- Secure work with clamps or a vise, freeing both hands to operate the tool.

- Avoid accidental starting. Do not hold fingers on the switch button while carrying a plugged-in tool.

- Maintain tools with care; keep them sharp and clean for best performance.

- Follow instructions in the user manual for lubricating and changing accessories.

- Be sure of good footing and maintain good balance when operating power tools

- Wear proper apparel for the task. Loose clothing, ties, or jewelry can become caught in moving parts.

- Remove all damaged portable electrical tools from use and tag them: "Do Not Use."

One of the most common power tools used on construction sites is a circular saw. Circular saws should never be used if they lack a safety guard. An upper guard should cover the entire blade of the saw, and a retractable lower guard should cover the teeth of the saw except where it makes contact with the wood. The lower guard should automatically return to its full covering position once the tool is withdrawn from the material it is cutting. These guards should never be disabled.

Electrical hazards

Electric power tools pose the threat of both burns and shocks. Under some circumstances, even a small amount of electric current can lead to death. Low voltage does not mean low hazard. A current of only 100 milliamperes can lead to muscular contraction and may not allow the victim to free himself or herself from the circuit. The longer the person remains in the electrical circuit, the greater the danger of serious injury. Electric shocks also startle people and can cause them to fall from a ladder or elevated work surface resulting in serious injury.

To prevent shocks and burns, power tools should be properly grounded and insulated. Electric tools should have a three-wire cord and should be plugged into a grounded receptacle. The third prong should never be removed from the plug. Electrical tools should never be used in damp or wet locations unless specifically approved for that use. If the skin is wet, or water is present in the environment increased caution is required.

Ladders

The safety supervisor and custodian should pay particular attention to the use of ladders. The unsafe use of ladders results in many serious injuries. Workers should be able to recognize hazards and follow procedures to minimize them. Training should focus on the following four points:

- the nature of hazards in the work area;

- the correct procedures for erecting, maintaining, and disassembling the ladders used;

- the proper construction, use, placement, and care in handling ladders; and

- the maximum intended load-carrying capacities of ladders used.

Common jobs around churches and schools that use ladders include painting, cleaning gutters, washing windows, hanging decorations and lights, changing light bulbs, and doing repairs that require getting on the roof. Pay particular attention to safety for any of these common uses of ladders.

The safety supervisor and custodian should be familiar with the following guidelines from OSHA that can help reduce accidents and injuries associated with the use of ladders:

- When ladders are used for access to an upper landing surface, the side rails of the ladder should extend at least 3 feet above the upper landing surface.

- Ladders must be maintained free of oil, grease, and other slipping hazards.

- Ladders must not be loaded beyond their maximum intended load for which they were built.

- Ladders must be used only on stable and level surfaces unless they are secured to prevent accidental movement.

- Ladders must not be used on slippery surfaces unless secured or provided with slip-resistant feet to prevent accidental movement.

- Ladders placed in areas such as passageways, doorways, or driveways, or where they can be displaced by workplace activities or traffic must be secured to prevent accidental movement or a barricade must be used to keep traffic or activities away from the ladder.

- The area around the top and bottom of the ladder must be kept clear.

- Ladders must not be moved, shifted, or extended while in use.

- Ladders must have nonconductive side rails if they are used where the worker or the ladder could contact exposed energized electrical equipment.

- The top or top step of a stepladder must not be used as a step.

- Crossbracing on the rear section of stepladders must not be used for climbing unless the ladders are designed and provided with steps for climbing on both front and rear sections.

- A competent person should inspect ladders for visible defects on a periodic basis and after any incident that could affect their safe use.

- When ascending or descending a ladder, the worker must face the ladder.

- Each worker must use at least one hand to grasp the ladder when climbing.

- A worker on a ladder must not carry any object or load that could cause him or her to lose balance and fall.

- Portable ladders with structural defects—such as broken or missing rungs, cleats, or steps, broken or split rails, corroded components, or other faulty or defective components—must immediately be marked defective, or tagged with "Do Not Use" or similar language and withdrawn from service until repaired.

When using ladders, it is always best to have two people present. One person should stay on the ground and keep the ladder steady. Two or more people, however, should not use a ladder at the same time.

10.4 Worker Safety for Teenagers

Many teens participate in church or school maintenance or construction projects. Adult supervision should be provided to youth who participate in these projects. It may come as a surprise to some leaders that the Fair Labor Standards Act prohibits assigning certain tasks to teen employees because of the large number of injuries that are associated with them such as the following:

- Driving a car or truck

- Using certain power equipment

- Operating a tractor or other heavy equipment

While these standards apply to paid employees and to churches that meet certain federal requirements, they are helpful in understanding a standard of care that the government has established for teenage safety. Teenagers who participate in church or school construction projects should receive a job orientation that includes the following components:

- Clear instructions on what they can and cannot do.

- A review of all safety precautions.

- A demonstration on how to perform the tasks they are being asked to do.

- Observation and feedback while they perform the task to show they know how to do it correctly.

- Clarifying any questions that they have.

Their work should be monitored on a regular basis to make sure no problems surface. Adults should set a good example by complying with all safety guidelines. The Secretary of Labor has determined that the following non-farm jobs are hazardous to youth below the age of 18 (this is not an exhaustive list, but includes those jobs that are most common in church or school projects):

- Driving a motor vehicle

- Power-driven wood working machines*

- Power-driven hoisting equipment

- Power-driven metal forming, punching, and shearing machines*

- Power-driven circular saws, band saws, and guillotine shears*

- Roofing operations*

* Limited exemptions are provided for apprentices and student-learners under specified standards.

Finally, churches and schools should not hire minors without first obtaining a proper work permit. Laws for hiring minors vary from one state to another and a variety of work conditions apply to hours of employment and duties.

10.5 First Aid

First-aid supplies should always be maintained at a construction site and at the church or school office. If a worker is seriously injured move him or her as little as possible. INDIVIDUALS WITH HEAD OR BACK INJURIES SHOULD NOT BE MOVED, unless essential to move them out of immediate danger. Two emergency techniques to move an injured person are the shirt drag (grabbing the shirt around the neck and pulling the person back a few feet in a straight line), and the blanket drag (same as shirt drag but the person is moved by pulling a blanket or carpet or something else they are lying on). Immediately call 911 and do not hang up until you are told to do so by the medical dispatcher.[2]

If a worker receives a cut or a wound and is bleeding, while wearing protective gloves, apply fingertip pressure directly over the wound. If that does not stop the bleeding apply direct pressure to the wound for at least 10 minutes using a gauze pad or some other clean material.[3] If the wound is to a limb, elevate the limb above the heart. For example, if the wound is to a leg, have the person lay down and prop up the leg.

The first aid kit should contain an eyewash in case sawdust or dust particles get in a worker's eye. Also, it is also good to always have someone available who can perform CPR.

Summary

Proper supervision and training can reduce work-related injuries at church and school construction or maintenance projects. Custodians and maintenance personnel should be familiar with safe work procedures. Each project should have a designated safety supervisor that monitors the work area for hazards, inspects the tools to make sure they are in good repair and are used properly, enforces the use of personal protective equipment, and provides training to the workers to minimize accidents and injuries. Attention should be given to the proper use of hand tools, power tools, electrical hazards, and ladders. Many volunteer workers on these projects are teenagers. Special precaution should be taken with these workers so that they do not take on responsibilities that are unsafe either for them or for their co-workers. A first aid kit should always be kept on the construction site. In case an accident should occur, the safety supervisor should have basic training to provide limited help until professional help arrives.

---

[2] Grant B. Goold, *First Aid in the Workplace*, (Upper Saddle River, New Jersey: Prentice-Hall, Inc., 1998), p. 16.
[3] Goold, p. 65.

In the next chapter, we explore two areas of risk management that emerge from the discipline of ergonomics: reducing injuries associated with computer workstations, and minimizing work-related back problems.

Additional Resources on the Internet

For additional information on making construction and maintenance projects safe, review the material found on the following web sites. Also, several publications are listed that are available from the Occupational Safety and Health Administration. These resources were used in the preparation of this chapter.

"Assessing the Need for Personal Protective Equipment: A Guide for Small Business Employers." U.S. Department of Labor, Occupational Safety and Health Administration Document #3151.
<http://www.osha-slc.gov/Publications/OSHA3151/Osha3151.html>.

"Controlling Electrical Hazards." U.S. Department of Labor, Occupational Safety and Health Administration Document #3075.

"Hand and Power Tools." U.S. Department of Labor, Occupational Safety and Health Administration Document #3080.

"How to Prepare for Workplace Emergencies." U.S. Department of Labor, Occupational Safety and Health Administration Document #3088.

"Job Hazard Analysis." U.S. Department of Labor, Occupational Safety and Health Administration Document #3071.

"Stairways and Ladders." U.S. Department of Labor, Occupational Safety and Health Administration Document #3124.
<http://www.osha-slc.gov/Publications/OSHA3124/osha3124.html>.

"Work Safe This Summer Employer's Guide to Teen Worker Safety, A Quick Look at the Fair Labor Standards Act."
<http"//www.dol.gov/dol/opa/public/summer/guide/flsa.htm>.

"Work Safe This Summer Employer's Guide to Teen Worker Safety, Employer's Teen Safety Checklist."
<http"//www.dol.gov/dol/opa/public/summer/guide/checklist.htm>.

"Work Safe This Summer Employer's Guide to Teen Worker Safety, Ideas from Other Employers."
<http"//www.dol.gov/dol/opa/public/summer/guide/ideas.htm>.

"Work Safe This Summer Employer's Guide to Teen Worker Safety, Preparing Teens to Work Safely."
<http"//www.dol.gov/dol/opa/public/summer/guide/preparing.htm>.

CHAPTER 11. REDUCING WORK-RELATED INJURIES AT CHURCH AND SCHOOL— ERGONOMIC CONSIDERATIONS

Workplace design has a profound influence on the productivity, morale, and health of workers. This is true not only in businesses but within churches and schools as well. Ergonomics, or the study of how to adapt work environments to the needs of workers, has become an important science. In recent decades, new understandings have emerged concerning the relationship between the physical arrangement of work space, the design of tools, how work is performed, and how certain injuries occur. The focus is upon the interaction between design, use, and safety.

Churches and schools can benefit by applying ergonomic knowledge to workplace design and performance. The most important benefit is maintaining the health and well-being of employees. In turn that contributes to less absenteeism, higher productivity, and less stress and turbulence in coping with potential problems.

While no statistics exist for churches, musculoskeletal disorders (MSDs) of the neck, shoulder, elbow, hand, wrist, and back probably represent the greatest number of work-related injuries in churches. The same is probably true for schools. During the past three decades extensive research has been conducted on the work-relatedness of these conditions, including the publication of more than 6,000 scientific articles on ergonomics and the workplace. In 1997, the U.S. Department of Health and Human Services published a critical review of the epidemiologic evidence for work-related musculoskeletal disorders of the neck, upper extremity, and low back. Specific attention was given to disorders of the neck, shoulder, elbow, hand, wrist, lower back, and psychosocial factors. Selected findings from that study, which provide a basis for understanding the application of ergonomic techniques in churches and schools, are presented below.

11.1 The Scope of the Problem

The Bureau of Labor Statistics conducts an annual survey of occupational injuries and illnesses. In 1994, 32 percent of all days away from work due to illness or injury were the result of overexertion or repetitive motion. Of that group, approximately 75 percent of the injuries or illnesses were due to overexertion in lifting, pulling, pushing, holding, carrying, or turning objects. A majority of these injuries affected the back, and about 9 percent affected the shoulder. Another 13 percent were due to repetitive motion including typing or key entry, repetitive use of tools, and repetitive placing, grasping, or moving objects other than tools. Of these injuries or illnesses, 55 percent affected the wrist, 7 percent affected the shoulder, and 6 percent affected the back. The average cost per case of an MSD claim is in the thousands of dollars. One case involves medical expenses, lost wages, lost production, cost of recruiting and training replacement workers, plus the cost of rehabilitation. Prevention is a far more cost-effective way to go.

11.2 Risk Factors and MSDs

A summary of the findings relevant to churches and schools indicates that a causal relationship exists between a number of risk factors and MSDs. Several categories were used to classify the evidence of work-relatedness including *strong evidence* and *evidence. Strong evidence* indicates that a causal relationship is very likely between intense and/or long duration exposure to a specific risk factor(s) and an MSD. The second category, *evidence*, indicates that convincing evidence exists for a causal relationship. The main risk factors studied included highly repetitive work, forceful work, posture, vibration, or a combination of these factors.

Neck and Neck/Shoulder. Evidence exists for a causal relationship between highly repetitive work and neck and neck/shoulder MSDs. Repetitive work for the neck includes work activities that involve continuous arm or hand movements which affect the neck/shoulder area. Strong evidence was found that posture is a risk factor for neck and neck/shoulder MSDs.

Shoulder. A causal relationship was also found between repetitive work and shoulder MSDs and posture and MSDs. Evidence was found for both risk factors.

Elbow. Strong evidence was found that a causal relationships exists between a combination of repetition, force and posture and elbow MSDs. Evidence exists that force alone affects the elbow.

Hand/wrist (carpal tunnel syndrome). Strong evidence was found indicating a causal relationship between a combination of force and repetition or force and posture and carpal tunnel syndrome. In addition, evidence was found of a positive association between highly repetitive work, forceful work, and hand/wrist vibration and carpal tunnel syndrome.

Hand/wrist (tendinitis). There is evidence of an association between any single factor (repetition, force, and posture) and hand/wrist tendinitis. There is strong evidence that job tasks that require a combination of risk factors (e.g., highly repetitious, forceful hand/wrist exertions) increase risk for hand/wrist tendinitis.

Low back. The review provided strong evidence that low-back disorders are associated with work-related lifting and forceful movements. There is also evidence for an association between back disorder and heavy physical work, and for work-related awkward postures and low back disorders.

Psychosocial factors. Overall, studies of upper extremity disorders (neck, shoulder, elbow, hand, wrist) suggest that certain psychosocial factors (including intensified workload, monotonous work, and low levels of social support) have a positive association with these disorders. Psychosocial factors were also associated with back disorders such as perceptions of increased workload or job dissatisfaction.

11.3 Application to Churches and Schools

While ergonomics has broad applications across many forms of work, our concern in this chapter is to apply ergonomic knowledge to two areas that deserve special attention in churches and schools. The first is the design and use of computer workstations. The use of computers can contribute to excessive fatigue, eye strain, blurred vision, headaches, stress, and neck, back, arm, and muscle pain. Computers are widely used within both churches and schools and these health problems can affect many workers. Musculoskeletal disorders to the neck, shoulder, elbow, hand, wrist, and back are becoming increasingly common in both churches and schools. The second area of concern is the lifting and handling of materials and supplies. Many church and school workers suffer from lower back pain. Training employees in proper lifting techniques can help prevent and reduce back problems.

11.4 Computer Workstations

To promote the healthy use of computers, churches and schools should pay attention to the positioning of each piece of equipment including the chair, keyboard, monitor, and mouse. The chair should be adjusted first, followed by the keyboard, mouse, and monitor. Other important factors include lighting and variation in the completion of computer tasks.

A workstation that is not oriented correctly can cause fatigue and soreness in the neck, shoulder, wrist, fingers, and other muscles. Shoulder pain, for example, may be associated with repetitive movements of the upper arm while using a mouse. Something as simple as having the mouse a few inches higher than the keyboard and off to one side can lead to considerable discomfort and pain in the shoulder and neck with repetitive use. The size of a mouse, or continually clicking buttons may contribute to finger pain. Sometimes changing the size of the mouse or substituting a different tracking device such as a trackball can solve the problem. The basic starting point, however, is setting up the workstation to maximize comfort.

Computer users should feel comfortable and be able to maintain a relaxed posture. Support should be maintained for the back, arms, legs, and feet. Items that are used frequently such as a phone, notepad, and wastebasket should be easy to reach. A document holder should be positioned so that it does not result in straining the eyes, neck, shoulders, or back muscles.

No single "ideal" position exists for comfort and posture for a computer workstation. That is not to say, however, that any position is okay. To be comfortable, people need to move around and adjust their sitting position. Workers should be encouraged to monitor and react to their own body. What is perfect for one person may not be for someone else. Some basic ergonomic principles, though, can guide that process.

Positioning equipment

Chair selection and adjustment

In creating a comfortable workstation, attention should first be given to the chair. The chair is one of the most important factors that affects comfort, and also has a direct impact on back pain. Use chairs that can be adjusted from the sitting position.

The critical distance in adjusting the height of the chair is the distance from the floor to the crease behind the knee. The chair height is correct when the entire sole of the foot can rest on the floor or footrest and the back of the knee is slightly higher than the seat of the chair. This height allows blood to circulate freely in the legs and feet. A footrest should be used only if the feet do not reach the floor. If a footrest is used, it should be large enough to permit the worker to shift his or her feet so that they do not remain in one single position while seated. Workers need to shift their entire sitting position periodically. Also, the footrest should have a non-slip surface and should not slide on the floor.

The seat of the chair should be comfortable and distribute the user's weight without causing the person to slide forward. The front of the seat should be rounded rather than having a sharp edge. Some seats slope gently down at the back to produce less stress on the lower back. Armrests should be low and short enough to fit under the work surface. If they are too high, they can prevent the worker from being close enough to the work surface. Many people prefer to rest their forearms on armrests while typing. In such cases, adjustable armrests should be used and they should be wide enough to provide comfortable support. The backrest should support the entire back, including lumbar support of the lower back. Some people find it helpful to use a back cushion to provide additional lumbar support. The backrest should be tilted slightly back. The Ergonomics Program at UC Berkeley recommends that the angle formed by the thighs and back should be at least 90 degrees or more. To be ergonomically acceptable, both the chair height and the backrest angle of the chair should be adjustable. Once the chair is adjusted, the work surface should be at about elbow level while using the keyboard. If the work surface cannot be adjusted and it is too high, raise the chair. That will mean, however, using a footrest to support the feet. Note: if more than one person uses the same workstation, adjustments should be made each time prior to beginning work.

The keyboard and mouse

The keyboard and the mouse should be located directly in front of the user. Many workstations have a keyboard tray that slides in and out from under the work surface. Such a tray may be required to maintain adequate comfort levels. While the keyboard should not rest on a person's legs, it is better to have it lower than higher. When it is at a proper height, a person's shoulders and neck muscles will feel relaxed while typing. The keyboard should be positioned so that it is flat. The preferred working position for most people is with the forearms parallel to the floor and elbows at the side. The wrist should be flat, in line with the forearm and should be maintained while typing. Rather than rotating wrists to reach some keys, the entire arm should be moved. Different opinions exist on the use of wrist rests. A common view is that typists should rest their wrists on a pad while using the computer keyboard. Many ergonomic experts now challenge this view. They claim that resting one's wrist on a pad while typing causes individuals to stretch their fingers, which in turn pulls on tendons all the way to the elbow. In addition, keeping the wrist on the pad causes the wrist to bend when reaching for certain keys. Computer keyboards have more keys than traditional typewriters which are harder to reach from a stationary wrist position. The ergonomics program at the University of California at Berkeley claims that a wrist pad should be used only to rest wrists between typing. They recommend that the worker type with the wrists floating above the keyboard. Others, claim that no conclusive evidence exists on the benefits of wrist pads.[1]

---

[1] Alan Hedge, *Ergonomic Guidelines for Arranging a Computer Workstation*, Cornell University, <http://ergo.human.cornell.edu/ergoguide.html>.

The mouse should be located right next to the keyboard, and at the same height. When in use, a straight line should be maintained between the hand and the foreman. The upper arm should not be extended or elevated when using a mouse. The shoulders should be relaxed, and the wrist should remain flat and not bent. Many people prefer to use a wrist pad with a mouse.

The monitor

Improper lighting, glare, and poor positioning of the screen can create visual problems. The topmost line of the screen should not be higher than the user's eyes. Lower levels are actually better. A recommended range for the viewing area of the monitor is between 20 to 50 degrees below horizontal eye level. Looking down also helps eyes from drying out as quickly. The top of the monitor should be slightly further away from the eyes than the bottom of the monitor. Monitors that are tilted toward the user tend to contribute to higher levels of neck discomfort. According to OHSA, the viewing distance to the monitor should fall within a range of 18 to 24 inches, although others recommend larger distances up to 40 inches away. Obviously, an important factor in selecting a distance is the readability of the text on the monitor. The first choice is to increase text size rather than bringing the monitor closer.

One problem that some churches and schools experience is the size of the monitor and the desk space available to accommodate it. Some monitors are so deep they take up almost all available space on top of the desk. For users to be 18 to 30 inches away from the front of the screen pushes them away from the keyboard. A keyboard extender mounted under the desk can help address this problem. New flat screen technology will solve this problem.

Some users place the monitor on top of the computer base unit. That is particularly true with older models where the base unit lies flat rather than stands on end. When the base unit stands on end, people tend to locate it on the floor next to or under the desk. With flat units, however, many churches and schools place them on the desktop and position the monitor on top of the base. That raises the monitor too high.

The traditional recommendation has been that if a document holder is used, it should be located as close as possible to the monitor and at the same distance from the user's eyes to avoid a change in focus. This view has been challenged in recent years claiming that eyestrain is not increased when the distances are different. The concern is that the monitor is brought too close to the user to align it up with documents that must be close by in order to read. Some believe that having the monitor farther away is not only better, but preferred.[2]

Glare is a problem for many computer users. To avoid glare, lighting should be indirect so that it does not shine directly into the user's eyes, but bright enough to enable the worker to read the screen and documents he or she is using. A small desk lamp may be helpful to illuminate documents. Overhead, diffused light sources are among the best for computer workstations. High illumination can cause the screen to appear "washed out." To reduce glare, screens can be placed at

---

[2] Dennis R. Ankrum, *Visual Ergonomics in the Office*, Nova Solutions, Inc., <http://ur-net.com/office-ergo/setting.htm>.

right angles to windows and light sources. Blinds and curtains can help reduce direct sunlight and most people find dark letters on a light background the easiest to read. If the desktop reflects light, place a blotter or mat on it with a non-reflective finish. Some users find a glare screen helpful, but while reducing glare, they also darken the screen and may make it more difficult to read. Use the brightness and contrast controls on the monitor to maximize readability and eye comfort.

Altering Posture

Computer users should take regular breaks to alter their posture. Once your workstation is set up properly, the next line of defense against fatigue, eye strain, and muscle soreness is to alter your posture on a regular basis while seated. Adjust your sitting position, stretch your arms and legs, and exercise your shoulders, neck, fingers and hand muscles. Keep the blood circulating throughout your body. Sitting in one position can reduce circulation. Periodically, give the eyes a break by refocusing on something about 20 feet away from the monitor. That provides the eye muscles with a chance to relax. Second, stand up and move around at least once every half-hour or so. Workers should be encouraged to notify church or school leaders as soon as possible if they begin to experience pain. Often, the source of the pain can be identified, and treatment is better earlier rather than later if an injury has occurred. Some pain may be the result of fatigue and will go away with one or two days of rest. Pain that persists, however, is a warning sign indicating the need for medical intervention.

11.5 Back Pain

Although back pain is common, it is also mysterious. It can be very difficult to pinpoint the source of back pain or know what causes it. Most people experience back pain, which is second only to headaches as the most frequent source of pain. Some individuals, such as those individuals in jobs that do frequent or heavy lifting, or who sit for extended periods, are at higher risk. Once lower back pain occurs for the first time, most people have recurring symptoms within a few years. The good news is that most people fully recover from each episode. For some, however, back pain is chronic and no simple solutions exist. According to the National Institute of Health, surgery is helpful in only 1 in 100 cases of lower back pain, and can cause even more problems for some people. People, though, are not without help. A prevention program is one of the best ways to address the problem of back pain. Proper lifting techniques are a vital component.

Lifting techniques

Since the risk of back pain is so high, churches and schools should provide basic guidelines to employees to avoid high-risk actions. A common cause of back injuries is the improper lifting of objects. Several simple rules should be followed:

1. Keep all lifted objects close to your body. Do not extend the arms while carrying something. Rather, keep them in close to the body.

2. Avoid lifting while twisting, bending forward, and reaching. Stand directly in front of the object to be lifted. Do not lift over obstacles.

3. Lift with your legs. Squat down to pick an object up rather than bend over. Use the leg muscles to lift rather than the back muscles.

4. Get help to lift heavy objects. Lifting heavy objects increases the risk for injury. Ask for help from another person, or use some form of mechanical assistance.

5. Take breaks. An increased frequency of lifting also impacts the potential for injury. Lifting many objects over a limited time creates an accumulative impact on the body. Taking breaks can help the body recuperate.

6. Plan ahead before moving materials. Make sure the pathway you will use is clear and accessible. Have a place ready to put down the object you are carrying.

Exercise

Exercising is one of the best ways to strengthen the back and to prevent back problems from occurring or reoccurring. As with all exercise programs, individuals should consult with their doctor before beginning. The Mayo Clinic provides a list of illustrated exercises with instructions to stretch and strengthen back muscles on their web site at www.mayohealth.org/mayo/9402/htm/pain_tab.htm.

Responding to back injuries

As with any work-related injury, a person who injuries his or her back should report the problem and seek assistance. A complete written report should be made of the circumstances surrounding the injury, including date, time, and cause of the injury. Sometimes back pain occurs for no apparent reason.

A mild case of back pain is usually treated at home. However, if the cause of the injury is an accident, a fall, a blow to the body, or if the pain is intense, spreads down the legs, results in tingling in the legs, or interferes with bladder control, immediate medical attention should be sought. In addition, if a mild case of pain does not improve within a few days, a doctor should be seen.

The three most common treatments for less severe cases of back pain are rest, medication and physical therapy. Most people recover at home in two weeks or less with bed rest, rehabilitative exercise, and over-the-counter medications such as aspirin or acetaminophen, or with prescription nonsteroidal anti-inflammatory drugs, or muscle relaxants. Physical therapy may include massages, exercises, and the use or cold or heat. Cold packs and heating pads can be used several times a day to increase comfort, but treatments should be limited to 20 minutes. During the first two days cold packs should be used. Cold packs can be placed on muscle spasms or on areas in pain. Heating pads or hot baths are used second, following the first two days, to help loosen tight muscles. Lying on a firm supportive mattress during the first two days can be helpful, but individuals should then begin to move about, gradually returning to normal activities. They should avoid sitting for extended periods and get moderate exercise. Massage should only be performed by a licensed professional such as a physical therapist. The Mayo Clinic reports that 80 to 90 percent of back pain becomes resolved within six weeks regardless of the treatment.[3]

---

[3] *Back Pain, Guide to Treatments*, 11-05-98, <www.mayohealth.org/mayo/9811/htm/backpain3.htm>.

Coping with back pain

Workers that have back problems can do several things to increase their comfort. The National Institute of Health makes the following recommendations:

- Wear comfortable, low-heeled shoes.

- Make sure your work surface is at a comfortable height.

- Use a chair with a good lower back support that may recline slightly.

- If you must sit for long periods of time, try resting your feet on the floor or on a low stool, whichever is more comfortable.

- If you must stand for long periods of time, try resting one foot on a low stool.

- If you must drive for long distances, try using a pillow or a rolled-up towel behind the small of your back. Also be sure to stop often and walk around for a few minutes.

11.6 Implementing an Ergonomics Program

Implementing a successful ergonomics program begins with a commitment of church and school leaders to care for their employees. This chapter has focused on two specific areas: computer workstations and lifting materials. The former focuses to a large degree on equipment design, placement, and use; the latter concern involves applying proper techniques to lifting and using good judgment.

All employees should have ergonomic chairs with adjustable heights and backs. Each person should receive training on how to adjust the chair, keyboard, mouse and monitor. Workstations should have indirect light and no user should look into direct light.

All employees should also receive training on proper lifting techniques. Custodians, teachers, and secretaries frequently lift supplies and other items. Back problems can occur at anytime, and using sound judgment and safe lifting techniques benefits everyone.

Summary

Ergonomics provides information that churches and schools can use to make their working environments more safe for both paid and volunteer workers. Special attention should be given to the use of computer workstations and work-related lower back injuries.

Overexertion and repetitive motion account for nearly one-third of all days away from work due to an illness or injury. Evidence published by the U.S. Department of Health and Human Services now confirms that a causal relationship exists between several musculoskeletal disorders (MSDs) and work-related injuries. Identified problem areas include disorders of the neck, shoulder, elbow, hand, wrist, and lower back. Psychosocial factors are also associated with such disorders.

Ergonomic knowledge can be applied to the use of computer workstations to reduce MSDs. Attention should be given to the proper selection and placement of the chair, keyboard, mouse, and monitor. While no single "ideal" position will work for everyone, ergonomic principles can guide the process. The first step is to adjust the chair, followed by the keyboard and mouse, and then the monitor. Improper adjustments can lead to neck, shoulder, elbow, wrist, and lower back problems, as well as eyestrain, fatigue, and headaches.

Back pain is the second most common source of pain following headaches. The causes of back pain can be difficult to diagnose and to treat. Individuals that do heavy or frequent lifting at work, or who sit for extended periods are at higher risk.

Churches and schools should train all employees and volunteers in proper lifting techniques. If an injury should occur, it should be reported immediately and appropriate care should occur. Most minor back injuries are treated at home with rest, medication, and exercises. More severe cases, and cases resulting from a fall, body blow, or accident need the attention of a doctor.

Churches and schools can reduce the likelihood of MSDs through training and education. Focusing on computer workstations and proper lifting techniques can enhance safety in two common problem areas that impact staff members at churches and schools.

The next chapter explores the issue of juvenile violence and examines steps that schools and churches can take to reduce this concern.

Additional Resources on the Internet

For additional information on ergonomics, review the material found on the following web sites. Also, several publications are listed that are available from the U.S. Department of Labor, Occupational Safety and Health Administration. These resources were used in the preparation of this chapter.

"Back Pain, Common and Uncommon Causes." Mayo Clinic Health Letter, November 5, 1998.
<http://www.mayohealth.org/mayo/9811/htm/backpain2.htm>.

"Back Pain, Guide to Prevention." Mayo Clinic Health Letter, November 5, 1998.
<http://www.mayohealth.org/mayo/9811/htm/backpain5.htm>.

"Back Pain, Guide to Treatments." Mayo Clinic Health Letter, November 5, 1998.
<http://www.mayohealth.org/mayo/9811/htm/backpain3.htm>.

"Back Pain, Overview." Mayo Clinic Health Letter, November 5, 1998.
<http://www.mayohealth.org/mayo/9402/htm/backcare.htm>.

"Back Pain, Test Help with Diagnosis." Mayo Clinic Health Letter, November 5, 1998. <http://www.mayohealth.org/mayo/9811/htm/backpain4.htm>.

"Carpal Tunnel Syndrome." National Institute for Occupational Safety and Health. <http://www.cdc.gov/niosh/ergtxt5a.html>.

"Elbow Musculoskeletal Disorders (Epicondylitis): Evidence for Work-Relatedness." National Institute for Occupational Safety and Health. <http://www.cdc.gov/niosh/ergtxt4.html>.

"Ergo Guidelines." <http://www.ergoequip.com/ergo2.htm>.

"Ergonomic Chairs." <http://www.office-ergo.com/ergonomi.htm>.

"Ergonomic Guidelines for Arranging a Computer Workstation." Cornell University Ergonomics Web. <http://ergo.human.cornell.edu/ergoguide.html>.

"Fourteen Things You Should Know About Back Pain." <http://www.office-ergo.com/12things/htm>.

"Hand/Wrist Musculoskeletal Disorders (Carpal Tunnel Syndrome, Hand/Wrist Tendinitis, and Hand-Arm Vibration Syndrome): Evidence for Work-Relatedness." National Institute for Occupational Safety and Health. <http://www.cdc.gov/niosh/ergtxt5.html>.

"Hand/Wrist Tendinitis." National Institute for Occupational Safety and Health. <http://www.cdc.gov/niosh/ergtxt5b.html>.

"How to Create a Comfortable Working Environment." <http://ww.ocean.odu.edu/ug/ergonomics.html>.

"Human Factors and Ergonomics Group: Selected Computer Keyboards Publications (1987-1999)." Cornell University Ergonomics Web. <http://ergo.human.cornell.edu/kbdpubs.html>.

"It's Your Body." University of California, San Francisco; University of California, Berkeley, Ergonomics Program. <http://me.berkeley.edu/ergo/services/tips.html>.

Johnson, Pete W. "Computer Workstation Self-Audit Checklist." University of California, San Francisco; University of California, Berkeley, Ergonomics Program. July 18, 1994. <http://me.berkeley.edu/ergo/services/tips/checklist.html>.

Johnson, Pete W. "Pointing Device Summary." University of California, San Francisco; University of California, Berkeley, Ergonomics Program. July 18, 1994. <http://me.berkeley.edu/ergo/services/tips/pdtips.html>.

Karp, Gary. "How Managers Can Reduce Cumulative Trauma." Onsight Technology Education Services. <http://www.sirius.com/~gkarp/onsight/articles/worktips.html>.

Karp, Gary. "Should You Wear a Wrist Rest?" Onsight Technology Education Services. <http://www.sirius.com/~gkarp/onsight/articles/wristrest.html>.

Karp, Gary. "What is Ergonomics?" Onsight Technology Education Services. <http://www.sirius.com/~gkarp/onsight/articles/ergomon.html>.

"Low Back Pain." Mayo Clinic Health Letter, July 1997. <http://www.mayohealth.org/mayo/9708/htm/o_myback.htm>.

"Low-Back Musculoskeletal Disorders: Evidence for Work-Relatedness." National Institute for Occupational Safety and Health. <http://www.cdc.gov/niosh/ergtxt6.html>.

"Musculoskeletal Disorders (MSDs) and Workplace Factors." National Institute for Occupational Safety and Health. <http://www.cdc.gov/niosh/ergosci1.html>.

"Musculoskeletal Disorders (MSDs) and Workplace Factors: Appendices." National Institute for Occupational Safety and Health. <http://www.cdc.gov/niosh/appendabc.html>.

"Neck Musculoskeletal Disorders: Evidence for Work-Relatedness." National Institute for Occupational Safety and Health. <http://www.cdc.gov/niosh/ergtxt2.html>.

"Prevention of Low Back Problems." Agency of Health Care Policy and Research (AHCPR). <http://www.vh.org/Patients/IHB/Ortho/BackPatient/Prevention.html>.

"Shoulder Musculoskeletal Disorders: Evidence for Work-Relatedness." National Institute for Occupational Safety and Health. <http://www.cdc.gov/niosh/ergtxt3.html>.

"Three Points to Healthy Computer Use." University of California, San Francisco; University of California, Berkeley, Ergonomics Program. <http://me.berkeley.edu/ergo/services/tips/3things.html>.

"Tips for Enhancing the Office Environment." University of Wisconsin-Milwaukee, Department of Environmental Health, Safety and Risk Management. <http://www.uwm.edu/Dept/EHSRM/GENINFO/genergotips.html>.

"Visual Ergonomics in the Office (Guidelines for Monitor Placement and Lighting)." <http://ur-net.com/office-ergo/setting.htm>.

"Warning Signs of Repetitive Strain Injury (RSI)." Repetitive Strain Injury Recovery Book. <http://www.rsihelp.com/warning.shtml>.

"What is Ergonomics." <http://www.ergoequip.com/ergo9.htm>.

"Work-Related Musculoskeletal Disorders and Psychosocial Factors." National Institute for Occupational Safety and Health. <http://www.cdc.gov/niosh/ergtxt7.html>.

"Working Safely with Video Display Terminals." U.S. Department of Labor. Occupational Safety and Health Administration Document #3092.

"Your Daily Back Routine." Mayo Clinic Health Letter, November 5, 1998. <http://www.mayohealth.org/mayo/9402.htm/pain_tab.htm>

CHAPTER 12. REDUCING THE POTENTIAL FOR JUVENILE VIOLENCE

Historically, both churches and schools have been viewed as safe places. In recent years, mass shootings at public schools and a few religious institutions have raised new questions concerning safety and security. The reality remains, however, that students are more safe at school than when they are not at school, and that violent acts at churches are rare. According to the U.S. Justice Department, school crime is not getting worse. Yet, a growing awareness exists that steps should be taken to make schools and churches as safe as possible from acts of violence. Extensive research has been done regarding violence and safety at schools and many new research projects are currently underway. Little research has been done with respect to safety at churches, in part because it simply has not been a problem. This chapter examines recent trends and statistics regarding juvenile and school violence and then reviews strategies for enhancing safety and security at both schools and churches.

12.1 Juvenile Violence

The mass media coverage of violent acts at schools and religious organizations has given many people a wrong perspective, both on the nature of violent activity among young people, and the degree to which young people are at risk with respect to violence. During the 1990s, violence among high school students actually declined. From the period 1991-1997, the percent of students involved in each of the following areas dropped: physical fights (14 percent decline); injuries from physical fights (20 percent decline); number of students carrying a weapon (30 percent decline); number of students carrying a gun (25 percent decline); and the number of students carrying a gun on school property (28 percent decline).[1] The rate of serious crime by juvenile offenders is less today than it was 20 years ago, although the number of juvenile female offenders has been increasing.[2]

This is not to say, however, that violence is not a problem. While the crime rate is down, since 1981 the arrest rate is up for both juvenile males and females. Teenagers are two and a half times more likely than adults to be victims of violence.[3] In addition, the most violent hour of the day for juvenile victims is the hour following the dismissal of school.[4] Many juvenile offenders begin violent behavior very young and one-fourth will already have a court record by their 14th birthday. Of the youth ages 12 to 16 who are arrested, 40 percent have two or more arrests. Acts of violence at school are often connected with drug use. Those students who use illicit drugs are far more likely to be a victim of a violent act than those students who do not. Furthermore, it is estimated that it costs society $2 million for every student who drops out of high school for a life of crime and drugs.

---

[1] Nancy D. Brener, et. Al., "Recent Trends in Violence-Related Behaviors Among High School Students in the United States, *Journal of the American Medical Association*, Vol. 282, No. 5, August 4, 1999, 440-446.

[2] *The 1999 National Report Notebook, Juvenile Offenders and Victims*, p. 2, <http://ojjdp.ncjrs.org/ojstatbb/qrptnote.html>.

[3] <www.cdc.gov/ncipc/dvp/yvpt/myths.htm>.

[4] *The 1999 National Report Notebook, Juvenile Offenders and Victims*, <http://ojjdp.ncjrs.org/ojstatbb/qrptnote.html>.

Extensive research has been conducted to identify and understand factors that affect juvenile violence. When certain factors are present, the probability for violence increases. Table 1 published by the National Center for Injury Prevention and Control, illustrates social and individual factors that affect violent behavior.[5]

Table 1: Social Factors that Affect Violent Behavior

Individual	Family	Peer/School	Neighborhood
history of early aggression beliefs supportive of violence social cognitive deficits	poor monitoring or supervision of children exposure to violence parental drug/alcohol abuse poor emotional attachment to parents or caregivers	associate with peers engaged in high-risk or problem behavior low commitment to school academic failure	poverty and diminished economic opportunity high levels of transiency and family disruption exposure to violence

In the remainder of this chapter, attention is given to the nature of juvenile violence and crime within our society with a special focus on violence and schools. Then, strategies are explored on what schools can do to reduce violence and to create safe environments for students, teachers, and staff.

12.2 Juvenile Offenders and Victims

The 1999 National Report on Juvenile Offenders and Victims provides the most comprehensive research findings currently available on juvenile violence.[6] Below is a summary of the findings from the 1999 Report as well as from other government sources on the following concerns:

- Homicide
- Suicide
- Violent crime
- Sexual assault
- School crime
- Physical fights
- Theft
- Gangs
- Fear
- Violence against teachers

Homicide

Homicide is the second leading cause of death for individuals ages 15 to 24 and third for children age 5 to 14. The largest number of deaths occurred in 1993, about 8 per day, and has been steadily declining. In 1997, 2,100 juveniles were

---

[5] *Youth Violence in the United States Fact Sheet*, <www.cdc.gov/ncipc/dvp/yvpt/newfacts.htm>.
[6] The report is available on the Internet at <http://ojjdp.ncjrs.org/ojstatbb/qrptnote.html>.

murdered, equaling about 6 per day. Fifty percent of the victims were between the ages of 15-17 and they were most likely killed with a gun. Eighty-five percent of juveniles were killed either by a family member (40 percent) or someone else they knew (45 percent). However, for those ages 15-17, only 5 percent were killed by a family member. Most of the victims over age 12 were male, but the death rate is about the same for males and females under age 13. The homicide rate for black youth is higher than for white youth, although same-race killings is prevalent among both groups: 94 percent for blacks and 91 percent for whites. About 25 percent of the time, the murderer is another juvenile.

Geographically, juvenile homicide tends to be concentrated in large urban areas. Over 85 percent of all counties in the United States that reported findings to the FBI in 1997 had no juvenile homicides, and another 8 percent had one death. Approximately 25 percent of all deaths occurred in just five counties. The cities with the most deaths were Los Angeles, Chicago, New York, Philadelphia, and Detroit which collectively represent 9 percent of the U.S. population.

Suicide

Suicide is a leading cause of death among young people age 19 and under. Juvenile suicide victims tend to be white and male. These two groups each account for 80 percent of all victims. Statistically, one suicide occurs for every two homicides among juveniles. The homicide rate is five times as high and the suicide rate is twice as high in the United States compared to 26 other industrialized countries.

Violent crime

The 1999 National Report indicated that juveniles experienced twice as much serious violent crime (i.e., rape, robbery, aggravated assault), and three times as much simple assault as the adult population. However, in recent years, the crime rate has declined from its peak in 1993. When violent crime did occur, the victim generally knew the offender who 34 percent of the time was a friend. However, about one-third of the time, the offender was a stranger.

Sexual assault

Over 1 child in 20 experiences a serious crime before the age of 13. Sexual assault is the most common serious crime perpetrated on children under the age 12 accounting for 32 percent of the total. Over one-third of the victims of sexual assault are under the age 7 with about 47 percent being female. The younger the victim, the more likely the offender is another juvenile. According to the FBI's findings, 43 percent of the offenders were juveniles when the victim was under age 7. The number was 34 percent for victims between ages 7 to 11 and 24 percent for victims ages 12 to 17. The vast majority of children under age 12 are sexually assaulted at home (84 percent), either by a family member (47 percent) or an acquaintance (49 percent). Strangers accounted for only about 4 percent of the sexual assault crimes perpetrated against children under the age 12. The most likely time for a sexual assault with a juvenile offender is between 3 P.M. and 4 P.M. on school days and between noon and 1 P.M. on nonschool days.

Dating violence also affects middle school and high school students. One study of 8th and 9th grade male and female students indicated that one in four had experienced nonsexual dating violence, while about one in twelve were victims of sexual dating violence.[7] College students are more likely to report being victims of dating violence than high school students, with more females reporting being victims than males. A high percentage of rapes (80 to 95 percent) occurring on college campuses are committed by someone known to the victim.

School crime

The 1999 National Report indicates that school crime is not on the increase. Based on studies for 1989 and 1995, the number of students reporting any victimization remained the same at 15 percent. During those periods, 12 percent of students experienced property crimes such as theft, while 3 to 4 percent of students reported violent crime. While the theft rate was about the same for both male and female students, males were twice as likely to be victims of violence. Furthermore, students living in urban areas experienced higher levels of serious violent crime than did students who lived in suburban or rural areas, although the theft rate was about the same regardless of where the student lived. Students at public and private schools reported higher rates of property theft than violent crime. Data from 1995 indicated, however, that the number of students who experienced violence was nearly twice as high in public schools (4 percent) compared to private schools (2 percent).

The media coverage of shootings in public schools during 1997-1999 has created an image in the minds of many people that violent death has reached epidemic proportions in schools. The reality is that violent death is rare, although serious violent crime is not. What is misleading, though, is the perception that these acts are widespread. They actually occur in only a small percentage of schools throughout the United States. While fighting and theft are common and occurred, for example, in about half of middle schools and high schools during the 1996-97 school year, only about 1 school in 5 reported a serious violent crime. Schools making such reports were more likely to be located in an urban area rather than in a small town or rural setting. During that same period, only about 16 percent of schools used formal security measures. A trend exists, however, for all schools to implement more formal security precautions, including hiring staff members to deal with issues of crime and security.

Physical fights

Fights are far less common on school property than off school property. In a 1997 study of high school students, about 15 percent reported being in a physical fight at school within a 12 month period, compared to 37 percent for both school and nonschool fights. Students in ninth and tenth grade, both males and females, were far more likely to get in fights than older students. Males were far more likely to be in a physical fight than females. The number of students actually injured was about 4 percent.

---

[7] *Fact Sheet on Dating Violence*, <www.cdc.gov/ncipc/dvp/yvpt/datviol.htm>.

Theft

Theft is more common at schools than physical violence with one-third of high school students claiming to be victims. More males reported crimes than did females, although there were no significant differences across grades or racial groups.

Gangs

The number of students reporting gang activity at their school significantly increased from 1989 to 1995 from 15 percent to 28 percent. During this period, reported gang activity increased at both public and private schools, although reported gang activity was higher at public schools (31 percent to 7 percent). Gangs are more likely to exist at urban high schools (41 percent) than at suburban (26 percent) or rural schools (20 percent), although they are present in all three categories.

Fear

About 1 student in 25 missed at least one day of school during a 30 period in 1997 because they felt it was unsafe to go to school. Black and Hispanic students were more likely to miss school for feeling unsafe than white students. During the 1990s, these feelings of being unsafe have increased, both concerning threats at school as well as on the way to and from school. Students develop perceptions that certain places at school are unsafe, and as those perceptions develop, they tend to avoid places they view as unsafe. It may be a bathroom, a gathering area outside the school, or a particular hallway. These perceptions provide insights as to how students perceive school safety.

Violence against teachers

Teachers, as well as students, are victims of crime while at school. Public school teachers are more likely to be victims of violent crime than teachers in private schools. In a 1993-94 study, 13 percent of public school teachers reported threats of injury and 4 percent had been physically attacked. That compares with 4 percent of teachers in private schools reporting threats and 2 percent being attacked. For the period, 1992-96, teachers in elementary and secondary schools experienced about the same rate of violent crime (4 incidents per 1,000 teachers). Middle school and junior high school teachers experienced the highest rates of violent crime, although those who work in urban schools were far more likely to be victims than teachers in suburban or rural schools. Male teachers experienced more violent crime than did female teachers. High school teachers experienced higher levels of theft.

12.3 Steps to Promote Safety and Prevent Violence at Churches and Schools

Reducing acts of violence is a multidimensional issue. First, as the above findings illustrate, the problem is one that affects the entire society and there are no simple solutions. The problem can be approached from many different perspectives including psychological, sociological, cultural, medical, or spiritual. For some, the root causes of violence are connected to childhood development and family life. Others look at patterns of social interaction and economic concerns. Issues such as the norms, values, and beliefs of high-risk populations rise to the surface for others that study the problem of violence. Some perpetrators have mental illness. Others engage in hate crimes or random acts of violence. Some crimes are premeditated. Others are spontaneous. While some acts of violence can be prevented, others will never be eliminated.

In responding to the problem of violence, churches and schools should develop common sense plans that take the problem of violence seriously. Yet differences will exist in prevention plans that reflect social and demographic differences. For most schools, and almost all churches, serious violent crime is not a problem. Yet no school or church wants to be caught off guard and then later blamed for having done nothing in light of today's environment concerning this problem. One incident, no matter how impossible it might be to prevent, thrusts a church, school and community into a national spotlight with relentless inspection and analysis. Schools, in particular, will be held to a standard of care that requires some advance planning both to prevent and respond to acts of violence. Two concerns exist: one that schools will do nothing, and second that they will overreact The debate on this issue will intensify as long as acts of mass violence occur. The irony is that these events are the most rare of all, and are arguably the most difficult to prevent when they are the acts of single individuals. The more common acts of physical fights and theft, which affect far more students on a daily basis, receive little attention from the media. In developing a prevention plan, leaders must address issues of both frequency and severity concerning acts of violence. Attention should be given to both those actions that are frequent but less severe (i.e., fights, theft), and those actions that are less frequent but more severe that involve violent serious crime (even if they are rare or have not even occurred). Failure to focus on the first keeps students at risk; failure to address the second could be catastrophic both in terms of student safety and also in terms of legal liability which is now a part of the risk facing every school and church.

Seven security measures were recently studied to determine what actions schools are currently taking to enhance their security.[8] The seven measures and the corresponding findings were as follows:

1. *Visitors were required to sign in.* This security measure is almost universally required by every school regardless of size, location, or instructional level. Ninety-six percent of the schools required visitors to sign-in before gaining access to school buildings.

2. *Access to school grounds was controlled.* Only 24 percent of schools controlled access to school grounds, although that percentage increased to 49 percent for large schools. On the other hand it dropped to 16 percent for small schools. Clear demographic differences surfaced in the study. Rural schools were far less likely to control access than urban schools (13 percent to 35 percent). Schools with high minority populations of 50 percent or more were far more likely to control access than schools with low minority enrollments of 5 percent or less.

---

[8] U.S. Department of Education, National Center for Education Statistics, Fast Response Survey System, "Principal/School Disciplinarian Survey of School Violence," FRSS 63, 1997; see School Efforts to Ensure Safety and Promote Discipline, <http://nces.ed.gov/pubs98/violence/98030009.html>.

3. *Access to the school building was controlled.* About half (53 percent) of schools controlled access to their school buildings. High schools (40 percent) were less likely to control access than were either middle schools (51 percent) or elementary schools (57 percent). Again, larger schools were more likely to control access than small schools, as were urban schools compared to towns or rural areas.

4. *School campuses were closed for most students during lunch.* Four out of five schools had a closed lunch period prohibiting students from leaving campus. This was more true for middle schools (93 percent) than either elementary schools (76 percent) or high schools (78 percent).

5. *Students had to pass through metal detectors daily.* Only one school in one hundred used metal detectors on a daily basis, and they tended to be schools with a history of violent crimes. Metal detectors are not foolproof, and students can find many ways to sneak weapons into a school if that is their goal.

6. *Random metal detector checks were performed.* The random use of metal detectors was also very low (4 percent), although 15 percent of larger schools or schools with a history of serious crime conducted random checks using metal detectors. These metal detectors may be hand held devices similar to those used at airports. Random detection is primarily used as a deterrent. When used, the goal is to keep students off guard on when and where the detection will occur.

7. *Schools conducted drug sweeps (e.g., locker searches, dog searches).* Nineteen percent of schools conducted drug sweeps, but they tended to be done at schools that had at least one serious discipline problem. Those schools tended to be high schools (45 percent or middle schools 36 percent), and a few elementary schools (5 percent). Drug searches serve more of a deterrent role than one of locating drugs, and as such, should be conducted without notice and with full enforcement if drugs are found.

One trend to promote safety in schools is to hire a School Resource Officer or SRO.[9] While no single shared meaning of an SRO exists, they tend to be law enforcement officers who engage in a wide range of student and school services ranging from counseling, teaching law, and carrying out law enforcement duties, including the authority to make an arrest. The role varies depending on the school and its needs.

According to the U.S. Department of Education, in 1997, slightly more than one school in twenty had a law enforcement person stationed at the school for 30 or more hours peer week. High schools were nearly twice as likely as middle schools and twenty times as likely as elementary schools to use law enforcement personnel. Most schools (78 percent), though, did not have law enforcement officials on school property. They were most likely found in large schools with 1,000 or more students, and schools with a history of at least one serious crime during the past school year. Having a law enforcement officer on school grounds can be helpful, but should not be viewed as the primary solution to the problem

---

[9] See School Resource Officers: What We Know, What We Think We Know, What We Need To Know, <www2.ncsu.edu/ncsu/cep/PreViolence/srowhatweknow.htm>.

of violence. Problems with respect to pay, authority, role clarification, status, and training can undermine the effectiveness of the position.

Many school leaders struggle in determining the best approach to respond to the problem of violence. Resources now exist to help schools develop a prevention plan (churches can also use the same resources).

12.4 Developing a Safety and Security Program for Schools

Safety is one dimension of risk management. Risks that arise from violent acts, however, are different from risks that arise from a hurricane or from playing on a slide. Physical violence is an intentional action designed to inflict injury and suffering. While safety concerns cut across all areas of risk including acts of violence, security focuses more on intentional acts that result in harm to others. In the remainder of this chapter, the focus is on developing both a safety and security program to reduce the potential for violence and crime in schools. The concern is both on safety and security. While the focus on security is different from other issues addressed in this book, the same risk management principles that are used regarding safety also apply to security. First, an assessment should be made of the risks a school faces. One approach is to conduct a normative needs assessment, a felt needs assessment, a comparative needs assessment, an environmental needs assessment and a future needs assessment. Each of these steps is described below.

The assessment process

While individual schools have unique needs, they also share much in common with other schools. In recent years considerable research has been done to identify needs and understand how schools can respond to the problem of violence. As a result, every school can benefit from this research and learn from the experiences, some of which have arisen from tragedies, of others. What risks should schools be prepared to respond to? Some of the more common problem areas are noted below:

- Bullying, intimidating, and threatening behaviors
- Possessing or using weapons
- Acts of physical violence (fights, hitting)
- Acts of serious physical violence (physical and sexual assault)
- Holding hostages on buses or on school property
- Acts of theft or robbery
- Bomb threats
- Threats or acts of suicide
- Vandalism and sabotage
- Gang activity
- Kidnapping or abduction
- Injuries and death
- Disciplinary problems
- Drug and alcohol use
- Campus access

Schools must also take reasonable care in selecting and supervising employees. Employees can also create safety and security problems. Attention should be given to the following concerns:

- Conducting criminal background checks
- Touching policies
- The proper use of discipline with students
- Appropriate and inappropriate use of force in responding to students

Schools should assess their needs with respect to each individual item listed above. Other needs will also surface during the assessment process. The assessment process should include the following components:

1. *Normative needs assessment.* What are the baseline standards that every school should meet in developing a safety and security program? What do the experts say and recommend concerning school safety? Fortunately, extensive work has been done in this area. The Departments of Education and Justice have released the most comprehensive document available as of today, *A Guide to Safe Schools,* that provides valuable information concerning the problem and practical steps that schools can take to address this concern. However, it must be recognized that schools are not in the business of security. Teachers did not train for, nor do they want the job of being a cop. Administrators are not risk managers. They are educators. As such, a normative needs assessment should also include experts in security who may have little background in education. A rapport needs to develop that brings together a synthesis where education is the driving force and security is part of the infrastructure.

2. *Felt Needs Assessment.* A safety program should respond to the felt needs of the local school community, including administrators, teachers, staff, students, and parents. The use of focus groups, questionnaires, forums, and town meetings can be used to surface concerns and pinpoint issues of particular concern that should shape how a school responds to safety concerns.

3. *Comparative Assessment.* Schools can learn from one another. No need exists to reinvent the wheel. Schools should collect written safety and security plans from other schools. Members of the planning team should visit other schools and learn from their experiences.

4. *Environmental Assessment.* An assessment should be made of the school and community environment. This is a two dimensional process. The first part of the process focuses on the physical environment of the school. First, a safety and security audit should be made of school facilities, property, the surrounding neighborhood, and the routes children use to and from school. This will require the assistance of trained professionals who understand security issues. This is not the same thing as conducting a property inspection for insurance purposes (although some overlap does occur). Attention should be given to facility design, traffic patterns, gathering areas, evacuation routes, lighting, locks, plus more. Second, an assessment should occur of trends related to acts of violence and crime that

impact the school. Data, if available, on school disciplinary trends should be examined. This will involve law enforcement personnel. School leaders should have a clear understanding of issues related to both the physical security needs of the school and its surroundings as well as trends within the "social environment" of the school. In essence, a complete ecological assessment is needed.

5. *Future Assessment.* School leaders cannot simply plan for the present, they must be looking ahead to the future. Issues related to funding, population trends, staffing, and many other concerns must be kept in mind.

Developing a planned response to identified needs

Responding to violence is not like responding to the safety concerns of a playground. A playground presents a set of well-defined problems. Agreement exists on how to make a playground safe. The social-psychological dimensions of violence create complex issues that are contextual and that require creative solutions. While some aspects of violent behavior are well understood, and it is clear that violence at schools can be reduced, neither the problem nor the solution is one dimensional. Multiple risk management techniques are needed that address biological, social, and emotional risks; psychological risks; economic risks; physical risks; property risks; and, legal risks. The scope of the problem illustrates the need for a team approach with experts from many different disciplines. As we will see below, responding to the problem of school violence is a community wide endeavor that requires extensive collaboration and expertise.

One innovative approach to responding to violence in schools is based upon recognizing *warning signs* and developing the knowledge and skills to intervene early enough to prevent escalation. To be effective, the entire school community must be involved: parents, students, teachers, staff, and administrators. Extensive training is required as well as the coordination and use of community resources. This is the approach advocated in *A Guide to Safe Schools*, published by The U.S. Department of Education. The guide is a public domain document and is available on the Internet.[10] The key points of the guide are summarized in the following sections.

12.5 Characteristics of a Safe and Responsive School

Safe schools share certain characteristics. First they focus on academic achievement. Not only do they stress academic excellence, they provide adequate resources and programs to help students. They establish expectations for the student, the school, and the home. Second, safe schools get families involved with the student's growth both at school and at home. They welcome parents at school and promote positive interaction between the school and the family. Third, safe schools build ties with community organizations such as social service organizations, the police, and religious organizations. Other important steps to take include the following:

● Emphasize positive relationships among students and staff. Having adult support is a critical factor in preventing student violence. Safe schools find

---

[10] <http://www.ed.gov/offices/OSERS/OSEP/earlywrn.html>.

ways to nurture supportive relationships between students and between students and staff.

- Discuss safety issues openly. Safe schools raise safety issues and train students on appropriate behaviors, how to respond to feelings of anger, and how to resolve conflicts.

- Treat students with equal respect. Students who feel isolated, discriminated against, or treated unfairly may respond in aggressive ways. Safe schools make a deliberate and systematic effort to nurture community and to help children and staff to show respect for one another.

- Create ways for students to share their concerns. Students may know about the potential for violence before it happens, but feel threatened to report it to school officials. Safe schools find ways to encourage children to share concerns and to protect them when they do share.

- Help children feel safe expressing their feelings. Safe schools help students to express fears, anger or anxieties to someone they trust, and try to prevent students from feeling isolated and rejected.

- Have somewhere to refer children who are suspected of being neglected or abused. Schools should work with local community organizations to provide safe environments for abused children.

- Offer extended day programs for children. Well-supervised programs that provide a range of activities can be effective in reducing violence. Such programs provide a service for many families as well as for the community and the children who participate in them.

- Promote good citizenship and character. Schools should provide moral teaching and promote values such as kindness, respect, and honesty.

- Identify problems and assess progress toward solutions. Leaders need to assess risks and respond with appropriate solutions. The process should be systematic, intentional, and sustained.

- Support students in making the transition to adult life and the workplace. Community service opportunities, work-study programs, and apprenticeships can all help students connect with caring adults that can foster both hope and direction for the future.

12.6 Early Warning Signs of Violence

While it is not always possible to predict violent behavior, certain warning signs point to the need for further observation and potential intervention. This is especially true if a cluster of indicators surface. No single indicator is sufficient to predict violent behavior, and if used indiscriminately, warning indicators can become misleading and cause harm to a child. Each child is unique and leaders need to assess warning signs in light of the background and circumstances of each individual situation. If warning signs appear, leaders should consult with trained professionals before developing any conclusions. *A Guide to Safe Schools* identifies the following sixteen warning signs:

Key point. All children are unique and express themselves in many different ways. The following warning signs do not indicate how a particular child may act. Rather, they identify a broad spectrum of behaviors that may indicate a troubled child, and that when present in increasing combinations provide a basis for observation, and when appropriate, intervention.

1. *Social withdrawal.* Gradual or complete social withdrawal may indicate that a child is troubled. Feelings of rejection, depression, and a lack of confidence are just a few of many factors that may cause a child to withdraw.

2. *Excessive feelings of isolation and being alone.* Most children who are isolated and appear to have few friends do not engage in violent behaviors. However, some do and it is just one factor among many to monitor.

3. *Excessive feelings of rejection.* Many young children experience rejection that is emotionally painful. Troubled children may become isolated from their peers. How they respond depends on many factors. Sometimes emotional distress becomes expressed in negative ways. Some aggressive children may express acts of violence.

4. *Being a victim of violence.* Some children who are victims of violence at home, in the community, or at school may displace feelings of anger on others.

5. *Feelings of being picked on and persecuted.* A child who is teased and ridiculed may withdraw. If no support is obtained, a child may respond in ways that can include aggression or violence.

6. *Low school interest and poor academic performance.* While many factors can cause poor school performance, a child that feels frustrated, denigrated, unworthy, and chastised may act out in ways that include aggressive behaviors.

7. *Expression of violence in writings and drawings.* In and of themselves, drawings and stories that include violence may signal little about potential violent behavior. Children are immersed in a world of violent shows and movies and it's a medium they know well. An overrepresentation of violence that is repetitious and directed towards specific individuals may indicate more deep feelings that suggest follow-up from a trained professional may be appropriate.

8. *Uncontrolled anger.* All children become anger. Frequent and intense anger that arises from minor irritants may indicate a potential for violent behavior.

9. *Patterns of impulsive and chronic hitting, intimidating, and bullying behaviors.* If left unattended, bullying behaviors that begin early in a child's life might continue to escalate over time.

10. *History of discipline problems.* Children with chronic discipline problems may manifest aggressive behaviors in many ways including breaking rules, defying authority, and violent actions toward others.

11. *Past history of violent and aggressive behavior.* Aggressive and violent behaviors are likely to be repeated unless proper intervention takes place. Setting fires and cruelty to animals may also occur. Violent behaviors may escalate, especially for children who engage in acts of violence before age 12.

12. *Intolerance for differences and prejudicial attitudes.* Intense and overt dislike or hatred toward others based on race, ethnicity, religion, language, gender, physical appearance, health problems, or other similar factors may lead to aggressive behaviors.

13. *Drug use and alcohol use.* Children who use drugs and alcohol are more likely to be victims as well as perpetrators of violence.

14. *Affiliation with gangs.* Youth who are involved with gangs that promote violent attitudes may engage in violent behaviors, including serious violent crimes.

15. *Inappropriate access to, possession of, and use of firearms.* Children with inappropriate access to firearms are at increased risk of becoming victims. Children with a history of aggressive behavior and other emotional problems should not have access to weapons or firearms.

16. *Serious threats of violence.* A detailed and specific threat of violence toward others or one's self must always be taken seriously. Professional intervention and follow-through should occur if and when such threats are made.

12.7 Responding to Imminent Warning Signs

Some warning signs require an immediate response. When they occur, intervention is required to prevent a situation from escalating into something worse. Again, while these warning signs do not indicate that worse violence will occur, they send a message that intervention is needed now. These warning signs include serious, overt, and hostile actions. Other students, several staff members, and the student's family members are usually aware of the escalating problem. *A Guide to Safe Schools* lists the following imminent warning signs:

- Serious physical fighting with peers or family members
- Severe destruction of property
- Severe rage for seemingly minor reasons
- Detailed threats of lethal violence
- Possession and/or use of firearms and other weapons
- Other self-injurious behaviors or threats of suicide

These behaviors require immediate intervention. Law enforcement officers should be involved when detailed threats of violence occur, or if a child carries a weapon, particularly a firearm.

Training students and staff

All school employees should be trained to identify early and imminent warning signs, and understand the differences and principles that accompany them. Early warning signs are not intended to be used as diagnostic tools to evaluate violent tendencies in children. Rather they present opportunities to monitor the needs of a child and to provide appropriate support. If multiple warning signs begin to surface as part of a constellation of behaviors, more serious intervention may be needed. Imminent warning signs, however, always indicate the need for immediate action. When they occur, intervention is required which may include law enforcement. Schools need to develop connections with experts and professionals who can provide assistance in both the diagnosis of problems, and the response to inappropriate behaviors. Dealing with troubled and aggressive students requires specialized knowledge and care.

Students should have clear expectations of what is expected of them, as well as the consequences of their behaviors. They should understand the goals of creating a safe school, their role within that plan, and view it as a positive contribution to their own education and development. Each student should receive a copy of the school handbook or other document that spells out the policies for students, and sign a form indicating they have read and understand the policies. The school should retain the signed forms.

Intervention: getting help for troubled children

Prevention programs are an important part of reducing violence and making schools safe, but some children need more direct personal intervention. Providing help to the 5 to 10 percent of children who engage in high risk behaviors does much more than decrease the potential for violence. Early intervention helps children to receive help and support that can improve their quality of life for years to come. Not only do they benefit from such intervention, but so does their family, friends, school and community. Research and expert experience indicates that when certain principles are followed, the potential for a positive outcome increases. *A Guide to Safe Schools* recommends that the following principles be followed regarding intervention.

1. *Share responsibility by establishing a partnership with the child, school, home, and community.* Effective intervention coordinates services using law enforcement, family service agencies, mental health agencies, businesses, churches and other ministries within the community.

2. *Inform parents and listen to them when early warning signs are observed.* Parents should be involved as early as possible. Communication between the school and the parents should be ongoing. School leaders should communicate specific steps that parents can take to support the coordinated intervention efforts.

3. *Maintain confidentiality and parents' rights to privacy.* Parental consent and involvement is necessary before sharing information with any other agency, except in cases of known or suspected abuse. The *Family Educational Rights and Privacy Act*, a federal law that addresses the privacy of education records, must be observed.

4. *Develop the capacity of staff, students, and families to intervene.* Every member of the school community—teachers, staff, students, and parents—should receive training on appropriate responses to imminent warning signs. Success depends upon a collaborative effort.

5. *Support students in being responsible for their actions.* Make efforts to help students understand they are responsible for their own actions. Get them involved in planning, implementing, and evaluating prevention strategies.

6. *Simplify staff requests for urgent assistance.* Develop ways to cut through the red tape when imminent warning signs appear.

7. Make interventions available as early as possible. Once problems are identified, formulate strategies to initiate help in a timely manner. Problems can escalate, and once they pass a certain threshold, intervention is both more difficult and more costly.

8. Use sustained, multiple, coordinated interventions. Children who are violent at school also cause problems elsewhere. For intervention to be effective, it should be comprehensive, involving family members and others that have direct contact with the child. A variety of resources and support, both from the family and the community, are needed. A fragmented, isolated, short-term approach to intervention will not be effective.

9. Analyze the contexts in which violent behavior occurs. In assessing the best approach to intervention, consideration should be given to the child's age, cultural background, family experiences, and values.

10. Build upon and coordinate internal school resources. Develop an infrastructure within the school that can coordinate internal resources to promote safety and provide support.

11. Provide direct training to children on problem solving skills, anger control skills, and factors that can exacerbate aggressive outbursts.

Research shows that while violence is less prevalent in schools than the media leads people to believe, pre-violent behaviors such as threats, bullying, and classroom disruptions are common. Early and systematic intervention is the best strategy to reduce the incidence of such behavior and to prevent it from escalating.

12.8 Create and Maintain a Safe Physical Environment

A safe school provides a sense of security while children are present. Based on input from experts, *A Guide to Safe Schools* recommends that school leaders take the following actions to enhance the physical security of a school.

1. Supervise access to the buildings and grounds.

2. Reduce class size and school size.

3. Adjust scheduling to minimize time in hallways or in potentially dangerous locations.

4. Conduct a building safety audit.

5. Close the school campus during lunch periods.

6. Adopt a policy on uniforms.

7. Arrange supervision at critical times.

8. Prohibit students from congregating in areas where they are likely to engage in rule breaking or intimidating and aggressive behaviors.

9. Have adults visibly present throughout the school building.

10. Stagger dismissal times and lunch periods.

11. Monitor the surrounding school grounds.

12. Coordinate with police to ensure there are safe routes to and from school.

13. Identify safe areas where students and staff should go in the event of a crisis.

14. Maintain a clean and safe building. More incidents of violence occur when schools are dirty, too hot or cold, filled with graffiti, and are in need of repair.

12.9 Develop Policies that Support Responsible Behavior

Schools that enact proactive strategies to promote and reinforce positive behavior find that they are able to reduce suspensions, expulsions, and office referrals. The goal is to develop and implement a positive approach to discipline. To be effective a program must be fair and consistently enforced. The entire school community should be involved in establishing rules and procedures. *A Guide to Safe Schools* recommends the following action steps:

1. *Develop a schoolwide disciplinary policy.* The policy should include a code of conduct along with specific rules and consequences. The policy should have some flexibility built into that can accommodate student differences on a case-by-case basis.

2. *Integrate community values and educational goals into the disciplinary policy.* The policy should be a tool to educate students on values such as honesty, respect for others, and personal integrity.

3. *Include students, staff, parents, and community leaders in the development of the policies.* Some ways to involve students include classroom discussions, school assemblies, student government, and participation on discipline teams. Some schools have found it helpful to use peer mediation and conflict resolution.

4. *Be fair in the application of rules.* Consequences should be commensurate with the offense. The rules should be in writing and applied in a way that is nondiscriminatory.

5. *Focus on positive strategies for change.* Rather than relying on forms of punishment alone, also use strategies for teaching positive behaviors. Identify values that can provide energy and a sense of hope to troubled children and that can help motivate students to change from negative to positive behaviors.

6. *Have a zero tolerance statement where appropriate.* A growing number of schools follow a zero tolerance policy for the illegal possession of weapons, alcohol, or drugs.

While the need to develop policies is fundamental, many schools already have policies, perhaps similar to those suggested above, and they are of little value. Schools and churches are similar in that unless policies become integrated into the fabric and life of the organization, they simply collect dust somewhere in a filing cabinet. On the other hand, policies that arise out of the values and deepest feelings of the school family have the potential to bring about change. This is more likely to occur when the policies are connected to positive outcomes, and connect with the dreams, aspirations, and hopes of students and teachers. Policies that focus on the negative, that create burdens and generate hostility cannot be sustained over time without authoritarian power. As a result school leaders should use planning methods such as appreciative inquiry to build the foundation for policies that give life to the institution. In their collective application, these policies should appeal to our hopes and not to our fears.

12.10 Develop a Prevention Plan

Every school should develop a written prevention plan that corresponds to its unique needs and environment. To be effective, a plan must become part of the very fabric and culture of the school itself. Parents, students, administrators, teachers, and support staff should embrace the goals and values that are reflected in the plan. The plan should provide specific information on its purpose and detail the responsibilities and expectations for each part of the school family. Finally, the plan should identify the network of agencies and services within the community with which the school will collaborate in the implementation of the plan, and explain how that collaboration will occur. *A Guide to Safe Schools* states that an effective written plan includes the following:

1. Descriptions of the early warning signs of potentially violent behavior and procedures for identifying children who exhibit these signs.

2. Descriptions of effective prevention practices the school community has undertaken to build a foundation that is responsive to all children and enhances the effectiveness of interventions.

3. Descriptions of intervention strategies the school community can use to help troubled children. These include early interventions for students who are at risk of behavioral problems, and more intensive, individualized interventions and resources for students with severe behavioral problems or mental health needs.

4. A crisis intervention plan that includes immediate responses for imminent warning signs and violent behavior, as well as a contingency plan to be used in the aftermath of a tragedy.

A local attorney should review all aspects of the plan to ensure it is consistent with federal, state, and local laws. Once the written plan is developed and approved, training should be provided to all members of the school community including administrators, teachers, support staff, and students.

12.11 Form a Prevention and Response Team

One proven way to develop and implement a safety program is to form a core team to oversee the process. Typically, members of this team include the building administrator, general and special education teachers, one or more parents, a school psychologist (or counselor or social worker), a school resource officer, and a drug-free schools program coordinator. If some of these individuals are not available from the school, seek the involvement of outside resource people. The core team members have the primary job of designing a program that will receive widespread support and achieve the goals of the safe school program. Different aspects of the plan can benefit by using additional resource people. For example, include students when formulating schoolwide policies. Law enforcement personnel can be helpful in developing a crisis management plan. A wide range of individuals can contribute to the work of the team including the following:

- school nurses
- school board members
- bus drivers
- secretaries
- custodians
- PTA officers
- attorneys, judges, probation officers
- clergy
- youth workers
- media representatives
- mental health workers
- physicians
- business leaders
- recreational specialists
- college faculty members
- influential community leaders

The work of the committee should be formally authorized and supported by the school board. Once the plan is developed, the committee should work with school administrators, teachers, and students to implement an orientation program, and an ongoing training program.

12.12 Responding to a Crisis

Chapter 4 examined strategies for crisis management. Few schools expect to have a crisis, but every school should be prepared to respond if one should occur. A crisis response plan for an act of violence should contain two components: (1) intervening during a crisis to ensure safety, and (2) responding in the aftermath of a crisis. *A Guide to Safe Schools* identifies four tasks that should be completed as part of school's crisis response plan::

1. Training for teachers and staff in a range of skills—from dealing with escalating classroom situations to responding to a serious crisis.

2. Reference to district or state procedures. Many states now have recommended crisis intervention manuals available to their local education agencies and schools.

3.	Involvement of community agencies, including police, fire, and rescue, as well as hospital, health, social welfare, and mental health services. The faith community, juvenile justice, and related family support systems also have been successfully included in such team plans.

4.	Provision for the core team to meet regularly to identify potentially troubled or violent students and situations that may be dangerous.

Intervening during a crisis

Some crises, such as a hurricane, provide advance notice. Acts of violence that impact a school may provide little or no notice. Some of these include the use of weapons in or around a school, a bomb threat, an explosion, or a suicide. These events require an immediate response. Being prepared with a written plan of action, a core team of leaders, and a trained faculty, staff, and student body can reduce both chaos and injury. To be effective, a crisis plan should address the following concerns:

1.	Evacuation procedures and other procedures to protect students and staff from harm. It is critical that schools identify safe places where students and staff can go in a crisis. It is also important to practice evacuating the premises in an orderly manner.

2.	An effective, fool-proof communication system. Individuals must have designated roles and responsibilities to prevent confusion.

3.	A process for securing immediate external support from law enforcement officials and other relevant community agencies.

To be adequately prepared for a crisis, a school must practice the concerns addressed above. To increase the likelihood of responding well, schools should do the following:

1.	Provide inservice training for all faculty and staff to explain the plan and exactly what to do in a crisis. Where appropriate, include police and other members of the community.

2.	Produce a written manual or small pamphlet or flip chart to remind teachers and staff of their duties.

Practice responding to imminent warning signs. Make sure all adults in the building have an understanding of what they might do to prevent violence (e.g., being observant, knowing when to get help, and modeling good problem solving, anger management, and/or conflict resolution skills) and how they can safely support each other.

Responding in the aftermath of a crisis

Crises produce a range of emotional responses which are often accompanied by high levels of stress. Members of the school's crisis management team should be familiar with and sensitive to the reactions of people who experience loss. If a crisis occurs, the school will need to draw upon community wide resources to respond adequately. Schools who have experienced tragedy have included the following provisions in their response plans:

1. *Help parents understand children's reactions to violence.* In the aftermath of violence, children may experience unrealistic fears of the future, have difficulty sleeping, become physically ill, and be easily distracted. Other symptoms may also be present.

2. *Help teachers and other staff members deal with their reactions to the crisis.* Debriefing and grief counseling is just as important for adults as it is for students.

3. *Help students and faculty adjust after the crisis.* Provide both short-term and long-term mental health counseling following a crisis.

4. *Help victims and their family members re-enter the school environment.* Often, school friends need guidance on how to act. The school community should work with students and parents to design a plan that makes it easier for victims and their classmates to adjust.

5. *Help students and teachers address the return of a previously removed student to the school community.* Whether the student is returning from a juvenile detention facility or a mental health facility, schools need to coordinate with staff from the facility to explore how to make the transition as uneventful as possible.

Summary

During the 1990s, violence among young people in America declined. The perception, though, is different. Mass shootings at several high schools have increased the national sensitivity to youth violence. As a result, no school can be unprepared in responding to acts of violence.

Violence and crime are often localized. Most American counties report no juvenile homicides on an annual basis. Juveniles, though, experience more serious crime than the adult population. Sexual assault affects children of all ages.

School crime is on the decrease. Students in urban schools experience more serious crime than do students in other locations. Public schools students experience more crime than do students in private schools. Fighting and theft are common in all schools, although fighting is more common off school property than on school property.

In responding to school violence, most schools require visitors to sign-in, about half control access to the building, and one-fourth control access to school property. A majority of schools close the campus for lunch. About one-fifth of schools conduct drug sweeps, but very few schools use metal detectors.

Developing a safety and security plan to reduce acts of crime and violence begins with assessing needs within the school or church. Responding to such needs, however, is not a well-defined problem. Many factors affect both the problem and the proposed solutions.

One approach to creating a safe and responsive school is to recognize early warning signs of violence and to intervene early. Such a program must involve the entire community and school family including parents, teachers, students, staff, and administrators. Imminent warning signs should be differentiated from early warning signs. Some imminent warning signs that include serious, overt, or hostile actions require an immediate response.

While teachers and students should not be expected to become experts in security, they should develop a threshold level of knowledge that enables them to respond appropriately to reduce risks when they occur. Prevention programs can help reduce violence. Some children, however, need more specialized attention than do others. Troubled children benefit from early intervention. Enhancing the physical security of the property and facilities can also create a heightened sense of safety.

Schools should develop policies that support responsible behavior, and that undergird a positive approach to discipline. A prevention plan is also needed that provides descriptions of warning signs and intervention strategies that can reduce violence. If an act of violence should occur, every school should have a crisis response plan ready to reduce chaos and injury.

In Part 3 of this handbook attention is turned to risks that impact both people and property. The next chapter addresses reducing the risk of fire.

Additional Resources on the Internet

For additional information on juvenile violence, review the material found on the following web sites. These resources were used in the preparation of this chapter.

"1999 National Report Notebook: Juvenile Offenders." Office of Juvenile Justice and Delinquency Prevention. <http://ojjdp.ncjrs.org/ojstatbb/qrptnote.html>.

"1999 National Report Notebook: Juvenile Population Characteristics" Office of Juvenile Justice and Delinquency Prevention.
<http://ojjdp.ncjrs.org/ojstatbb/qrptnote.html>.

"1999 National Report Notebook: Juvenile Victims." Office of Juvenile Justice and Delinquency Prevention. <http://ojjdp.ncjrs.org/ojstatbb/qrptnote.html>.

"1999 National Report Notebook: Law Enforcement and Juvenile Crime." Office of Juvenile Justice and Delinquency Prevention.
<http://ojjdp.ncjrs.org/ojstatbb/qrptnote.html>.

"Early Warning Timely Response: A Guide to Safe Schools." U.S. Department of Education, Special Education and Rehabilitative Services.
<http://wwwed.gov/offices/OSERS/OSEP/earlywrn.html>.

"Emerging Research: Research on Very Young Offenders." Office of Juvenile Justice and Delinquency Prevention.
<http://ojjdp.ncjrs.org/pubs/makingadiffer/emerging_1.html>.

"Facts About Violence Among Youth and Violence in Schools." National Center for Injury Prevention and Control.
<http://www.cdc.gov/ncipc/dvp/schoolvi.htm>.

"Indicators of School Crime and Safety, 1998." National Center for Education Statistics. <http://nces.ed.gov/pubs98/safety/index.html>.

"Preventing Violence & Suicide Enhancing Futures: Suicide in the United States." National Center for Injury Prevention and Control. <http://www.cdc.gov/ncipc/dvp/yvpt/suicide.htm>.

"Preventing Violence & Suicide Enhancing Futures: Fact Sheet on Dating Violence." National Center for Injury Prevention and Control. <http://www.cdc.gov/ncipc/dvp/yvpt/datviol.htm>.

"Preventing Violence & Suicide Enhancing Futures: Facts & Myths About Youth Violence." National Center for Injury Prevention and Control. <http://www.cdc.gov/ncipc/dvp/yvpt/myths.htm>.

"Preventing Violence & Suicide Enhancing Futures: Resource Organizations." National Center for Injury Prevention and Control. <http://www.cdc.gov/ncipc/dvp/yvpt/partner.htm>.

"Preventing Violence & Suicide Enhancing Futures: Solutions, An Interdisciplinary Approach to Violence." National Center for Injury Prevention and Control. <http://www.cdc.gov/ncipc/dvp/yvpt/solution.htm>.

"Preventing Violence & Suicide Enhancing Futures: Theories on Causation of Youth Violence." National Center for Injury Prevention and Control. <http://www.cdc.gov/ncipc/dvp/yvpt/theory.htm>.

"Preventing Violence & Suicide Enhancing Futures: Youth Violence in the United Sates Fact Sheet." National Center for Injury Prevention and Control. <http://www.cdc.gov/ncipc/dvp/yvpt/newfacts.htm>.

"Preventing Violence & Suicide Enhancing Futures: Youth Violence." National Center for Injury Prevention and Control. <http://www.cdc.gov/ncipc/dvp/yvpt/yvpt.htm>.

"Recent Trends in Violence-Related Behaviors Among High School Students in the United States." JAMA. <http://jama.ama-assn.org/issues/v282n5/abs/joc90430.html>.

"Research on Girls." Office of Juvenile Justice and Delinquency Prevention. <http://ojjdp.ncjrs.org/pubs/makingadiffer/emerging_5.html>.

"School Efforts to Ensure Safety and Promote Discipline." National Center for Education Statistics. <http://nces.ed.gov/pubs98/violence/98090009.html>.

"School Resource Officers and Safe School Planning." North Carolina State University. <http://www2.ncsu.edu/ncsu/cep/PreViolence/sroplan.htm>.

"School Resource Officers: Job Descriptions." North Carolina State University. <http://www2.ncsu.edu/ncsu/cep/PreViolence/srojob.htm>.

"School Resource Officers: What They Know, What We Think We Know, What We Need to Know." North Carolina State University. <http://www2.ncsu.edu/ncsu/cep/PreViolence/srowhatweknow.htm>.

"School Violence Incident Reporting in the United States." North Carolina State University. <http://www2.ncsu.edu/ncsu/cep/PreViolence/usincident.htm>.

"School Violence." Office of Juvenile Justice and Delinquency Prevention. <http://ojjdp.ncjrs.org/pubs/makingadiffer/emerging_3.html>.

CHAPTER 13. REDUCING THE RISK OF FIRE

In a typical year, it is estimated that over 10,000 churches and related ministries file a claim arising from a fire. While fires represent about 10 percent of all church insurance claims, they account for over 25 percent of the monies paid out for losses. The greatest fire hazards to churches are lightning, electrical problems, open flames, appliances, and arson.

Lightning is one of the most common causes of church fires (and also electrical surges). Yet fires that result from lightning tend to do less damage than fires that originate from electrical problems, open flames, or from arson. While arson accounts for about 4 percent of the fires, the losses from those fires represent about 20 percent of the total. Fires that originate from electrical problems and open flames account for under 15 percent of claims, but over 50 percent of the losses.

13.1 The Fire Triangle

The fire triangle is a well understood concept with respect to fire safety. For a fire to start and continue, three factors must be present: an ignition source, fuel, and oxygen. If one component is removed, a fire will not occur. Prevention focuses on removing at least one component.

13.2 Principles of Fire Prevention

Two main strategies should be followed as part of the prevention program. One is to implement a regular inspection program and the second is to initiate a maintenance program

Inspections

A walk-through inspection of the entire church or school facility should be conducted regularly, preferably at least quarterly. The inspection should focus on three areas: ignition sources, fuel sources, and responding to a fire. The main principle of fire prevention is to remove at least one component of the fire triangle (an ignition source, fuel, or oxygen). In almost every case, the removal of oxygen is impossible. Churches and schools should therefore focus their inspection efforts on identifying and removing either hazardous ignition sources or sources of fuel. In addition, the inspection should also check fire fighting equipment and escape routes.

Sources of ignition

The main sources of ignition in a church or school can be identified quickly. The purpose of the inspection is to identify and correct unsafe conditions. The furnace room, kitchen, printing room, and any other room containing gas appliances, heating equipment, electrical appliances, or open flames should be carefully inspected. Electrical outlets should be checked for potential overload.

One purpose of the inspection is to remove ignition sources that pose a hazard to the church or school. What sources of ignition can be removed or mitigated? Several important ones include lightning, unsafe wiring, and unsafe open flames. For example, the use of lightning rods, replacing unsafe wiring, cleaning and repairing chimneys, flues and furnaces, and reducing or controlling the use of open flames with candles, propane torches and gas appliances such as heaters can increase safety. In addition, establishing security procedures can reduce the likelihood of arson.

Sources of fuel

The inspection should also identify and remove sources of fuel that pose a hazard. Careful custodial care can contribute greatly to the reduction of fuels that contribute to fires in churches and schools. The proper storage of hazardous chemicals, the removal of rubbish, and keeping areas around ignition sources clean and free from fuel sources can reduce fires.

Fire fighting equipment and escape routes

Inspectors should check that fire extinguishers are fully charged and located in their proper positions. Smoke detectors and alarm systems should tested. Fire escape routes should also be inspected, including doors, stairways, fire escapes, ladders, and emergency lighting. In large facilities, exits, stairways, and floors should be identified with a letter or number so that they can be easily identified in an emergency. In addition, a fire drill should be practiced periodically.

Maintenance

Maintenance plays an important role in fire prevention. Attention should be given to the maintenance of equipment, storage practices, and good housekeeping.

Electrical equipment, gas appliances, and heating equipment

Routine maintenance of equipment can prevent fires. The problem is that many churches and schools do not have the staff or procedures in place to see that maintenance is done. A problem with a piece of equipment may go unattended for months, even years. It may be that it is not reported, or that no one takes responsibility to correct it. It's one thing if the problem does not pose a risk, but if it can start a fire then it is a serious hazard and deserves immediate attention. One way for churches and schools to cope with this problem is to develop service contracts for some of the more important areas that require ongoing maintenance. This is especially important with respect to heating and air conditioning equipment. Having an inspection and service call at least twice a year can extend the life of the equipment and reduce the potential for fire and other hazards. Any gas or electrical appliance that develops a problem should receive prompt attention. The cost of routine maintenance should be included in the church's or school's annual budget.

Storage

Special attention should be given to the storage of hazardous chemicals, gasoline, paint thinner, insecticides and other flammable liquids. Storage procedures should be carefully spelled out and enforced. All employees and staff members should be trained on how to follow them. What may appear as an unimportant decision, such as where to keep a cleaning fluid, may have serious consequences if it should become a source of fuel for a fire.

Good housekeeping

Many fires are fueled by clutter and debris that accumulate over time in places such as furnace rooms and garages. Leaders should take special care to promote good housekeeping practices throughout church and school facilities giving special attention to areas such as kitchens, printing rooms, science labs, and furnace rooms where a fire is more likely to ignite.

13.3 Facility Design and Location

Fire safety should be an important consideration in the design or remodeling of church or school buildings. The type of construction materials should take into account fire hazards. The use of firewalls, fire divisions, fire doors, the nature of wall openings, and automatic fire detection and suppression systems can help churches and schools control their exposure to fire.

13.4 Responding to Key Problem Areas

Church and school leaders can significantly reduce the potential for fire through inspections and preventive maintenance in several key problem areas. Attention should be given to the following concerns.

Lightning

As noted earlier, lightning is the number one cause of church fires. Arson and electrical fires, though, do more damage. Lightning, however, does more harm than just starting fires. It can also create power surges that damage electrical equipment such as organs, telephone systems, computers, and fax machines (see chapter 15 for reducing the risk of personal injury from lightning and thunderstorms). Rural churches in open areas are particularly vulnerable. Often, a volunteer fire department is miles away. In such cases, a fire from lightning can result in a total loss. Church and school buildings with bell towers, steeples, or spires are also vulnerable. The installation of lightning rods can significantly reduce these fires. If your church or school already has one or more lightning rods that were installed many years ago, do not assume that they are working properly. Make sure that the wires are unbroken. If they appear damaged, hire a professional to check them.

Electrical wiring and appliances

Unsafe electrical wiring causes fires every year in churches and schools resulting in considerable damage. This is particularly true in older facilities where the likelihood of unsafe wiring dramatically increases. Unsafe conditions can include worn-out insulation or components, overloaded circuits, and the use of extension cords as a substitute for permanent wiring. The insulation around wiring can become brittle with age. The wire may be embedded within walls, or may be something as simple as a cord to an old lamp. Short circuits can lead to fires. Perhaps a more common problem is overloading circuits. Some churches and schools, especially older ones, simply do not have enough electrical outlets. As a result, adapters are used to increase the number of cords that can be plugged into an outlet. A dangerous action is to replace fuses so the circuit will accommodate higher amps. The fuse box should be checked to make certain that the correct fuses are in use. Unplug appliances that are not used regularly. Make sure that the church organ is turned off following each service. Under certain conditions, they can ignite. Also check light fixtures and make sure that the light bulb wattage does not exceed the recommended wattage. If your building is more than 20 years old, have a professional inspect the wiring for potential problems.

Cold weather problems

Cold weather increases fire hazards. The improper use of kerosene or electrical space heaters, wood burning stoves or fireplaces, propane torches to unfreeze pipes, or furnaces and boilers can all lead to a fire. These concerns are addressed in the next chapter on risks related to cold weather.

Halogen Floor Lamps

The Consumer Product Safety Commission has identified halogen torchiere floor lamps as a potential fire and safety hazard. These floor lamps are about six feet tall and contain a bowl shaped light fixture at the top of the bowl. The glass bulb located at the very top of the lamp becomes extremely hot and flammable materials that come in contact with it can catch on fire. Since February 5, 1997, manufactured lamps come with a glass or wire shield designed to prevent contact with the bulb. However, over 40 million lamps were sold without such protection prior to 1997. A careful inspection should be made of church and school facilities, especially offices, libraries, and other locations that might use floor lamps to determine if any of these lamps are being used. If so, make sure it has a protective cover and if not, discontinue its use until it a cover shield is installed. Free shields are available at many hardware stores.

Kitchens

Fellowship is central to the life of every church, and that includes regular use of the church kitchen. School kitchens are used on a daily basis. The kitchen poses a number of fire risks that can be reduced through basic maintenance and care of equipment. Since many people tend to use the typical church kitchen, training plays an important role in reducing the risk of fire. School employees should also be provided training on safety concerns. Also, posters and signs can help guide behaviors to lower risks.

Cooking equipment is associated with a significant number of fires. Electrical equipment tends to pose more of a risk than does gas equipment. Some basic risk management guidelines include the following:

1. Make sure a fire extinguisher is located near the kitchen exit, preferably one with a Class BC rating.

2. Keep the area near and above the range stop free of flammable items such as paper towels, dish towels, plastic bowls or utensils, and potholders. Remove packages and empty ingredient boxes away from the burners. Put the lids on bottles (such as cooking oil) and put them away. Keep the range hood clean and remove any accumulated grease.

3. While cooking, do not leave the stove unattended.

4. Avoid gas build up prior to lighting a pilot light. First light the match, then turn on the gas. If you must first vent the gas line to remove air, do not try to light the pilot light until adequate time has passed to remove any build up of gas from around the pilot.

5. Do not attempt to carry something that has caught on fire. Grease may catch on fire or something near the stove may catch on fire. Quickly remove anything near the fire that can burn. Liquids that are on fire can spill and spread quickly. If the fire is in a pot, cover it with a lid. A wet cloth or fire blanket can be used to smoother an isolated fire. If the fire starts in a trash can cover the top to cut off the oxygen supply. Use something like a tray or a cutting board. Never hesitate to use a fire extinguisher on a small fire.

Flammable liquids

Over time, churches and schools often accumulate a supply of flammable liquids that are left over from a variety of work projects. Furthermore, since many churches and schools are short on storage space, these items often end up in a furnace room or utility room with a water heater, which significantly increases the potential for fire. The most common liquids include gasoline (the most dangerous of all), acetone, benzene, lacquer thinner, alcohol, turpentine, contact cements, paint thinner, kerosene, and charcoal lighter fluid. Many flammable liquids produce vapors that can ignite even though the containers in which they are stored are located a considerable distance away from where a spark may occur. These liquids should not be stored in the same room with furnaces, water heaters, ranges and gas appliances. In addition, they should be kept in tightly sealed, non-breakable containers which are properly labeled and kept out of the reach of children. Be on guard if the church or school is going through a remodeling project or is being painted. Rags soaked in thinner and other flammable liquids can create a hazard.

Candles

Many churches use candles as a routine part of worship, and for other activities. Wherever possible, electric candles should be substituted for open flames. Candles should be used only with direct supervision and should be extinguished once the service is finished. They should not be located on or near any flammable item. Keep candles away from young children. Paraffin wax poses a health risk.

Burning trash

Trash burning occurs with regularity on construction sites and in many rural settings. Churches or schools that burn trash should consult with their fire department concerning proper safety precautions. They should also make sure they are not violating any zoning codes. Trash burning requires supervision, a water supply or other means to extinguish a fire, and proper containment and clearance so that the fire cannot jump to a secondary and unintended source of fuel.

Arson

Arson creates major financial losses for churches and schools and severe destruction to property. People set church buildings or schools on fire for many reasons. One of the most common is to destroy evidence following a burglary, or as an act of vandalism. Sometimes it is an accident. A homeless person may slip into the building through an unlocked door and start a fire with a candle or a cigarette. In one instance a girl age 13 started a church on fire as part of an occult ritual. An angry church member or student may commit arson. Some church fires are hate crimes. In some cases pastors or church leaders have started fires so the church can collect insurance money. Churches and schools that implement efforts to reduce crime, also reduce the likelihood of arson (see chapter 16).

In response to the wave of church burnings in the 1990s, the federal government issued the following *Church Threat Assessment Guide* to church leaders to reduce the problem of arson and bombing attacks.[1] The guide notes that it should not be considered all-inclusive.

Area of vulnerability

The guide identifies the following churches as being at a higher risk:

- Churches located in isolated or rural areas.

- Churches left unattended for extended periods of time.

- Churches with unsecured doors and/or uncovered windows leave weak points for forced entry by intruders.

- The absence of an adequate burglar alarm system provides a determined criminal with additional time for criminal activity.

- Heavy shrubs and outside vegetation, and/or the absence of sufficient perimeter lighting, provides security for criminals, not victims.

Affirmative actions to reduce vulnerability

Based on an analysis of church fires, the guide makes the following recommendations to church leaders to reduce the risk of arson or bombing. These recommendations also apply to schools and also help reduce the potential for crime or vandalism.

1. *Install perimeter floodlights outside the building.* Criminals can conceal their presence and activity from witnesses at night. Adequate lighting that illuminates all points of entry (doors, windows, skylights, etc.) discourages them. Interior lights in areas visible through exterior windows should be left on during all hours of darkness. Exterior lights should have protective screens over them to prevent vandalism. All lights should be checked weekly for serviceability. Relatively inexpensive motion activated and/or timing equipment may be purchased to automatically turn lights on and off.

2. *Install an adequate fire and burglar alarm system.* Alarms should be installed by reputable local companies that can service and properly maintain the equipment. Please note that some municipalities or police departments have enacted burglar alarm standards and will not respond to false alarms by inferior systems that frequently cause false alarms. Check with your local police or sheriff's department.

[1] See "National Church Arson Task Force." U.S. Department of the Treasury, U.S. Department of Justice, Bureau of Alcohol, Tobacco and Firearms, Federal Bureau of Investigation. <http://www.atf.treas.gov/pub/arsonrpt.htm>.

3. *Solid wood or sheet metal doors provide extra integrity that a hollow core wooden door cannot.* Metal security grates or screens that cover the entire door and frame also provide added security. A steel door frame that properly fits the door is as important as the construction of the door. With the proper foundation of a sufficient door and frame, the most obvious consideration, door locks, can be addressed. Long throw dead bolts of hardened steel are excellent deterrents to forced entry. Many standard locks are easy to pick or break open. Do remember that exits must remain operable for fire and life safety reasons.

4. *Install burglar-proof bars on screens, and large roof vents to prohibit access through them.* However, it should be noted that aesthetic or fire safety considerations often preclude their use. If bars are used, they should be operable from the interior and not limit the exit or evacuation of the building. *Local ordinances should be researched BEFORE costly security renovations are undertaken.*

5. *Use outside lights around windows.* Windows, regardless of their height from the ground, are common points of entry for criminals. Burglars can open unlocked windows, break glass and unlock locked windows, saw through metal or wooden frames, or pry entire window frames from exterior walls.

6. *Trim shrubs and vines.* Heavy shrubs and vines should be kept low to the ground to reduce their potential to conceal criminals or incendiary or explosive devices. Large trees or vines should be removed to prevent criminals from climbing to upper windows, large vents, or onto the roof.

7. *Become active in community programs.* Participate in formal Neighborhood Watch type programs organized by local authorities.

8. *Meet with your neighbors and security personnel assigned to your neighboring businesses.* Explain your situation and ask them to keep an eye on your facilities.

9. *Educate personnel on methods to deal with telephoned threats and conducting bomb searches.* Develop a written protocol for threats and keep it posted.

10. *Document any strange or threatening phone calls.* Talk with the phone company about tracing your lines or installing Caller ID to identify your callers if you are receiving threats.

11. *Be on guard for suspicious packages.* If a suspicious package or letter is received, immediately call your local police or sheriff's department. Do not touch or manipulate the object in any manner. Be alert for letters or packages that display an excessive amount of postage, contain grease stains, or have unfamiliar or missing return addresses.

12. *Keep the handling of threatening correspondence, once identified, to an absolute minimum.* Place envelopes, letters or the packages in clear plastic bags and do not compress the bag. Store them in another location until they can be turned over to law enforcement.

13. *Check the property.* On a rotating basis, have a member of the congregation, who is at least 18 years of age check on the church facilities daily. Evaluate the need for a security guard for nights and weekends.

14. Report suspicious people. Obtain as detailed a physical description as possible of any suspicious person(s) noticed in or around your facility, including a description of vehicles and license numbers.

15. Duplicate all documents, computer disks, and records that are stored at the church or school. Complete a comprehensive inventory of all furniture and equipment, to include serial numbers and value. Evaluate insurance coverage frequently.

16. Remove fire hazards. Remove all potential fire hazards from the grounds, such as trash, lawn clippings and debris. Store all combustible materials in a locked room or shed.

Cautionary notes

While leaders can take affirmative steps to reduce arson, there are some things that should not be done. Churches that feel they are at a high risk should observe the following cautionary notes:

1. DO NOT allow watch persons to sleep inside the church.

2. The carrying of firearms, nightsticks, mace, or any type of weapon while conducting surveillance or participating in watch programs should not be permitted.

3. DO NOT approach a suspicious person, challenge anyone, or otherwise place yourself in jeopardy. If a suspicious situation is found, report it to the nearest law enforcement agency. Take detailed legible notes of the activity, which may be used later for court or police purposes.

4. DO NOT pursue vehicle or suspects.

5. Remember, you do not possess police powers and you are liable as an individual for civil and criminal charges should you exceed your authority. The key is to OBSERVE and REPORT.

6. If possible, conduct any watch patrols in pairs.

7. Conduct watches in a random fashion and not in an observable pattern.

Realize that a perfect security system does not exist and that some of these recommendations may or may not be practical for a place of worship. However, these suggestions can reduce the potential for arson, bombing, vandalism or burglary at your church or school. Many of the listed security measures are quite expensive and may be beyond the means of many churches or schools. Local police crime prevention sections are excellent sources for security evaluations and suggestions. Also, local fire departments can provide on-site fire safety and arson prevention inspections. They will assist you in prioritizing your needs within your budget constraints.

13.5 Responding to a Fire

The most important concern if a fire should occur is to protect human life. The response of humans to a fire is based upon a number of factors including age and maturity. For example, a group of preschool children will respond differently than adults. A response plan should take into account who occupies church or school facilities at any given time, what roles individuals should take if a fire should occur, and how building design and facility location will impact evacuation.

Occupants and evacuation

Some church facilities stay empty for most of the week while others remain in almost constant use. The nature and use of the facilities plays a major role in formulating a response plan to a fire. Churches and schools that sponsor programs for children, senior citizens or individuals that lack mobility and potential awareness of the facilities need detailed evacuation plans with at least two evacuation routes. Leaders who oversee these programs should be familiar with evacuation procedures, and be prepared to take a leadership role to protect human life from fire. Periodically include a diagram in your church bulletin or newsletter that illustrates evacuation routes. Few churches ever practice a fire drill, but members should be familiar with escape routes. Special training should be provided to those who work in the church nursery. All schools, preschools, and day care programs should practice fire drills.

Fire response roles

Many large organizations form a fire brigade with individuals assigned clearly defined roles to respond to a fire. Most churches have a small staff of only a few people and forming such a brigade will often be impractical. Schools tend to have more employees. Yet, church staff members should and can fulfill important roles if a fire should occur. One person should have an immediate responsibility to sound an alarm and notify others. Someone else may call 911. Naturally, judgment must be used depending on the magnitude and location of the fire in responding to each duty. It may make sense to make the call quickly from inside the building. Then again, circumstances may dictate the need for immediate evacuation before the call is made. If the call is made from outside church facilities, it should be planned in advance from where the call should be made. Similarly, another person may have a responsibility to secure important files. Any person that may be leading a group within the church should know how to evacuate the building, and how to do so as safely as possible. These, and other roles and responsibilities, should be clarified and rehearsed as part of a response plan. All nursery workers should know how to evacuate the children in their care.

13.6 Controlling Exposure to Fires

Once a fire starts, the use of smoke detectors, fire alarms, fire extinguishers, sprinkler systems and other fire suppressant systems can help control and limit potential losses. A church or school that has a fire response plan in place can benefit through advanced preparation, training and practice.

Smoke detectors

Churches and schools should install smoke detectors in strategic locations giving special attention to locations that pose a higher risk of fire or loss such as furnace rooms, kitchens, printing areas, storage areas, offices and locations that might be used for sleeping. A good chance exists that if your church has a smoke detector, that it does not work. Many smoke detectors receive little or no maintenance. As a result the batteries become dead, the units malfunction due to corrosion or dirt, or they simply fail due to age. In other cases, the units are disconnected or the batteries are removed to avoid nuisance alarms. Smoke detectors are important, both in reducing property loss and in protecting human life. Inspections should be made on a monthly basis, and batteries should be replaced at least annually, or more frequently if necessary. The grills should be kept free of dust or other debris.

Fire extinguishers

All staff members should receive basic training and actual practice in the use of fire extinguishers. Not all fires can be extinguished with water. Pouring water on some fires can actually make the situation worse. As a result, fires are classified according to how they should be extinguished. The three classifications relevant to churches and schools include the following:

Fire Classification	Nature of the Fire	How extinguished
Class A	Ordinary combustible materials such as wood, paper and cloth.	Water
Class B	Flammable liquids such as gasoline, oil, or grease.	A dry chemical powder, carbon dioxide
Class C	Electrical fires involving live electrical equipment such as appliances, wiring, switches, and fuse boxes.	A nonconductive dry chemical powder

Fire extinguishers are rated for the class of fire that they can extinguish. For example, a Class A fire extinguisher contains water, while Class B and C extinguishers generally contain a dry powder, but are designed for different uses.

Multipurpose fire extinguishers are available that can be used on all three classifications of fire. These ABC rated extinguishers eliminate the risk of trying to put out a grease fire, for example, with water. To reduce the risk of misclassification, insurance companies recommend that churches and schools use Class ABC fire extinguishers. A Class BC extinguisher is often preferred for the kitchen area. Fire extinguishers should be recharged on an annual basis.

Invite someone from the local fire department help you determine the number of fire extinguishers you need and where they should be located. In general, you need one extinguisher for every 2,500 square feet of space, and at least one for every floor.

Using a fire extinguisher

Staff members should receive basic training on how to use a fire extinguisher. It should begin with each person removing the fire extinguisher from its mounted position so that he or she has a sense of its weight and how to hold it. Some extinguishers can be heavy. The top should be no higher than five feet off the floor. The training should then include actual practice in using the extinguisher to put out a controlled fire in a safe outdoor setting. Staff members should understand the differences between each fire classification. For example, if the fire is electrical turn off the power source as quickly as possible before trying to extinguish the fire. Discharge the extinguisher toward the base of the fire.

Sprinkler systems

Sprinkler systems can significantly reduce the damage of a fire. Several different types of sprinkler systems are available including both wet and dry ones. Wet systems should use an alarm system that detects leaks. Temperature settings must be controlled in unoccupied buildings that have wet sprinkler systems so the pipes do not freeze. Church and school leaders should consult with at least two different companies as well as with their insurance carrier to explore what the best option is for their facility. Installing a sprinkler system may also reduce insurance costs. Any new building program should include a sprinkler system, regardless of the size of the church or school facility. Also check local zoning ordinances regarding the use of sprinklers.

Standpipe systems

High rise buildings and some older buildings may have a standpipe system with rolled or folded hoses to fight fires. The systems operate by distributing water throughout a building to fight fires using large quantities of water. Churches and schools should have the local fire department inspect standpipe systems.

Summary

Fire accounts for approximately one-fourth the costs of church insurance losses in a typical year. Churches and schools that conduct regular inspections and engage in routine maintenance can reduce the potential for fires.

Inspections should focus on three key factors: (1) identify sources of ignition and correct any unsafe conditions; (2) identify and remove sources of fuel that pose a hazard; and (3) make sure that the church or school has adequate and operational fire fighting equipment, and that fire escape routes are unobstructed and easy to identify.

Routine maintenance should also focus on three areas: (1) make sure that electrical equipment, gas appliances, and heating equipment are all in good repair; (2) see that hazardous chemicals and flammable liquids are stored properly; and (3) follow good housekeeping rules by removing all clutter and debris.

Special attention should be given to inspecting and maintaining electrical wiring, electrical and gas appliances, kitchen areas, furnace rooms, the use and storage of flammable liquids, the use of lightning rods, and burning trash. In the late 1990s, a series of church fires heightened the problem of arson. In response, the government published a guide to assist churches to assess their vulnerability to arson. The guide also provides affirmative steps that churches and schools can take to reduce their vulnerability.

If a fire should occur, the foremost concern is the protection of human life. Evacuation plans should exist that include two possible evacuation routes for each area of the building. In the event of a fire, each staff member should have a clearly defined role. Important tasks include contacting 911 to report the fire, sounding alarms, and securing important files.

The use of smoke alarms, fire alarms, fire extinguishers, and sprinkler systems can help control losses. All staff members should have training and practice in using a fire extinguisher.

In the next chapter, the focus is on reducing risks associated with cold weather.

Additional Resources on the Internet

For additional information on fire prevention, review the material found on the following web sites. Also, several publications are listed that are available from the Consumer Product Safety Commission. These resources were used in the preparation of this chapter.

"Annual Fire Statistics." Consumer Product Safety Review / Spring 1997.

"Carbon Monoxide (or CO) Kills!" Michigan State University Extension. <http://www.orcbs.msu.edu/AWARE/safetynews/octnov95.html>.

"Carbon Monoxide Detectors Can Save Lives CPSC Document #5010." Consumer Product Safety Commission. <http://www.cpsc.gov/cpscpub/pubs/5010.html>.

"Carbon Monoxide Fact Sheet CPSC Document #4466." Consumer Product Safety Commission. <http://www.cpsc.gov/cpscpub/pubs/466.html>.

"CPSC and NKHA Stress Kerosene Heater Safety CPSC Document #5052." Consumer Product Safety Commission. <http://www.cpsc.gov/cpscpub/pubs/5052.html>.

"CPSC Warns of Carbon Monoxide Poisoning with Camping Equipment CPSC Document #5008." Consumer Product Safety Commission. <http://www.cpsc.gov/cpscpub/pubs/5008.html>.

"Dangers of Burning Charcoal Indoors." Consumer Product Safety Review / Summer 1996.

"Dangers of Carbon Monoxide." Consumer Product Safety Review / Winter 1997.

"Fire Safety Tips." Office of the Illinois State Fire Marshall. <http://ww.state.il.us/osfm/fst.htm>.

"Gas & Fuel-Burning Appliances." Consumer Product Safety Review, Fall 1997, Vol. 2 No. 2.

"Heating Boiler Safety." <http://www.freenet.edmonton.ab.ca/absa/boilsafe.html>.

"Heating Tape Hazard." U.S. Department of Transportation U.S. Coast Guard. <http://www.uscg.mil/hq/g-m/moa/docs/sa0296.htm>.

"Home Fire-Safety Alert Check Chimneys and Smoke Detectors." Emergency Management Branch, Division of Public Safety, Office of Research Services, Public Safety News - Issue 98-23, November 1998. <http://www.nih.gov/od/ors/newsltrs/psn/psn98-23.htm>.

"Home Heating Safety." Virtual Children's Hospital of Iowa.
<http.www.vh.org/Patients/IHB/Peds/Safety/SpaceHeaters.html>.

"Installation Safety." National Resources Canada.
<http://www.nrcan.gc.ca/es/erb/reed/wood/05_e.html>.

"Maintaining Your Wood Heating System." National Resources Canada.
<http://www.nrcan.gc.ca/es/erb/reed/wood/13_e.html>.

"New Electric Heat Tapes Help Prevent Fires: Safety Alert CPSC Document
#5045." Consumer Product Safety Commission.
<http://www.cpsc.gov/cpscpub/pubs/5045.html>.

"Reducing Injuries from Multi-Purpose Lighters." Consumer Product Safety
Review / Winter 1997.

"Safety Tips for Winter Storms."
<http://www.coastalnet.com/weather/nwsmhx/wntrsafe.htm>.

"Safety: Fires - Disaster Services." American Red Cross.
<http://www.redcross.org/disaster/safety/resfires.html>.

"UL Reminds Consumers to Use Space Heaters Safely This Heating Season."
Underwriters Laboratories Inc. January 13, 1998.
<http://www.ul.com/about/newsrel/heater.htm>.

CHAPTER 14. REDUCING RISKS ASSOCIATED WITH COLD WEATHER

Cold weather poses five specific types of risks to churches and schools: (1) risks that arise from heating systems, including portable heaters and wood burning stoves; (2) freezing pipes that burst and create water damage; (3) snow and ice build-up that contribute to roof leaks and structural damage; (4) slick sidewalks and stairs that contribute to slips and falls; and (5) potential harm to humans due to exposure to cold.

14.1 Heating Systems

Heating systems pose several different risks to churches and schools. The period from September to March represents increased risk to fire and carbon monoxide poisoning. Each year fires that arise from poorly maintained heating systems create extensive property damage and loss of life. The good news is that most fires and other risks associated with heating systems can be prevented through simple maintenance procedures and inspections regarding gas and fuel burning appliances.

Gas and fuel burning appliances

The most common heating systems found in churches or schools use gas or other fuel burning appliances. A qualified professional should conduct an annual inspection of the heating system to reduce the risk of fire, explosions, and carbon monoxide poisoning. The inspection of the heating system should not be left to a volunteer. Rather, churches and schools should purchase an annual service contract that includes both a safety inspection of the equipment and routine maintenance. Not only is the life of the equipment prolonged, but the church or school may be transferring certain risks to the service company in case a problem or accident does occur. Inspections should be done for all appliances, including furnaces, stoves, and water heaters, that burn natural or propane gas, heating oil, wood, or other fuel. Kerosene and gas space heaters should be cleaned annually. Chimneys, flues, and vents should also be inspected.

Gas leaks

A number of hazards arise with the use of gas or fuel burning appliances. For example, a gas leak can lead to an explosion. Flexible connectors manufactured prior to the late 1970s have been associated with incidents that have led to serious injuries resulting from explosions. Such connectors should be replaced. In addition, avoid gas build up prior to lighting a pilot light. First light the match, then turn on the gas. If you must first vent the gas line to remove air, do not try to light the pilot light until adequate time has passed to remove any build up of gas from around the pilot.

Carbon monoxide

Carbon monoxide (CO) poisoning is another risk tied to the use of fuel burning appliances that affects thousands of people each year. Carbon monoxide is an odorless and colorless gas that results from the incomplete combustion of fuels. Any fossil fuel burning appliance (i.e., wood, oil, kerosene, propane, natural gas, charcoal, pressed woodchip logs) poses a threat. Since the gas cannot be detected through normal sensory perception, no warning exists that unsafe levels may be present. Exposure to the gas can result in headaches, dizziness, fatigue, breathing difficulties, nausea, and death. Many people mistake these symptoms with a case of the flu. Long-term exposure to a low concentration of CO can have a similar impact as a short-term exposure to high concentrations. Children, senior citizens, pregnant women, and individuals with heart disease are at a greater risk than other members of the population. Even very small amounts of CO can create health problems for these most vulnerable groups. The Consumer Product Safety Commission recommends the use of CO detectors near any sleeping area. Detectors should contain labels showing they meet the Underwriters Laboratories, Inc. (UL) voluntary standard UL 2034. Such detectors provide the highest margins of safety. Since most deaths occur at night while people sleep, a church should install detectors in or directly outside the bedrooms of a church owned parsonage, rectory, or manse or in any other facility where people sleep that may be exposed to CO. In addition, churches and schools should prohibit the inside use of charcoal grills and also consider installing CO detectors in kitchen areas that use a gas range or oven.

Kerosene heaters

Sometimes, kerosene heaters are used in church or school offices to supplement the main heating system. Kerosene heaters pose significant risks, and are generally looked on with disfavor from safety experts. Before using a kerosene heater, always check with your local fire department to see if any restrictions exist on their use in your state or community. For the reasons noted above, CO detectors should also be used with kerosene heaters. Purchase only 1-K kerosene and use a reputable dealer. Other grades of kerosene can cause additional health problems due to higher sulfur dioxide emissions. Never substitute or mix gasoline with kerosene. Even a small amount of gasoline can increase volatility and significantly increase the risk of fire. Kerosene fuel should not be stored near a furnace, water heater, stove, or other gas appliance. It should be stored outside the building in a tightly sealed, properly labeled, non-breakable container, preferably in a fire-resistant storage shed. In addition, never store kerosene in a gasoline container. Normally, kerosene containers are blue while gasoline containers are red. Using a red container can cause confusion and possibly lead to someone unwittingly using gasoline rather than kerosene with disastrous results. The heater should not be placed in doorways or hallways and should be located at least three feet away from anything that could catch on fire. Make sure that it is stable and will not tip over. It is also a good idea to maintain a screen around the heater to avoid accidental burns, especially to children. The room in which the heater is located should be properly ventilated with fresh air coming in from the outside. Before moving a kerosene heater it should first be turned off and it should also be off while it is being filled. Always fill the heater outside in case a spill should occur. Do not fill the tank above the full mark since that space is needed for fuel expansion during operation. If the tank is too full, the kerosene can overflow. Each time the tank is filled, check the wick to make sure that it is clean and in good operating condition. If a heater should flare up during operation, do not attempt to move it. That can spread the fire. First, attempt to shut the heater off using a manual shut off switch. If necessary call 911. Also have a fire extinguisher available that is rated for flammable liquids.

Electric space heaters

Space heaters are often used in church or school offices during the winter months to supplement the main heating system. Any church or school that uses electric space heaters should consider the following precautions. First, make sure that any portable space heater that you buy or use has been inspected and evaluated for safety from Underwriters Laboratories (the UL mark will be present on such heaters). Do not use electric space heaters near water, such as in a bathroom, break room, or kitchen, unless the manufacturer intends it for such use. Space heaters should be keep at least three feet away from combustible materials. Make sure they are not near curtains or paper that may be stored on the floor. When not in use, the space heater should be turned off and unplugged. For example, make sure they are turned off before leaving the church or school facilities at the end of the day. Since many space heaters use a thermostat, it becomes easy to forget that they are even turned on if they are not operating when it is time to leave for the day. They should never be left unattended for any extended period. Preferably, extension cords should not be used with space heaters. If one is used, make sure it corresponds to the necessary wire gauge size of your heater. Never use a damaged cord that is frayed, has loose connections, or has exposed wiring. Finally, fires are more likely to result when space heaters are used for purposes for which they are not intended. For example, do not use a space heater to dry wet clothes or shoes or to thaw frozen pipes. While space heaters can supplement a heating system, they are not intended to replace it.

Wood burning stoves

Some churches use wood burning stoves. The use, design, and installation of wood burning stoves have significantly improved over the years. Yet, wood burning stoves still require special attention. First, wood burning stoves require professional installation. Do not leave the installation to a volunteer. Connections must be secure, the chimney liner must be properly installed (and maintained), and proper attention must be given to other details such as the hearth, gaskets, doors, and the flue. Second, not all wood burning systems are the same, and different systems require specialized knowledge and expertise, both in terms of installation as well as in use. Once the system is installed, a smoke detector and a fire extinguisher should always be installed in the same room with the stove. The Consumer Product Safety Commission recommends that wood burning stoves be inspected twice monthly. Older systems may need to be cleaned as frequently as every three weeks. Creosote builds up in chimney flues and poses a risk of a chimney fire. Professional chimney sweeps should be used to inspect and clean chimneys. A major inspection is best done in the spring, following the heating season. That also provides time to obtain replacement parts that may be needed for repairs. Wood stoves should not be used to burn trash or paper or any other item that can cause the stove to over heat. Green wood should also be avoided. When starting a fire, do not use gasoline or other flammable liquids. In addition, use coal only in compliance with the manufacturer's instructions. When cleaning your stove, use a metal container to collect the ashes. Ashes may contain a live ember that can ignite and should not be disposed off where they can come in contact with combustible material. Finally, always contact your insurance company before installing a wood burning stove. It may affect your premiums.

Boilers

Many churches and schools use boilers to heat their facilities. Boiler accidents can cause serious and expensive damage including the loss of life, but in almost every case, problems can be prevented through simple maintenance. One of the most common and dangerous problems is a defective low water fuel cut-off control. Low water in a boiler can cause overheating and result in permanent damage. If overheating does occur, an explosion can result if the safety value does not adequately release the pressure. Low water can be caused by a variety of factors including something as simple as a blown fuse or a tripped breaker. Every church or school that uses a boiler should have it inspected before the heating season begins. Routine maintenance using certified technicians is vital for the safe operation of this heating system.

Chimneys and flues

Chimneys and flues should be inspected prior to the heating season to make sure they have no cracks or blockage. If your church or school has a fireplace, a professional chimney sweep should be used to remove creosote build-up. Cleaning should occur following the use of three cords of wood.

14.2 Freezing Pipes, Insulation and Heat Tape

Each year churches and schools experience significant losses due to water damage from freezing pipes that burst. Floors become warped, stains appear on walls and ceilings, and carpets become ruined. Sometimes flooding occurs that damages furnishings and electrical equipment. Shut off the water and drain the pipes to buildings that are unoccupied during the winter months (be careful to check for leaks when the water is turned back on again). For all other cases, water pipes that are exposed to cold temperatures such as those in crawl spaces or attics should be properly insulated. Also, know where to shut off the water valves if a break should occur. If a pipe should freeze, open all faucets, remove the insulation and wrap the pipe in rags. Then thaw it by pouring hot water over the frozen pipe. Never try to thaw pipes using a blow torch or a space heater. Sometimes churches and schools use electric heat tapes to prevent water pipes from freezing. While heat tapes can reduce the risk of pipes bursting, they can also pose a fire hazard, and are a source of possible ignition. To reduce this risk use only certified heat tapes recognized by Underwriters Laboratories (UL), the Canadian Standards Association (CSA) or Factory Mutual Research Company (FMRC). The Consumer Product Safety Commission offers the following tips concerning purchasing, installing, and maintaining heat tapes:[1]

- Replace uncertified heat tapes more than 3 years old with new heat tapes certified to meet recognized voluntary standards. All new heat tapes will have a 3-prong plug.

- Always plug the 3-prong plug into a 3-prong outlet to make sure the heat tape is grounded.

---

[1]*New Electric Heat Tapes Help Prevent Fires: Safety Alert*, Consumer Product Safety Commission, Document #5045, <www.cpsc.gov/cpscpub/pubs/5045.html>.

- Use a ground-fault circuit-interrupter (GFCI) wherever heat tapes are plugged in.

- Do not wrap heat tape over itself unless specifically permitted in the manufacturer's instructions.

- Apply heat tapes directly on the pipe to be protected, never on top of the insulation covering the pipe.

- Do not cover the heat tape with insulation unless advised by the manufacturer. Use nonflammable insulation such as fiber glass. Do not use foam or vinyl insulation that could catch fire from a failing heat tape.

- Keep the end-cap sealed and off the ground to prevent water from getting in. Moisture can lead to a fire.

- Do not use heat tapes designed for water pipes on gutters, driveways, or fuel lines.

- If a heat tape has a thermostat, check instructions to see if the thermostat should be placed against the pipe and covered with insulation or if it should be left hanging and uncovered.

- Inspect heat tapes each year and replace them if you notice signs of deterioration. Look for discolored surfaces (especially at the plug), charring, cuts or breaks in the insulation, or bare wires.

- Check installation instructions when you change types or brands of heat tape because different heat tapes have different installation requirements.

14.3 Snow and Ice Buildup

Church and school roofs face the greatest problem from snow and ice buildup. Snow and ice can stay on a roof for days, melting and freezing, weakening shingles and creating water problems that can result in serious damage. Plus, heavy snow buildup can put great stress on a roof. The first strategy to combat snow and ice buildup begins in the fall. Clean the gutters and make sure that all drains are free of debris. If any roof leaks exist, see that they are repaired. Evaluate the strength of your roof to support a heavy snow load. Once snow and ice buildup occur, the main strategy is to remove it. To help this process occur naturally, once again, make sure the drains and gutters are clean and free of debris. It may be necessary to clear a path on the roof to help the snow melt and drain properly. At times, the snow buildup can be so great that it becomes necessary to remove it from the roof. Such removal is hard work and physically strenuous, and it can be very dangerous. When such occasions arise, a professional should be hired who has the experience and equipment to do the job properly. Request a certificate of insurance to make sure any individual or company that does such work is fully covered.

Hills and mounds of snow created from plowing church or school parking lots can also create visibility problems. Slick driving conditions accompanied by poor visibility and glare can lead to accidents. Educate and remind employees, staff, church members, and students to take extra precautions while driving and walking in the parking lot when such conditions arise. Mounds of snow attract children who use them to play on and to slide down. These children can become invisible to a driver and the risk of an accident is higher in such situations.

14.4 Slips and Falls

Slips and falls reach their peak during the winter months due to slick sidewalks and stairs. Make sure that outdoor handrails are clear of ice buildup. Clear sidewalks of snow and ice and use salt to help ice from forming (or to melt) and sand to provide traction. Create a team within the church or school to respond to slick conditions. Have someone inspect all sidewalks and outdoor stairs prior to any meeting, and to take the necessary measures to make sidewalks and stairs safe to use. When necessary use warning signs to help people identify slippery conditions or actually close off an area if it is unsafe. Keep an adequate supply of sand and salt on hand during the winter months to respond to the needs of your area. Since elderly people are more vulnerable to slips and falls, provide escort services to members of the church who may require special assistance.

14.5 Cold Weather Exposure and Harm to Humans

While cold weather poses many risks to church and school property, it also poses risks to human beings. Churches and schools need to develop cold weather policies that address concerns related to exposure to cold weather for staff members, students, and for church members. Advance planning is needed concerning the cancellation of services or school, guidelines for outdoor activities, and use of vehicles.

Outdoor activities

Church and school leaders should remain alert to three potential health risks that surface during cold weather: (1) overexertion, (2) frostbite, and (3) hypothermia. In particular, special attention should be given to those at higher risk including the elderly, those who already have health problems, and to children.

Overexertion

Overexertion can occur in many ways, but two of the more common ones in the winter are from shoveling snow and from pushing stalled or stuck cars. Any employee or volunteer who shovels snow should be in good physical shape and use to physical exertion. Shoveling snow can be a life-threatening activity for those at risk for a stroke or heart attack. Breathing cold air causes some blood vessels to constrict. At the same time, the loss of body heat, combined with the strenuous physical activity, causes the heart to work harder as it must pump blood through more narrow arteries. Shortness of breath, chest pain, or tightness in the chest are all warning signs. If they occur, the person should immediately stop and seek help. In addition to putting strain on the heart, shoveling snow can also cause back problems. Train those who shovel snow to lift with their leg muscles and not with their back. A wet shovel full of snow can weigh eight or more pounds. Before shoveling, stretching exercises should be done. Some basic guidelines to reduce risks associated with shoveling snow include the following:

- Work in pairs—it reduces the workload and provides someone who can seek help if a problem should arise.

- Pace yourself and take frequent rest breaks.

- Only use people who engage in regular exercise. Do not use anyone who is at risk for a heart attack or stroke, or who has back problems.

- Do not shovel snow on a full stomach. Wait at least one hour to begin work after eating a meal, or shovel before eating.
- Use a snow blower or hire a snow removal service.

Snow blowers

According to the Consumer Product Safety Commission, snow blowers are the fourth leading cause of finger amputations, and that in a typical year, over 5,000 people go to hospital emergency rooms with injuries sustained from using a snow blower. The main cause of finger amputations is attempting to clear the auger or discharge chute with one's hands. The heavier and more wet the snow, the more likely the snow blower will become clogged. The engine should always be turned off prior to unclogging the machine, and clear instructions should be given to keep hands and feet away from all moving parts. Hands should never be used to clean the machine even if it is turned off. Avoid wearing loose fitting clothing, such as a scarf, that might get caught in the machine. Snow blowers with gasoline engines also pose a threat of carbon monoxide poisoning. A machine should never be left running in an enclosed area or left unattended while the engine is on. Start the machine outside and do not add gas to a running or hot engine. Some machines are electric. Careful attention must be maintained at all times while using an electric snow blower to keep the power cord away from all moving parts of the machine.

Frostbite and hypothermia

In addition to overexertion, frostbite and hypothermia also pose health risks. Many churches and schools sponsor outdoor activities such as ski trips during the winter months, especially for youth. Scouting troops often go on winter campouts. Guidelines should be established that dictate when outdoor activities should be suspended based upon the forecast, temperature and wind chill factors. For example, a *winter storm watch* indicates severe winter conditions are possible within the next 48 hours. A *winter storm warning* means that severe winter conditions have begun or are about to begin very soon.

Provide individuals who participant in outdoor activities during cold weather, or employees who must work outside, guidance on how to dress. Recommend multiple layers of loose fitting cotton or wool clothing with an outside layer that is water repellent and wind resistant. Layers can be removed as needed to prevent perspiration or chill. Since the head and neck lose body heat faster than any other part of the body, it is important to keep them covered, preferably with a hood, or with a hat and scarf. Generally, mittens provide greater warmth than gloves, and woolen socks are also a good choice. Train leaders and employees to be on the alert for signs of frostbite or hypothermia. The cheeks, ears, and nose are especially vulnerable to frostbite. Symptoms of frostbite include a loss of feeling and a pale or white appearance in the fingers, toes, ears, cheeks, or nose. Hypothermia occurs when the body temperature drops too low. Any person with a temperature below 95 degrees (F) needs immediate medical help. Symptoms of hypothermia include uncontrollable shivering, slow speech, memory lapses, stumbling, drowsiness, and exhaustion. Wet clothing should be changed to avoid the loss of body heat. If a person develops hypothermia, warm the trunk of the body first, followed by the arms and legs. Remove any clothing that could restrict blood flow. Wrap the person in a blanket and avoid giving caffeine (coffee or tea), alcohol, drugs, hot beverages, or food. The best choice is warm broth. Caffeine is a stimulant and can cause the heart to beat too fast while alcohol is a depressant and can cause the heart to beat too slow. Either one can accelerate the impact of cold on the body. For frostbite, apply a gentle, steady pressure with a warm hand, but DO NOT rub or massage. Hold the frostbitten area against a warm body and gently breathe warm air on it. DO NOT rub the area, apply snow, or thrust the area into hot or cold water. If the injured parts of the body are immersed in warm water, the water should be between 102 and 106 degrees (F). If the water is too hot or too cold it can cause additional damage. A thermometer must be used to monitor the water temperature. For either hypothermia or frostbite, seek medical attention as soon as possible.

Transportation safety

Winter driving poses increased risks. Icy and snow packed roads can be killers. Individuals who regularly drive church or school vehicles during cold weather should receive specialized driver's training. Others who volunteer or who drive on a limited basis should follow a written checklist and understand church or school policies on how to respond to an emergency. Before departing, examine the vehicle, fluid levels (oil, antifreeze, windshield washer), tires, and check to see that all emergency equipment is accounted for (see below). Make sure the spare tire is in good repair and that a jack is present. It is also a good idea to have a portable 12 volt air pump as well as a spare set of keys which are kept by a second person. As a standard policy, vehicles should be properly serviced prior to a trip and always begin with a full tank of gas both coming and going. Fill up with gas as soon as you arrive at your destination to avoid ice in the tank. If more than one vehicle is being used for the trip, stay in visible contact with one another once you are on the road. Obtain a weather report before departing. Schedule driving during daylight hours and use major roads. Don't try to save time by using secondary roads. Have a designated person to contact if a problem should arise. Drivers should wear sunglasses to cut down on glare. Conditions can become hazardous rapidly, and all vehicles should have equipment such as blankets, flashlight with fully charged batteries, a cell phone, shovel, windshield scraper and brush, flares, water proof matches, tool kit, booster cables, tow-line, a knife, bag of sand, portable radio, a red distress flag, maps, and emergency rations. It is best to create an emergency kit in a sturdy, easy to carry container that contains most of these items. If driving conditions become so hazardous that it is unsafe to continue, or if the vehicle becomes disabled, pull off the road to the safest location possible. Turn on the flashing hazard lights, and set up flares and other warning markers. Place the distress flag on the antenna or hang it out the window. Remain in the vehicle and wait for help unless a building is clearly visible and which you can reach safely on foot. Use your cell phone to call 911. Do not wander off in extremely cold weather or in a snowstorm. While waiting in the vehicle, drivers must stay alert to the possibility of carbon monoxide poisoning if the engine is left running to generate heat. Generally, the engine should run about 10 minutes per hour. Keep a window slightly cracked while the engine is running to get a fresh supply of air, and make sure the tail pipe does not become clogged with snow. If the wind is blowing, make sure that the exhaust is not blowing into the vehicle. Exercise to stay warm. At least one person should stay awake at all times.

Cancellation of church services or of school

Heavy snow, ice storms, or extreme temperatures can cause the cancellation of church services or school. Most schools have a plan in place to respond to the cancellation of school. Few churches do. Churches need established guidelines concerning when to cancel services due to inclement weather. While a few inches of snow may mean nothing in some parts of the country, in others it can shut down entire communities. Having guidelines in place concerning wind chill factors, snow totals, and freezing rain can assist church leaders to act promptly and decisively when bad weather hits. Part of the problem that most congregations face is communicating such decisions to congregational members. Today, voice mail systems and the Internet provide new and powerful ways to communicate such decisions to congregational members directly and efficiently. Members can call the church and get a message or visit the church's web site for updated information that can be easily modified from almost any location. Make arrangements in advance with local media outlets to announce your cancellation.

Summary

Cold weather poses increased risks to churches and schools in at least five ways: (1) damage that can arise from heating systems; (2) freezing pipes; (3) structural damage from snow build-up; (4) icy conditions that cause slips and falls; and (5) potential harm to humans exposed to the cold.

Heating systems pose numerous risks ranging from fire to carbon monoxide poisoning. All heating systems including gas and fuel burning appliances and stoves, electric space heaters, and boilers need regular inspections and routine maintenance. All chimneys and flues should be professionally cleaned. An annual contract with a heating and air conditioning company is one of the best ways to keep equipment properly serviced. Carbon monoxide detectors should be used with heating systems that burn fossil fuels (e.g., wood, oil, kerosene, propane, natural gas, pressed woodchip logs).

Freezing pipes should never be thawed using a blowtorch or a space heater. Hot water should be poured over the freezing pipe. Use only certified heat tape to protect pipes from freezing.

Snow and ice build-up can cause structural damage, especially to roofs. Churches and schools should have roofs and gutters cleaned every fall to remove leaves and debris. If an outside company is used to remove snow from the roof, obtain a certificate of insurance to make sure that any individual or company that does the work is fully covered.

Keep all sidewalks, stairs, and handrails free from ice and snow. Inspect all walkways prior to church services or the beginning of school. Use warning signs to notify people of unsafe conditions.

Cold weather poses direct risks to humans. Churches and schools should take steps to minimize the potential of overexertion, frostbite, or hypothermia. Shoveling snow and pushing stuck cars can lead to overexertion. If a snow blower is used, clear procedures should be followed to unclog it from packed snow to avoid the amputation of fingers.

Churches and schools often sponsor winter trips for youth, and may have employees who work outside in cold weather. Special care should be taken to avoid hypothermia and frostbite. Guidelines should be provided on how to dress for cold weather using multiple layers of loose fitting cotton or wool clothing. The head and neck lose heat faster than any other part of the body so a hat and scarf or hood is recommended. If signs of hypothermia or frostbite occur, medical help should be sought immediately.

Winter weather also increases driving risks. Churches and schools that sponsor winter trips should use a written checklist for the driver and vehicle and have an emergency plan in place if a problem should occur.

The next chapter examines how churches and schools can reduce risks associated with natural disasters and severe weather.

Additional Resources on the Internet

For additional information on reducing risks associated with cold weather, review the material found on the following web sites. Also, several publications are listed that are available from Consumer Product Safety Commission. These resources were used in the preparation of this chapter.

"Annual Fire Statistics." Consumer Product Safety Review / Spring 1997.

"Carbon Monoxide (or CO) Kills!" Michigan State University Extension. <http://www.orcbs.msu.edu/AWARE/safetynews/octnov95.html>.

"Carbon Monoxide Detectors Can Save Lives CPSC Document #5010." Consumer Product Safety Commission. <http://www.cpsc.gov/cpscpub/pubs/5010.html>.

"Carbon Monoxide Fact Sheet CPSC Document #4466." Consumer Product Safety Commission. <http://www.cpsc.gov/cpscpub/pubs/466.html>.

"CPSC and NKHA Stress Kerosene Heater Safety CPSC Document #5052." Consumer Product Safety Commission. <http://www.cpsc.gov/cpscpub/pubs/5052.html>.

"CPSC Warns of Carbon Monoxide Poisoning with Camping Equipment CPSC Document #5008." Consumer Product Safety Commission. <http://www.cpsc.gov/cpscpub/pubs/5008.html>.

"Dangers of Burning Charcoal Indoors." Consumer Product Safety Review / Summer 1996.

"Dangers of Carbon Monoxide." Consumer Product Safety Review / Winter 1997.

"Fact Sheet: Winter Storms." Federal Emergency Management Agency. http://166.112.200.140/library/stormsf.htm>.

"Fire Safety Tips." Office of the Illinois State Fire Marshall. <http://ww.state.il.us/osfm/fst.htm>.

"Gas & Fuel-Burning Appliances." Consumer Product Safety Review, Fall 1997, Vol. 2 No. 2.

"Heating Boiler Safety." <http://www.freenet.edmonton.ab.ca/absa/boilsafe.html>.

"Heating Tape Hazard." U.S. Department of Transportation U.S. Coast Guard. <http://www.uscg.mil/hq/g-m/moa/docs/sa0296.htm>.

"Home Fire-Safety Alert Check Chimneys and Smoke Detectors." Emergency Management Branch, Division of Public Safety, Office of Research Services, Public Safety News - Issue 98-23, November 1998. <http://www.nih.gov/od/ors/newsltrs/psn/psn98-23.htm>.

"Home Heating Safety." Virtual Children's Hospital of Iowa. <http.www.vh.org/Patients/IHB/Peds/Safety/SpaceHeaters.html>.

"Installation Safety." National Resources Canada. <http://www.nrcan.gc.ca/es/erb/reed/wood/05_e.html>.

"Maintaining Your Wood Heating System." National Resources Canada. <http://www.nrcan.gc.ca/es/erb/reed/wood/13_e.html>.

"New Electric Heat Tapes Help Prevent Fires: Safety Alert CPSC Document #5045." Consumer Product Safety Commission. <http://www.cpsc.gov/cpscpub/pubs/5045.html>.

"Reducing Injuries from Multi-Purpose Lighters." Consumer Product Safety Review / Winter 1997.

"Safety Tips for Winter Storms." <http://www.coastalnet.com/weather/nwsmhx/wntrsafe.htm>.

"Safety: Fires - Disaster Services." American Red Cross. <http://www.redcross.org/disaster/safety/resfires.html>.

"Snow Shoveling With Care." Mayo Clinic Health Letter, February 18, 1997. <http://www.mayohealth.org/mayo/ptrd/htm/snow_sh2.htm>.

"Snow Thrower Safety Alert CPSC Document #5117." Consumer Product Safety Commission. <http://www.cpsc.gov/cpscpub/pubs/5117.html>.

"Surviving the Cold Weather." National Safety Council. <http://www.nsc.org/lrs/lib/fs/health/cold.htm>.

"Tips to Help Make Winter Safer." Ohio Department of Health. <www.odh.state.oh.us/headlines/headline-5.htm>.

"UL Reminds Consumers to Use Space Heaters Safely This Heating Season." Underwriters Laboratories Inc. January 13, 1998. <http://www.ul.com/about/newsrel/heater.htm>.

"Winter Preparedness Safety Tips." Federal Emergency Management Agency. <http://www.fema.gov/library/wntsft.htm>.

"Winter Safety Tips for School Staff, #9042." University of Maine, Cooperative Expension. <http://www.umext.maine.edu/emergency/9042.htm>.

"Winter Storms...the Deceptive Killers." U.S. Department of Commerce. <http://www.nws.noaa.gov/om/wntrstm.htm>.

Tatnall, Holly. "Cold Weather Safety." Colorado State University Cooperative Extension 4-H Youth/Consumer & Family Education, Eagle County, November 1997.
<http://www.colostate.edu/Depts/CoopExt/PUBS/COLUMNHA/ha9711.htm>.

CHAPTER 15. REDUCING RISKS FROM NATURAL PERILS

Natural perils pose a threat to every church and school, but perils differ significantly in both frequency and severity. Following the general principle on evaluating risks, church and school leaders need to take into account both frequency and severity for any given risk. For example, a congregation in Oklahoma does not need to worry about a class 4 hurricane, but it must be concerned about a tornado. Even then, while the odds of being hit by a tornado are small, the possibility is significant enough and the severity is so high that every church and school needs protection from that risk. A school in Miami, Florida does not have to worry about snow on the roof, but it may have a problem with mold. Whether or not the mold is a serious risk or simply an irritation depends on many factors. Each risk is unique and requires independent analysis and evaluation.

A comprehensive list of natural perils to church and school property would be quite extensive. Our purpose here is not to identify and discuss every risk, but rather to review general risk management strategies that can be used to prevent or control property losses, and to apply those strategies to the most significant property risks facing churches and schools today. Attention is given to earthquakes, floods, tornadoes, hurricanes, landslides, and thunderstorms. These reflect the most substantive risks facing the typical congregation or school today with respect to natural perils that pose risks to property. A section also is devoted to volcanoes, which affect states along the West Coast, including Alaska.

15.1 Earthquakes

Unlike hurricanes, earthquakes cannot be predicted in advance. They can strike at any time with devastating results. Churches and schools located in earthquake zones can take measures with respect to both loss prevention and loss control.

Loss prevention measures

Today, construction technology has helped to make buildings in earthquake zones safer and more secure. Churches and schools at risk for earthquakes should have their facilities inspected, and make whatever modifications feasible to enhance the structural integrity of the buildings. Find out if your community has established seismic building standards. The Federal Emergency Management Agency recommends the following precautions with respect to facilities:[1]

- Shelves should be fastened securely to the wall.
- Avoid mounting items to walls such as mirrors and large pictures directly over places where people sit. Check offices, reception areas, classrooms, parlors, and libraries for potential hazards.
- Make sure that hanging overhead light fixtures are properly secured.
- Have electrical wiring and all gas connections inspected. If an earthquake should occur, faulty wiring or gas leaks can create fires or explosions.
- Water heaters should be strapped to the wall studs and bolted to the floor.

---

[1] <http://www.fema.gov/library/quakef.htm>.

- Examine the foundation for cracks and defects. See that needed repairs are made.

- Store flammable liquids and pesticides in sturdy and secured located cabinets, preferably on the bottom self. Check to see that all containers are tightly sealed.

Training also plays an important role to minimize losses when responding to an earthquake. Churches and schools located in earthquake zones should have a written emergency plan on what to do if an earthquake should occur. Staff members, employees, congregational members, and students should receive periodic training and instruction on how to respond if an earthquake should occur. A person's natural instincts may lead them to make bad decisions in a moment of crisis. It is better to have a plan in place that is understood by everyone affected. The Federal Emergency Management Agency recommends the following procedures in preparing a response plan:

- Identify the safe places inside church or school facilities. Examine every room. The safest places include under sturdy furniture such as a pew, heavy table, or desk; against an inside support wall; and away from items such as glass or mirrors that could shatter, or from furnishings that could tip over and fall on someone.

- Identify safe places outside the church or school facilities. These include the most open places that are away from buildings, telephone poles, power lines, and trees.

Every school teacher, Sunday School teacher, church leader, employee, and volunteer should know where to go and where to lead others if an earthquake should occur, including if they are driving a church or school vehicle. Leaders should provide periodic instructions concerning the response plan to congregation members. Articles should be included in the church newsletter and bulletin. The church and school should store emergency first aid supplies including bandages and antibacterial ointment. In addition, churches and schools should form and train an emergency team to respond if an earthquake should occur. Their duties are part of the overall crisis management strategy (see chapter 4).

Loss control measures

If an earthquake should occur during a church or school activity, leaders and members must be prepared to act quickly at a time when confusion will reign. If adequate preparation and training have occurred, losses can be reduced. The Federal Emergency Management Agency recommends the following procedures during an earthquake:

- If you are inside church or school facilities while shaking occurs, do not attempt to flee the building. Move immediately to a safe place (which has been previously identified as part of the response plan). People who try to get outside are at risk from falling objects.

- If you are outside church or school facilities, immediately move to an open area and stay there until the shaking stops.

- If you are driving a church or school vehicle, immediately stop and pull over to an open area. Have all passengers remain in the vehicle. Once the shaking stops proceed with caution and avoid bridges and ramps until they have been inspected.

Once the earthquake is over, the response team should go into immediate action. The following steps should be taken:

- Implement the church's or school's shutdown procedures (see Appendix 4D at the end of chapter 4). Have someone designated to shut off gas and power until a proper inspection of gas lines and electrical wiring occurs. A gas leak or electrical problems pose risks of fires and explosions.

- Provide immediate assistance to trapped or injured persons. Call 911 for help. Do not move seriously injured people unless other risks pose greater harm to them. Apply whatever first aid you can.

- Keep people away from damaged buildings. After shocks are normal and can cause additional damage, especially if a building has already sustained structural damage.

- Cleanup any spills of flammable liquids, but stay out of any building in which you smell fumes of gases.

- Items stored in cabinets, closets, and cupboards may fall out when the doors are opened. Be careful.

- Inspect all chimneys before igniting any fires. Any structural damage could result in a fire.

15.2 Floods

Floods are the number one weather-related killer in the United States and they also cause severe property damage to churches and schools. In 1990, 4 inches of rain fell in less than 2 hours in Shadyside, Ohio creating a 30-foot high wall of water leaving 26 people dead, and between $6-8 million in damages. Just a year later, 15 people died in Texas from flooding caused by 17 inches of rain over a two month period resulting in damages of $100 million. In 1999, flooding caused from two hurricanes in less than a 30 day period ravaged North Carolina leaving dozens dead and over a billion dollars in damages.

Floods can occur anywhere in the United States and with little warning. Different areas of the country, however, do face different levels and types of risks. Most floods are caused by slow moving thunderstorms, repeated rain storms, or heavy rains from hurricanes. Often rivers overflow and dams may break releasing additional torrents of water. Floods can also cause mudslides. Flood insurance is not included in a standard insurance policy, but flood insurance is available through government sponsored programs. Contact your insurance agent and ask about the National Flood Insurance Program.

As with all disasters, the church or school should have a disaster response team that takes the initiative for both loss prevention and loss control measures.

A congregation or school that has considered the possibility of a flood in advance, and has a plan in place to reduce risks prior to and after a flood will be in a better position to recover than one that has done no preparation at all.

Loss prevention measures

Every church or school can take some simple measures before a flood occurs to reduce potential losses, both to people and to property. Start by assessing your flood risk. Contact your local office of the Red Cross or the National Weather Service and ask for information about the risk of floods in your area. If your church or school is located in a high risk area, be prepared in advance by stockpiling certain emergency supplies and materials such as sandbags, rolls of plastic sheeting, plywood, hammers, nails, and shovels. During flooding, water can backup into church or school buildings through drains. Have valves installed in all drains to prevent backup. It is also a good idea to stockpile plugs that can be inserted into the drains as an additional safety measure to prevent water from backing up from sewer lines. Take precautions to protect electrical and mechanical equipment, providing permanent locations that are as high off the ground as feasible. It is best to install ground-fault circuit-interrupters (GFCI) to reduce the risk of electrical shock. Landscape church or school property to redirect water away from the buildings. However, if you redirect water to adjacent property and it causes damage, your church or school may be liable. Have a plan to use sandbags to protect entrances to church or school facilities, as well as for critical rooms inside the facilities. If a flood warning occurs and time permits, move valuable property to upper floors. Second, have both an evacuation plan and a shut down plan in place for your church or school. Third, make sure you have an appropriate level of insurance coverage.

One part of the church's crisis management plan should be to care for vulnerable members of the congregation such as the elderly who live alone and do not have family members to help them during times of crisis. Maintain a list of individuals who will need crisis assistance. Have designated volunteers assigned to each vulnerable person who will see to their safety and personal needs. Have them collect medications, prescriptions, and any other medical supplies or equipment that the person may need if an evacuation should occur.

Loss control measures

If you live in a flood prone area, or if a flood should occur, a number of steps should be taken to control potential losses. Be extremely carefully about electrical hazards and flammable materials. Do not enter any building that has standing water around it. The combination of standing water and electricity can be deadly. If you suspect that electrical problems exist, turn off the main breaker and contact an electrician. If a puddle of water is around the main fuse box or circuit breaker, do not attempt to reach it. Leave the job to an electrician. In addition, flammable liquids such as kerosene, gasoline, or oil may be present as well as gas vapors that can ignite and create explosions or fires. Fire hazards include leaking gas, flooded electrical circuits, submerged appliances, and flammable materials, some of which may enter the church or school through the flood waters coming from upstream. Do not use a lantern, blow torch or matches when returning to inspect or repair any flooded building until you know it is safe to enter. When you do enter, use a flashlight. If you smell the odor of gas, turn off the gas valve if possible and leave immediately. Call the gas company from a nearby residence or business. Do not re-enter the building until you have received clearance from the gas company.

The cleanup following a flood is a major task with inherent dangers. Examine the structure of the church or school building including the foundation, walls, floors, and windows. Look for cracks or other signs that damage has occurred. A flooded building can collapse. Also keep an eye open for animals and snakes that may have entered the building during the flood. Do not use bare hands to sort through debris. Use a stick, shovel or rake. Also, watch your step to avoid exposed nails and other sharp objects. Wear shoes with thick soles. Throw away all food from the church or school kitchen that has come in contact with flood waters. If the church or school has a well, have the water tested before it is used. Also, do not drink city tap water until you receive notice that it is safe to do so. Begin the clean-up process as soon as it is safe and feasible to do so. Initiate whatever salvage operations that are possible and document all of your losses in writing and with photographs. Make sure that electrical equipment such as furnaces, freezers, refrigerators and other appliances get a chance to dry thoroughly before they are used. All electrical appliances that have been exposed to water should be inspected and tested by a qualified technician. If you vacuum water from the floor using a wet-dry cleaner, carefully read the manufacturer's instructions. Make sure that it is properly grounded and use a vacuum with a ground-fault circuit-interrupter (portable GFCIs are available which you can plug directly into an outlet). Check to see that smoke and carbon monoxide detectors are working properly. Any furnishing that has been covered with water is a possible source of bacterial contamination. Such items, including carpeting, must either be thrown out or steam cleaned, sanitized, and dried. Water damaged furnishings from a church nursery should be replaced to avoid any risk to children. In addition, wet insulation must also be replaced since it can harbor biological pollutants. Floods can bring down trees and cause considerable damage to the church's or school's landscaping. The use of chain saws can be extremely hazardous. Permit only experienced individuals to use chain saws on church or school property while assisting with the cleanup.

Far more important than property losses are the human losses that occur in a flood. Flood victims will experience anger, fear, depression, and potential economic losses. Part of the survival mission of the church in a time of crisis is to minister to the needs of its members. These will include base needs of food, shelter, and clothing, to emotional, psychological, and spiritual needs necessary to cope with the losses that have occurred. Many people will have no insurance and the economic losses can be overwhelming. Church leaders should recognize that following a flood, church income is likely to decline at a time when financial needs will increase, both for the church as well as for its members. At best, insurance may pay for part of the losses and the church will likely be dependent upon contributions, often from other congregations outside of the flooded area, and sometimes from across the country. At this time, implement your communication plan to stay in touch with both your congregational members as well as other congregations that can provide important support during a time of crisis. Many congregational members may be facing their own personal disasters and a coordinated relief effort will be needed. Different age groups will reflect different needs, both emotionally and physically. It is likely that alternative facilities will be needed for meetings. These facilities should have been identified in advance as part of a written disaster strategy (see chapter 4). Recognize that recovery is an ongoing process that takes time, often years, before the impact of a flood recedes.

Church or school vehicles and floods

Unfortunately, many people who die in floods are attempting to cross rising water in an automobile. In these cases, poor judgment leads to tragic results. Drivers of church or school vehicles should have clear and unequivocal instructions never to drive across roads with moving water during flood conditions. The car can easily stall and be swept away in a matter of seconds even in what appears to be shallow water. According to the National Oceanic and Atmospheric Administration, the typical momentum of water flowing downstream creates 500 lbs. of lateral force for each foot the water rises. Simultaneously, for each foot the water increase, a car displaces 1,500 lbs. of water, with the effect that the car is 1,500 lbs. lighter. The combination of the lateral force of the water and the buoyancy of the car means that two feet of water will carry away most automobiles. Similarly, 6 inches of water can sweep people off from their feet.

15.3 Tornadoes

Most tornadoes occur in the spring and summer months, although they can occur anytime and anywhere. In a typical year, over 800 tornadoes occur in the United States resulting in over 1,500 injuries and 80 deaths.[2] Most tornadoes occur east of the Rocky Mountains. Often they are associated with thunderstorms and occasionally accompany tropical storms and hurricanes that move over land. The peak time for tornadoes in the southern states is from March through May. For the northern states it is during the summer months. While a tornado can occur at anytime of day, they are most likely to occur between 3 P.M. and 9 P.M. Typically they move from southwest to northeast, but they can move in any direction. The average speed is 30 mph, but they can be stationary and have been known to travel at 70 mph.

If conditions are favorable for a tornado, the national weather service issues a *tornado watch*. A tornado watch means that tornadoes are possible in your area. A *tornado warning* means that a tornado has been sighted or indicated by weather radar. Watch for a dark, often greenish sky. A "wall cloud," large hail, or a loud roar are additional signs of a tornado. Some tornadoes are visible as a funnel cloud, but others are obscured by rain or clouds. Once a warning has been issued, if the sky becomes threatening or other clues appear, shelter should be sought immediately. Sometimes the air becomes very still before a tornado hits. Sunlit skies may actually appear behind the tornado. Floods, hail, and strong winds can cause severe and life threatening damage.

About 70 percent of tornadoes have wind speeds of less than 110 mph and last from 1 to 10 minutes. These are considered weak tornadoes and account for less than 5 percent of tornado deaths. Nearly 30 percent of tornado deaths come from strong tornadoes with winds between 110 to 205 mph. About 29 percent of all tornadoes fall into this category. These tornadoes may last 20 minutes or longer.

---

[2] Tornadoes....Nature's Most Violent Storms, National Oceanic and Atmospheric Administration, <http://www.nws.noaa.gov/om/tornado.htm>.

Violent tornadoes have wind speeds in excess of 205 mph and can last over one hour. While violent tornadoes account for only 2 percent of all tornadoes, they cause about 70 percent of tornado deaths. Flying debris from tornadoes causes most of the deaths and injuries. The Fujita-Pearson Tornado Scale is used to classify tornadoes according to wind speed.

The Fujita-Pearson Tornado Scale

F-0 (Gale tornado)	40-72 mph wind	Chimney damage, tree branches broken
F-1 (Moderate tornado)	73-112 mph wind	Mobile homes pushed off foundation or overturned
F-2 (Significant tornado)	113-157 mph wind	Considerable damage, mobile homes demolished, tress uprooted
F-3 (Severe tornado)	158-206 mph wind	Roofs and walls torn down, trains overturned, cars thrown
F-4 (Devastating tornado)	207-260 mph wind	Well-constructed houses leveled, large missiles generated
F-5 (Incredible tornado)	261-318 mph wind	Homes lifted off foundation and carried considerable distances

Loss prevention measures

Churches and schools can take several steps to enhance safety prior to a tornado. The first step is to have a tornado response plan for when school or church is in session, and also to have a plan for outdoor activities. Both churches and schools should practice tornado drills. Monitor weather reports. All schools and church offices should maintain a NOAA Weather Radio. The National Weather Service continuously broadcasts updated weather warnings. Many weather radios broadcast a tone which indicates that a warning or watch has been issued.

If a warning is issued and threatening weather is approaching, take shelter in a pre-designated safe location. Underground shelters are the best choice, but if one is not available, move to an interior hallway or room on the lowest floor and get under a sturdy piece of furniture. Stay away from the corners of the room since they tend to attract debris. Do not be directly under a room on the floor above in which heavy items are stored such as a piano. Stay away from windows. Flying debris can cause serious injuries. If possible, protect your head and body with a coat.

A school should have a registered engineer or architect inspect school facilities and designate tornado shelter areas. A school should have a compressed air horn or megaphone to activate an alarm in case electrical power goes off. If a warning occurs near the time of normal dismissal, keep the children at the school. Being on a bus is not safe. Keep children away from cafeterias, gymnasiums, theaters, indoor swimming pools, or large rooms if severe weather is anticipated. Delay lunches and gym classes if necessary. A church sanctuary is not safe. Tornado-strength winds can cause walls and ceilings to collapse.

Many schools and churches use mobile classrooms. These buildings are not safe during a tornado. Occupants should seek shelter in the main building in designated safe areas.

Automobiles and buses are not safe during a tornado. Do not try to outrun a tornado, but seek shelter inside. If no shelter is available, try to lie flat in a ditch or ravine or the lowest spot available with your arms over your head. Do not get under the vehicle or by a tree. Be alert for the potential of flooding.

Both church and school offices should maintain basic disaster supplies including a flashlight and extra batteries, a portable, battery-operated radio, and first aid kit.

Loss control measures

Once the tornado passes, implement disaster loss control measures. The first task is to protect human life and help any that are injured. One of the goals is to mitigate further damage. Do not enter any damaged building. Shut off gas and power. Do not use matches or any open flames until buildings have been inspected. Immediately clean up any flammable liquids that have spilled. If you smell gas or chemicals, open a window and immediately leave the building. Keep people away from any downed power lines, or broken electrical lines.

15.4 Hurricanes

The hurricane season for the Atlantic, Gulf of Mexico, and the Caribbean begins in June and continues through November. The peak period is from mid-August until late October. The season begins about a month earlier in the eastern Pacific. On average, about six hurricanes form each year in the Atlantic, Gulf of Mexico and Caribbean. According to the National Oceanic and Atmospheric Administration (NOAA), about five hurricanes hit the mainland every three years with two of them being major hurricanes (category 3 or higher)

Hurricanes are classified according to sustained wind speed. The Saffir-Simpson Hurricane scale breaks hurricanes down into five categories with each category reflecting higher levels of potential damage.

Category	Sustained Winds	Damage
1	74-95 mph	Minimal
2	96-110 mph	Moderate
3	111-130 mph	Extensive
4	131-155 mph	Extreme
5	> 155 mph	Catastrophic

Modern technology has greatly enhanced weather forecasting. Today forecasters can monitor and track tropical depressions which, under the proper conditions, can escalate into tropical storms and hurricanes. The ability to provide advance warnings greatly reduces deaths and injuries, and provides people with an opportunity to better protect property as well. Even so, major hurricanes create severe property losses. The damage is the result of storm surges, storm tides, strong winds, heavy rains, flooding, and tornadoes, all of which can result from a hurricane. Over 45 million Americans live in hurricane zones, and these numbers more than double during the summer months as vacationers make their way to coastal areas. These coastal areas experience the greatest loss of life and property damage when hurricanes do occur.

Loss prevention measures

One problem immediately surfaces with respect to loss prevention and hurricanes. It is the perception that hurricanes pose no real danger. This perspective arises when people fail to differentiate a category 1 or 2 hurricane from those that are higher and far more destructive. A hurricane may occur and the news coverage indicates that little damage occurred. People do not evacuate and make it through the storm without a problem. Or they do evacuate and little damage is done. An attitude develops that hurricanes are tolerable—why go through all the inconvenience of vast preparations and relocation when nothing is likely to happen anyway? The vast majority of people who live along the coast have not experienced a major hurricane. A false sense of security can develop that underestimates the severe damage and injuries that can result from a hurricane.

Understand the difference between a *hurricane watch* and a *hurricane warning*. The National Weather Service issues a hurricane watch to indicate the threat of hurricane conditions for a specific area within the next 24-36 hours. A hurricane warning means that hurricane conditions are expected in 24 hours or less. Once a watch is issued, leaders should initiate immediate action to safeguard church or school property. Time must be factored in to allow individuals to take care of their own personal needs as well as those of the church or school. If church or school property is to be protected, action must be initiated early.

For the typical church or school, the primary concern related to hurricanes is property damage. Since advance warnings are now typical, few people will occupy church or school facilities during a hurricane unless the church or school is serving as a hurricane shelter (see below). Leaders can prepare for a hurricane by initiating the following precautions. First, if you live in a hurricane prone region, prepare a written crisis management plan. Prior to each hurricane season, do routine maintenance on facilities. Make sure the roof is in good shape. Repair any leaks and replace shingles as needed. Clean all gutters and downspouts. Maintain a stockpile of emergency supplies such as plywood, rolls of plastic sheeting, hammers, and nails. Trim dead limbs from trees. Pine trees are especially susceptible to breaking or uprooting during hurricanes and can do significant damage if they hit church or school facilities. Consider removing such trees and replacing them with other landscaping choices that do not pose a serious risk. Identify safe evacuation routes. Often, individuals may need to drive a substantial distance to find a shelter, a hotel room, or other housing. A drive that may take 30 minutes or an hour under normal driving conditions may take hours if a full scale evacuation is underway. An early decisive response is the best course of action.

If you have not done so, review your insurance policy with your agent and clearly understand what type of coverage you have if your church or school sustains damage from a hurricane. Have your agent help you to identify the risks you are retaining, and ask if additional coverages are available that may be helpful to you. Remember, floods that are caused by a hurricane are not covered in your regular policy and must be purchased through the National Flood Insurance Program as a separate policy.

If a hurricane watch or warning should occur, initiate a shutdown of church or school facilities. Clear the property of all items that could be blown away by the storm such as outdoor furniture. Fill-up vehicles with gas and, if possible, park them in a garage or in a sheltered location. If the church or school has a freezer, turn it to the coldest setting. Put up storm shutters where feasible or cover windows with plywood. The Federal Emergency Management Association recommends using 1/2 inch marine plywood. The plywood should be cut to fit the windows. Using predrilled holes, the plywood should be installed using screws that are positioned 18 inches apart. Each plywood shutter should be given an identification mark so it can be stored and used in the future for the same window. The shutters should be cut and the holes predrilled as part of a general response strategy. Then if a hurricane should occur, they will be ready to install. If church or school facilities are susceptible to storm surge, take the same precautions that would be used for a flood (see above).

If you are at church or school facilities when a hurricane strikes, make sure that all exterior doors are secured. Turn off the gas and electricity. Take cover in an interior room or basement and close interior doors. Stay away from windows or from objects that could fall on you. Take refuge in a closet or under a table or other protected area. Do not use elevators since they may become stuck if the power suddenly goes off.

One part of the church's crisis management plan should be to care for vulnerable members of the congregation such as the elderly who live alone and do not have family members to help them during times of crisis. Maintain a list of individuals who will need crisis assistance. Have designated volunteers assigned to each vulnerable person who will see to their safety and personal needs. Have them collect medications, prescriptions, and any other medical supplies or equipment that the person may need if an evacuation should occur.

Serving as a shelter

If your church or school has the potential to be used as a shelter, consult with your local county emergency response office on the best way to proceed. Organizations such as the Red Cross can provide assistance and guidance on how to organize and run the shelter. Discuss your plans with your insurance agent.

Loss control measures

As with any natural disaster, the most important concern is to respond first to any personal injuries. Do not move people that have been injured unless they face additional threats. Call 911 for help (since the loss of power often occurs following a hurricane, the church or school should own at least one battery powered, portable phone). Check on the well-being of vulnerable members of the congregation who have remained in their homes. Volunteers should be pre-assigned to do this task.

Water and high winds cause most of the property damage that results from a hurricane. Often trees are down and roofs are damaged. If damage has occurred, it is not always immediately visible. A careful visual inspection should be done of the roof and of the overall structure of the buildings. Take pictures of all damage and immediately notify your insurance company. Avoid any downed power lines and if you smell gas, shut off the main gas supply, open windows, and leave the building immediately. Call the gas company once you have reached a safe location. Check all drains for sewage backup. If damage has occurred, initiate temporary repairs on the building to prevent more damage due to exposure to the elements. A large roll of plastic sheeting and tarps often come in very handy. In addition, the same loss control measures identified previously for a flood should also be followed for a hurricane (see above).

15.5 Landslides and Mudflows

While landslides and mudflows affect very few churches or schools, those at risk can experience extreme damage that occurs without warning. If you have facilities located in a known landslide or mudflow area, check with your county planning department to evaluate your risk.

Loss prevention measures

Churches or schools located in danger zones should have a written plan to respond to a landslide or mudflow. Normally a landslide or mudflow requires individuals in the danger zones to evacuate. Furthermore, since roads can become quickly blocked, more than one escape route should be planned in advance. According to the Federal Emergency Management Agency, several measures can be taken to reduce the potential impact of a landslide or mudflow. One simple landscaping task is to plant ground cover and build retaining walls. Takes steps to prevent erosion. Use landscaping techniques to redirect rocks or flowing mud away from your buildings. However, if they are channeled onto adjacent property and do damage your church or school may be liable. Monitor your buildings for potential warning signs of stress or problems including the following:[3]

- Windows and doors that begin to stick.
- The appearance of cracks in walls, floors, ceilings, and foundations.
- Outside walls, walks, or stairs begin to separate from the building.
- Cracks appear in paved or unpaved areas and they continue to get wider.
- Underground utility lines break.
- Ground begins to bulge at the bottom of a slope.
- Water breaks through the surface of the ground.
- Fences, walls, utility poles or trees begin to move or tilt.

A combination of these warning signs requires a professional evaluation. Do not wait for conditions to become worse.

Check with your insurance agent concerning the coverage you have for landslides and mudflow. Insurance for mudflow must be obtained through the National Flood Insurance Program and is available through your local insurance agency.

Loss control measures

The first task following a landslide or mudflow is to help anyone who is injured. Seek medical assistance as quickly as possible. Do not move injured victims unless additional threats to their safety are present. Check on vulnerable members of the congregation who may require assistance.

---

[3] FEMA:<www.fema.gov/library/landslf.htm>.

Keep away from the slide area until professionals have inspected it and proclaimed it safe to re-enter. At that point, inspect facilities for damage. Examine foundations, roofs, chimneys, gas lines, water lines, and power lines. If gas leaks are present, shut off the main gas line, open windows and leave the building as quickly as possible. Once you reach a safe location, notify the gas company. Similarly, notify the power company if power lines are down or electrical hazards are present. Make sure that smoke detectors and carbon monoxide detectors are operating. Make temporary repairs to protect church or school facilities from further exposure to the elements. If erosion has occurred, plant a ground cover to reduce the potential impact of future mudslides.

15.6 Volcanoes

Currently, over 500 active volcanoes exist worldwide with a majority being located in a region that encircles the Pacific Ocean known as the "Ring of Fire." Hawaii, Alaska, Washington, Oregon, and California are located in that ring and all have volcanoes. The populations at greatest risk are in Hawaii and Alaska. While volcanic eruptions are fairly rare events, churches or schools located within a 20 mile radius of a volcano face some risk even if the volcano is dormant. Mount St. Helens in Washington erupted after being dormant for more than 100 years. While the number of churches and schools located in these areas will be small, the need to have a risk management plan for an eruption is critical. Volcanoes have enormous explosive power and can hurl hot rocks for 20 miles. These rocks are hot enough to start fires. Ash and noxious fumes can affect people within a 100 mile radius. A volcanic eruption automatically triggers an evacuation of affected areas and individuals may be required to leave at a moment's notice. Staff members and leaders in danger zones should be prepared in advance to respond to this natural disaster. When a volcano occurs, other natural disasters such as earthquakes, floods, landslides, mudflows, thunderstorms, and tsunamis can follow.

Loss prevention measures

Churches and schools located in danger zones should have a written plan to respond to a volcano. Since volcanoes can erupt unexpectedly, leaders and members should understand the warning signals that will be used to notify the public of an eruption. As part of your advance planning, identify multiple escape routes that go away from the volcano in several different directions. If a volcano should erupt, the evacuation route used should be upwind of the volcano to avoid airborne ash and toxic fumes. It is very possible that a church that operates a day care or a school will have children that become separated from their parents if an evacuation takes place. Church or school leaders and parents should know in advance how to contact one another if an evacuation should occur. For example, a church or school outside the danger zone may be designated as the emergency contact center. Both leaders and parents can contact the designated center to provide information on where they are and how they can be contacted. Such arrangements will need to be made in advance and everyone who could be affected needs to understand how to respond under emergency circumstances. Provide parents with a brochure that describes the procedures and includes the evacuation routes and destinations, and the phone number for the emergency control center.

While it is better to evacuate than to stay in a building, that is not always possible. If you are indoors, close all windows and doors. Do not go outside and try to watch the eruption. The lateral force of a volcano can be so powerful that it can level an entire forest. Stay away from windows. Seek shelter under tables or desks. If you are outdoors, seek shelter inside as soon as possible. If shelter is not available, stay away from low lying areas—move to higher ground. Volcanoes release toxic gases that can accumulate in low lying areas. Try to keep your body from being exposed to falling ash and debris. Cover your mouth and nose with a damp cloth in order to breathe better. People have died from breathing volcanic ash. Also, stay away from streams and rivers where floods and mudslides can occur. Do not cross a bridge if a mudflow is approaching or is passing underneath it. The force of a mudflow is extremely powerful and can cause a bridge to collapse in a matter of minutes. Finally, do not attempt to drive while heavy ash is falling. The engine can become clogged and the vehicle can stall leaving you stranded.

One part of the church's crisis management plan should be to care for vulnerable members of the congregation such as the elderly who live alone and do not have family members to help them during times of crisis. Maintain a list of individuals who will need crisis assistance. Have designated volunteers assigned to each vulnerable person who will see to their safety and personal needs. Have them collect medications, prescriptions, and any other medical supplies or equipment that the person may need if an evacuation should occur.

Check with your insurance agent concerning the coverage you have for damage created by a volcano. Insurance for mudflows must be obtained through the National Flood Insurance Program and is available through your local insurance agency.

Loss control measures

As with any natural disaster, the first task is to help anyone who is injured. Seek medical assistance as quickly as possible. Do not move injured victims unless additional threats to their safety are present. Check on vulnerable members of the congregation who may require assistance.

Inspect church or school facilities for damage. Examine foundations, roofs, chimneys, gas lines, and power lines. If gas leaks are present, shut off the main gas line, open windows and leave the building as quickly as possible. Once you reach a safe location, notify the gas company. Similarly, notify the power company if power lines are down or electrical hazards are present. Make sure that smoke detectors and carbon monoxide detectors are operating. Make temporary repairs to protect the facilities from further exposure to the elements. If erosion has occurred, plant a ground cover to reduce the potential of mudslides. If your buildings are at risk due to a possible landside, seek help immediately from professionals. If you are uncertain of whom to contact, seek help from your insurance agent and the Federal Emergency Management Agency.

15.7 Thunderstorms and Lightning

More people are killed on an annual basis from lightning strikes than from tornadoes. More church fires start from lightning than from any other cause. It is estimated that nearly 1,800 thunderstorms are occurring at any moment around the world.[4] While the typical thunderstorm lasts 30 minutes and is 15 miles in diameter, it can create flash floods, strong winds, and hail. The intense stage of the storm generally lasts from 10 to 20 minutes. A thunderstorm is considered severe if it has wind speeds of at least 58 mph or produces hail of at least 3/4-inch in diameter. The National Weather Service issues a *thunderstorm watch* when the weather conditions are such that a severe thunderstorm is likely to develop. A *thunderstorm warning* is issued when a severe thunderstorm has been sighted or indicated by weather radar.

Loss prevention measures

Thunderstorms can occur quickly without warning. Others can be seen approaching. To estimate the distance in miles to a flash of lightning, count the seconds between the lightning and the thunder and divide by five. Danger signs for thunder storms include dark, towering, or threatening clouds and distant thunder and lightning. If a thunderstorm watch is issued, church and school leaders should be prepared to respond. A thunderstorm warning indicates a need to remain in a safe place. A severe thunderstorm can spawn a tornado. Some steps that churches and schools can take prior to severe thunderstorms include the following:[5]

- Install lightning rods.

- Routinely trim dead branches off trees. Strong winds can cause branches to fall and do considerable damage.

- Secure outdoor objects that can blow in strong winds.

- Keep a battery-powered radio available in the church or school office with extra batteries.

- Install surge protectors for sensitive electrical equipment such as organs, computers, telephones, copy machines, and fax machines. Make sure that electrical circuits are properly grounded.

If a thunderstorm occurs, take the following precautions:

- Do not handle electrical equipment or telephones when lightning is striking. The lightning can follow the wire.

- Turn off electrical appliances such as air conditioners. Power surges from lightning can overload the compressors.

- Avoid water faucets and sinks because metal pipes can transmit electricity.

- Students in gym classes should not take showers during thunderstorms.

Use the following safety precautions if you are caught outdoors in a thunderstorm:

- Attempt to get into a building or car.

- If no structure is available, get to an open space and squat as close to the ground as possible.

---

[4] *Thunderstorms and Lightning…The Underrated Killers*, National Oceanic and Atmospheric Administration, <http://www.nws.noaa.gov/om/trwbro.htm>.
[5] ibid., p. 2f.

- If in a woods, find an area protected by a low clump of trees—never stand underneath a single large tree in the open.

- Be alert of the potential for flooding in low-lying areas.

- Avoid tall structures such as towers, tall trees, fences, telephone lines, or power lines.

- Stay away from natural lightning rods such as gold clubs, tractors, fishing rods, bicycles, or camping equipment.

- Stay away from rivers, lakes, or other bodies of water.

- If you are isolated in a level field or prairie and you feel your skin tingle or your hair stand on end (which indicates that lightning is about to strike), bend forward, putting your hands on your knees. A position with feet together and crouching while removing all metal objects is recommended. Do not lie flat on the ground. Rather, minimize your contact with the ground.

- If you are in a car, pull safely to the shoulder of the road away from any tress. Stay inside the car and turn on the emergency flashers until it is clear to drive.

If lightning or thunder occurs, those outdoors, such as grounds keepers or children participating in athletic events, should come inside. It does not need to be raining for lightning to strike. It may occur as far away as 10 miles from any rainfall. Rubber-soled shoes and rubber tires provide no protection from lightning.

Loss control measures

Once the thunderstorm is over, check for injuries. If a person has been struck by lightning, they do not carry an electrical shock. A lightning strike can cause a person's heart to stop beating. In such cases, cardiopulmonary resuscitation (CPR) should be performed until medical help arrives. Look for downed power lines and any obvious building damage. A common problem is loose or missing shingles. Pick up downed tree limbs or other debris that is on walkways or outdoor stairways.

15.8 Extreme Heat or Sun Exposure

Two additional weather-related concerns are excessive heat and sun exposure. Churches and schools both sponsor many outdoor activities. Staying too long in the sun or in excess heat can cause illnesses. Adults and children should be reminded to wear sunscreen when they participate in outdoor activities. Avoid extended periods in the sun during the strongest heat of the day, from 10 A.M. to 2:00 P.M. If you must be outdoors during those periods, try to stay in the shade as much as possible, wear lightweight, reflective clothing, and use sunscreen. Drink plenty of water and avoid drinks with caffeine. Drink water even if you are not thirsty.

Common heat disorders include sunburn, heat cramps, heat exhaustion, and heat stroke. The Federal Emergency Management Agency notes the following about each disorder:[6]

---

[6] Fact Sheet: Extreme Heat, Federal Emergency Management Agency, <http://www.fema.gov/library/heatf.htm>.

- *Sunburn.* Symptoms include skin redness and pain, possible swelling, blisters, fever, and headaches. Treatment includes taking a shower and to use soap to remove oils that may block pores preventing the body from cooling naturally. If blisters occur, medical help should be sought.

- *Heat cramps.* Symptoms include heavy sweating and painful spasms, usually in the leg and abdominal muscles. First aid can be given by gently massaging the muscles to relieve the spasm. Sips of water can be taken but should be discontinued if nausea occurs.

- *Heat exhaustion.* Symptoms include heavy sweating, weakness, a weak pulse, pale and clammy skin, fainting, and vomiting, although a normal temperature is possible. First aid includes having the victim to lie down in a cool place. Loosen the clothing and apply wet, cool cloths. Fan or move the person to a room with air conditioning. Give sips of water but if nausea occurs discontinue. If vomiting occurs, seek immediate medical attention.

- *Heat stroke.* Symptoms include a body temperature of 106 degrees, hot dry skin, a rapid pulse, and possible unconsciousness. The victim is not likely to sweat. Heat stroke is a severe medical emergency that requires immediate medical attention. Call 911 or get the victim to an emergency room immediately. Delay can be fatal. Cool the person with cool sponging, fans, and the removal of clothing. DO NOT GIVE FLUIDS.

Summary

Natural perils pose a threat to every church and school, but differ significantly in frequency and severity. Church and school leaders should identify those perils that pose a significant risk and develop a crisis management plan based upon the principles discussed in chapter 4. The most common and severe natural perils include earthquakes, floods, tornadoes, hurricanes, landslides and mudflows, and thunderstorms and lightning. Volcanoes also threaten some church and schools.

In developing a crisis management plan for each threat, attention should be given to both loss prevention and loss control measures. Leaders should recognize the warning signs of each threat, understand the potential for damage, and know what safety precautions to take to protect human life and property. When a natural disaster is imminent, building shutdown procedures should be implemented including shutting off gas and electrical power, securing backup data from computers, and safeguarding important documents and records. Vulnerable members of the congregation should be helped if an evacuation is necessary and they should always be checked upon following any natural disaster.

If a natural disaster strikes, special precautions should be taken if property damage has occurred. Immediately report any downed power lines. Stay away from damaged electrical circuits. Evacuate any building if there is the smell of gas and open a window on the way out. Call the gas company from a location outside of the building and immediately report the problem.

Thunderstorms occur frequently and can cause severe damage including death. Stay indoors when thunder and lightning are present. If outdoors, take shelter in low-lying areas. Crouch with hands on the knees, but do not lie on the ground.

Excessive heat can cause several medical disorders including sunburn, heat cramps, heat, exhaustion, and the most serious of all—heat stroke which is a life threatening problem that requires immediate medical attention.

The next chapter examines the problems of crime and vandalism and provides ways churches and schools can reduce these risks.

Additional Resources on the Internet

For additional information on reducing risks associated with natural disasters and severe weather, review the material found on the following web sites. Also, several publications are listed that are available from Consumer Product Safety Commission and the Red Cross. These resources were used in the preparation of this chapter.

"After a Flood: The First Steps." American Red Cross.

"Backgrounder: Volcanoes." Federal Emergency Management Agency. <http://www.fema.gov/library/volcano.htm>.

"Building Evacuation Plan: Geological Sciences." <http://www.geo.utexas.edu/geosafety/building_evacuation_plan.htm>.

"Earthquakes: Be Ready 1-2-3." American Red Cross.

"Evacuation and Emergency Plans." <http://help.jsc.nasa.gov/s40/tipevac.htm>.

"Fact Sheet: Earthquakes." Federal Emergency Management Agency. <http://www.fema.gov/library/quakef.htm>.

"Fact Sheet: Floods and Flash Floods." Federal Emergency Management Agency. <http://www.fema.gov/library/floodf.htm>.

"Fact Sheet: Hurricanes." Federal Emergency Management Agency. <http://www.fema.gov/library/hurricaf.htm>.

"Fact Sheet: Landslides and Mudflows." Federal Emergency Management Agency. <http://www.fema.gov/library/landslif.htm>.

"Fact Sheet: Post-Disaster Water Treatment." American Red Cross.

"Fact Sheet: Using a Generator When Disaster Strikes." American Red Cross.

"Fact Sheet: Volcanoes." Federal Emergency Management Agency. <http://www.fema.gov/library/volcanof.htm>.

"Fact Sheet: Water Storage Before Disaster Strikes." American Red Cross.

"Flash Floods and Floods…the Awesome Power!" U.S. Department of Commerce National Oceanic and Atmospheric Administration National Weather Service. July 1992. <http://www.nws.noaa.gov/om/ffbro.htm>.

"Home Evacuation Drills." <http://www.stfd.com/EvacPlans.html>.

"Hurricanes...Unleashing Nature's Fury." U.S. Department of Commerce National Oceanic and Atmospheric Administration National Weather Service. March 1994. <http://www.nws.noaa.gov/om/hurrbok.htm>.

"Living With Our Faults: An Earthquake Preparation Guide." <http://www.ci.campbell.ca.us/famevac.html>.

"Planning for a Municipal Emergency and Evacuations." <http://town.maniouwadge.on.ca/emergency.htm>.

"Safety Tips for Flood Victims: Safety Alert CPSC Document #5035." Consumer Product Safety Commission. <http://www.cpsc.gov/cpscpub/pubs/5035.html>.

"Safety: California Preparedness Materials - Earthquake Tips for People with Disabilities." American Red Cross. <http://www.redcross.org/disaster/safety/eqtips.html>.

"Safety: California Preparedness Materials - Earthquake Tips for People with Visual Disabilities." American Red Cross. <http://www.redcross.org/disaster/safety/eyes.html>.

"Safety: California Preparedness Materials - Earthquake Tips for People Who Are Hearing Impaired." American Red Cross. <http://www.redcross.org/disaster/safety/deaf.html>.

"Safety: California Preparedness Materials - Earthquake Tips for People with Mobility Disabilities." American Red Cross. <http://www.redcross.org/disaster/safety/eqtmdis.html>.

"Safety: California Preparedness Materials - Earthquake Tips for People with Communication and Speech Related Disabilities." American Red Cross. <http://www.redcross.org/disaster/safety/eqtcoms.html>.

"Safety: California Preparedness Materials - Earthquake Tips for People with Cognitive Disabilities." American Red Cross. <http://www.redcross.org/disaster/safety/cogdis.html>.

"Safety: California Preparedness Materials - Earthquake Tips for People with Psychiatric Disabilities." American Red Cross. <http://www.redcross.org/disaster/safety/eqtpsyd.html>.

"Safety: California Preparedness Materials - People with Special Medical Needs." American Red Cross. <http://www.redcross.org/disaster/safety/pwsmn.html>.

"Safety: California Preparedness Materials - Tips for Collecting Emergency Documents." American Red Cross. <http://www.redcross.org/disaster/safety/doctip.html>.

"Safety: California Preparedness Materials - Tips for Creating an Emergency Health Information Card." American Red Cross. <http://www.redcross.org/disaster/safety/tipcrd.html>.

"Safety: Checklist for Mobility Problems." American Red Cross. <http://www.redcross.org/disaster/safety/checklst.html>.

"Safety: Disaster Preparedness for Seniors - What We Can Do to Save Our Lives." American Red Cross. <http://www.redcross.org/disaster/safety/seniors.html>.

"Safety: Disaster Supplies Kit." American Red Cross. <http://www.redcross.org/disaster/safety/supplies.html>.

"Safety: Earthquakes - Disaster Services." American Red Cross. <http://www.redcross.org/disaster/safety/earth.html>.

"Safety: Emergency Preparedness Checklist." American Red Cross. <http://www.redcross.org/disaster/safety/emerprep.html>.

"Safety: Helping Children Cope with Disaster." American Red Cross. <http://www.redcross.org/disaster/safety/chilcope.html>.

"Safety: Preparing Financially for a Disaster - Before Disaster Strikes." American Red Cross. <http://www.redcross.org/disaster/safety/before.html>.

"Safety: Talking About Disaster - Flood and Flash Flood." American Red Cross. <http://www.redcross.org/disaster/safety/guide/flood.html>.

"Safety: Your Evaculation Plan." American Red Cross. <http://www.redcross.org/disaster/safety/evac.html>.

"Safety: Your Family Disaster Plan." American Red Cross. <http://www.redcross.org/disaster/safety/displan.html>.

CHAPTER 16. REDUCING THE RISK OF CRIME AND VANDALISM

I was visiting a large, but poor inner city congregation. As I pulled up to the run down church facilities, I noticed it was surrounded by a tall cyclone fence with razor wire across the top. It gave the impression of a military compound. Later in a meeting with church leaders I wondered about the fence and asked if crime was a problem. "Oh no," they exclaimed. "The people in the neighborhood respect the church. They know how much we do for the poor." Following the meeting, once everyone had left, the pastor said, "I want to tell you something. I've had to buy a gun. The truth is that crime on the property is a problem. Just this month, two batteries have been stolen out of the church car. I have to fire the gun in the air at night to scare these thieves away."

Crime and vandalism are problems for all churches and schools, regardless of size or location. In part, churches are targets of crime because they are often vacant and unprotected. Sometimes doors and windows are left unlocked. Thieves are attracted to churches and schools for many reasons. The Sunday offering may be left in the church office in a file cabinet for a Monday deposit. The church or school office generally contains computers, printers, a fax machine, and other electronic equipment. Musical instruments and sound equipment are often left in a sanctuary or a music room. A shed may house a riding lawn mower and power tools. These items attract thieves. They may burglarize cars in the parking lot during a church service and then enter the sanctuary and steal coats off racks in the foyer. In one church, thieves, dressed as workmen, walked into the church library in broad daylight, while staff members watched, and stole a Persian rug claiming they were taking it to be cleaned. In many schools, students experience theft on a regular basis.

In addition to burglary, churches and schools also experience vandalism. Windows are broken, equipment is smashed, graffiti is painted on walls, and vehicles are damaged. While robbery is less of a problem, it is not unheard of. Many secretaries express concern about leaving the office at night during the winter months when it is dark, and then walking alone to their car in an abandoned parking lot. Church secretaries often work alone with no one else in the building. These secretaries are self-conscious about security concerns, and feel uncomfortable or threatened when strangers, transients, or homeless people come to the church seeking help. Some of the individuals seeking help have emotional or mental problems, and others are experienced con-artists. Church secretaries often feel torn between a desire to provide help on the one hand, and a feeling of fear on the other. Frequently, they do not have the resources to provide help and yet are afraid of offending someone who seems desperate.

Burglary, vandalism, and feelings of insecurity by secretaries are all common problems that deserve attention.

16.1 Crime Prevention through Environmental Design

While no statistics are available, one can postulate that casual, nonprofessional criminals commit most church and school crime. Churches and schools can develop a crime prevention program that can reduce problems in all areas.

One rapidly developing approach to this concern is Crime Prevention Through Environmental Design (CPTED). The basic idea behind CPTED is that proper design and use of the environment can reduce crime and the fear that is associated with it. CPTED revolves around a few simple ideas:

- *Surveillance.* The property and building design should promote clear and unobstructed views from activity areas.

- *Access Control.* Entry points should be carefully designed to maximize safety and security.

These principles can be applied to a wide spectrum of problems that impact churches and schools. In developing a crime prevention program, leaders should give attention to burglary, robbery, vandalism, safety on trips, and personal safety while at work.

16.2 Burglary Prevention

Burglary prevention involves controlling access to church facilities and property, maintaining an effective surveillance system, and maintaining sufficient lighting to deter the casual thief.

Controlling access to property and buildings

Controlling access to the building and to the property is a central part of an effective burglary prevention plan. Make sure that all doors fit snugly and that the frame structures are solid and secure. Use one inch deadbolt locks on exterior doors and also on inside doors that require higher levels of security. Door hinges should be located on the interior side of doors. Windows should use burglar resistant glass and have good locks. Make sure that all basement windows are secure, possibly using a grill if zoning permits. Note: if the church is locked during working hours, employees should always be able to exit through any door in case of fire. Other burglary prevention measures include the following:

- Never leave a spare key outside the office.

- Use a burglar resistant safe that is fireproof and securely anchored. Change the combination periodically, especially after a turnover in employees. Keep cash stored on the property in the safe.

- If you use padlocks, they should be of a high quality hardened steel.

- Use landscape designs and plants to make a break-in more difficult. Thorny or prickly plants such as a holly under a first floor window can discourage potential burglars. Plants, however, should not obstruct the view through windows or doors.

- Use landscaping, fences, and screens to control access to church property.

- Do not have easy access to the roof.

- Use a metal bar or a piece of wood in the track of sliding doors to provide additional security.

- Keep all vehicles locked and parked in an area with bright lights. Never leave any valuables or the keys in a vehicle.

- Try to make parking spaces visible from the street, or from the main offices of the church building.

- All church or school keys should be numbered. Maintain an accurate list of who has a church key. Limit the distribution of keys to the fewest number of people possible. Store keys in a key safe.

- Do not give out sensitive information or credit card numbers over the phone unless you have initiated the call, or you know the person with whom you are speaking.

Surveillance systems

Increasingly, churches and schools use surveillance systems for security reasons. Some of the key factors to keep in mind are noted below:

Monitor church parking lots during church services. Burglars may break into cars during the service. Also monitor the church foyer once the service has started. Individuals will enter the church and steal coats or other valuables during the service.

Use an alarm system as a compliment to basic security measures. Many different alarm systems are available for a wide range of prices and monitoring fees. Meet with representatives from several different companies. Have them evaluate your needs and provide a written proposal and description of what they recommend. Then select and install a system that best needs your needs. Alarm systems make use of a phone line to notify of an intruder. Check with the security company on how they protect the phone line. Most alarm systems have a built in delay in order to allow staff members to disarm them when they enter the building. The delay should be as short as possible. In addition, only one entry should be used to disarm the system. All other entrances should immediately trigger the alarm. An increasing number of churches and schools use a combination of video surveillance and alarms. Make sure any would be criminal knows that you have an alarm system. Deterrence is the best policy. Place stickers on windows and doors and place signs at strategic locations on the property warning of your alarm system.

Create a natural surveillance system. Maximize visibility between offices and the outside of the church or school, especially parking lots and entrances. Make sure proper lighting exists. Do not create natural hiding areas around the buildings. Train employees to be observant about people who enter the facilities, especially strangers. Look for signs of illegal entry such as screens that have been slit or broken windows. Employees should be prepared to contact the police if warranted.

Lighting

Lighting is one of the best and least expensive forms of deterrence that a church or school can use. Installing protective lighting, though, is not the same thing as having outside lights. Lights must have sufficient illumination to deter vandals and the casual criminal. Criminals do not like being seen and sufficient lighting in the right places makes criminals feel uneasy. Install protective lighting around locations that someone might use to enter the facilities such as doors, windows, or skylights. The parking lot and street entrances into the parking lot should also have good illumination. Protect outside lights with a cover so someone will not be able to break the bulb easily. Consult with the local power company to determine the proper level of illumination for security purposes.

Additional measures

Here are some additional measures that churches and schools can take to reduce crime and burglary:

- Mark church or school equipment with an indelible identification mark or number. Maintain an inventory of all equipment and their corresponding identification marks or numbers.

- Store important documents in a safe deposit box at a bank.

- Keep backup copies of computer data and important documents off of church or school property.

16.3 Preventing Robbery

Robbery is different from burglary in that it involves a personal threat or the actual use of force. Robbery occurs less frequently than burglary and is not a significant problem in most churches. It does occur periodically, though, primarily to church secretaries who are working alone at the church. In addition, individuals have been assaulted in church parking lots, especially at night following church activities. The need for adequate lighting in parking lots is vital. In high risk areas, a security guard may be warranted. Violent crimes, including robbery, do occur in schools. Schools should refer to the chapter in this book on preventing juvenile violence for additional information. Here are some controls that can be used against robbery.

- Keep doors locked during regular office hours. Install a remote controlled door lock that the secretary can activate from the church office. The secretary should be able to see who is at the door through a window, a peephole, or through video surveillance.

- Create a physical barrier between the reception space used to greet visitors and the secretary. For example, the secretary may be in a locked office that has a sliding window that opens up to the reception area. Or the office may have a counter that separates the secretary from people in the office. Some churches install a "Dutch door" in the secretary's office. The bottom half of the door remains locked while the top half is open. The secretary should be seated in a location that enables a natural surveillance of who is outside the office, or who is entering the office.

- Install a panic button in the office. The button should activate an alarm in other parts of the building that summons help.

- Do not keep large amounts of money at the church or school. Make arrangements with the bank to make deposits on the same day that collections are made.

- Maintain adequate lighting in the church or school parking lot and around the facilities. Use a buddy system when going to a parked car.

- Instruct drivers of church or school vehicles not to pick up hitchhikers.

- Train employees not to resist a robber. Seek advice from local enforcement on how to respond to a robbery.

16.4 Preventing Vandalism

Vandalism is generally the work of young people. Each year, churches and schools experience significant losses due to vandalism. Vandals often act impulsively. Some steps to prevent vandalism include the following:

- Establish the same safeguards that are listed to prevent burglary, especially preventive lighting.

- Control access to playgrounds that may attract potential vandals.

- Keep the property clear of any rubbish.

- Report every act of vandalism to the police, no matter how minor.

- Quickly respond to any act of vandalism. Make repairs or remove graffiti. Take steps to prevent future acts such as improving lighting or using shrubs and bushes next to the building to prevent graffiti.

- Organize a neighborhood watch program around the church or school. Work with local law enforcement officers.

16.5 Preventing Computer Crime

Increasingly, churches and schools are dependent on databases, records and files maintained on office computer equipment. The loss or destruction of that information could generate serious problems, as well as financial losses for a church or school. Furthermore, an increasing number of churches and schools are on the Internet. Receiving e-mail opens computers up to the potential of viruses that can cause serious damage and harm. Several precautionary steps can be taken to reduce computer crime.

- Maintain current virus protection software. The software must be updated on a regular basis to identify new viruses.

- Limit the use of office computers to authorized staff members. Use passwords to gain access to sensitive information.

- Back-up data on a daily basis and store copies in safe locations.

16.6 Preventing Crime on Trips

Many churches and schools sponsor trips for both youth and adults. Some trips are outside the United States and the participants may not be well prepared to reduce crime. In some parts of the world, pick pockets and thieves are common and precautions are needed. Groups that go on these trips should take the following precautions:

- Use traveler's checks rather than cash. Leave a list of the ID numbers for the traveler's checks at home with someone you can contact in case they become lost or stolen. Also keep a list with you on the trip.

- For trips outside the United States, take along a photocopy of your passport and keep it in a safe place separate from the original.

- Clean your billfold or purse of all nonessential items prior to the trip. If you have more than one credit card, keep them separate from one another. That way if one becomes lost or stolen, a backup card will still be available for use. Also, take along the phone numbers of your credit card company so you can contact them in case a card is lost or stolen.

- Use a money belt. Do not wear a purse over your shoulder. Place the strap over the head and under the arm so that it cannot be grabbed and taken away. Keep wallets in a front pocket or inside coat pocket rather than in a back pocket.

- Use ATM machines during the day when there are plenty of people around.

- Do not display expensive items that may attract attention.

- Avoid dark streets and isolated areas. Always stay with a buddy. Use streets that are well-traveled. If you feel you are being followed, immediately go to a place where there are other people.

- Do not accept rides from strangers.

- Do not bring jewelry and valuables.

- Never resist a robber.

- Do not leave purses or valuable items hanging on a chair while seated in a public place. Do not leave valuable items sitting on top of a table while seated in a public place. A well-known scheme is for one person to come to the table and create a sudden diversion while a second person grabs the valuables and runs off. This can happen quickly, in just a matter of seconds.

16.7 Personal Safety in Responding to Transients

Compassion, anxiety, bewilderment . . . these are just a few of the words that describe how church secretaries and other staff members feel about working with transients and others who come to the church seeking personal help. Often, church secretaries work alone at the church office and when confronted by a street person seeking money, they are caught between a desire to help and personal fear for their own safety.

Helping the poor is central to the church's mission. But that does not mean that such help should be done thoughtlessly or without concern for the welfare and safety of those who work with the needy. To avoid problems, church staff members need training and guidance in responding to transients and to other individuals seeking help. Church leaders should take the initiative to see that their church has developed an adequate set of policies and procedures to respond to those who come to the church seeking assistance. Often, the secretary is at the church alone when these situations occur. Clearly, such scenarios require advanced planning. The following suggestions may be of help to some church staff members who respond to the needs of transients, the homeless, and street people.

1. Define each staff member's role with respect to the church's ministry of caring for the needy. Clarify tasks such as interviewing, making referrals, giving vouchers, and following up.

2. Establish procedures to enhance personal safety in responding to the needs of transients. As churches become an increasing target for theft, and the number of people seeking financial assistance increases, church staff members are becoming more concerned about safety issues as the comments below illustrate.

- *One morning my buzzer sounded letting me know that someone had entered the building. A man came into my office and asked for a place to spend the night. I tried to locate a place for him, but each agency I called responded using an answering machine. In the meantime, the man was becoming more agitated. I finally called a member of the congregation, trying to remain cool, but at the same time letting this member know that I was alone in the building and that I, while not fearing for my life, felt very uncomfortable. The member relayed this information to the police department, and an officer just happened by for a visit. The policeman took the transient to a hotel. The room was billed to our church.*

- *Within a few months of beginning my job as church secretary I learned a good lesson on trusting human nature as opposed to being a good steward of my own and church property. I had my wallet stolen out of my purse (which was in a desk drawer) by a transient who came in for help from our food pantry. Our church has always maintained an open door policy. We have been without a pastor for seven months and there have been times when I have felt personally threatened by transients who arrive when I am alone in the building. I do wish the church would put their words into actions when they say they're concerned about me being alone, but I don't think they will unless something drastic were to happen.*

- *For a time we were having some rather harrowing experiences with transients coming into our church, including one very large man who claimed he needed only $13.75 more for bus fare to get home. He told me he had been in jail for two years for killing a man, and that while in jail he had become a drug addict, and now had AIDS. He even showed me the scars on his wrists where he had tried to kill himself. He was extremely nervous and agitated as he waited for me to do something for him. The pastor was away. Nine calls later I found there was not one source who could help. The man finally left and I never saw him again.*

3. Provide training to church secretaries and other staff members on how to respond to transients. For many church secretaries, their introduction to working with transients occurs when the first needy person arrives at the church office. Have staff members engage in role-playing to practice how they would respond in a true-life situation. Here are some training tips:

- Staff members should know what information to collect and how to verify it from those requesting help.

- Staff members should be able to make referrals. Create a brochure that lists the type of assistance programs available in your community. Provide one to each person who requests help.

- Tell people what you can do rather than what you cannot do. Keep coming back to "Let me tell you what we can do." This may be only making a referral.

Too often training in responding to such situations is often nonexistent as illustrated by the following comment:

- *I have been a parish secretary for almost one year now. My last job was retail management, so you can imagine my shock the first time someone came to the office door asking for food! For some reason this possibility had not occurred to me, nor had the Rector (who was on vacation) or the former secretary brought it up during my training.*

Security issues

Cases have occurred where church secretaries have been assaulted during daylight hours. Church leaders should give more attention to security in general and more precaution should be taken to safeguard secretaries who work in the building alone. Consider the following points.

1. When a secretary is working alone at the church, the building should be locked. An electronic lock can be installed in the door, which allows the secretary to unlock the entrance without leaving the office. Even if the electronic security system is not possible, the doors should remain locked and a doorbell should be used. Some churches maintain an open-door policy. In this case, control access to the office. Do not let strangers into the work area.

2. In high crime areas access to the building should be controlled during office hours even if the secretary is not alone in the building.

3. An intercom system should be installed between the secretary's office and the pastor's office. While that has value far beyond security concerns, it does allow the secretary to contact the pastor if a problem is developing. A code word can be used indicating that immediate assistance is required in the church office. Also install a panic button in the church office. The button should activate an alarm in other parts of the building that summons help. If the phone system permits, program speed dial numbers for emergency phone numbers such as the police.

4. If a church employee is working at the church alone, he or she should not indicate that to someone over the phone, or to a stranger who drops in.

5. Employees who work alone should let others know their schedule. Church secretaries, for example, can call someone to let them know they are leaving work before they walk out into a dark parking lot and drive home. The church should maintain adequate lighting in all areas around the church and in the parking lot. Employees should have parking spaces as close to the door as possible.

6. Do not allow strangers to enter the church office. If the only access to the office is through the door (as opposed to a business window) and a counter does not separate the workspace from the reception area, consider installing a Dutch door. The top half can be left open while the bottom remains locked. Sometimes a person will ask to use the office phone. Some churches provide access to a pay phone, or to a phone in the reception area that can be used for local calls only. Some secretaries make the call on the other person's behalf. The point is to be safety conscious.

7. Keep personal valuables locked-up. Thefts can occur quickly such as when the secretary leaves for a few minutes to use the rest room.

8. Do not keep large amounts of cash at the church.

9. If a staff member feels that an unsafe situation is developing, he or she should not hesitate to contact the police. If your phone system has speed dialing, program the local police number into it for quick access.

10. Some people have serious emotional problems or needs that go far beyond the secretary's ability to help. Staff members should know their limits, and be prepared to make referrals when necessary.

Responding to the con-artist

Any organization that provides resources to those in need will also attract those who attempt to abuse the system. This is especially true of churches. The Christian emphasis upon caring and compassion can be viewed by the con-artist as an invitation for easy pickings.

Often, those who try to con church staff members are in as much need as are others who seek help. The difference, however, is that the con-artist uses lying and deception to swindle staff members. Consider the following example:

> *A man and woman came into my office explaining that they had just made a 2,000-mile trip to attend the funeral of her father. However, just before they left home their car was wrecked. The insurance company provided a rental car for temporary use. They had just enough time to attend the funeral and return home before the car was due back. On the trip out her purse was taken from the car while they were at a rest stop. They had just enough cash to make it to the funeral, but not enough to make the return trip home. Hence, they wanted help for gas, food, and lodging. A few phone calls on my part indicated that indeed, the man described as her father had died, but that he had no daughter. When confronted with the facts, the couple requesting help become hostile and defensive and bolted out of the office.*

When the con-artist succeeds in securing financial assistance, it perpetuates dishonesty and takes away limited resources from others who deserve help. What's the solution? Easy answers are not available. However, below are some suggestions that may be helpful in responding to this concern.

1. Do not give cash. Use a voucher system.

2. To the extent possible, provide food assistance to all that request it based on reasonable frequency guidelines. Food is a basic human need and often the person

requesting help has children. The local church can maintain a food pantry, know where to make referrals, or provide vouchers which explicitly state what can and cannot be purchased with them.

3. Ask for identification (driver's license, etc.) and references. Don't be afraid to make a few phone calls to gain more information.

4. Verify the need. Ask for names, addresses, phone numbers, statements and other relevant information. If the person is evasive, take note of it and raise your level of caution.

5. Inquire concerning the person's religious background. Do they have a minister you can contact? Why did they come to your church? Have other churches helped them?

6. Be aware if the person attempts to use guilt to manipulate you—"If you were really a Christian..." Don't allow yourself to be manipulated by guilt; it's often a tactic of the con-artist.

7. The con-artist often stresses the urgency of the need and presents it in a life or death context. If you don't help the world will come to an end. Legitimate requests may also contain an element of urgency. Look for other factors such as manipulation and evasiveness if you believe it may be a con.

8. The con-artist often has no local ties. He or she is from out of town and has been waylaid by a series of unfortunate circumstances. When you ask for names and references they have none. However, they have plenty of excuses.

9. Unless you have discussed it with a lawyer, do not hire transients for part-time work. Some churches operate with the assumption that work will separate the truly needy who have the right attitude and commitments from the freeloaders. However, once the church begins to pay a transient to do work for the church a number of legal concerns arise related to liability, workers compensation insurance, social security, and withholding taxes. Make sure you understand the legal implications before hiring a transient.

10. Develop a community wide program with a centralized referral system. Often this is done through the local ministerial association in cooperation with the police and other social service agencies.

Summary

Burglary and vandalism are problems for all churches and schools. One approach to reducing these problems is through environmental design. Create clear and unobstructed views from all areas. Limit the number of entry points to maximize safety and security.

Burglary prevention involves controlling access to property and maintaining an effective surveillance system. Lighting is one of the most important and least expensive deterrents a church or school can use to prevent crime. Robbery is different from burglary in that it involves a personal threat or use of force. Church and school employees should not resist a robber.

Computer crime is on the increase. Churches and schools should use anti-virus software on their computer systems and maintain regular back-up copies of data.

Schools and churches that sponsor mission or educational trips should take special precautions to reduce the potential for crime. Provide instructions to all participants on safety measures. Trips outside of the country pose higher risks.

Church staff members need training in responding to requests for help from transients and other persons in need. Church secretaries often are alone at the church office when these requests for assistance occur. Church leaders should clarify procedures on how to respond and maintain a safe environment for staff members who work alone at the church office.

In the next chapter, we examine the crime of embezzlement.

Additional Resources on the Internet

For additional information on reducing crime and vandalism, review the material found on the following web sites. These resources were used in the preparation of this chapter.

"Alarms." City of Overland Park. <http://www.opkansas.org/html/alarms.html>.

"Annoying Phone Calls." <http:www.jetlink.net/~jgarner/anoycall.htm>.

"Commercial Properties." <http://www.cpted-watch.com/commercial.htm>.

"Crime Prevention Through Environmental Design." City of Overland Park. <http://www.opkansas.org/html/cpted.html>.

"Fraud Against Seniors." <http:www.jetlink.net/~jgarner/seniorf.htm>.

"National Church Arson Task Force." U.S. Department of the Treasury, U.S. Department of Justice, Bureau of Alcohol, Tobacco and Firearms, Federal Bureau of Investigation. <http://www.atf.treas.gov/pub/arsonrpt.htm>.

"Self, Home, and Family: Crime Prevention for Small Business." ." National Crime Prevention Council. <http://www.ncpc.org/1smbus.htm>.

"Self, Home, and Family: Protecting Company Information." National Crime Prevention Council. <http://www.ncpc.org/1coinfo.htm>.

"Self, Home, and Family: Protecting Yourself - Auto Theft." National Crime Prevention Council. <http://www.ncpc.org/1pro2dc.htm>.

"Self, Home, and Family: Protecting Yourself - Family Travel Safety Tips." National Crime Prevention Council. <http://www.ncpc.org/1pro3dc.htm>.

"Self, Home, and Family: Protecting Yourself - Home Security." National Crime Prevention Council. <http://www.ncpc.org/1sec1dc.htm>.

"Self, Home, and Family: Protecting Yourself - Preventing Fraud." National Crime Prevention Council. <http://www.ncpc.org/1pro6dc.htm>.

"Self, Home, and Family: Protecting Yourself - Rural Crime Prevention." National Crime Prevention Council. <http://www.ncpc.org/1sec4dc.htm>.

"Self, Home, and Family: Protecting Yourself - Street Smarts." National Crime Prevention Council. <http://www.ncpc.org/1pro1dc.htm>.

"Self, Home, and Family: Taking Crime Prevention to Work." National Crime Prevention Council. <http://www.ncpc.org/1towork.htm>.

Waggoner, Kim. "Focus on Crime Prevention Creative Solutions to Traditional Problems." FBI Law Enforcement Bulletin. <http://www.fbi.gov/library/leb/1997/aug973.htm>.

CHAPTER 17. REDUCING THE RISK OF EMBEZZLEMENT

Our research indicates that over 5 percent of churches have had funds embezzled at some time in the past. For larger churches the number is much higher—up to 15 percent. These statistics reflect known cases only. The actual numbers are no doubt much higher, since those who embezzle church funds do their best to conceal their misconduct.

17.1 Embezzlement Defined

The definition of embezzlement varies slightly from state to state, but in general it refers to the wrongful conversion of property that is lawfully in your possession. The idea is that someone has legal control or custody of property or funds, and then decides to convert the property or funds to his or her own personal use.

Most people who embezzle funds insist that they intended to pay the money back and were simply "borrowing" the funds temporarily. An intent to pay back embezzled funds is not a defense to the crime of embezzlement. Most church employees who embezzle funds plan on repaying the church fully before anyone suspects what has happened. One can only imagine how many such schemes actually work without anyone knowing about it. The courts are not persuaded by the claims of embezzlers that they intended to fully pay back the funds they misappropriated. The crime is complete when the embezzler misappropriates the church's funds to his or her own personal use. As one court has noted:

> The act of embezzlement is complete the moment the official converts the money to his own use even though he then has the intent to restore it. Few embezzlements are committed except with the full belief upon the part of the guilty person that he can and will restore the property before the day of accounting occurs. There is where the danger lies and the statute prohibiting embezzlement is passed in order to protect the public against such venturesome enterprises by people who have money in their control.

In short, it does not matter that someone intended to pay back embezzled funds. This intent in no way justifies or excuses the crime. The crime is complete when the funds are converted to one's own use—whether or not there was an intent to pay them back.

What if the embezzled funds are returned? The crime of embezzlement has occurred even if the embezzled funds in fact are paid back. Of course, it may be less likely that a prosecutor will prosecute a case under these circumstances. And even if the embezzler is prosecuted, this evidence may lessen the punishment. But the courts have consistently ruled that an actual return of embezzled funds does not purge the offense of its criminal nature or absolve the embezzler from punishment.

> *Key point. Even if an embezzler is caught or confesses, and then agrees to "pay back" the embezzled funds, church officials seldom know if all embezzled funds are being returned. They are relying almost entirely on the word of the embezzler.*

17.2 Why Churches Often are Vulnerable to Embezzlement.

Many churches refuse to adopt measures to reduce the risk of embezzlement out of a fear of that such measures will reflect a lack of trust in those persons who handle church funds.

> *Example. Tom has counted the church offering at his church for 25 years. The church board has discussed this arrangement several times, but fails to stop it out of a fear of offending Tom.*

Why should church leaders take this risk seriously? For several reasons, including the following:

Survey data. Our survey data (mentioned above) demonstrates that embezzlement is a risk that every church should take seriously.

Removing temptation. Churches that take steps to prevent embezzlement remove a source of possible temptation from church employees and volunteers who work with money.

Protecting reputations. By taking steps to prevent embezzlement a church protects the reputation of innocent employees and volunteers who otherwise might be suspected of financial wrongdoing when financial irregularities occur.

Avoiding confrontations. By taking steps to prevent embezzlement a church avoids the unpleasant task of confronting individuals who are suspected of embezzlement.

Avoiding church division. By taking steps to prevent embezzlement a church avoids the risk of congregational division that often is associated with cases of embezzlement—with some members wanting to show mercy to the offender and others demanding justice.

Avoiding the need to inform donors. By taking steps to prevent embezzlement a church reduces the risk of having to tell donors that some of their contributions have been misappropriated by a church employee or volunteer.

Protecting the reputation of church leaders. By taking steps to prevent embezzlement a church reduces the damage to the reputation and stature of its leaders who otherwise may be blamed for allowing embezzlement to occur.

Preserving accountability. Churches that take steps to prevent embezzlement help to create a "culture of accountability" with regard to church funds.

These are powerful motivations for addressing the issue of embezzlement.

17.3 How Embezzlement Happens

Let's look at a few cases of actual embezzlement of church funds to see how it can occur.

> *Example. An usher collected offerings each week in the church balcony, and pocketed all loose bills while carrying the offering plates down a stairway to the main floor.*

Church officials later estimated that he embezzled several thousands of dollars over a number of years, before being caught.

Example. *The same two persons counted church offerings for many years. Each week they removed all loose coins and currency (not in offering envelopes) and split it between them. This practice went on for several years, and church officials later estimated that the two had embezzled several tens of thousands of dollars.*

Example. *A church left its Sunday offering, along with the official count, in a safe in the church office until Monday. On Monday morning a church employee deposited the offering. The employee ignored the official counts, and deposited the offering less loose coins and currency (which she retained). The deposits were never checked against the offering counts.*

Example. *A church bookkeeper embezzled several thousand dollars by issuing checks to a fictitious company. He opened an account in the name of a fictitious company, issued church checks to the company for services that were never performed, and then deposited the checks in the fictitious company's account. He later withdrew the funds and purchased two automobiles which he gave to a friend. A court ruled that the friend had to give the cars back to the church, since they had been purchased with embezzled church funds. The point here, as noted by the court, is that one who acquires property that was purchased with embezzled church funds may be required to transfer the property to the church.*

Example. *A minister received an unauthorized kickback of 5% of all funds paid by a church to a contractor who had been hired to build a new church facility. The minister received over $80,000 from this arrangement, in exchange for which he persuaded the church to use the contractor. The minister's claim that the $80,000 represented a legal and nontaxable "love offering" was rejected by a federal court that found the minister guilty of several felony counts. This arrangement was not disclosed to the church board, and obviously amounted to an unauthorized diversion of church funds back to the minister.*

Example. *A church accountant embezzled $212,000 in church funds. This person's scheme was to divert to his own use several designated offerings, and to inflate the cost of equipment that he paid for with his own funds and that the church later reimbursed at the inflated amounts. The interesting aspect of this case was that the accountant was not only found guilty of embezzlement, but he was also convicted for tax evasion because he had failed to report any of the embezzled money as taxable income, and was sentenced to prison.*

Example. *A court ruled that an insurance company that paid out $26,000 to a charity because of an act of embezzlement could sue the embezzler for the full amount that it paid. This is an important case, for it demonstrates that a church employee who embezzles church funds may be sued by the church insurance company if it pays out a claim based on the embezzlement. In other words, the fact that the church decides not to sue the embezzler does not mean that the person will be free from any personal liability. If the church has insurance to cover the loss, the insurance company can go after the embezzler for a full recovery of the amount that it paid out on account of the embezzlement.*

17.4 Reducing the Risk of Embezzlement

Can the risk of embezzlement be reduced? If so, how? The good news is that there are number of steps that church leaders can take to reduce this risk, and most of them are quite simple as noted below.

Implement an effective system of internal control

The first and most effective deterrent to embezzlement is a strong system of "internal control." Internal control is an accounting term that refers to policies and procedures adopted by an organization to safeguard its assets and promote the accuracy of its financial records. What procedures has your church adopted to insure that cash receipts are properly recorded and deposited, and that only those cash disbursements that are properly authorized are made? These are the kinds of questions that are addressed by a church's system of internal control. Key steps to take include the following:

- Check to be sure that more than one person collects church offerings, and that no one has unsupervised possession of an offering plate at any time.

- Make sure that more than one person counts the offering.

- Check that there is regular turnover or rotation among the persons who collect and count church offerings.

- Check to be sure that different persons count and deposit church offerings.

- Check to be sure that a person who neither counts offerings nor deposits them with a bank is assigned the responsibility of reconciling offering counts with the bank deposit slips.

- Check to be sure that offering counts and bank deposit slips are reconciled for every service. Or, reconcile offering counts with monthly bank statements.

- Check to be sure that monthly bank statements are reviewed by a church official or employee having no responsibility for handling cash or writing checks.

Key point. The most important point to emphasize is "division of responsibilities." The more that tasks and responsibilities are shared or divided, the less risk there will be of embezzlement.

Key point. Many churches refuse to implement basic principles of internal control out of a fear of "offending" persons who may feel that they are being suspected of misconduct. The issue here is not one of hurt feelings, but accountability. The church, more than any other institution in society, should set the standard for financial accountability. After all, its programs and activities are rooted in religion, and it is funded entirely with donations from persons who rightfully assume that their contributions are being used for religious purposes. The church has a high responsibility to promote financial accountability. This duty is simply not met when the practices described above are followed.

Screen persons with financial responsibility

Some churches screen bookkeepers, accountants, and other employees who will have access to funds or be involved in financial decisions. Screening can consist of obtaining references from employers, prior employers, and other churches or charities with which the person has been employed or associated.

Conduct annual audits

A church can reduce the risk of embezzlement by having an annual audit of its financial records by a CPA firm. An audit accomplishes three important functions:

1. An audit promotes an environment of accountability in which opportunities for embezzlement (and therefore the risk of embezzlement) are reduced.

2. The CPA (or CPAs) who conducts the audit will provide the church leadership with a "management letter" that points out weaknesses and inefficiencies in the church's accounting and financial procedures. This information is invaluable to church leaders.

3. An audit contributes to the integrity and reputation of church leaders and staff members who handle funds.

Key point. Don't confuse an audit with a more limited engagement that CPAs will perform, such as a "compilation."

Key point. Audits can be expensive, and this will be a very relevant consideration for smaller churches. Of course, the time involved in performing an audit for a smaller church will be limited, which will result in a lower fee. Churches can control the cost of an audit by obtaining bids. Also, by staying with the same CPA firm, most churches will realize a savings in the second and succeeding years since the CPA will not have to spend time becoming familiar with the church's financial and accounting procedures.

Key point. Smaller churches that cannot afford a full audit may want to consider two other options: (1) Hire a CPA to conduct a review, which is a simpler and less expensive procedure. If the review detects irregularities, a full audit may be considered worth the price. (2) Create an internal audit committee if there are accountants or business leaders within the church who have the ability to review accounting procedures and practices and look for weaknesses. These people often are very familiar with sound internal control policies, and will quickly correct weaknesses in the church's financial operations. An added bonus—such a committee will serve as a deterrent to those who might otherwise be tempted to embezzle church funds.

Bond persons who handle funds

Churches can address the risk of embezzlement by bonding the church treasurer and any bookkeeper or accountant that is on staff. You can also purchase a blanket policy to cover all employees and officers. It is important to note that insurance policies vary. Some require that the embezzler be convicted before it will pay a claim, while others do not. The period of time covered by the policy will also vary. These are important points to be discussed by your church board in consultation with your insurance agent.

Key point. Insurance is not a substitute for implementing a sound system of internal control.

17.5 Responding to Allegations of Embezzlement.

Sometimes a person who has embezzled church funds will voluntarily confess—usually out of a fear that he or she is about to be "caught." But in many cases the embezzler does not confess—at least initially. Discrepancies or irregularities may occur which cause church leaders to suspect this person. Consider the following examples.

Example. The same person has counted church offerings for many years. The pastor inadvertently notices that offerings are always higher when this person is absent (due to illness, business, or vacation).

Example. Church officials noticed that a church bookkeeper was living a higher standard of living than was realistic given her income. Among other things, she purchased an expensive home and a luxury car.

Example. Church offerings have remained constant, or increased slightly, despite the fact that attendance has increased.

Example. A church treasurer notices that a church official with sole signature authority on the church checking account has purchased a number of expensive items from unknown companies without any documentation to prove what was purchased and why.

Church leaders often are unsure how to address suspected cases of embezzlement. The suspected embezzler is almost always a trusted member or employee, and church leaders are reluctant to accuse such a person without irrefutable evidence that he or she is guilty. Seldom does such evidence exist. The pastor may confront the person about the suspicion, but in many cases the individual will deny any wrongdoing—even if guilty. This compounds the frustration of church officials, who do not know how to proceed.

Here is a checklist of steps that church leaders can take to help resolve such difficult cases:

1. *Confront the suspected embezzler.* Based on the evidence of a good faith investigation, the pastor and at least one other church leader should confront the suspected embezzler. Inform the person that the church has evidence indicating that he or she has embezzled church funds. Seek a confession or explanation. Inform the person that if no one confesses or there is no explanation, the church will be forced to call in a CPA firm to confirm that embezzlement has occurred and to identify the probable embezzler.

Tip. Embezzlement is a criminal offense. Depending on the amount of funds or property taken, it may be a felony that can result in a sentence in the state penitentiary. This obviously would have a devastating impact on the embezzler, and his or her family. If the evidence clearly indicates that a particular member or employee has embezzled church funds, but this person denies any wrongdoing, inform him or her that the church may be forced to turn the matter over to the police for investigation and prosecution.

2. Have a local CPA conduct an audit to establish that embezzlement has occurred, and provide an estimate of how much was embezzled. If the suspected embezzler denies any wrongdoing (or if embezzlement is suspected but it is not clear who is guilty), church leaders should consider hiring a local CPA firm to look for evidence of embezzlement. There is a good possibility that the embezzlement will be detected, and that the perpetrator will be identified.

> *Tip. CPAs can also help the church establish a strong system of internal control to reduce the risk of embezzlement in the future.*

Many church leaders have found that turning the investigation over to a CPA firm is much more acceptable than conducting the investigation internally. The CPA firm is completely objective, and ordinarily will not know the suspected embezzler. Further, few church members will object to the church hiring a CPA firm to detect wrongdoing and help establish a sound system of internal control.

3. Contact the police or local prosecutor. If the suspected embezzler does not confess, or if embezzlement is suspected but it is not clear who is guilty, church leaders must consider turning the matter over to the police or local prosecutor. This is a very difficult decision, since it may result in the prosecution and incarceration of a member of the congregation.

4. The embezzler confesses. In some cases the embezzler eventually confesses. Often, this is to prevent the church from turning the case over to the IRS or the police, or to a CPA firm. Embezzlers believe they will receive "better treatment" from their own church than from the government. In many cases they are correct. It often is astonishing how quickly church members will rally in support of the embezzler once he or she confesses—no matter how much money was stolen from the church. This is especially true when the embezzler used the embezzled funds for a "noble" purpose, such as medical bills for a sick child. Many church members demand that the embezzler be forgiven. They are shocked and repulsed by the suggestion that the embezzler—their friend and fellow church member—be turned over to the IRS or the police! But is it this simple? Should church leaders join in the outpouring of sympathy? Should the matter be dropped once the embezzler confesses?

These are questions that each church will have to answer for itself, depending on the circumstances of each case. Before forgiving the embezzler and dropping the matter, church leaders should consider the following points:

1. A serious crime has been committed, and the embezzler has breached a sacred trust. The church should insist, at a minimum, that the embezzler must:

- disclose how much money was embezzled;
- make full restitution by paying back all embezzled funds within a specified period of time; and,
- immediately and permanently be removed from any position within the church involving access to church funds.

> *Tip. Closely scrutinize and question the amount of funds the embezzler claims to have taken. Remember, you are relying on the word of an admitted thief. Is it a realistic amount? Is it consistent with the irregularities or discrepancies that caused church*

leaders to suspect embezzlement in the first place? If in doubt, consider hiring a local CPA to review the amount the embezzler claims to have stolen.

2. *In many cases the embezzler will insist that he or she is not able to pay back the embezzled funds.* They have been spent. This presents church leaders with a difficult decision, since the embezzler has received unreported taxable income from the church. The embezzler should be informed that the embezzled funds must either be returned within a specified time, or a promissory note must be signed promising to pay back the embezzled funds within a specified period of time. The embezzler should be informed that failure to agree to either alternative will force the church to issue him or her a 1099 (or a corrected W-2 if the embezzler is an employee) reporting the embezzled funds as taxable income. Failure to do so will subject the church to a potential penalty (up to $10,000) for aiding and abetting in the substantial understatement of taxable income under section 6701 of the tax code.

> **Tip.** *An embezzler's biggest problem ordinarily will not be with the church or even with the local prosecutor. It will be with the IRS for failure to report taxable income. There are only two ways to avoid trouble with the IRS: (1) the embezzler pays back the embezzled funds, or (2) the church reports the embezzled funds as taxable income on a 1099 or corrected W-2.*

3. *Church leaders must also remember that they owe a fiduciary obligation to the church and that they are stewards of the church's resources.* Viewing the offender with mercy does not necessarily mean that the debt must be forgiven and a criminal act ignored. Churches are public charities that exist to serve religious purposes, and they are funded entirely out of charitable contributions from persons who justifiably assume that their contributions will be used to further the church's mission. These purposes may not be served when a church forgives and ignores cases of embezzlement.

> **Tip.** *The federal Employee Polygraph Protection Act prohibits most employers from requiring or even suggesting that an employee submit to a polygraph exam. Employers also are prevented from dismissing or disciplining an employee for refusing to take a polygraph exam. There is an exception that may apply in some cases—an employer may require that an employee take a polygraph exam if the employee is suspected of a specific act of theft or other economic loss and the employer has reported the matter to the police. However, the employer must follow very strict requirements to avoid liability. A church should never suggest or require that an employee submit to a polygraph exam, even in cases of suspected embezzlement, without first contacting a local attorney for legal advice.*

17.6 The Consequences of Embezzlement

Persons who embezzle church funds face a number of consequences. Some of them may come as unpleasant surprises. Here are four of them.

1. *Felony conviction.* Embezzling church funds is a felony in most states, and conviction can lead to a term in a state penitentiary.

2. *Tax evasion.* In many cases the embezzler's biggest concern is not the possibility of being prosecuted for the crime of embezzlement. Rather, it is the possibility of

being prosecuted by the IRS for tax evasion. Embezzlers never report their illegally obtained "income" on their tax returns. Nor do they suspect that failure to do so may subject them to criminal tax evasion charges. In fact, in some cases it is actually more likely that the IRS will prosecute the embezzler for tax evasion than the local prosecutor will prosecute for the crime of embezzlement.

> **Example.** *A church accountant embezzled $212,000 in church funds. His scheme was to divert to his own use several designated offerings, and to inflate the cost of equipment that he paid for with his own funds and that the church later reimbursed at the inflated amounts. The accountant not only was found guilty of embezzlement, but he was also convicted of tax evasion because he had failed to report any of the embezzled money as taxable income. He was sentenced to a 2-year prison term, followed by 2 years of probation.*

3. *Recovery of property purchased with embezzled funds.* Persons who receive property purchased by the embezzler with embezzled funds may be required to return the property to the church.

4. *Insurance company lawsuits.* As if the three consequences summarized above are not enough, embezzlers face an additional consequence—they may be sued by an insurance company that pays a claim based on the embezzlement. Many churches purchase insurance to cover financial losses due to theft or embezzlement. Insurance companies that pay out claims based on such losses are free to sue the persons responsible.

> **Example.** *A court ruled that an insurance company that paid out $26,000 to a charity because of an act of embezzlement could sue the embezzler for the full amount that it paid. Such cases illustrate an important point—a church employee or volunteer who embezzles church funds may be sued by the church insurance company if it pays out a claim based on the embezzlement.*

17.7 Confidentiality and Privileged Communications

Sometimes ministers learn of embezzlement through a confession by the embezzler in the course of confidential counseling. This presents the minister with a dilemma—either protect the confidentiality of the confession and refuse to disclose it, or ignore confidentiality and disclose the confession. This dilemma is compounded by the fact that some ministers have been sued for disclosing confidential information without the consent of the other person. Embezzlers may claim that they confessed their crime to their minister in confidence and in the course of spiritual counseling, with no thought that the minister would disclose the information to others.

> **Tip.** *Ministers who disclose confidential information without permission risk being sued for breaching their duty of confidentiality. When an employee or volunteer approaches a minister and confesses to embezzling church funds, there normally will be an expectation that the minister will keep that information in confidence. There is no sign above the minister's desk that says, "warning, confessions of criminal activity will be promptly shared with the board or with the civil authorities." Ministers who violate this expectation need to understand that they face potential legal liability for doing so—unless they have the employee's permission, in writing.*

Ministers who receive a confidential confession of embezzlement from a church employee or volunteer should not disclose this information to others, including the church board, without the person's written permission. If the embezzler does not consent to the disclosure of the confession, and refuses to meet with the board, the minister should not disclose the information to any other person. Disclosure under these circumstances could result in a lawsuit being brought against the minister and church. If such a situation should arise, the minister should seek legal counsel.

Does this mean that the minister should drop the matter? Not necessarily. The minister is free to gather independent evidence that embezzlement occurred, so long as this is done without disclosing the confession. For example, the minister could persuade the church board to hire a CPA to conduct an audit of the church's financial records. Such a procedure may reveal that embezzlement has occurred. The minister also should attempt to persuade the embezzler to confess to the board.

Key point. Closely related to the concept of confidentiality is the clergy-penitent privilege. Ministers cannot be compelled to disclose in court the contents of confidential communications shared with them in the course of spiritual counseling.

Example. Late one night, a church treasurer arranged a meeting with her priest after informing him that she "had done something almost as bad as murder." The treasurer, after requesting that their conversation be kept confidential, informed the priest that she had embezzled $30,000 in church funds. The priest, with the permission of the treasurer, sought the assistance of the church board. The board decided that the embezzlement had to be reported to the local police. The treasurer was later prosecuted for embezzling church funds, and she was convicted and sentenced to four months in jail despite the fact that she fully repaid the church prior to her trial. She appealed her conviction on the ground that it had been based on her confidential statements to the priest which, in her opinion, were "penitential communications" that were privileged against disclosure in court. The appeals court concluded that the statements made by the church treasurer to the priest were not privileged since they involved a "problem-solving entreaty" by the treasurer rather than a request to make a true confession seeking forgiveness or absolution—the very essence of the spiritual relationship privileged under the statute. That is, the treasurer sought out the priest not for spiritual counseling, but to disclose her embezzlement and to seek his counsel on how to correct the problem. The court also emphasized that the treasurer had "released" the priest from his assurance of confidentiality by consenting to his disclosure of the facts of the case to the church board members.

Informing the congregation

Church leaders often refuse to disclose to the congregation any information about an incident of embezzlement for fear of being sued for defamation. This concern is understandable. However, serious problems can occur when the pastor or church board dismisses a long-term employee or volunteer for embezzlement and nothing is disclosed to the membership. Church leaders under these circumstances often are accused of acting arbitrarily, and there is a demand for an explanation. Refusal to respond to such demands may place the church leadership in an even worse light.

There is a possible answer to this dilemma. Many states recognize the concept of "qualified privilege." This means that statements made to others concerning a matter of common interest cannot be defamatory unless made with malice.

Statements are made with malice if they are made with a knowledge that they are false, or with a reckless disregard as to their truth or falsity. In the church context, this privilege protects statements made by members to other members concerning matters of common interest. Such communications cannot be defamatory unless malice is proven. Church leaders who decide to disclose why an embezzler was dismissed can reduce the legal risk to the church and themselves by following a few basic precautions:

- Only share information with active voting members of the church—at a membership meeting or by letter. The qualified privilege does not apply if the communication is made to non-members.

- Adopt procedures that will confirm that no non-member received the information.

- Limit your remarks to factual information and do not express opinions.

- Prepare in advance a written statement that is communicated with members, and that is approved in advance by an attorney.

Key point. In some cases, it is helpful to obtain a signed confession from an individual who has been found guilty or who has confessed. If the individual consents to the communication of the confession to church members, then you can quote from the confession in a letter that is sent to members of the congregation, or in a membership meeting. Be sure that this consent is in writing.

Key point. One court ruled that a church could be sued for defamation for sharing suspicions regarding a church treasurer's embezzlement with members in a congregational meeting. The court concluded that the treasurer should have been investigated and dismissed by the board, without informing the congregation. While no other court has reached a similar conclusion, this case suggests that church leaders should disclose cases of embezzlement to the church membership only if (1) absolutely necessary (for example, to reduce congregational unrest), and (2) an attorney is involved in making this decision.

17.8 Avoiding False Accusations

In some cases it is not certain that embezzlement has occurred, or that a particular individual is guilty. A church must be careful in how it proceeds in these cases to avoid possible liability for defamation or emotional distress.

Example. A church convened a special business meeting at which the church treasurer was accused of embezzling church funds. Following this meeting the treasurer was shunned by church members who viewed her as guilty. This case is tragic, since the treasurer had been a long and devoted member of the church. Her life was ruined by the allegation, and she had to leave the church. It was later proven that she was completely innocent. She later filed a lawsuit, accusing the pastor and members of the church board of defamation. A court agreed with her, and awarded her a substantial verdict. The court pointed out that the accusation of embezzlement was based on flimsy evidence and could have easily been refuted with any reasonable investigation. The court concluded that church leaders are liable for defamation if they charge a church worker with embezzlement without first conducting a good faith investigation.

The court also pointed out that the charges should not have been disclosed to the congregation, but rather should have been discussed among the church board and a decision made at that level on whether or not to dismiss the treasurer.

This case provides church leaders with very helpful guidance in handling suspicions of embezzlement. Do not rush to judgment. Conduct a deliberate and competent investigation, and let the church board resolve the issue without involving or informing the congregation, if possible. In some cases, congregational outrage may occur following the dismissal of an embezzler by the pastor or church board, especially if nothing is communicated to the congregation about the basis for the action. In these cases the board may decide that the membership must be informed. If so, refer to the above discussion on "informing the congregation."

Summary

The definition of embezzlement varies slightly from state to state, but in general it refers to the wrongful conversion of property that is lawfully in your possession. The idea is that someone has legal control or custody of property or funds, and then decides to convert the property or funds to his or her own personal use. Churches are vulnerable to embezzlement, and often fail to detect it or even suspect that it could occur. The key to reduce the risk of embezzlement is to implement an effective system of internal control. If embezzlement does occur church leaders must take action and respond to the problem. Responding appropriately is often a difficult task because the embezzler is almost always a trusted member of the congregation. Embezzlement, however, is a felony in most states, and also has tax consequences. When embezzlement does occur, leaders must maintain confidentiality in communicating with the congregation, and avoid possible liability for defamation or emotional stress.

In the next chapter, we focus on reducing the risk of defamation.

CHAPTER 18. REDUCING
THE RISK OF DEFAMATION

Defamation is a form of legal liability associated with words. Church leaders frequently make public statements orally and in official publications. They must recognize that they, and their church, may be liable on the basis of defamation for public statements that are false and that damage the reputation of another person. This chapter will review the definition of defamation, two important defenses to defamation, and several examples illustrating this important basis of liability.

18.1 Definition of Defamation

Defamation consists of the following elements:

(1) oral or written statements about another person

(2) that are false

(3) that are "published" (that is, communicated to a sufficient number of other persons to affect the other person's reputation), and

(4) that injure the other person's reputation

If the words are oral, the defamation is sometimes called *slander*. If the words are written, the defamation may be referred to as *libel*. Although this terminology is still widely used, there is a tendency to refer to both slander and libel as defamation.

Defamation involves injury to another's reputation rather than feelings. Not every derogatory statement is defamatory.

18.2 Ministers May Be Sued for Defamation

Ministers may be liable for defamation if they communicate false statements to other persons that injure the reputation of another. To illustrate, in one case a minister publicly stated that a member of his congregation had a "vile spirit and utter disrespect for leadership," and declared that another member had associated himself with a pastor who "under the role of minister of Jesus, is one of Satan's choicest tools." A court found such remarks to be defamatory.[1] In another case, a Roman Catholic archbishop was found guilty of defaming a priest by publicly referring to him as an "irresponsible and insane" person who was "morally blind" and "disobedient to the laws of the church."[2]

Here are some examples of actual cases in which ministers were sued on the basis of defamation because of statements they made.

> *Example. A minister left a pastoral position in Alaska and accepted a call as minister of a church in Tennessee. When he presented himself to the church to begin his duties, he was informed by church officials that because of derogatory information the church had received from a denominational official (a "presbyter") in Alaska, the church would not hire him. The presbyter had informed church leaders that the minister was divorced, dishonest, unable to perform pastoral duties because of throat surgery, and*

---

[1] Brewer v. Second Baptist Church, 197 P.2d 713 (Cal. 1948).
[2] Hellstern v. Katzer, 79 N.W. 429 (Wis. 1899).

that he had made an improper sexual advance to a church member in Alaska. The minister sued the presbyter for defamation and interference with contract.[3]

Example. A minister wrote an article in a church publication that addressed the church's newly developed doctrine on divorce and remarriage. The article contained statements that allegedly defamed the former spouse of a prominent church official.[4]

Example. A conflict arose in a church between a pastor and some members of the congregation. A denominational official intervened in an attempt to resolve the problem. The official prepared a report to the church council that stated, "A significant number of members have experienced the pastor as being aloof; as being the boss; as being dogmatic; as not being open to the persons who disagree or have different viewpoints, even to the point of feeling that they are dismissed from friendship; as not always hearing what the other person is trying to say; as having particular difficulty in appreciating women as equals; as one who talks negatively about persons to others (behind their backs), sometimes close to the point of breaking confidentiality." The pastor alleged that this statement was defamatory, as was a bishop's disclosure to members of the congregation that the pastor was going to a psychiatric hospital for treatment.[5]

Example. A Catholic priest became upset when he suspected that a monument company that did work at a church cemetery was guilty of using church utilities without paying for them. He wrote a letter to the owner of the monument company which stated, in part, "Stated simply, your workers entered our property, and used [church] utilities without permission, and that is theft. I could have them arrested and charged, for your information." A copy of the letter was sent to the diocese. A week later, the priest published the following statement in a church newsletter (that was mailed to 362 families): "For your information, I have been obliged [to inform the monument company] that it is forbidden . . . to perform work of any kind in [the cemetery]. The company has persisted in ignoring my cemetery policies, and has a 'come as you please, go as you please' attitude and uses our electrical utilities without permission. The utilities come out of cemetery funds (e.g., your pocket)." The monument company sued the priest for defamation when it learned of the statement in the newsletter.[6]

Example. A youth pastor who made statements to members of his congregation about an alleged affair between an associate pastor and a church employee was sued for defamation.[7]

Example. A minister wrote a letter to another minister, recommending that a foreign missionary's endorsement be withdrawn. In the letter, the minister stated that the missionary in question was a liar; that he failed to pay his debts; that he was engaged in a program of destruction, hatred, and "tyrancy"; that his nature was to rule as a dictator; that his aim was to divide and split the churches; and that he was carrying

---

3 Marshall v. Munro, 845 P.2d 424 (Alaska 1993).

4 McNair v. Worldwide Church of God, 242 Cal. Rptr. 823 (2d App. Dist. 1987).

5 Yaggie v. Indiana-Kentucky Synod, 860 F. Supp. 1194 (W.D. Ky. 1994).

6 Redmond v. McCool, 582 So.2d 262 (La. App. 1991).

7 St. Luke Evangelical Lutheran Church v. Smith, 568 A.2d 35 (Md. 1990).

8 Murphy v. Harty, 393 P.2d 206 (Ore. 1964).

out Satan's plan of division and destruction. The missionary sued the pastor for defamation.[8]

These examples suggest that ministers should refrain from making public remarks that might diminish the reputation, respect, goodwill, or esteem of other persons.

School teachers and administrators may be sued for defamation as a result of public statements they make. The above discussion of pastoral liability is relevant to teachers and school officials. Here are some examples of cases in which private school officials were sued for defamation.

Example. An eighth-grade student at a church school was disciplined for engaging in behavior involving inappropriate touching of girls. The student's parents sued the school, claiming that their son had been excessively and unfairly punished for his "youthful indiscretions." They also claimed that their son was defamed when school officials described the student's behavior to other students, the police, and a state agency.[9]

Example. A church operated a private school. Its minister of education, who also served as principal of the school, resigned after admitting that he misappropriated church funds, destroyed church records, forged signatures, and committed other criminal acts. He later pleaded guilty to criminal charges for his admitted conduct in misappropriating school funds. He informed the church that a woman who served as a secretary at the school participated in the misappropriations. After an audit confirmed the principal's accusations the church asked the secretary to resign. The church issued (1) a letter to its members claiming that the secretary misappropriated school funds; (2) a letter to the school children's parents claiming that the secretary deposited tuition funds into the wrong accounts and later used the funds for her personal benefit, destroyed checks and bank records; forged signatures, covered up these indiscretions, received seventy dollars extra per pay period for nearly two years as well as other undocumented "reimbursements," and (3) a report to the church members reporting the secretary's resignation and claiming that she deposited tuition funds into the wrong account and then used the funds to support programs and individuals outside of and over the budget adopted by the congregation. At a meeting of church members, church officials orally accused the secretary of depositing tuition funds into the wrong account and then using the funds for her personal benefit or for other people or projects as she and the principal saw fit; destroying checks, bank records, and financial records; forging signatures; and covering up many of these indiscretions. The secretary later sued the church and the individual members of the church audit committee, claiming that the church's actions defamed her and inflicted emotional distress.[10]

18.3 Defenses to Defamation

Ministers who do communicate disparaging remarks about another person may be able to assert one of the following defenses to a charge of defamation.

---

[9] Iwenofu v. St. Luke School, 1999 WL 61007 (Ohio App. 1999).
[10] Hanssen v. Our Redeemer Lutheran Church, 938 S.W.2d 85 (Tex. App. 1997).

Truth

If an allegedly defamatory remark is true, it is simply not regarded as defamatory by most courts. This defense is based on the principle that the dissemination of truth should not be restricted by the fear of defamation lawsuits.

However, note that in recent years the courts have devised a new tort ("invasion of privacy") to punish statements which, though true, disclose private facts about another person in a way that would be highly offensive to a reasonable person. As a result, while truth is a defense to defamation, it does not necessarily insulate one from all legal liability.

Matters of "common interest"

Several courts have ruled that church members are protected by a *qualified privilege* when sharing with other church members about matters of mutual concern or common interest. This means that such communications cannot be defamatory unless they are made with malice. Malice in this context means that the person who made the allegedly defamatory remark knew that it was false, or made it with a reckless disregard as to its truth or falsity. This is a difficult standard to prove, which means that communications between church members will be defamatory only in exceptional cases. The same rule has been applied by a number of courts to statements made in the course of church disciplinary proceedings.

To illustrate, statements made under the following circumstances have been held not to be defamatory: a communication made between officers of a church or denomination on any subject in which they both have an interest;[11] communications between members of a religious organization concerning the conduct of other members or officers;[12] charges made against a church member during a church investigation into his character;[13] reading a sentence of excommunication of a church member in the presence of a church congregation;[14] an article in a publication produced by a religious denomination describing difficulties in missions work in an area under the control of a particular minister;[15] charges made by an officer of a church against the church's minister;[16] and disparaging statements made by several church members concerning their minister during a church disciplinary proceeding.[17]

> *Example. Church board members who wrote a letter asking their pastor to resign on account of his failing health were not guilty of defamation. The letter requested that the pastor either retire or resign and stated that if he did not elect one of these alternatives, the deacons would recommend to the church congregation that his services as pastor be terminated. The pastor responded to the deacons' request by informing them that he would neither retire nor resign. The deacons then called for a*

---

11 Church of Scientology v. Green, 354 F. Supp. 800 (S.D.N.Y. 1973).

12 Willenbucher v. McCormick, 229 F. Supp. 659 (D. Colo. 1964).

13 Cimijotti v. Paulsen, 219 F. Supp. 621 (N.D. Iowa 1963), *appeal dismissed*, 323 F.2d 716 (8th Cir. 1963).

14 *Id.*

15 Herndon v. Melton, 105 S.E.2d 531 (N.C. 1958).

16 Browning v. Gomez, 332 S.W.2d 588 (Tex. 1960).

17 Joiner v. Weeks, 383 So.2d 101 (La. App. 1980).

special meeting of the congregation and distributed copies of the letter they had sent the pastor. At this meeting, the congregation requested that the pastor retire and approved the terms and conditions of his retirement package. The pastor retired at this meeting. He later sued the board of deacons for defamation. A state appeals court ruled that even if the letter signed by the deacons was defamatory, it was protected by a "qualified privilege" since it "concerned various church interests" including the pastor's perceived inability to perform his pastoral duties, it was written by members of the congregation (the deacons), and communicated exclusively to other members of the church. The court stressed that there was no evidence that any nonmembers "were either given or otherwise received a copy of the letter." The court concluded that the pastor failed to prove that the deacons acted with malice, and as a result the letter was not defamatory.[18]

Example. An Ohio appeals court ruled that a former teacher at a church-operated school could not sue school officials for defamation since the allegedly defamatory statements made by the school officials concerned a matter of "common interest" and accordingly were privileged. The court also found that the school officials had not acted with malice in making their statements.[19]

Example. A Texas appeals court ruled that statements made by church leaders during a church investigation were not defamatory. It observed, "Statements made in the context of a church investigatory proceeding are protected by a qualified privilege. If a qualified privilege exists, the defamed party has the burden of establishing that the privilege has been abused. A qualified privilege is abused when the person uttering the statement knows the matter to be false or does not act for the purpose of protecting the interest for which the privilege exists."[20]

Example. A Texas court ruled that a church was not liable for defaming a former secretary as a result of statements made to church members claiming that she had misappropriated church funds. The court ruled that the secretary had not been defamed because the church was protected by a qualified privilege and she failed to prove malice. It observed, "All of the members of [the church] have a common interest in the church's use of their financial contributions to the church; thus, the members have a common interest in information about those funds. The members who made the statements in question reasonably believed that the misappropriation took place and that the board, the members, and the parents shared a common interest in the use of the funds and information about those funds."[21]

Key point. These defenses also are available to teachers and administrators employed by church schools.

---

[18] Mosley v. Evans, 630 N.E.2d 75 (Ohio App. 11 Dist. 1993).

[19] McCartney v. Oblates of St. Francis de Sales, 609 N.E.2d 216 (Ohio App. 6 Dist. 1992).

[20] Kelly v. Diocese of Corpus Christi, 832 S.W.2d 88 (Tex. App. Corpus Christi 1992).

[21] Hanssen v. Our Redeemer Lutheran Church, 938 S.W.2d 85 (Tex. App. 1997).

Summary

Ministers and lay church leaders occasionally communicate potentially defamatory statements to their congregations. Examples include statements concerning suspected embezzlement by a church employee, allegations of sexual misconduct by a staff member or volunteer, or explanations of why a church employee was dismissed. Before making any statements to the congregation in such cases, church leaders should consider the following points:

- Such statements may be defamatory.

- Such statements will not be protected by the qualified privilege if nonmembers are present when they are made.

- Such statements may be protected by a qualified privilege if they are made to members only. This means that church leaders take steps to ensure that only members are present when the statements are made. This can be accomplished in a number of ways. For example, a special meeting of members is called and only persons whose names are on the church's current list of active voting members are admitted. As an additional precaution, members present at such a meeting should be asked to adopt a resolution of confidentiality, agreeing not to discuss the information with any non-member under any circumstances. Persons dissenting from this vote should be excused from the meeting. Alternatively, the statements are set forth in a letter that is sent to active voting members (with the notation "privileged and confidential" on both the letter and envelope).

- Consult with an attorney before making any potentially defamatory statement to the congregation (in a meeting or through correspondence).

In the next chapter we explore the topic of undue influence and provide steps that can be taken to reduce that risk.

CHAPTER 19. REDUCING THE RISK OF UNDUE INFLUENCE

Gifts to churches occasionally are challenged by disinherited heirs on the ground that the pastor "unduly influenced" the donor into making the gift. There are several factors the courts will consider in deciding whether or not undue influence occurred, including the age and mental health of the donor, and the presence of independent legal advice. Undue influence generally must be proven by "clear and convincing" evidence.

This chapter will focus on ministers who engage in undue influence. There have been no cases of teachers or administrators at church schools unduly influencing a donor into making a gift to the school.

19.1 Definition

If a minister unduly influenced a donor in making a gift to the church, the donor (or the donor's heirs) may have the gift canceled. This rule applies both to direct gifts made during one's lifetime and to gifts contained in documents (such as wills) which take effect at the donor's death. Undue influence is more than persuasion or suggestion. It connotes total dominion and control over the mind of another. As one court noted, "undue influence is that influence which, by force, coercion or overpersuasion destroys the free agency" of another.[1]

Undue influence generally must be inferred from the circumstances surrounding a gift, since it seldom can be proven directly. Circumstances commonly considered in determining whether a donor was unduly influenced in the making of a gift include the following:

- whether the gift was the product of hasty action
- whether the gift was concealed from others
- whether the person or organization benefited by the gift was active in securing it
- whether the gift was consistent or inconsistent with prior declarations and planning of the donor
- whether the gift was reasonable rather than unnatural in view of the donor's circumstances, attitudes, and family
- the donor's age, physical condition, and mental health
- whether a confidential relationship existed between the donor and the recipient of the gift
- whether the donor had independent advice

Most courts have held that undue influence must be proven by "clear and convincing" or "clear and satisfactory" evidence. Proof by a mere preponderance of the evidence will not suffice. However, some courts have ruled that a "presumption" of undue influence may arise when a gift is made by a church member directly to his or her minister, or when an attorney who drafts a will leaving a gift to a church is a member of the same church. This presumption is rebuttable.

---

[1] In Matter of Soper's Estate, 598 S.W.2d 528, 538 (Mo. 1980).

19.2 Cases Recognizing Undue Influence

In a number of cases the courts have nullified gifts to churches on the basis of undue influence. A few representative examples are set forth below.

Example. A 70-year-old invalid dying from cancer was visited several times a week by a pastor of her church. Three days before her death, the pastor persuaded her to execute a will leaving most of her property to him. The pastor's personal attorney was called upon to draft the instrument. Two days later, the pastor attempted to have the donor give him additional property by a deed of gift, but by this time the donor was in a stupor and was physically unable to sign her name. She died a day later. The gift to the pastor was challenged on the ground that it was the product of undue influence. The court concluded that undue influence was established by the age and feeble mental and physical condition of the donor, the involvement of the pastor in procuring the gift to himself, the confidential "clergyman-parishioner" relationship that existed between the pastor and the donor, and the lack of any independent advice.[2]

Example. Gifts to an Episcopal rector and his church were invalidated on the basis of undue influence since the donor was a 76-year-old woman suffering from arteriosclerosis, senility, and severe loss of memory.[3]

Example. The Oklahoma Supreme Court ruled that a provision in a deceased church member's will leaving the bulk of her estate to her church was invalid since it was a product of the pastor's "undue influence." A 96-year-old woman died, leaving the bulk of her estate to the Baptist church she had attended for the last several years of her life. For many years, the woman suffered from alcoholism and during the 1970's her health and living conditions deteriorated. From 1980 to 1983 the pastor of a local Baptist church became closely acquainted with her and visited with her in her home several times. By 1984 all of the woman's friends were members of this church. The pastor arranged for several of them to regularly assist the woman by cleaning her home. Through this process the woman became very dependent upon the pastor and reposed great trust in him. Although in 1983 the woman attended several sessions of an estate planning seminar at her church, she failed to make the last session where a "will information guide" was distributed. In 1984, when the woman was 89 years of age, the pastor brought her a copy of the "will information guide" and spent several hours assisting her in cataloging her assets. The pastor later asked a church member who was an attorney to contact the woman and discuss her will's preparation. This attorney had not represented the woman in any other legal matters. Before the attorney drafted the will he had one 15-minute telephone conversation with her in which he discussed the contents of her estate using the "will information guide" provided him by the pastor. A few weeks later the woman was taken to the attorney's office by a church member. She reviewed her will and signed it. All of the subscribing witnesses were church members chosen by the pastor. Seven years after the will was signed the woman died. Her nephew claimed that the gift to the church should not be honored since it was based on "undue influence." The supreme court invalidated the gift on the basis of undue influence. The court applied a "2-prong test" to determine

---

[2] In re Miller's Estate, 60 P.2d 492 (Cal. 1936).
[3] Tallahassee Bank and Trust Co. v. Brooks, 200 So.2d 251 (Fla. App. 1967). *See also* Hensley v. Stevens, 481 P.2d 694 (Mont. 1971) (gift to minister held to be product of undue influence and fraud since minister induced gift by falsely representing that he would reconvey a portion of the property to the donor's husband but never did).

whether undue influence invalidates a provision in a will: First, does a "confidential relationship" exist between the deceased and another person; and second, did the stronger party in the relationship assist in the preparation of the weaker person's will. Factors to be considered in applying this 2-prong test include (1) whether the person charged with undue influence was not a natural object of the maker's bounty; (2) whether the stronger person was a trusted or confidential advisor or agent of the will's maker; (3) whether the stronger person was present or active in the procurement or preparation of the will; (4) whether the will's maker was of advanced age or impaired faculties; (5) whether independent and disinterested advice regarding the will was given to its maker. The court rejected the pastor's claim that he could not have unduly influenced the woman since he received nothing under her will.[4]

Example. A gift by a 79-year-old single woman to her church was invalidated because the evidence demonstrated that the church's minister visited the donor daily and preyed upon her fear that other churches in the community might exceed her own in size and prosperity.[5]

19.3 Cases Rejecting Undue Influence

In the great majority of cases, however, gifts to churches have been upheld despite the claim that they were the product of undue influence. To illustrate, in one case, a court in upholding a gift to a church observed:

If a determined old lady, who knows her own mind and without consulting her children, carries out her own wishes in that regard and buys an annuity contract, can have her wishes held for naught and the contract set aside . . . then no such annuity can stand in this state against such attack. The entire evidence discloses that the conduct of the officer of this church or organization was above reproach, for, even after she sought them out and asked for the investment, they did not press the matter, but gave her every opportunity to seek other advice and change her desires.[6]

Example. A gift of property by an 82-year-old single woman to a Catholic church to assure the saying of masses for deceased members of her family was upheld despite the claims of her nearest relatives that such was not her real intention and that she had been unduly influenced by the church without her family's knowledge or consent. In upholding the validity of the gift, the court noted the following factors: (1) the donor's desire to make provision for the saying of masses for her family preceded the date of the gift; (2) the donor's will, which had been executed prior to the gift to the church, left nothing to surviving family members; (3) the donor did not conceal the gift; (4) there was no evidence that the donor was in a weakened condition of mind or body at the time of the gift; and (5) she reaffirmed the gift in subsequent letters, one of which was written five years after the day of the gift.[7]

Example. A South Carolina court rejected a claim that an elderly decedent's will, which left the bulk of her estate to the Lutheran Church in America (LCA), was the

---

[4] Suagee v. Cook, 897 P.2d 268 (Okla. 1995).
[5] Whitmire v. Kroelinger, 42 F.2d 699 (W.D.S.C. 1930).
[6] Wixson v. Nebraska Conference Association of Seventh-Day Adventists, 241 N.W. 532 (Neb. 1932).
[7] Guill v. Wolpert, 218 N.W.2d 224 (Neb. 1974).

product of "undue influence" and accordingly invalid. The decedent executed her first will at the age of 78. This will left 10 percent of her estate to her local church, 40 percent to various relatives, and 50 percent to another charity. At the age of 87, the decedent began changing her will. The fourth and final amendment of her will, executed when she was 88 years old, placed the bulk of her estate in a charitable trust, the income from which was distributed to the LCA. The final will was challenged by a beneficiary whose share of the estate had been reduced. The beneficiary argued that the final will was invalid since it had been the product of undue influence. The court acknowledged that undue influence can invalidate a will, but it denied that the decedent's final will had been the result of undue influence. The court observed that undue influence must be proven by the person challenging a will, and that it consists of "influence amounting to coercion destroying free agency on the part of the [decedent]" so that the will was the result of "force and fear." The court, in rejecting the allegation of undue influence, observed that the final version of the decedent's will had been executed "when she was in reasonably good health, and during her latter years [when] she continued to work in her yard, talk with her neighbors, do some cooking and go to a grocery store . . . ." In short, she still possessed sufficient independence and health to support the conclusion that "she was the ultimate decision maker." Accordingly, the allegation of undue influence was rejected and the validity of the will upheld.[8]

Other courts have rejected a charge of undue influence where a donor, though 90 years of age, was well-educated and predisposed to making a gift to her church;[9] where an elderly donor had long considered making a gift to his church and was not close to his parish priest;[10] where an elderly donor was mentally competent and experienced in business affairs, and was the first to suggest making a gift to his church;[11] where a donor's lifetime gifts to her church and minister left her with ample assets for her own support, were not the result of active solicitation by her minister, and were acknowledged with satisfaction several times by the donor during her life;[12] where a donor frequently gave to her church, was capable of making independent business decisions, and was not close to any of her relatives;[13] and where an 84-year-old single woman left the bulk of her estate to a minister who was a friend and not the minister of the church she attended.[14]

Persons who would challenge a gift made to a church on the basis of undue influence must not delay in seeking redress for an unreasonable length of time, since unreasonable delay will bar any recovery.[15]

Summary

Ministers should refrain from soliciting gifts to themselves from aged or mentally infirm church members, and should be very cautious in soliciting gifts for the church. However, gifts to a church ordinarily will be valid if a minister merely

8 First Citizens Bank & Trust v. Inman, 370 S.E.2d 99 (S.C. App. 1988).
9 Klaber v. Unity School of Christianity, 51 S.W.2d 30 (Mo. 1932).
10 Coughlin v. St. Patrick's Church, 209 N.W. 426 (Iowa 1926).
11 Severson v. First Baptist Church, 208 P.2d 616 (Wash. 1949).
12 Lindley v. Lindley, 356 P.2d 455 (N.M. 1960).
13 Umbstead v. Preachers' Aid Society, 58 N.E.2d 441 (Ind. 1944).
14 Succession of Easterly, 563 So.2d 1006 (La. App. 1990).
15 Nelson v. Dodge, 68 A.2d 51 (R.I. 1949).

suggests and does not actively solicit a gift, the donor is mentally competent, the donor was predisposed to conveying the gift, and the donor had independent advice and assistance in implementing the gift.

Many wills leaving substantial portions of estates to churches have been challenged by "disinherited heirs" on the basis of undue influence. Persons bringing such lawsuits often recognize that they have a weak case, but they sue anyway, hoping that the church will quickly "settle" with them in order to avoid the potential "adverse publicity" associated with such lawsuits. After all, what church wants to be accused publicly of coercing elderly members into making gifts to the church? If your church receives a gift under a will that is challenged on the basis of undue influence, be sure to bear in mind a couple of considerations. First, undue influence usually is very difficult to prove, particularly when the decedent was in reasonably good mental and physical health at the time the will was executed. Second, in many states, undue influence must be proven by "clear and convincing evidence"—a more difficult burden of proof than the ordinary "preponderance of the evidence" standard. A church that becomes aware that an elderly or infirm person is considering leaving a portion of his or her estate to the church can reduce the possibility of undue influence even further by ensuring that the person obtains the independent counsel of an attorney in drafting the will or trust. Ideally, the attorney should not be a member of the same church. Finally, church leaders should recognize that they have a moral obligation to assist in implementing the estate plans of deceased members so long as they are satisfied that no improper influence was exercised. If a former member in fact intended that a portion of his or her estate be distributed to the church, and church leaders too quickly succumb to threats of attorneys hired by disgruntled family members, then they have violated a sacred trust.

In the following chapter, we turn our attention to invasion of privacy and explore how that risk can be reduced.

CHAPTER 20. REDUCING THE RISK OF THE INVASION OF PRIVACY

In chapter 18 we learned that truth is a defense to defamation. This means that a pastor who publicly discloses confidential information cannot be liable for defamation, so long as the pastor is telling the truth. It does not matter how much the information harms another person's reputation. In recent years several courts have expressed discomfort with this rule, and have allowed persons to sue pastors and others who publicly disclose private facts about them. Liability in such cases is a form of invasion of privacy, and is called "public disclosure of private facts." Pastors should be familiar with this form of liability, since it can expose them to unexpected liability for the disclosure of truthful information.

20.1 Public Disclosure of Private Facts

Those who give publicity to the private life of another are subject to liability for invasion of privacy if the matter publicized is of a kind that would be highly offensive to a reasonable person and is not of legitimate concern to the public.[1] The key elements of this form of invasion of privacy are (1) publicity, (2) of a highly objectionable kind, (3) given to private facts about another. *Publicity* is defined as a communication to the public at large, or to so many persons that the matter is substantially certain to become one of public knowledge. It is not an invasion of privacy to communicate a fact concerning another's private life to a single person or even to a small group of persons.[2] But a statement made to a large audience, such as a church congregation, does constitute "publicity."

The facts that are publicly disclosed must be *private*. There is no liability if one merely repeats something that is a matter of public record or has already been publicly disclosed. Thus, a minister who makes reference in a sermon to the prior marriage or prior criminal acts of a particular church member has not invaded the member's privacy, since such facts are matters of public record. Many other facts—such as dates of birth, military service, divorce, licenses of various kinds, pleadings in a lawsuit, ownership of property, and various debts—are matters of public record. References to such facts ordinarily will not invade another's privacy.

The matter that is communicated must be such that a reasonable person would feel justified in feeling seriously aggrieved by its dissemination.

This type of invasion of privacy is especially relevant to ministers, who frequently are apprised of private facts about members of their congregations, and who have many opportunities to divulge such information. Ministers must exercise caution in divulging private facts about members of their congregations, even when the communication is positive in nature and contains information that is factually true (and accordingly would not be defamatory). For example, a minister publicly comments on the sordid immorality of a recent convert to his church, intending his remarks to be complimentary. He has publicized private facts about the member under circumstances that may be highly offensive. The minister under these circumstances may well have invaded the privacy of the church member.

---

[1] Restatement (Second) of Torts § 652D.

[2] *Id.* at § 652D comment "a".

Example. A Michigan court ruled that a minister may invade the privacy of a church member by disclosing to the congregations information that was communicated to him by the member in the course of a confidential counseling session.[3] A church member (the "plaintiff") confessed to his pastor that he had previously committed adultery with prostitutes. The pastor decided to communicate this information to the entire congregation, including the member's wife, family, and friends. The pastor insisted that he did not believe in confidential communications and that church doctrine required exposing sins to the congregation. The member claimed that the pastor had been motivated not by religious doctrine but by ill will and the intent to humiliate him and create dissension within his family. The disgraced member sued his pastor and church, alleging that the pastor's disclosure amounted to an invasion of privacy. The court concluded, "[W]e believe that plaintiff has pleaded that [the pastor] disclosed to the congregation plaintiff's previous contacts with prostitutes, that this information was of no legitimate concern to the public and was conveyed to the congregation with the intent to embarrass plaintiff and cause him severe emotional distress. Whether [the pastor's] conduct was sufficiently outrageous or extreme is a question best left to the jury." The court cautioned that it was assuming that the plaintiff was not a member of the church as of the date of the pastor's disclosure. If the plaintiff were a member on that date, then the court insinuated that the first amendment would prevent it from resolving any "intentional tort claims."

20.2 False Light in the Public Eye

Some courts have recognized a second kind of invasion of privacy when one gives publicity to a matter that places another before the public in a "false light." However, the false light in which the person was placed must be highly offensive to a reasonable person, and it must have been publicized either with a knowledge that it was false or with a reckless disregard concerning its truth or falsity.[4]

A minister who ascribes beliefs or positions to others that they do not in fact hold may have invaded their privacy. In preparing sermons or articles, ministers must be careful not to attribute to other persons opinions, statements, or beliefs that are not in fact held.

Example. A New Jersey court allowed a woman to sue a pastor of her church for invasion of privacy for informing the congregation about a sexual relationship she had with another pastor of the same church.[5]

Example. An Oregon court ruled that a pastor was guilty of invading the privacy of a church member and his wife by making public statements placing them in a false light.[6] A church member's three children were injured when the car they were driving was struck by the daughter of another church member. The pastor informed the church board, and the congregation itself, that the father whose children were injured was having his children pretend to be injured in order to obtain a larger settlement from the other driver's insurance company. Neither the pastor, nor any other church member, ever investigated the facts to ascertain the extent of damage done to the car

---

[3] Smith v. Calvary Christian Church, 592 N.W.2d 713 (Mich. App. 1998).

[4] *Id.* at § 652E (1977).

[5] F.G. v. MacDonell, 677 A.2d 258 (N.J. Super. 1996).

[6] Muresan v. Philadelphia Romanian Pentecostal Church, 962 P.2d 711 (Or. App. 1998).

or the injuries suffered by the passengers. The pastor did not know whether the children, in fact, were injured by the accident. The children's parents sued the pastor, claiming that he had defamed them and invaded their privacy. They also sued the church as the pastor's employer. The jury determined that the pastor's statements placed the parents in a false light by repeatedly accusing them of falsifying their children's condition to obtain a larger insurance settlement. The court defined "false light" invasion of privacy as follows: "One who gives publicity to a matter concerning another that places the other before the public in a false light is subject to liability to the other for invasion of his privacy, if (a) the false light in which the other was placed would be highly offensive to a reasonable person, and (b) the actor had knowledge of or acted in reckless disregard as to the falsity of the publicized matter and the false light in which the other would be placed."[7] The pastor insisted that he could not be liable for "false light" invasion of privacy because the parents failed to prove the element of publication. According to the pastor, to prevail on a false light invasion of privacy claim, the parents had to establish that he published false information about them "to the public at large." The court disagreed, noting that publication is established by proof that "the false information reached or was sure to reach either the public generally or a large number of persons in [the parents'] work community." In this case, "there was evidence that plaintiffs' entire community of friends, relatives and acquaintances were members of the church and that [the pastor] made false statements about [them] in church meetings of hundreds of members at a time. We conclude that the evidence was sufficient as to the element of publication." The pastor also claimed that the parents failed to prove the element of malice, which he insisted requires evidence of actual intent to harm. Once again, the court disagreed. It noted that "in this case, there is evidence that [the pastor] repeatedly made false statements with no regard for their truth or falsity."

Example. Three female church members claimed that their pastor sexually harassed and abused them over a period of several months. The district superintendent of a state denominational agency (the "Conference") learned of the allegations, and asked the three women to appear before a "staff-parish relations committee" of their church. At the meeting each woman was given an opportunity to describe the pastor's allegedly inappropriate behavior. After hearing the accusations against their pastor, the committee gave the pastor a vote of "no confidence" and submitted the charges to the Conference for a full review. The pastor then requested six weeks' paid vacation followed by a leave of absence, and the committee granted his request. The pastor spoke to the church congregation the following Sunday, and explained he was taking a paid vacation. The women claimed that the Conference and district superintendent invaded their privacy by the following actions: (1) they asked the women to appear before a church committee to disclose their accusations; (2) they permitted the pastor to make some final remarks to the congregation, at which time he made it appear that he was being falsely accused; (3) they "acquiesced" in the decision of the staff-parish relations committee to permit the pastor to go on paid vacation after his final service, and this further implied that the women's charges were groundless; and (4) they failed to inform the congregation of the true reason for the pastor's resignation. A South Carolina court ruled that neither the Conference nor the district superintendent was guilty of invasion of privacy. In concluding that there had been no "public disclosure of private facts" the court observed, "[The women] made their disclosures

---

[7] Restatement (Second) of Torts § 652E.

expecting and intending that both the committee and [Conference] would act on those complaints. [They] therefore intended that their complaints should become public to the limited extent that occurred under these circumstances." With regard to the women's claim that the Conference and district superintendent invaded their privacy by publicly placing them in a "false light," the court simply noted that no South Carolina case has recognized this theory of liability. And, even if it were to be recognized, neither the Conference nor district superintendent did anything to "give rise to such a claim under these circumstances."[8]

20.3 The Privacy Act of 1974

Much confusion surrounds the scope of the Privacy Act of 1974. The Privacy Act was enacted to permit persons (1) to know of any records about them the government is collecting, maintaining, and distributing; (2) to prevent government records about them from being used without consent and for purposes other than those for which the records were first acquired; and (3) to correct and amend such records if necessary. The Privacy Act applies only to records maintained by the federal government and some federal contractors. It has no relevance to church records, and is not a basis for pastoral liability.

Summary

Ministers should recognize the risks associated with the disclosure of confidential information. If such disclosures would seriously offend the average person, then they expose the minister to liability based on invasion of privacy—even if the information that is disclosed is true. Truth is not a defense to invasion of privacy, unlike defamation. Ministers also should realize that publicly ascribing positions to persons that they do not hold is another form of invasion of privacy that has been recognized by some courts. In the next chapter we examine risks associated with counseling, and how they can be reduced.

---

[8] Brown v. Pearson, 483 S.E.2d 477 (S.C. App. 1997).

CHAPTER 21. REDUCING RISKS ASSOCIATED WITH COUNSELING

Most churches offer some form of counseling services. The most common example would be counseling of church members by a minister. Many churches also offer lay counseling services. Some limit these services to members of the congregation, while others target the general public and promote their counseling ministry in the local media and telephone directory. Some churches use counselors or psychologists who are licensed by the state, while others use unlicensed laypersons with little if any professional training. Counseling ministries can provide an excellent and needed service, and represent a "point of contact" with the community. However, there are a number of important legal concerns that should be considered by any church that offers such services, or that is considering doing so in the future. The more important concerns are summarized in this chapter.

Key point. Many of the principles and risk management strategies in this chapter apply equally to persons who counsel students in church-operated schools.

21.1 Negligent Counseling (malpractice)

Malpractice generally is defined as a failure to exercise an accepted degree of skill in the performance of professional duties that results in injury to another person. In the past, malpractice suits were restricted almost exclusively to doctors and lawyers—a doctor prescribed the wrong medication or made a faulty diagnosis; a lawyer missed a pleading deadline or made an error in a title search. But in recent years a small number of malpractice suits have been brought against ministers. Most courts have rejected clergy malpractice as a basis for liability in all cases. A few courts have found clergy guilty of malpractice for engaging in sexual misconduct with an adult or minor, or if they engage in "non-religious" counseling. This important topic is addressed more fully in chapter 25.

21.2 Sexual Misconduct

There have been a number of lawsuits brought by women who were seduced or sexually assaulted by male clergy and mental health professionals. Often the misconduct occurred in the course of a counseling relationship. This important basis of liability is addressed in chapter 24.

21.3 False Accusations

In some cases false accusations are brought against counselors by persons seeking a legal settlement or pursuing some other ulterior motive. It is imperative for counselors to recognize that a false accusation can be as devastating as a true one. Because of the unique temptations that counseling can present, and the possibility of false accusations, "defensive measures" should be taken by those who engage in counseling. Some precautions are presented later in this chapter.

21.4 Child Abuse Reporting

Ministers who are mandatory reporters of child abuse under state law may be criminally and civilly liable for failing to report child abuse to civil authorities. This important basis of liability is addressed in chapter 23.

Churches that use lay counselors should apprise them of the child abuse reporting requirements under state law. Keep in mind that these statutes are amended frequently, so updated copies should be obtained at least annually.

Whether or not the child abuse reporting statute requires a church counselor to report known or reasonably suspected instances of abuse, the counselor (and perhaps the church) would risk potential civil liability for failing to report abuse. For example, a minor who is being abused by a step-parent learns that a church counselor was aware of the abuse but did not report it. The minor may sue the counselor (and the church) arguing that the failure to report the abuse aggravated the injury. The "statute of limitations" on such claims does not even begin to run until the minor reaches the age of majority, meaning that contingent liability for such claims can persist for many years. Further, many states have enacted laws suspending the statute of limitations until an adult survivor of child abuse "discovers" that he or she was injured by the abuse. This can extend the statute of limitations for a significant amount of time.

Some states permit adults who were abused as children to sue clergy or lay counselors who were aware of the abuse but chose not to report it.

It is essential that any church counselor be apprised of his or her legal obligations under state law with respect to this important issue.

21.5 Confidentiality

Another very important consideration in church counseling is the concept of confidentiality. Counselors (and the church) can be sued if they intentionally or inadvertently disclose confidential information to third parties. Obviously, this can occur in several ways—for example, the counselor directly communicates the information, or the counselor's counseling notes are accessible to church staff. Counselors need to be strictly admonished to maintain the confidences shared with them. Some states recognize limited exceptions to this rule in cases of child abuse reporting, or when a counselee threatens to harm others.

The concepts of privilege and confidentiality are closely related. Generally, "confidentiality" refers to a duty not to disclose to *anyone* the substance of communications shared in confidence. While the impropriety of disclosing confidential information is universally acknowledged, few ministers have been found legally accountable for unauthorized disclosures. This is because, until recently, the duty to preserve confidences was considered to be moral rather than legal in nature. However, in recent years some ministers have been sued for divulging confidences.

> *Tip. Be sure to distinguish between the concepts of privilege and confidentiality. The clergy-penitent privilege provides that clergy cannot be compelled to disclose in court the content of communications shared with them in confidence while acting as a spiritual adviser. The related concept of confidentiality imposes upon clergy a duty not to disclose to others any communications shared with them in confidence.*

> *Tip. Clergy who disclose confidential information shared with them in counseling sessions may be exposing themselves, as well as their church, to legal liability on the basis of malpractice, invasion of privacy, breach of fiduciary duty, and infliction of*

emotional distress. This conclusion may apply even when clergy share confidential information in order to discipline a member for violating church standards. The point is this—would members disclose confidential information if they suspected that their minister would report it to the church board or congregation in order to discipline them? Clearly, the answer is "no." Therefore, it is essential for clergy to refrain from disclosing information obtained during confidential counseling sessions—even if it relates to a person's qualifications or eligibility for membership. Of course, the church board can still discipline the individual, but not on the basis of any information shared with the minister in the course of a confidential counseling session. Another alternative is for a minister to obtain the permission of the counselee to share confidential information with the board or with some other person. If this permission is obtained (in writing), this will serve as a defense in the event that the minister is later sued for disclosing the information.

Example. A bishop who confessed to church leaders that he had committed adultery sued his church when church leaders disclosed the confession without the bishop's consent.[1] The bishop had specifically asked his church leaders to keep his confession in confidence, and they promised to do so. However, the bishop alleged that they later disclosed his confession to a local church's board of elders, a church congregation, and numerous other persons. As a result of these disclosures, the bishop was shunned by friends, family, and members of his church and denomination. He sued the church and various church officials. A state appeals court ruled that the church could be sued for emotional distress and related claims, and it ordered the case to proceed to trial. The court acknowledged that it could find no previous case in which "a counselee or communicant has sought to hold a religious officer liable in tort for [an unauthorized disclosure of confidential communications]." However, it saw no reason why clergy and church leaders should not be held legally accountable for injuries they inflict when they disclose confidential information to others without consent.

Example. A woman (the "victim") was referred to a pastor for counseling because of his many years of counseling experience. The victim later joined the pastor's church, and continued to meet with him for counseling, relating to him highly personal and private matters including the fact that her father had sexually molested both her and a sister. The victim's sister attended the same church, and married the pastor's son. The marriage between the sister and the pastor's son deteriorated after the sister learned that her husband was having an affair with another woman. When the pastor's son publicly blamed his wife for the breakup of their marriage, the victim met with the pastor to defend her sister and to present evidence showing that the husband (the pastor's son) was the one who had been unfaithful. The pastor responded by defending his son to the church board and congregation. He informed both the board and congregation that the sister could not be believed because her family was "incestuous" and "dysfunctional." The victim and her sister sued the pastor and the church on a number of grounds, including invasion of privacy, defamation, malpractice, and breach of fiduciary duty. The court concluded that the pastor offered "no good reason for insulating a counselor from liability for betraying clients' confidences to their detriment merely because the counselor is a clergy member and unlicensed, and the counseling as well as wrongful disclosure takes place in a religious setting."[2]

---

[1] Snyder v. Evangelical Orthodox Church, 264 Cal. Rptr. 640 (Cal. App. 1989).
[2] Barnes v. Outlaw, 937 P.2d 323 (Ariz. App. 1996).

Example. A Michigan court ruled that a minister could not be sued for breaching a "duty of confidentiality" by disclosing to the congregations information that was communicated to him by a member in the course of a confidential counseling session.[3] A church member (the "plaintiff") confessed to his pastor that he had previously committed adultery with prostitutes. The pastor decided to communicate this information to the entire congregation, including the member's wife, family, and friends. The pastor insisted that he did not believe in confidential communications and that church doctrine required exposing sins to the congregation. The member claimed that the pastor had been motivated not by religious doctrine but by ill will and the intent to humiliate him and create dissension within his family. The disgraced member sued his pastor and church, alleging that the pastor's disclosure amounted to a breach of the duty of confidentiality. The plaintiff insisted that the clergy-penitent privilege imposes upon clergy a "duty of confidentiality," and that clergy who disclose confidences without permission may be sued for breaching this duty. The court disagreed, noting that the clergy-penitent privilege is a "rule of evidence that did not create a cause of action for disclosure of private or privileged communications."

Example. A New York court ruled that two rabbis could be sued for divulging information shared with them by a counselee in a conversation protected by the clergy-penitent privilege.[4] A woman obtained counseling, individually, from two rabbis. During her counseling sessions, she revealed information of an extremely personal and confidential nature. The woman later brought a lawsuit seeking to divorce her husband and obtain custody of their four minor children. In the course of this lawsuit, the woman's husband introduced an affidavit from each of the rabbis to support his claim for custody of the children. In the affidavits the rabbis disclosed some of the confidential information that had been shared with them in confidence by the woman. The woman immediately sued both rabbis, claiming that they violated the clergy-penitent privilege. The court ruled that ministers who breach the clergy-penitent privilege by disclosing information shared with them in confidence may be sued by the counselee for breaching a fiduciary duty of confidentiality. The court further concluded that imposing liability on clergy in such cases does not violate the first amendment guaranty of religious freedom.

21.6 The Unauthorized Practice of Counseling or Psychology

All fifty states have enacted statutes regulating the practice of psychology. These statutes prohibit persons from practicing psychology or representing that they are psychologists unless they are certified or licensed by the state. The purpose of such statutes is to protect the public against "charlatans and quacks who, despite inadequate training and professional experience, guarantee easy solutions to psychological problems."[5]

Psychologist regulation statutes fall into two general categories. *Certification laws* do not prevent persons from practicing psychology, but rather prohibit use of the title "psychologist" or any of its derivatives by persons who are not certified psychologists. *Licensure laws* prohibit the practice of psychology by anyone who is not a licensed psychologist. Certification laws have been criticized for not

---

[3] Smith v. Calvary Christian Church, 592 N.W.2d 713 (Mich. App. 1998).

[4] Lightman v.Flaum, 687 N.Y.S.2d 562 (Sup. 1999).

[5] National Psychologist Association v. University of New York, 203 N.Y.S.2d 821 (1960).

adequately protecting the public against unqualified practitioners. Licensure statutes have been criticized as being too restrictive.

Certification is obtained from state authorities through an application process. Applicants ordinarily must demonstrate that they are at least 21 years of age, of good moral character, and a citizen of the United States. In addition, they must have earned a specified degree in psychology and have practiced psychology for a minimum number of years.

Licensure statutes prohibit any person from engaging in the practice of "psychology" without a valid license. A typical licensing statute provides, "No person shall practice as a psychologist . . . unless he is validly licensed and registered."[6] Licensing statutes differ in their definition of the phrase "practice of psychology." Some statutes define the term broadly. For example, one statute provides:

> The "practice of psychology" . . . is defined as rendering to individuals, groups, organizations, or the public any psychological service involving the application of principles, methods, and procedures of understanding, predicting and influencing behavior, such as the principles pertaining to learning, perception, motivation, thinking, emotion, and interpersonal relationships; the methods and procedures of interviewing, counseling, behavior modification, and psychotherapy; of constructing, administering, and interpreting tests of mental abilities, aptitudes, interests, attitudes, personality characteristics, emotion, and motivation; and of assessing public opinion.[7]

Other statutes define *practice of psychology* more narrowly.

All licensing statutes exempt certain activities from the definition of *practice of psychology.* Exemptions vary from state to state, but the following exemptions are common: (1) professional activities of lawyers, physicians, social workers, sociologists, and counselors; (2) activities of government employees in the ordinary course of their employment; (3) activities of a student, intern, or resident in psychology, pursuing a course of study at an accredited university; (4) educational activities of teachers in public and private schools, or the authorized duties of guidance counselors.

Most states also exempt certain activities of clergy from the "practice of psychology." Here are some examples:

- "duly recognized members of any bona fide religious denomination shall not be restricted from functioning in their ministerial capacity provided they do not represent themselves as being clinical psychologists or providing clinical psychological services."[8]

- "nothing contained in this act shall be construed to prevent qualified . . . ministers . . . from doing work of a psychological nature consistent with their training and consistent with any code of ethics of their respective

---

[6] Mo. Rev. Stat. § 337.015.

[7] *Id. See also* Colo. Rev. Stat. § 12-43-108; Ga. Ann. Code § 84-3101; Ky. Rev. Stat. § 319.010; Okla. Stat. Ann. Title 59, § 1352.

[8] Ill. Ann. Stat. ch. 111, § 5353.

professions so long as they do not hold themselves out to the public by any title or description of services incorporating the words 'psychologic,' 'psychological,' 'psychologist' or 'psychology.'"[9]

- "nothing in this chapter shall be construed to limit . . . a duly ordained minister, priest, rabbi, Christian Science practitioner, or other clergyman from carrying out his responsibilities while functioning in his ministerial capacity within a recognized religious organization serving the spiritual needs of its constituency, provided he does not hold himself out as a psychologist."[10]

- "nothing [in this statute] shall in any way limit qualified members of other professional groups such as . . . clergymen . . . from doing work of a psychological nature consistent with their training and consistent with any code of ethics of their respective professions."[11]

- "the provisions of the Psychologists Licensing Act shall not apply to qualified members of other professions, including but not limited to . . . pastoral counselors doing work of a psychological nature consistent with their training and consistent with the code of ethics of their respective professions provided they do not hold themselves out to the public by any title or description incorporating the work psychological, psychologist, or psychology."[12]

- "nothing in this chapter shall be construed to limit the professional pursuits of teachers in public and private schools, [or] clergymen . . . from full performance of their professional duties."[13]

- "nothing in this Act shall be construed to apply to . . . duly ordained religions [sic] doing work of a psychological nature consistent with their training and consistent with any code of ethics of their respective professions, provided they do not represent themselves by any title or in any manner prohibited by this Act."[14]

An application for a license to practice psychology must satisfy various requirements. Ordinarily, these are similar to the requirements for obtaining a certificate, and generally include a minimum age (typically 21), good moral character, being a resident of the state and citizen of the United States, professional experience of a prescribed duration, and the prescribed academic degree. Some states require that the academic degree be a doctoral degree based on a program of studies that were primarily psychological. Others permit a masters degree in psychology plus a longer number of years of professional experience.

Several states have combined certification and licensure statutes. Such statutes prohibit anyone from practicing psychology without a license, and also prohibit

---

[9] Kan. Stat. Ann. § 74-5344.
[10] Ky. Rev. Stat. Ann. § 319.015.
[11] Mo. Rev. Stat. § 337.045.
[12] OKLA. STAT. title 59, § 1353.
[13] TENN. Code ANN. § 63-11-206.
[14] Tex. Rev. Civ. Stat. Ann. art. 4512c.

use of the term *psychology* or any of its derivatives by any person who is not a licensed psychologist.

In conclusion, ministers who are employed full-time in a pastoral ministry by a church congregation are free to counsel with church members and others in the course of their church employment. The same rule ordinarily will apply to ministers who are hired by a church specifically for a counseling ministry. In neither case, however, may a minister use the term *psychology* or any of its derivatives in connection with such counseling ministry unless he or she is in fact a licensed psychologist. Ministers who establish a full-time or part-time *counseling* ministry independent of a church ordinarily should not engage in professional counseling unless (1) they are specifically exempted from the prohibition against the unlicensed practice of psychology; (2) their state board of psychologist examiners does not prosecute unlicensed counselors; (3) the term *practice of psychology* is not defined broadly enough (under applicable state law) to include counseling; or (4) their state has a professional counselor licensing statute under which the counselor is licensed or exempt.

21.7 Risk Management Strategies

Summarized below are some risk management strategies that are being used by some churches to reduce the risks associated with counseling ministries.

Counseling policy

Churches that use pastoral or lay counselors can prepare a brochure or statement clearly communicating to each counselee that the church considers counseling to be an essential aspect of its ministry, and that it is important for persons seeking counseling to recognize that certain conditions and considerations apply, including some or all of the following:

- The counselors are engaged solely in spiritual counseling based on their understanding of the Bible, and they are not engaged in the practice of psychology, professional counseling, or psychotherapy.

- State law may require a counselor to report allegations of child abuse to civil authorities.

- Statements made in confidence to a pastor in the course of counseling ordinarily are "privileged," meaning that neither the counselee nor the pastor can be compelled to disclose in a court of law any statements made in the course of the counseling. However, the presence of a third party during a counseling session may jeopardize the privilege, since the counseling may no longer be considered "confidential." To illustrate, statements made in the course of pastoral counseling may not be privileged if a counselee brings a friend along to the counseling session.

- Any statements made in confidence in the course of counseling will be kept in strict confidence by the counselor. As noted above, the duty to maintain confidences may not apply in the context of child abuse. Further, the counselor may reserve the right to disclose confidential information in specified situations (such as threats of suicide, or an intent to harm another person).

Avoid controversial therapies

Counselors should be instructed to avoid any controversial counseling techniques that have been associated in recent years with staggering levels of liability (such as age regression therapy or multiple personality disorders).

Referrals

Counselors should have a clear understanding of those cases that need to be referred to a professional counselor.

> **Key point.** *When referring counselees to a professional counselor, it is important to avoid endorsing the person. Simply inform the counselee that the counselor is state licensed (as a counselor, psychologist, or psychiatrist), and has satisfactorily served a number of other members of the congregation.*

Insurance

Does the counselor have counseling insurance? If so, what are the coverage amounts? What exclusions exist? These are questions that should be addressed prior to the time the counselor begins counseling. Also check to see if the church's liability insurance policy covers the counseling activities.

Legal agreement

Consider executing a legal agreement with the counselor that expresses the conditions of the arrangement.

Use of the terms "counseling" or "psychology"

It is unlawful in most states for unlicensed persons to use the terms *counselor, psychologist, counseling,* or *psychology* in connection with their services. Pastors who engage in counseling of church members in the course of performing their pastoral duties are exempted from this limitation in most states, but this exemption does not apply to lay counselors even though they are working in a church.

> **Example.** *B is an insurance salesman who feels called to be a counselor. He persuades his church to let him use a vacant office to conduct his counseling ministry. Some counselees are members of the church, but B recruits several counselees from outside the church by advertising himself as a "professional counselor" in the newspaper and telephone directory. B's use of the term "professional counselor" would be unlawful in most states. Not only would this expose B to liability, but it also increases the church's risk.*

> **Example.** *Same facts as the previous example, except that B is an ordained minister. The result is the same. B would not be permitted in most states to use the term "professional counselor" for a counseling ministry that is promoted publicly. This also would be true if B opens an office away from the church to conduct his counseling ministry.*

Child abuse reporting

Be sure that pastoral and lay counselors are familiar with the child abuse reporting requirements under state law. Remember that these laws are subject to change, and so it is essential for counselors to be familiar with the most recent version.

Other risk management strategies

Other risk management strategies designed to reduce the risk of sexual contact by pastoral counselors with counselees (and false accusations of such contact) are addressed in chapter 24.

Summary

Any church-based ministry that involves people will create some degree of risk. Counseling ministries are no different. This chapter has described many of the risks associated with counseling ministries. Legal risks should not necessarily cause church leaders to abandon a valuable ministry. In many cases, risks can be reduced by the implementation of risk management strategies. There are many strategies that can reduce the risks associated with counseling ministries. Many of these strategies are summarized in this chapter. In the chapter that follows, we examine how to reduce risks associated with contracts.

CHAPTER 22. REDUCING RISKS ASSOCIATED WITH CONTRACTS

Ministers generally will not be personally liable for a contract they sign if the following conditions are satisfied:

(1) the *contract was authorized* by appropriate church action in accordance with the church's governing documents

(2) the *minister is authorized to sign* the contract on the basis of either the church's governing documents or by action of the church board

(3) the identity of the employing church is *disclosed* in the contract, and

(4) the minister signs in a *representative capacity,* such as "Pastor John Smith, President," or "Pastor John Smith, authorized agent."

The absence of any one or more of these conditions can expose ministers to personal liability on contracts they sign. Each of these conditions is addressed more fully below.

22.1 The Contract was Authorized by Church Action

Before signing a contract, a minister or other church officer should confirm that the contract was approved or authorized by appropriate church action. In many cases, a church's articles of incorporation, constitution, bylaws, or other governing document will specify how contracts are authorized. Some church governing documents prescribe different kinds of authorization for different kinds of contracts. For example, a church's constitution specifies that a contract for the sale of church property must be approved by a two-thirds majority of the members in a duly called membership meeting. Some church governing documents authorize the senior pastor to enter into contracts for low-cost items. It is important for ministers and church officers to be familiar with all of these provisions, so that contracts are properly authorized.

> *Example. A church's bylaws specify that all purchases of real estate must be authorized by majority vote of the membership. The church's board of directors independently approves a purchase of a home adjacent to the church's parking lot. The contract to purchase the home is unauthorized. The senior pastor, or anyone else signing the contract, may be personally liable for the obligation.*

22.2 The Minister is Authorized to Sign

Even if a contract is authorized by appropriate church action, this does not necessarily mean that the senior pastor is legally authorized to sign it. Once again, the church's governing documents must be reviewed to determine if the pastor is authorized to sign the contract.

In no event should ministers or church officers assume that they are authorized to enter into contracts on behalf of their church simply by virtue of their position. One court has observed:

The mere proclaiming of [oneself] as the religious superior of the congregation may suffice to establish that fact in spiritual matters of his church, but it does not effect legal superiority in secular matters. There must be clear and convincing evidence of congregational acknowledgement of and acquiescence in the concept of legal superiority and authority over church business and property matters.[1]

Example. The senior pastor of a church assumes that he has the legal authority to sign a contract for the purchase of church equipment on the basis of his status as president of the church corporation. In fact, the bylaws require that such a contract be signed by the pastor and a church officer. The pastor lacked the legal authority to sign the contract, and will be personally liable for honoring it if the church declines or is unable to do so.

Example. A church's bylaws authorize the board to authorize purchases of vehicles and other items of personal property up to $30,000 in value. The bylaws further specify that such contracts must be approved by the board, and signed by the senior pastor and either the church secretary or the church treasurer. The pastor signs a contract for the purchase of a new church van without board approval. If the church refuses to honor or ratify this contract, the pastor will be personally responsible for it since (1) the contract was not properly authorized by the church board, and (2) the pastor did not have the sole authority to sign the contract.

Example. A Massachusetts appeals court ruled that a church treasurer was without legal authority to sign a real estate sales contract for the sale of church property.[2] The treasurer (who also was a member of the church board) was the only person to sign the contract on behalf of the church. She signed her name without any reference to her official or representative capacity. The church constitution specified that sales of church property had to be authorized by the church board. However, the board never authorized the sale in question. The church refused to honor the contract, and the buyer sought a court order compelling the church to comply. The court ruled that the church could not be compelled to honor the contract. It concluded that a treasurer has no legal authority to sign contracts unilaterally on behalf of a church corporation. The court noted that the treasurer "was not authorized to sign the agreement by virtue of her office as treasurer. The power of an officer of a charitable corporation to bind the corporation is narrowly construed in Massachusetts, and it most certainly does not extend to agreements to dispose of real estate owned by the corporation . . . ." The court also rejected the buyer's argument that the treasurer had "apparent authority" to sign the contract on behalf of the church. Apparent authority exists whenever a corporation leads others to believe that a particular individual is authorized to execute contracts on behalf of the corporation when in fact no such authority exists. The court, in rejecting the application of the apparent authority doctrine in this case, noted that "where the sale of corporate real estate is outside the scope of the corporation's usual activity, the doctrine of apparent authority does not apply. The constitution of this corporation recites the 'nature and end of the congregation' to be 'the perfection of the love of God and man,' and that the congregation is to minister

---

[1] Gospel Tabernacle Body of Christ Church v. Peace Publishers & Co., 506 P.2d 1135, 1138 (Kan. 1973). *See also* American Legion v. Southwest Title and Insurance Co., 207 So.2d 393 (La. 1968), *reversed on other grounds*, 218 So.2d 612 (La. 1969) (lease entered into by minister without knowledge of church was held to be a "nullity"); Hill v. Hill, 241 S.W.2d 865 (Tenn. 1951).

[2] Biscegelia v. Bernadine Sisters, 560 N.E.2d 567 (Mass. App. 1990).

'to the needs of contemporary society in domestic and foreign missions through Christian education, health care services, spiritual and corporal works of mercy.' These purposes and activities are obviously unrelated to the sale of real estate." As a result, the court refused to order the church to honor the real estate contract. Of course, the treasurer could be personally liable for the contract.

Example. The New Hampshire Supreme Court ruled that a land sales contract executed by a church secretary and treasurer was not legally enforceable.[3] The court observed that the officers of a corporation "have only those powers conferred on them by the bylaws of the corporation or by the resolution of the directors." Neither the bylaws of the church nor any resolution by the board vested the secretary and treasurer with authority to enter into contracts on behalf of the church.

Example. The New Hampshire Supreme Court ruled that a nun did not have the legal authority to enter into a contract for the sale of land owned by her religious order.[4] The nun entered into a contract with a real estate broker to sell him 8 acres owned by her order. The broker made no effort to verify the authority of the nun to execute the contract on behalf of the order. The nun later informed the broker that she wished to cancel the contract. The broker sued her for damages, and requested a court order compelling the enforcement of the agreement. A trial court ruled in favor of the nun, and the state supreme court agreed. The court emphasized that the nun had no actual or implied authority to sign contracts. It added: "Trustees or similar officers of unincorporated religious organizations must have the consent of their organization in order to convey its property. . . . [We] see no evidence that [the nun] had obtained any authorization or consent for the proposed land sale from any membership group." The court further noted that the broker made no attempt to verify the nun's authority to sign the contract, and observed that "when a . . . broker signs a purchase and sale agreement without making any attempt to verify either the existence of the corporation with which he is contracting, or the authority of the person with whom he is dealing . . . he fails to exercise reasonable diligence." The court acknowledged that the broker could sue the nun individually, but added that "we doubt the technical or practical merit of such a claim in light of the fact that the defendant would be an eighty-year-old nun who had long before taken a vow of poverty." This case demonstrates that a single officer or trustee cannot sign legal documents on behalf of a church without authorization. It also demonstrates that an individual officer or trustee who unsuccessfully attempts to sell church property to a third party can be personally sued for damages incurred by the third party as a result of the unsuccessful sale.

Example. The Wisconsin Supreme Court ruled that an officer of a church-sponsored relief agency was personally liable on a contract that he signed without authorization.[5] The agency needed some plumbing work done, and an officer negotiated and signed a contract with a plumbing company. The name of the agency was mentioned prominently in the contract, as was the fact that the officer was signing in his capacity as director of the agency. The agency was unable to pay the plumbing bill, and the plumbing company sued the officer personally. The court observed: "This court has long adhered to the general rule that, where an agent merely contracts on behalf of a disclosed principal, the agent does not become personally

---

[3] Daniel Webster Council v. St. James Association, 553 A.2d 329 (N.H. 1987).
[4] Shakra v. Benedictine Sisters of Bedford, 553 A.2d 1327 (N.H. 1989).
[5] Benjamin Plumbing, Inc. v. Barnes, 470 N.W.2d 888 (Wis. 1991).

liable to the other contracting party. . . . [H]owever, an agent will be considered a party to the contract and held liable for its breach where the principal is only partially disclosed. A principal is considered partially disclosed where, at the time of contracting, the other party has notice that the agent is acting for a principal but has no notice of the principal's corporate or other business organization identity. . . . The general rule that agents are contractually liable where the principal is partially disclosed has produced the rule that an agent is liable where the contracting party is not aware of the corporate status of the principal." The court concluded that the director, by mentioning the agency's name in the contract but not whether or not it was incorporated, assumed personal liability on the contract under this rule. The court noted that the fact that the plumbing company was aware that the director was acting on behalf of a named agency "reveals nothing of its awareness of the type of business organization it was dealing with. All business entities are not corporations." Further, the court stressed that the plumbing company "had no affirmative duty to investigate" whether or not the agency was a corporation. The court also rejected the officer's claim that he was exempt from liability under a state law granting limited legal immunity to the uncompensated directors of nonprofit organizations. The court stressed that a director "cannot be granted immunity unless his liability related solely to his status as a director." In this case, however, the director's contractual liability to the plumbing company "stems from his position as an agent to a partially disclosed corporate principal and not from his status as a director."

A church may be legally obligated by contracts entered into without authorization by its pastor or a church officer if there is a history of the pastor or officer entering into unauthorized contracts that the church honored. If the dollar amount of a contract is small, there may be little concern. But this establishes a pattern that may be carried over to a higher cost transaction that the church may have no choice but to accept. In some cases, if there is not a pattern of accepting unauthorized contracts, the church may be able to repudiate the contract, but this has the potentially undesirable effect of transferring liability to the pastor or officer. Obviously, this is no way to enter into contracts. Here are some suggestions that will reduce the risk of such problems:

1. Review the church's organizational documents to determine the authority of the pastor or other officers to unilaterally enter into contracts on behalf of the church. Church leaders should have a clear understanding of such authority.

2. Often, a church's organizational documents do not give the pastor or any other officer unilateral authority to enter into contracts. This can cause problems in the future, since pastors and officers sometimes assume they are authorized to execute contracts for the purchase of low cost items on behalf of the church. When church leaders routinely accept such contracts, the church is in effect investing the pastor or officer with "apparent authority" to enter into unauthorized contracts. This may not be a concern for small cost items, but it may be a real problem for larger cost items. As a result, a church should consider two options. First, amend the organizational documents to give the pastor or some other designated officer limited authority to unilaterally execute contracts on behalf of the church. For example, some church bylaws authorize the pastor to purchase items up to $500 or some other amount without prior approval by the congregation or board. Such a

provision can reduce the risk of establishing a pattern of church acceptance of unauthorized contracts. Second, if the church elects not to amend its organizational documents, then it needs to periodically caution the pastor and other officers that they have no authority to unilaterally enter into contracts on behalf of the church, and instruct them to seek appropriate approval before entering into any contract.

3.   If a pastor or other officer makes an unauthorized purchase of a product or service of substantial cost, church leaders should recognize that the church has no legal obligation to accept the contract if it has not invested the pastor or officer with "apparent authority" by its practice of routinely accepting unauthorized contracts. The church may either repudiate the contract, or ratify it. Repudiation means that the church refuses to accept the purchased product or service. In such a case, the pastor or officer will be personally liable for paying the purchase price. Ratification is an acceptance of the contract by accepting the purchased product or service without objection. If the church accepts the product or service that was acquired by the pastor or officer in an unauthorized transaction, then the church will be legally obligated to honor the contract.[6]

22.3 The Church's Identity is Disclosed

A church's identity should be disclosed in a contract in order for ministers and other church officers to avoid personal liability for contracts they sign on behalf of their church. A respected legal treatise on corporation law states that "if there is no disclosure of the [corporation] in the body of the contract, the mere appending of words descriptive of the signer as, for example, the word 'president,' would not be sufficient of itself to relieve the signer of individual liability."[7]

> *Example. A senior pastor is authorized to sign a contract on behalf of the church. He signs the contract as "Pastor Bob Black, President," but he fails to disclose the church's name anywhere in the contract. The pastor may be personally liable on the contract if the church refuses to honor or ratify it, or if it is unable to do so.*

22.4 The Minister Signs in a Representative Capacity

Ministers should sign contracts in a "representative capacity" in order to reduce the risk of personal liability. This means that they should use such language as "president," "agent," or "authorized representative" when signing their name to a contract. They should never sign their names without a clear indication that they are signing as representatives of their church.

> *Example. A corporate officer signed a check in the amount of $43,000 on behalf of his company. The company's name was imprinted on the check, so there was no doubt that it was an obligation of the company. However, the officer's signature did not indicate that he was signing in a "representative capacity"—that is, as a representative of the company rather than in his personal or individual capacity. A bank dishonored the check on the basis of insufficient funds, and the recipient sued the officer directly. The officer insisted that he could not be personally liable for the*

[6] Butler v. Sacred Heart of Jesus English Rite Catholic Church, 680 N.Y.S.2d 909 (Civ. Ct. 1998).
[7] Fletcher CYC. CORP. § 3034 (1978 & Supp. 1999).

amount of the check, since the company's name had been imprinted on it. The court disagreed. It referred to a state law specifying that an authorized representative who signs his or her name to an instrument "is personally obligated if the instrument names the [company] represented but does not show that the representative signed in a representative capacity." In summary, the officer was personally liable for payment of the check even though the company's name was imprinted on it, since the officer did not indicate clearly that he was signing in a representative capacity.[8]

Summary

Persons who sign contracts on behalf of their church may become personally liable for fulfilling the contract, if the church elects not to honor the contract or if the church is financially unable to do so. This is a very real risk, as the examples in this chapter demonstrate. The good news is that ministers and church officers can avoid this risk by not signing a contract on behalf of their church unless they are certain that (1) the contract has been properly authorized; (2) they are authorized to sign on behalf of the church; (3) the church is clearly identified in the contract as the party to the agreement; and (4) the minister signs in a "representative capacity." In the chapter that follows, we explore risks associated with the failure to report known or suspected cases of child abuse.

---

[8] Hind-Marsh v. Puglia, 665 So.2d 1091 (Fla. App. 1995).

CHAPTER 23. REDUCING RISKS ASSOCIATED WITH THE FAILURE TO REPORT CHILD ABUSE

It is common for ministers to learn that a minor is being abused. This can occur in a number of ways, including a confession by the perpetrator, or a disclosure by a friend or relative of the victim or perpetrator. Often, ministers want to resolve such matters internally through counseling with the victim or the alleged offender, without contacting civil authorities. Such a response can have serious legal consequences, including the following: (1) ministers who are *mandatory reporters* under state law face possible criminal prosecution for failing to comply with their state child abuse reporting law; (2) some state legislatures have enacted laws permitting child abuse victims to sue ministers for failing to report child abuse; and (3) some courts have permitted child abuse victims to sue ministers for failing to report child abuse. Each of these theories of liability is addressed below.

Key point. This chapter also is relevant to nonminister church staff. Counselors, child care workers, and private school teachers are mandatory reporters in most if not all states. All church staff (minister and nonminister) will be mandatory reporters in a state that makes everyone a mandatory child abuse reporter who has reason to believe that a child has been abused.

23.1 Criminal Liability

In general

All fifty states have enacted child abuse reporting statutes in an effort to protect abused children and prevent future abuse.[1] Child abuse is defined by most statutes to include physical abuse, emotional abuse, neglect, and sexual molestation. A child ordinarily is defined as any person under the age of 18 years. Some states specifically limit the definition of "child abuse" to abuse that is inflicted by a parent or other person legally responsible for the minor's care. Such a statute, if interpreted narrowly, might not require clergy to report incidents of abuse inflicted by teachers, child care workers, custodians, associate ministers, adolescents, or volunteer youth workers—even if they otherwise are under a mandatory duty to report child abuse under state law.

All fifty states enumerate categories of persons who are under a legal duty to report abuse to designated civil authorities. In most states, such "mandatory reporters" must report both actual and reasonably suspected cases of child abuse. Failure to do so is a crime (usually a misdemeanor). Some states define *mandatory reporters* to include any person having a reasonable belief that child abuse has occurred. Obviously, clergy will be mandatory reporters under these statutes. The remaining states define *mandatory reporters* by referring to a list of occupations which generally includes physicians, dentists, hospital employees, nurses, coroners, school employees, nursery school workers, law enforcement officers, and licensed psychologists. Ministers are specifically identified as mandatory reporters under a

---

[1] See generally I. SLOAN, CHILD ABUSE: GOVERNING LAW & LEGISLATION (1983); Mitchell, Must Clergy Tell? Child Abuse Reporting Requirements Versus the Clergy Privilege and Free Exercise of Religion, 71 MINN. L. REV. 723 (1987).

few of these statutes.[2] But even if they are not, they may be mandatory reporters if they fall within a listed classification, such as school or child care workers and administrators, or counselors. In summary, many clergy have a mandatory duty to report child abuse. Clergy should not assume that they have no duty to report.

Clergy who are not mandatory reporters under their state law generally are considered "permissive reporters," meaning that they may report cases of abuse to the designated civil authorities but are not legally required to do so.

The clergy-penitent privilege

Ministers who are mandatory reporters of child abuse under state law are under a profound ethical dilemma when they receive information about child abuse in the course of a confidential counseling session that is subject to the clergy-penitent privilege. They have to chose between fulfilling their legal obligation to report, or honoring their ecclesiastical duty to maintain the confidentiality of privileged communications. A number of states have attempted to resolve this dilemma by specifically exempting clergy from the duty to report child abuse if the abuse is disclosed to them in the course of a communication protected by the clergy-penitent privilege.[3] Other states, while not specifically excluding clergy from the duty to report, do provide that information protected by the clergy-penitent privilege is not admissible in any legal proceeding regarding the alleged abuse.[4] Some state child abuse reporting statutes do not list the clergy-penitent privilege among those privileges that are abolished in the context of child abuse proceedings.[5] The intent of such statutes may be to excuse clergy from the testifying in such cases regarding information they learned in the course of a privileged communication.

Even if the clergy-penitent privilege applies in the context of child abuse reporting, it is by no means clear that the privilege will be a defense to a failure to report, since (1) the information causing a minister to suspect that abuse has occurred may not have been privileged (that is, it was not obtained in confidence, or it was not obtained during spiritual counseling); and (2) a privilege ordinarily applies only to courtroom testimony or depositions, and not to a statutory requirement to report to a state agency.

Unfortunately, the failure by many states to recognize the clergy-penitent privilege in the context of child abuse reporting disregards the therapeutic purpose of the privilege. Many child abusers will be discouraged from seeking spiritual counsel if the privilege does not assure the confidentiality of their communications. This will

---

[2] *See, e.g.,* CONN. GEN. STAT. § 17-38(b) ("clergyman"); MISS. CODE ANN. §§ 43-21-353 and 43-23-9 ("minister"); NEV. REV. STAT. § 432B.220(2)(d) ("a clergyman, practitioner of Christian Science or religious healer, unless he has acquired the knowledge of the abuse or neglect from the offender during a confession"); N.H. REV. STAT. ANN. § 169-C:29 ("priest, minister, or rabbi").

[3] *See, e.g.,* Ariz. Rev. Stat. § 13-3620A; Fla. Rev. Stat. § 415.512; Ky. Rev. Stat. § 620.050(2); La. Rev. Stat. § 14:403B(4)(b); Md. Code § 5-705(a)(3); Minn. Stat. § 626.556(3)(a)(1); Mont. Code § 41-3-201(4)(b); Nev. Rev. Stat. § 432B.220(2)(d); Or. Rev. Stat. § 418.750; S.C. Code § 20-7-550; Utah Code § 62A-4-503(2).

[4] See, *e.g.,* Ark. Stat. § 12-12-511; Ky. Rev. Stat. § 620.050(2); Pa. Stat. Title 23, § 6381(c); S.C. Code § 20-7-550.

[5] *See, e.g.,* Ind. Rev. Stat. § 31-6-11-8; N.C. Stat. § 7A-551; Tenn. Rev. Stat. § 37-1-411; Va. Stat. § 63.1-248.11.

only compound the problem. If, on the other hand, the privilege were preserved, many child abusers would seek out ministers for spiritual counseling, and the underlying causes of such behavior could be isolated and in some cases corrected.

Making a report

Persons who are legally required to report generally make their report by notifying a designated state agency by telephone and confirming the telephone call with a written report within a prescribed period of time. The reporter generally is required to (1) identify the child, the child's parents or guardians, and the alleged abuser by name, and provide their addresses; (2) give the child's age; and (3) describe the nature of the abuse. Most states have toll-free numbers that receive initial reports of child abuse.

Immunity for making a report

Every state grants legal immunity to reporters of child abuse. This means that a reporter cannot be sued simply for reporting child abuse. However, several states require that the report be based on "reasonable cause to believe" that abuse has occurred.[6] The purpose of extending legal immunity to reporters obviously is to encourage child abuse reporting. However, several studies indicate that numerous false reports have also been encouraged.[7] Such studies have raised serious legal questions concerning the propriety of legal immunity. One expert has observed that the many false reports "invite the intolerable situation of falsely accusing large numbers of parents of abuse."[8] Persons who maliciously transmit false reports are subject to civil liability in most states and criminal liability in some.

Penalty for not reporting

While persons who are legally required to report child abuse are subject to criminal prosecution for failure to do so, instances of actual criminal prosecution are rare. However, some clergy have been prosecuted for failing to file a report when they were in a mandatory reporting classification and they had reasonable cause to believe that abuse had occurred. Criminal penalties for failing to file a report vary, but typically involve short prison sentences and small fines.

23.2 Civil Liability Based on Statute

A few states have enacted statutes that create civil liability for failure to report child abuse.[9] In these states, victims of child abuse can sue adults who failed to report

---

[6] The courts generally have interpreted "reasonable cause to believe" very liberally, thereby reducing the risk of being sued for making a report that turns out to have been false. *See, e.g.,* Cream v. Mitchell, 264 Cal. Rptr. 876 (Cal. App. 1989) (a doctor who misdiagnosed chicken pox as venereal disease, and reported his diagnosis to the state, was found to have had a reasonable suspicion of abuse); Thomas v. Chadwick, 274 Cal. Rptr. 128 (Cal. App. 4 Dist. 1990) (a doctor who misdiagnosed a congenital defect as child abuse, and who reported his diagnosis to the state, was immune from liability).

[7] *See, e.g.,* A. Sussman & S. Cohen, Reporting Child Abuse and Neglect: Guidelines for Legislation (1975) (56% of all reports are valid).

[8] R. Light, Abused and Neglected Children in America: A Study of Alternative Policies, 43 HARVARD EDUCATIONAL REVIEW 556, 569 (1973).

[9] *See, e.g.,* ARK. CODE § 12-12-504(b) ("[a]ny person . . . required by this subchapter to make

the abuse. Not only are adults who fail to report abuse subject to possible criminal liability (if they are mandatory reporters), but they also can be sued for money damages by the victims of abuse. In each state, the statute only permits victims of child abuse to sue *mandatory reporters* who failed to report the abuse. No liability is created for persons who are not mandatory reporters as defined by state law.

> **Key point.** *Persons who are "mandatory" child abuse reporters in some states can be sued by victims of child abuse for failure to comply with state child abuse reporting requirements. These lawsuits may be brought in some states many years after the failure to report. It is possible that other state legislatures will enact laws giving victims of child abuse the legal right to sue mandatory reporters who failed to comply with their reporting obligations. It is also possible that the courts in some states will allow victims to sue mandatory reporters (and perhaps those who are not mandatory reporters) for failing to report child abuse even if no state law grants them the specific right to do so. These potential risks must be considered when evaluating whether or not to report known or suspected incidents of child abuse.*

23.3 Civil Liability Based on Court Rulings

Several courts have refused to allow child abuse victims to sue ministers on the basis of a failure to comply with a child abuse reporting law. A few courts have reached the opposite conclusion.

> **Example.** *A California appeals court upheld the conviction of two pastors for failing to report an incident of child abuse. A girl was sexually molested by her stepfather, and informed two pastors of her church who also served as president and principal of a church-operated school the girl attended. The pastors did not report the abuse to civil authorities, even though as school administrators they were mandatory child abuse reporters, because they wanted to handle the matter within the church. They viewed the matter as "a pastoral one" involving the girl's inability to forgive her stepfather. The pastors also insisted that they considered the stepfather's actions to be a sin rather than child abuse, and that as pastors they were required to follow the scriptures concerning the discipline of a fellow Christian. A jury found the pastors guilty of violating the state child abuse reporting law, and a state appeals court upheld the convictions. The court rejected the pastors' claim that their conviction amounted*

---

notification of suspected child maltreatment who willfully fails to do so, shall be civilly liable for damages proximately caused by that failure"); COLO. STAT. § 19-3-304(4)(b) (any person who is a mandatory reporter of child abuse and who willfully fails to report known or reasonably suspected incidents of abuse "shall be liable for damages proximately caused thereby"); IOWA CODE § 232.75 ("[a]ny person . . . required . . . to report a suspected case of child abuse who knowingly fails to do so is civilly liable for the damages proximately caused by such failure"); MICH. COMP. LAWS § 722.633 ("[a] person who is required by this act to report an instance of suspected child abuse or neglect and who fails to do so is civilly liable for the damages proximately caused by the failure"); MONT. CODE § 41-3-207 ("[a]ny person . . . required by law to report known or suspected child abuse or neglect who fails to do so or who prevents another person from reasonably doing so is civilly liable for the damages proximately caused by such failure or prevention"); N.Y. SOC. SERV. § 420 ("[a]ny person . . . required by this title to report a case of suspected child abuse or maltreatment who knowingly and willfully fails to do so shall be civilly liable for the damages proximately caused by such failure"); R.I. GEN. LAWS § 40-11-3 (a mandatory reporter who fails to report a reasonably suspected incident of child abuse "shall be civilly liable for the damages proximately caused by that failure").

to a violation of the first amendment guaranty of religious freedom by forcing them to report incidents of abuse rather than "handling problems within the church." The court concluded, "The mere fact that a [minister's] religious practice is burdened by a governmental program does not mean an exception accommodating that practice must be granted. The state may justify an inroad on religious liberty by showing it is the least restrictive means of achieving some compelling state interest. Here, if [the pastors] are held to be exempt from the mandatory requirements of the [child abuse reporting law] the act's purpose would be severely undermined. There is no indication teachers and administrators of religious schools would voluntarily report known or suspected child abuse. Children in those schools would not be protected. The protection of all children cannot be achieved in any other way."[10]

Example. An Indiana appeals court ruled that an adult who had been abused as a minor could sue his pastor on the basis of negligence for failing to report the abuse. A minor (the "victim") was sexually abused by his foster father and a number of other adults. When he was an adult, the victim sued a minister who had knowledge of the abuse but failed to report it to the authorities. He claimed that the minister was legally responsible for his injuries on the basis of a negligent failure to report. The court noted that negligence consists of the following elements: a duty to exercise reasonable care with respect to another, a breach of that duty, and injury to the other. In determining whether or not one has a duty to exercise reasonable care with respect to another, the court considered three factors—the existence of a "special relationship," the foreseeability of injury, and public policy. The court concluded that it often will be foreseeable that a victim of child abuse will suffer further injury if the abuse is not reported. It also conceded that public policy does not support the imposition of legal liability on adults who fail to report incidents of child abuse absent a state law creating such liability. In short, the second factor often supports the recognition of a duty, while the third factor often does not. This makes the first factor (the existence of a special relationship) determinative. The court acknowledged that no satisfactory definition of a "special relationship" exists. However, it concluded that such a relationship may have existed between the victim and the pastor, as a result of the following allegations made by the victim: (1) he met the pastor when he was fourteen years of age; (2) over the next four years he spoke with the pastor more than fifty times; (3) he sought help from the pastor concerning the sexual abuse he was suffering from his foster father and others; and (4) the pastor did provide some counsel to him regarding his abuse. The court concluded, "[The pastor] knew of the alleged abuse and could have reasonably foreseen that it would continue absent adult intervention. In addition, there is a genuine issue of material fact as to whether [he] enjoyed a special relationship with [the victim]. When the level of interaction or dependency between an abused child and an adult results in a special relationship, the adult necessarily assumes a greater responsibility for that child. The special relationship imbues to the child a sense of security and trust. For the child, the stakes are high. For the adult, making a good faith report to a local child protection service is neither burdensome nor risky. In such circumstances, the adult is committing an even greater disservice to the child when the adult fails to make a report of the alleged abuse."[11]

Example. The Iowa Supreme Court ruled that a priest was not legally responsible for damages suffered by a victim of child abuse as a result of his decision not to report the

---

[10] People v. Hodges, 13 Cal. Rptr.2d 412 (Cal. Super. 1992).
[11] J.A.W. v. Roberts, 627 N.E.2d 802 (Ind. App. 5 Dist. 1994).

abuse to civil authorities. A child (the victim) and her parents met with their parish priest on a number of occasions for family counseling. The priest was not a licensed counselor. The victim did not tell the priest that her father had sexually abused her but did tell him that he had "hurt" her. The physical and sexual abuse of the victim stopped when her father left home when she was in eighth grade. The victim attempted suicide a month later. The victim later sued her former priest and church. She claimed that the priest failed to report her abuse to the civil authorities, and that as a result the abuse continued and her injuries were aggravated. She conceded that the priest was not aware that abuse had occurred, but she insisted that he should have been aware of the abuse based on her statement to him that her father had "hurt her." A trial court dismissed the claim against the priest on the ground that he was not a mandatory child abuse reporter under state law and as a result had no duty to report the abuse even if he suspected it. The state supreme court affirmed the trial court's decision. This case demonstrates that members of the clergy are not necessarily mandatory child abuse reporters under a state law that makes "counselors" mandatory reporters. And, it illustrates that clergy who are not mandatory reporters, and who fail to report an incident of child abuse, will not necessarily be liable for the victim's injuries.[12]

Example. *A Texas court ruled that ministers who are mandatory child abuse reporters under state law cannot be sued by child abuse victims on account of their failure to report. A 12-year-old boy was sexually molested by the children's music director at his church. At first, the victim told no one. However, over the next few years the victim told five pastors in his church about the molestation. Although pastors are "mandatory reporters" of child abuse under Texas law, none of them reported the allegations to civil authorities or to the victim's parents. The victim sued his church when he was an adult. He claimed that the church was responsible for his injuries because of its "inadequate response" to his "cries for help," and because of the failure by the 5 pastors to report the abuse to civil authorities. The court concluded that the church was not liable for the victim's injuries on account of the 5 pastors' failure to comply with the state child abuse reporting law. The 5 pastors in this case were mandatory reporters under Texas law, and the victim claimed that their failure to report his allegations of abuse made them and the church legally responsible for his injuries. The court disagreed, noting that the state child abuse reporting law is a criminal statute and that "nothing in the statute indicates that it was intended to create a private cause of action."*[13]

Example. *The Washington state supreme court ruled that an ordained minister could not be prosecuted criminally for failing to file a report despite his knowledge that a child was being abused. The minister was informed by a female counselee that her husband had sexually abused their minor child. The minister discussed the matter with both the husband and daughter in an attempt to reconcile the family, but filed no report with civil authorities within 48 hours as required by state law. The minister was prosecuted and convicted for violating the state child abuse reporting statute. He received a deferred sentence coupled with one year's probation and a $500 fine, and in addition was required to complete a "professional education program" addressing the ramifications of sexual abuse. The minister appealed his conviction, and the state supreme court reversed the conviction and ruled that the state child abuse reporting statute could not apply to clergy acting in their professional capacity as spiritual advisers. The court noted that the state legislature's 1975 amendment of the*

---

[12] Wilson v. Darr, 553 N.W.2d 579 (Iowa 1996).

[13] Marshall v. First Baptist Church, 949 S.W.2d 504 (Tex. App. 1997).

Washington child abuse reporting statute deleting a reference to "clergy" among the persons under a mandatory duty to report known or reasonably suspected cases of child abuse "relieved clerics from the reporting mandate. Logically, clergy would not have been removed from the reporting class if the legislature still intended to include them." The court further observed, "Announcing a rule that requires clergy to report under all circumstances could serve to dissuade parishioners from acknowledging in consultation with their ministers the existence of abuse and seeking a solution to it. . . . [But] simply establishing one's status as clergy is not enough to trigger the exemption in all circumstances. One must also be functioning in that capacity for the exemption to apply. . . . Thus we hold as a matter of statutory interpretation that members of the clergy counseling their parishioners in the religious context are not subject to the reporting requirement [under the state child abuse reporting law]." However, the court concluded that two "religious counselors" who were not ordained or licensed ministers could be prosecuted criminally for failure to report incidents of abuse that had been disclosed to them. The court concluded that the criminal conviction of the non-clergy "religious counselors" did not violate the first amendment guaranty of religious freedom.[14]

Example. A federal district court in Wisconsin ruled that a church was not legally responsible for the molestation of a young boy by a teacher at the church's school. It rejected the victim's claim that the church was responsible on the basis of a failure to report the abuse to civil authorities as required by state law. The court conceded that the school administrator had "reasonable cause to suspect" that one of his teachers had committed child sexual abuse, and was obligated to alert the authorities under the state child abuse reporting law. However, the court emphasized that the church's breach of its duty to report the suspected abuse to civil authorities could not have been the cause of the victim's injuries since the victim could not prove that any of the acts of molestation occurred after the time a child abuse report should have been filed.[15]

23.4 Steps Clergy Should Take after Receiving an Allegation of Child Abuse

Clergy who learn of allegations of child abuse should consult with a local attorney and address the following questions:

- Am I a mandatory or a permissive reporter under state law?

- If the allegations are true, do they constitute child abuse as defined under state law? Remember, in some states the definition of child abuse is limited to abuse inflicted by a parent or person responsible for a child's care.

- Do I have reasonable cause to believe that abuse has occurred? Be sure to interpret this broadly. An alleged offender's denial of any wrongdoing does not preclude reasonable cause. Remember, offenders typically deny any wrongdoing.

---

[14] State v. Motherwell, 788 P.2d 1066 (Wash. 1990). *See also* Wilson v. Darr, 553 N.W.2d 579 (Iowa 1996), in which the Iowa Supreme Court observed, "The legislature did not include members of the clergy among those that are required to report child abuse under [state law]. Because it is common knowledge that clergymen engage in activities within a religious context that might unearth abusive situations, that omission must be deemed to have been a conscious choice to exclude this profession from the reporting requirements of the statute."

[15] Kendrick v. East Delavan Baptist Church, 886 F. Supp. 1465 (E.D. Wis. 1995).

- Did I receive the information in the course of spiritual counseling? If so, does the clergy-penitent privilege protect me from disclosing this information? In a few states, it does.

- How severe was the abuse? Evaluate the severity of the alleged abuse and the possible existence of other victims of the same perpetrator.

- Did the alleged abuse involve pedophilic behavior (sexual contact with a pre-adolescent child)? If so, respond aggressively since pedophilia is often considered to be incurable and many pedophiles have hundreds of victims over the course of a lifetime.

- Do I have any risk of civil liability under state law if I choose not to report the abuse? It is possible that abuse victims will be permitted to sue clergy who fail to report (even if they are not mandatory reporters) if their injuries are aggravated and perpetuated because of the failure to report.

- Should I candidly (but anonymously) discuss the available evidence with the state agency that receives child abuse reports to determine whether the agency believes that a report should be filed?

- Should I try to persuade the informant to report the abuse? If the informant is unwilling, offer to accompany him or her to the police station or state agency that receives reports of abuse. If this does not work, then ask for the informant's permission to file a report yourself.

- Can child abuse be reported to law enforcement officials in my state? Some states permit this. If you are in such a state, and you have a law enforcement officer in your congregation, consider reporting to that person.

Summary

Child abuse is a serious problem in our society. Ministers and other church staff members should recognize that they may be legally required to report known or reasonably suspected incidents of abuse to civil authorities. This requirement should not be viewed as governmental meddling in church affairs, but rather as an effective way to combat this social evil. Church leaders often are inclined to treat accusations of abuse as an internal church matter. This chapter demonstrates that such an attitude not only will help to perpetuate abuse, but also may lead to criminal and civil liability on the part of those persons who are mandatory reporters under state law and who failed to report. The first amendment guaranty of religious freedom does not insulate ministers and lay church leaders from the reporting obligation, if they are mandatory reporters under state law. However, the clergy-penitent privilege will protect ministers in some states from the obligation to report child abuse if they learned of the abuse in the course of a conversation that is protected by the privilege. In the next chapter, we examine the legal concerns associated with clergy sexual misconduct and steps that can be taken to minimize that risk.

CHAPTER 24. REDUCING THE RISK OF SEXUAL MISCONDUCT

A number of ministers have been sued for engaging in sexual relations with adult counselees or minors. To illustrate, many cases have involved sexual relations between male ministers and female counselees. The woman later sues the minister for intentional infliction of emotional distress, battery, breach of fiduciary duty, and malpractice, among other theories of liability. Suing ministers for sexual misconduct presents a number of problems for adult victims.

First, ministers often will assert the "consent" defense—meaning that the "victim" consented to the relationship and accordingly should not be permitted to sue. Victims will allege that a minister's unique position of authority and respect overcame their free will and made their conduct non-consensual.

Second, any theory of liability based on intentional behavior by a minister is potentially excluded from coverage under the church's general liability insurance policy. If a minister's conduct is excluded from insurance coverage, and the minister has little if any financial resources, then the victim will be left without a remedy unless she can sue the minister's church or denomination. However, lawsuits brought by victims of clergy sexual misconduct against a minister's employing church or denomination have been rejected by the courts in most cases unless the victim can prove that the church or denomination had actual knowledge of previous incidents of sexual misconduct by the same minister and did nothing to monitor or restrict the minister's activities. The issue of church liability for clergy sexual misconduct is addressed fully in a later chapter.

Third, the first amendment guaranty of religious freedom affords some protection for clergy conduct.

Fourth, the abolition by most states of any liability for "seduction" or "alienation of affections" may restrict if not eliminate lawsuits brought against clergy based upon sexual misconduct.

Ministers can be liable in such cases on the basis of a number of legal principles. These principles, along with possible defenses, are summarized below.

24.1 Theories of Liability

Malpractice

Some courts have found clergy liable on the basis of malpractice for sexual misconduct with an adult or minor. These cases are addressed in chapter 25.

Fiduciary duty

A few courts have concluded that clergy, in some situations, owe a "fiduciary duty" toward members of their congregation, and that they can be liable for breaching this duty when they engage in sexual misconduct with a member of their congregation. For example, a few courts have concluded a fiduciary duty arises when clergy "hold themselves out" to their church and community as a skilled marriage counselor. Many of these cases have occurred in one state—Colorado.

Example. *A federal appeals court ruled that a pastor who had engaged in sexual relations with two female church employees who had sought him out for marriage counseling could be sued by the women for breaching a fiduciary duty he owed them. This case suggests that clergy who act as marriage counselors may be deemed fiduciaries, and as such they are held to a very high standard of ethical behavior with regard to those they counsel. This duty is breached when a counselor engages in sexual relations with a counselee. The court also ruled that it may be breached by "betraying confidences" obtained in a "relation of trust" (such as a counseling relationship). In other words, apart from the sexual misconduct, the former minister was liable to the two women for disclosing confidences he obtained during counseling sessions with them. This aspect of the ruling illustrates the importance of maintaining the confidentiality of information shared during counseling sessions. Disclosing such information without permission may lead to legal liability based on a breach of the counselor's fiduciary duties.*[1]

Example. *The Colorado Supreme Court ruled that a victim of clergy sexual misconduct could sue the minister for breaching his fiduciary duty. A married couple who were experiencing marital problems sought marriage counseling from their parish priest. The husband and wife were both Catholics and "had faith and confidence" in their priest. During the course of counseling, the priest developed an intimate relationship with the wife that contributed directly to the dissolution of her marriage. The wife alleged that the priest, as one who held himself out to her as a professional and trained marriage counselor, breached his "fiduciary duty" to her. The court noted that a marriage counselor has a "fiduciary duty" toward a counselee to act "with utmost good faith and solely for the benefit of" the counselee. The court concluded that the priest violated his fiduciary duty toward the wife if the allegations in her complaint were true.*[2]

Example. *The Colorado Supreme Court ruled that an Episcopal diocese and bishop were responsible for a pastor's sexual misconduct with a female member of the congregation who had sought him out for counseling. The court concluded that the bishop and diocese breached their "fiduciary duty" to the victim. The court noted that a fiduciary relationship exists when there is a special relationship of trust, confidence and reliance between two persons, and when one of them assumes a duty to act in the other's best interests. The court acknowledged that the clergy-parishioner relationship "is not necessarily a fiduciary relationship." However, the clergy-parishioner relationship often involves "the type of interaction that creates trust and reliance" and in some cases will constitute a fiduciary relationship. The court concluded that a fiduciary relationship existed between the bishop and the victim on the basis of the following factors: (1) The bishop was in a superior position and was able to exert substantial influence over the victim. An unequal relationship between two parties can be evidence of a fiduciary relationship, since the party with the greater influence and authority often assumes a duty to act in the dependent party's best interests. (2) The bishop, in his meeting with the victim, served as a counselor to the victim and not as a representative of the diocese. If he was acting only as a representative of the diocese, he failed to convey that fact to the victim and led her to believe that he was acting in her interest. The court concluded that the bishop and diocese had breached their fiduciary duty to the victim by not acting in her "utmost good faith" (by taking no*

---

[1] Sanders v. Casa View Baptist Church, 134 F.3d 331 (5th Cir. 1998).
[2] Destefano v. Grabian, 763 P.2d 275 (Colo. 1988).

action to help her, not assisting her in understanding that she was not solely responsible for the sexual relationship, and not recommending counseling for her).[3]

Example. *A Colorado court ruled that a minister could be sued by a woman with whom he had sexual contacts. A woman (the victim) attended a church for a few years, and began to volunteer her services for a variety of activities including the remodeling of a classroom. She engaged in these volunteer services on the recommendation of a therapist who suggested that she work in a "safe environment" to overcome her fears of the workplace. The victim's volunteer work caused her to come in contact with her minister after normal working hours. On one occasion the minister approached her while she was remodeling a classroom, began caressing her back, and told her "I love you Dianne, you mean so much to me." Following this incident the victim became physically ill and cried. A few days later, the minister called the victim into his office where the two of them sat next to each other on a small couch. The minister again caressed her and expressed his love for her. Following a third incident, the victim informed two other women in the church about the minister's behavior, and one responded, "Oh my God, not you too." The victim later sued the minister, claiming that he had breached his fiduciary duty toward her. A state appeals court rejected the claim that no fiduciary relationship existed between the victim and the minister. The court noted that the minister had counseled the victim on personal and intimate matters, and that such counseling was enough to establish a fiduciary relationship.*[4]

Example. *The Colorado Supreme Court ruled that a pastor who molested a young boy could be sued for his behavior on the basis of a breach of a fiduciary duty. A 7-year-old boy (the "victim"), who was experiencing emotional trauma, was encouraged by his pastor to enter into a counseling relationship with him. The boy's mother approved, and the counseling sessions lasted for a number of years. From the very first counseling session the victim claimed that the pastor engaged in sexual contact with him, including having him sit on the pastor's lap while the pastor massaged his thighs and genitals. While these "massages" were occurring the pastor would tell the victim that "your father loves you, your mother loves you, God loves you, and I love you." Two other adult males claimed that the pastor had engaged in similar behavior with them when they were minors, including a physical inspection of their genitals to see if they had been "properly circumcised." The court ruled that the victim could sue the pastor for breaching a fiduciary duty.*[5]

Example. *An Oregon state appeals court ruled that a victim of clergy sexual misconduct could sue her minister.*[6] *The woman sued the minister for "breach of confidential relationship." The woman alleged that her minister abused his pastoral and counseling relationships with her by "manipulating" her into having sexual relations with him. She claimed to have suffered sexual abuse, extreme emotional distress, physical illness, loss of sleep and memory, clinical depression, and loss of her "ability to trust other adults, to trust authority, and to deal with religion and faith in God." A state appeals court concluded that the woman's lawsuit stated facts which, if proven true, could possibly result in legal liability. The court concluded that the facts alleged in the lawsuit stated a claim for breach of confidential relationship. It rejected*

---

[3] Moses v. Diocese of Colorado, 863 P.2d 310 (Colo. 1993).

[4] Winkler v. Rocky Mountain Conference, 923 P.2d 152 (Colo. App. 1995).

[5] Bear Valley Church of Christ v. DeBose, 928 P.2d 1315 (Colo. 1996).

[6] Erickson v. Christenson, 781 P.2d 383 (Or. App. 1989).

the minister's argument that the claims against him were really an attempt to sue him for "seduction"—a legal theory that had been eliminated by the Oregon legislature in 1973. The fact that the minister allegedly used seduction as a means of breaching his confidential relationship with the woman, and to intentionally cause her emotional distress, did "not convert her claim into one for seduction."

Most courts have refused to hold ministers liable for their sexual misconduct on the basis of a fiduciary duty. In some cases this is because the court refuses to recognize breach of fiduciary duty as a basis for legal liability. In other cases, the ministers did not hold themselves out as marriage counselors or engage in other behavior giving rise to a fiduciary duty.

Example. A Florida court ruled that it was barred by the first amendment from resolving a woman's claim that her priest and church were responsible on the basis of a breach of a fiduciary duty for the priest's acts of sexual misconduct.[7] The woman had sought out a priest for marital counseling and alleged that the priest engaged in sexual contacts with her. The woman sued her church and diocese, claiming that they were aware of prior incidents involving sexual misconduct during counseling by the same priest. Despite this knowledge, nothing was done to address the problem. She claimed that the priest breached a fiduciary duty by becoming romantically involved with her, and that the church and diocese had a fiduciary relationship with her (because she reported the priest's misconduct to them) that was breached. A state appeals court concluded that resolving the woman's breach of fiduciary duty claims (against the priest, church, and diocese) would constitute excessive entanglement between church and state in violation of the first amendment: "Taking the allegations of [her] complaint as true, [she] alleged the church defendants owed her a fiduciary duty, yet definition of that duty necessarily involves the secular court in church practices, doctrines, and belief. To establish a breach of the fiduciary duty allegedly owed to [her] by the church defendants, [she] would need to establish the church remained inactive in the face of her allegations against [the priest]. However, the church's policies undoubtedly differ from the rules of another employer, and may require the nonsecular employer to respond differently when faced with such allegations. When a secular court interprets church law, policies, and practices it becomes excessively entangled in religion. We align ourselves with those courts finding a first amendment bar to a breach of fiduciary duty claim as against church defendants, concluding resolution of such a claim would necessarily require the secular court to review and interpret church law, policies, and practices."

Example. An Illinois court ruled that a husband whose wife was seduced by her pastor could not sue the pastor for breach of a fiduciary duty. The court noted that Illinois law prohibits "the recognition of an action for breach of fiduciary duty premised upon the counseling relationship between a cleric and a church member with whom the cleric had been sexually involved." The court further noted that courts in a few states have reached the opposite conclusion, but it insisted that "when a parishioner lodges such a claim, religion is not merely incidental to a plaintiff's relationship with a defendant, it is the foundation for it. . . . The fiduciary relationship is inescapably premised upon the cleric's status as an expert in theological and spiritual matters."[8]

---

[7] Doe v. Evans, 718 So.2d 286 (Fla. App. 1998).

[8] Amato v. Greenquist, 679 N.E.2d 446 (Ill. App. 1997).

Example. The Nebraska Supreme Court ruled that a priest was not liable on the basis of a breach of any fiduciary duty for his sexual contacts with a woman who had come to him for counseling. The woman claimed that the priest had a fiduciary obligation to refrain from doing anything that might harm her relationship with her husband and children, and that he breached this duty. The court acknowledged that "[s]everal cases have allowed recovery on the theory of breach of fiduciary duty with regard to sexual misconduct of a member of the clergy with a parishioner." However, it stressed that this theory of liability has been rejected by other courts because of "constitutional difficulties with regard to defining a standard of care."[9]

Example. A federal court in New York refused to find a pastor liable for his alleged sexual seduction of a church member he had counseled for several years.[10] The woman sued the pastor on the basis of an alleged breach of a fiduciary duty. The court noted that this basis of liability was simply a variation of clergy malpractice. It pointed out that neither the state legislature nor any court had recognized clergy malpractice as a basis for liability, and therefore the woman's lawsuit had to be dismissed.

Example. The Ohio Supreme Court rejected a woman's attempt to sue her church and pastor for injuries she allegedly suffered because of a sexual relationship with her pastor.[11] A husband and wife who had been experiencing marital problems went to a Lutheran minister for counseling. They selected him because "he held himself out to the public . . . as a minister and counselor trained and able to provide counseling for marital difficulties." During the final three or four weeks of counseling, the minister allegedly engaged in consensual sexual relations with the wife. These relations, and the counseling, ended when the husband learned of the affair. The husband, who was later divorced from his wife, sued both the minister and his church. The suit against the minister alleged a breach of fiduciary duty, among other things. The state supreme court dismissed all of the husband's claims. It noted that the breach of fiduciary claim, like the husband's other claims, had to be dismissed since they all sought damages based on the minister's seduction of the wife, and as such were barred by the state law prohibiting lawsuits based on "alienation of affections."

Example. The Oklahoma Supreme Court ruled that a pastor was not liable on the basis of a breach of a fiduciary duty for sexual contacts he had with a woman during counseling. In rejecting this basis of liability, the court noted that only "[o]ne court has followed this view" and that "[o]ther courts have declined to use this fiduciary or trust theory for various reasons." The court concluded that "[w]e need not determine if the fiduciary theory applies to the facts before us, because . . . the underlying conduct at issue does not invade a legally recognized right of the husband. . . . We conclude that the husband's claims arising from the affair are not cognizable." The court noted that the Oklahoma legislature had abolished the torts of alienation of affections.[12]

---

[9] Nebraska Supreme Court issues an important ruling; Schieffer v. Catholic Archdiocese, 508 N.W.2d 907 (Neb. 1993).

[10] Schmidt v. Bishop, 779 F. Supp. 321 (S.D.N.Y. 1991). *Accord* Langford v. Roman Catholic Diocese, 677 N.Y.S.2d 436 (A.D. 1998).

[11] Stock v. Pressnell, 527 N.E.2d 1235 (Ohio 1988).

[12] Bladen v. First Presbyterian Church, 857 P.2d 789 (Okla. 1993).

Emotional distress ("outrageous conduct")

Some clergy who have engaged in sexual misconduct have been sued by their victims on the basis of intentional infliction of emotional distress (sometimes referred to as "outrageous conduct"). This is a very difficult wrong to prove. The elements of an intentional infliction of emotional distress claim are (1) the defendant acted intentionally or recklessly; (2) the conduct was extreme and outrageous; (3) the actions of the defendant caused the victim emotional distress; and (4) the emotional distress suffered by the victim was extreme and severe. Generally, liability is proven "only when the conduct has been so outrageous in character, and so extreme in degree, as to go beyond all possible bounds of decency, and to be regarded as atrocious, and utterly intolerable in a civilized community."[13] One court has further explained that

> [t]here must be substantial evidence of extreme conduct: It has not been enough that the defendant has acted with an intent which is tortious or even criminal, or that [he or she] has intended to inflict emotional distress, or even that [his or her] conduct has been characterized by malice, or a degree of aggravation that would entitle the plaintiff to punitive damages for another tort.[14]

Example. The Colorado Supreme Court ruled that a victim of clergy sexual misconduct could sue the minister for intentional infliction of emotional distress (or "outrageous conduct"). The court concluded that the wife could sue the priest for outrageous conduct if she could establish that the priest was guilty of "extreme and outrageous conduct" that intentionally caused the wife "severe emotional distress." [15]

Example. An Illinois court ruled that a husband whose wife was seduced by her pastor could sue the pastor for intentionally inflicting emotional distress as a result of marital counseling he performed for the husband without disclosing the affair. The court noted that for the pastor to be guilty of intentional infliction of emotional distress, the former husband had to prove facts "establishing that the [pastor's] conduct was extreme and outrageous and that [he] either intended his conduct to inflict severe emotional distress or knew that there was a high probability that the conduct would cause such distress." Such a basis of liability exists "only where the conduct complained of is so outrageous as to go beyond all bounds of decency, and to be regarded as atrocious, and utterly intolerable in a civil community." The court noted that the former husband had sought counseling from the pastor "concerning his failing marriage," and it concluded that the pastor "acted in an extreme and outrageous manner by counseling the [husband] while [he] was involved with [the wife] and by counseling in a manner designed to covertly undermine the couple's marriage."[16]

---

[13] Hanssen v. Our Redeemer Lutheran Church, 938 S.W.2d 85 (Tex. App. 1997). *See also* Bear Valley Church of Christ v. DeBose, 928 P.2d 1315 (Colo. 1996); Doe v. Hartford Roman Catholic Diocesan Corporation, 716 A.2d 960 (Conn. Super. 1998); Singleton v. Christ the Servant Evangelical Lutheran Church, 541 N.W.2d 606 (Minn. App. 1996); Brown v. Pearson, 483 S.E.2d 477 (S.C. App. 1997). Most courts refer to section 46 of the Restatement (Second) of Torts, a respected legal treatise.

[14] John v. Estate of Hartgerink, 528 N.W.2d 539 (Iowa 1995).

[15] Destefano v. Grabian, 763 P.2d 275 (Colo. 1988).

[16] Amato v. Greenquist, 679 N.E.2d 446 (Ill. App. 1997).

Example. The Nebraska Supreme Court ruled that a priest could not be sued for infliction of emotional distress by a woman with whom he engaged in sexual relations. The woman alleged that the conduct of her priest was outrageous and extreme and caused her severe emotional distress. As a direct result of that conduct, the woman allegedly suffered severe and permanent emotional injury and incurred current and future medical expenses. She also claimed that she had lost faith in the Catholic Church and in God. The court observed that intentional infliction of emotional distress requires proof of the following three elements: (1) intentional or reckless conduct; (2) the conduct is so outrageous in character and so extreme in degree as to go beyond all possible bounds of decency and is to be regarded as atrocious and utterly intolerable in a civilized community; and (3) the conduct caused emotional distress so severe that no reasonable person should be expected to endure it. In rejecting this theory of liability the court observed, "A sexual relationship between two consenting adults is not outrageous conduct such as to give rise to a claim for intentional infliction of emotional distress. This seems especially true given the fact that the [woman and the priest] engaged in an approximate 7-year sexual relationship."[17]

Example. An Oregon state appeals court ruled that a victim of clergy sexual misconduct could sue her minister.[18] The woman sued the minister for "intentional infliction of emotional distress." The woman alleged that her minister abused his pastoral and counseling relationships with her by "manipulating" her into having sexual relations with him. She claimed to have suffered sexual abuse, extreme emotional distress, physical illness, loss of sleep and memory, clinical depression, and loss of her "ability to trust other adults, to trust authority, and to deal with religion and faith in God." A state appeals court concluded that the woman's lawsuit stated facts which, if proven true, could possibly result in legal liability. The court concluded that the facts alleged in the lawsuit stated a claim for intentional infliction of emotional distress by the minister. It rejected the minister's argument that the claims against him were really an attempt to sue him for "seduction"—a legal theory that had been eliminated by the Oregon legislature in 1973. The fact that the minister allegedly used seduction as a means of breaching his confidential relationship with the woman, and to intentionally cause her emotional distress, did "not convert her claim into one for seduction."

Assault and battery

Clergy who engage in inappropriate sexual contacts with others may be subject to civil and criminal liability for their actions. Assault and battery not only are crimes, but they also are intentional torts (meaning that they can be the basis for civil lawsuits seeking money damages).

Sexual harassment

Sexual harassment is a form of "sex discrimination" prohibited by Title VII of the Civil Rights Act of 1964. Equal Employment Opportunity Commission (EEOC) regulations define sexual harassment as follows:

---

[17] Nebraska Supreme Court issues an important ruling; Schieffer v. Catholic Archdiocese, 508 N.W.2d 907 (Neb. 1993).
[18] Erickson v. Christenson, 781 P.2d 383 (Or. App. 1989).

Unwelcome sexual advances, requests for sexual favors, and other verbal or physical conduct of a sexual nature constitute sexual harassment when (1) submission to such conduct is made either explicitly or implicitly a term or condition of an individual's employment, (2) submission to or rejection of such conduct by an individual is used as the basis for employment decisions affecting such individual, or (3) such conduct has the purpose or effect of unreasonably interfering with an individual's work performance or creating an intimidating, hostile, or offensive working environment.

This definition confirms the conclusion reached by numerous state and federal courts that sexual harassment includes *at least two separate types of conduct:*

- *"quid pro quo" harassment,* which refers to conditioning employment opportunities on submission to a sexual or social relationship, and

- *"hostile environment" harassment,* which refers to the creation of an intimidating, hostile, or offensive working environment through unwelcome verbal or physical conduct of a sexual nature.

Many states have enacted similar statutes. Clergy may be personally liable for sexual harassment under some of these laws.

Example. An Ohio appeals court ruled that a minister could be sued for his alleged acts of sexual harassment.[19] A woman served some ten years as parish secretary of a church prior to the arrival of a new minister. Soon after the arrival of the new minister, the secretary began alleging that the minister was engaging in acts of sexual harassment against her. Initially, the secretary contacted the bishop of the diocese with her complaint. He promised to make an investigation and apparently did, but concluded that, although he believed she was sincere in her allegations, there was nothing that he could do because the minister denied any wrongdoing, and the bishop felt he could not resolve the credibility issue. The bishop did, during the investigation, order the work hours of the minister and secretary to be so staggered that they would not be working at the same time. After hearing that the bishop would take no further action, the woman wrote to the minister in question, the standing committee of the diocese, the vestry, the warden, and the bishop in an attempt to resolve what she called "this terrible problem." Upon receipt of this letter, the minister called the chancellor of the diocese, who advised him to fire the secretary. The minister thereafter was instructed by the vestry of the church to notify the congregation that the secretary had been fired and to give a reason. Accordingly, the minister published in the parish newsletter a statement that the secretary had been engaging in an open malicious endeavor to discredit him. Following her dismissal, the former secretary filed a lawsuit against the minister, her church, and the diocese. She based her lawsuit on several legal grounds, including sexual harassment. A state appeals court ruled that there was sufficient evidence of sexual harassment by the minister to allow the case to proceed to trial.

Criminal and statutory liability

Sexual contact between clergy and a counselee may constitute a crime under state law. Many states have enacted legislation making it a crime for "psychotherapists" to engage in sexual contact with a counselee, and some of these laws define the

---

[19] Davis v. Black, 591 N.E.2d 11 (Ohio App. 1991).

term *psychotherapist* to include clergy.[20] Other states have enacted legislation giving counselees a statutory right to sue counselors for sexual misconduct.

Example. A federal appeals court ruled that a pastor could be liable under a state law imposing liability on "psychotherapists" for engaging in sexual contact with counselees.[21] A woman sued a pastoral counselor alleging that the counselor had engaged in sexual relations with her. The court permitted the woman to sue the pastor for violating the Illinois Sexual Exploitation in Psychotherapy Act. This Act permits counselees to sue a psychotherapist for sexual contact. While the Act excludes "counseling of a spiritual or religious nature" from liability, the court noted that this exclusion would not apply to purely "secular" counseling by a pastor.

Example. A Minnesota appeals court ruled that a minister could be criminally liable for sexually seducing a female counselee.[22] The minister was approached by a married female church member who desired counseling. At the conclusion of one counseling session that explored the subject of grief, the pastor gave the woman a brief hug. The following week she asked the pastor if they were engaged in "normal counseling," and he replied that he loved her. The session ended with the two engaged in hugging and passionate kissing. Two days later, the woman went back to clarify that their relationship would remain "platonic" and non-sexual. At that meeting, the two engaged in hugging and kissing. The pastor gave the woman a rose as a symbol that their relationship would forever remain "pure and chaste from afar" and that he would "maintain her virginity." A month later, the two went to a motel and engaged in sexual intercourse for the first time. The woman testified that the pastor assured her that it was a "good" sexual encounter because he was unselfish. He also informed her that sex between a counselor and counselee was a felony in Minnesota. The two engaged in sexual intercourse on at least two other occasions over the next few months. The woman testified that the pastor assured her that sexual contact and intercourse was consistent with her "treatment" because it would remove her inhibitions about sex and "set her free" from her sexual "hang-ups." The pastor was later prosecuted for criminal sexual contact under a state law prohibiting sexual contact by a "psychotherapist" with an "emotionally dependent" patient, or sexual contact by a psychotherapist with a patient occurring by means of "therapeutic

---

[20] *See, e.g.,* IOWA CODE § 709.15 (makes "sexual abuse by a counselor or therapist" a crime, and defines "counselor or therapist" to include a "member of the clergy" who "provides or purports to provide mental health services"); MINN. STAT. § 609.345 (makes it a felony for a "psychotherapist" to engage in "sexual contact" with a counselee during a counseling session, or at any time if the counselee is "emotionally dependent upon the psychotherapist" or the sexual contact occurred by means of "therapeutic deception," and defines "psychotherapist" to include clergy who engage in counseling activities); N.D. CENT. CODE § 12.1-20-06.1 (makes it a felony for a therapist to have sexual contact with a counselee and defines the term "therapist" to include a "member of the clergy" who engages in counseling or any other effort to treat a mental or emotional condition); TEX. CIV. PRACT. & REM. CODE, title 4, § 81.001 et seq. (makes "sexual exploitation" of a patient by a "mental health services provider" a felony, and defines a mental health services provider to include a "member of the clergy" not engaged in "religious, moral, or spiritual counseling, teaching, and instruction"); WIS. STAT. § 940.22 (makes "sexual contact" between a "therapist" and a counselee a felony offense, and defines "therapist" to include a "member of the clergy" who engages in counseling or any other effort to treat a mental or emotional condition).
[21] Dausch v. Rykse, 52 F.3d 1425 (7th Cir. 1994).
[22] State v. Dutton, 450 N.W.2d 189 (Minn. App. 1990).

deception." A jury convicted the pastor on four felony counts, and he appealed. In upholding the conviction, a state appeals court concluded that the pastor was a psychotherapist since he had assumed the role of a counselor, and that he had in fact committed both sexual contact and sexual intercourse with an "emotionally dependent" patient, and that the sexual contact and intercourse occurred because of "therapeutic deception."

Example. *A minister was sentenced to two consecutive life sentences for 3 acts of rape and 8 first-degree sexual offenses perpetrated on 4 women. The minister professed his innocence during his trial, but the prosecutor introduced into evidence several "love letters" the minister had written to at least one of the victims, along with several pornographic magazines and videos found in the minister's apartment. The magazines and videos were introduced by the prosecutor to rebut the minister's attempt to portray himself as an exemplary "family man" and minister. A North Carolina appeals court rejected the minister's claim that the 2 consecutive life sentences constituted "cruel and unusual punishment" in violation of the Constitution. This case illustrates the significant criminal liability that clergy face for acts of sexual misconduct. Of course, this is in addition to civil liability.*[23]

"Loss of consortium" or alienation of affections

This basis of liability has been consistently rejected by the courts. It is discussed below under "defenses to liability."

24.2 Defenses to Liability

Clergy who are sued for sexual misconduct may be able to assert one or more defenses.

Consent

The courts have reached different conclusions regarding the legal effect of a person's "consent" to a sexual relationship with a minister. Some courts have concluded that sexual relations between two consenting adults cannot be the basis for liability. Other courts have reached the opposite conclusion, usually on the ground that the pastor's unique authority and status precludes voluntary consent.

Several courts have referred to section 892A of the *Restatement of Torts* (a respected legal treatise), which provides:

(1) One who effectively consents to conduct of another intended to invade his interests cannot recover in an action of tort for the conduct or for harm resulting from it.

(2) To be effective, consent must be

   (a) by one who has the capacity to consent or by a person empowered to consent for him, and

   (b) to the particular conduct, or to substantially the same conduct.

---

[23] State v. Woodard, 404 S.E.2d 6 (N.C. App. 1991).

(3) Conditional consent or consent restricted as to time, area or in other respects is effective only within the limits of the condition or restriction.

(4) If the actor exceeds the consent, it is not effective for the excess.

(5) Upon termination of consent its effectiveness is terminated, except as it may have become irrevocable by contract or otherwise, or except as its terms may include, expressly or by implication, a privilege to continue to act.

An official comment in the *Restatement of Torts* further explains this language:

> Except in the case of persons whom the law protects for reasons of policy, such as those who are mentally immature or otherwise incompetent, no one suffers a legal wrong as the result of an act to which, unaffected by fraud, mistake or duress, he freely consents or to which he manifests apparent consent. This principle is expressed in the ancient legal maxim, *volenti non fit injuria,* meaning that no wrong is done to one who consents. . . .

> To be effective, the consent must be given by one who has the capacity to give it or by a person empowered to consent for him. If the person consenting is a child or one of deficient mental capacity, the consent may still be effective if he is capable of appreciating the nature, extent and probable consequences of the conduct consented to, although the consent of a parent, guardian or other person responsible is not obtained or is expressly refused. If, however, the one who consents is not capable of appreciating the nature, extent or probable consequences of the conduct, the consent is not effective to bar liability unless the parent, guardian or other person empowered to consent for the incompetent has given consent, in which case the consent of the authorized person will be effective even though the incompetent does not consent; or unless there is a privilege to take emergency action . . . .

> *Example. A Colorado court ruled that consent is not a defense to a pastor's sexual contacts with a minor. It observed that such a defense would be "premised on the assumption that a child is capable of giving the kind of consent the law should recognize to a sexual relationship with an adult religious counselor." The court insisted that "a child is in no position to exercise independent judgment and evaluate on an equal basis the consequences of such a relationship." The court also rejected the argument that the victim became capable of consenting to the relationship as she matured, since this "ignores that dependence, transference, and the resulting vulnerability do not cease merely because a child physically matures while sexual abuse in secrecy by an adult in a position of trust continues unabated."*[24]

> *Example. The Nebraska Supreme Court ruled that a priest could not be sued by a woman with whom he engaged in sexual relations since her consent to the relationship was a complete bar to any recovery. The court observed, "What is involved in this case is conduct between consenting adults. There is no allegation that the [priest] used force or fraud to accomplish his sexual relations with the [woman]." The court continued, "In tort law, consent ordinarily bars recovery for intentional interferences with person or property. . . . [I]t is a fundamental principle of common law that 'to one who is willing,*

---

[24] Bohrer v. DeHart, 943 P.2d 1220 (Colo. App. 1996).

no wrong is done.'" The court concluded that "[a] sexual relationship between two consenting adults is not outrageous conduct such as to give rise to a claim for intentional infliction of emotional distress. This seems especially true given the fact that the [woman and the priest] engaged in an approximate 7-year sexual relationship." The court referred to section 892A of the Restatement of Torts (a respected legal treatise), which provides, "One who effectively consents to conduct of another intended to invade his interests cannot recover in an action of tort for the conduct or for harm resulting from it." An official comment in the Restatement of Torts further explains this language: "Except in the case of persons whom the law protects for reasons of policy, such as those who are mentally immature or otherwise incompetent, no one suffers a legal wrong as the result of an act to which, unaffected by fraud, mistake or duress, he freely consents or to which he manifests apparent consent."[25]

Statute of limitations

Every state has enacted various "statutes of limitation" that prescribe the deadlines for filing legal claims. Clergy who are sued for sexual misconduct often assert that the lawsuit must be dismissed because it was filed after the deadline prescribed by the applicable statute of limitations expired. Some courts have recognized this defense.[26] Other courts (and some legislatures) have extended the statute of limitations deadline in cases of sexual misconduct, recognizing that in some cases victims are not fully capable of associating the misconduct with their emotional injuries until many years after the statute of limitations deadline has expired.

Example. A Maryland court ruled that a 34-year-old adult's lawsuit against two priests who molested him when he was a minor was barred by the statute of limitations. The victim was repeatedly molested by the two priests while serving as an altar boy over a period of 6 years. The victim claimed that it was not until he was 33 years old when his marriage was "falling apart" that he first became aware that he had been injured as a result of the priests' actions. He sued the priests the next year. A state appeals court concluded that the victim's lawsuit was barred by the Maryland statute of limitations, which requires personal injury lawsuits to be filed within 3 years of the date a victim "knew or, with due diligence, reasonably should have known of the wrong." The victim claimed that he was aware of the priests' conduct but did not appreciate the offensiveness of it or realize that he had been harmed until he began experiencing marital difficulties, and therefore the statute of limitations should not start running until that date. A state appeals court disagreed, concluding that "if any memory of sexual abuse suffered during childhood survives into adulthood, the statute of limitations begins to run when the victim reaches the age of majority." Further, "even if no memory at all survives into adulthood, the limitations period still begins to run on the date the victim reaches the age of majority."[27]

Example. A federal court in New York refused to find a pastor liable for his alleged sexual seduction of a church member he had counseled for several years.[28] The woman sued the pastor some 30 years after the pastor began engaging in sexual contact with

---

[25] Nebraska Supreme Court issues an important ruling; Schieffer v. Catholic Archdiocese, 508 N.W.2d 907 (Neb. 1993).

[26] *See, e.g.,* Doe v. Maskell, 679 A.2d 1087 (Md. 1996).

[27] Doe v. Archdiocese of Washington, 689 A.2d 634 (Md. App. 1997).

[28] Schmidt v. Bishop, 779 F. Supp. 321 (S.D.N.Y. 1991).

her. The court noted that the statute of limitations for negligence and malpractice, under New York law, is 3 years. Since the alleged malpractice first occurred nearly 30 years ago, the woman's claims obviously were barred by the statute of limitations. The woman attempted to avoid the application of the statute of limitations in three ways, each of which was rejected by the court. First, she asked the court to apply the "delayed discovery" doctrine. By this she meant that the statute of limitations should not start until a person "knows or should have known of the injury and the defendant's role in causing that injury." The court acknowledged that some states have adopted such a rule, particularly in the context of child sexual abuse cases. It noted that "the argument for a delayed discovery rule in this context, simply stated, is that victims of child sexual abuse often do not realize until years later either that they have been abused at all or the scope of their injuries." However, the court rejected this view: "Persuasive though this argument may be, there is not authority for the adoption of such a rule in child sex abuse cases in New York. . . . [The New York courts] have steadfastly declined to alter the traditional New York rule that the statute of limitations commences to run when a cause of action accrues, even though the plaintiff is unaware that he has a cause of action." Next, the woman argued that the pastor should be prohibited from relying on the statute of limitations because of his "misrepresentations." The court agreed that the statute of limitations can be suspended if a party's fraud or "active concealment" prevents a plaintiff from filing a timely claim. However, it disagreed that this rule applied in the present case, since the pastor had done nothing to prevent the woman from filing a timely lawsuit. Finally, the woman argued that the statute of limitations should be suspended because she "was under duress." The court rejected this claim as well, since "it is extremely doubtful whether any reasonable juror could find that [she] was under constant legal duress for a 31-year period, during most of which she lived half a continent away from the [pastor]."

Example. *The Ohio Supreme Court dismissed a lawsuit brought by a 25-year-old man who had been repeatedly molested as a minor by a church choir director. The victim had been molested by his church choir director on nearly 300 occasions over a period of 3 years (from 1981 through 1984) when he was between 15 and 18 years of age. He turned 18 in July of 1984. In July of 1991, shortly after his 25th birthday, the victim filed a lawsuit against the choir director and his church. This was long after the applicable statute of limitations had expired, but the victim insisted that he did not "discover" the nature and extent of his injuries until he sought psychological help as an adult. The court ruled that the statute of limitations began to run on the victim's 18th birthday and not when he claimed to have "discovered" that his emotional injuries were caused by the abuse. The court observed, "Here, the facts clearly establish that at the time [the victim] reached the age of majority, [he] knew that he had been sexually abused by [the choir director]. [The choir director] allegedly initiated homosexual conduct with [the victim] on two hundred to three hundred separate occasions without [his] consent. During the period of sexual abuse, [the victim] was fourteen to seventeen years of age. . . . [U]pon reaching the age of majority, [the victim] knew that he had been sexually abused, and he knew the identity of the perpetrator. Although [he] may not have discovered the full extent of his psychological injuries until [later] the fact that [he] was aware upon reaching the age of majority that he had been sexually abused by [the choir director] was sufficient to trigger the commencement of the statute of limitations for assault and battery."*[29]

---

[29] Doe v. First United Methodist Church, 629 N.E.2d 402 (Ohio 1994).

First Amendment

Does the first amendment guaranty of religious freedom protect clergy from being sued as a result of their sexual misconduct? Most courts have said that it does not, although a few courts have reached the opposite conclusion.

Example. The Colorado Supreme Court ruled that an Episcopal diocese and bishop were responsible for a pastor's sexual misconduct with a female member of the congregation who had sought him out for counseling. It rejected the bishop's claim that the first amendment's guaranty of religious freedom prevented a civil court from addressing the victim's claims. The court acknowledged that the first amendment prevents civil courts from resolving controversies involving church doctrine. However, the court insisted that churches have no absolute immunity from being sued in cases not involving doctrine: "Civil actions against clergy members and their superiors that involve claims of a breach of fiduciary duty, negligent hiring and supervision, and vicarious liability are actionable if they are supported by competent evidence in the record. . . . [The victim's] claims in this case do not involve disputes within the church and are not based solely on ecclesiastical or disciplinary matters . . . . Our decision does not require a reading of the Constitution and Canons of the Protestant Episcopal Church or any other documents of church governance. Because the facts of this case do not require interpreting or weighing church doctrine and neutral principles of law can be applied, the first amendment is not a defense against [the victim's] claims."[30]

Example. The Colorado Supreme Court ruled that a pastor who molested a young boy could be sued for his behavior, and that the first amendment guaranty of religious freedom was no defense. The pastor had argued that any touching of the victim that might have occurred was not designed to satisfy any sexual desires, but was intended to facilitate the minor's communication with God. The court concluded that the pastor's "massage technique" was not entitled to constitutional protection as an exercise of religion: "Although his ultimate goal . . . was for counselees to receive help from God in resolving their problems . . . his choice to use massage with children had no biblical, doctrinal, or spiritual basis . . . . Despite the religious setting, the described massage technique simply reflects [the pastor's] choice of a relaxation and communication method between himself and his counselees."[31]

Example. An Illinois court ruled that a pastor could be sued by a woman he had sexually seduced during marriage counseling, and that the lawsuit was not barred by the first amendment guaranty of religious freedom. The court acknowledged that "[a] court's authority to resolve disputes involving a church is narrowly circumscribed by the first amendment's guarantee that the right to the free exercise of religion will not be abridged." However, "where doctrinal controversy is not involved in a church dispute, mandatory deference to religious authority is not required by the first amendment, and the court may choose from a variety of approaches in resolving the dispute." It noted that the courts can resolve disputes over control of church property so long as they can do so on the basis of "neutral principles of law" requiring no examination of religious doctrine. The court applied the same "neutral principles of law" approach in this case involving alleged church liability for the sexual misconduct of its pastor.[32]

---

[30] Moses v. Diocese of Colorado, 863 P.2d 310 (Colo. 1993).

[31] Bear Valley Church of Christ v. DeBose, 928 P.2d 1315 (Colo. 1996).

[32] Bivin v. Wright, 656 N.E.2d 1121 (Ill. App. 1995).

Example. A Minnesota appeals court ruled that the first amendment guaranty of religious freedom was no defense to a minister's criminal conviction for engaging in sexual contact with a vulnerable counselee.[33] The court ruled that no constitutional right protects a pastor who engages in sexual activity as part of religious counseling. The court observed, "These statutes are meant to protect vulnerable persons and allow them to reposit trust in those who can help them. The legislature has recognized the emotional devastation that can result when a psychotherapist takes advantage of a patient."

Example. The Ohio Supreme Court rejected a woman's attempt to sue her church and pastor for injuries she allegedly suffered because of a sexual relationship with her pastor.[34] A husband and wife who had been experiencing marital problems went to a Lutheran minister for counseling. They selected him because "he held himself out to the public . . . as a minister and counselor trained and able to provide counseling for marital difficulties." During the final three or four weeks of counseling, the minister allegedly engaged in consensual sexual relations with the wife. These relations, and the counseling, ended when the husband learned of the affair. The husband, who was later divorced from his wife, sued both the minister and his church. The suit against the minister alleged a breach of fiduciary duty, among other things. The state supreme court dismissed all of the husband's charges against the minister. The court began its decision by acknowledging that clergy are not immune from legal liability for their actions. It observed that "religious leaders have been held liable for obtaining gifts and donations of money by fraud; for undue influence in the transfer of property; for the kidnapping of a minor; for unlawful imprisonment; and for homosexual assault." The first amendment guaranty of religious freedom did not prevent liability in these cases, and did not protect the minister in the present case, since "we find it difficult to conceive of pastoral fornication with a parishioner or communicant as a legitimate religious belief or practice in any faith."

The court next addressed the question of "whether a member of the clergy, who holds himself out as being trained and capable of conducting marital counseling, is immune from any liability for harm caused by his counseling by virtue of the first amendment" guaranty of religious freedom. Both the priest and the diocese argued that the first amendment required the dismissal of the lawsuit since "the performance of pastoral duties by a Catholic priest, including sacramental counseling of parishioners, is a matter of ecclesiastical cognizance and policy with which a civil court cannot interfere." The court acknowledged that "marital counseling by a cleric presents difficult questions" and "may implicate first amendment rights." However, it concluded that the priest could not argue that his conduct was protected by the constitutional guaranty of religious freedom since "when the alleged wrongdoing of a cleric clearly falls outside the beliefs and doctrine of his religion, he cannot avail himself of the protections afforded by the first amendment." In particular, the court noted that "sexual activity by a priest is fundamentally antithetical to Catholic doctrine," and "by definition is not an expression of a sincerely held religious belief."

---

[33] State v. Dutton, 450 N.W.2d 189 (Minn. App. 1990).
[34] Stock v. Pressnell, 527 N.E.2d 1235 (Ohio 1988).

Insurance

Clergy who are sued as a result of sexual misconduct often assume that the church's insurance policy will provide a legal defense and pay for any judgment or settlement up to the insurance limits. Such an assumption may be incorrect, since most insurance policies exclude coverage for any "intentional" or criminal acts, and some exclude coverage for sexual misconduct. As a result, a number of clergy have had to retain and pay for their own attorney, and pay any judgment or settlement attributable to their misconduct.

> **Key point.** *Ministers who engage in sexual misconduct may be guilty of a number of "intentional wrongs" including battery, breach of a fiduciary duty, and intentional infliction of emotional distress. Generally, intentional wrongs are not covered under a church's liability insurance policy, and so ministers who commit such acts may find that they must pay for their own attorney and any portion of a judgment or settlement attributable to their conduct.*

> **Example.** *A Colorado court ruled that a church insurance policy could not be tapped to pay a judgment rendered against a minister in a sexual misconduct case. A woman sued her former minister and her church on the basis of injuries she suffered as a result of the minister's sexual misconduct. A jury ruled that the minister was liable for the woman's injuries and awarded a monetary judgment in her favor. The minister insisted that the judgment against him was covered under a church insurance policy. A state appeals court disagreed. The court noted that "if the meaning of the insurance policy is expressed in plain, certain, and readily understandable language, it must be enforced as written." The church's insurance policy provided, "The company will pay on behalf of the insured all sums which the insured shall become legally obligated to pay as damages because of injury to any person arising out of sexual misconduct or sexual molestation which occurs during the policy period." Exclusions to the policy, however, specifically provided that the insurance did not apply "[t]o any person who personally participated in any act of sexual misconduct or sexual molestation." The minister claimed that by denying coverage to the perpetrator of the sexual misconduct, the exclusion rendered any coverage under the policy for sexual misconduct "illusory." The court disagreed, noting that coverage existed under the policy for the church. The court also rejected the minister's claim that the insurance company had "waived" its right to deny coverage by providing a defense to the minister under a "reservation of rights."[35]*

> **Example.** *A Minnesota appeals court ruled that a church insurance policy did not require the insurance company to defend a pastor who was sued by a woman he had seduced. The court also ruled that the insurance company would not have to pay any portion of a jury verdict against the pastor. The pastor turned the lawsuit over to the church's insurance company, assuming that the insurer would defend him and pay any verdict against him up to the policy limits. The insurer rejected the pastor's request, and informed him that it would neither defend him against the claims of the lawsuit nor pay any portion of a verdict attributable to his misconduct. The pastor sued the insurance company in an attempt to force it to defend him. A state appeals court noted that the church's insurance policy specified that the insurer was liable for any personal injury "caused by an occurrence to which this insurance applies." The policy defined*

---

[35] Church Mutual Insurance Company v. Klein, 940 P.2d 1001 (Colo. App. 1996).

the term "occurrence" as an act that "results in bodily injury . . . neither expected nor intended." The court concluded that the pastor's repeated sexual exploitation of the victim resulted in personal injuries that were both "expected and intended," and accordingly they did not constitute an "occurrence" for which insurance coverage was available. The court observed, "We conclude [that the victim's] allegations that [the pastor] used his authority as a pastor and counselor to facilitate his sexual abuse of a psychologically vulnerable person creates an inference of an intent to injure and relieves [the insurance company] of its duty to defend." [36]

Elimination of "loss of consortium" and "alienation of affection" claims

A number of courts have concluded that a husband whose wife is seduced by a pastor cannot sue the pastor since any basis for liability was effectively abolished when "alienation of affections" was eliminated as a basis for liability by the state legislature. [37]

> *Example. A Louisiana appeals court ruled that a husband whose wife had allegedly been seduced by his pastor could not sue the pastor or his church. The court noted that the state of Louisiana abolished the tort of "alienation of a wife's affections" in 1927, and that this prevented the husband from suing his priest for clergy malpractice. However, the court stressed that it was not addressing the issue of whether or not a wife who is seduced by a priest can maintain a lawsuit for clergy malpractice. Second, the court rejected the husband's claim that the priest was guilty of intentional infliction of emotional distress, since such a claim may only be brought by the intended victim (in this case, the wife). The court also concluded that the four minor children could not sue the priest for alienation of their mother's affections. [38]*

> *Example. The Nebraska Supreme Court ruled that a husband could not sue a priest for "loss of consortium" as a result of the priest's sexual relationship with the man's wife. The husband claimed that as a result of the priest's actions he had lost the care and comfort of his wife and had been deprived of her comfort and companionship and incurred pain, suffering, and mental anguish. The court rejected this theory of liability, noting that it was essentially a claim for "alienation of affection" and that such claims are specifically prohibited by a Nebraska statute. [39]*

> *Example. The Oklahoma Supreme Court ruled that a pastor was not liable on the basis of "seduction" for sexual contacts he had with a woman during counseling. In rejecting this basis of liability, the court noted that the state legislature had abolished any liability for seduction. A state statute provides that the "seduction of any person of sound mind and legal age is hereby abolished as a civil cause of action in this state." It concluded that "[w]e are not at liberty to recognize a cause of action by the wife against her minister for engaging in a consensual sexual affair." [40]*

---

[36] Houg v. State Farm Fire and Casualty Company, 481 N.W.2d 393 (Minn. App. 1992).

[37] *See, e.g.,* Cherepski v. Walters, 913 S.W.2d 761 (Ark. 1996); R.E.R. v. J.G., 552 N.W.2d 27 (Minn. App. 1996).

[38] Greene v. Roy, 604 So.2d 1359 (La. App. 3 Cir. 1992).

[39] Nebraska Supreme Court issues an important ruling; Schieffer v. Catholic Archdiocese, 508 N.W.2d 907 (Neb. 1993).

[40] Bladen v. First Presbyterian Church, 857 P.2d 789 (Okla. 1993).

24.3 Church Liability

This chapter addresses the liability of pastors who engage in sexual misconduct. Churches also may be liable for a pastor's acts of sexual misconduct, this basis of liability is addressed in another chapter.

24.4 Establish Boundaries for Ministers and Other Staff Members

Because of the unique temptations that counseling can present, and the possibility of false accusations, "defensive measures" should be taken by pastors and others who engage in counseling. While no congregation can *eliminate* the risk of sexual misconduct, the good news is you can *reduce* it. When you make a commitment to do so, you are helping your staff members and your church. Sexual misconduct creates tremendous pain and trauma for everyone involved. Below are suggestions that can help your church reduce the risk of sexual misconduct.

Provide guidance and engage in dialogue

First, recognize that sexual misconduct is a congregational problem, not simply the moral failing of an individual. Often, when a church learns that a leader has engaged in sexual misconduct, the blame is placed totally upon the individual. In many cases, the misconduct could have been prevented if the church would have become more involved in establishing boundaries for its leaders. Ministers, like all professionals, need guidance and accountability in establishing and maintaining boundaries in their service to the congregation. Church leaders should work cooperatively with their staff members in establishing boundaries for ministry. Use the following suggestions to create dialogue and as a point of departure in establishing your own boundary conditions.

Establish restrictions on the time and location of counseling services

The focus is to maintain *accountability* and to lower *isolation*. Some churches require individual counseling activities to occur during regular office hours, or at times when other staff members are present within the building. Counseling may be prohibited, for example, in isolated locations, such as a home, when only two adults are present. Boundaries should be established that clarify both when and where counseling should occur. Similar consideration should be given to visitation or any other ministry activity that creates isolated interaction and personal involvement. The goal is not to thwart ministry, but to create conditions that maintain accountability.

Establish limits on the length and number of counseling sessions

Some ministers and churches limit counseling sessions to 50 minutes with no more than 6-8 sessions. After that, if more counseling is required, a referral is made. While some churches have professional counselors on their staff, most do not. The time and expertise required to engage in long-term counseling often cannot be provided by the typical minister or staff member.

Place restrictions on the frequency of counseling sessions

One meeting per week is fairly standard.

Create guidelines for telephone counseling

Telephone counseling should have similar boundaries as if it were occurring in person. Boundary conditions should be established for time, length and frequency of calls.

Have guidelines on the purpose of counseling and the people who are involved

Many church leaders assume that all pastors are trained as counselors. That is not true. While some pastors have extensive training as counselors, others have very little. The counseling services provided should reflect the expertise and training of your church staff. Consider a "third person" rule. Some churches prohibit any male minister or counselor on staff from counseling privately with an unaccompanied female (i.e., opposite sex counseling) unless a third person is present. The third person may be the minister's or counselor's spouse, another minister on staff, or a mature and trusted church staff member (preferably female). Since the vast majority of cases of inappropriate sexual behavior involve male counselors and female counselees, churches can significantly reduce their risk by using women to counsel women. The key concern is to maintain accountability in situations that pose a higher risk, including the risk of false allegations.

Establish guidelines on appropriate and inappropriate touching

For example, your church may encouraging hugging before and after church services. However, is hugging appropriate in a counseling or visitation setting when only two adults are present? What about holding hands and praying? Church leaders should openly discuss appropriate and inappropriate touching. Also, have guidelines on age-related touching involving children. Touching should always respond to the need of the child and not to the need of the adult.

Have polices in place for making referrals

Church leaders should help staff members discover referral resources and to know when to use them. A limit in the number of sessions, or the need of the counselee may trigger an automatic referral.

Create accountability through proper supervision

Ministers and church staff members should be accountable to other church leaders for their counseling and visitation activities. While confidentiality between a minister and a parishioner is vital, supervision is also needed. Staff members can provide regular reports on their ministry activities to other designated leaders. If boundaries are being violated, these leaders can examine the basis for such violations and work with the church staff to maintain the best interests of the church's ministry.

Establish policies concerning socializing and accepting gifts from counselees

For example, is it okay for a minister to have a private lunch or dinner with a counselee? What about accepting a gift, or giving a gift? What role does socializing have in the ministry of visitation or counseling and what boundaries should govern it? These are important issues that church leaders should discuss.

Maintain visibility

Windows, open doors, and the use of video cameras, under the proper conditions, can lower the risk of sexual misconduct. Not all counseling sessions require strict privacy. The following options can be helpful under such circumstances. Consider the use of windows to make sessions clearly visible to office staff. Some counselors conduct counseling sessions in a room with an open door, so that office staff can clearly see the counselor or counselee. Of course, such precautions are effective only if other staff are present and visible throughout the counseling session. This means that the church should implement a policy limiting counseling sessions to office hours when other staff are present and visible.

Some churches have installed video cameras in offices and church nurseries, largely to reduce the risk of false allegations. If sessions are recorded, tapes should be retained indefinitely, or until they are reviewed by two designated church members who prepare a written summary stating whether or not they observed any inappropriate acts. This review can be performed in "fast forward" mode, and should not take long.

Obtain sample policies from other organizations

Discuss boundaries concerns with other professional organizations that provide counseling services. Invite a doctor, psychologist, or social worker to discuss this issue with your staff.

Screen workers that serve as counselors or who have unsupervised access to children

This includes checking references and conducting a criminal background check. An employment verification service can assist you in doing this. Screening should be done prior to hiring such workers.

Have more than one adult present in high risk settings

As noted above, some counseling sessions may require that three people be present. Also, some visitation activities might be done in pairs that are regularly rotated. Having multiple adults present to supervise children is always a good idea.

Train workers to understand and follow policies

Once your church establishes policies, provide training for all of your staff members. Periodically review each policy and solicit feedback on how well they are working. Make changes when necessary. Also, always respond to inappropriate conduct.

24.5 Watch For Red Flags

Sexual misconduct generally does not occur quickly. Often, warning signs exist that indicate something is wrong. When you spot a red flag, respond to it. Keep your eyes open for the following:

A pattern of boundary violations

For example, 50 minute sessions continue to be extended to 90 minutes. Rather than meeting once a week, sessions now occur more frequently, or the location changes so it is more isolated. Address each boundary violation. Recognize that multiple and frequent violations indicate a red flag.

Depression

Church staff members who are depressed may be more vulnerable to sexual misconduct. While this is not true for everyone, it is for some. If a staff member appears depressed or manifests symptoms of high stress, take action to provide support.

Family problems

Ministers and staff members have family problems like everyone else. Often, they feel pressure to keep every problem hidden. Let your staff members know in advance that if they or any member of their family have problems, the church wants to help. Make counseling services available for them with individuals they can trust.

Financial concerns

Finances impact all families and can play a role in sexual misconduct. A staff member who feels underpaid and taken-for -granted can become demoralized. Payment can be sought in other ways, including emotionally and sexually. Churches should care about the financial well-being of their staff members, and provide not only adequate financial support, but emotional support as well.

Transference and Infatuation

Sometimes a staff member openly expresses feelings of love or infatuation. For example, the staff member may say, "I feel like I'm falling in love with someone I'm counseling (or someone they may be working with)." Such comments provide an opportunity for appropriate intervention and a rechecking of boundaries.

Another problem is the inability to recognize transference. Many courts have recognized the psychological principle of "transference." To illustrate, one court defined transference as "a phenomenon that occurs that is similar to a state of dependency in which the client begins to project the roles and relationships and the images and experiences that they have had with other people previously in their life, especially other significant people such as mother, father, brothers, sisters, early teachers and adult models, upon the therapist."[41] Another court defined transference as "a process whereby a patient undergoing psychotherapy for a mental or emotional disturbance (particularly a female patient being treated by a male psychotherapist) develops such overwhelming feelings of warmth, trust, and dependency towards the therapist that she is deprived of the will to resist any sexual overtures he might make."[42] Similarly, another court observed, "Transference is the term used by psychiatrists and psychologists to denote a

---

[41] Doe v. Samaritan Counseling Center, 791 P.2d 344 (Alaska 1990).
[42] Alpharetta First United Methodist Church v. Stewart, 473 S.E.2d 532 (Ga. App. 1996).

patient's emotional reaction to a therapist and is generally applied to the projection of feelings, thoughts and wishes onto the analyst, who has come to represent some person from the patient's past . . . . Transference is crucial to the therapeutic process because the patient unconsciously attributes to the psychiatrist or analyst those feelings which he may have repressed towards his own parents.... [I]t is through the creation, experiencing and resolution of these feelings that [the patient] becomes well. . . . Understanding of transference forms a basic part of the psychoanalytic technique."[43]

Pastoral and lay counselors often are tempted to engage in inappropriate sexual contact with a counselee because of unfamiliarity with this phenomenon. They misinterpret transference as affection, and fail to engage in anti-transference precautions that reduce the risk of inappropriate physical or emotional bonding.

Poor judgment or rationalization

A staff member may seek approval or support for actions that are inappropriate, but which have been rationalized as serving a valid purpose. For example, the staff member may say, "This person really needs more support and since she works all day, the only time I can see her is at night. I don't see any problem meeting her at her apartment. She's invited me over for dinner. I believe I can really help her and a little more relaxed setting would help her to share. My wife doesn't get home from her job until almost midnight, so I'm generally free in the evenings anyway."

Previous misconduct

Church leaders may learn that a staff member has engaged in previous sexual misconduct. Once such information is obtained, church leaders must evaluate to what degree the prior misconduct places the church at risk, and determine a reasonable course of action based upon the facts as well as advice and input from professionals. This is not an easy task, but church leaders should be aware that once such knowledge is obtained, if the misconduct is repeated, the church may face a charge of negligent retention if it did nothing to prevent further misconduct. Once church leaders learn about previous misconduct, they should seek the advice of a competent attorney. The church's insurance carrier can help the church locate such an individual. Also, the church should seek the input of denominational leaders (if the church is part of a denomination). All information should be handled with the strictest confidence. If the misconduct involved child sexual molestation or if more than one incident of sexual misconduct occurred, retention places the church at high risk. Increasingly, such violations mean a permanent removal from ministry. Some other forms of sexual misconduct pose a lower risk, but such evaluations require outside professional input. A church should always seek outside assistance from denominational leaders, their insurance carrier, professional counselors, and a knowledgeable attorney in evaluating the implications of prior sexual misconduct.

Summary

Several lawsuits have been brought by women who were seduced or sexually assaulted by male clergy and mental health professionals. Often the misconduct

---

[43] Bladen v. First Presbyterian Church, 857 P.2d 789 (Okla. 1993).

occurred in the course of a counseling relationship. As much as we would like to deny it, private counseling sessions involving dependent or emotionally vulnerable persons can present unique and sometimes formidable temptations. If inappropriate sexual contacts are initiated, there can be substantial damage to the victim and the victim's family. But this is not all. Such behavior often devastates the counselor as well, leading to criminal charges, loss of professional credentials, future unemployability, and unavailability of any insurance coverage for either a legal defense or payment of damages. Clearly, steps must be taken to reduce or eliminate this risk.

But there is another risk associated with counseling—the risk of false accusations of inappropriate behavior. Unfortunately, in some cases false accusations are brought against counselors by persons seeking a legal settlement or pursuing some other ulterior motive. It is imperative for counselors to recognize that a false accusation can be as devastating as a true one.

Ministers who engage in counseling should seriously consider the risk management strategies addressed in this chapter. These strategies can reduce the risks of both sexually inappropriate behavior, and false accusations. The next chapter examines the issue of clergy malpractice.

CHAPTER 25. REDUCING THE RISK OF CLERGY MALPRACTICE

Malpractice generally is defined as a failure to exercise an accepted degree of skill in the performance of professional duties that results in injury to another. In the past, malpractice suits were restricted almost exclusively to doctors and lawyers— a doctor prescribed the wrong medication or made a faulty diagnosis; a lawyer missed a pleading deadline or made an error in a title search. But in recent years a small number of malpractice suits have been brought against ministers. Most of these cases have involved sexual misconduct, but a small number have involved other forms of misconduct.

25.1 The Majority View — Clergy cannot be Liable for Malpractice

Most courts have concluded that ministers cannot be liable on the basis of malpractice for either the content of their preaching or counseling, or acts of sexual misconduct. In the most significant ruling addressing "clergy malpractice," the California Supreme Court ruled that a church and certain of its ministers were not legally responsible for the death of a suicide victim who had been a member of the church and who had counseled with the ministers.[1] The court based its rejection of clergy malpractice on two grounds. First, by exempting clergy from the licensing requirements that apply to other counselors, the state legislature recognized that "the secular state is not equipped to ascertain the competence of [pastoral] counseling." Second, "it would certainly be impractical, and quite possibly unconstitutional, to impose a duty of care on pastoral counselors" since such a duty "would necessarily be intertwined with the religious philosophy of the particular denomination or ecclesiastical teachings of the religious entity."

A number of other courts, in rejecting clergy malpractice as a basis for legal liability, have relied on either or both of these grounds.

> *Example.* A Colorado court, in concluding that a pastor and his employing church were not responsible for the pastor's sexual misconduct with a counselee on the basis of clergy malpractice, observed: "[The courts of this state have] joined substantially all of the other courts that have passed upon the issue in rejecting the notion that a claim will lie against a pastoral counselor or the pastor's church based upon the pastor's failure to observe any particular standard of care in providing the counseling; no claim for "clergy malpractice" can be asserted. The judicial rejection of such a claim has been based, in large part, upon the effect that recognition of such a claim would have upon the right of religious expression guaranteed by the first amendment. In order to adjudicate a claim based upon the "malpractice" of a religious counselor, courts would first have to establish the degree of skill and learning normally exercised by members of the clergy in similar circumstances and, then, to determine whether such standard had been violated. . . . To attempt to require members of the clergy to comply with such a standard, however, could very well restrict their right freely to exercise and practice their religion."[2]

---

[1] Nally v. Grace Community Church, 253 Cal. Rptr. 97 (1988).

[2] DeBose v. Bear Valley Church of Christ, 890 P.2d 214 (Colo. App. 1994). *See also* Schieffer v. Catholic Archdiocese, 508 N.W.2d 907 (Neb. 1993) ("[s]o far as we have been able to determine, no jurisdiction to date has recognized a claim for clergy malpractice"); Bladen v. First Presbyterian

Example. The Colorado Supreme Court refused to recognize the theory of "clergy malpractice" in a case involving the seduction of a female church member by a Catholic priest.[3] The woman had claimed that the priest "negligently performed his duty as a marital counselor." The court viewed this theory as a claim of malpractice, which it defined as "any professional misconduct, unreasonable lack of skill or fidelity in professional or fiduciary duties, evil practice, or illegal or immoral conduct." Since a priest was involved, the court characterized the malpractice claim as a claim of "clergy malpractice." However, the court ruled that the lower courts had properly dismissed this claim since "to date no court has acknowledged the existence of such a tort" and it raises "serious first amendment issues." The court acknowledged that psychologists and psychiatrists may be sued for malpractice if they engage in sexual relations with counselees. However, a Colorado statute specifically excluded clergy from the list of counselors who can be sued for malpractice on the basis of such conduct, and accordingly the court ruled that the priest could not be sued for malpractice.

Example. An Illinois court ruled that a husband whose wife was seduced by her pastor could not sue the pastor, or denominational agencies, for malpractice. The former husband asserted that (1) the pastor had approximately 11 years experience in preaching and counseling; (2) his professional counseling experience included marriage counseling, faith counseling, and general family counseling; (3) he "held himself out as a skilled professional in matters of counseling"; (4) the pastor and denominational agencies "encouraged congregants to seek counseling from the church and its clergy before seeking secular professionals in order to promote unity, closeness and interdependence within members of the congregation in accordance with stated church doctrine"; and (5) the pastor "was acting within the scope and parameters of his employment duties on behalf of the church defendants and in furtherance of stated church doctrine when he counseled" the husband and wife. A state appeals court rejected the former husband's claim that the pastor and bishop were guilty of clergy malpractice: "Our courts have refused to entertain [clergy malpractice] claims because the first amendment's free exercise clause prohibits courts from considering claims requiring the interpretation of religious doctrine. To permit claims for clergy malpractice would require courts to establish a standard of reasonable care for religious practitioners practicing their respective faiths, which necessarily involves the interpretation of doctrine." The former husband insisted that if the pastor could not be sued for malpractice, he could be sued for "psychotherapy malpractice." The court disagreed, at least to the extent that this claim was in reality alleging malpractice by the pastor in his role as a member of the clergy. If, on the other hand, the former husband was addressing conduct outside of the performance of ministerial duties, then his claims could be redressed by a civil court. The court observed: "In essence, the plaintiff's complaint alleges that [the pastor], while counseling him in accordance with duties established by church doctrine, breached his duty as a professional marriage counselor. We believe there is an inherent contradiction in this core allegation which exposes the problem with claims of malpractice against members of the clergy, even when couched in terms of professional or psychotherapy malpractice." [4]

Church, 857 P.2d 789 (Okla. 1993) ("[c]laims for clergy malpractice for improper sexual conduct have so far been rejected by the courts").

[3] Destefano v. Grabian, 763 P.2d 275 (Colo. 1988).

[4] Amato v. Greenquist, 679 N.E.2d 446 (Ill. App. 1997).

Example. *A federal court in New York refused to find a pastor guilty of malpractice on the basis of his alleged sexual seduction of a church member he had counseled for several years. A woman (the "victim") began a counseling relationship with a pastor when she was a child of 12. The relationship continued for nearly 30 years. The victim alleged that the pastor engaged in repeated sexual contact with her over the years, and that she terminated the relationship with him only after seeing a psychotherapist who convinced her that the pastor's behavior had been wrong. The victim later sued the pastor, claiming that his acts amounted to clergy malpractice. The court dismissed this claim, along with all of the victim's other claims of liability against the pastor and her former church. In addressing the claim of malpractice, the court observed: "It would be impossible for a court or jury to adjudicate a typical case of clergy malpractice, without first ascertaining whether the cleric, in this case a Presbyterian pastor, performed within the level of expertise expected of a similar professional (the hypothetical "reasonably prudent Presbyterian pastor"), following his calling, or practicing his profession within the community. . . . Any effort by this court to instruct the trial jury as to the duty of care which a clergyman should exercise, would of necessity require the court or jury to define and express the standard of care to be followed by other reasonable Presbyterian clergy of the community. This in turn would require the court and the jury to consider the fundamental perspective and approach to counseling inherent in the beliefs and practices of that denomination. This is as unconstitutional as it is impossible. It fosters excessive entanglement with religion."*[5]

Example. *A New York court ruled that a church and diocese could not be sued on the basis of malpractice for the alleged sexual misconduct of a priest. The priest allegedly molested a minor pupil at a church-operated secondary school. A state appellate court rejected the malpractice claim, noting that malpractice is based on negligent rather than intentional behavior, and that the sexual assault alleged in this case was an intentional act. The court also pointed out that "we are unaware of any authority supporting the proposition that sexual abuse by a member of the clergy is cognizable as clergy malpractice." The court referred to the Nally case.*[6]

Example. *The Ohio Supreme Court refused to recognize the alleged tort of "clergy malpractice" in a case involving the sexual seduction of a wife during marital counseling. A husband and wife who had been experiencing marital problems went to a minister for counseling. They selected him because "he held himself out to the public . . . as a minister and counselor trained and able to provide counseling for marital difficulties." During the final three or four weeks of counseling, the minister allegedly engaged in consensual sexual relations with the wife. These relations, and the counseling, ended when the husband learned of the affair. The husband, who was later divorced from his wife, sued both the minister and his church. The suit against the minister alleged "clergy malpractice" among other theories of liability. The Ohio Supreme Court dismissed all of the husband's claims. It concluded that the minister could not be guilty of clergy malpractice since malpractice implies negligent conduct, and the minister's actions were intentional in nature. The court observed: "The reluctance of courts to embrace the tort of clergy malpractice may be attributed to the*

---

[5] Schmidt v. Bishop, 779 F. Supp. 321 (S.D.N.Y. 1991). *See also* Jones by Jones v. Trane, 591 N.Y.S.2d 927 (Sup. 1992) ("It is when what is sought is an evaluation of a member of the clergy while acting as a spiritual counselor that courts have refrained from undertaking to define a standard of care.").

[6] Joshua S. v. Casey, 615 N.Y.S.2d 200 (A.D. 1994).

many, and often complex, questions that arise under it. For example, what exactly are the "professional services" rendered by a cleric? And does the standard of the professional vary with the ecclesiastical office? In other words, is a rabbi, priest, pastor, or lay elder held to the same standard of care regardless of training or wide variances in the authority and obligation of religious offices? Also, where a "professional service," such as the marriage counseling involved in this case, is not unique to the cleric, should the cleric be held to the same duty of care as secular counselors? Finally if a legal duty is imposed on clergy to perform or not to perform in a particular way, will this clash with the religious beliefs of some faiths and thus violate the free exercise clause of the first amendment to the United States Constitution?[7]

Example. *The Oklahoma Supreme Court rejected clergy malpractice as a basis for liability in a case brought by a husband for "bad advice" he had received from a minister. The court concluded: "Once a court enters the realm of trying to define the nature of advice a minister should give a parishioner serious first amendment issues are implicated. We decline to determine the nature of the advice a minister must give during counseling sessions with a parishioner, and we decline to recognize a claim for bad advice from a minister under the facts before us."*[8]

Example. *A Texas court, in refusing to recognize "clergy malpractice" as a basis for liability, made the following observation: "Because the [civil courts] must abstain from ecclesiastical disputes involving questions of doctrine or practice, state courts have rejected uniformly claims for clergy malpractice. This is because such a claim requires definition of the relevant standard of care. Defining that standard could embroil courts in establishing the training, skill, and standards applicable for members of the clergy in a diversity of religions with widely varying beliefs. Furthermore, defining such a standard would require courts to identify the beliefs and practices of the relevant religion and then to determine whether the clergyman had acted in accordance with them. Thus, as these courts have correctly concluded, to recognize a claim for clergy malpractice would require courts to identify and apply the teachings of a particular faith, thereby making the judiciary responsible for determining what conduct and beliefs are part of a particular religion."*[9]

25.2 The Minority View — Clergy can be Liable for Malpractice

A few courts have recognized malpractice claims against clergy in either or both of the following two situations:

(1) sexual misconduct with an adult or minor

(2) "non-religious" counseling

Example. *A federal appeals court concluded that two female church employees could sue the minister who had seduced them since he had "held himself out" as a qualified marital counselor. The minister's duties did not include counseling, and he knew that he was not responsible for providing spiritual counseling to church members. He also knew that the church had a written policy of referring church members in need of*

---

[7] Stock v. Pressnell, 527 N.E.2d 1235 (Ohio 1988).

[8] Bladen v. First Presbyterian Church, 857 P.2d 789 (Okla. 1993).

[9] Sanders v. Casa View Baptist Church, 134 F.3d 331 (5th Cir. 1998).

non-pastoral counseling to a licensed professional counselor. Nevertheless, the minister began counseling with two women after assuring them that he was qualified by both education and experience to provide marital counseling. The women assumed that he was authorized by the church to provide counseling. The minister entered into a sexual relationship with both women, and hired both of them as church employees. When the women learned that they both were having affairs with the same minister, they informed a church deacon. The minister resigned, and the two women were dismissed. The women later sued the minister for malpractice. The court refused to recognize a claim for clergy malpractice, but it did conclude that the women could sue the minister for malpractice as a "marriage counselor." The former minister insisted that he could not be guilty of malpractice as a marriage counselor unless his counseling was purely secular in nature. And, since he occasionally discussed scripture in his counseling sessions with the two women, his counseling was not purely secular. The court disagreed, noting that the minister's marriage counseling was "essentially secular" in nature and that this was enough for him to be guilty of malpractice as a marriage counselor. The court concluded that the first amendment did not prevent the former minister from being sued for malpractice as a marriage counselor or for breach of fiduciary duties "not derived from religious doctrine." It explained its reasoning as follows: "[B]ecause the jury found that [the former minister] held himself out as possessing the education and experience of a professional marriage counselor, his counseling activities with the [two women] were judged, not by a standard of care defined by religious teachings, but by a professional standard of care developed through expert testimony describing what a reasonably prudent counselor would have done under the same or similar circumstances."[10]

Example. A federal appeals court ruled that a church and denominational agency were not legally responsible for a pastoral counselor's sexual contacts with a female counselee. However, it concluded that the pastor could be sued for professional negligence with regard to purely secular counseling, and could be liable with respect to such counseling under a state law imposing liability on "psychotherapists" for engaging in sexual contact with counselees. A woman alleged that a pastor told her that she needed "secular psychological" and not religious counseling, and that he was qualified to provide it. The pastor allegedly assured the woman that such treatment was included in his job description at the church. The woman attended counseling sessions with the pastor at his office in the church for more than two years. Over time the pastor increased the frequency and length of the sessions. The woman claimed that he told her that "religion does not apply here. Your problems are so deep you need more psychological treatment from me." She stated that she became very involved in the therapy and attached to the pastor. He allegedly represented to her that he was a capable, trained professional on whom she could rely to assist her with her personal problems. However, the pastor eventually gave the woman an ultimatum: "I have been giving to you, and I need something back for my services. You must give back to me or I will not work with you anymore." From that date on the woman claimed that her therapy sessions began with sexual relations with the pastor. The woman later sued her pastor, church, and a denominational agency. She asserted that the pastor was responsible for her injuries on the basis of professional negligence, breach of fiduciary duty, negligent infliction of emotional distress, and violation of the Sexual Exploitation of Psychotherapy Act. A federal appeals court ruled that the woman

---

[10] Sanders v. Casa View Baptist Church, 134 F.3d 331 (5th Cir. 1998).

could sue the pastor for professional negligence. It acknowledged that no court has permitted clergy to be sued for malpractice, but it limited such cases to the context of religious counseling. The court observed: "Therefore, if a complaint alleges that the psychological services that were provided were "secular" in nature, or that the provider held himself out to be providing the services of a psychological counselor, the negligence claim cannot be characterized as one for clergy malpractice. Tort claims for behavior by a cleric that does not require the examination of religious doctrine are cognizable. Under these circumstances, the claim is for professional malpractice by a psychological counselor, not clergy malpractice."[11]

Example. An Arizona court ruled that a pastor and his church could be sued on the basis of "therapist" malpractice as a result of the pastor's disclosure of confidential information shared with him by a counselee during counseling. The counselee sought out the pastor to help her through emotional difficulties and depression "because of his 40 years counseling experience." The pastor relied on several cases rejecting clergy malpractice claims because of first amendment concerns about determining a standard of care for pastors. The court concluded that these cases were not relevant because the victim sued the pastor for therapist malpractice rather than clergy malpractice, and her claim was based on a psychological therapist's duty not to disclose confidential information revealed in counseling sessions. The court noted that "the inclusion of biblical passages on the chart [used by the pastor] did not convert the session into religious counseling, especially when the purpose of the meeting was not to provide her with religious or spiritual guidance, the church's precepts and practices were not part of the counseling, and [the victim] was not a church member when she sought help from [the pastor]." The court concluded, "[The pastor and church] offer no good reason for insulating a counselor from liability for betraying clients' confidences to their detriment merely because the counselor is a clergy member and unlicensed, and the counseling as well as wrongful disclosure takes place in a religious setting."[12]

Example. A Colorado court, in concluding that a pastor and his employing church were not responsible for the pastor's sexual misconduct with a counselee on the basis of clergy malpractice, observed: "[W]hile the services performed by a therapeutic counselor and those provided through pastoral counseling often overlap, so long as the cleric providing pastoral counseling is not held out as a therapeutic counselor, the standards of care applicable to therapeutic counseling cannot be applied to a pastoral counselor.[13]

Example. An Illinois court ruled that a husband whose wife was seduced by her pastor could not sue the pastor for malpractice. The court acknowledged that the pastor had 11 years experience in preaching and counseling; his professional counseling experience included marriage counseling and general family counseling; and he "held himself out as a skilled professional in matters of counseling." However, the court concluded that the wife had sought out the pastor in his role as a pastoral counselor rather than a secular counselor. The court conceded that if the former husband was addressing conduct outside of the performance of ministerial duties, then his claims could be redressed by a civil court. It concluded: "In essence, the plaintiff's

---

[11] Dausch v. Rykse, 52 F.3d 1425 (7th Cir. 1994).
[12] Barnes v. Outlaw, 937 P.2d 323 (Ariz. App. 1996).
[13] DeBose v. Bear Valley Church of Christ, 890 P.2d 214 (Colo. App. 1994).

complaint alleges that [the pastor], while counseling him in accordance with duties established by church doctrine, breached his duty as a professional marriage counselor. We believe there is an inherent contradiction in this core allegation which exposes the problem with claims of malpractice against members of the clergy, even when couched in terms of professional or psychotherapy malpractice."[14]

Example. A New Jersey court allowed a woman to sue her church for clergy malpractice as a result of a sexual relationship that was initiated by her pastor. The woman's lawsuit alleged that she had sought counseling from a pastor of her church, and that the pastor became aware of her emotional vulnerabilities and exploited them by inducing her to engage in sexual acts with him. The woman filed a complaint with a "standing committee on clergy ethics" of her denomination, and the committee later determined that the minister had "violated his pastoral relationship" with the victim by engaging in "inappropriate sexual behavior toward her." The committee "sanctioned" the minister. The woman then sued her church, claiming that the pastor's actions amounted to clergy malpractice. A state appeals court ruled that the woman could sue the church for clergy malpractice. The court acknowledged that a number of courts have rejected liability based on clergy malpractice, but it refused to reach the same conclusion. It observed that "malpractice" is nothing more than the negligent performance of a professional service and "a deviation from the standards of performance applicable to the professional service in question." The court expressed concern over potential first amendment violations when civil courts apply the concept of malpractice to members of the clergy. However, it was unwilling to conclude (as many other courts have done) that the first amendment bars recognition of civil liability for clergy malpractice in all cases. It concluded, "In the present case, it is unlikely that [the church] will assert that sex with a counselee by a pastoral counselor is sanctioned by or somehow involves tenets of the . . . church, or would otherwise create an entanglement with religious beliefs or rituals of first amendment concern."[15]

25.3 Risk Management Strategies

Many of the risk management strategies summarized in chapter 24 will be helpful in reducing the risk of clergy malpractice claims.

Summary

Ministers who engage in counseling as a part of their ministry should be aware of the following conclusions regarding "clergy malpractice":

(1) No court has found a minister liable on the basis of malpractice for the content of his or her counseling.

(2) Most courts have refused to find ministers liable on the basis of malpractice for sexual misconduct with counselees, on the basis of either or both of the following two grounds: First, by exempting clergy from the licensing requirements that apply to other counselors, the state legislature recognized that "the secular state is not equipped to ascertain the competence of [pastoral] counseling." Second, "it would certainly be

---

[14] Amato v. Greenquist, 679 N.E.2d 446 (Ill. App. 1997).
[15] F.G. v. MacDonell, 677 A.2d 258 (N.J. Super. 1996).

impractical, and quite possibly unconstitutional, to impose a duty of care on pastoral counselors" since such a duty "would necessarily be intertwined with the religious philosophy of the particular denomination or ecclesiastical teachings of the religious entity."

(3) A few courts have recognized malpractice claims against clergy in either or both of the following two situations—sexual misconduct with an adult or minor, or "non-religious" counseling.

(4) It is advisable for churches to obtain counseling liability or malpractice insurance. While the likelihood of a church being successfully sued for clergy malpractice is very remote, the likelihood of being sued for clergy malpractice is conceivable. With malpractice insurance, the insurer will be responsible to retain and pay for the church's legal defense.

In the next part of this handbook, we focus our attention on director and officer liability. The next chapter examines ten theories of liability with which directors and officers should be familiar.

CHAPTER 26. COMMON FORMS OF LIABILITY

In recent years a number of lawsuits have attempted to impose personal liability on directors of churches and other religious organizations. In some cases, directors are sued because of statutes that provide limited legal immunity to churches (discussed in chapter 27).

As a general rule, directors are not responsible for actions taken by the board prior to their election to the board (unless they vote to ratify a previous action). Similarly, directors ordinarily are not liable for actions taken by the board after their resignation. Again, they will continue to be liable for actions that they took prior to their resignation.

A number of state laws permit nonprofit corporations to amend their bylaws to indemnify directors for any costs incurred in connection with the defense of any lawsuit arising out of their status as directors.

Ten theories of personal liability are summarized below.

26.1 Theory 1 — Tort Liability

Perhaps the most common basis of legal liability relates to the commission of torts. A *tort* is an act that causes personal injury or property damage. Examples include negligence (e.g., careless operation of a church-owned vehicle), defamation, fraud, copyright infringement, and wrongful termination of employees.

Church board members are not automatically liable by virtue of their official position for the torts committed by the church or the church's agents and employees. Rather, they will be liable only for those torts that they commit, direct, or participate in, even though the corporation itself may also be liable.

To illustrate, directors may be personally liable if they:

- knowingly permit an unsafe condition to exist on church property that results in death or injury
- cause injury as a result of the negligent operation of a vehicle in the course of church business
- negligently fail to adequately supervise church activities resulting in death or injury
- terminate an employee for an impermissible reason
- utter a defamatory remark about another individual
- authorize an act that infringes upon the exclusive rights of a copyright owner
- engage in fraudulent acts
- knowingly draw checks against insufficient funds
- knowingly make false representations as to the financial condition of the church to third parties who, in reliance on such representations, extend credit to the church and suffer a loss

In all of these cases the director must personally commit, direct, or participate in the tort. A director ordinarily will not be liable for the torts committed by other board members without his or her knowledge or consent. Obviously, board members having any question regarding the propriety of a particular action being discussed at a board meeting should be sure to have their dissent to the proposed action registered in the minutes of the meeting.

26.2 Theory 2 — Contract Liability

Church board members may be personally liable on contracts that they sign in either of two ways. First, board members may be personally liable on a contract that they sign without authority. Second, board members may be personally liable on a contract that they are authorized to sign but which they sign in their own name without any reference to the church or to their representative capacity. To prevent this inadvertent assumption of liability, board members who are authorized to sign contracts (as well as any other legal document) should be careful to indicate the church's name on the document and clearly indicate their own representational capacity (agent, director, trustee, officer, authorized representative, etc.).

26.3 Theory 3 — Breach of the Fiduciary Duty of Care

The board members of business corporations are under a duty to perform their duties "in good faith, in a manner they reasonably believe to be in the best interests of the corporation, and with such care as an ordinarily prudent person in a like position would use under similar circumstances." This duty commonly is referred to as the "prudent person rule" or the "duty of due care." In recent years, some courts have extended this duty to the board members of nonprofit corporations. To illustrate, a federal district court ruled that the directors of a nonprofit corporation breached their fiduciary duty of care in managing the corporation's funds.[1] For nearly 20 years, management of the corporation had been dominated almost exclusively by two officers, whose decisions and recommendations were routinely adopted by the board. The corporation's finance committee had not convened in more than 11 years. Under these facts, the court concluded:

> Total abdication of [a director's] supervisory role, however, is improper . . . . A director who fails to acquire the information necessary to supervise . . . or consistently fails even to attend the meetings . . . has violated his fiduciary duty to the corporation . . . . A director whose failure to supervise permits negligent mismanagement by others to go unchecked has committed an independent wrong against the corporation.

A ruling of the bankruptcy court in the "PTL" ministry bankruptcy case addressed the liability of directors and officers.[2] The court agreed with the bankruptcy trustee that televangelist Jim Bakker (as both an officer and director) had breached his legal duty of care to PTL. It quoted a South Carolina statute (PTL was located in South Carolina) that specifies the duty of care that a director or officer owes to his or her corporation:

---

[1] Stern v. Lucy Webb Hayes National Training School for Deaconesses & Missionaries, 381 F. Supp. 1003 (D.D.C. 1974).
[2] Heritage Village Church and Missionary Fellowship, Inc., 92 B.R. 1000 (D.S.C. 1988).

A director or officer shall perform his duties as a director or officer, including his duties as a member of any committee of the board of directors upon which he may serve, in good faith, in the manner he reasonably believes to be in the best interest of the corporation and of its shareholders, and with such care as an ordinary prudent person in a like position would use under similar circumstances.[3]

The court, in commenting upon this provision, observed:

> Good faith requires the undivided loyalty of a corporate director or officer to the corporation and such a duty of loyalty prohibits the director or an officer, as a fiduciary, from using this position of trust for his own personal gain to the detriment of the corporation. In this instance, there are no shareholders of the corporation; however, even though there are no shareholders, the officers and directors still hold a fiduciary obligation to manage the corporation in its best interest and not to the detriment of the corporation itself.

The court concluded that "the duty of care and loyalty required by [Bakker] was breached inasmuch as he (1) failed to inform the members of the board of the true financial position of the corporation and to act accordingly; (2) failed to supervise other officers and directors; (3) failed to prevent the depletion of corporate assets; and (4) violated the prohibition against self-dealing."

With respect to Bakker's defense that his actions had been "approved" by the board, the court observed that Bakker "exercised a great deal of control over his board" and that "a director who exercises a controlling influence over co-directors cannot defend acts committed by him on the grounds that his actions were approved by the board." The court acknowledged that officers and directors cannot be "held accountable for mere mistakes in judgment." However, it found that "the acts of [Bakker] did not constitute mere mistakes in judgment, but constituted gross mismanagement and a neglect of the affairs of the corporation. Clearly the salaries, the awards of bonuses and the carte blanche exercised over PTL checking accounts and credit cards were excessive and without justification and there was lack of proper care, attention and circumspection to the affairs of the corporation. [Bakker] breached [his] duty to manage and supervise . . . ."

In support of its conclusions, the court cited numerous findings, including the following:

- Bakker failed to require firm bids on construction projects though this caused PTL substantial losses
- capital expenditures often greatly exceeded estimates, though Bakker was warned of the problem
- Bakker rejected warnings from financial officers about the dangers of debt financing
- many of the bonuses granted to Bakker were granted "during periods of extreme financial hardship for PTL"
- Bakker "let it be known that he did not want to hear any bad news, so people were reluctant to give him bad financial information"

---

[3] *Id.* at 1014-1015, quoting S.C. STAT. ANN. § 33-13-150(a).

- "it was a common practice for PTL to write checks for more money than it showed in its checkbook; the books would often show a negative balance, but the money would eventually be transferred or raised to cover the checks written—this 'float' often would be three to four million dollars"

- most of the events and programs at PTL that were made available to the public were operated at a loss; since 1984, "energy was placed into raising lifetime partner funds rather than raising general contributions"

- Bakker "during the entire period in question, failed to give attention to financial matters and the problems of raising money and cutting expense."

Though at the time of Bakker's resignation in 1987 PTL had outstanding liens of $35 million, and general contributions were in a state of decline, "millions of dollars were being siphoned off by excessive spending." Such spending, noted the court, "is shocking to the conscience to the extent that it is unbelievable that a religious ministry would be operated in such a manner."

The court concluded that "Mr. Bakker, as an officer and director of PTL . . . approached the management of the corporation with reckless indifference to the financial consequences of [his] acts. While on the one hand [he was] experiencing inordinate personal gain from the revenues of PTL, on the other hand [he was] intentionally ignoring the extreme financial difficulties of PTL and, ironically, [was], in fact, adding to them." To illustrate, Bakker accepted huge bonuses at times of serious financial crisis at PTL. "Such conduct," noted the court, "demonstrates a total lack of fiduciary responsibility to PTL." The court emphasized that *"trustees and corporate directors for not-for-profit organizations are liable for losses occasioned by their negligent mismanagement."*

Discharging the fiduciary duty of due care

There are a number of ways that church board members can reduce the risk of liability for breaching the fiduciary duty of due care, including the following:

- attending all of the meetings of the board and of any committees on which they serve

- thoroughly reviewing all interim and annual financial statements and reports, and seeking clarification of any irregularities or inconsistencies

- affirmatively investigating and rectifying any other problems or improprieties

- thoroughly reviewing the corporate charter, constitution, and bylaws

- dissenting from any board action with which they have any misgivings, and insisting that their objection be recorded in the minutes of the meeting

- resigning from the board if and when they are unable to fulfill these duties.

As one court has observed, "the law has no place for dummy directors."

Example. A Minnesota court dismissed a lawsuit brought by Lutheran pastors against a denominational pension board for allegedly breaching their fiduciary duty to participants by not investing in companies that did business in South Africa. The Evangelical Lutheran Church in America (ELCA) established a board of pensions in

1988 to manage and operate a pension fund for Lutheran pastors and lay employees "exclusively for the benefit of and to assist in carrying out the purposes of the ELCA." The ELCA adopted the position that the system of apartheid in South Africa was so contrary to Lutheran theology that it had to be rejected as a matter of faith. The ELCA passed a resolution to "see that none of our ELCA pension funds will be invested in companies doing business in South Africa." A dissenting group of Lutherans opposed the ELCA's decision to use its assets as a political weapon and asked to withdraw their pension funds. When their request was denied they sued the board of pensions and the ELCA, claiming that both groups had violated their fiduciary duties to participants in the pension program by elevating social concerns over sound investment strategy. A state appeals court dismissed the lawsuit on the ground that a resolution of the lawsuit would require the court to interpret religious doctrine in violation of the first amendment's nonestablishment of religion clause. The court concluded that the "ELCA enacted the [apartheid] policy in an effort to further its social and doctrinal goals . . . . Accordingly, any review of the Board of Pensions' [investment policy] would entangle the court in reviewing church doctrine and policy."[4]

Example. *A New York appeals court ruled that directors of a charitable trust could be sued for breaching their fiduciary duties. A child of the founder of the trust filed a lawsuit seeking to remove 8 of the trust's 11 directors. He asserted that the 8 directors breached their fiduciary duties, mismanaged the trust's investments, and negligently selected the trust's investment advisor. The court ruled that the 8 directors could be sued. It noted that "it is well established that, as fiduciaries, board members bear a duty of loyalty to the corporation and may not profit improperly at the expense of their corporation." In this case, the lawsuit alleged that the 8 directors breached their fiduciary duties by investing a substantial portion of the trust's assets in speculative securities and in the stock of a company with direct ties to the directors. The court concluded that the "business judgment rule" (which protects directors from any liability for their reasonable and good faith decisions) did not apply in this case, since it was not available "when the good faith or oppressive conduct of the officers and directors is in issue."[5]*

Example. *An Ohio court refused to allow church members to sue board members personally for breaching their fiduciary duties by failing to oust a pastor who allegedly had engaged in financial improprieties. It observed, "[I]nquiry into the relationship between the trustees and the congregation in matters concerning the pastorship would require the courts to consider each party's view of who should preach from the pulpit. Review of such matters would further require the court to determine the issue of whether the trustees' performance of their duties met the standards of the congregation and would therefore involve an inquiry into ecclesiastical concerns. Therefore . . . civil courts lack . . . jurisdiction to entertain such matters. . . . [We] hold that the lower court has no jurisdiction over the claims brought by the individual members of the congregation seeking to . . . hold the board liable for breach of fiduciary duty to the congregation."[6]*

4 Basich v. Board of Pensions, 540 N.W.2d 82 (Minn. App. 1995).
5 Scheuer Family Foundation, Inc. v. 61 Associates, 582 N.Y.S.2d 662 (A.D. 1 Dept. 1992).
6 State v. Meagher, 1997 WL 180266 (Ohio App. 1997).

26.4 Theory 4 — Breach of the Fiduciary Duty of Loyalty

Church board members have a fiduciary duty of loyalty to the corporation. This duty generally requires that any transaction between the board and one of its directors be

(1) fully disclosed

(2) approved by the board without the vote of the interested director, and

(3) fair and reasonable to the corporation

In most cases, a director breaches the duty of loyalty only through some secret or undisclosed interest in a transaction with the corporation. To illustrate, a director who owns a business (e.g., insurance, real estate, furnishings) may violate the duty of loyalty by inducing the board to enter into a transaction with his company without fully disclosing to the board his personal interest in the transaction. Additionally, the director ordinarily should abstain from voting on the transaction, and the transaction should be fair and reasonable to the corporation.

26.5 Theory 5 — Violation of Trust Terms

Church board members may be legally accountable for violating the terms or restrictions of properties and funds held in trust by the church. To illustrate, the trustees of one church were sued by church members when they attempted to sell church assets contrary to the restrictions specified in the church charter.[7] The original charter of the church stated that it was formed "for the purpose of religious worship . . . at the corner of Fifth Street and E Street, Southeast, in the City of Washington." In 1982, after the safety of the historic church building became an issue, the pastor and board of trustees decided to close the church and move to a new location. For at least ten years prior to the sale of the church property, relations between the board of trustees and a segment of the congregation became increasingly hostile. After the sale of the church building, a group of the dissidents filed a lawsuit alleging that the trustees and pastor had violated their fiduciary duty as trustees to hold church properties for the purposes specified in the corporate charter (i.e., to conduct religious worship "at the church building on the southeast corner of Fifth Street and E Street"). The dissidents claimed they were attempting to "salvage the historic old Mount Jezreel church building." The dissidents pointed out that title to the church's properties was in the name of the trustees who held church properties "in trust" for the members of the congregation, and that church members were "trust beneficiaries" who could sue the trustees for improper or unauthorized transactions with respect to those properties.

A trial court dismissed the lawsuit, but an appeals court ruled in favor of the dissidents. The appeals court observed:

> Although title to the church property is vested in the trustees or directors, the property itself is held in trust for the uses and purposes named and no other.

---

[7] Mt. Jezreel Christians Without a Home v. Board of Trustees of Mount Jezreel Baptist Church, 582 A.2d 237 (D.C. App. 1990).

Because the church was incorporated for the purpose of religious worship, and because the property was held in trust for that purpose, the members of the congregation are indeed the beneficiaries of the trust. As such, they have standing to sue the trustees in the event that the trust property is used or disposed of in a manner contrary to the stated purposes of the trust. . . . We therefore hold that, as a general principle, bona fide members of a church have standing to bring suit as trust beneficiaries when there is a dispute over the use or disposition of church property.

The same principle may apply to board members who authorize the diversion of designated funds from their intended purposes or projects. For example, assume that a member donates $10,000 to a church's new building fund, and that the church later decides not to build a new facility. Can the church board divert the $10,000 to another use, or must it return the funds to the donor? Or, assume that the church raises several contributions totaling $250,000 for a new building fund and later decides to abandon the project. Does the board have an obligation to track down all of the donors and offer to return their contributions?

Church board members may be liable for diverting designated gifts to other purposes only if someone has the legal right to enforce the original designation. Some courts have ruled that the donor has such a right, but others have not. Even if a donor cannot enforce a designated gift, this does not make it unenforceable. In most states the following persons are authorized to enforce a designated gift: (1) the state attorney general; (2) a donor who reserves a right to enforce a designated gift in a written instrument; or (3) a trustee of a written trust that contains the designated gift.

> **Example.** *The Connecticut Supreme Court ruled that donors who make designated gifts to charity ordinarily do not have a legal right to enforce their designations.*[8] *A foundation contributed $250,000 to a university with the stipulation that the funds be used to provide scholarships to needy students in the nursing program. A few years later the university closed its nursing school. The foundation sued the university, and asked a court to order the university to segregate the gift from its general fund and set it aside once again for the gift's original purpose. If that purpose could no longer be fulfilled, then the foundation asked the court to compel the university to return the gift. The court ruled that donors who make designated gifts to charity have no legal right to enforce their designations unless they specifically reserve the right to do so. The court acknowledged that a designated contribution is held in trust by a charity for the specified purpose. And, while the donor cannot enforce a designated gift, there are others who can. These include the state attorney general, a trustee of a written trust, or anyone with a "special interest" in the enforcement of the designation.*

Since designated gifts generally can be enforced by someone (even if not the donor), church board members may be legally responsible for diverting designated gifts to other purposes. As a result, it is essential for church leaders to consult with a local attorney before using a donor's designated funds for some other purpose. To reduce the risk of personal liability, church leaders should consider the following precautions if they decide to use designated gifts for other purposes:

---

[8] Herzog Foundation v. University of Bridgeport, 699 A.2d 995 (Conn. 1997).

Donors can be identified

If donors can be identified, they should be asked if they want their contributions returned or retained by the church and used for some other purpose. Ideally, donors should communicate their decision in writing to avoid any misunderstandings. Churches must provide donors with this option in order to avoid violating their legal duty to use designated funds only for the purposes specified. Of course, churches should advise these donors that they may need to file amended tax returns if they claimed a charitable contribution deduction for their contributions in a prior year.

> *Key point. Often, donors prefer to let the church retain their designated contributions rather than go through the inconvenience of filing an amended tax return.*

Donors cannot be identified

A church may not be able to identify all donors who contributed to the building fund. This is often true of donors who contributed small amounts, or donors who made anonymous cash offerings to the building fund. In some cases, designated contributions were made many years before the church abandoned its building plans, and there are no records that identify donors. Under these circumstances the church has a variety of options. One option would be to address the matter in a meeting of church members. Inform the membership of the amount of designated contributions in the church building fund that cannot be associated with individual donors, and ask the church members to take an official action with regard to the disposition of the building fund. In most cases, the church membership will authorize the transfer of the funds to the general fund. Note that this procedure is appropriate only for that portion of the building fund that cannot be traced to specific donors. If donors can be identified, then use the procedure described above.

Other options are available. Churches should be sure to consult with a local attorney when deciding how to dispose of designated funds if the specified purpose has been abandoned.

Some donors can be identified, and some cannot

In most cases, some of the building fund can be traced to specific donors, but some of it cannot. Both of the procedures summarized above would have to be used.

> *Key point. This discussion has focused on building funds. The same analysis is relevant to contributions that designate any other specific purpose or activity. Other examples include contributions designating a new organ, a missions activity, or a new vehicle.*

Uniform Management of Institutional Funds Act (UMIFA)

This Act is designed to provide the boards and trustees of charitable organizations (including churches) with guidance in handling *institutional funds*. The Act defines an institutional fund as a fund that is "not wholly expendable by the institution on a current basis under the terms of the applicable gift instrument." An official interpretation of the Act, adopted by its drafters, further clarifies that an endowment fund is an institutional fund . . . which is held in perpetuity or for a term and which is not wholly expendable by the institution. Implicit in the definition is the continued maintenance of all or a specified portion of the original gift. . . . If a governing board has the power to spend all of a fund but, in its discretion, decides to invest the fund and spend only the yield or appreciation therefrom, the fund does not become an endowment fund under this definition . . . .

According to these provisions, the Act would not apply to church building funds (or other designated funds) that exist for a specific project requiring the expenditure of the entire fund. However, some churches have established perpetual endowment funds that will meet the Act's definition of an institutional fund. These churches should be familiar with the key provisions of the Act. An introductory note to the Act states:

It is established law that the donor may place restrictions on his largesse which the donee institution must honor. Too often, the restrictions on use or investment become outmoded or wasteful or unworkable. There is a need for review of obsolete restrictions and a way of modifying or adjusting them. The Act authorizes the governing board to obtain the acquiescence of the donor to a release of restrictions and, in the absence of the donor, to petition the appropriate court for relief in appropriate cases.

The Act contains the following relevant provisions:

§ 7. (a) With the written consent of the donor, the governing board may release, in whole or in part, a restriction imposed by the applicable gift instrument on the use or investment of an institutional fund.

(b) If written consent of the donor cannot be obtained by reason of his death, disability, unavailability, or impossibility of identification, the governing board may apply in the name of the institution to the [appropriate] court for release of a restriction imposed by the applicable gift instrument on the use or investment of an institutional fund. The [attorney general] shall be notified of the application and shall be given an opportunity to be heard. If the court finds that the restriction is obsolete, inappropriate, or impracticable, it may by order release the restriction in whole or in part. A release under this subsection may not change an endowment fund to a fund that is not an endowment fund.

(c) A release under this section may not allow a fund to be used for purposes other than the educational, religious, charitable, or other eleemosynary purposes of the institution affected.

(d) This section does not limit the application of the doctrine of *cy pres*.

An official comment to this section of the Act contains the following additional guidance:

One of the difficult problems of fund management involves gifts restricted to uses which cannot be feasibly administered or to investments which are no longer available or productive. There should be an expeditious way to make necessary adjustments when the restrictions no longer serve the original purpose. . . . This section permits a release of limitations that imperil efficient administration of a fund or prevent sound investment management if the governing board can secure the approval of the donor or the appropriate court.

Although the donor has no property interest in a fund after the gift, nonetheless if it is the donor's limitation that controls the governing board and he or she agrees that the restriction need not apply, the board should be free of the burden. . . . If the donor is unable to consent or cannot be identified, the appropriate court may upon application of a governing board release a limitation which is shown to be obsolete, inappropriate or impracticable.

This section of the Act, which remains largely unknown to church leaders and their advisers, provides important guidance in the event that the purpose of a perpetual endowment fund is frustrated and the church would like to expend the gift for another purpose.

Example. The Connecticut Supreme Court ruled that the Uniform Management of Institutional Funds Act (UMIFA) does not give donors the authority to enforce designated gifts to charity. The court acknowledged that UMIFA permits a charity to avoid an obsolete designation in a gift without resort to the courts by obtaining the donor's consent: "With the written consent of the donor, the governing board may release, in whole or in part, a restriction imposed by the applicable gift instrument on the use or investment of an institutional fund." However, the court pointed out that the drafters of UMIFA made the following official comments: "It is established law that the donor may place restrictions on his largesse which the donee institution must honor. Too often, the restrictions on use or investment become outmoded or wasteful or unworkable. There is a need for review of obsolete restrictions and a way of modifying or adjusting them. The Act authorizes the governing board to obtain the acquiescence of the donor to a release of restrictions and, in the absence of the donor, to petition the appropriate court for relief in appropriate cases. . . . The donor has no right to enforce the restriction, no interest in the fund and no power to change the [charitable] beneficiary of the fund. He may only acquiesce in a lessening of a restriction already in effect." The court noted that these "clear comments regarding the power of a donor to enforce restrictions on a charitable gift" were based on a concern by the drafters of UMIFA that donors would be exposed to "potential adverse tax consequences" if UMIFA "was interpreted to provide donors with control over their gift property after the completion of the gift." The court explained this concern as follows: "The drafters' principal concern in this regard was that the matter of donor restrictions not affect the donor's charitable contribution deduction for the purposes of federal income taxation. In other words, the concern was that the donor not be so tethered to the charitable gift through the control of restrictions in the gift that the donor would not be entitled to claim a federal charitable contribution exemption for the gift." In resolving these concerns, the drafters of UMIFA clearly stated their position as follows: "No federal tax problems for the donor are anticipated by permitting release of a restriction. The donor has no right to enforce the restriction, no interest in the fund and no power to change the [charitable] beneficiary of the fund. He may only acquiesce in a lessening of a restriction already in effect." The court concluded, "[W]e find no support in any source for the proposition that the drafters of UMIFA intended that a donor or his heirs would supplant the attorney general as the designated enforcer of the terms of completed and absolute charitable gifts. Indeed, it would have been [inconsistent] for the drafters of UMIFA to strive to assist charitable institutions by creating smoother procedural avenues for the release of restrictions while simultaneously establishing standing for a new class of litigants, donors, who would defeat this very purpose by virtue of the potential of lengthy and complicated litigation."

The "cy pres" doctrine

Note that Section 7(c) of the Uniform Management of Institutional Funds Act (quoted above) specifies that the Act does not limit the application of the *cy pres* doctrine. This is a potentially significant provision. The "cy pres" doctrine (which has been adopted by most states) generally specifies that if property is given in trust to be applied to a particular charitable purpose, and it is or becomes impossible or impracticable or illegal to carry out the particular purpose, and if the donor manifested a more general intention to devote the property to charitable purposes, the trust will not fail but the court will direct the application of the property to some charitable purpose which falls within the general charitable intention of the donor.

Example. A New Jersey court ruled that church funds earmarked by a donor for a specific purpose could be used by the church for other, related purposes.[9] In 1911, a Quaker church established a fund for the care and maintenance of its graveyard, and began soliciting contributions for the fund. By 1988, the fund had increased to nearly $200,000, and had annual income far in excess of expenses. In 1985, the church discussed the possibility of using the excess income for purposes other than graveyard maintenance, and ultimately expressed a desire to use excess income from the fund for general church purposes (including upkeep and maintenance of church properties). A church trustee who administered the fund took an unbending position that the fund could not be used for any purpose other than graveyard maintenance. The court ruled that the excess income could be used for general church purposes other than graveyard maintenance. The court observed that the cy pres doctrine was created "for the preservation of a charitable trust when accomplishment of the particular purpose of the trust becomes impossible, impractical, or illegal." The court concluded that "if income from a charitable trust exceeds that which is necessary to achieve the donor's charitable objective, cy pres may be applied to the surplus income since there is an impossibility of using the income to advance any of the charitable purposes of the [donor]." Therefore, to the extent that the graveyard fund in question "exceeds maintenance and preservation costs, application of cy pres is appropriate since there is an impossibility of using the excess income to advance the particular purpose expressed by the donors." The only remaining question was whether or not the donors manifested an intention to devote excess income to a charitable purpose more general than graveyard maintenance. The court concluded that the donors to the graveyard fund in fact manifested such an intent: "The only sensible conclusion to be reached is that the donors did not intend that the trusts would grow while the [church] itself may cease to exist because of lack of funds. We are also convinced that use of the funds for

---

[9] Sharpless v. Medford Monthly Meeting of the Religious Society of Friends, 548 A.2d 1157 (N.J. Super. 1988).

general meeting purposes is sufficiently similar to the particular purpose of the [donors] to apply the cy pres doctrine." [10]

Example. *An elderly man drafted a will in 1971 that left most of his estate "in trust" to his sisters, and upon the death of the surviving sister, to a local Congregational church with the stipulation that the funds be used "solely for the building of a new church." The man died in 1981, and his surviving sister died in 1988. Since the Congregational church had no plans to build a new sanctuary, it asked a local court to interpret the will to permit the church to use the trust fund not only for construction of a new facility but also "for the remodeling, improvement, or expansion of the existing church facilities" and for the purchase of real estate that may be needed for future church construction. The church also asked the court for permission to use income from the trust fund for any purposes that the church board wanted. The state attorney general, pursuant to state law, reviewed the church's petition and asked the court to grant the church's requests. However, a number of heirs opposed the church's position, and insisted that the decedent's will was clear, and that the church was attempting to use the trust funds "for purposes other than building a new church." The Iowa Supreme Court ruled in favor of the church. Applying the cy pres rule, the court concluded: "The will gave the property in trust for a particular charitable purpose, the building of a new church. The evidence clearly indicated that it was impractical to carry out this particular purpose. Furthermore, the [decedent] did not provide that the trust should terminate if the purpose failed. A trust is not forfeited when it becomes impossible to carry out its specific purpose, and there is no forfeiture or reversion clause." The court concluded that the trial court's decision to permit the church to use the trust fund for the remodeling, improvement, or expansion of the existing church facilities "falls within the [decedent's] general charitable intention." Accordingly, the trial court's decision represented a proper application of the cy pres rule.* [11]

26.6 Theory 6 — Securities Law

Section 410(b) of the Uniform Securities Act (adopted in about 40 states) imposes civil liability on every officer or director of an organization that (a) offers or sells unregistered, nonexempt securities; (b) uses unlicensed agents in the offer or sale of its securities (unless the agents are specifically exempted from registration under state law); or (c) offers or sells securities by means of any untrue statement of a material fact or any omission of a material fact. In recent years, a number of churches have violated some or all of these requirements. Such violations render each officer and director of the church potentially liable. Section 410(b) does provide that an officer or director of an organization that sells securities in violation of any of the three provisions discussed above is not liable if he "sustains the burden of proof that he did not know, and in the exercise of reasonable care could not have known of the existence of the facts by reason of which the liability is alleged to exist."

26.7 Theory 7 — Wrongful Discharge of an Employee

Historically, employment agreements of *unspecified* duration were considered to be terminable at the will of either the employer or the employee. No "cause" was

---

[10] *Id.* at 1160 (citations omitted).
[11] Matter of Trust of Rothrock, 452 N.W.2d 403 (Iowa 1990).

necessary. In recent years, several courts have permitted discharged "at will" employees to sue their former employer on the basis of several grounds, including

- wrongful discharge in violation of public policy (e.g., employee terminated for filing a workmen's compensation claim, or for reporting illegal employer activities)

- intentional infliction of emotional distress (e.g., discharge accompanied by extreme and outrageous conduct)

- fraud (e.g., employee accepts job in reliance on employer misrepresentations)

- defamation (e.g., malicious and false statements made by previous employer to prospective employers)

- breach of contract terms (e.g., employer made oral representations, or written representations contained in a contract of employment or employee handbook, that were not kept)

Directors may be personally liable to the extent that they participate in the wrongful termination of an employee.

26.8 Theory 8 — Willful Failure to Withhold Taxes

Section 6672 of the Internal Revenue Code specifies that

> any person required to collect, truthfully account for, and pay over any [income tax or FICA tax] who willfully fails to collect such tax, or truthfully account for and pay over such tax, or willfully attempts in any manner to evade or defeat any such tax or the payment thereof, shall, in addition to other penalties provided by law, be liable for a penalty equal to the total amount of the tax evaded, or not collected, or not accounted for and paid over.

Stated simply, this section says that any corporate officer, director, or employee who is responsible for withholding taxes and paying them over to the government is liable for a penalty in the amount of 100% of such taxes if they are either not withheld or not paid over to the government. This penalty is of special relevance to church leaders, given the high rate of noncompliance by churches with the payroll reporting procedures.

Does the penalty imposed by section 6672 apply to churches and other nonprofit organizations? The answer is yes. Consider the following 3 points:

IRS Policy Statement P-5-60

In Policy Statement P-5-60 (part of the Internal Revenue Manual), the IRS states:

> The 100% penalty (applicable to withheld income and social security taxes) will be used only as a collection device. If a corporation has willfully failed to collect or pay over income and employment taxes, or has willfully failed to pay over collected excise taxes, the 100% penalty may be asserted against responsible officers and employees of the corporation, including volunteer members of boards of trustees of organizations referred to in section 501 of the Internal Revenue Code [e.g., churches], whenever such taxes cannot be

immediately collected from the corporation itself. . . . When the person responsible for withholding, collecting and paying over taxes cannot otherwise be determined, the Service will look to the president, secretary, and the treasurer of the corporation as responsible officers.

The IRS has been criticized for attempting to assess the 100% penalty against volunteer directors of charitable organizations having little if any control over finances. The IRS responded to this criticism by amending Policy Statement P-5-60 to include the following significant statements:

Determination of Responsible Persons

Responsibility is a matter of status, duty, and authority. Those performing ministerial acts without exercising independent judgment will not be deemed responsible. In general, non-owner employees of the business entity, who act solely under the dominion and control of others, and who are not in a position to make independent decisions on behalf of the business entity, will not be asserted the trust fund recovery penalty. *The penalty shall not be imposed on unpaid, volunteer members of any board of trustees or directors of an organization referred to in section 501 of the Internal Revenue Code to the extent such members are solely serving in an honorary capacity, do not participate in the day-to-day or financial operations of the organization, and/or do not have knowledge of the failure on which such penalty is imposed.*

In order to make accurate determinations all relevant issues should be thoroughly investigated. An individual will not be recommended for assertion if sufficient information is not available to demonstrate he or she was actively involved in the corporation at the time the liability was not being paid. However, this shall not apply if the potentially responsible individual intentionally makes information unavailable to impede the investigation.

This language indicates that the IRS will not assert the 100% penalty against uncompensated, volunteer board members of a church who (1) are solely serving in an honorary capacity, (2) do not participate in the day-to-day or financial operations of the organization, and (3) do not have knowledge of the failure to withhold or pay over withheld payroll taxes.

Court decisions

The courts have recognized that church officers can be liable for the section 6672 penalty. Consider the following two cases:

- *Carter v. United States, 717 F. Supp. 188 (S.D.N.Y. 1989).* A church-operated charitable organization failed to pay over to the IRS withheld income taxes and the employer's and employees' share of social security and Medicare taxes for a number of quarters. The IRS assessed a penalty in the amount of 100% of the unpaid taxes ($230,245.86) against *each* of the four officers of the organization pursuant to section 6672 of the Internal Revenue Code. The officers challenged the validity of the IRS actions. A court observed that a person is liable for the full amount of taxes under section 6672 if "(1) he or she was under a duty to collect, account for, and pay over the taxes (i.e., a 'responsible person'), and (2) the failure to pay the taxes was 'willful.'" The court concluded that the four officers of the church-related charitable organization satisfied both requirements, and so they were personally liable for the unpaid taxes under section 6672. The officers were "responsible persons" since (1) they were directors as well as officers, (2) they had the authority to sign checks (including payroll checks), and (3) they were involved in "routine business concerns such as corporate funding, bookkeeping, salaries, and hiring and firing." The fact that a nonprofit organization was involved, and that the officers donated their services without compensation, did not relieve them of liability. The court also ruled that the officers acted "willfully" and accordingly met the second requirement of section 6672. It defined "willful action" as "voluntary, conscious and intentional—as opposed to accidental—decisions not to remit funds properly withheld to the government." There need not be "an evil motive or an intent to defraud." The court specifically held that "the failure to investigate or to correct mismanagement after having notice that withheld taxes have not been remitted to the government is deemed to be willful conduct." Further, the court concluded that payment of employee wages and other debts with the knowledge that the payment of payroll taxes is "late" constitutes willful conduct.

● *In re Triplett, 115 B.R. 955 (N.D. Ill. 1990).* A federal bankruptcy court in Illinois ruled that a church treasurer was not personally liable for his church's failure to withhold and pay over to the IRS some $100,000 in payroll taxes, but that the pastor and chairman of the board of deacons might be. The court concluded that the church treasurer did not have sufficient control over the finances of the church to be liable for the 100% penalty. It noted that the chairman of the board of deacons made all decisions regarding which bills would be paid, and he (and the pastor) were alone responsible day-to-day church operations. While the treasurer did not satisfy the definition of a "responsible person," the court suggested that the pastor and chairman of the deacon board would. It observed that "ample evidence exists to indicate that other church employees, like [the pastor and chairman of the deacon board] may be liable. It is fortuitous that the treasurer's assessment has been litigated before assessments against these other persons." This case illustrates that the IRS is committed to assessing the 100% penalty under Code section 6674 against church leaders in appropriate cases. While the treasurer in this case did not have sufficient control over church finances to be a "responsible person," there is little doubt that many church treasurers would satisfy the court's definition of a "responsible person."

Taxpayer Bill of Rights 2 (TBOR2)

Congress enacted the Taxpayer Bill of Rights 2 in 1996. This law contains four important limitations on the application of the penalty under section 6672:

1. Notice requirement. The IRS must issue a notice to an individual the IRS had determined to be a responsible person with respect to unpaid payroll taxes at least 60 days prior to issuing a notice and demand for the penalty.

2. Disclosure of information if more than one person subject to penalty. TBOR2 requires the IRS, if requested in writing by a person considered by the IRS to be a responsible person, to disclose in writing to that person the name of any other person the IRS has determined to be a responsible person with respect to the tax liability. The IRS is required to disclose in writing whether it has attempted to collect this penalty from other responsible persons, the general nature of those collection activities, and the amount (if any) collected. Failure by the IRS to follow this provision does not absolve any individual from any liability for this penalty.

3. Contribution from other responsible parties. If more than one person is liable for this penalty, each person who paid the penalty is entitled to recover from other persons who are liable for the penalty an amount equal to the excess of the amount paid by such person over such person's proportionate share of the penalty. This proceeding is a federal cause of action and is separate from any proceeding involving IRS collection of the penalty from any responsible party.

4. Volunteer board members of churches and other charities. TBOR2 clarifies that the responsible person penalty is not to be imposed on volunteer, unpaid members of any board of trustees or directors of a tax-exempt organization to the extent such members are solely serving in an honorary capacity, do not participate in the day-to-day or financial activities of the organization, and do not have actual knowledge of the failure. However, this provision cannot operate in such a way as to eliminate all responsible persons from responsibility.

TBOR2 requires the IRS to develop materials to better inform board members of tax-exempt organizations (including voluntary or honorary members) that they may be treated as responsible persons. The IRS is required to make such materials routinely available to tax-exempt organizations. TBOR2 also requires the IRS to clarify its instructions to IRS employees on application of the responsible person penalty with regard to honorary or volunteer members of boards of trustees or directors of tax-exempt organizations.

> *Example. Bill serves as treasurer of his church. Due to financial difficulties, a decision is made by the pastor to use withheld payroll taxes to pay other debts. The IRS later asserts that the church owes $25,000 in unpaid payroll taxes. The church has no means of paying this debt. The IRS later insists that Bill and the other members of the church board are personally liable for the debt. It is likely that Bill is a responsible person who may be liable for the 100 percent penalty since he has authority over the day-to-day financial activities of the church. The new law will not protect him. However, the new law will protect those members of the church board who (1) are volunteer, unpaid members; (2) serve solely in an honorary capacity; (3) do not participate in the day-to-day or financial activities of the organization; and (4) do not have actual knowledge of the failure to pay over withheld taxes to the government.*

Example. A church board votes to use withheld taxes to pay other debts of the church. Over a three year period the church fails to deposit $100,000 in withheld taxes. The IRS claims that the board members are personally liable for the 100 percent penalty for failing to deposit withheld taxes. All of the members of the board claim they are protected by the provisions of the new law. They are not correct, since the new law specifies that its provisions cannot operate in such a way as to eliminate all responsible persons from responsibility.

Conclusions

The precedent summarized above demonstrates that church officers and directors (and in some cases employees such as administrators or bookkeepers) can be *personally liable* for the payment of income taxes and social security and Medicare taxes that they fail to withhold, account for, or pay over to the government. It does not matter that they serve without compensation, so long as they satisfy the definition of a "responsible person" and act willfully. Many church officers and directors (and in some cases employees such as administrators or bookkeepers) will satisfy the definition of a "responsible person," and such persons can be personally liable for unpaid payroll taxes if they act under the liberal definition of "willfully" described above. Clearly, church leaders must be knowledgeable regarding a church's payroll tax obligations, and insure that such obligations are satisfied.

Key point. Congress enacted legislation in 1998 permitting personal delivery, as an alternative to delivery by mail, of a preliminary notice that the IRS intends to assess a 100-percent penalty upon a financially responsible person under section 6672 of the tax code.

26.9 Theory 9 — Exceeding the Authority of the Board

Occasionally, it is asserted that a church board has taken an action that exceeded its authority or power. Some courts have held that directors of nonprofit corporations have a fiduciary relationship with the members of the corporation that requires them to follow the corporate charter and bylaws. For example, one court held that directors who attempted to amend the bylaws of a nonprofit corporation without the knowledge or approval of the membership violated their fiduciary duty to the corporation: "[I]n seeking to disenfranchise the members of the corporation, some or all of the officers and directors of the corporation failed to meet their fiduciary obligation to the members."

26.10 Theory 10 — Loans to Directors

The Model Nonprofit Corporations Act, as well as various other laws under which many churches are incorporated, prohibit church boards from making loans (out of corporate funds) to either directors or officers. Directors who vote in favor of such loans can be liable for them in the event that the loan is unauthorized or otherwise impermissible. Church boards must check the state law under which they are incorporated before considering any loans to a minister.

Summary

Church board members often are concerned about their personal liability for serving on the church board. As this chapter illustrates, they should be concerned.

In recent years it has become common for board members to be named as defendants in lawsuits brought against a church. In most of these cases, board members are sued personally for either or both of two reasons: (1) the church has inadequate insurance to cover the potential claim, or (2) the church's liability is limited by state law. Church board members should recognize that they face the threat of personal liability as a result of serving on the board. This suggests the following responses:

(1) *Review the liability limits in your church insurance policy.* All insurance policies cover losses only up to a specified amount. Church board members should be familiar with these amounts, and periodically determine whether or not they are adequate. Remember, one of the reasons that church board members are sued personally is that the church's insurance coverage is inadequate.

(2) *Review the exclusions in your church insurance policy.* All church insurance policies contain exclusions. An exclusion is a specified loss that is not covered under the policy. Church board members should be familiar with these exclusions, and periodically determine whether or not some or all of them should be covered under a separate policy or endorsement. Remember, one of the reasons that church board members are sued personally is that the church's insurance coverage is inadequate.

(3) *Review any state limitations on church liability.* Does your state limit the liability of churches? Some do. For example, a few states impose limits on the amount of money damages that can be awarded against a church. Other states recognize a form of "charitable immunity" that prohibits churches from being sued by "beneficiaries" of their services. If your state contains any limitation on the liability of churches, it is more likely that you will be sued personally. Remember, one of the reasons that church board members are sued personally is that the church's liability is limited by state law.

(4) *Education.* Church board members should be familiar with the ten kinds of personal liability summarized in this chapter. This knowledge can assist church boards in taking steps to manage the risk of personal liability.

(5) *Insurance.* Legal risks can be managed or reduced, but seldom eliminated. As a result, it is a prudent practice for churches to obtain "directors and officers insurance." Such a policy will cover board members in some cases when they are sued personally. Directors and officers insurance is addressed in chapter 34.

(6) *Review your state's limitations on church board member liability.* All states have enacted legislation that provides "limited immunity" to uncompensated church board members. These laws contain exceptions that vary from state to state. Most states, for example, do not provide immunity to board members who engage in willful or wanton misconduct, intentional or criminal acts, or gross negligence. The limited liability of church board members under state and federal law is addressed in chapter 27.

The following table summarizes the ten theories of liability discussed in this chapter. In the next chapter we examine immunity statutes and their application to church officers and directors.

Table 26-1: Personal Liability of Church Officers, Directors, and Trustees

theory of liability	definition	examples
tort	conduct that injures another's person or property	• negligent operation of a church vehicle • negligent supervision of church workers and activities • copyright infringement • wrongful termination of employees
contract	executing a contract without authorization, or with authorization but without any indication of a representative capacity	• a church board member signs a contract without indicating he or she is signing in a representative capacity, on behalf of a named church • a church board member signs a contract without authorization
breach of the fiduciary duty of care	every officer or director has a fiduciary duty of due care to the corporation; a breach of this duty can result in liability	• failure to attend board meetings; question irregularities; review the church's financial records; and dissenting from questionable actions
breach of the fiduciary duty of loyalty	every officer or director has a fiduciary duty of loyalty to the corporation; a breach of this duty can result in liability	• a church board votes in favor of a contract with a member of the board (unless the conflict is fully disclosed, the contract is fair to the church, and is approved by a disinterested majority of the board)
violation of trust terms	board members may be liable for violating or disregarding the terms of an express trust	• a donor contributes money to a church's building fund, and the church board approves the use of the fund for other purposes unrelated to a building (cf. cy pres doctrine)
securities law	selling securities without registering as an agent (if required by state law); engaging in fraudulent activities in the offer or sale of church securities	• church board members sell church securities to members of the congregation without registering as an agent under state securities law • church board members make unfounded guarantees in the sale of church securities. • church board members make material misrepresentations of fact, or fail to disclose material facts, in the offer or sale of church securities
wrongful discharge of employees	dismissing without "good cause" an employee hired for a definite term of employment prior to the expiration of the term; dismissing an "at will" employee in violation of public policy	• a church board dismisses an employee prior to the end of a 2-year term, without good cause • a church board dismisses an "at will" employee for refusing to backdate tax records

theory of liability	definition	examples
willful failure to withhold taxes	section 6672 of the Internal Revenue Code imposes a 100 percent penalty upon any "responsible person" who willfully fails to withhold federal payroll taxes, or who withholds them but fails to pay them over to the government	• a church treasurer uses withheld federal taxes to meet a church's payroll obligations
exceeding the authority of the board	church board members may be accountable for taking action they are not authorized to perform	• a church board purchases real estate on behalf of the church (without congregational approval as required by the church charter)
loans to directors	many state nonprofit corporation laws specify that church board members may be liable for approving a loan to an officer or director	• a church board approves a $15,000 loan to the senior minister to enable him to make the down payment on a home

CHAPTER 27. IMMUNITY STATUTES

27.1 In General

Most states have enacted laws limiting the liability of church officers and directors. In some states, these laws protect all church volunteers. In some cases, the statute may protect only officers and directors of churches that are incorporated under the state's general nonprofit corporation law. The most common type of statute immunizes *uncompensated* directors and officers from legal liability for their ordinary negligence committed within the scope of their official duties. These statutes generally provide no protection for "willful and wanton" conduct, intentional or criminal acts, or "gross negligence."

In some states, "compensation" does not include the reimbursement of travel expenses incurred while serving as a director or officer. Churches that compensate their directors and officers over and above the reimbursement of travel expenses should reconsider such a policy if they are located in a state that grants limited immunity to uncompensated officers and directors. Obviously, these statutes will not protect ministers who receive compensation from their church.

> *Tip. Churches should consider adopting an appropriate resolution clarifying that a minister's annual compensation package is for ministerial duties rendered to the church, and not for any duties on the church board. Like any other church officer or director, the minister serves without compensation. Such a provision, if adopted, might qualify the minister for protection under the legal immunity law. It is worth serious consideration.*

Statutes immunizing the directors and officers of nonprofit organizations from liability do not prevent the organization itself from being sued on the basis of the negligence of an officer or director. The immunity statutes only protect the officers or directors themselves. Many of the immunity statutes apply only to the directors and officers of organizations exempt from federal income tax under section 501(c) of the Internal Revenue Code. Some of them appear to apply only to *incorporated* organizations.

Why have states enacted such laws? The primary reason is to encourage persons to serve as directors of nonprofit organizations. In the past, many qualified individuals have declined to serve as directors of such organizations out of a fear of legal liability. The immunity statutes respond directly to this concern by providing directors of nonprofit organizations with limited immunity from legal liability.

27.2 Gross Negligence

Church leaders should be familiar with the concept of gross negligence, for the following three reasons:

(1) Punitive damages

Courts can award "punitive damages" for conduct that amounts to gross negligence. Punitive damages are damages awarded by a jury "in addition to compensation for a loss sustained, in order to punish, and make an example of, the wrongdoer." They are awarded when a person's conduct is particularly reprehensible and outrageous. This does not necessarily mean intentional misconduct. Punitive damages often are associated with reckless conduct or conduct creating a high risk of harm. To illustrate, in one case a punitive damage award was based on the fact that church officials repeatedly and knowingly placed a priest in situations where he could sexually abuse boys and then failed to supervise him and disclose his sexual problem. Clearly, church officials did not intend for the priest to molest anyone. But, under the circumstances, the jury concluded that the church's actions were sufficiently reckless to justify an award of punitive damages. Church leaders must understand that reckless inattention to risks can lead to punitive damages, and that such damages may not be covered by the church's liability insurance policy. It is critical to note that many church insurance policies exclude punitive damages. This means that a jury award of punitive damages represents a potentially uninsured risk. Accordingly, it is critical for church leaders to understand the basis for punitive damages, and to avoid behavior which might be viewed as grossly negligent.

(2) Loss of limited immunity under state law

State and federal laws provide uncompensated officers and directors of nonprofit corporations (including churches) with immunity from legal liability for their ordinary negligence. This is an important protection. However, such laws do not protect officers and directors from liability for their gross negligence.

(3) Personal liability

Church leaders who are guilty of gross negligence are more likely to be sued personally than if their behavior is merely negligent. Indifference by church leaders to information that clearly demonstrates improper behavior by a staff member or volunteer worker can be viewed by a court as gross negligence, and this will make it more likely that the church leaders will be sued personally.

> **Example.** A Colorado court ruled that a denominational agency could be sued by a woman with whom a minister had sexual contacts, and that a state statute providing limited immunity to uncompensated officers and directors of nonprofit corporations was not a defense.[1] The statute specifies, "No member of the board of directors of a nonprofit corporation or nonprofit organization shall be held liable for actions taken or omissions made in the performance of his duties as a board member except for wanton and willful acts or omissions."[2] The court concluded that this provision did not apply in this case, since there was no evidence that the agency "accomplished its work through unpaid volunteers."

> **Example.** The Minnesota Supreme Court rejected the argument that a state limited immunity statute only protected board members when acting collectively as a board.[3] It acknowledged that "it is a longstanding tenet of corporation law that a member of the board has no authority to act individually unless specifically authorized by the corporate bylaws or articles of incorporation." However, the court noted that the statute protects more than directors. It also protects officers, trustees, members, and

---

[1] Winkler v. Rocky Mouton Conference, 923 P.2d 152 (Colo. App. 1995).
[2] Colo. Rev. Stat. § 13-21-116.
[3] Rehn v. Fischley, 557 N.W.2d 328 (Minn. 1997).

agents, and these individuals (unlike directors) can act individually rather than collectively. The court concluded that "a director acting outside the specific scope of his or her duty as a member of the board will receive the statute's protection so long as the director is acting on behalf of the nonprofit corporation."

Example. *A New York court ruled that a "charitable immunity" law granting limited legal immunity to the uncompensated directors of a nonprofit organization did not protect a church's trustees from liability for the sexual misconduct of their minister. An unincorporated church and its trustees were sued as a result of their minister's alleged rape of a number of minor females in the church. Among other things, the lawsuit alleged that the church and trustees were responsible for the victims' suffering as a result of their "negligent supervision" of the minister's actions. In their defense, the trustees relied on a state law granting uncompensated directors of nonprofit organizations limited immunity from liability for their actions. The court rejected this defense for two reasons: "The [trustees] did not present presumptive evidence of uncompensated status in that they did not present an affidavit of a chief financial officer of the [church]. Further, there is a reasonable probability that the specific conduct of such [trustees] constitutes gross negligence. If the [trustees] did act as the [victims] allege, they may be found to have proceeded in reckless disregard of the consequences of their acts."*[4]

Example. *The Wisconsin Supreme Court ruled that a state law providing limited immunity to the uncompensated officers and directors of nonprofit corporations only provided protection for acts arising from one's status as an officer or director.*[5] *A church-sponsored relief agency needed some plumbing work done. Its director negotiated and signed a contract with a plumbing company. The name of the relief agency was mentioned prominently in the contract, as was the fact that the director was signing in his capacity as director of the agency. The agency was unable to pay the plumbing bill, and the plumbing company sued the director personally. The director claimed that he was immune from liability on the basis of a state law protecting uncompensated officers and directors of nonprofit corporations for "monetary liabilities arising from a breach of, or failure to perform, any duty resulting solely from his or her status as a director or officer." The court disagreed. It noted that a director "cannot be granted immunity unless his liability related solely to his status as a director." In this case, however, the director's contractual liability to the plumbing company "stems from his position as an agent to a partially disclosed corporate principal and not from his status as a director."*

27.3 Volunteer Protection Act

In 1997 Congress enacted the Volunteer Protection Act[6] based on the following findings: (1) the willingness of volunteers to offer their services is deterred by the potential for liability actions against them; (2) as a result, many nonprofit organizations have been adversely affected by the withdrawal of volunteers from boards of directors and service in other capacities; and (3) due to high liability costs and unwarranted litigation costs, volunteers and nonprofit organizations face higher costs in purchasing insurance, through interstate insurance markets, to cover their activities.

---

[4] Karen S. v. Streitferdt, 568 N.Y.S.2d 946 (A.D. 1 Dept. 1991).
[5] Benjamin Plumbing, Inc. v. Barnes, 470 N.W.2d 888 (Wis. 1991).
[6] 42 U.S.C. § 14501

The Act clarifies that it "preempts the laws of any state to the extent that such laws are inconsistent with this [Act] except that this [Act] shall not preempt any state law that provides additional protection from liability relating to volunteers or to any category of volunteers in the performance of services for a nonprofit organization or governmental entity."

Here is a summary of the Act's main provisions:

- No volunteer of a nonprofit organization shall be liable for harm caused by an act or omission of the volunteer on behalf of the organization or entity if—(1) the volunteer was acting within the scope of the volunteer's responsibilities in the nonprofit organization or governmental entity at the time of the act or omission; (2) if appropriate or required, the volunteer was properly licensed, certified, or authorized by the appropriate authorities for the activities or practice in the state in which the harm occurred, where the activities were or practice was undertaken within the scope of the volunteer's responsibilities in the nonprofit organization or governmental entity; (3) the harm was not caused by willful or criminal misconduct, gross negligence, reckless misconduct, or a conscious, flagrant indifference to the rights or safety of the individual harmed by the volunteer; and (4) the harm was not caused by the volunteer operating a motor vehicle, vessel, aircraft, or other vehicle for which the state requires the operator or the owner of the vehicle, craft, or vessel to possess an operator's license or obtain insurance.

- The Act provides no protection to nonprofit organizations themselves.

- Punitive damages may not be awarded against a volunteer unless the victim proves by clear and convincing evidence that the harm was caused by the volunteer's willful or "criminal misconduct, or a conscious, flagrant indifference to the rights or safety of the individual harmed."

Summary

Church board members should be familiar with the concept of limited immunity under applicable state and federal law, as well as the exceptions that apply. Such familiarity will provide church board members with a more realistic assessment of their exposure to personal liability as a result of their service on the board. It also will highlight behavior that may result in personal liability, which in turn should prompt appropriate risk management strategies. In the next part of this handbook, we focus on church and school liability. The next chapter examines the topic of copyright law and provides suggestions on how to prevent copyright violations.

CHAPTER 28. COPYRIGHT LAW VIOLATIONS

28.1 The Copyright Owner's Exclusive Rights

Section 106 of the Copyright Act gives a copyright owner the following five "exclusive rights":

- making copies of the copyrighted work

- preparing derivative works based upon the copyrighted work

- distributing copies or phonorecords of the copyrighted work to the public by sale or other transfer of ownership, or by rental, lease, or lending

- performing publicly any performable literary, musical, dramatic, choreographic, or audiovisual work

- displaying publicly any literary, musical, dramatic, choreographic, or audiovisual work

These five exclusive rights comprise the "bundle of rights" that constitute or define copyright. It is unlawful for anyone to violate any of the exclusive rights of a copyright owner. These rights, however, are not unlimited in scope. The approach of the Copyright Act is to set forth the copyright owner's exclusive rights in broad terms in section 106, and then to provide various limitations, qualifications, or exemptions.

28.2 Infringement

Section 501 of the Copyright Act states that "[a]nyone who violates any of the exclusive rights of the copyright owner . . . is an infringer of the copyright." Of the five exclusive rights, the one causing the most difficulties for churches is the copyright owner's exclusive right to *reproduce* the work (i.e., make copies). Obviously, an infringement occurs when someone makes a verbatim copy of copyrighted material. But what if someone produces a work that is similar but not identical to another's copyrighted work? Can this constitute infringement on the copyright owner's exclusive right of reproduction? For example, does infringement occur if a reproduction does not contain any "word-for-word" copying of original material but merely paraphrases it? Probably so, since a number of courts have held that "paraphrasing is tantamount to copying in copyright law."[1] Another court has observed that copying "cannot be limited literally to the text, else a plagiarist would escape by immaterial variations."[2]

Another difficult question is the verbatim copying of only small portions of copyrighted material. When does such use constitute infringement on the copyright owner's exclusive right of reproduction? There is no easy answer to this question. Courts generally evaluate both the quantity of copyrighted material that is copied verbatim, and its quality. That is, what percentage of the copyrighted work was copied, and how much of the allegedly infringing work consisted of the

---

[1] *See, e.g.,* Davis v. E.I. duPont de Nemours & Co., 240 F. Supp. 612 (S.D.N.Y. 1965).
[2] Nichols v. Universal Pictures Co., 45 F.2d 119 (2nd Cir. 1930).

copied material? Further, how significant was the "quality" of the copied material? Was it the essence of the work as a whole, or was it incidental or insignificant? To illustrate, the courts have found copying of the following amounts of copyrighted material to constitute copyright infringement: (1) two identical bars of a musical work;[3] (2) four notes and two words, which comprised the "heart of the composition;"[4] (3) three sentences (that were used for advertising purposes);[5] (4) three sentences;[6] (5) eight sentences;[7] (6) less than one percent of the copyrighted work;[8] and (7) the phrase "put on a happy face."[9]

However, copying of the following portions of copyrighted material was held not to constitute infringement upon the copyright owner's exclusive right of reproduction: (1) a sentence and a half;[10] (2) sixteen words;[11] and (3) two sentences.[12]

Such precedent leaves little doubt that most reproductions of copyrighted materials by churches will constitute an infringement of the exclusive right of copyright owners to reproduce their works. To cite just a few examples—the copying of copyrighted chorus or hymn lyrics onto a transparency or bulletin insert ordinarily will amount to an infringement, since a substantial quantity of the original work is reproduced, the amount reproduced is significant in terms of quality, and the copy serves the same function as the original work. To illustrate, in one case a publisher reproduced the chorus lyrics of two famous copyrighted songs in songsheet pamphlets, maintaining that the reproduction of only chorus lyrics of copyrighted songs was so trivial in nature and amount as to constitute noninfringing fair use. The court found such reproductions to be an infringement, and rejected the publisher's claim that its reproductions constituted fair use. Though only the chorus lyrics were reproduced (and not the regular verse lines or music), the court found that "the chorus of a musical composition may constitute a material and substantial part of the work and it is frequently the very part that makes it popular and valuable."[13] Similarly, another court found the reproduction of chorus lyrics in a song sheet magazine to be an infringement rather than fair use, since the reproduction "met the same demand on the same market" as the original.[14] The courts in each of these two cases gave a narrow interpretation of fair use because the function served by the infringing use directly satisfied a function that was served by the copyright owner's sheet music.

---

[3] Robertson v. Batten, Barton, Durstine and Osborn, Inc., 146 F. Supp. 795 (S.D. Cal. 1956).

[4] Elsmere Music, Inc. v. National Broadcasting Co., 482 F. Supp. 741 (S.D.N.Y. 1980), *aff'd*, 623 F.2d 252 (2nd Cir. 1980).

[5] Henry Holt & Co. v. Liggett & Myers Tobacco Co., 23 F. Supp. 302 (E.D. Pa. 1938).

[6] Amana Refrigeration, Inc. v. Consumers Union of the United States, Inc., 431 F. Supp. 324 (N.D. Iowa 1977).

[7] Martin Luther King, Jr. Center for Social Change, Inc. v. American Heritage Products, Inc., 508 F. Supp. 854 (N.D. Ga. 1981).

[8] Hedeman Products Copr. v. Tap-Rite Products Corp., 228 F. Supp. 630 (D.N.J. 1964).

[9] American Greetings Corp. v. Kleinfab Corp., 400 F. Supp. 228 (S.D.N.Y. 1975).

[10] Toulmin v. The Rike-Kumler Co., 316 F.2d 232 (6th Cir. 1963).

[11] Suid v. Newsweek Magazine, 503 F. Supp. 146 (D.D.C. 1980).

[12] Jackson v. Washington Monthly Co., 481 F. Supp. 647 (D.D.C. 1979).

[13] Johns & Johns Printing Co. v. Paull-Pioneer Music Corp., 102 F.2d 282 (8th Cir. 1939).

[14] Leo Feist, Inc. v. Song Parodies, Inc., 146 F.2d 400 (2nd Cir. 1944).

Obviously, verbatim copying of the lyrics and melody of a copyrighted musical work (for use by the choir, a soloist, an accompanist, or an instrumental group) would constitute infringement.

Often overlooked is the fact that both the musical score and lyrics of a hymn or chorus are eligible for copyright protection. Section 102(a) of the Copyright Act states that copyright protection subsists in original "musical works, including any accompanying words," that are reduced to a tangible form. Persons who compose both the music and lyrics of an original hymn are entitled to copyright protection for both. This has important consequences. It means, primarily, that no one can make copies of either the music or lyrics without authorization. To illustrate, a church will infringe upon this copyright protection if it inserts only the words of a particular song in a booklet or on a songsheet, or types them on a piece of paper and projects them onto a screen.

It is also important to recognize that one of the copyright owner's exclusive rights is the right to prepare derivative works based upon the copyrighted work. Derivative works include musical arrangements. Therefore, it is not permissible for anyone other than the copyright owner or one whom the copyright owner has authorized to create an arrangement of a copyrighted musical work. To illustrate, one church choir director who made a choral arrangement of a copyrighted hymn without authorization was found to be guilty of copyright infringement.[15] The director's arrangement consisted of the entire score of the copyrighted hymn plus the insertion of a four-measure introduction. The director made several copies of his arrangement on the church's duplicating machine. Each copy contained the director's name and identified him as the arranger. The copyright owner brought a lawsuit against the director and his church, alleging copyright infringement. A federal appeals court found the director and his employing church jointly liable for copyright infringement. The court found the director's lack of intent to infringe to be irrelevant, and concluded that the copying of all or substantially all of a copyrighted musical work could not be considered "fair use."

28.3 Penalties for Infringement

What legal remedies are available to a copyright owner whose copyrighted work has been infringed? A copyright owner whose work has been infringed may elect to recover statutory damages or actual damages plus the infringer's profits. Because of the difficulty in proving actual damages and infringer's profits, copyright owners frequently prefer to pursue statutory damages. As a general rule, when a copyright owner elects to recover statutory damages, a court is obliged to award between $500 and $20,000. However, if infringement was willful, a court may increase the award of statutory damages to $100,000.

Section 504(c)(1) specifies that a copyright owner may elect to recover statutory damages "for all infringements involved in the action, with respect to any one work, for which any one infringer is liable individually . . . ." As a result, a copyright owner may recover only a single award of statutory damages despite repeated infringements of a particular copyrighted work by the same infringer.

---

[15] Wihtol v. Crow, 309 F.2d 777 (8th Cir. 1962).

Example. A music pastor makes a copy (without authorization) of a copyrighted song for each of the 50 members of the church choir. If the copyright owner elects statutory damages, then only a single award of statutory damages is available. The copyright owner cannot receive a separate award for each of the 50 separate copies that were made of the same copyrighted work.

28.4 Exceptions to Copyright Infringement

The "religious service" exemption

Section 110(3) of the Copyright Act specifies that the "performance of a nondramatic literary or musical work or of a dramatico-musical work of a religious nature, or display of a work, in the course of services at a place of worship or other religious assembly" is not an infringement of copyright.

Performance of a nondramatic literary work means reading from a book or periodical in a nondramatic manner. As a result, a copyrighted translation of the Bible can be quoted publicly in the course of religious services, as can any book or periodical of a religious nature. Without the exception contained in section 110, such readings might constitute copyright infringement since one of a copyright owner's exclusive rights is the right to perform his work publicly.

Section 110 also permits the performance of a copyrighted musical work of a religious nature in the course of services at a place of worship or other religious assembly. Therefore copyrighted hymns, solo materials, orchestrations, and choral arrangements of a religious nature may be performed in religious services. Without the exception contained in section 110, such performances might constitute copyright infringements.

Dramatico-musical works of a religious nature may also be performed in the course of religious services. Such works include certain performances of sacred music that may be regarded as dramatic, such as oratorios and cantatas.

Also exempted from copyright infringement are displays of works of all kinds in the course of religious services.

These exemptions are not intended to cover performances of secular operas, musical plays, motion pictures, and the like, even if they have an underlying religious or philosophical theme and take place in the course of religious services.

To be exempted under section 110, a performance or display must be "in the course of services," and so activities at a place of worship that are for social, educational, fundraising, or entertainment purposes are excluded. Some performances of these kinds may be exempted under section 110(4). This section exempts from copyright infringement certain performances of nondramatic literary or musical works that are performed without admissions charge or that are performed with an admissions charge if the proceeds are used exclusively for educational, religious, or charitable purposes and not for private financial gain, unless the copyright owner has served notice of objection to the performance at least seven days before the performance.

Since the performance or display must also occur "at a place of worship or other religious assembly," the exemption would not extend to religious broadcasts or other transmissions to the public at large, even if the transmissions were sent from a place of worship. Nor would the exemption apply to the public distribution of tape recordings of religious services containing any copyrighted materials. Thus, while a copyrighted religious musical work may be performed at a religious service, publicly distributed tape recordings of the service that reproduce the copyrighted work do not constitute a performance of the work in the course of services at a place of worship and, accordingly, such recordings are not exempt under section 110. On the other hand, as long as services are being conducted before a religious assembly, the exemption would apply even if they were conducted in such places as auditoriums and outdoor theaters.

The exemption provided by section 110 exempts only religious performances in the course of religious services from copyright infringement. The Act states that to *perform* a work means to recite or render it. Performance of a copyrighted hymn or choral arrangement thus means to sing it, and performance of a copyrighted cantata means to present it. There is therefore no license to copy a copyrighted work, such as by duplicating a single piece of music for all of the members of a choir, since duplication does not constitute a performance even though the duplicated copies may eventually be used in a performance. Only the copyright owner has the right to reproduce a copyrighted work by making copies. Similarly, a church may not assemble a booklet of copyrighted hymns or choruses (lyrics or music) for use by its members in the course of religious services since this would necessitate copying the protected works. Of course, a church can duplicate a musical work or lyrics whose copyright term has expired or that never was subject to copyright protection since such works are considered to be in the public domain.

Fair use

Section 107 of the Copyright Act specifies that

> the fair use of a copyrighted work, including such use by reproduction in copies or phonorecords or by any other means specified [in section 106], for purposes such as criticism, comment, news reporting, teaching (including multiple copies for classroom use), scholarship, or research, is not an infringement of copyright. In determining whether the use made of a work in any particular case is a fair use the factors to be considered shall include—(1) the purpose and character of the use, including whether such use is of a commercial nature or is for nonprofit educational purposes; (2) the nature of the copyrighted work; (3) the amount and substantiality of the portion used in relation to the copyrighted work as a whole; and (4) the effect of the use upon the potential market for or value of the copyrighted work.

Fair use is one of the most common defenses invoked by persons charged with copyright infringement. Unfortunately, it is very difficult to define. Even section 107 does not define the term but rather recites "factors to be considered" in determining if a particular use is a fair use.

There is little doubt that many reproductions of copyrighted materials by churches will fail to constitute noninfringing fair use. Certainly any verbatim copying of an entire work will almost never constitute fair use. Examples of this type of copying include the duplication of a musical work for members of the choir, a bulletin insert, a soloist, accompanist, instrumental group, or for use as a transparency or slide. Even copying of a significant portion (in terms of either quantity or quality) of a copyrighted work ordinarily will fail to constitute noninfringing fair use. An example here would be the copying of only the lyrics (and not the melody) of a copyrighted chorus or hymn. In all of these cases, a finding of fair use will be unlikely because (1) such acts of copying constitute mere reproductions of a work in order to use it for its intrinsic purpose; (2) the nature of the work involved does not suggest a broad definition of fair use; (3) the amount of copyrighted material that is copied is significant in terms of both quantity and quality; (4) similar acts of copying by other churches would "adversely affect the market for or value of the copyrighted work." In other words, none of the four fair use factors ordinarily will support a finding of fair use.[16]

The "fair use guidelines"

One of the most common fair use issues concerns the reproduction of copyrighted materials for educational purposes. In 1975, negotiating teams representing authors, publishers, and educational institutions reached an agreement known as the Agreement on Guidelines for Classroom Copying in Not-For-Profit Educational Institutions with Respect to Books and Periodicals. The House Report on the Copyright Act of 1976 reprinted the Agreement in full, and further noted that the guidelines set forth in the Agreement "are a reasonable interpretation of the minimum standards of fair use."

The educational guidelines are very restrictive, and rarely will apply to churches. They apply primarily to copying by teachers in not-for-profit educational institutions for their own research or class preparation, and also to limited copying for classroom use. There are strict requirements as to the amount of material that can be copied under the guidelines for classroom use. For example, in the case of literary works ("prose"), teachers are limited to (a) either a complete article, story or essay of less than 2,500 words, or (b) an excerpt from any prose work of not more than 1,000 words or 10 percent of the work, whichever is less, but in any event a minimum of 500 words. Other requirements apply. The guidelines also warn that "copying shall not substitute for the purchase of books, publishers' reprints or periodicals."

---

[16] *But cf.* New Era Publications International v. Carol Publishing Group, 904 F.2d 152 (2nd Cir. 1990). A federal appeals court ruled that the use of several extended quotations of a religious leader reproduced without permission in an uncomplimentary biography constituted fair use. The court evaluated each of the four "fair use factors" and concluded that all of them supported the finding of fair use. With regard to the first factor, the court concluded that biographies, and particularly critical biographies, generally constitute fair use. The proposed book used quotations from the religious leader's published writings "for the entirely legitimate purpose of making his point that [the leader] was a charlatan and his church a dangerous cult." While the author no doubt expected to make a profit, this was a secondary purpose. As to the second factor, the court again emphasized that the proposed book was a biography, and that biographies generally constitute fair use. The court observed that "biographies, of course, are fundamentally personal histories and it is both reasonable and customary for biographers to refer to and utilize earlier works dealing with the subject of the work and occasionally to quote directly from such works." The third fair use factor asks how much of the copyrighted work is quoted—both in terms of quantity and quality. The court concluded that only small portions of several works were quoted, rather than larger selections of any one work. Further, the portions quoted were not "key portions" of any of the books. Finally, the court concluded that the fourth factor led to a finding of fair use, since the biography would have little if any impact on the sale of the copyrighted works.

Shortly after the guidelines for books and periodicals were formulated, representatives of music publishers and music educators met to draft guidelines relative to music. The House Report on the Copyright Act of 1976 reprinted the guidelines in full and noted that the guidelines "are a reasonable interpretation of the minimum standards of fair use." Like the guidelines for books and periodicals, the music guidelines are very restrictive and rarely will apply to churches. Perhaps most importantly, these guidelines permit "emergency photocopying to replace purchased copies which for any reason are not available for an imminent performance provided purchased replacement copies shall be substituted in due course." Clearly, this provision will be of little use to churches, since it requires that (1) copies of music have been purchased, (2) they are unavailable for an imminent performance because they are suddenly destroyed or lost, and (3) the church purchases replacement copies in due course.

Religious displays

Section 109(c) provides that "the owner of a particular copy lawfully made . . . is entitled, without the authority of the copyright owner, to display that copy publicly, either directly or by the projection of no more than one image at a time, to viewers present at the place where the copy is located."

This section is of considerable relevance to churches, and especially those that use transparencies and slides of copyrighted music in the course of worship services. Recall that one of the exclusive rights of a copyright owner is the right to display a copyrighted work publicly. Section 109(c) limits this exclusive right by adopting the general principle that the *lawful owner* of a copy of a copyrighted work should be able to put the copy on public display without the consent of the copyright owner.

Section 109(c) would authorize the use of an opaque projector to display a copy of a musical work in the course of choir rehearsals or church services since the opaque projector displays an image of a lawfully made copy consisting ordinarily of either sheet music or a page in a hymnal. But if a church makes a transparency of an existing copyrighted musical work without authorization, such a transparency would not be a lawfully made copy and thus could not be displayed without infringing the owner's copyright. Section 109(b) would authorize the display of a transparency in the course of choir rehearsals or church services if the transparency constituted a lawfully made copy. This could occur in three ways. First, a transparency purchased from an authorized vendor would be a lawful copy and could be displayed publicly. Second, a transparency of a public domain work could be fabricated and displayed. Third, a transparency made with the express permission of the copyright owner would be a lawful copy.

The nonprofit performance exception

Section 110(4) contains a general exception to the exclusive right of a copyright owner to publicly perform his or her copyrighted work. It provides:

> [P]erformance of a nondramatic literary or musical work otherwise than in a transmission to the public, without any purpose of direct or indirect commercial advantage and without payment of any fee or other compensation for the performance to any of its performers, promoters, or organizers, [does not constitute copyright infringement] if—(A) there is no

direct or indirect admission charge; or (B) the proceeds, after deducting the reasonable costs of producing the performance, are used exclusively for educational, religious, or charitable purposes and not for private financial gain, except where the copyright owner has served notice of objection to the performance under the following conditions; (i) the notice shall be in writing and signed by the copyright owner or such owner's duly authorized agent; and (ii) the notice shall be served on the person responsible for the performance at least seven days before the date of the performance, and shall state the reasons for the objection; and (iii) the notice shall comply, in form, content, and manner of service, with requirements that the Register of Copyrights shall prescribe by regulation.

Let's consider a number of important aspects of this important exemption.

(1) The performance must not have a profit motive.

(2) No fee or compensation can be paid to the performers (or promoters or organizers) for the performance. This condition does not prevent performers from receiving a salary for duties that include a particular performance. For example, performances by a school band do not lose the benefit of this exemption merely because the band conductor is a music teacher who receives an annual salary for performing his duties, so long as he receives no fee or payment for any particular performance.

(3) There must either be no direct or indirect admissions charge, or alternatively, if an admissions charge is assessed, then any amounts left after deducting the reasonable costs of producing the performance must be used solely for educational, religious, or charitable purposes. If there is an admissions charge, then the copyright owner is given the authority to "veto" the performance by serving upon the person responsible for the performance a notice objecting to the performance. Such a notice must be in a writing that is signed by the copyright owner; it must be served upon the person responsible for the performance at least seven days before the date of the performance; and, it must state the reasons for the objection. The impact of this provision is limited severely by the fact that section 110(4) does not require that the copyright owner be notified that his or her work is going to be performed at a nonprofit event with an admissions charge.

Authorization from copyright owner

Even if none of the exceptions to copyright infringement applies, a particular use of copyrighted material may be authorized by the copyright owner. For example, assume that a church choir director wishes to perform a particular song during a worship service, that he has a single octavo, and that he cannot obtain additional copies locally and it is too late to order copies by mail. While this "emergency need" to make unauthorized copies is not a recognized exception to copyright infringement, the director is free to contact the copyright owner directly and request permission to make copies. If permission is granted, then the making of copies will not constitute infringement.

Many music publishers have very liberal policies with respect to church music. Some music publishers grant "blanket licenses" to churches, authorizing them to make copies of any song in the publisher's repertory for an annual fee. Occasionally, several publishers and composers will assign the right to license the use of their works to a single company in return for the payment of a royalty. The company acts as a clearinghouse on behalf of the publishers and composers, granting blanket licenses to churches in exchange for a fee that is apportioned among the various publishers and composers. This approach is offered by Christian Copyright Licensing, Inc. (CCLI) of Portland, Oregon. CCLI has publishers and composers enter into nonexclusive assignments of their musical works with CCLI. While CCLI acts as a clearinghouse for several publishers and composers, the publishers and composers remain free to directly market and license their works to individual churches. Churches that purchase a blanket license from CCLI are authorized to make copies of any song in the CCLI repertory (which includes the works of several publishers and composers) for congregational use, for the duration of the license period (ordinarily one year). This means, for example, that churches are free to make bulletin inserts and transparencies. Churches also are authorized to make audio and video recordings of services that contain copyrighted music (in the CCLI repertory), provided that copies of the recording are distributed for less than a specified cost, and do not exceed a specified number. The making of certain musical arrangements is also permitted.

Churches must make a record of what songs they sing or perform in the course of a year, and file reports with CCLI. These reports help CCLI allocate royalties to the various publishers and composers. The fee that a church pays is based on a number of variables, including the size of the church and the kind of copying involved. In principle, the CCLI approach has the advantage of making compliance with copyright law much easier. Of course, the success of the project will depend upon four key factors—the number of songs in the CCLI repertory, the number of churches that obtain a CCLI license, the fee that CCLI will charge, and the degree of voluntary compliance by churches with the terms and conditions of the CCLI license. Churches wishing to contact CCLI may write them at the following address: Christian Copyright Licensing, Inc., 17201 NE Sacramento Street, Portland, Oregon 97230-5941. The CCLI toll-free telephone number is 1-800-234-2446. Further, note that CCLI licenses only apply to limited cases of reproduction and performance of religious musical works. They do not convey any authorization with respect to duplication of literary works (books and articles), and they do not apply in all cases to reproduction or performance of music. Accordingly, even if CCLI licenses are widely accepted, they must not be viewed as a solution to all of a church's copyright concerns.

What a CCLI license does and does not permit

A CCLI license *does* authorize a church to do the following:

- Print songs and hymns in bulletins, programs, liturgies, and songsheets.
- Create your own customized songbooks or hymnals.
- Create overhead transparencies, slides, or use any other format whereby songs are visually projected, such as computer graphics and projection.
- Arrange, print and copy your own arrangements, vocal and instrumental, of songs where no published version is available.
- Record your worship services by audio or video means, provided you only record "live" music (instrumental and vocal). Accompaniment "tracks"

cannot be reproduced. You may also charge up to $4.00 each for audio tapes (cassettes) and $12.00 each for video tapes.

A CCLI license *does not* authorize a church to do the following:

- Photocopy or duplicate octavos, cantatas, musicals, handbell music, keyboard arrangements, vocal scores, orchestrations, or other instrumental works.

- Translate songs from English into another language. This can only be done with the approval of the respective publisher.

- Rent, sell, or lend copies made under the license to groups outside the church or to other churches. (It is permissible to distribute tapes to shut-ins, missionaries, or others outside the church.)

- Assign or transfer the license to another church or group without CCLI's approval.

28.5 Works Made for Hire — A Checklist of Important Points

A "work made for hire" is any book, article, or piece of music created by an employee in the course of employment. Factors to consider in deciding whether or not a work was created in the course of employment include the following: (1) Was the work written or composed during office hours? (2) Was the work created on church property? (3) Was the work created using church equipment? (4) Was the work created using church personnel? The employer owns the copyright in a work made for hire.

An employer, by a signed writing, can transfer copyright in a work made for hire to the employee who created it. A church that transfers the copyright in a work made for hire to the employee who created it is jeopardizing its tax-exempt status, since this may constitute "inurement" of its assets to a private individual. A church that transfers the copyright in a work made for hire to the employee who created it may also be exposing the employee to intermediate sanctions.

Summary

As this chapter demonstrates, copyright law has numerous applications to common church practices. Unfortunately, churches frequently engage in conduct that infringes upon the exclusive rights of the copyright owner, and such infringements expose churches to potential liability. Church leaders should recognize that any damages a church is required to pay as a result of acts of copyright infringement are not covered by the church's general liability insurance policy. The risk to the church can be reduced in many ways, including the following:

- *Familiarity with the law.* Church leaders should have a clear understanding of the exclusive rights of copyright owners as well as the exceptions to copyright infringement, and take steps to ensure that their church is in substantial compliance with the copyright law.

- *Education of church staff.* Church staff should be familiar with the material in this chapter.

- *Copy machines.* Place a notice by every copy machine warning church staff that it is unlawful for employees and volunteer workers to make unlawful copies on church equipment. Here is a sample:

Under the United States copyright law, copyright owners have the exclusive right to print, publish, copy and sell their protected works. The copyright owners of the books and music you purchase are indicated on those publications.

That means that it may be illegal for you to copy a publication without the written permission of the copyright owner.

The making of unlawful copies on this machine is strictly prohibited by the church.

- *Software policy.* If a computer program is copyrighted, then it may not be duplicated without the permission of the copyright owner. This means that a church employee cannot make duplicate copies of a program for use on different computers. It also means that an employee cannot make a copy of a program for use at home. The key thought is this—you should not be able to operate a program simultaneously on two or more computers. If you can, then ordinarily a copy has been made and unless authorization has been obtained from the copyright owner, this copying infringes on the owner's exclusive right to make copies. Note that there are many public domain and "share-ware" programs that are available, and these ordinarily can be copied (with some restrictions in some cases). And, even copyrighted programs occasionally authorize limited copying (see owner's manuals for details). Church leaders should consider adopting a computer use policy for their church. Such a policy informs employees of practices that violate the copyright law and that are prohibited by the church.

- *Works made for hire.* Advise employees to create their literary and musical works at home on their own time.

- *Permission from copyright owners.* Obtain written permission from copyright owners before copying their works.

- *The CCLI license.* Obtain a license from CCLI.

- *The MPLC license.* Obtain a license from Motion Picture Licensing Corporation ("MPLC"). This will authorize the church to show any video in the MPLC catalog on church premises or during a church activity. You can purchase a license from MLC at 1177 Summer Street, Stamford, Connecticut 06905-0838 (telephone 203-353-1600). Churches using video tapes should definitely consider this license.

CHAPTER 29.   SECURITIES LAW VIOLATIONS

29.1 In General

Laws regulating the sale of securities have been enacted by the federal government[1] and by all 50 states.[2] The term *security* is defined very broadly by such laws. The Uniform Securities Act, which has been adopted by a majority of the 50 states, defines a *security* broadly to include many instruments utilized in church fundraising efforts, including bonds, notes, and trust agreements.

Securities laws were enacted to protect the public against fraudulent and deceptive practices in the sale of securities and to provide full and fair disclosure to prospective investors. To achieve these purposes, most securities laws impose the following conditions on the sale of securities:

1. registration of proposed securities with the federal or state government in advance of sale

2. filing of sales and advertising literature with the federal or state government

3. registration of agents and broker-dealers who will be selling the securities

4. prohibition of fraudulent practices

Although the federal government and most states exempt securities offered by any organization "organized and operated not for private profit but exclusively for a religious . . . purpose" from registration,[3] it is important to note that some states do not exempt the securities of religious organizations from registration;[4] others impose conditions on the exemption;[5] many require that an application for exemption (or "notice" of exemption) be submitted and approved before a claim

---

[1] Securities Act of 1933, 15 U.S.C. §§ 77a-77aa.

[2] Nearly 40 states have enacted all or significant portions of the Uniform Securities Act.

[3] Section 3(a)(4) of the federal Securities Act of 1933 and section 401(a)(10) of the Uniform Securities Act exempt the securities of nonprofit religious organizations from registration. Section 401(a)(10) of the Uniform Securities Act, which has been adopted by several states, specifies that "[t]he following securities are exempted from the [securities registration and sales literature filing requirements] . . . a security issued by a person organized and operated not for private profit but exclusively for a religious, educational, benevolent, charitable, fraternal, social, athletic, or reformatory purpose, or as a chamber of commerce or trade or professional association."

[4] As of the date of publication of this text, the following states do not exempt the debt securities (i.e., bonds and notes) of religious organizations from registration: California, Florida, Georgia, Indiana, Louisiana, Minnesota, Oregon, and Wisconsin.

[5] For example, § 451.802(a)(8) of the Michigan Securities Act exempts from registration the securities of nonprofit organizations, including religious organizations, but only if the securities are "part of an issue having an aggregate sales price of $250,000 or less and are sold only to bona fide members of the issuing organization and are sold without payment of a commission or consulting fee." Securities issued by a charity or religious organization that do not meet these conditions are exempt only if (1) ten days before an offer or sale of the security it files with the administrator an offering circular with a filing fee of $50, and the administrator does not disallow the exemption; (2) no commission or consulting fee is paid to any person except a registered broker-dealer in connection with the offer or sale of the security; and (3) it offers and sells the

of exemption will be recognized;[6] a few states require churches and religious denominations that "issue" their own securities to be registered as issuers or issuer-dealers;[7] and all securities laws subject churches and other religious organizations to the antifraud requirements. Churches therefore must not assume that any securities that they may offer are automatically exempt from registration or regulation.

Key point. Church securities always will be subject to some degree of regulation. The question in each case is how much.

Key point. Research conducted by your authors reveals that securities violations represent one of the most significant sources of church liability in terms of the size of verdicts. This is a risk that church leaders must take seriously.

29.2 Registration of Securities

In those states in which a church must register its securities, registration ordinarily is accomplished by filing a registration statement with the state securities commission setting forth the following information: the name and address of the church; the date of incorporation; a description of the general character of the church's operations; a description of the church's properties; the name, address, and occupation of each director, and the compensation, if any, that each receives from the church; the kind and amount of securities to be offered; the proposed offering price for each security; estimated commissions and finding fees; and estimated cash proceeds to the church from the sale of registered securities. In addition, the following materials must accompany the registration statement: a copy of any prospectus, offering circular, or other sales literature; a specimen copy of the securities being registered; a copy of the church's articles of incorporation and bylaws; a copy of any trust indenture under which the securities are being offered; a signed opinion of legal counsel as to the legality of the security being registered; written consent of any accountant having prepared or certified a report or valuation which is used in connection with the registration statement; a balance sheet; profit and loss statements for each of the preceding three fiscal years; a check to cover the filing fee; and such other material as the securities commission may require.[8]

---

securities only through registered securities broker-dealers or through persons exempted from the definition of the term *agent*. The securities exemption in some states (including Colorado, North Carolina, South Dakota, and Virginia) exempt only those churches that are organized under local law. Many states require churches to notify the state securities commission of a proposed offer or sale of securities as a prerequisite to exemption. Church securities are exempt from registration in some states only if no "commission" or other remuneration is paid to those individuals who offer or sell the securities.

[6] Iowa Code § 502.202.9; Kan. Stat. Ann. § 17-1261(h); Md. Corps. & Ass'ns Code Ann. § 11-601(9); Mo. Ann. Stat. § 409.402(a)(9); Mont. Code Ann. § 30-10-104(8); Nev. Rev. Stat. § 90.520.2(j); N.Y. Gen. Bus. § 359-f(1)(e); N.C. Gen. Stat. § 78A-16(9); Okla. Stat. title 71, § 401(b)(15) (transactional exemption only); Pennsylvania Securities Act of 1972 § 203(p); S.C. Code Ann. § 35-1-310(8); Tenn. Code Ann. § 48-2-103(a)(7); Wash. Rev. Code § 21.20.310(11).

[7] *See, e.g.*, Rule 3E-400.002 of the Rules of the Department of Banking and Finance, Division of Securities, State of Florida.

[8] Uniform Securities Act § 304.

The method of registration described above is referred to as registration by *qualification*. Most states provide for at least two other methods of registration: registration by *coordination* and registration by *notification*. Churches will rarely if ever utilize registration by coordination, since this method assumes registration of an issuer's securities under the federal Securities Act of 1933 and churches are exempt from registration under this Act. Registration by notification is available to securities issued by a corporation that has been in continuous operation for at least five years if the corporation satisfies a minimum net earnings test. A registration statement similar to that described in connection with registration by qualification must be filed for a registration by notification.

The registration statement ordinarily is prepared on a form provided by the state securities commission. Considerable effort has been expended to standardize securities laws and related forms among the 50 states. Most states now permit issuers to register their securities on a uniform application developed by the American Bar Association. This uniform application is called Form U-1.

Generally, the filing of a registration statement with a state securities commission constitutes registration of the security unless the commission objects to the registration statement within a prescribed period. A state securities commission retains the authority to suspend or revoke a registration of securities on the basis of a variety of grounds, including fraud, unreasonable commissions, illegality, omission of a material fact in the registration statement, and willful violation of any rule, order, or condition imposed by the securities commission.[9] Registration of securities generally is effective for one year, although some state laws stipulate that a registration will expire when the securities described in the registration statement have been sold.

The North American Securities Administrators Association has developed guidelines for a church to follow in drafting a prospectus or offering circular. In general, these guidelines require certain basic information on the cover page, and in addition require a full description of the history and operations of the church; the church's prior borrowing experience; risk factors associated with investment in the church's securities; how funds will be held during the offering period; anticipated use of proceeds; current financial condition of the church, accompanied by financial statements for the past three years; the church's properties; the type and amount of the securities to be offered, including interest rates, maturity dates, payment dates, and paying agent; the plan of distribution; pending or threatened legal proceedings against the church; tax aspects of ownership of the church's securities; and the church's leadership.

29.3 Registration of Salespersons

It is important to observe that most states require that persons who sell or offer to sell securities be registered with the state securities commission. Registration involves submitting a detailed application[10] and, in most cases, the successful

---

[9] *Id.* at § 306.

[10] Most states accept the uniform Form U-4 prepared by the National Association of Securities Dealers. *See generally* § 4-07, *supra*.

completion of a securities law examination. A few states that exempt the securities of religious organizations from registration do not exempt persons selling or offering to sell such securities from the salesman registration requirements.

29.4 Prohibition of Fraud

No state securities law exempts religious organizations from the antifraud provisions. The antifraud provisions of the Uniform Securities Act are set forth in section 501:

> In connection with an offer to sell, sale, offer to purchase, or purchase, of a security, a person may not, directly or indirectly:
>
> (1) employ a device, scheme, or artifice to defraud;
>
> (2) make an untrue statement of a material fact or omit to state a material fact necessary in order to make the statements made not misleading, in the light of the circumstances under which they are made; or
>
> (3) engage in an act, practice, or course of business that operates or would operate as a fraud or deceit upon a person.

This section is substantially the same as section 17(a) of the federal Securities Act of 1933. Section 17 expressly states that the Act's exemption of nonprofit organizations from the registration requirements does not apply to the antifraud provisions.

The antifraud provisions of federal and state securities laws are very broad. They have been construed to prohibit a wide variety of activities, including the following:

- making false or misleading statements about church securities
- failing to disclose material risks associated with securities
- manipulating the church's financial records in order to facilitate the sale of securities
- failing to establish a debt service or sinking fund reserve out of which church securities will be retired
- making false predictions
- recommending the sale of securities to investors without regard to their financial condition
- inducing transactions that are excessive in view of an investor's financial resources
- borrowing money from an investor
- commingling investors' funds with the personal funds of another, such as a salesman
- deliberately failing to follow an investor's instructions; making unfounded guarantees
- misrepresenting to investors the true status of their funds
- representing that funds of investors are insured or "secure" when in fact they are not

- representing that investments are as safe as if they had been made in a bank, when this is not the case

- representing that securities have been approved of or recommended by the state securities commission or that the commission has passed in any way on the merits or qualifications of the securities or of any agent or salesman

Key point. There are two additional considerations that churches should consider before offering securities. First, some securities may be regulated under state and federal banking law. For example, it is possible that the issuance of "demand notes" (notes redeemable by investors "on demand") would violate state and federal banking laws. Demand notes are basically deposit arrangements which may trigger banking regulation. Second, complex accounting principles apply to some securities programs. It is essential for churches to work with a CPA firm with experience in representing nonprofit organizations that issue securities.

In a leading case, the federal Securities and Exchange Commission brought an action in federal court seeking to enjoin a church and its leader from violating the antifraud provisions of the Securities Act of 1933.[11] The church had solicited funds through investment plans consisting essentially of the sale of interest-bearing notes to the general public. The notes were promoted through advertising literature extolling the security of the investment. For example, one advertisement stated in part:

> You may be a Christian who has committed his life into the hands of God, but left his funds in the hands of a floundering world economy. Financial experts everywhere are predicting a disaster in the economy. They say it is only a matter of time. . . . God's economy does not sink when the world's economy hits a reef and submerges! Wouldn't it be wise to invest in His economy?

The Securities and Exchange Commission argued that the church had defrauded investors by such representations when in fact it had a substantially increasing operating deficit that had jumped from $42,349 to $203,776 in the preceding three years. This fact was not disclosed to investors.

The church argued that religious organizations are protected by the first amendment from the reach of securities laws. In rejecting this contention, the court observed: "Defendants constantly emphasize that they are engaged in 'God's work.' No court has ever found that conduct, by being so described, is automatically immunized from all regulation in the public interest."[12] The court quoted with approval the United States Supreme Court's earlier observation that "[n]othing we have said is intended even remotely to imply that, under the cloak of religion, persons may, with impunity, commit frauds upon the public."[13] The court found it irrelevant that investors had a "religious" motivation, that most

---

[11] Securities and Exchange Commission v. World Radio Mission, Inc., 544 F.2d 535 (1st Cir. 1976).

[12] *Id.* at 539 n.7.

[13] *Id.* at 537 n.3, quoting Cantwell v. Connecticut, 310 U.S. 296, 306 (1940). The court was "surprised . . . by defendants' recitation of the parable of the servants entrusted with their master's talents. We do not question the parable, but insofar as it indicates a duty to make loans, it

investors were "believers," and that the church did not intend to defraud or deceive anyone.

A number of churches and other religious organizations have been investigated by the federal Securities and Exchange Commission and by state securities commissions. In most cases, the investigation was prompted by the complaint of an investor.

29.5 Consequences of Violating Securities Law

Churches that violate state securities laws face a variety of potential consequences under state and federal securities laws. These include investigations, hearings, subpoenas, injunctions, criminal actions, cancellation of sales, suits for monetary damages by aggrieved investors, monetary fines, and revocation of an exemption, or registration, of securities.

> *Key point. It is important to recognize that "good faith" (a lack of an intention to deceive, or lack of knowledge that a particular transaction is either fraudulent or otherwise in violation of securities law) does not necessarily protect against liability. To illustrate, some courts have ruled that the sale of unregistered securities in violation of state securities law is punishable despite the innocent intentions of the seller.[14] However, civil lawsuits by investors alleging fraud in the sale of securities must demonstrate an actual intent to deceive or defraud.[15]*

29.6 Examples

The following examples illustrate the application of securities law to church practices.

> *Example. A church issues $200,000 in 10-year promissory notes to its members and spends all of the proceeds on a new education building. The failure to establish a "sinking fund" out of part of the proceeds received from the sale of these securities, and out of which the securities will be repaid at maturity, constitutes securities fraud. This is a good example of how churches can unwittingly engage in securities fraud.*

> *Example. A church issues 10-year, 10 percent promissory notes to several of its members. No prospectus, offering circular, or other literature is filed with the state securities commission or made available to investors. The failure to provide prospective investors with a prospectus (also called an "offering circular") constitutes securities fraud. Once again, this illustrates how churches can innocently commit securities fraud.*

---

is to make profitable ones. A servant contemplating lending to a possibly shaky enterprise would do well to note the final verse." *Id.* at 538 n.6.

[14] Moerman v. Zipco, Inc., 302 F. Supp. 439 (E.D.N.Y. 1969), *aff'd*, 422 F.2d 871 (2nd Cir. 1970); Trump v. Badet, 327 P.2d 1001 (Ariz. 1958).

[15] The United States Supreme Court so held in Ernst & Ernst v. Hochfelder, 425 U.S. 185 (1976). While the *Ernst* decision dealt only with proof of an intent to deceive under the antifraud provisions of federal securities law, the decision has been held to apply by implication to private actions under the antifraud provisions of state securities laws. *See, e.g.*, Greenfield v. Cheek, 593 P.2d 293 (Ariz. 1978).

Example. A church plans to issue $300,000 in promissory notes. It composes a prospectus describing much of the financial background of the church. The prospectus also contains the following four statements: (1) "The membership of the church has increased during each of the past ten years, so it can be expected that membership growth will continue to occur." (2) "These securities have been exempted from registration by the state securities commission and thus you are assured that they have been carefully studied and approved by the state." (3) "A copy of this prospectus shall at all times be maintained in the church office for the benefit of any prospective investor." (4) "Interest on these obligations is guaranteed." Each of these statements may constitute securities fraud.

Example. A church decides not to include the following information in its prospectus out of a concern that this information might make the church's securities less attractive: (1) A lawsuit is pending against the church alleging malpractice on the part of the pastor. (2) The total dollar value of securities to be offered. (3) A statement that no sinking fund reserve exists. (4) A statement that for two of the past five years the church's expenses exceeded revenues. Omitting any of this information from the church's prospectus may constitute securities fraud.

Example. A church finance company failed to comply with the provisions of the Indiana Securities Act regarding the registration of securities prior to the offering and sale of certain securities to Indiana residents. As a result, the company and state securities commission entered into a settlement agreement which required the company to pay a fine and make rescission offers to all Indiana residents who purchased unregistered, non-exempt securities.[16]

Example. In 1992, the Michigan Corporations and Securities Bureau revoked the exemptions of a denominational church loan fund, and ordered it to discontinue the sale of any securities, because of the offer and sale of unregistered, nonexempt securities from 1987 though 1991 in violation of state securities law. In 1993, the loan fund registered $10 million in securities. Following the expiration of this registration in 1994, the loan fund sold more than $1.3 million in unregistered, nonexempt securities to 95 Michigan residents. Because of this second violation of state securities law, the Bureau took the following steps: (1) It revoked and denied the availability of any exemption for the loan fund's securities for a period of five years. All securities issued during that five-year period would have to be registered under state law. (2) The Bureau ordered the loan fund to give written notice to its investors that they may have certain rights to have their money refunded because of the loan fund's violations of state securities law. (3) The Bureau ordered the loan fund to "retain an experienced securities attorney" before any future attempt to register its securities.[17]

Example. A church engaged in a chain distributor scheme of marketing ministerial credentials was found guilty of a fraudulent practice.[18] The church, whose archbishop

---

[16] In the Matter of Church Extension Plan (Lifeline Extension Pool), 1997 WL 2449 (Ind. Div. Sec. 1997).

[17] In the Matter of the Missions and Church Extension Trust Fund, 1996 WL 173463 (Mich. Corp. Sec. Bureau 1996). *See also* In re Lutheran Association for Church Extension, Inc., 1993 WL 304762 (Fla. Dept. Banking and Finance 1993).

[18] People v. Life Science Church, 450 N.Y.S.2d 664 (1982).

was an attorney who had been disbarred for tax fraud in connection with the activities of the church, encouraged persons to become members by purchasing ministerial credentials for $3,500. Once the fee was paid, the new minister would name and establish his own church chartered by the parent church. He could then either make donations to his "church" or take a vow of poverty placing all his property in the name of his church and then pay all personal and family expenses through the church's account, thereby avoiding all taxes. Each minister was given the right to act as a "missionary representative" and was entitled to a 10 percent commission for each new member he recruited into the church. After recruiting two fully paid members in one month, the missionary representative was granted advancement to the "missionary supervisor" level and thereby became eligible to receive a special bonus of $500 for each new fully paid minister recruited. After the missionary supervisor level, one could become a "director" and receive a 40 percent commission. Ministers were enticed through a demonstration of number doubling. Two became four, eight became sixteen, thirty-two became sixty-four, and commissions mounted from $350 to a total of $1,023,500 when 2,047 new recruits were added. A chart was prepared to give dramatic visual impact on how to become a millionaire. A court summarily concluded that such a scheme was fraudulent, and that application of state securities law to the church did not violate the first amendment.

Example. A securities dealer offered for sale and sold securities in a local church's mortgage bond investment program. The offering materials for such securities contained a letter which indicated that the bonds were "A" rated when, in fact, they had not received any independent rating. The Texas securities commission determined that this representation was misleading, and it ordered the dealer to discontinue any further references to "ratings" unless it obtained an independent rating from a recognized securities rating agency. It also ordered the dealer to pay a fine, and make "rescission offers" to all persons who invested in any securities accompanied by materials containing the misleading representation. A rescission offer is an offer by an issuer of securities to an investor, offering to buy back the investor's securities.[19]

Example. The Virginia Division of Securities investigated a church's securities program, and concluded that the church violated state securities law by selling unregistered securities in the form of bonds called "Certificates of Faith," and using unregistered agents in the sale of the securities. The church entered into a settlement offer with the Division, which required it to make a rescission offer to all bondholders including an explanation for the reason for the rescission offer. The church also agreed to offer only securities that are registered under the Virginia Securities Act or are exempted from registration, and to offer and sell such securities only through agents who are registered under the Virginia Securities Act or who are exempted from registration.[20]

Example. A state corporation commission launched an investigation into a church's bond program as a result of the following allegations: (1) the church's prospectus omitted disclosure of defaults by the church on bonds it issued in 1984 and 1987; (2) the financial statements included with the church's prospectus failed to properly

---

[19] In the Matter of California Plan of Church Finance, Inc., 1997 WL 403287 (Tex. State Securities Board 1998).
[20] Commonwealth of Virginia v. Unity Christ Church, 1996 WL 392586 (Va. Corp. Com. 1996).

reflect the total accrued interest on outstanding bonds; and (3) the prospectus issued to investors falsely represented that the church was current in its sinking fund payments for prior bond offerings. The commission entered into a settlement with the church which contained a number of terms, including the following: (1) payment of a fine; (2) an assurance that the church would not engage in any further practices in violation of state securities law; (3) an audit of the church's financial records; (4) the formulation of a financial plan by which all holders of outstanding bonds will be paid full principal and interest in accordance with the terms of their bond agreements; and (5) distribute to all bondholders a disclosure document, approved by the commission, disclosing all previous omissions, the church's current financial status, and its plan for the full repayment of all outstanding bonds.[21]

Summary

There are many options available to churches that need to raise funds for capital improvements or other purposes. Church leaders must recognize that the issuance or sale of securities as a means of raising funds presents legal risks that can expose the church to substantial liability. In many cases, churches that issue securities encourage members to invest their retirement savings and other resources in the church project. This can result in financial hardship, hard feelings, and lawsuits if the church for any reason encounters difficulty in meeting its legal obligation to repay the securities with interest at maturity. It is often the very members whose securities are dishonored who contact the state securities commission for help. This may result in an investigation that in many cases will reveal noncompliance on the part of the church with state securities law.

Church leaders should not even consider the use of securities to raise funds without taking the following precautions:

1. *Legal counsel.* The most important precaution that church leaders can take is to retain an attorney who specializes in securities law, and who has experience in working with nonprofit organizations. Such a person can be invaluable in helping a church to avoid inadvertent violation of state and federal securities law.

2. *State registration requirements.* Determine whether or not your state requires church-issued securities, and persons who offer or sell such securities, to be registered. Your attorney will know the answer to this question, and will assist you in complying with any registration requirements that may apply. Many church leaders erroneously assume that churches are "exempted" from securities regulation. Nothing could be further from the truth. Church securities are not exempt from registration in some states, and many states do not exempt clergy or church board members who offer or sell church securities from the "salesperson" registration requirements.

3. *Be familiar with the concept of securities fraud.* One of the most important precautions that church leaders can take is to be familiar with the

[21] Commonwealth of Virginia v. Zion Apostolic Christian Memorial Church, 1998 WL 514271 (Va. Corp. Com. 1998).

definition of securities fraud. Churches are not exempt in any state from the prohibition of fraud in the offer or sale of securities. This fact, coupled with the expansive definition of "fraud" in state securities laws, can quickly lead to inadvertent liability. The materials in this chapter will be helpful in understanding the concept of securities fraud. Your attorney can amplify upon this information.

4. *Consider other forms of fundraising.* Other means of raising funds should be seriously considered. Churches that issue securities to raise funds because they do not qualify for conventional financing often find themselves in violation of securities law.

In the next chapter we examine premises liability.

CHAPTER 30. PREMISES LIABILITY

30.1 In General

Persons can be injured on church premises in a number of ways. Many parishioners have slipped on icy sidewalks or parking lots, fallen down stairs, tripped on wet floors, walked through plate glass windows, or been assaulted on church parking lots. Many churches allow outside groups to use their premises, and it is not uncommon for injuries to occur during such activities. What is a church's liability in such cases?

30.2 Liability Based on Status as Invitee, Licensee, or Trespasser

In most states, the liability of a church for injuries caused on its premises depends upon the status of the victim, since the degree of care which a church must exercise in safeguarding and inspecting its premises depends entirely upon the status of the victim. Most courts hold that a person may be on another's property as an *invitee*, a *licensee*, or a *trespasser*. An *invitee* may be either a public invitee or a business visitor. Section 332 of the *Restatement (Second) of Torts*, which has been adopted in many states, specifies that:

(a) An invitee is either a public invitee or a business visitor.

(b) A public invitee is a person who is invited to enter or remain on land as a member of the public for a purpose for which the land is held open to the public.

(c) A business visitor is a person who is invited to enter or remain on land for a purpose directly or indirectly connected with business dealings with the possessor of the land.

Landowners owe the greatest duty of care to *invitees*, since invitees by definition are on a landowner's property because of an express or implied invitation. Most courts hold that landowners owe invitees a duty to use reasonable and ordinary care to keep their premises safe, including the responsibility of correcting those concealed hazards of which they know or reasonably should know, or at least warning invitees of such hazards. Even so, a landowner is not a guarantor of the safety of invitees. So long as a landowner exercises reasonable care in making the premises safe for invitees or if adequate warning is given about concealed perils, a landowner will not be responsible for injuries that occur. Many courts have refused to hold landowners responsible for an invitee's injuries caused by an obvious hazard or by a concealed hazard of which the invitee was aware. Some courts have concluded that church members attending church services or activities are invitees because they satisfy the definition of *public invitee*. For example, one court concluded that a church member who was injured when she tripped and fell over a wooden cross that had been used in a skit presented at a church meeting was a public invitee since she had been invited to enter the premises as a member of the public for a purpose for which the property was held open to the public.[1]

---

[1] Stevens v. Bow Mills Methodist Church, 283 A.2d 488 (N.H. 1971). *See also* Hedglin v. Church of St. Paul, 158 N.W.2d 269 (Minn. 1968).

A *licensee* generally is defined as one who is privileged to enter or remain on property because of the owner's express or implied consent. It is often said that invitees enter one's property by invitation, either express or implied, and that licensees are not invited but their presence is tolerated or merely permitted. In most states a landowner is responsible for warning licensees of hidden dangers of which the landowner is actually aware and to refrain from willfully or wantonly injuring them or recklessly exposing them to danger. The landowner has no duty to protect a licensee against hidden dangers of which the landowner is unaware. Thus, landowners are under no duty to make their premises safe for licensees by inspecting for and correcting hidden conditions that may cause injury.

A *trespasser* is a person who enters another's property without invitation or consent. In general, a landowner owes no duty to an undisclosed trespasser, and thus trespassers have no legal remedy if they are injured by a dangerous condition on another's property.[2] However, landowners who are reasonably apprised of the presence of trespassers ordinarily must refrain from willfully or wantonly injuring them, and, according to some courts, must warn them of concealed hazards of which the owner is actually aware.[3]

A few states in recent years have abandoned the prevailing view of assessing a landowner's liability for injuries occurring on his premises by focusing on the status of the victim. These states have substituted a simple standard of reasonable care that a landowner owes to all lawful visitors. In determining a landowner's liability, the status of a victim is still relevant but not controlling. For example, the fact that an injured victim was a trespasser will reduce the landowner's duty of care since a reasonable person would not take the same steps to ensure the safety of trespassers that he would for invitees.

The great majority of cases involving accidents on church property have determined the church's liability on the basis of the status of the victim. Often, an accident victim's recovery of monetary damages against the church depends on his or her characterization as an invitee by a court, since this status creates the highest duty of care on the part of the church. If the victim is deemed to be a mere licensee, then often any monetary recovery is precluded. Many courts have concluded that accident victims are invitees of a church.

30.3 Cases Recognizing Invitee Status

A number of courts have ruled that members and certain other persons who are injured on church property are entitled to recover damages because of their status as invitees.

> **Example.** *An Indiana appeals court concluded that a member who tripped over a plastic runner covering an aisle in a synagogue was an invitee rather than a licensee, and accordingly that the synagogue was legally responsible for his injuries. The court concluded that persons who are invited to enter upon premises for a purpose*

---

[2] Adams v. Atlanta Faith Memorial Church, 381 S.E.2d 397 (Ga. 1989); Richards v. Cincinnati West Baptist Church, 680 N.E.2d 191 (Ohio App. 1996).

[3] *See, e.g.,* Reider v. city of Spring Lake Park, 480 N.E.2d 662 (Minn. App. 1992) (a church has a duty to warn trespassers of danger on its property if trespassers regularly use portions of the property).

for which the premises are held open to the public or for business dealings with the owner of the premises are invitees who may recover for such injuries. The court concluded that members who attend activities at a church or synagogue are invitees under this test, since they are invited to enter the premises for the purposes for which they are held open to the public. Accordingly, a church or synagogue has a duty to protect them against negligent conditions on the premises, including improperly maintained aisle runners.[4]

Example. The Iowa Supreme Court ruled that the president of a state organization of church women who was injured when she fell down a darkened church stairway was an invitee of the church because she had been invited to appear and preside over a women's meeting, and her presence was of mutual benefit to herself and the church. Since she was an invitee, the court concluded that the church owed her a duty to exercise ordinary care to keep the premises in reasonably safe condition and that this duty had been breached.[5]

Example. The Mississippi Supreme Court ruled that a church and its board of trustees could be sued by a member who was injured when she slipped and fell on a waxed floor while leaving a Sunday school class. The member argued that she was an invitee and accordingly that the church had a duty "to exercise reasonable care to keep the premises in a reasonably safe condition and, if the [church] knows of, or by the exercise of reasonable care should have known of, a dangerous condition, which is not readily apparent to the invitee, the [church] is under a duty to warn the invitee of such condition." The member claimed that the church breached this duty of care. On the other hand, the church maintained that the member was merely a licensee to whom it owed a minimal duty of refraining from willfully and wantonly injuring her through active negligence. The state supreme court ruled that the member was an invitee at the time of her injury: "Members of religious associations, in general . . . fall within the category of public invitees. Religious bodies do expressly and impliedly invite members to come and attend their services and functions. They hold their doors open to the public. While they do not charge admission fees . . . churches do depend on contributions . . . in order that they may continue to be open to the public. Therefore, a church member who does not exceed the scope of the church's invitation, is an invitee while attending a church for church services or related functions." As a result, the member who slipped and fell on the waxed floor was an invitee to whom the church owed a high degree of care, rather than a mere licensee to whom the church owed only a minimal duty of care.[6]

Example. The Missouri Supreme Court ruled that a woman who was injured when she slipped and fell on a freshly waxed floor inside a church while on a tour at the invitation of her son was an invitee to whom the church was liable because of its failure to remedy the dangerous condition. The church's contention that the victim was not an invitee because the church received no benefit from her presence was rejected by the court: "Not only was she welcome, but her status as a potential member and future contributor provided a benefit to the church in an economic sense. That benefit so derived is not speculative but is comparable to, and no less than, that where the

---

[4] Fleischer v. Hebrew Orthodox Congregation, 504 N.E.2d 320 (Ind. App. 1987).
[5] Sullivan v. First Presbyterian Church, 152 N.W.2d 628 (Iowa 1967).
[6] Clark v. Moore Memorial United Methodist Church, 538 So.2d 760 (Miss. 1989). *Accord* Heath v. First Baptist Church, 341 So.2d 265 (Fla.App.1977), *cert. denied*, 348 So.2d 946 (Fla.1977).

customer shops but does not buy. This was sufficient to give her all the required attributes of an invitee."[7]

Example. *The New Jersey Supreme Court rejected a church's claim that a Sunday school teacher who was injured when she slipped and fell on an icy sidewalk in front of the church was not entitled to recovery as an invitee since she was a mere social guest. The court acknowledged that those who enter another's property as guests, whether for benevolent or social reasons, are licensees to whom the landowner owes a very minimal duty of care. The court concluded that the operation of a church is more than a mere social gathering: "To very many people it concerns a business of extreme moment, however unworldly." The court also insisted that the injured teacher's presence on church property was primarily for the benefit of the church, for "despite the voluntary and unrecompensed status of the plaintiff, she entered these premises as a matter of duty to the [church], and for the furtherance of the important interest, albeit a spiritual one, of the church, as distinguished from her own." The court accordingly held that the teacher was a business invitee to whom the church had breached its duty of reasonable care.[8]*

Example. *The Washington state supreme court concluded that a church member who was injured in a fall from a negligently assembled scaffolding while donating his labor in the construction of a church building was an invitee of the church since the business or purpose for which he had entered the premises was of economic benefit to the church. Accordingly, the church was found liable for breaching its duty of exercising reasonable care to render its premises safe from, or at least warn of, dangerous conditions of which the church knew or could discover with reasonable diligence.[9]*

30.4 Cases Recognizing Licensee Status

In other cases, courts have concluded that a particular accident victim was present on church premises as a licensee. In most cases, a finding that an accident victim is a licensee will insulate the church from liability, since the only duty that a church owes to a licensee in most states is the duty to refrain from injuring a licensee willfully or wantonly and to exercise ordinary care to avoid imperiling the licensee by any active conduct. In some states, a church also owes a licensee a duty to correct concealed hazards of which it is actually aware or at least to warn a licensee of such hazards. But a church does not owe a licensee a duty to exercise reasonable care in maintaining church premises in a reasonably safe condition, and it does not have a duty to make inspections for dangerous conditions. This latter duty is owed only to invitees.

To illustrate, courts have found the following persons to be licensees and as a result have denied a legal remedy for injuries suffered on church premises: a member of an industrial basketball league that played its games in a church gymnasium;[10] a five-year-old girl who was visiting a church at which her grandmother was employed;[11] a church member who was injured while walking across a church

---

[7] Claridge v. Watson Terrace Christian Church, 457 S.W.2d 785 (Mo. 1970).
[8] Atwood v. Board of Trustees, 98 A.2d 348 (N.J. 1953).
[9] Haugen v. Central Lutheran Church, 361 P.2d 637 (Wash. 1961).
[10] Turpin v. Our Lady of Mercy Catholic Church, 202 S.E.2d 351 (N.C. 1974).
[11] Lemon v. Busey, 461 P.2d 145 (Kan. 1969).

lawn seeking entrance into a church to light a candle for her daughter;[12] a policeman who was investigating a complaint that a church was being broken into;[13] and a child who was burned by a fire while playing on church property.[14]

> *Example. The Alabama Supreme Court ruled that a church was not responsible for injuries sustained by a visiting choir member who slipped and fell on church premises. The court based its decision on the status of the choir member while present as a guest on the other church's property. It concluded that a person attending a church service is a licensee while on the church premises, and not an invitee. It noted that a choir member visiting another church to participate in a special service is not an invitee since the person's presence does not provide a "material benefit" to the other church. It further observed that special church services are common, and that guests who participate in such services are "in much the same position as social guests enjoying unrecompensed hospitality in a private home by invitation." As such, they are licensees. The court concluded that the church did not breach any duty it owed to the choir member as a licensee, since it did not willfully or wantonly injure her, and it was not aware of any condition of the floor that would cause an injury.[15]*

30.5 Trespassing Children

It is common for neighborhood children to play on church property. This may include skateboarding, bicycling, use of motorized recreational vehicles, basketball, baseball, or several other activities. Some of these activities expose minors to a significant risk of harm. Is the church legally responsible for injuries that may result? The answer depends on whether the victim entered onto church property because of an "artificial condition."

Injuries caused by an artificial condition

If a minor is injured because of an artificial condition on church property, then the church's potential liability is described in section 339 of the *Restatement (Second) of Torts*, a respected legal treatise that is recognized in most states:

> A possessor of land is subject to liability for physical harm to children trespassing thereon caused by an artificial condition upon the land if:
>
> (a) the place where the condition exists is one upon which the possessor knows or has reason to know that children are likely to trespass, and
>
> (b) the condition is one of which the possessor knows or has reason to know and which he realizes or should realize will involve an unreasonable risk of death or serious bodily harm to such children, and
>
> (c) the children because of their youth do not discover the condition or realize the risk involved in intermeddling with it or in coming within the area made dangerous by it, and

---

[12] Coolbaugh v. St. Peter's Roman Catholic Church, 115 A.2d 662 (Conn. 1955).
[13] Scheurer v. Trustees of Open Bible Church, 192 N.E.2d 38 (Ohio 1963).
[14] Wozniczka v. McKean, 247 N.E.2d 215 (Ind. 1969).
[15] Hambright v. First Baptist Church, 638 So.2d 865 (Ala. 1994). *Accord* Prentiss v. Evergreen Presbyterian Church, 644 So.2d 475 (Ala. 1994); Davidson v. Highlands Church, 673 So.2d 765 (Ala. App. 1995).

(d) the utility to the possessor of maintaining the condition and the burden of eliminating the danger are slight as compared with the risk to children involved, and

(e) the possessor fails to exercise reasonable care to eliminate the danger or otherwise to protect the children.

An artificial condition is any condition that does not naturally exist. For example, the following conditions would be artificial: a basketball court, swimming pool, parking lot, or playground equipment.

Example. *A New Jersey court ruled that a church may be liable for injuries sustained by a neighborhood child while playing on church premises. A church was located on a large lot without a fence.[16] The lot contained a low point where rain water accumulated. One day it rained quite heavily and a deep pond-like puddle formed in the low area. A 3-year-old child who lived across the street often played on the church's property. She looked out the window of her home and noticed her tricycle on the church's property and wanted to bring it out of the rain. Her mother (the "victim") instructed the little girl to stay in the house and told her that she would retrieve the tricycle. The mother crossed the street to get the tricycle and noticed the large pond-like puddle that had accumulated on the church's property as a result of the rain. The tricycle was on the other side of puddle and the mother began walking around the puddle to retrieve it. Suddenly, she heard her little girl behind her saying that she would get the tricycle. The mother instantly realized that her daughter had walked into the large puddle and was in the middle of it. The mother was fearful that due to the young age of the child and given the depth of the water that the child was in danger. She immediately walked towards the child, but before she could reach her, she slipped in the mud under the water, fracturing her leg. The mother sued the church. A state appeals court concluded that the church could be sued for the mother's injuries. It quoted the general rule from section 339 of the Restatement (Second) of Torts, and concluded that each of these conditions was met. First, the pastor knew that children played on the church's property. Second, the pastor was aware of the accumulation of water on the property after a heavy rain, and the risk this posed to small children. Third, the pastor should have realized that the flooding condition on the property created an unreasonable risk of serious harm to young children. Fourth, the burden of eliminating the danger was slight compared with the risk to children. The pastor testified that the cost of installing a fence to keep children from walking in the area was approximately $2,000. The court pointed out that the church in fact did install a fence following the incident. Fifth, the church failed to exercise reasonable care to eliminate the danger or otherwise to protect the children. At the time of the incident, "the church had taken no steps to remove the condition or to warn children of the danger." The court noted that the Restatement addresses liability of property owners associated with injuries to children caused by artificial conditions on their property. It concluded that the "ponding effect" was an artificial condition: "The church buildings and the parking lot had been constructed on the property. The engineer testified that rain water from portions of the roof and from the stone driveway area contributed to the accumulation of water in the low area. The church building, with the resulting flow of rain water from the roof and the stoned parking lot were not natural conditions of the land, but instead were artificial conditions contributing to*

---

16 Blackburn v. Broad Street Church, 702 A.2d 1331 (N.J. Super. 1998).

the accumulation of rain water on the property." The court concluded that if a church owes a duty of care to a trespassing child under the Restatement analysis summarized above, it also owes a duty of care to an adult rescuer. As a result, the church could be responsible for the mother's injuries incurred while attempting to save her child from the dangerous condition on the property.

Injuries not caused by an artificial condition

Churches owe a minimal degree of care to trespassing children who are injured due to a natural condition (such as a tree or naturally occurring pond or lake). In general, the church must refrain from wantonly or willfully injuring such children.

> **Example.** *An Ohio court ruled that a church was not responsible for injuries sustained by a minor who was injured while trespassing on church property.[17] A church owned a "water drenching machine" that was used at various church activities. The machine was designed to be connected to a hose, and anyone who hit a lever on the machine with a ball caused an individual in the machine to be drenched with water. When not in use, the church stored the machine against a wall in the back of the church. A "no trespassing" sign was posted by the church. In addition, neighborhood children were not permitted to play on church premises during the week. The pastor and his wife frequently chased uninvited children off the property. One day a 6-year-old boy entered the church's premises, walked around to the back of the church, and crawled onto the machine. He was injured when it fell on him. The boy's parents sued the church. They claimed that they were not aware that neighbor children were not allowed to play on church property, although they did acknowledge that they were aware of the "no trespassing" sign. A state appeals court ruled in favor of the church. It noted that the boy was a trespasser, and that a property owner's only duty with respect to a trespasser is to "refrain from wantonly or willfully injuring him." The parents admitted that the church had not acted wantonly or willfully, but they insisted that the church was liable for their son's injuries on the basis of the "dangerous instrumentality" rule. Under this rule, a property owner has a higher duty of care to a child trespasser when it operates hazardous equipment "the dangerousness of which is not readily apparent to children, on or immediately adjacent to a public place." The court concluded that this exception did not apply in this case, since the machine was not "on or immediately adjacent to a public place." To the contrary, the machine was "private property, behind the church building and up against a wall. It was not within easy reach of a child in a public area."*

30.6 Use of Church Property by Outside Groups

Churches often let outside groups use their premises. Examples include scout troops, preschools, aerobics classes, substance abuse groups, childbirth classes, and music classes. Can a church be legally responsible for injuries occurring on its premises while being used by such groups? Possibly.

> **Example.** *An Indiana court ruled that a church was liable for an injury occurring on its premises while being used by an outside group. A church permitted a local community group to use its facilities for an annual one-day celebration. The event was advertised in the church bulletin, and included a religious ceremony. After the ceremony, guests were ushered into another room for a reception where refreshments*

---

[17] Richards v. Cincinnati West Baptist Church, 680 N.E.2d 191 (Ohio App. 1996).

were served. While refreshments were being served, volunteers disassembled the tables and chairs in the room where the ceremony occurred. Although the guests were asked to proceed to the reception immediately following the ceremony, a few guests remained behind to socialize. As one of these guests proceeded to the reception area a few minutes later, she tripped and fell over some of the disassembled tables. She later sued the church. The church claimed that it was not responsible for the guest's injuries since it had not retained any control over its facilities while they were being used by the community group for its celebration. The church also pointed out that the group was permitted to use the facilities without charge, that it was responsible for cleaning up the facilities following its activities, and that the church did not retain any control over the facilities during the celebration. A state appeals court noted that "the church is correct in observing that control of the premises is the basis of premises liability." However, the court concluded that there was ample evidence of control by the church. It observed: "[The priest] testified . . . that if he chose to do so, he could have decided not to allow the [community group] to hold their function there; that there was a janitor on the premises to make sure the buildings were locked; that the [organization] was not in charge of securing the premises; that the church placed an announcement in the church bulletin regarding when and where the celebration was to take place; that the church conducted a religious ceremony as a part of the celebration; and that he would not say that the church relinquished control over the property. This testimony was enough to create an issue of fact as to whether the church retained control over the premises."[18]

Example. *A charity permitted an outside group to use its facility for a Christmas party. During the party, a woman suffered serious injuries when she fell on a slippery floor. As a result of her injuries the woman underwent surgery for a complete hip replacement. She later sued the charity, claiming that it was responsible for her injuries because it had retained control over the premises during the party. She claimed that the floor was unreasonably slippery, and this dangerous condition caused her to fall. One witness testified, "It was obvious that floor was slippery. It was just waxed or something. I mean it wasn't dirty. It was clean. Probably too clean." The charity asked the court to dismiss the case, but its request was denied. On appeal, a state appeals court suggested that there was sufficient evidence that the charity retained control over its premises during the party to send the case to a jury. The court began its opinion by acknowledging that a property owner may be legally responsible for injuries that occur on its premises when they are under its custody or control. The court suggested that the charity had retained control over its premises during the Christmas party on the basis of the following factors: (1) the charity was responsible for setting up tables for the party; (2) the charity provided a custodian during the entire party; and (3) the charity was responsible for opening the premises at the beginning of the party and locking the premises at the conclusion of the party. The charity's custodian admitted that he had cleaned the floor prior to the party and that he was on duty and responsible for cleaning the floor during the party.[19]*

---

[18] St. Casimer Church v. Frankiewics, 563 N.E.2d 1331 (Ind. App. 1990).

[19] Aufrichtig v. Progressive Men's Club, 634 So.2d 947 (La. App. 2 Cir. 1994).

30.7 Assaults in Church Parking Lots

Some persons have been assaulted in church parking lots. To illustrate, a member is assaulted and robbed while walking to her car in a church parking lot after leaving an evening function. Is the church liable for such injuries?

Example. A female college student (the victim) worked as a summer waitress in a local restaurant. One evening she left work and walked to the far end of the parking lot where her car was parked. A busboy accompanied her part of the way, but returned to the restaurant when they were in the vicinity of the car. The victim entered her car, started the engine, rolled down her window, and waited several seconds for the engine to "warm up" (the car had been experiencing engine problems). As she waited, an assailant reached through the open window, unlocked the door, and forced his way into the car. The assailant punched the victim in the face and drove off while holding her in a "headlock." He drove to a nearby cornfield, raped her, tied her with jumper cables, and then fled with her car keys. The victim managed to free herself and run to a nearby farmhouse where she called for help. She later sued her employer, claiming that it was responsible for her injuries because of its failure to provide adequate security and lighting in its parking lot. A jury agreed, and awarded her $600,000 in damages. The employer appealed this verdict, and the state supreme court upheld the award. The court noted that other waitresses had complained to the restaurant's owner about the inadequate lighting in the parking lot. It also noted that 14 minor property crimes (mostly vandalism) had occurred on the parking lot in the 4 years preceding the assault. Under these circumstances, the court concluded that it was appropriate to find the employer responsible for the victim's injuries on the basis of negligence.[20]

Example. A South Carolina court ruled that a church was not liable for injuries sustained by a person when he was attacked on church property.[21] A church owned an apartment complex that is used as low income housing. Despite the fact that the apartment building was in a high-crime area, and church leaders were aware of numerous incidents of criminal behavior occurring within the building, the church did not provide a security guard. A man (the "victim") was injured when he was attacked while visiting a friend in the apartment building. The victim sued the church, claiming that it was responsible for his injuries on the basis of negligence. A state appeals court disagreed. The court observed: "A [property] owner has a duty to take reasonable care to protect invitees. However, this duty does not extend to protection from criminal attacks from third persons unless the owner knew or had reason to know the criminal attack would occur. . . . In this case [the victim and his mother] stated they knew of criminal activity that had occurred at [the apartment building] in the past, including an alleged shooting. In addition [the victim] asserted he knew [his attacker] was a violent person and that he had seen [him] involved in other fights at the complex. However, there is no evidence in the record that [the church] was aware of [the attacker's] previous fights or of any incident that day that would put management on notice the attack [on the victim] might occur. Therefore [the church] had no duty to protect [the victim] from an intentional attack."

---

[20] Koutoufaris v. Dick, 604 A.2d 390 (Del. 1992).
[21] Goode v. St. Stephens United Methodist Church, 494 S.E.2d 827 (S.C. 1998).

30.8 Reducing the Risk of Assaults on Church Property

Unfortunately, church members occasionally are assaulted on church property. Some members have been assaulted on church parking lots while walking toward their car at night after a service or event at their church. A church may be responsible for such assaults if it was aware of previous assaults on its premises, or in the immediate area. Church leaders should recognize that their church is exposed to a much higher degree of care for the protection of members and visitors if one or more assaults has occurred on church premises or in the immediate vicinity of the church. However, the church can reduce its risk of liability by demonstrating that it used reasonable care in protecting against such attacks. How can a church do so? Churches have used some or all of the following measures:

- Provide adequate illumination of the parking lot.

- Designate "escorts" who will accompany persons to their car upon request. Be sure that this option is communicated to church members and visitors.

- Station volunteers in the parking lot.

- Install a wide-angle video camera on the church roof.

- Have a uniformed security guard, or off-duty police officer, monitor the parking lot. For more suggestions, church leaders should contact their insurance agent.

30.9 Defenses to Liability

Churches have been found innocent of wrongdoing in several cases regardless of the status of the person injured on their property because the condition or activity that caused the injury could not under any circumstances serve as a basis for legal liability. For example, the courts have held that a church is under no duty to illuminate its parking lot when no church activities are in process;[22] to remove oil and grease from its parking lot;[23] to place markings on a sliding glass door;[24] to begin removing snow from church stairways before the end of a snowstorm;[25] or to remove every square inch of snow and ice from its parking lot following a storm.[26] The parents of an infant whose eye was seriously injured in a church nursery during worship services were denied any recovery since no one witnessed the accident and there was no evidence that it was caused by any negligence on the part of the church.[27] Similarly, a church member doing volunteer work for his church was denied recovery for injuries sustained when a ladder fell on him. The court noted that the member was an invitee, and that the church owed him a legal duty to correct or give notice of concealed, dangerous conditions of which it was or should have been aware. However, the court denied recovery on the ground that the member was aware of the unsecured ladder and the danger it presented, and

---

[22] Huselton v. Underhill, 28 Cal. Rptr. 822 (1963).

[23] Goard v. Branscom, 189 S.E.2d 667 (N.C. 1972), *cert. denied*, 191 S.E.2d 354 (N.C. 1972).

[24] Sullivan v. Birmingham Fire Insurance Co., 185 So.2d 336 (La. 1966), *cert. denied*, 186 So.2d 632 (La. 1966).

[25] Hedglin v. Church of St. Paul, 158 N.W.2d 269 (Minn. 1968).

[26] Byrne v. Catholic Bishop, 266 N.E.2d 708 (Ill. 1971).

[27] Helton v. Forest Park Baptist Church, 589 S.W.2d 217 (Ky. App. 1979).

this knowledge excused the church from its duty of correcting the condition or notifying the member of its existence.[28]

One or more defenses may be available to a church that is sued by a person who is injured on church premises.

> *Example. The Florida Supreme Court held that a church member who was injured when she fell while walking in a dark hallway connecting the sanctuary with a social hall was precluded from suing the church by her own contributory negligence. The court observed that darkness is in itself sufficient warning to signal caution to one entering an unfamiliar situation, and that if one fails to heed the signal, he is guilty of contributory negligence.[29]*

> *Example. A Georgia court ruled that a church was not responsible for injuries suffered by a woman who slipped and fell on church property. The woman had taken her daughter up a wooden ramp to the entrance of a church school, and was injured when she slipped and fell on the way down. It was raining at the time of the accident, and the ramp was wet. Immediately after she fell the woman told the church's pastor that "it's not your fault . . . it was just raining and I was in a hurry and slipped and fell." The woman had slipped before on the same ramp, and was aware that it was slippery even under dry conditions. She later sued the church as a result of her injuries. A state appeals court, in upholding the trial court's dismissal of the lawsuit, observed: "Everyone knows that any wet surface may be slippery. [The woman] has slipped on the ramp when it was dry. She had knowledge of its danger equal and perhaps superior knowledge to [that of the church], and she fell either because she was hurrying or because she chose to negotiate the ramp despite the danger which was obvious to her. The mere fact that a dangerous condition exists, whether caused by a building code violation or otherwise, does not impose liability on the [property owner]."[30]*

> *Example. A Michigan court ruled that a church could be sued by the estate of an individual who was killed as a result of a defective ladder while performing work on church property. The decedent was engaged in performing repair and maintenance of a church building when he fell from a church-owned ladder and was killed. His estate sued the church, claiming that its negligence was the cause of the decedent's death. The court concluded that the decedent was an "invitee" on the church's premises. It noted that "an invitor must warn of hidden defects; there is no duty to warn of open and obvious dangers unless the [property owner] anticipates harm to the invitee despite the invitee's knowledge of the defect." The court concluded that "an extension ladder is an essentially uncomplicated instrument which gains a propensity for danger only because it will allow the user to reach great heights. This danger is most obvious to all but children of tender years . . . ." As a result, a church cannot be legally responsible for injuries suffered by workers who are injured when they fall from a ladder. However, the court cautioned that this rule did not necessarily apply in this case, since the estate of the decedent claimed that the decedent's fall was caused not by the general nature of the ladder itself but rather by a missing or malfunctioning safety latch. The court*

---

[28] Fisher v. Northmoor United Methodist Church, 679 S.W.2d 305 (Mo. App. 1984). *Contra* Coates v. W.W. Babcock Co., 560 N.E.2d 1099 (Ill. App. 1990).

[29] Trinity Episcopal Church v. Hoglund, 222 So.2d 781 (Fla. 1969).

[30] Patterson v. First Assembly of God, 440 S.E.2d 492 (Ga. App. 1994).

observed, "The real inquiry is whether this defect must be deemed an open and obvious danger. We think not. The danger that an extension ladder might slip and telescope down because of inadequate bracing at its base . . . is a danger readily apparent to persons of ordinary intelligence and experience. However, the fact that a safety latch is missing or malfunctioning creates a different, or at least an additional, danger that is not so obvious absent specific knowledge of the defect."[31]

Example. A Minnesota court concluded that a church member who slipped and fell on an icy stairway while leaving a church service was not entitled to recover damages from the church because her failure to use an available handrail made her contributorily negligent.[32]

Example. A Minnesota court concluded that a church was not responsible for injuries sustained by a member who tripped on a dark stairway. The court noted that "evidence of the church's negligence was minimal. [The member] did not establish that the lights were turned off by a person for whose negligence the church could be held vicariously liable."[33]

Example. A New York court dismissed a lawsuit brought against a church by a woman who was injured during a church-sponsored activity. The woman and her husband attended a "country fair and barbecue" sponsored by her church. Following dinner, the couple took a raft ride on a nearby lake. After the ride, they were directed to walk on a back lawn area to return to the front of the church building. As the woman walked up a sloping lawn around the outside of a large tree, she slipped and fell, injuring her leg. She claimed that she slipped on ice cubes that were on the ground. A state appeals court dismissed the case. The court concluded that "plaintiff was required to demonstrate . . . that the condition was caused by [the church's] agents or existed for a sufficient period of time to require [the church] to have corrected it." Since the woman offered no evidence that an agent of the church caused the ice to be discarded on the lawn, or that the ice had been on the lawn for an unreasonable amount of time without being corrected, the lawsuit had to be dismissed.[34]

Example. A New York court ruled that a church was not legally responsible for injuries sustained by a woman who slipped on a patch of ice in the church parking lot. The woman had attended a meeting of a local community group on the church's premises.

---

[31] Eason v. Coggins Memorial Christian Church, 532 N.W.2d 882 (Mich. App. 1995).

[32] Hedglin v. Church of St. Paul, 158 N.W.2d 269 (Minn. 1968). *But cf.* Davis v. Church of Jesus Christ of Latter Day Saints, 796 P.2d 181 (Mont. 1990). In the *Davis* case, the Montana Supreme Court upheld a jury's award of more than $400,000 to a young woman who was injured when she slipped and fell on an icy church sidewalk. The church argued that it was not responsible for "natural accumulations" of snow and ice and that it had no duty to warn of a danger that was clearly apparent to a reasonable person. The court concluded that "a property owner may be held liable for falls on accumulations of ice and snow where the hazard created by the natural accumulation is increased or a new hazard is created by an affirmative act of the property owner. Even where such a condition is actually known or obvious, a property owner may be held liable if he should have anticipated that injuries would result from the dangerous condition." The court concluded that the church janitor's act of shoveling the sidewalk without applying any salt left the sidewalk covered with a "sheen of ice" that constituted a new hazard different from the natural accumulation of snow and ice that existed previously. It was this hazard, along with the dangerous slope of the sidewalk (without a railing), that constituted negligence on the part of the church.

[33] Thies v. St. Paul's Evangelical Lutheran Church, 489 N.W.2d 277 (Minn. App. 1992).

[34] Torani v. First United Methodist Church, 558 N.Y.S.2d 272 (A.D. 3 Dept. 1990).

On her way to her car, she slipped and fell on a patch of snow-covered ice and sustained serious injuries. She sued the church. The court ruled that the church was not responsible for the accident, since it was not aware of the ice and snow accumulation (no church employees were present at the time of the meeting) and the church did not have a reasonable opportunity to remove the snow and ice. The icy condition developed only two hours before the accident, and the snow (that concealed the ice) began falling only 15 minutes prior to the accident. Under these circumstances the court concluded, "[The church] as the owner of the premises, had a duty to exercise reasonable care under the circumstances. In order to impose liability upon [the church] there must be evidence that it knew, or in the exercise of reasonable care should have known, that an icy condition existed in its parking lot. Additionally, a party in possession or control of property is afforded a reasonable time after the cessation of the storm or temperature fluctuation which created the dangerous condition to exercise due care in order to correct the situation." There simply was not sufficient time in this case for the church to have removed the snow or ice prior to the accident, and accordingly the church was not legally responsible for the woman's injuries.[35]

Example. A Pennsylvania court ruled that a Catholic church and diocese were not responsible for the injuries sustained by a woman who slipped and fell on an icy church parking lot. The woman, who was attending the church to participate in a bingo game, alleged that the parking lot was covered with a sheet of ice and also 5 inches of new snow. She alleged that the church had been negligent in failing to "implement some remedial measure (placing salt or ashes, warning visitors of the presence of ice, or barricading the icy area)," and accordingly the church was responsible for her injuries. A state appeals court ruled that the church was not responsible for the woman's injuries. It observed, "[A]n owner or occupier of land is not liable for general slippery conditions, for to require that one's walks be always free of ice and snow would be to impose an impossible burden in view of the climatic conditions in this hemisphere. Snow and ice upon a pavement create merely a transient danger, and the only duty upon the property owner or tenant is to act within a reasonable time after notice to remove it when it is in a dangerous condition. . . . [I]n order to recover for a fall on an ice or snow covered sidewalk, a plaintiff must prove (1) that snow and ice had accumulated on the sidewalk in ridges or elevations of such size and character as to unreasonably obstruct travel and constitute a danger to pedestrians traveling thereon; (2) that the property owner had notice, either actual or constructive, of the existence of such condition; (3) that it was the dangerous accumulation of snow and ice which caused the plaintiff to fall." The court concluded that the injured woman had failed to satisfy this test, and accordingly the church was not responsible for her injuries.[36]

Example. The Rhode Island Supreme Court ruled that a church was not responsible for the death of a parishioner who was killed when she was struck by a vehicle while

---

[35] Byrd v. Church of Christ, 597 N.Y.S.2d 211 (A.D. 3 Dept. 1993). *But see* Graff v. St. Luke's Evangelical Lutheran Church, 625 N.E.2d 851 (Ill. App. 1993), in which the court concluded that "there is generally no duty to remove natural accumulations of ice and snow" and that "[t]he mere removal of snow leaving a natural ice formation underneath does not constitute negligence." However, a church or other property owner can be legally responsible for injuries in at least two situations: (1) snow is removed in a negligent manner, or (2) "an injury occurred as the result of snow or ice produced or accumulated by artificial causes or in an unnatural way, or by the defendant's use of the premises."

[36] Harmotta v. Bender, 601 A.2d 837 (Pa. Super. 1992).

crossing a street to enter a parking lot. Three adult members of a Catholic church drive to the church to attend midnight mass on Christmas Eve. As was the practice of many parishioners, they parked their car in a small parking lot across the street from the church. The parking lot was owned by a neighboring commercial establishment, but church members were allowed to use the parking lot during church services by common consent. The parking lot was separated from the church by a public street. After mass ended, the three members left the church and proceeded to cross the street to reach their car in the parking lot. While in a crosswalk they were struck by a vehicle driven by a drunk driver. One of the members was killed, and another received severe and permanent injuries. On prior occasions the church had asked the city police to provide a traffic officer to control traffic after church services. The police occasionally provided officers in response to the church's requests if any were available. At no time did the church have a contract with the police to provide traffic officers. No representative of the church had asked the police to provide a traffic officer on the night of the accident. A lawsuit was brought against the church by the injured member and the estate of the member who was killed (the "plaintiffs"). The state supreme court dismissed the lawsuit on the ground that "the duty to control traffic has traditionally rested squarely with the government." Further, "[t]he fact that a landowner may request public traffic control on a public street does not vest in that landowner the personal right or obligation to control such a public way."[37]

Summary

Physical injuries occurring on church premises or in the course of church activities represent the most common basis of church liability. This chapter illustrates a number of ways that such injuries may arise, and the legal principles the courts apply in determining whether or not the church is legally responsible.

In most cases, the liability of a church for injuries occurring on its premises depends upon how a court defines the term *invitee*. As the cases in this chapter illustrate, there is some difference of opinion regarding the definition of this term. Clearly, however, those states that have adopted the *Restatement (Second) of Torts* definition of an invitee ordinarily will regard most participants in church activities and services to be invitees. The United States Supreme Court has observed:

> In an effort to do justice in an industrialized urban society, with its complex economic and individual relationships, modern common-law courts have found it necessary to formulate increasingly subtle verbal refinements, to create subclassifications among traditional common-law categories, and to delineate fine gradations in the standards of care which the landowner owes to each. Yet even within a single jurisdiction, the classifications and subclassifications bred by the common law have produced confusion and conflict. . . . Through this semantic morass the common law has moved, unevenly and with hesitation, towards "imposing on owners and occupiers a single duty of reasonable care in all the circumstances."[38]

The courts generally deviate from the "invitee" and "licensee" analysis in evaluating the liability of churches for injuries sustained by neighborhood or

---

[37] Ferreria v. Strack, 636 A.2d 682 (R.I. 1994).
[38] Kermarec v. Compagnie Cenerale, 358 U.S. 625, 630-31 (1959).

"trespassing" children while on church property, and focus on whether or not the injury was caused by an "artificial condition." If the injury was caused by an artificial condition (any condition that does not naturally exist) then the church may be liable if it was aware of the trespassing children, the artificial condition involves a risk of death or serious bodily harm, the children do not discover the condition or realize the risk, the "utility" in maintaining the condition and the burden of eliminating the danger are slight as compared with the risk to children, and the church fails to exercise reasonable care to eliminate the danger or otherwise to protect the children. An artificial condition is any condition that does not naturally exist. For example, the following conditions would be artificial: a basketball court, swimming pool, parking lot, or playground equipment.

Churches owe a minimal degree of care to trespassing children who are injured due to a natural condition (such as a tree or naturally occurring pond or lake). In general, the church must refrain from wantonly or willfully injuring such children.

Churches often let outside groups use their premises, and they may be legally responsible for injuries occurring on their premises while they are being used by such groups.

There is another class of personal injuries that may occur on church premises. Some persons have been assaulted in church parking lots. Churches may be responsible in some cases for these injuries.

In the next chapter, our attention turns to the topic of employment discrimination.

CHAPTER 31. EMPLOYMENT DISCRIMINATION

Congress has enacted a number of employment and civil rights laws regulating employers. These laws generally apply only to employers that are engaged in interstate commerce. This is because the legal basis for such laws is the constitutional power of Congress to regulate interstate commerce. As a result, religious organizations that are not engaged in commerce generally are not subject to these laws. In addition, several of these laws require that an employer have a minimum number of employees. The courts have defined "commerce" very broadly, and so many churches will be deemed to be engaged in commerce.

Most states have enacted various forms of nondiscrimination laws that apply to some employers. These laws are more likely to apply to churches, since there is no "interstate commerce" requirement, and the minimum number of employees that an employer must have to be governed by these laws generally is fewer than under comparable federal laws.

Church leaders should understand a very practical aspect of employment discrimination claims. Most church liability insurance policies provide no coverage for such claims. As a result, most churches that are sued for employment discrimination are responsible for retaining and compensating their own attorney, and paying the full amount of a judgment or settlement. This "financial" risk should be considered when evaluating the need to manage the risk of employment discrimination.

31.1 The "Interstate Commerce" Requirement

Congress has enacted a variety of employment and civil rights laws that apply to some churches and religious organizations. These include:

- Title VII of the Civil Rights Act of 1964

- Age Discrimination in Employment Act

- Americans with Disabilities Act

- Employee Polygraph Protection Act

- Family Medical Leave Act

- Uniformed Services Employment and Reemployment Rights Act

A table in this chapter summarizes most of these laws.

Is a church engaged in a business, industry, or activity affecting commerce? This is a complex question for which no simple answer can be given. In general, the answer in a particular case will depend upon how narrowly or expansively a court construes the term *affecting commerce*, and upon the size of the church and the nature of its operations. Small churches employing no more than one or two persons ordinarily are not engaged in an activity affecting commerce. They are not involved in commercial activities; they sell no product or service; they are financed through voluntary contributions; they exist to fulfill noncommercial purposes; and they function outside the economic marketplace. Further, governmental regulation of such churches carries with it the hazard of excessive governmental entanglement with religion, which is prohibited by the first amendment.[1]

A church or other religious organization engaged in significant commercial activities may be considered to be affecting commerce. To illustrate, a federal appeals court concluded that a church-operated school was engaged in commerce.[2] A disabled woman who was turned down for a job at the school filed a lawsuit claiming that the school discriminated against her in violation of the federal Americans with Disabilities Act. The ADA prohibits employers engaged in an activity "affecting commerce" *and* having at least 15 employees from discriminating in any employment decision on account of the disabled status of an employee or applicant for employment who is able to perform the essential functions of the job with or without reasonable accommodation by the employer. Was the school engaged in an industry affecting commerce? The court noted that the ADA defines this crucial term as "any activity, business, or industry in commerce or in which a labor dispute would hinder or obstruct commerce or the free flow of commerce." The church insisted that it was not an "industry affecting commerce" under this definition, but the court concluded that it was. It relied on an earlier case in which a federal appeals court found that an employer affected commerce since (1) it purchased products and supplies from out of state; (2) its employees traveled out of state on the employer's business; and (3) its employees made interstate telephone calls.[3] The court concluded:

> The school and its employees have engaged in activities that affect commerce. The school purchased supplies and books from companies outside of the District of Columbia. . . . Approximately five of its employees commuted to the school from outside of the District. Employees made interstate telephone calls and mailed letters to locations outside of the District of Columbia.

However, the court cautioned that the woman had not provided any evidence that the church had engaged in activities affecting interstate commerce, and so "this issue is inconclusive." The court added that "[we] presume that some of the same factors exist with respect to the church." There is little doubt that the court believed that the church was engaged in commerce.

Is a church engaged in commerce?

There are a number of factors indicating that a church or other religious organization is engaged in commerce. These include any one or more of the following:

- operation of a private school
- sale of products (such as literature or tapes) to persons or churches in other states
- purchase of products (Sunday School literature, office equipment, etc.) from out-of-state vendors

---

[1] NLRB v. Catholic Bishop of Chicago, 440 U.S. 490 (1979).
[2] Equal Employment Opportunity Commission v. St. Francis Xavier Parochial School, 117 F.3d 621 (D.C. Cir. 1997).
[3] Martin v. United Way, 829 F.2d 445 (3d Cir.1987).

- persons from other states attend your church
- operation of a "web page" on the internet
- operation of a commercial or "unrelated trade or business"
- employees travel out-of-state
- employees make out-of-state telephone calls
- the church sends mail out-of-state
- television or radio broadcasts

Example. A church is accused of engaging in sex discrimination in violation of Title VII of the Civil Rights Act of 1964. The church insists that it is not covered by Title VII since it is not engaged in commerce. The church operates a web page on the internet. This single factor may persuade a court that the church is engaged in commerce.

Example. A church is accused of engaging in age discrimination in violation of federal law. The church insists that it is not covered by this law since it is not engaged in commerce. The church conducts a weekly 15-minute radio broadcast. This single factor indicates that the church is engaged in commerce.

Key point. The United States Supreme Court issued a ruling in 1997 that defined commerce very broadly. The case is important because it involved a religious organization (a church-affiliated summer camp). This case makes it more likely that churches and other religious organizations will be deemed to be engaged in commerce. The Court observed: "Even though [the] camp does not make a profit, it is unquestionably engaged in commerce, not only as a purchaser . . . but also as a provider of goods and services. . . . The attendance of these campers necessarily generates the transportation of persons across state lines that has long been recognized as a form of "commerce" . . . . Our cases have frequently applied laws regulating commerce to not-for-profit institutions. . . . The nonprofit character of an enterprise does not place it beyond the purview of federal laws regulating commerce. We have already held that the commerce clause is applicable to activities undertaken without the intention of earning a profit. . . . We see no reason why the nonprofit character of an enterprise should exclude it from the coverage of [the commerce clause]."[4]

Example. The National Labor Relations Board has ruled that the publishing and distribution of Sunday school literature by a religious denomination is an activity affecting commerce.[5]

Example. The United States Supreme Court has ruled that an evangelistic association was engaged in activities affecting commerce since it was engaged in several commercial enterprises, including advertising, landscaping, service stations, restaurants, manufacture and sale of candy and clothing, record keeping, construction, plumbing, sand and gravel, electrical contracting, hog farms, feed and farm supplies, real estate development, and freight hauling.[6]

---

[4] Camps Newfound/Owatonna v. Town of Harrison, 117 S. Ct. 1590 (1997).
[5] Sunday School Board of the Southern Baptist Convention, 92 N.L.R.B. 801 (1950). *But cf.* Lutheran Church Missouri Synod, 109 N.L.R.B. 859 (1954).
[6] Tony and Susan Alamo Foundation v. Secretary of Labor, 471 U.S. 290 (1985).

Example. A federal appeals court concluded that a religious organization that operated a hotel on a commercial basis was engaged in a business or activity affecting commerce.[7]

The United States Department of Labor has enacted a regulation specifying that

[a]ctivities of eleemosynary, religious, or educational organizations may be performed for a business purpose. Thus, where such organizations engage in ordinary commercial activities, such as operating a printing and publishing plant, the business activities will be treated under the Act the same as when they are performed by the ordinary business enterprise.[8]

31.2 Counting Employees

Some federal civil rights and employment laws apply only to employers having a minimum number of employees. To illustrate, employers must have 15 or more employees to be subject to the Americans with Disabilities Act and Title VII of the Civil Rights Act of 1964. An employer must have at least 20 employees to be subject to the federal age discrimination law.

Federal nondiscrimination laws generally require that an employer have the minimum number of employees "for each working day in each of 20 or more calendar weeks in the current or preceding year." The United States Supreme Court has applied the "payroll method" for counting employees.[9] Under this approach, an "employee" is any person with whom the employer has an *employment relationship* during the week in question.

Example. A Louisiana court dismissed a Title VII sex discrimination claim brought against a church by a dismissed female choir director. The court noted that the church had fewer than 15 employees and therefore it was not subject to Title VII's ban on sex discrimination.[10]

Tip. In summary, in determining whether an employer has 15 or more employees "for each working day in each of 20 or more calendar weeks in the current or preceding year," each week in which an employer has an employment relationship with 15 or more employees is counted.

Tip. The Supreme Court has acknowledged that self-employed persons will appear on an employer's payroll, and that they should not be counted. It clarified that in counting employees under the "payroll method," only those persons who in fact are employees are counted.

Employees of affiliated ministries

Should the employees of an affiliated or subsidiary organization be combined with the employees of a parent organization when counting employees? That is, should the employees of a school, preschool, retirement facility, or other church-affiliated ministry be combined with the employees of the church when counting employees

---

[7] NLRB v. World Evangelism, Inc., 656 F.2d 1349 (9th Cir. 1981).

[8] 29 C.F.R. § 779.214.

[9] Walters v. Metropolitan Educ. Enterprises, Inc., 117 S. Ct. 660 (1997).

[10] Steed v. St. Paul's United Methodist Church, 1999 WL 92626 (La. App. 1999).

Application of Selected Federal Employment and Civil Rights Laws to Religious Organizations

Statue	Main Provisions	Covered Employers
Title VII of 1964 Civil Rights Act	bars discrimination in employment decisions on the basis of race, color, national origin, sex, or religion	• 15 or more employees + interstate commerce • religious employers can discriminate on the basis of religion
Age Discrimination in Employment Act	bars discrimination in employment decisions on the basis of age (if 40 or over)	• 20 or more employees + interstate commerce
Americans with Disabilities Act	bars discrimination against a qualified individual with a disability who can perform essential job functions with or without reasonable employer accommodation (that does not impose undue hardship)	• 15 or more employees + interstate commerce • religious employers can discriminate on the basis of religion
Employee Polygraph Protection Act	employers cannot require, request, suggest, or cause any employee or applicant to take a polygraph exam	• interstate commerce (no minimum number of employees)
Immigration Reform and Control Act	I-9 form must be completed by all new employees demonstrating identity and eligibility to work	• all employers
Fair Labor Standards Act	requires minimum wage and overtime pay to be paid to employees	• employers who employ employees who are engaged in commerce or in the production of goods for commerce, as well as any employee "employed in an enterprise engaged in commerce or in the production of goods for commerce"
Family and Medical Leave Act of 1993	eligible employees qualify for up to 12 weeks unpaid leave per year because of (1) birth or adoption of child, including care for such child, or (2) caring for spouse, child, or parent with a serious health condition, or (3) the employee's serious health condition	• 50 or more employees + interstate commerce
Occupational Safety and Health Act	mandates a safe and healthy workplace for covered employees	an organization "engaged in a business affecting commerce who has employees"
Older Workers Benefit Protection Act of 1991	bars employees at least 40 years old from "waiving" their rights under age discrimination law unless the waiver meets strict legal standards	20 or more employees + interstate commerce

for purposes of applying federal civil rights and employment laws? This is an important question, given the large number of churches that operate affiliated ministries. Under the "single employer" doctrine, separate entities that represent a "single, integrated enterprise" may be treated as a single employer for purposes of meeting the 15 employee test. A federal appeals court, in deciding whether or not a church and its affiliated school and preschool were a "single, integrated enterprise," applied a four-part test.[11] This test, originally announced by the Supreme Court in 1965,[12] focuses on the following four factors: (1) interrelation of operations; (2) common management; (3) centralized control of employment relations; and (4) common ownership or financial control. The court clarified that "the absence or presence of any single factor is not conclusive," and that "control over the elements of labor relations is a central concern." The court cautioned that a plaintiff "must make a substantial showing to warrant a finding of single employer status," and that "there must be sufficient indicia of an interrelationship between the immediate corporate employer and the affiliated corporation to justify the belief on the part of an aggrieved employee that the affiliated corporation is jointly responsible for the acts of the immediate employer." The court suggested that it would be much more likely for an affiliate's employees to be added to the parent corporation if the affiliate and parent were one corporate legal entity.

31.3 The "Clergy Exemption" under Federal Civil Rights Laws

Many courts have ruled that the first amendment guaranty of religious freedom prevents civil rights laws from applying to the relationship between a church and its ministers. Here are some examples:

> *Example. A federal appeals court made the following observation in a case involving a dismissed minister's claim of unlawful discrimination: "This case involves the fundamental question of who will preach from the pulpit of a church, and who will occupy the church parsonage. The bare statement of the question should make obvious the lack of jurisdiction of a civil court. The answer to that question must come from the church. The court acknowledged that the government's interest in preventing employment discrimination "is compelling," but it concluded that such an interest "does not override" the protection that the church claims under the constitutional guaranty of religious freedom."[13]*

> *Example. A minister-employee of the Salvation Army alleged that her employer had violated the Civil Rights Act of 1964 by paying female officers smaller salaries than similarly situated males. A federal appeals court concluded that the relationship of the Salvation Army to its officers was a church-minister relationship, and that the application of the provisions of Title VII to the employment relationship existing between a church and its minister would result in an impermissible encroachment by the government into an area of purely ecclesiastical concern.[14]*

---

[11] Equal Employment Opportunity Commission v. St. Francis Xavier Parochial School, 117 F.3d 621 (D.C. Cir. 1997).

[12] Radio Union v. Broadcast Services, 380 U.S. 255 (1965).

[13] Minker v. Baltimore Annual Conference of the United Methodist Church, 894 F.2d 1354 (D.C. Cir. 1990).

[14] McClure v. Salvation Army, 460 F.2d 553 (5th Cir. 1972), *cert. denied*, 409 U.S. 896 (1972).

Example. A female sued a religious denomination alleging sex discrimination in violation of Title VII when her application to serve as an "associate in pastoral care" was rejected. In rejecting this lawsuit, the court observed: "[C]ourts must distinguish incidental burdens on free exercise in the service of a compelling state interest from burdens where the inroad on religious liberty is too substantial to be permissible. . . . This case is of the latter sort: introduction of government standards to the selection of spiritual leaders would significantly, and perniciously, rearrange the relationship between church and state. While an unfettered church may create minimal infidelity to the objective of Title VII, it provides maximum protection of the first amendment right to the free exercise of religious beliefs. In other words, in a direct clash of highest order interests, the interest in protecting the free exercise of religion embodied in the first amendment to the Constitution prevails over the interest in ending discrimination embodied in Title VII."[15]

Example. A black female sued her religious denomination, claiming both sex and race discrimination when her application for appointment as a member of the clergy was denied. A federal appeals court rejected her claim, noting that "religious bodies may make apparently arbitrary decisions affecting the employment status of their clergy members and be free from civil review having done so." The court added: "[The minister's] argument, that Title VII may be applied to decisions by churches affecting the employment of their clergy, is fruitless." The court concluded: "To accept [the minister's] position would require us to cast a blind eye to the overwhelming weight of precedent going back over a century in order to limit the scope of the protection granted to religious bodies by the free exercise clause."[16]

Example. A federal appeals court dismissed a lawsuit by a nun claiming that her employer, the Catholic University of America, discriminated against her on the basis of her sex in violation of Title VII of the Civil Rights Act of 1964. The nun was employed as a professor of canon law. She applied for academic tenure after 6 years of teaching, and her application was denied. She sued the University, claiming that its decision to deny her tenure amounted to sex discrimination. The court upheld a federal district court's dismissal of the lawsuit, concluding that it was barred by the first amendment guaranty of religious freedom: "The Supreme Court has shown a particular reluctance to interfere with a church's selection of its own clergy. . . . Relying on these and other cases [a number of federal courts] have long held that the free exercise [of religion] clause exempts the selection of clergy from Title VII and similar statutes and, as a consequence, precludes civil courts from adjudicating employment discrimination suits by ministers against the church or religious institution employing them." The court pointed out that the so-called "ministerial exemption" has not been limited to members of the clergy, but "has also been applied to lay employees of religious institutions whose primary duties consist of teaching, spreading the faith, church governance, supervision of a religious order, or supervision or participation in religious ritual and worship." Employees whose positions are "important to the spiritual and pastoral mission of the church should be considered clergy." The court concluded that "the ministerial exception encompasses all employees of a religious institution, whether ordained or not, whose primary functions serve its spiritual and pastoral mission," and this included a nun who taught in the canon law department of

---

[15] Rayburn v. General Conference of Seventh Day Adventists, 772 F.2d 1164 (4th Cir. 1985).
[16] Young v. Northern Illinois Conference of the United Methodist Church, 21 F.3d 184 (7th Cir. 1994).

the Catholic University. The court noted that the canon law department performs "the vital function of instructing those who will in turn interpret, implement, and teach the law governing the Roman Catholic Church and the administration of its sacraments."[17]

Example. *A New Jersey court ruled that a lay teacher could sue a Catholic high school for age and sex discrimination. The teacher had been employed to teach English and history. After several years of teaching, she was informed that her position was being eliminated due to "budget problems." The teacher sued the school, claiming that the real reason she was being terminated was because of her gender and age. As proof, she alleged that the school later replaced her with a younger, male teacher. The school defended itself by insisting that all teaching positions at a Catholic high school are "religious" in nature, and that the first amendment prohibits the civil courts from applying civil rights laws to such positions. In support of its position, the school noted that the contract signed by its teachers stated that all teachers are to "exemplify Christian principles and ideals" in the performance of their duties, and are to open each class with prayer. Further, the school asserted that "parochial school teachers, no matter what the subject matter being taught, are performing a ministerial function . . . inculcating faith, values, and moral precepts into the students" and that "secular subjects in a parochial school are important vehicles for the propagation of the faith." The court acknowledged that civil rights laws cannot be applied to ministers or lay employees performing ministerial functions for a church or religious school. However, the court concluded that the lay teacher in this case did not satisfy this test. It observed: "[T]he fact that faculty members serve as exemplars of practicing Christians does not automatically make their duties ministerial. . . . A teacher of secular subjects need not be considered a religious leader. Here . . . enforcing the prohibition against discrimination would have no impact on religious belief, doctrine, or practice. . . . Thus, since the underlying dispute does not turn on doctrine or polity, the court should not abdicate its duty to enforce secular rights."[18]*

Example. *A Wisconsin court ruled that a lawsuit brought by a former church employee claiming that her dismissal constituted unlawful sex discrimination had to be dismissed since the employee's position was "ministerial" and "ecclesiastical."[19] A female employee of a Catholic seminary, who served as "director of field education," claimed that the seminary's decision not to renew her contract of employment was based on her sex in violation of a state civil rights law. The law prohibits discrimination in employment decisions on the basis of an employee's "age, race, creed, color, handicap, marital status, sex, national origin, ancestry, arrest record, or conviction record." A state court rejected the seminary's claim that the civil courts lack jurisdiction to resolve employment discrimination suits brought against religious organizations. The court relied in part on a 1986 decision of the United States Supreme Court finding that the civil courts are not prohibited from "merely investigating" the circumstances of an employee's dismissal by a religious school.[20] The court observed that giving religious organizations immunity from employment discrimination laws "would dangerously encroach upon the [nonestablishment of religion] clause's prohibition against furthering religion by providing a benefit exclusively to a religious association." However, the court ruled that the first*

---

[17] E.E.O.C. v. Catholic University of America, 83 F.3rd 455 (D.C. Cir. 1996).

[18] Gallo v. Salesian Society, Inc., 676 A.2d 580 (N.J. Super. 1996).

[19] Jocz v. Labor and Industry Review Commission, 538 N.W.2d 588 (Wis. App. 1995).

[20] Ohio Civil Rights Commission v. Dayton Christian Schools, Inc., 477 U.S. 619 (1986).

amendment's protection of the free exercise of religion provides religious organizations with substantial protections that must be considered. These include the enforcement of state civil rights laws in cases involving employment decisions by religious organizations with respect to employees who perform a "ministerial" or "ecclesiastical" function. If an employee performs such a function, then "further enforcement of the [state civil rights law] against the religious association is constitutionally precluded, and the complaint should be dismissed." The court concluded that the employee in this case performed ministerial functions since her duties consisted of "teaching, spreading the faith, church governance, supervision of a religious order, or supervision or participation in religious ritual or worship."

31.4 Title VII of the Civil Rights Act of 1964

Title VII of the Civil Rights Act of 1964 bars certain employers from discriminating in employment decisions on the basis of any of the following factors:

- race
- color
- national origin
- sex
- pregnancy
- religion

Only those employers that are engaged in an activity "affecting interstate commerce" and having at least 15 employees are subject to this law. What about churches? Most churches have fewer than 15 employees and so they are not covered. Churches with 15 or more employees are covered only if they are engaged in an activity affecting interstate commerce. In general, whether or not a church meets this requirement will depend upon the frequency and nature of its interstate transactions. To illustrate, a church that sells several tapes of its weekly services to persons living in other states almost certainly is engaged in interstate commerce. On the other hand, a church that does not sell any products across state lines, that is not engaged in any commercial activities, and that makes few if any out-of-state purchases probably is not engaged in interstate commerce and would not be subject to Title VII.

Key point. *Churches that are not covered by Title VII of the Civil Rights Act of 1964 may be subject to a similar state law.*

Application to churches

Title VII contains an important exception—churches can discriminate on the basis of religion in their employment decisions. This means that churches can consider only persons of their own faith when hiring both ministers and nonminister employees.

Example. *A church needs to hire a new office secretary. It only considers persons who are members of its faith. Persons who are members of other faiths are not considered. While this policy "discriminates" on the basis of religion against persons of other faiths, it is a permitted form of discrimination under Title VII.*

Key point. *Churches cannot use religion as a "pretext" for engaging in discrimination against a protected class. To illustrate, a church that is subject to Title VII and that adopts a policy prohibiting employees from engaging in adultery could not apply its policy only to female employees.*

Consistency

A number of courts have ruled that Title VII's exemption of religious organizations from the ban on religious discrimination in employment does not apply if a religious organization uses religion as a "pretext" to discriminate against a member of a protected class. This is a very important qualification. Religious organizations can discriminate in their employment decisions on the basis of religion, but they must be consistent. To illustrate, a church that dismisses only female employees on the basis of adultery could not justify this practice on the basis of the Title VII exemption.

Example. *A federal appeals court ruled that a church-operated preschool did not violate federal law when it dismissed an unmarried, pregnant preschool teacher. The school required its teachers to adhere to its religious tenets, including a prohibition against sex outside of marriage. The dismissed worker knew that the school was a church-related school and indicated on her employment application that she had a Christian background and believed in God. The worker insisted that she was never told that she would be terminated if she engaged in sex outside of marriage. However, the school's faculty handbook (given to the worker after she was hired) reads: "Christian character, as well as professional ability, is the basis for hiring teachers at [the school]. Each teacher . . . is expected in all actions to be a Christian example for the students." When school administrators learned that the unmarried worker was pregnant, a decision was made to terminate her employment. The school's president claimed that the woman was dismissed not because of pregnancy, but because the facts indicated that she engaged in sex outside of marriage. The woman sued the school, claiming that it committed unlawful sex discrimination when it fired her. The court ruled that the school lawfully dismissed the woman on the basis of her violation of its religious teachings against premarital sex and not because she was pregnant. The court rejected the woman's claim that the school applied its policy against premarital sex in a discriminatory way that was more strict when women were involved. The court observed that "although Title VII requires that [the school's] code of conduct be applied equally to both sexes, [the school] presented uncontroverted evidence . . . that [the administrator] had terminated at least four individuals, both male and female, who had engaged in extramarital sexual relationships that did not result in pregnancy." Further, the court acknowledged that the school's policy occasionally may have been violated because the administrator was unaware of every instance of premarital sex by his staff, but it insisted that "isolated inconsistent application" of the policy "was not sufficient to show that [the school's] articulated nondiscriminatory reason was not the real reason for [the woman's] termination."[21]*

Violations of "moral teachings"

Can a church lawfully discriminate against an employee or applicant for employment on the basis of moral teachings? In some cases, religious

---

[21] Boyd v. Harding Academy of Memphis, Inc., 88 F.3d 410 (6th Cir. 1996).

organizations will be able to demonstrate that their moral teachings are integral to their religious beliefs, and therefore employment discrimination based on moral teachings is a form of religious discrimination that is permitted by Title VII. To avoid any confusion, religious organizations that take an adverse employment action against an employee or applicant for employment as a result of the organization's moral teachings should word their determination with references to relevant passages from scripture. This will make it more likely that a court will view the decision as a protected form of religious discrimination.

> *Example.* *A federal district court in California refused to dismiss a lawsuit brought by a former church employee who was dismissed after church leaders learned that she was pregnant out of wedlock. A church operated a private school, and required all employees to be "born again believers living a consistent and practical Christian life." Employees were required to sign a statement of faith, and to commit themselves to the mission of the church and to a Christian lifestyle that emulates the life of Christ. The school's librarian, a female, signed an annual affirmation agreement in which she agreed that she would be bound by the moral values and religious beliefs of the church. As an employee, the librarian received an employee manual that repeatedly stressed the importance of employees living a life in conformity to the beliefs and values of the church. The librarian was fired when church leaders learned that she was pregnant out of wedlock. The librarian filed a lawsuit in federal court, asserting that the church and school discriminated against her on account of her pregnancy in violation of Title VII. The church and school filed a motion to dismiss, alleging that the librarian had been fired "for the sin of being pregnant without benefit of marriage" (a condition inconsistent with the religious values of the church and school). However, the church and school later asserted that the librarian's dismissal had nothing to do with her pregnancy, but rather was based on her adulterous relationship. Her pregnancy was evidence of the adultery but had nothing to do with the religious reason for her dismissal. A federal court acknowledged that the "new position" of the church and school—that the librarian was fired for adultery, and not on account of her pregnancy—would not give rise to a Title VII claim since Title VII specifically permits religious employers to discriminate on the basis of religion in employment decisions. However, the "old position" of the church and school—that the librarian was fired because she was pregnant and not married—raised the possibility of sex discrimination. This case illustrates the importance of accurately describing the basis for terminating an employee. There is a critical legal difference between dismissing an employee on account of pregnancy (even if out of wedlock) and dismissing an employee on account of adultery (of which pregnancy is merely evidence).[22]*

Dismissing an employee for violation of a church's moral teachings

Before dismissing an employee for violating the church's moral teachings, church leaders should ask the following questions:

(1) Is there sufficient evidence to support our decision?

(2) Did we inform the employee, in an employee handbook or other document, that he or she would be subject to dismissal for engaging in behavior in violation of our moral teachings?

---

[22] Vigars v. Valley Christian Center, 805 F. Supp. 802 (N.D. Cal. 1992).

(3) How will we describe the basis for our decision? The best description will refer to the church's doctrinal tenets, and scriptural citations. Stay away from words such as "pregnancy" that can have a "secular" meaning, and that diminish the "religious exemption" available to churches under most federal and state civil rights and employment laws.

(4) How have we treated other employees in the past who were guilty of the same kind of misconduct? Have we treated all employees equally? Or, have we treated some employees less favorably than others. For example, have we dismissed female employees who were guilt of extramarital sexual relations, but only warned or reprimanded males employees guilty of the same behavior? Before dismissing an employee for misconduct, church leaders should review all other known cases involving similar misconduct by other employees. Be sure that the church's actions are consistent with its previous practice, and that an employee who is protected against discrimination by state or federal law not be treated less favorably than other employees.

(5) Have we contacted an attorney before taking final action?

Other forms of discrimination

While churches that are covered by Title VII are exempted from the ban on religious discrimination in their employment decisions, they are not exempted from the ban on discrimination based on race, color, national origin, or sex. Many courts have ruled that the first amendment guaranty of religious freedom prevents civil rights laws (including Title VII) from applying to the relationship between a church and its *ministers*. However, most courts have not extended this exception to nonminister church employees. As a result, churches involved in interstate commerce and having at least 15 employees should assume that Title VII protects their nonminister employees.

Key point. The "interstate commerce" and minimum number of employee requirements are addressed earlier in this chapter.

Sexual harassment

Sexual harassment is a form of "sex discrimination" prohibited by Title VII of the Civil Rights Act of 1964. Equal Employment Opportunity Commission (EEOC) regulations define sexual harassment as follows:

(a) *Harassment on the basis of sex is a violation of Sec. 703 of Title VII.* Unwelcome sexual advances, requests for sexual favors, and other verbal or physical conduct of a sexual nature constitute sexual harassment when (1) submission to such conduct is made either explicitly or implicitly a term or condition of an individual's employment, (2) submission to or rejection of such conduct by an individual is used as the basis for employment decisions affecting such individual, or (3) such conduct has the purpose or effect of unreasonably interfering with an individual's work performance or creating an intimidating, hostile, or offensive working environment.

This definition confirms the conclusion reached by numerous state and federal courts that sexual harassment includes *at least two separate types of conduct:*

(1) *"quid pro quo"* *harassment*, which refers to conditioning employment opportunities on submission to a sexual or social relationship, and

(2) *"hostile environment"* *harassment*, which refers to the creation of an intimidating, hostile, or offensive working environment through unwelcome verbal or physical conduct of a sexual nature.

> **Key point.** *A woman's "consent" is not a defense to an allegation of sexual harassment. The United States Supreme Court has observed: "[T]he fact that sex-related conduct was voluntary in the sense that the complainant was not forced to participate against her will, is not a defense to a sexual harassment suit . . . . The gravamen of any sexual harassment claim is that the alleged sexual advances were unwelcome . . . . The correct inquiry is whether [the victim] by her conduct indicated that the alleged sexual advances were unwelcome, not whether her actual participation in sexual intercourse was voluntary." In other words, a female employee may engage in voluntary sexual contact with a supervisor because of her belief that her job (or advancement) depends on it. While such contact would be voluntary, it is not necessarily welcome. Sexual harassment addresses unwelcome sexual contact, whether or not that contact is voluntary.*

When is an employer liable for sexual harassment? Consider the following rules:

Rule #1 – quid pro quo harassment

If a supervisor conditions employment opportunities on an employee's submission to a sexual or social relationship, and the employee's "compensation, terms, conditions or privileges of employment" are adversely affected because of a refusal to submit, this constitutes quid pro quo sexual harassment for which the employer will be legally responsible. This is true whether or not the employer was aware of the harassment.

Rule #2 – harassment committed by nonsupervisory employees

EEOC regulations address employer liability for the sexual harassment of nonsupervisory employees as follows:

> With respect to conduct between fellow employees, an employer is responsible for acts of sexual harassment in the workplace where the employer (or its agents or supervisory employees) knows or should have known of the conduct, unless it can show that it took immediate and appropriate corrective action.

Rule #3 – harassment committed by non-employees

EEOC regulations address employer liability for the sexual harassment of non-employees as follows:

> An employer may also be responsible for the acts of non-employees, with respect to sexual harassment of employees in the workplace, where the employer (or its agents or supervisory employees) knows or should have known of the conduct and fails to take immediate and appropriate corrective action. In reviewing these cases the Commission will consider the extent of the employer's control and any other legal responsibility which the employer may have with respect to the conduct of such non-employees.

Rule #4 – hostile environment harassment by a supervisor, with a tangible employment decision

If a supervisor creates an intimidating, hostile, or offensive working environment through unwelcome verbal or physical conduct of a sexual nature, this is "hostile environment" sexual harassment for which the employer will be legally responsible if the supervisor takes any "tangible employment action" against the employee. A tangible employment action includes "a significant change in employment status, such as hiring, firing, failing to promote, reassignment with significantly different responsibilities, or a decision causing a significant change in benefits." The employer is liable under such circumstances whether or not it was aware of the harassment.[23]

Rule #5 – hostile environment harassment by a supervisor, with no tangible employment decision

If a supervisor creates an intimidating, hostile, or offensive working environment through unwelcome verbal or physical conduct of a sexual nature, this is "hostile environment" sexual harassment for which the employer will be legally responsible even if the supervisor takes no "tangible employment action" against the employee.[24]

Rule #6 – the employer's "affirmative defense" to liability for a supervisor's hostile environment sexual harassment not accompanied by a tangible employment decision

If a supervisor engages in hostile environment sexual harassment but takes no "tangible employment decision" against a victim, the employer may assert an "affirmative defense" to liability. This defense consists of two elements:

(1) The employer "exercised reasonable care to prevent and correct promptly any sexually harassing behavior." This generally means that the employer adopted a written sexual harassment policy that was communicated to employees, and that contains a complaint procedure.

(2) The victim "unreasonably failed to take advantage of any preventive or corrective opportunities provided by the employer or to avoid harm otherwise." This generally means that the victim failed to follow the complaint procedure described in the employer's sexual harassment policy.[25]

It is essential for any church having employees to adopt a sexual harassment policy, since this will serve as a defense to liability for a supervisor's acts of "hostile environment" sexual harassment to the extent that a victim of such harassment does not follow the policy.

> **Key point.** *A written sexual harassment policy does not insulate a church from all sexual harassment liability. It will not serve as a defense in any of these situations: (1) a "tangible employment decision" has been taken against an employee; (2) incidents of quid pro quo sexual harassment; or (3) a victim of a supervisor's hostile*

---

[23] Burlington Industries, Inc. v. Ellerth, 118 S. Ct. 2257 (1998); Faragher v. City of Boca Raton, 118 S. Ct. 2275 (1998).

[24] *Id.*

[25] *Id.*

environment sexual harassment pursues his or her remedies under the employer's sexual harassment policy.

What terms should be included in a sexual harassment policy? Unfortunately, the Supreme Court has not addressed this question directly. However, other courts have. Here is a list of some of the terms that should be incorporated into a written sexual harassment policy:

- Define sexual harassment (both quid pro quo and hostile environment) and state unequivocally that it will not be tolerated and that it will be the basis for immediate discipline (up to and including dismissal).

- Contain a procedure for filing complaints of harassment with the employer.

- Encourage victims to report incidents of harassment.

- Assure employees that complaints will be investigated promptly.

- Assure employees that they will not suffer retaliation for filing a complaint.

- Discuss the discipline applicable to persons who violate the policy.

- Assure the confidentiality of all complaints.

In addition to implementing a written sexual harassment policy, a church should also take the following steps:

- Communicate the written policy to all workers.

- Investigate all complaints immediately. Some courts have commented on the reluctance expressed by some male supervisors in investigating claims of sexual harassment. To illustrate, a federal appeals court observed: "Because women are disproportionately the victims of rape and sexual assault, women have a stronger incentive to be concerned with sexual behavior. Women who are victims of mild forms of sexual harassment may understandably worry whether a harasser's conduct is merely a prelude to violent sexual assault. Men, who are rarely victims of sexual assault, may view sexual conduct in a vacuum without a full appreciation of the social setting or the underlying threat of violence that a woman may perceive."

- Discipline employees who are found guilty of harassment. However, be careful not to administer discipline without adequate proof of harassment. Discipline not involving dismissal should be accompanied by a warning that any future incidents of harassment will not be tolerated and may result in immediate dismissal.

- Follow up by periodically asking the victim if there have been any further incidents of harassment.

Key point. EEOC guidelines contain the following language: "Prevention is the best tool for the elimination of sexual harassment. An employer should take all steps necessary to prevent sexual harassment from occurring, such as affirmatively raising the subject, expressing strong disapproval, developing appropriate sanctions, informing employees of their right to raise and how to raise the issue of harassment under Title VII, and developing methods to sensitize all concerned."

Key point. Most states have enacted their own civil rights laws that bar sexual harassment in employment, and it is far more likely that these laws will apply to churches since there is no "commerce" requirement and often fewer than 15 employees are needed to be covered by the law.

Tip. The assistance of an attorney is vital in the drafting of a sexual harassment policy.

Tip. Church insurance policies generally do not cover employment related claims, including sexual harassment. If your church is sued for sexual harassment, you probably will need to retain and pay for your own attorney, and pay any judgment or settlement amount. This often comes as a shock to church leaders. You should immediately review your policy with your insurance agent to see if you have any coverage for such claims. If you do not, ask how it can be obtained. You may be able to obtain an endorsement for "employment practices." Also, a "directors and officers" policy may cover these claims.

Example. An associate pastor engaged in sexual relations with two female employees in the course of a counseling relationship. The women later informed the senior pastor. As a result, the two women were dismissed, and the associate pastor was forced to resign. The women later sued the church on the basis of several legal theories, including sexual harassment. A trial court threw out the sexual harassment claim, and the women appealed. A federal appeals court concluded that the church was not guilty of "hostile environment" sexual harassment. It noted that in order for the two women to establish "hostile environment" sexual harassment they needed to "produce evidence showing, among other things, that [the church] knew or should have known of the harassment in question and failed to take prompt remedial action." However, since it was established that the church "took prompt remedial action upon learning of [the minister's] misconduct," the two women had to prove that the church should have known of the minister's behavior before it was disclosed. The court concluded that the women failed to do so. The women claimed that the former minister had offended a few other women by complimenting them on their appearances and hugging them. This evidence, even if true, was not enough to demonstrate that the church "knew or should have known" of a "hostile environment." The court also rejected the women's claim that the church had engaged in "quid pro quo" sexual harassment. It noted that for the women to establish quid pro quo sexual harassment, they "were required to produce evidence showing, among other things, that the harassment complained of affected tangible aspects of their compensation, terms, conditions, or privileges of employment. In addition, they were required to develop evidence demonstrating that their acceptance or rejection of the harassment was an express or implied condition to the receipt of a job benefit or the cause of a tangible job detriment. [But the women's] own testimony—that they were subjected to mild criticism of their work and told that they would not be promoted to positions they knew did not exist—indicates that their jobs were not tangibly and detrimentally affected by their decisions to end their sexual relationships with [the minister] . . . . Further, there is no objective evidence in the record supporting the [women's] claims that they engaged in sex with [the minister] under an implied threat of discharge if they did not."[26]

---

[26] Sanders v. Casa View Baptist Church, 134 F.3d 331 (5th Cir. 1998).

Example. A federal appeals court ruled that a church-operated school was guilty of sexual harassment as a result of its failure to address its principal's offensive behavior with several female employees. A denominational agency operated a residential school for emotionally and physically impaired children. Over the course of several years, the principal of the school was accused on many occasions of sexual harassment by female employees. There was substantial evidence that school officials were aware of many of these complaints. School officials launched an investigation into the sexual harassment charges. They found that there was a significant basis to the harassment complaints. The school suspended the principal for five days without pay, ordered him to submit to a psychological assessment, and placed him on three months' probation. It also invited an outside consultant to conduct several days of seminars on sexual harassment. Even after this corrective action, there were several instances of inappropriate behavior involving the principal. During this same year, the principal was given a satisfactory performance evaluation and a raise. Several female employees who had been harassed by the principal sued the denominational agency on the ground that it was legally responsible for the principal's acts because of its failure to respond adequately to the accusations against him. A trial court ruled in favor of the women, and awarded them $300,000 in damages. A federal appeals court upheld this ruling. It referred to the "long-term, ostrich-like failure" by denominational and school officials to "deal forthrightly with [the principal's] treatment of female employees." The court observed that "the jury was entitled to conclude that [the agency] not only looked the other way for many years but that its corrective action was woefully inadequate, as demonstrated by [the principal's] later conduct." This case illustrates the importance of dealing promptly with complaints of sexual harassment. Letting years pass without addressing complaints of harassment will only increase significantly a church's risk of liability. After several years of complaints, the agency finally suspended the principal for five days, ordered a psychological assessment, imposed a three-month probationary period, and invited consultants to conduct sexual harassment training. These acts may seem thorough and adequate, but the court concluded that they were not sufficient to avoid liability for sexual harassment, because (1) the complaints against the principal had occurred over so many years; (2) the principal's acts of harassment were so pervasive; (3) the agency waited years before acting; (4) the agency's response was insufficient, since the principal continued to engage in harassment even after he was disciplined; and (5) the principal received a satisfactory employee evaluation and a raise during the same year that he was disciplined for harassment.[27]

Example. A woman was hired as an associate pastor of a church in Minnesota. A year later, she filed a discrimination charge with the state department of human rights against her supervising pastor. She claimed that her supervising pastor repeatedly made unwelcome sexual advances toward her. He allegedly referred to themselves as "lovers," physically contacted her in a sexual manner, and insisted on her companionship outside the work place despite her objections. The woman informed her local church leaders as well as her synod before filing the complaint with the state. Although the church and synod investigated the woman's allegations, no action was taken to stop the alleged harassment. Less than three months after the complaint was filed with the state, the church held a congregational meeting at which it voted to dismiss the woman as pastor. The reason stated for the discharge was the woman's

---

[27] Jonasson v. Lutheran Child and Family Services, 115 F.3d 436 (7th Cir. 1997).

"inability to conduct the pastoral office efficiently in this congregation in view of local conditions." A state appeals court ruled that the woman could sue her former supervising pastor for sexual harassment. The court also rejected the supervising pastor's claim that the woman was prevented from suing because she had "consented" to the supervising pastor's conduct.[28]

Example. A North Carolina appeals court ruled that the first amendment did not prevent it from resolving a sexual harassment lawsuit brought by three female church employees against their church and denominational agencies. Three female church employees (the "plaintiffs") sued their Methodist church and various Methodist agencies as a result of the sexual misconduct of a pastor. The lawsuit alleged that the pastor "committed inappropriate, unwelcome, offensive and nonconsensual acts of a sexual nature against the plaintiffs, variously hugging, kissing and touching them, and made inappropriate, unwelcome, offensive and nonconsensual statements of a sexually suggestive nature to them." The plaintiffs further alleged that the pastor's actions amounted to sexual harassment and assault and battery, causing them emotional distress, embarrassment, humiliation, and damage to their reputations and career potential. The lawsuit alleged that the local church and Methodist agencies "knew or should have known" of the pastor's propensity for sexual harassment as well as assault and battery upon female employees and that they failed to take any actions to warn or protect the plaintiffs from his wrongful activity. A state appeals court concluded that if a resolution of the plaintiffs' legal claims did not require the interpretation of church doctrine, then "the first amendment is not implicated and neutral principles of law are properly applied to adjudicate the claim."[29]

Example. An Ohio court ruled that an Episcopalian minister and his employing church could be sued for the minister's alleged acts of sexual harassment. A woman served some ten years as parish secretary of an Episcopal church prior to the arrival of a new minister. Soon after the arrival of the new minister, the secretary began alleging that the minister was engaging in acts of sexual harassment against her. Initially, the secretary contacted the bishop of the diocese with her complaint. He promised to make an investigation and apparently did, but concluded that, although he believed she was sincere in her allegations, there was nothing that he could do because the minister denied any wrongdoing. The bishop did order the work hours of the minister and secretary to be so staggered that they would not be working at the same time. After hearing that the bishop would take no further action, the woman wrote to the minister in question, the standing committee of the diocese, the vestry, the warden, and the bishop in an attempt to resolve what she called "this terrible problem." Upon receipt of this letter, the minister called the chancellor of the diocese, who advised him to fire the secretary. The minister thereafter was instructed by the vestry of the church to notify the congregation that the secretary had been fired and to give a reason. Accordingly, the minister published in the parish newsletter a statement that the secretary had been engaging in an open malicious endeavor to discredit him. Following her dismissal, the former secretary filed a lawsuit against the minister, her church, and the diocese. She based her lawsuit on a number of grounds, including sexual harassment. The appeals court ruled that the woman's claims were credible. It rejected the claim that the church could not be responsible for the minister's alleged actions since they were not performed within the "scope of his employment." It noted

---

[28] Black v. Snyder, 471 N.W.2d 715 (Minn. App. 1991).
[29] Smith v. Privette, 495 S.E.2d 395 (N.C. App. 1998).

that "it is quite clear that the alleged sexual harassment did occur within the scope of [the minister's] employment with [the church]. He was the supervisor of [the secretary], and most of the alleged sexual harassment took place during working hours at the work place."[30]

Summary

This chapter addresses the application of employment discrimination laws to churches. Church leaders should be familiar with the following points:

- Several federal laws prohibit discrimination in any employment decision, including hiring, firing, promotions, demotions, and fringe benefits. These laws only apply to churches that are engaged in interstate commerce. The courts have interpreted "interstate commerce" very broadly, and so church leaders should assume that they meet this requirement. Some federal laws banning employment discrimination only apply to employers having a minimum number of employees.

- Federal laws ban employment discrimination based on race, color, national origin, gender, religion, age, disability, and military status.

- Most states have enacted laws banning various forms of employment discrimination. These laws are more likely to apply to churches, since there is no "interstate commerce" requirement and often a smaller number of employees are required to trigger coverage.

- Churches are exempt from the ban on "religious discrimination" in employment under federal law, and comparable state laws.

- The exemption of churches from the ban on "religious discrimination" in employment extends to employment decisions based on scriptural standards. However, it is essential that a church be consistent in applying its scriptural standards, and treat "similar cases similarly." For example, churches that treat male employees who engage in extramarital sexual relations more leniently than females who engage in such conduct will not qualify for the exemption from employment discrimination based on religion.

- Most courts have refused to apply employment discrimination laws to the relationship between a church and its ministers.

- Church liability insurance policies generally provide no coverage for employment discrimination claims. As a result, churches that are sued for discrimination will need to retain and compensate their own attorney, and pay for any judgment or out-of-court settlement.

The next chapter focuses on the negligent selection and retention of volunteers and employees.

---

[30] Davis v. Black, N.E.2d, 70 Ohio App. 3d 359 (Ohio App. 1991).

CHAPTER 32. NEGLIGENT SELECTION AND RETENTION OF VOLUNTEERS AND EMPLOYEES

32.1 Negligent Selection of Church Workers—In General

One of the most significant legal risks facing churches today is negligent selection. The term negligence means carelessness or a failure to exercise reasonable care. Negligent selection, then, means carelessness or a failure to exercise reasonable care in the selection of a worker.

Why sexual misconduct is the greatest legal risk facing churches today

The problem of negligent selection often occurs in cases involving sexual misconduct. Furthermore, church liability for the sexual misconduct of employees and volunteers is the most significant risk facing churches today for a number of reasons, including the following:

1. *Many opportunities.* There ordinarily are many opportunities within the church for persons to engage in sexual misconduct with adults or children. Churches have many children involved in a variety of programs, and many pastors engage in extensive counseling.

2. *Trust.* Churches are institutions of trust, and many members and leaders cannot conceive of acts of sexual misconduct occurring on their premises. As a result, they do not see a need to institute procedures and policies that will reduce the risk of such behavior.

3. *Money damages.* The amount of money damages that courts award in such cases can be substantial.

4. *Limited insurance coverage.* Most church insurance policies either exclude sexual misconduct claims, or significantly reduce the amount of coverage. This means that many churches face a potentially large and underinsured risk.

5. *Other damages.* The damage that such claims cause to victims, victims' families, offenders, congregations, and church leaders is considerable.

6. *Board liability.* Board members face personal liability in such cases if they refused to take steps to address this risk or ignored danger signals, and their conduct amounts to "gross negligence."[1]

7. *Punitive damages.* Churches face the possibility of being assessed punitive damages if church leaders willfully refused to address this risk or ignored danger signals. Punitive damages are designed to "punish" wrongdoers for reckless or grossly negligent conduct. They are not covered by church insurance policies.

8. *Polarization.* Congregations often are polarized in the aftermath of an incident of sexual misconduct. Some members insist that the offender be forgiven, while others focus on issues of justice, accountability, and protection.

---

[1] *See* Chapter 26.

Key point. Some courts use the term "negligent hiring" instead of "negligent selection." This text uses the term negligent selection since it is a broader term that encompasses the selection of both employees and uncompensated volunteers. Technically, volunteers are not "hired," and so the narrower term "negligent hiring" would not apply to them.

32.2 Negligent Selection of Church Workers—Sexual Misconduct Cases Involving Minor Victims

In recent years, hundreds of churches have been sued as a result of the sexual molestation of minors by church workers on church property or during church activities. Common examples include the molestation of male and female children and adolescents by youth pastors, camp counselors, Sunday school teachers, church custodians, volunteer youth workers, and others. In many of these cases, the victim alleges either or both of the following two theories: (1) the church was negligent in hiring the offender without adequate screening or evaluation, or (2) the church was negligent in its supervision of the offender. The second of these theories ("negligent supervision") is discussed in the next chapter.

The term negligence refers to conduct that creates an unreasonable risk of foreseeable harm to others. It connotes carelessness, heedlessness, inattention, or inadvertence. It is important to recognize that churches are not "guarantors" of the safety and well-being of children. They are not absolutely liable for every injury that occurs on their premises in the course of their activities. Generally, they are responsible only for those injuries that result from their negligence. Negligent selection simply means that the church failed to act responsibly and with due care in the selection of workers (both volunteer and compensated) for positions involving the supervision or custody of minors. Victims of molestation who have sued a church often allege that the church was negligent in not adequately screening applicants. The typical church uses just about anyone who expresses an interest in working in a volunteer capacity with the youth in the church. Even applicants for compensated positions are not screened by many churches. Often, when an incident of molestation occurs the senior minister is later asked to testify in court regarding steps that the church took to prevent the incident. The victim's lawyer asks, "What did you or your staff do to prevent this incident from occurring—what procedures did you utilize to check the molester's background and suitability for work with children?" All too often, the minister's answer is "nothing." The jury's reaction to such a response is predictable.

A single incident of abuse or molestation can devastate a church. Parents often become enraged, the viability of the church's youth and children's programs is jeopardized, and church leaders may be blamed for allowing the incident to happen. But far more tragic is the emotional trauma to the victim and the victim's family, and the enormous potential legal liability the church faces.

There is good news, however. Church leaders can take relatively simple yet effective steps to significantly reduce the likelihood of such an incident occurring. This chapter will review some of the more significant reported court rulings, and then suggest a number of preventive measures that any church can implement in order to reduce the risk of such incidents.

Tip. No one understands or appreciates risk better than insurance companies. Risk evaluation is their business. As a result, it is very important to observe that a number of church insurance companies have reduced the insurance coverage they provide for sexual misconduct, and in some cases they have excluded it entirely. Some companies are suggesting that these incidents are excluded under the provision in most policies excluding damages based on intentional, criminal conduct (most acts of sexual molestation involve criminal activity). Church leaders should immediately review their church liability insurance policy to determine whether the church has any coverage for acts of sexual misconduct, and if so, whether such coverage has been limited in any way. If you fit within either category, the risk management recommendations in this chapter are of even greater relevance.

Court decisions recognizing negligent selection claims

Some courts have found churches liable on the basis of negligent selection for the molestation of a minor by a church worker if the church failed to exercise reasonable care in the selection of the worker. Representative cases are summarized below.

Example. The Alaska Supreme Court ruled that a church could be legally responsible for the alleged sexual abuse of a 3-year-old child that occurred in a church nursery.[2] The court concluded that the church could be responsible on the basis of "negligent hiring" since it did not exercise a sufficiently high degree of care in selecting the volunteer worker who allegedly committed the abuse. In particular, the court emphasized that the church had not interviewed the volunteer regarding her own background, and did not conduct any "background check." The court observed, "[T]he employer, in selecting an employee, must exercise a degree of care commensurate with the nature and danger of the business in which he is engaged and the nature and grade of services for which the employee is intended. In the present case, [the church] was in the business of providing a safe place for the care of young children whose parents were attending church services. It engaged [the attendant] to make sure that those children were properly cared for. We consider it self-evident that the selection of individuals to whom the care and safety of young children will be entrusted requires a relatively high level of care before it may be considered reasonable. [The church] did not interview [the attendant] or conduct a background check, nor has it offered any evidence that [the attendant's] past sexual abuse did not affect her competency." The court rejected the church's claim that it was not required to conduct an interview of background check on the nursery attendant since she was a mere volunteer rather than an employee. It noted simply that a volunteer "may be subject to the same interview and background checks" as any other worker, so long as the volunteer is subject to the control of the employer. In summary, the court concluded that a church can be legally responsible on the basis of negligent selection for acts of sexual molestation inflicted by a nursery attendant if the church did not conduct any background investigation into the attendant's suitability and fitness as a child care worker.

Example. A California court ruled that a church was responsible on the basis of "negligent hiring" for the sexual molestation of a 13-year-old boy by his pastor.[3] However, the court concluded that the church was not responsible for the victim's

---

[2] Broderick v. King's Way Church, 808 P.2d 1211 (Alaska 1991).
[3] Evan F. v. Hughson United Methodist Church, 10 Cal. Rptr.2d 748 (Cal. App. 3 Dist. 1992).

molestation of his 6-year-old sister. The pastor was hired after being suspended from the ministry for a number of years because of allegations that he had molested a child. He later molested a 13-year-old boy who attended the church. The court noted that "in California, an employer can be held liable for negligent hiring if he knows the employee is unfit, or has reason to believe the employee is unfit or fails to use reasonable care to discover the employee's unfitness before hiring him." The court noted that the local church's pastoral search committee was aware that the pastor previously had "stepped down" from the ministry for some reason. Yet, the church did not "investigate or make any inquiry" regarding the pastor's fitness to serve. The court observed that the local church's pastoral selection committee was aware of "some difficulty with [the pastor's] reappointment to the active ministry and understood he had been on a sabbatical of some kind. . . . Nevertheless, [the church] did not investigate or make any inquiry regarding [the pastor's] fitness to serve as pastor." The court rejected the sister's claim that the church was liable for her brother's acts of molestation. At the trial, a child psychiatrist testified that the 13-year-old brother had molested his sister because of his experience with the pastor. The psychiatrist explained that abused and molested children often abuse and molest others. She noted that the brother had not previously engaged in any incidents of child molestation, and that the pastor's assaults had triggered a premature sexual stimulation and "awakening" of the boy (who was then an early adolescent entering puberty). The psychiatrist concluded that the boy, in molesting his sister, was "re-enacting" or "acting out" his own molestation experience of a larger person overpowering a smaller one. The court, in rejecting the sister's claim, observed, "[T]he theory of negligent hiring here encompasses the particular risk of molestation by an employee with a history of this specific conduct. It does not encompass acts done by non-employees, such as the 13-year-old brother, or consequences involving less particular, even speculative, hazards. To conclude otherwise would impose liability on the person who hired the person who molested the person who molested the person in the sister's position. This convoluted syntax alone argues against imposing liability in this situation."

Example. *A Colorado court dismissed a lawsuit brought by a woman alleging that her church acted improperly and unlawfully when it dismissed her after she made complaints of sexual harassment and child molestation against another minister.[4] The woman alleged that between 1968 and 1975, when she was a minor, her stepfather committed various acts of sexual assault against her when they resided together. Her stepfather was a minister at the time, and later became president of his denomination. The woman pursued ministerial studies and was licensed as a minister. After serving as a minister in the State of Washington she moved to the Denver area to start a new church. She later learned that her stepfather, with whom she had severed all ties, was also pastoring a church in the Denver area. She learned that her stepfather was allegedly sexually harassing women church employees and a woman parishioner in his Denver church. She reported this alleged harassment, as well as the sexual abuse she had suffered from her stepfather as a minor, to denominational officers. In response, the stepfather filed charges with the denomination against the woman, claiming that her allegations were false and demanding a full investigation. After an investigation, denominational officers revoked the woman's license and denied her the opportunity to open a new church. The woman responded by filing a lawsuit against*

---

[4] Van Osdol v. Vogt, 892 P.2d 402 (Colo. App. 1994). Accord Bear Valley Church of Christ v. DeBose, 928 P.2d 1315 (Colo. 1996).

her stepfather and her denomination alleging several theories of liability including illegal retaliation by denominational officials in response to her charges of sexual harassment, and negligent hiring of her stepfather by denominational officials. The court acknowledged that "[a]n employer may be liable for harm to others for negligently employing an improper person for a task that may involve risk to others." The woman claimed that her stepfather had been involved in an extramarital affair with a parishioner at another church prior to his present assignment and that denominational officials failed to investigate this allegation. The court concluded that "the extramarital affair was sufficiently different from [the woman's] allegations against [her stepfather] and, thus, did not create a duty on the part of the church to foresee [his] conduct." Further, the court noted that during the time the woman was allegedly abused as a child, her stepfather was not a minister, and that she did not allege that denominational officials knew or should have known of the stepfather's alleged sexual abuse of his stepdaughter when they hired him."

Example. *A New York court ruled that a Catholic church and diocese could be sued on the basis of negligent hiring as a result of the sexual molestation of an 11-year-old boy by a Catholic priest.[5] The victim and his sister were both enrolled in a parochial school operated by the church. An associate pastor at the church (who also served as director of religious education for the school) obtained permission from the victim's mother to take him to an athletic facility at a local college to play racquetball and basketball and go swimming. While in the shower room prior to entering the pool, the pastor allegedly removed all his clothing and made the victim do the same. He then molested the victim. The boy's mother later sued the pastor, church, and diocese, claiming that her son had suffered substantial emotional injuries. She alleged that the church and diocese were liable on the basis of negligent hiring. Specifically, she asserted that the church and diocese were liable for the misconduct of the pastor on the basis of their own negligence in hiring and placing him in contact with boys with inadequate investigation of his background and with actual or "constructive" knowledge of his propensities. The court rejected the argument of the church and diocese that permitting the civil courts to find religious organizations liable on the basis of negligent hiring of clergy would constitute excessive governmental interference with church autonomy in violation of the first amendment guaranty of religious freedom. The court observed, "[If the mother is] successful in establishing that, with knowledge that the priest was likely to commit sexual abuse on youths with whom he was put in contact, his employers placed or continued him in a setting in which such abuse occurred, the fact that the placement occurred in the course of internal administration of the religious units does not preclude holding the institutions accountable to the victim of their neglect in administration. Indeed, a contrary holding—that a religious body must be held free from any responsibility for wholly predictable and foreseeable injurious consequences of personnel decisions, although such decisions incorporate no theological or dogmatic tenets—would go beyond first amendment protection and cloak such bodies with an exclusive immunity greater than that required for the preservation of the principles constitutionally safeguarded."*

Example. *The Virginia Supreme Court ruled that a church and its pastor could be sued by a mother whose child was sexually assaulted by a church employee.[6] A*

---

[5] Jones by Jones v. Trane. 591 N.Y.S.2d 927 (Sup. 1992).
[6] J. v. Victory Baptist Church, 372 S.E.2d 391 (Va. 1988).

mother sued a church and its pastor, alleging that her 10-year-old daughter had been repeatedly raped and assaulted by a church employee. She asserted that the church and minister were legally responsible on the basis of several grounds, including "negligent hiring" (referred to as negligent selection in this chapter). Specifically, she alleged that when the employee was hired, the church and minister either knew or should have known that he had recently been convicted of aggravated sexual assault on a young girl, that he was on probation for the offense, and that a condition of his probation was that he not be involved or associated with children. Despite these circumstances, the individual was hired and entrusted with duties that encouraged him to come freely into contact with children, and in addition was given keys to all of the church's doors. The mother alleged that the employee in fact came into contact with her daughter on the church's premises, and had sexual intercourse with her on numerous occasions. The court ruled that the church could be sued on the basis of negligent selection. It rejected the church's contentions that the theory of negligent selection either was not recognized under Virginia law, or was not recognized in the context of church employers. The court also rejected the church's contention that it could not be responsible for criminal acts of employees: "To say that a negligently hired employee who acts willfully or criminally thus relieves his employer of liability for negligent selection when willful or criminal conduct is precisely what the employer should have foreseen would rob the tort of vitality . . . ." The court also rejected the church's contention that it could not be liable for the employee's acts of molestation since they had not occurred within the scope of employment. It acknowledged that church liability based on respondeat superior required that the employee's acts be committed within the scope of employment. However, "negligent hiring is a doctrine of primary liability; the employer is principally liable for negligently placing an unfit person in an employment situation involving an unreasonable risk of harm to others. Negligent hiring, therefore, enables plaintiffs to recover in situations where respondeat superior's scope of employment limitation previously protected employers from liability.

Court decisions rejecting negligent selection claims

Some courts have found churches not liable on the basis of negligent selection for the molestation of a minor by a church worker since the church exercised reasonable care in the selection of the worker. Representative cases are summarized below.

Example. A federal appeals court ruled that an archdiocese was not responsible for the alleged molestation of a minor by a priest.[7] The victim claimed that the archdiocese should have known that the priest had a history of sexual improprieties and that he would continue to pursue those activities when under its employ. He insisted that a minimal background check would have revealed the priest's pattern of sexual activity with minors. The court, in rejecting this argument, observed, "The record, however, permits of no conclusion that the [archdiocese] suspected that [the priest] had engaged in sexual improprieties or might do so in the future. It is doubtful that the archdiocese . . . knew anything about [his] darker side. [He] was diligent in guarding his secrets. He did not disclose his extracurricular activities to anyone at anytime in the course of his employment and, from his perspective, with good reason.

---

[7] Tichenor v. Roman Catholic Church, 32 F.3d 953 (5th Cir. 1994).

No tangible evidence in the form of a criminal history or discipline exists that would have been uncovered in a background check."

Example. The Alabama Supreme Court concluded that a church-operated preschool was not responsible for the kidnapping of a three-month-old infant by three adolescent sisters employed by the preschool.[8] At the time of the kidnapping, there was no qualified adult teacher, other than the administrator herself, directly supervising the sisters. The administrator later testified that the other teachers had "gone for the day" and that she thought one of the sisters had intentionally distracted her while the other two slipped the baby out the front door undetected. The local police and the Federal Bureau of Investigation investigated the incident, eventually found the baby, and reunited her with her parents. The parents experienced severe shock as a result of the kidnapping, and later sued the preschool. They claimed that the preschool was legally responsible for the kidnapping on the basis of negligent hiring of the three sisters. They pointed out that the preschool used girls who were only 12, 14, and 17 years of age to care for infants. And, there was evidence that the two older sisters had been physically (and perhaps sexually) abused by members of their family, and that the oldest sister lied to the center's administrator by telling her that she was pregnant. The court rejected the parents' claim that this evidence demonstrated that the preschool had been guilty of negligent hiring.

Example. A California court ruled that a Catholic church was not responsible on the basis of negligent hiring for a priest's acts of child molestation, since it had not been aware of any similar incidents of misconduct at the time the priest was employed.[9] The court acknowledged that "an employer may be liable to a third person for the employer's negligence in hiring or retaining an employee who is incompetent or unfit." However, the court qualified this rule by noting that "one who employs another to act for him is not liable . . . merely because the one employed is incompetent, vicious, or careless. If liability results it is because, under the circumstances, the employer has not taken the care which a prudent man would take in selecting the person for the business in hand. . . . Liability results . . . not because of the relation of the parties, but because the employer . . . had reason to believe that an undue risk of harm would exist because of the employment." The court noted that the harm the victim suffered was criminal sexual abuse of a minor by her priest. It observed, "There is nothing in the record to indicate [the priest] had a criminal history or had been previously implicated in sexual abuse of a minor. Thus the church could not have had antecedent knowledge of [his] purported criminal dangerousness." That is, evidence that the priest had engaged in sexual misconduct with adults did not necessarily make him a risk to children. The court observed that the victim failed to prove any facts "showing an undue risk of harm that [the priest] would commit criminal child sexual abuse if he were employed by the church." But even if evidence of sexual misconduct with adults would be relevant in evaluating a priest's risk of committing similar acts upon children, the church "had no actual knowledge of [his] sexual activity with [her] or anyone else until it heard [her] mother's report and [the priest's] admissions." In other words, the church could not be responsible for the priest's molestation of the victim on the basis of negligent hiring if it had no knowledge of any prior misconduct by the priest at the time he was hired or ordained. The court noted further noted that "the legal duty of inquiry [the victim]

---

[8] Hargrove v. Tree of Life Christian Day Care Center, 699 So.2d 1242 (Ala. 1997).
[9] Roman Catholic Bishop v. Superior Court, 50 Cal. Rptr.2d 399 (Cal. App. 1996).

seeks to impose on the church as an employer would violate the employee's privacy rights. Privacy is a fundamental liberty implicitly guaranteed by the federal Constitution and is explicitly guaranteed under the California Constitution as an inalienable right. The right encompasses privacy in one's sexual matters and is not limited to the marital relationship. Although the right to privacy is not absolute, it yields only to a compelling state interest. Here there was no compelling state interest to require the employer to investigate the sexual practices of its employee. Moreover, the employer who queries employees on sexual behavior is subject to claims for invasion of privacy and sexual harassment. Similarly [the victim's] contention that the church should have required [the priest] to undergo a psychological evaluation before hiring him is unavailing. An individual's right to privacy also encompasses mental privacy. We conclude the church did not fail to use due care in hiring [the priest]."

Example. *An Illinois court ruled that a church and a parent denomination were not legally responsible for a pastor's sexual assault of three boys.[10] The boys' parents sued the pastor, his church, and a denominational agency, claiming that the boys had suffered severe emotional damage. The parents claimed that the denominational agency negligently assigned the pastor to the church, knowing of a prior assault on another boy several years earlier. A jury returned a verdict against the agency in the amount of $450,000 ($150,000 per boy) on the basis of its alleged negligence. However, a state appeals court reversed the verdict and dismissed the negligence verdict against the agency. It is significant to note that the court observed that "the jury could well have determined that the [agency] took adequate precaution in having [the pastor] counseled and should not have been held to have reasonably foreseen that [he] would be likely to commit the acts of sexual assault." This case suggests that churches and denominations may be legally responsible on the basis of negligent hiring if they hire or retain a minister after learning that he or she was guilty of sexual misconduct in the past. However, the court emphasized that mere knowledge of previous incidents of sexual misconduct does not automatically create legal liability. Liability for negligent hiring or retention requires that the actions of the church or denomination created a foreseeable and unreasonable risk of harm to others.*

Example. *A Louisiana appeals court ruled that a church-affiliated hospital was not liable on the basis of negligent selection for the sexual misconduct of an employee who had been thoroughly screened and supervised. The hospital hired a male nursing assistant for a psychiatric ward after conducting a thorough background check that showed no criminal record and no unfavorable references from former employers. After working for six months, this employee raped a 16-year-old girl. The victim sued the hospital. The appeals court concluded that the hospital could not be liable for the assault on the basis of negligent hiring, because of the thorough nature of its pre-employment investigation.[11]*

Example. *A Minnesota court ruled that a church and denominational organization were not legally responsible on the basis of negligent hiring for a pastor's acts of child molestation.[12] The molester served as pastor of a church and was accused of sexually abusing numerous young boys during his tenure. He admitted abusing some of the*

---

[10] Mt. Zion State Bank v. Central Illinois Conference of the United Methodist Church, 556 N.E.2d 1270 (Ill. App. 1990).

[11] Samuels v. Southern Baptist Hospital 594 So.2d 571 (La. App. 1992).

[12] M.L. v. Magnuson, 531 N.W.2d 831 (Minn. App. 1995).

children, including a 10-year-old boy (the "victim"). *The victim later sued the pastor and his former church. The court defined "negligent hiring" as "the negligence of an employer in placing a person with known propensities, or propensities which should have been discovered by reasonable investigation, in an employment position in which, because of the circumstances of employment, it should have been foreseeable that the hired individual posed a threat of injury to others." In ruling that the church had not been negligent in hiring the pastor, the court observed, "There is no evidence [the church] had actual knowledge of [the pastor's] propensities to commit sexual abuse before he was hired. Moreover, it would have been contrary to the evidence for the jury to have concluded that [the church] should have learned of [his] propensities through reasonable investigation. The regional church body had direct knowledge that [the pastor] had sexually abused a child two years before he was hired by [the church]. But it is undisputed that the regional church did not tell [the church] about this incident and took no action against [the pastor] that might have been discovered by [the church]. The record does not permit an inference that [the church] could have learned about [the pastor's] propensities from the regional church, which was unwilling to disclose this information voluntarily. . . . . [T]he trial court suggested that if [the church] had simply called [the pastor's] previous employer it might have learned that [he] had been accused of sexual abuse at that church. If this search is reasonably seen as a part of the hiring process in this church organization in 1964, a proposition we do not review, we find no evidence in the record to show that [the pastor's] previous employer was aware of any accusations of sexual abuse against him. [The victim] has not presented any evidence of another source that [the church] might reasonably have investigated to discover [the pastor's] dangerous propensities, so the jury could not have determined that [it] negligently hired [him]."*

Example. A Washington state appeals court ruled that a church-operated school was not legally responsible for damages resulting from an alleged sexual relationship between a teacher and a student.[13] *The student's parents had sued the school and church for "negligent hiring" and "negligent supervision." The court rejected both allegations. With regard to the school's alleged negligent hiring, the court observed that "the hiring process employed by the school suggests it took reasonable care in hiring [the teacher]. . . . The process appears sufficient as a matter of law to discover whether an individual is fit to teach at [the school]."*

32.3 Negligent Selection of Church Workers—Sexual Misconduct Cases Involving Adult Victims

In recent years, hundreds of churches have been sued as a result of sexual contact by clergy with adults. Most of these cases have involved sexual contact with church employees or with counselees. Nearly all of the cases have involved sexual contact between male clergy and adult female employees or counselees. The personal liability of ministers for engaging in such acts is addressed in a previous chapter. This chapter will address the question of whether the minister's employing church can be legally responsible for the minister's acts on the basis of its negligent selection of the minister.

As noted earlier in this chapter, the term negligence refers to conduct that creates an unreasonable risk of foreseeable harm to others. It connotes carelessness,

---

[13] Scott v. Blanchet High School, 747 P.2d 1124 (Wash. App. 1987).

heedlessness, inattention, or inadvertence. Negligent selection of a minister means that the church failed to act responsibly and with due care in the selection of a minister who later engages in some form of foreseeable misconduct. To illustrate, assume that a church hires a minister without any background check, and fails to discover that the minister had been dismissed by another church because of committing adultery with two women. A year later, it is discovered that the minister has engaged in adultery with a married woman in the course of marital counseling. The woman sues the church, claiming that the minister's conduct caused her emotional and psychological harm, and that her church is legally responsible for the minister's acts on the basis of negligent selection. She insists that had church leaders contacted the other church they would have discovered the minister's background and would not have hired him.

Church leaders can take relatively simple yet effective steps to significantly reduce the likelihood of such incidents occurring. This section will review some of the more significant reported court rulings, and then suggest a number of preventive measures that any church can implement in order to reduce the risk of such incidents.

Tip. No one understands or appreciates risk better than insurance companies. Risk evaluation is their business. As a result, it is very important to observe that a number of church insurance companies have reduced the insurance coverage they provide for sexual misconduct, and in some cases they have excluded it entirely. Some companies are suggesting that these incidents are excluded under the provision in most policies excluding damages based on intentional, criminal conduct (most acts of sexual molestation involve criminal activity). Church leaders should immediately review their church liability insurance policy to determine whether the church has any coverage for acts of sexual misconduct, and if so, whether such coverage has been limited in any way. If you fit within either category, the risk management recommendations in this chapter are of even greater relevance.

Some courts have found churches liable on the basis of negligent selection for the sexual misconduct of a church worker involving another adult if the church failed to exercise reasonable care in the selection of the worker.

Example. A Colorado court ruled that a minister and a denominational agency could be sued by a woman with whom the minister had sexual contacts.[14] A woman (the victim) attended a church for a few years, and began to volunteer her services for a variety of activities including the remodeling of a classroom. She engaged in these volunteer services on the recommendation of a therapist who suggested that she work in a "safe environment" to overcome her fears of the workplace. The victim's volunteer work caused her to come in contact with her minister after normal working hours. On one occasion the minister approached her while she was remodeling a classroom, began caressing her back, and told her, "I love you Dianne, you mean so much to me." A few days later, the minister called the victim into his office where the two of them sat next to each other on a small couch. The minister again caressed her and expressed his love for her. Following a third incident, the victim informed two other women in the church about the minister's behavior, and one responded, "Oh my God, not you too." A few months later a denominational agency with which the church was affiliated held a meeting in response to a formal complaint it had received regarding

---

[14] Winkler v. Rocky Mouton Conference, 923 P.2d 152 (Colo. App. 1995).

the minister's conduct. Six women attended this meeting, and all described similar incidents of unwelcome verbal comments and physical contact involving the minister. As a result of this meeting, the minister was suspended. The victim later sued her church and a denominational agency on the basis of several theories of liability, including negligent hiring of the minister. She alleged that the agency had been made aware of at least one prior act of sexual misconduct involving the minister, and was aware that he had a problem with alcohol abuse. The court ruled that the agency could be liable on the basis of negligent hiring, despite the agency's argument that the ordination and discipline of ministers is an ecclesiastical matter involving theological concerns over which the civil courts cannot exercise jurisdiction. The court noted simply that neither the minister nor the agency claimed that the minister's "method of communicating with parishioners by touching, hugging, and expressing affection was based on any religious tenet or belief."

Some courts have ruled that churches were not liable on the basis of negligent selection for the sexual misconduct of a minister or other church worker involving another adult since the church exercised reasonable care in the selection of the worker. Many of these courts have concluded that the first amendment's "nonestablishment of religion" and "free exercise of religion" clauses prevent the civil courts from resolving negligent selection claims involving clergy misconduct. Representative cases are summarized below.

Example. A Florida court ruled that it was barred by the first amendment from resolving a woman's lawsuit claiming that she had been the victim of a priest's sexual misconduct.[15] The court began its opinion by noting that the first amendment prohibits any governmental practice (including judicial resolution of internal church disputes) that would lead to an "excessive entanglement" between church and state. The court noted that excessive entanglement occurs "when the courts begin to review and interpret a church's constitution, laws, and regulations." The court concluded that the resolution of a negligent hiring, supervision, or retention claim against a church or diocese would amount to an excessive entanglement in violation of the first amendment: "Our examination of case law presenting both sides of this question leads us to conclude the reasoning of those courts holding the first amendment bars a claim for negligent hiring, retention, and supervision is the more compelling. In a church defendant's determination to hire or retain a minister, or in its capacity as supervisor of that minister, a church defendant's conduct is guided by religious doctrine and/or practice. Thus, a court's determination regarding whether the church defendant's conduct was 'reasonable' would necessarily entangle the court in issues of the church's religious law, practices, and policies. 'Hiring' in a traditional sense does not occur in some religions, where a person is ordained into a particular position in the church, and assigned to one parish or another. A court faced with the task of determining a claim of negligent hiring, retention, and supervision would measure the church defendants' conduct against that of a reasonable employer; a proscribed comparison."

Example. A Georgia court dismissed a lawsuit brought by a woman against her church and a denominational agency as a result of injuries she allegedly sustained during a sexual relationship with her pastor.[16] The court observed, "An employer may not be held

15 Doe v. Evans, 718 So.2d 286 (Fla. App. 1998).
16 Alpharetta First United Methodist Church v. Stewart, 473 S.E.2d 532 (Ga. App. 1996).

liable for negligent hiring or retention unless the [victim] shows the employer knew or should have known of the employee's violent and criminal propensities. Specifically, the [couple] must show that the church and the [denominational agency] knew or should have known of [the associate pastor's] propensity for sexual misconduct. . . . . There is nothing in the record before us to show the church or [denominational agency] should have been on notice prior to ordaining [the associate pastor] that he had a propensity for sexual misconduct." As proof that the church and denominational agency had been negligent in ordaining or hiring the associate pastor, the couple noted that he had been suspended for a year while in seminary for cheating on a Hebrew examination, and that his psychological evaluation indicated certain problems, such as difficulty controlling his impulses, a tendency to use poor judgment, a tendency to disregard the rights of others, and a likelihood to express aggression in a physical manner. The court disagreed that these facts proved that either the church or denominational agency was guilty of negligent selection: "These types of generalized findings, without more, are not sufficient to put the church and [denominational agency] on notice of a propensity for sexual misconduct." The court pointed out that the psychological evaluation (which consisted of the Minnesota Multiphasic Personality Inventory, the Interpersonal Behavior Survey, the Strong-Campbell Interest Inventory, and the Sentence Completion Test) also showed several positive characteristics such as, "He is very social and interested in leadership in service to other people. . . . He shows a pattern of interest moderately like those of successful ministers or social workers." The court also summarized the many precautions that were taken prior to the time the pastor was ordained, including a 2-year internship, letters of recommendation, psychological testing, and extensive interviews by an ordination committee.

Example. An Indiana court ruled that neither a church nor a denominational agency could be sued on the basis of negligent hiring for injuries suffered by a woman who was molested by her pastor when she was a minor.[17] The woman claimed that the pastor began molesting her when she was 7 years old, and that the molestation continued until she was 20. The court concluded that neither the church nor the denominational agency could be liable on the basis of negligent selection of the pastor. The court observed that the pastor was hired by the church in 1954, and that there was no evidence whatsoever that would indicate a risk.

Example. A Louisiana court ruled that an Episcopal diocese was not legally responsible for the suicide of a woman allegedly caused by a sexual relationship with an Episcopal priest.[18] The husband of a woman who committed suicide sued a priest and diocese, claiming that his wife's suicide had been caused by the sexual misconduct of the priest. The lawsuit alleged that the priest was guilty of malpractice by taking advantage of an emotionally dependent woman and then abusing his position of trust to engage in sexual intercourse with her on numerous occasions. The husband claimed that the priest's behavior violated the teachings of the Episcopal Church as well as the ninth commandment ("thou shalt not covet they neighbor's wife") and the sixth commandment ("thou shalt not commit adultery"). The husband claimed that the diocese was responsible for his wife's suicide on the basis of several grounds, including a failure to adequately investigate the priest as to his emotional, psychological, and moral fitness to be a minister of the Episcopal Church. In dismissing the husband's

---

17 Konkle v. Henson, 672 N.E.2d 450 (Ind. App. 1996).
18 Roppolo v. Moore, 644 So.2d 206 (La. App. 4 Cir. 1994).

allegation of "negligent selection" of the priest by the diocese, the court observed, "[A]ny inquiry into the policies and practices of [churches] in hiring or supervising their clergy raises . . . first amendment problems of entanglement . . . which might involve the court in making sensitive judgments about the propriety of [churches'] supervision in light of their religious beliefs."

Example. *A federal court in New York refused to find a church or denomination agency liable on the basis of "negligent placement, retention, or supervision" for a pastor's sexual contacts with a woman during marital counseling.[19] The court made the following statement in rejecting the woman's claim that the church and denomination had been guilty of negligence: "[A]ny inquiry into the policies and practices of the church defendants in hiring or supervising their clergy raises . . . first amendment problems of entanglement . . . which might involve the court in making sensitive judgments about the propriety of the church defendants' supervision in light of their religious beliefs."*

Example. *The Oklahoma Supreme Court ruled that a married couple could not sue their church and former pastor for damages they allegedly incurred as a result of an adulterous affair between the former pastor and the wife.[20] The husband and wife sued the church and former pastor as a result of the pastor's conduct. The lawsuit alleged that the church was negligent in the selection of the pastor since it knew or should have known about the wife's affair and a previous affair in Texas. The church insisted that it did not know of the affair or of the alleged incident in Texas, and that it did not condone such behavior. The court concluded that the church was not responsible for injuries resulting from the minister's conduct. It observed that the first amendment guaranty of religious freedom did not shield churches from liability for personal injuries arising "from acts unrelated to religious practices protected by the first amendment." However, it insisted that all of the couple's claims against the church had to be dismissed. It observed, "Neither the claims by the husband nor the wife against the minister are cognizable in Oklahoma. . . . Because their claims against the minister also serve as the basis for the claims against the church for its negligent hiring and supervision of the minister, that claim is also not cognizable."*

32.4 Negligent Selection of Church Workers—Other Cases

Negligent selection claims are not limited to cases involving sexual misconduct. They can arise anytime that a church's failure to exercise reasonable care in the selection of an employee or volunteer leads to a foreseeable injury. Here are some examples:

- Using adolescents as attendants in the church nursery.

- Selecting adult workers without any training in CPR or other resuscitation techniques to accompany a youth group to any event involving swimming or boating.

- Selecting lay counselors with inadequate professional training.

- Selecting drivers for any church-sponsored activity without checking their driving record. For example, if a church uses a driver with a suspended drivers license, or with a history of traffic offenses, then it may be

---

[19] Schmidt v. Bishop, 779 F. Supp. 321 (S.D.N.Y. 1991).
[20] Bladen v. First Presbyterian Church, 857 P.2d 789 (Okla. 1993).

responsible on the basis of negligent selection for injuries caused by the driver's negligence. To reduce the risk of liability in this context, churches should refrain from using any driver without taking the following steps:

1. Have each prospective driver complete an application form that asks for the person's drivers license number, type of drivers license and expiration date, a description of any driving restrictions, and a history of traffic accidents and moving violations.

2. Ask the church's liability insurance carrier to check on the individual's driving record. Often, insurance companies will perform this task if requested, at no charge. The insurance company should be requested to update its research on all drivers of church vehicles periodically, to screen out persons with a recent history of unsafe driving.

3. Discontinue using any driver if reports are received that he or she is operating a church vehicle in a negligent manner. Fully investigate such reports, and do not use the individual again unless the investigation clearly demonstrates that the complaints were without merit.

4. If the prospective driver is a new member, then ask for the names and addresses of other churches in which he or she has worked as a driver. Contact those other churches and ask if they are aware of facts that would indicate that the individual should not be used as a driver. Make a written record of such contacts.

5. Periodically invite a local law enforcement officer to speak to all drivers concerning safety issues.

6. Require all drivers to immediately inform the church of any traffic convictions.

32.5 Negligent Retention of Church Workers—In General

A church may use reasonable care in selecting ministers or other church workers but still be responsible for their misconduct if it "retained" them after receiving information indicating that they posed a risk of harm to others. Some courts have concluded that churches can be sued on the basis of negligent retention for the sexual misconduct of ministers and other church staff. Representative cases are summarized below.

Example. A federal appeals court concluded that two female church employees could sue the minister who had seduced them since he had "held himself out" as a qualified marital counselor.[21] However, the court dismissed all of the employees' claims against the church, including negligent retention. The court acknowledged that "an employer that negligently retains in his employ an individual who is incompetent or unfit for the job may be liable to a third party whose injury was proximately caused by the employer's negligence." However, to prove negligent retention, the two women had to show that the church "knew or should have known that [the former minister's] conduct as a supervisor or counselor presented an unreasonable risk of harm to others." The court concluded that there was no evidence that the church "know or should have known" that the former minister was engaging in marital counseling or that he was likely to engage in sexual misconduct or disclose confidences as a marriage counselor.

---

21 Sanders v. Casa View Baptist Church, 134 F.3d 331 (5th Cir. 1998).

Example. A North Carolina court ruled that the first amendment did not prevent it from resolving a sexual harassment lawsuit brought by three female church employees against their church and denominational agencies.[22] The court began its opinion by noting that the key issue was whether the first amendment prevents "the filing of a negligent retention and supervision claim against a religious organization, when that claim is based on the conduct of a cleric of that organization." The court concluded that if a resolution of the plaintiffs' legal claims did not require an interpretation of church doctrine, then "the first amendment is not implicated and neutral principles of law are properly applied to adjudicate the claim." The court then noted that North Carolina recognizes negligent supervision and retention as separate bases of legal liability. To support a claim of negligent retention and supervision against an employer, a plaintiff must prove that "the incompetent employee committed a tortious act resulting in injury to plaintiff and that prior to the act, the employer knew or had reason to know of the employee's incompetency." The court concluded, "We acknowledge that the decision to hire or discharge a minister is inextricable from religious doctrine and protected by the first amendment from judicial inquiry. We do not accept, however, that resolution of the plaintiffs' negligent retention and supervision claim requires the trial court to inquire into the church defendants' reasons for choosing [the pastor] to serve as a minister. The plaintiffs' claim, construed in the light most favorable to them, instead presents the issue of whether the church defendants knew or had reason to know of [the pastor's] propensity to engage in sexual misconduct, conduct that the church defendants do not claim is part of the tenets or practices of [their religion]. Thus, there is no necessity for the court to interpret or weigh church doctrine in its adjudication of the plaintiffs' claim for negligent retention and supervision. It follows that the first amendment is not implicated and does not bar the plaintiffs' claim against the church defendants."

Example. A Minnesota court ruled that a church could be sued as a result of the pastor's acts of child molestation.[23] The court concluded that the church had been negligent in permitting the sexual abuse to occur. This conclusion was based in part on the fact that during the time the victim was being molested: (1) A church trustee saw the pastor kissing another adolescent boy on the mouth. The pastor, upon seeing the trustee, blushed and ran back to his apartment. The trustee informed another trustee of this incident, along with two members of the church council. No action was taken. (2) Another church trustee was approached by a local teacher and asked if the pastor was a child molester. This same trustee's uncle told him that he heard something went on at a cabin at church camp and asked if the pastor was "straight." (3) A church trustee's son had to make up some work for confirmation classes at the pastor's home. When he returned home, he told his father that the pastor wanted him "to get under the sheets" with him. (4) A student in the confirmation class testified that during a confirmation class at the church she thought she saw the pastor engage in an act of child abuse. She told her parents and the church's "intern pastor" what she saw. The girl and her parents quit attending the church after this incident. (5) Another confirmation student told the church's intern pastor that the pastor had "put his arm around him all of the time" and showered with the boys. The church claimed that the intern's "knowledge" could not be imputed to the church, since he was not an employee. In rejecting this defense, the court observed, "Regardless of whether [the intern pastor's] knowledge may be imputed to [the church, the church's] own

---

[22] Smith v. Privette, 495 S.E.2d 395 (N.C. App. 1998).
[23] Doe v. Redeemer Lutheran Church, 531 N.W.2d 897 (Minn. App. 1995).

council members and trustees were aware that [the pastor] had been engaging in sexual improprieties, but they turned a blind eye and did nothing to address the problem. The jury clearly could have found that [the church] should have taken action and failure to do so amounted to negligence."

Some courts have concluded that the first amendment prevents churches from being sued on the basis of negligent retention for the sexual misconduct of ministers.

Example. A federal court in Connecticut dismissed a lawsuit brought by two adult brothers against their church and diocese for injuries they allegedly sustained when they were sexually molested while minors by a priest.[24] The brothers alleged that the church and diocese were legally responsible for the priest's acts on the basis of negligent retention because they were aware that the priest had received treatment sessions for sexual abuse of minors over a 15-year period at Catholic treatment centers in New Mexico and Maryland. The court accepted affidavits from church officials claiming that they had no knowledge (or reason to suspect) that the priest had ever participated in any retreat or treatment for sexual abuse of any kind. The court concluded, based on these affidavits, that the church and diocese had no prior knowledge of any sexual misconduct on the part of the offending priest, and so the negligence claim had to be dismissed.

Example. A Georgia appeals court dismissed a daughter's lawsuit against a priest and Catholic diocese claiming that her father murdered her mother and then killed himself as a result of an adulterous affair between the mother and a priest.[25] The daughter claimed that her mother had been seduced by the priest, and that her father shot and killed her mother and then shot himself after finding out about it. The daughter claimed that the diocese was responsible for her parent's deaths on the basis of negligent hiring and retention of the priest. She insisted that if the diocese had adequately investigated the matter and "defrocked" the priest, the deaths would not have occurred. The court concluded that the diocese did not have sufficient proof that the priest had acted improperly. It observed, "To the contrary, all signs point to the unreliability of [the mother's] declarations. She told a friend that she did not have an affair with [the priest] and in an official church investigation by the church she denied any involvement with the priest. She wrote a letter to [her] archbishop in which she stated that she had fantasized an affair with [the priest] because her husband was away on business and she was lonely. She asked the archbishop for forgiveness and stated that she was seeking professional help." The court concluded that the priest and diocese "produced evidence demonstrating that [the priest] did not have a sexual relationship with [the mother]. [The daughter] has failed to come up with evidence to the contrary."

Example. A federal district court in Michigan ruled that a church school and various church agencies were not liable on the basis of negligent hiring, supervision, or retention for the sexual molestation of a minor student by a priest.[26] The court, in summarily rejecting the victim's claim that the school and church agencies had been guilty of "negligent hiring," observed, "Questions of hiring and retention of clergy

---

[24] Nutt v. Norwich Roman Catholic Diocese, 921 F. Supp. 66 (D. Conn. 1995). See also Martinelli v. Bridgeport Roman Catholic Diocese, 989 F. Supp. 110 (D. Conn. 1997).
[25] Boehm v. Abi-Sarkis, 438 S.E.2d 410 (Ga. App. 1993).
[26] Isely v. Capuchin Province, 880 F. Supp. 1138 (E.D. Mich. 1995).

necessarily will require interpretation of church canons, and internal church policies and practices. It is well-settled that when a court is required to interpret canon law or internal church policies and practices, the first amendment is violated because such judicial inquiry would constitute excessive government entanglement with religion. . . . [An] inquiry into the decision of who should be permitted to become or remain a priest necessarily would involve prohibited excessive entanglement with religion. Therefore [the victim's] claims of negligence predicated upon a negligent hiring theory will be dismissed."

Example. A Minnesota court ruled that a church and denominational organization were not legally responsible on the basis of negligent retention for a pastor's acts of child molestation.[27] The victim pointed to the following facts in supporting his claim that the church had been guilty of negligent retention: (1) some church members knew the pastor had an interest in children and youth ministry; (2) some church members knew the pastor was counseling children in private, including discussions of sexual and relationship issues; (3) some church members knew that, as part of his confirmation curriculum, the pastor discussed sexuality with children during the final interview; (4) some church members knew the pastor taught the boys about circumcision in confirmation classes, though a parent was always present during these lectures; (5) other incidents of sexual abuse occurred at the church at a time when other people would normally be around and the pastor took no special precautions to hide the abuse. The court concluded that the church was not guilty of negligent retention, since "[t]here is no evidence [it] had actual knowledge of [the pastor's] propensities to commit sexual abuse prior to the time [the victim] was abused." It observed, "There is no evidence that members in 1973 should have foreseen abuse because their clergyperson was interested in youth ministry or counseled children in private. We are mindful that most personal counseling occurs in private. And by itself, evidence of a youth ministry interest and counseling activity does not show that the congregation should suspect the pastor is engaging in sexual abuse. Nor is it reasonable to infer, at least without other evidence, knowledge in 1973 that a pastor will engage in sexual abuse merely because he or she counsels children on sexual issues. There is no evidence that counseling on sexual issues was outside a pastor's purview or so unusual that it should have raised suspicions of sexual abuse. We agree that the details of some of [the pastor's] discussions on sexuality were highly unusual and perhaps would have alerted [the church] to a problem. But there is no evidence that anyone reported the contents of these discussions to [the church's] decision makers nor has [the victim] explained how these [church] members could otherwise have learned the details of these conversations. . . . Finally, the jury could not conclude that [the church] should have known about other incidents of abuse simply because they occurred at the church when other people were probably in the building. The incidents all occurred in private, and there is no evidence that people who may have been in the building knew anything more than the fact that counseling sessions occurred. . . . If this evidence alone is sufficient to support a negligent retention verdict, it would appear impossible for a church to avoid liability without prohibiting pastors from counseling children in private or prohibiting discussion of sexual issues. We are not prepared to hold that every church must take these measures to avoid liability for negligent retention, much less that this standard can govern church practices retroactive to a time more than two decades past."

---

[27] M.L. v. Magnuson, 531 N.W.2d 831 (Minn. App. 1995). Accord Mulinix v. Mulinix, 1997 WL 585775 (Minn. App. 1997).

Example. A federal court in New York refused to find a church or denomination agency liable, on the basis of "negligent placement, retention, or supervision," for a pastor's sexual contacts with a woman during marital counseling.[28] The court made the following statement in rejecting the woman's claim that the church and denomination had been guilty of negligence: "[A]ny inquiry into the policies and practices of the church defendants in hiring or supervising their clergy raises . . . first amendment problems of entanglement . . . which might involve the court in making sensitive judgments about the propriety of the church defendants' supervision in light of their religious beliefs. Insofar as concerns retention or supervision, the pastor of a Presbyterian church is not analogous to a common law employee. He may not demit his charge nor be removed by the session, without the consent of the presbytery, functioning essentially as an ecclesiastical court. The traditional denominations each have their own intricate principles of governance, as to which the state has no rights of visitation. Church governance is founded in scripture, modified by reformers over almost two millennia. As the Supreme Court stated [long ago]: 'It is not to be supposed that the judges of the civil courts can be as competent in the ecclesiastical law and religious faith of all these bodies as the ablest men in each are in reference to their own. It would therefore be an appeal from the more learned tribunal in the law which should decide the case, to the one which is less so.'[29] It would therefore also be inappropriate and unconstitutional for this court to determine after the fact that the ecclesiastical authorities negligently supervised or retained the [pastor]. Any award of damages would have a chilling effect leading indirectly to state control over the future conduct of affairs of a religious denomination, a result violative of the text and history of the [first amendment]."

Summary

This chapter addresses two of the most significant legal risks faced by churches today—negligent selection and negligent retention. It is essential for church leaders to be familiar with these bases of liability so that preventive measures can be evaluated and implemented. Here are some important points to remember:

- Negligence is conduct that creates an unreasonable risk of foreseeable harm to the person or property of another, and that results in the foreseeable harm. The important point to recognize is that negligence need not be intentional. For example, negligence may include conduct that is simply careless, heedless, or inadvertent.

- A church may be liable on the basis of negligent selection for a worker's molestation of a minor if the church was negligent in the selection of the worker. Liability based on negligent selection may be imposed upon a church for the acts of employees and volunteers.

- A church may be liable on the basis of negligent selection for a worker's molestation of an adult if the church was negligent in the selection of the worker. Liability based on negligent selection may be imposed upon a church for the acts of employees and volunteers.

---

[28] Schmidt v. Bishop, 779 F. Supp. 321 (S.D.N.Y. 1991).
[29] Watson v. Jones, 80 U.S. 679 (1872).

- Negligent selection claims are not limited to cases involving sexual misconduct. They can arise anytime that a church's failure to exercise reasonable care in the selection of an employee or volunteer leads to a foreseeable injury. Examples include using adolescents as attendants in the church nursery; selecting adult workers without any training in CPR or other resuscitation techniques to accompany a youth group to any event involving swimming or boating; selecting lay counselors with inadequate professional training; and, selecting drivers for any church-sponsored activity without checking their driving record.

- A church may exercise reasonable care in selecting ministers or other church workers but still be responsible for their misconduct if it "retained" them after receiving information indicating that they posed a risk of harm to others.

- Churches can reduce the risk of liability based on negligent selection and retention by adopting appropriate risk management policies and procedures.

In the next chapter, we examine negligent supervision.

CHAPTER 33. NEGLIGENT SUPERVISION

Churches can use reasonable care in selecting workers, but still be liable for injuries sustained during church activities on the basis of negligent supervision. The term negligence means carelessness or a failure to exercise reasonable care. Negligent supervision, then, refers to a failure to exercise reasonable care in the supervision of church workers and church activities. Churches have been sued on the basis of negligent supervision in a variety of contexts.

Key point. Churches are not "guarantors" of the safety and well-being of those persons who participate in their programs and activities. Generally, they are responsible only for those injuries that result from their negligence.

33.1 Negligent Supervision of Church Workers—Sexual Misconduct Cases Involving Minor Victims

Many of the cases in which churches have been sued for negligent supervision involve incidents of child molestation. A child is molested on church premises, or during a church activity, and the child's parents sue the church. While the parents may allege that the church was negligent in selecting or retaining the offender, they also may assert that the church was negligent in supervising the offender and its premises and activities. One court defined negligent supervision of children as follows:

> The measure of duty of a person undertaking control and supervision of a child to exercise reasonable care for the safety of the child is to be gauged by the standard of the average responsible parent; such person is not an insurer of the safety of the child and has no duty to foresee and guard against every possible hazard. The measure of precaution which must be taken by one having a child in his care, who stands in no relation to the child except that he has undertaken to care for it is that care which a prudent person would exercise under like circumstances. As a general rule, a person who undertakes the control and supervision of a child, even without compensation, has the duty to use reasonable care to protect the child from injury. Such person is not an insurer of the safety of the child. He is required only to use reasonable care commensurate with the reasonably foreseeable risk of harm.[1]

Examples of court decisions finding churches and schools liable on the basis of negligent supervision for a worker's acts of child molestation are summarized below.

Example. A Minnesota court ruled that a church could be sued on the basis of negligent supervision as a result of a pastor's acts of child molestation.[2] The pastor served as both pastor and youth program teacher at the church. He lived in a third floor apartment at the church's youth center. The victim attended confirmation classes at the church, and the pastor was his instructor. The victim so admired the pastor that he wanted to become a pastor himself. The victim often went with the pastor to make calls or visit other churches. He also attended church camp during the summer and at

---

[1] Wallace v. Boys Club of Albany, Georgia, Inc., 439 S.E.2d 746 (Ga. App. 1993).
[2] Doe v. Redeemer Lutheran Church, 531 N.W.2d 897 (Minn. App. 1995).

times stayed overnight at the pastor's apartment. When the victim was 13 to 16 years old, he was molested by the pastor. The court concluded that the church had been negligent in permitting the sexual abuse to occur. This conclusion was based in part on the following facts: (1) During the time the victim was being molested, a church trustee saw the pastor kissing another adolescent boy on the mouth. The pastor, upon seeing the trustee, blushed and ran back to his apartment. The trustee informed another trustee of this incident, along with two members of the church council. No action was taken. (2) During the time the victim was being molested, another church trustee was approached by a local teacher and asked if the pastor was a child molester. This same trustee's uncle told him that he heard something went on at a cabin at church camp and asked if the pastor was "straight." (3) During the time the victim was being molested, a church trustee's son had to make up some work for confirmation classes at the pastor's home. When he returned home, he told his father that the pastor wanted him "to get under the sheets" with him. (4) During the time the victim was being molested, a student in the confirmation class testified that during a confirmation class at the church she thought she saw the pastor engage in an act of child abuse. She told her parents and the church's "intern pastor" what she saw. The girl and her parents quit attending the church after this incident. (5) During the time the victim was being molested, another confirmation student told the church's intern pastor that the pastor had "put his arm around him all of the time" and showered with the boys.

Example. A New York court ruled that a school was liable on the basis of negligent supervision for the rape of a 12-year-old girl that occurred when she left a school outing without permission.[3] The victim and her class of 30 students were attending a school outing at a public park. She left the group to have lunch at a nearby pizza restaurant. Upon returning to the park, she discovered that her class had left. Instead of returning to school, she walked home. While walking home, she was abducted and raped by two adolescent males. The victim sued the school, claiming that her injuries were caused by its negligent supervision of the class outing. A jury found the school negligent, and awarded the victim $3 million in damages. The verdict was based in part on the testimony of an expert in school safety that the school had departed from "safe and common practices." In particular, he noted the following: (1) there should have been at least one more adult supervising the group of 30 elementary-age children (only two adults were present during the outing); (2) students were not "paired off" as buddies; (3) arrangements were not made to have the class meet together at least once each hour while at the park; (4) students were not told that they could not leave the park alone; and (5) students were not told that they would only be dismissed from the outing after they returned to school. The safety expert also testified that the teacher in charge of the outing should have taken several steps immediately upon discovering that a child was missing. These included (1) notifying the school immediately to seek guidance from his superiors; (2) notifying the park police; (3) asking another teacher to take the children back to school so he could continue the search for the missing child; (4) remaining in the park until shortly before dismissal time to give the victim more time to return; and (5) notifying school officials upon his return that the victim was still missing. The case was appealed, and the state's highest court affirmed the trial court's judgment in favor of the victim. The court concluded, "[W]e cannot say that the intervening act of rape was unforeseeable as a matter of law. A rational jury hearing the trial testimony could have determined, as the jury did

---

[3] Bell v. Board of Education, 687 N.Y.S.2d 1325 (A.D. 1997).

in this case, that the foreseeable result of the danger created by [the school's] alleged lack of supervision was injury such as occurred here. A [jury] could have reasonably concluded that the very purpose of the school supervision was to shield vulnerable schoolchildren from such acts of violence. As we have previously recognized, when the intervening, intentional act of another is itself the foreseeable harm that shapes the duty imposed, the defendant who fails to guard against such conduct will not be relieved of liability when that act occurs."

Example. *A New York court found a school liable on the basis of negligence for the molestation of a kindergarten student in a school restroom.*[4] *The student was permitted to go to the bathroom alone, where he was molested by an older student. The child's parents sued the school, and a jury found that the child's kindergarten teacher had been negligent in allowing the child to go to the bathroom unaccompanied. The school appealed, and a state appeals court upheld the finding of negligence. The court began its opinion by noting that "[w]hile we recognize the general rule that educational institutions are not the insurers of the safety of their students and cannot be held liable for every instance in which one pupil injures another, schools are, however, under a duty to adequately supervise their students and are liable for foreseeable injuries which are [directly] caused by the absence of such supervision." The court noted that this duty "derives from the fact that the school, once it takes over physical custody and control of the children, effectively takes the place of their parents and guardians." The court noted that in this case the child was sent from his classroom (while class was in session) to the school bathroom, alone and unsupervised, where the assault occurred. Further, "[t]his was done despite two separate school memoranda, circulated amongst the school's staff, which explicitly provided security procedures to the contrary." The first memoranda stated that "teachers are instructed to send all pupils under third grade to the bathroom with a partner." The second memorandum stated that "to further insure security any child leaving your room or corridor area must have a pass. Young children should go in pairs." The court concluded that the school "did not act with ordinary prudence in allowing the five-year old plaintiff to proceed to the bathroom alone." The court acknowledged that schools generally must have notice of prior similar misconduct to be liable for assaults upon older students, since school personnel "cannot reasonably be expected to guard against all of the sudden, spontaneous acts that take place among students daily." However, in the case of a young child who is sent by his teacher to a public bathroom unescorted, the potential danger to the child "can be reasonably foreseen and could have been prevented by adequate supervision of the school." As a result, "while it would be reasonable to allow high school students to go to a public bathroom unaccompanied, the same practice surely does not apply to a five-year old child, who is unable to resist, is defenseless against attack, and poses an easy target for sexual molestation or other assaults. Stated another way, even the most prudent parent will not guard his or her teen at every moment in the absence of some foreseeable danger of which he or she has notice; but a five-year-old child in a public bathroom should be supervised or, at the very least, be accompanied by another child."*

Some courts have found churches not liable on the basis of negligent supervision for a worker's acts of child molestation on the ground that the church exercised reasonable care in the supervision of the victim and of its own programs and activities. Representative cases are summarized below.

---

[4] Garcia v. City of New York, 646 N.Y.S.2d 508 (A.D. 1996).

Example. A federal appeals court ruled that an archdiocese was not responsible for the alleged molestation of a minor by a priest.[5] An adult male sued a priest, a local Catholic church, and an archdiocese claiming that while he was a minor the priest performed illicit sexual acts upon him. The plaintiff alleged that the archdiocese and church were liable because they knew or should have known that illicit acts were being performed on their premises and at the priest's home. He charged that they failed to protect him or take appropriate measures to ascertain or correct the situation. Moreover, he alleged that they knew or should have known that they were fostering the priest's illicit activities and providing him with the means with which to conduct such activities. In rejecting the plaintiff's claim that the archdiocese was responsible for his injuries on the basis of negligent supervision, the court observed: "[E]mployers do not have a duty to supervise their employees when the employees are off-duty or not working. Employers also are not liable for failure to supervise when the employee engages in independent criminal conduct which results in the plaintiff's injuries. Moreover, an employer's duty to supervise does not include a duty to uncover his employees' concealed, clandestine, personal activities. . . . It is unfortunate, to say the least, that the frequency with which these cases have surfaced suggests that the clergy at [the local church] were naive. There is, however, nothing to indicate that the archdiocese or [church] knew or should have known of what was taking place in [the priest's] private world."

Example. A California court ruled that a Catholic church was not responsible on the basis of negligent supervision for a priest's acts of child molestation, since "nearly all" of the acts of molestation occurred when the priest "took the victim from her home to various public places and hotels."[6]

Example. A federal court in Connecticut dismissed a lawsuit brought against a church and diocese by two adults who had been sexually molested by a priest when they were minors.[7] The court ruled that the church and diocese were not responsible for the victims' injuries on the basis of negligence. The court cautioned that churches and denominational agencies are potentially liable on the basis of negligence for injuries sustained by victims of sexual molestation if they have knowledge of prior sexual misconduct by the molester. However, since the victims could prove that church officials either knew or should have known of any previous sexual misconduct by the offending priest, the negligence claims had to be dismissed. The court ruled that the first amendment guaranty of religious freedom does not necessarily protect a church or denominational agency from liability in a lawsuit based on negligent hiring, retention, or supervision if the victim's claims do not implicate issues of ecclesiastical concern.

Example. A federal district court in Michigan ruled that a church school and various church agencies were not liable on the basis of negligent hiring, supervision, or retention, for the sexual molestation of a minor student by a priest.[8] The court found that there was no constitutional prohibition to the recognition of a negligent supervision claim against a church school or agency, since such claims "can be decided without determining questions of church law and policies." However, the court refused to find the school or church agencies liable on this basis since "only a few jurisdictions"

---

[5] Tichenor v. Roman Catholic Church, 32 F.3d 953 (5th Cir. 1994).

[6] Roman Catholic Bishop v. Superior Court, 50 Cal. Rptr.2d 399 (Cal. App. 1996).

[7] Nutt v. Norwich Roman Catholic Diocese, 921 F. Supp. 66 (D. Conn. 1995).

[8] Isely v. Capuchin Province, 880 F. Supp. 1138 (E.D. Mich. 1995).

recognize "negligent supervision" as a basis of liability, and no court in Wisconsin (where the molestation occurred) had ever recognized negligent supervision as a basis of liability. The court made the following additional observation: "The precise issue, as this court sees it . . . is not whether now—20 years after the occurrences upon which plaintiff's claims are predicated—the Wisconsin Supreme Court would adopt the tort of negligent supervision, but rather whether, had the claim been presented to the Wisconsin Court in 1974-78 [when the acts of molestation occurred] would the court have recognized it then? This is consistent with the generally accepted principle that a tort action is to be determined by application of the law which existed at the time of the occurrence of the events upon which the action is predicated. . . . This reflects this court's concern . . . that it would be unfair to juxtapose contemporary mores and contemporary causes of action upon parties for events which occurred in a different era with a different level of social awareness of problems."

Example. A Minnesota appeals court ruled that a church and denominational organization were not legally responsible on the basis of negligent supervision for a pastor's acts of child molestation.[9] The molester was accused of sexually abusing numerous young boys during his tenure as senior pastor at a church. He admitted abusing some of the children, including a 10-year-old boy (the "victim"). The victim sued the pastor, his former church, and national and regional church bodies. The trial court concluded that the church had been negligent in supervising the pastor, but a state appeals court reversed this judgment. The court defined "negligent supervision" as "the failure of the employer to exercise ordinary care in supervising the employment relationship, so as to prevent the foreseeable misconduct of an employee from causing harm to other employees or third persons." The court added that negligent supervision "derives from the doctrine of respondeat superior" so the victim "must prove that the employee's actions occurred within the scope of employment in order to succeed on this claim." It is important to note that the court stressed the difficulty inherent in supervising clergy: "Even assuming that [the pastor's] abuse of [the victim] occurred within his scope of employment, there was insufficient evidence for the jury to conclude that [the church] failed to exercise ordinary care in supervising [him]. By the nature of the position, a clergyperson has considerable freedom in religious and administrative leadership in a church. The clergy also require privacy and confidentiality in order to protect the privacy of parishioners. There was no evidence that the supervision provided by [the church] differed from the supervision a reasonable church would provide. Nor was there any evidence of further reasonable supervision that could have prevented [the pastor] from abusing [the victim]. There was not enough evidence from which a reasonable jury could conclude that [the church] negligently supervised [the pastor]."

Example. The Missouri Supreme Court ruled that a diocese could not be liable for the sexual misconduct of a priest.[10] A Catholic priest served as associate pastor of a church. He invited a young boy and one of the boy's friends to spend the night and watch movies in the church parsonage. One of the boys later alleged that the priest sexually molested him. The parents sued the diocese, claiming that it was responsible for the priest's acts on the basis of several grounds, including negligent supervision. The parents asserted that after the priest was ordained the diocese had a duty to supervise his activities, which it failed to do. The parents claimed that the diocese

---

[9] M.L. v. Magnuson, 531 N.W.2d 831 (Minn. App. 1995).
[10] Gibson v. Brewer, 952 S.W.2d 239 (Mo. 1997).

"knew or reasonably should have known of prior sexual misconduct and a propensity to such conduct" by the priest. Once again, the court disagreed: "Adjudicating the reasonableness of a church's supervision of a cleric—what the church 'should know'—requires inquiry into religious doctrine. . . . [T]his would create an excessive entanglement, inhibit religion, and result in the endorsement of one model of supervision. Not recognizing the cause of negligent failure to supervise clergy is not an establishment of religion because it is a 'nondiscriminatory religious-practice exemption.'[11] It achieves 'a benevolent neutrality which will permit religious exercise to exist without sponsorship and without interference.'[12] Nonrecognition of this negligence tort preserves 'the autonomy and freedom of religious bodies while avoiding any semblance of established religion.'"

Example. *An Ohio court ruled that a church was not responsible for the rape of a 6-year-old boy occurring on church property during Sunday school.[13] The boy attended a Sunday school class of about 45 first and second graders. One adult female teacher was present on the day of the rape along with two teenage volunteers (one male and one female). During "story time," the victim became disruptive, and the teacher allowed the male volunteer to "take him back and color" in an unused room. The adult teacher did not check on the boy for the remainder of the Sunday school session. The boy's mother alleged that the male volunteer took her son to an unused room, raped him, and threatened to kill him if he "told anyone." The boy and his mother later sued the church, claiming that the boy's injuries were a result of the church's "negligent supervision" of its agents. The court noted that "negligence does not consist of failing to take extraordinary measures which hindsight demonstrates would have been helpful." The court further observed that a church is "not an insurer of the safety" of persons on its premises, but rather has only a "duty of ordinary care to avoid injury consistent with [existing] facts and circumstances." The court emphasized that the victim and his mother "have presented no evidence that [the church] knew, or in the exercise of reasonable diligence should have known of or anticipated a criminal sexual assault by [the alleged rapist] upon another." The victim and his mother placed great significance upon evidence that "a similar incident had occurred several years earlier." In rejecting the relevance of this evidence the court observed simply that "there is no evidence that the church or its agents knew, or in the exercise of diligence, should have known of such prior activity."*

Example. *A Pennsylvania court ruled that a church and diocese could not be legally responsible for a priest's repeated acts of child molestation occurring off of church premises.[14] A Catholic priest repeatedly molested a number of boys. His pattern was to befriend young boys, lure them into a sense of trust, and then molest them. He often would take boys out to meals, do special favors for them, and take them shopping or on trips. One victim, who had been molested more than fifty times by the priest, sued the church and diocese on the basis of negligent supervision. The court ruled that the church and diocese could not be guilty of negligent supervision since all of the priest's acts of molestation occurred off of church premises. The court noted that the Restatement of Torts (an authoritative legal text) imposes liability for negligent supervision upon employers only for misconduct occurring on their premises. It*

---

[11] Employment Division v. Smith, 494 U.S. 872, 879 (1990).
[12] Walz v. Tax Commission, 393 U.S. 664 (1970).
[13] Bender v. First Church of the Nazarene 571 N.E.2d 475 (Ohio App. 1989).
[14] Hutchinson v. Luddy, 683 A.2d 1254 (Pa. Super. 1996).

pointed out that all of the priest's acts of molestation occurred in motel rooms while on trips, and not on church premises.

Example. *A Tennessee court ruled that a church-operated preschool was not legally responsible for a sexual assault committed by a 4-year-old boy on another 4-year-old boy, since the assault was not foreseeable.*[15] *The court noted that there can be liability for negligence unless a victim's injuries were a reasonably foreseeable result of the negligent behavior. This test was simply not met. The court observed, "[T]he acts alleged in the complaint are unforeseeable as a matter of law. The alleged acts would be considered vile and reprehensible between two adults, but between two four-year-old boys, the alleged acts are even more shocking and appalling. We do not believe that a reasonable person would ever foresee this type of behavior between boys of that age. The possibility of an accident of this general character could not have been foreseen by [the church or school]. [The school] presented affidavits showing that a sexual assault had never occurred in the school, and that the school had no reason to suspect this behavior from [the assailant]. Moreover, we should consider the fact that the teacher could not reasonably foresee that a child that had just used the restroom facilities would return to the restroom instead of the classroom after getting a drink of water in the school hall."*

Example. *A Texas court rejected a parent's claim that a church was responsible on the basis of negligent supervision for the molestation of her daughter by a youth pastor.*[16] *A mother enrolled her daughter in a private school operated by a local church. A few months later, the mother discovered three sexually explicit letters which she believed were correspondence between her daughter and the youth pastor (who also taught at the school). These letters, along with explicit entries in the daughter's diary, led the mother to believe that her daughter and the youth pastor were engaging in sexual activities. She took the evidence to the senior minister of the church, asking for his assistance. Unsatisfied with the investigation, the mother sued the church and a national denominational agency. She claimed that the national church was responsible for the youth pastor's acts on the basis of negligent supervision. In rejecting this claim, the court noted that negligence requires proof that someone's conduct actually caused injuries to another, and it concluded that the national church's act of ordaining or licensing clergy in no way was the cause of the girl's injuries. Further, in rejecting the plaintiff's claim that the national church used "less than ordinary care" in discharging its "continuing duty" to monitor and supervise its clergy, the court observed that the national church "exercises no supervisory powers over the local ministers" and "is not responsible for the day-to-day oversight of the ministers." Since the national church had no duty to supervise clergy, "it is impossible that lack of supervision . . . was a substantial factor in causing plaintiff's injuries."*

Example. *A Washington state court ruled that a church school was not legally responsible for damages resulting from an alleged sexual relationship between a teacher and student.*[17] *In rejecting the claim of the victim's parents that the school had been guilty of negligent supervision, the court agreed that "schools have a duty to supervise their students," and to take precautions to protect students from dangers that may reasonably be anticipated. However, "at some point the event is so distant in*

---

[15] Roe v. Catholic Diocese of Memphis, 950 S.W.2d 27 (Tenn. App. 1996).
[16] Eckler v. The General Council of the Assemblies of God, 784 S.W.2d 935 (Tex. App. 1990).
[17] Scott v. Blanchet High School, 747 P.2d 1124 (Wash. App. 1987).

time and place that the responsibility for adequate supervision is with the parents rather than the school." Such was the case here, concluded the court, since the alleged misconduct occurred off school property during noninstructional hours.

33.2 Negligent Supervision of Church Workers—Sexual Misconduct Cases Involving Adult Victims

Many of the cases in which churches have been sued for negligent supervision involve incidents of sexual contact with adults. The most common example includes sexual contact between a male pastor and a female counselee in the course of a counseling relationship. While the counselee may allege that the church was negligent in selecting or retaining the pastor, she also may assert that the church was negligent in supervising the pastor. Summarized below are representative court decisions finding churches liable on the basis of negligent supervision for a minister's acts of sexual misconduct with adults.

Example. The Colorado Supreme Court found an Episcopal diocese and bishop legally responsible for a pastor's sexual misconduct with a female parishioner on the basis of a number of grounds, including negligent supervision.[18] The court observed, "An employer may therefore be subject to liability for negligent supervision if he knows or should have known that an employee's conduct would subject third parties to an unreasonable risk of harm. . . . Both the diocese and [the bishop] had previous exposure to the problem of sexual relationships developing between priests and parishioners because the problem had arisen seven times before. The psychological reports gave notice that further supervision may be required. The reports indicate problems of sexual identification ambiguity, depression and low self-esteem. [The pastor's] file also indicated he had problems with authority. [He] had an inability to respond to superior authority. A reasonable person would have inquired further into [his] known difficulty in dealing with superior authority, and would have assumed a greater degree of care in monitoring his conduct. In light of its knowledge, it was reasonable for the jury to determine the [bishop and diocese] should have been alert to the possibility of problems with [the pastor] and taken adequate steps to insure [he] was not in a position where he could abuse the trust he enjoys as a priest conducting counseling."

Example. An Illinois court ruled that a church could be sued by a woman who was sexually seduced by her pastor during marriage counseling.[19] The court acknowledged that "Illinois courts have generally refused to decide cases that require a judicial interpretation of religious doctrine or church law." However, "where doctrinal controversy is not involved in a church dispute, mandatory deference to religious authority is not required by the first amendment, and the court may choose from a variety of approaches in resolving the dispute." It noted that the courts can resolve disputes over control of church property so long as they can do so on the basis of "neutral principles of law" requiring no examination of religious doctrine. The court applied the same "neutral principles of law" approach in this case involving alleged church liability for the sexual misconduct of its pastor. It observed, "Although the neutral principles of law approach is usually applied to disputes over church property, we cannot conclude from plaintiffs' complaint that the instant cause cannot be decided using neutral principles of negligence law, developed for use in all negligence disputes,

---

[18] Moses v. Diocese of Colorado, 863 P.2d 310 (Colo. 1993).
[19] Bivin v. Wright, 656 N.E.2d 1121 (Ill. App. 1995).

without interpretation of religious doctrine or church law, just as would be a secular dispute in a negligence case. . . . We cannot conclude from plaintiffs' complaint that their cause of action against [the church] will infringe upon, or place a burden upon, the church's freedom to exercise its religion. Inquiring into whether the church was negligent in its failure to protect plaintiffs from the sexual misconduct of its minister may not call into question the church's religious beliefs or practices or subject them to analysis or scrutiny. As we have pointed out, the minister's sexual misconduct was not rooted in the church's religious beliefs and was outside the boundaries of the church's ecclesiastical beliefs and practices. Thus, resolving this dispute may not require any interpretation of church doctrine or any regulation of ecclesiastical activity."

Example. *A North Carolina court ruled that the first amendment did not prevent it from resolving a sexual harassment lawsuit brought by three female church employees against their church and denominational agencies.[20] The court noted that the key issue was whether the first amendment prevents "the filing of a negligent retention and supervision claim against a religious organization, when that claim is based on the conduct of a cleric of that organization." The court noted that the local church and denominational agencies asserted that the civil courts were without jurisdiction to resolve plaintiffs' claims against them because the courts' resolution of these claims requires inquiry into religious doctrine. The court disagreed. It noted that the first amendment "does not grant religious organizations absolute immunity from liability. For example, claims against religious organizations have long been recognized for premises liability, breach of a fiduciary duty, and negligent use of motor vehicles." The court concluded that if a resolution of the plaintiffs' legal claims did not require the interpretation of church doctrine, then "the first amendment is not implicated and neutral principles of law are properly applied to adjudicate the claim."*

Example. *An Oregon court ruled that a woman who was sexually seduced by her minister in the course of a counseling relationship could sue her church on the basis of negligent supervision.[21] The woman alleged that the church "knew or should have known that [the minister] was not adequately trained as a counselor and that it knew or should have known that he had misused his position in the past to take advantage or parishioners and counseled persons . . . [and] failed to investigate claims of his sexual misconduct [or] warn parishioners of his misuse of his position . . . ." The court stressed that it was not finding the church responsible. Rather, it simply was rejecting the trial court's conclusion that the lawsuit failed to state facts for which the law provides a remedy.*

Many courts have concluded that the first amendment's "nonestablishment of religion" and "free exercise of religion" clauses prevent the civil courts from resolving negligent supervision claims involving clergy misconduct. To illustrate, the United States Supreme Court observed in a landmark case more than a century ago: "It would therefore also be inappropriate and unconstitutional for this court to determine after the fact that the ecclesiastical authorities negligently supervised or retained the defendant Bishop. Any award of damages would have a chilling effect leading indirectly to state control over the future conduct of affairs of a religious denomination, a result violative of the text and history of the establishment clause."[22]

---

[20] Smith v. Privette, 495 S.E.2d 395 (N.C. App. 1998).
[21] Erickson v. Christenson, 781 P.2d 383 (Or. App. 1989).
[22] Watson v. Jones, 80 U.S. 679 (1871).

Some courts have noted the inherent difficulty of supervising ministers in the performance of their duties, and in particular their counseling activities. As one court observed:

> By the nature of the position, a clergyperson has considerable freedom in religious and administrative leadership in a church. The clergy also require privacy and confidentiality in order to protect the privacy of parishioners. There was no evidence that the supervision provided by [the church] differed from the supervision a reasonable church would provide. Nor was there any evidence of further reasonable supervision that could have prevented [the pastor] from abusing [the victim]. There was not enough evidence from which a reasonable jury could conclude that [the church] negligently supervised [the pastor].[23]

Summarized below are representative cases in which the courts have ruled that a church cannot be liable on the basis of negligent supervision for the sexual misconduct of a minister involving an adult victim.

> ***Example.*** *A federal appeals court ruled that a religious order was not responsible for the alleged seduction of a female parishioner by a Catholic priest.[24] The woman sued the religious order claiming that it was responsible for her injuries on the basis of several grounds, including negligent supervision. The court concluded that the order was not responsible for the priest's misconduct on the basis of negligent supervision, since it had no duty to supervise him. While it was true that the order had received a complaint about the priest's behavior with another woman some 8 years before, the priest performed his duties under the direction and control of the archbishop and was accountable to the archbishop. Accordingly, the order had no duty to supervise the priest's actions.*

> ***Example.*** *The Colorado Supreme Court ruled that a diocese was not responsible for a priest's sexual contacts with a woman during counseling.[25] The woman sued the diocese on the basis of a number of grounds, including negligent supervision. Specifically, she alleged that the diocese had knowledge of previous indiscretions by the same priest, which had the effect of imposing upon the diocese a duty to supervise him. The court observed that a religious organization may be liable for negligent supervision if it has reason to know that a minister is likely to harm others. Liability results "because the employer antecedently had reason to believe that an undue risk of harm would exist because of the employment." The court concluded that "a person who knows or should have known that an employee's conduct would subject third parties to an unreasonable risk of harm may be directly liable to third parties for harm proximately caused by his conduct."*

> ***Example.*** *A Florida court ruled that it was barred by the first amendment from resolving a woman's lawsuit claiming that she had been the victim of a priest's sexual misconduct.[26] The court noted that the first amendment prohibits any governmental practice (including judicial resolution of internal church disputes) that would lead to an "excessive entanglement" between church and state. It continued, "Our*

---

[23] M.L. v. Magnuson, 531 N.W.2d 831 (Minn. App. 1995).
[24] Doe v. Cunningham, 30 F.3d 879 (7th Cir. 1994).
[25] Destefano v. Grabian, 763 P.2d 275 (Colo. 1988).
[26] Doe v. Evans, 718 So.2d 286 (Fla. App. 1998).

examination of case law presenting both sides of this question leads us to conclude the reasoning of those courts holding the first amendment bars a claim for negligent hiring, retention, and supervision is the more compelling. In a church defendant's determination to hire or retain a minister, or in its capacity as supervisor of that minister, a church defendant's conduct is guided by religious doctrine and/or practice. Thus, a court's determination regarding whether the church defendant's conduct was 'reasonable' would necessarily entangle the court in issues of the church's religious law, practices, and policies. 'Hiring' in a traditional sense does not occur in some religions, where a person is ordained into a particular position in the church, and assigned to one parish or another. A court faced with the task of determining a claim of negligent hiring, retention, and supervision would measure the church defendants' conduct against that of a reasonable employer; a proscribed comparison."

Example. *A Louisiana court ruled that an Episcopal diocese was not legally responsible for the suicide of a woman allegedly caused by a sexual relationship with an Episcopal priest.[27] The woman's husband claimed that the diocese was responsible for his wife's suicide on the basis of several grounds, including negligent supervision. In rejecting this basis of liability, the court observed, "[A]ny inquiry into the policies and practices of the church defendants in hiring or supervising their clergy raises . . . first amendment problems of entanglement . . . which might involve the court in making sensitive judgments about the propriety of the church defendants' supervision in light of their religious beliefs. . . . The traditional denominations each have their own intricate principles of governance, as to which the state has no rights of visitation. Church governance is founded in scripture, modified by reformers over almost two millennia. As the Supreme Court stated long [ago]: 'It is not to be supposed that the judgment of the civil courts can be as competent in the ecclesiastical law and religious faith of all these bodies as the ablest men in each are in reference to their own. It would therefore be an appeal from the more learned tribunal in the law which should decide the case, to one which is less so.'"[28]*

Example. *A federal court in New York refused to find a pastor guilty of malpractice on the basis of his sexual seduction of a church member he had counseled for several years.[29] The woman sued the church and a denominational agency on the basis of several grounds, including negligent supervision. In rejecting this basis of liability, the court observed, "[A]ny inquiry into the policies and practices of the church defendants in hiring or supervising their clergy raises . . . first amendment problems of entanglement . . . which might involve the court in making sensitive judgments about the propriety of the church defendants' supervision in light of their religious beliefs. Insofar as concerns retention or supervision, the pastor of a Presbyterian church is not analogous to a common law employee. He may not demit his charge nor be removed by the session, without the consent of the presbytery, functioning essentially as an ecclesiastical court. The traditional denominations each have their own intricate principles of governance, as to which the state has no rights of visitation. Church governance is founded in scripture, modified by reformers over almost two millennia. As the Supreme Court stated [long ago]: 'It is not to be supposed that the judges of the civil courts can be as competent in the ecclesiastical law and religious faith of all these bodies as the ablest men in each are in reference to their own. It would therefore be an*

---

[27] Roppolo v. Moore, 644 So.2d 206 (La. App. 1994).
[28] Watson v. Jones, 80 U.S. 679 (1871).
[29] Schmidt v. Bishop, 779 F. Supp. 321 (S.D.N.Y. 1991).

appeal from the more learned tribunal in the law which should decide the case, to the one which is less so.'[30] *It would therefore also be inappropriate and unconstitutional for this court to determine after the fact that the ecclesiastical authorities negligently supervised or retained the [pastor]. Any award of damages would have a chilling effect leading indirectly to state control over the future conduct of affairs of a religious denomination, a result violative of the text and history of the [first amendment]."*

Example. *The Oklahoma Supreme Court ruled that a married couple could not sue their church and former pastor for damages they allegedly incurred as a result of an adulterous affair between the former pastor and the wife.*[31] *The couple claimed that the church was liable for the pastor's acts on the basis of several grounds, including negligent supervision. The court concluded that the church was not responsible for injuries resulting from the minister's conduct, since none of the couple's claims against the pastor were viable. It observed, "Neither the claims by the husband nor the wife against the minister are cognizable in Oklahoma. . . . Because their claims against the minister also serve as the basis for the claims against the church for its negligent hiring and supervision of the minister, that claim is also not cognizable."*

33.3 Negligent Supervision of Church Workers—Other Cases

Other circumstances in which courts have found churches guilty of negligent supervision include a youth activity in which a 9-year-old boy was killed when a utility pole crushed him;[32] a church picnic during which a 15-year-old boy was rendered a quadriplegic when he fell out of a tree;[33] a church picnic at which a child drowned;[34] allowing a dangerous condition to continue in a crowded church service, which resulted in injury to a member;[35] permitting a snowmobile party on farmland without making an adequate inspection for dangerous conditions;[36] and failing to adequately supervise the activities of a church-sponsored scout troop.[37]

Example. *A Louisiana court ruled that a church was liable for injuries sustained by a youth group member who was struck by a vehicle while crossing a busy street.*[38] *A church's youth minister took a group of 37 teenagers and 4 adult chaperones to an out-of-town youth evangelism conference. Most attendees were high school age. After checking into their motel, the group went to a McDonald's restaurant, which was located on a heavily traveled four-lane road. By then it was getting dark, although the area was well lighted. The arrival of the youth group immediately crowded the McDonald's, filling all serving lines. Some of the boys noticed a small pizza parlor in a strip mall across the street with apparently no waiting. Several of the boys in the*

---

30 Watson v. Jones, 80 U.S. 679 (1872).

31 Bladen v. First Presbyterian Church, 857 P.2d 789 (Okla. 1993).

32 Glorioso v. YMCA of Jackson, 540 So.2d 638 (Miss. 1989).

33 Logan v. Old Enterprise Farms, Ltd., 544 N.E.2d 998 (Ill. App. 1989).

34 Herring v. R.L. Mathis Certified Dairy Co., 162 S.E.2d 863 (Ga. 1968), *aff'd in part and rev'd in part,* Bourn v. Herring, 166 S.E.2d 89 (Ga. 1969). *See also* L.M. Jeffords v. Atlanta Presbytery, Inc., 231 S.E.2d 355 (Ga. 1976); Brown v. Church of Holy Name of Jesus, 252 A.2d 176 (R.I. 1969).

35 Bass v. Aetna Insurance Co., 370 So.2d 511 (La. 1979).

36 Sullivan v. Birmingham Fire Insurance Co., 185 So.2d 336 (La. 1966), *cert. denied,* 186 So.2d 632 (La. 1966).

37 Kearney v. Roman Catholic Church, 295 N.Y.S.2d 186 (N.Y. 1968).

38 Bell v. USAA Casualty Insurance Company, 707 So.2d 102 (La. App. 1998).

group decided they would prefer to eat pizza without the wait. Three of the boys asked the youth minister if they could leave, cross the street, and get pizza. The minister said "yes," and walked them to the street to make sure they crossed safely. He did not lead the boys to a nearby traffic light because he considered that more dangerous. Meanwhile, three younger boys decided they wanted pizza. They assumed it was okay for them to cross the street since they saw the other three older boys doing so. The younger boys exited the McDonald's and ran across the street, passing the first group in the middle of the street in an effort to be first in line for pizza. One of the boys was "buzzed" by a speeding minivan when he was in the middle of the street. One of the members of the youth group was a 12-year-old boy with cerebral palsy (the "victim"). When he saw the other boys going to get pizza, he decided he was too hungry to wait at McDonald's. He did not ask the youth minister or any of the chaperones for permission to leave; he just left the restaurant and started across the street, without stopping or looking. In the middle of the street, he saw headlights. He lifted his arm defensively and was knocked to the ground, sustaining serious injuries. The victim and his parents sued their church. They asserted that the accident had been caused by the negligent supervision of the event by the youth minister and church. Specifically, they claimed that the youth minister and the chaperones did not prevent the 12-year-old victim from leaving the group; they did not notice him going out the door, crossing the parking lot and proceeding across the street; and they did not escort the boys to the street to assure safe crossing or lead them to the traffic light where the crossing would be safer. They also claimed that the youth minister and the adult chaperones made no plans for the boys to return safely to McDonald's after they finished their pizza. In essence, they "abandoned" the boys across the street. The court ruled that the church was guilty of negligent supervision. It observed, "Temporary custodians of children, such as school personnel and day care workers, are charged with the highest degree of care towards the children left in their custody, but are not insurers of the children's safety; supervisors must follow a standard of care commensurate with the age of the children under the attendant circumstances. The duty does not require individual supervision of each child at all times and places. However, fairly close supervision is required when students take a walking trip across a major thoroughfare." The court noted simply that "it is negligent for the adult leader to abandon the children."

Example. *A Pennsylvania court ruled that a seminary was responsible for the drowning death of a 12-year-old boy.*[39] *The victim was swimming with a group of altar boys from a Catholic church at a seminary-owned pool. The victim's mother sued the seminary, alleging that it had been negligent in allowing the boys to use the pool without a qualified lifeguard on duty. At the time of the drowning, the pool was under the supervision of a priest. The jury concluded that both the seminary and church were negligent, and it awarded more than $1 million in damages. A state appeals court affirmed this judgment. The court observed that "it is clear that [the evidence] was sufficient to support the jury's finding that the seminary had breached a duty owed to the minor decedent. The seminary, as owner of the pool, had a duty to exercise those precautions which a reasonably prudent owner would have taken to prevent injury to those persons whom it knew or should have known were using the pool. . . . A jury could have found, in view of the evidence, that the seminary knew or should have known that its pool was being used by children and that it failed to exercise reasonable care to prevent injury to them." The court further observed that "it was for*

---

[39] Rivera v. Philadelphia Theological Seminary, 580 A.2d 1341 (Pa. Super. 1990).

the jury to determine whether the seminary had been negligent in failing to take reasonable precautions to prevent access to its pool when a competent lifeguard was not present and whether the seminary could reasonably rely upon [the priest] to supervise the activities of the boys while they were using the pool."

Summary

This chapter addresses one of the most significant legal risks faced by churches today—negligent supervision. It is essential for church leaders to be familiar with this basis of liability so that preventive measures can be evaluated and implemented. Here are some important points to remember:

- Negligence is conduct that creates an unreasonable risk of foreseeable harm to the person or property of another, and that results in the foreseeable harm. The important point to recognize is that negligence need not be intentional. For example, negligence may include conduct that is simply careless, heedless, or inadvertent.

- Churches can use reasonable care in selecting workers, but still be liable for injuries sustained during church activities on the basis of negligent supervision.

- A church may be liable on the basis of negligent supervision for a worker's molestation of a minor if the church was negligent in supervising the worker. Liability based on negligent supervision may be imposed upon a church for the acts of employees and volunteers.

- A church may be liable on the basis of negligent supervision for a worker's molestation of an adult if the church was negligent in the supervision of the worker.

- Several courts have ruled that the first amendment guarantees of religious freedom and the nonestablishment of religion prevent the civil courts from resolving claims that a church was negligent in the supervision of a minister.

- Some courts have noted the inherent difficulty of supervising ministers in the performance of their duties, and in particular their counseling activities.

- Negligent supervision claims are not limited to cases involving sexual misconduct. They can arise anytime that a church's failure to exercise reasonable care in the supervision of an employee or volunteer leads to a foreseeable injury.

- Churches can reduce the risk of liability based on negligent supervision by adopting appropriate risk management policies and procedures, such as those discussed in Part 2 of this handbook.

The next chapter examines insurance and risk financing.

CHAPTER 34. INSURANCE AND RISK FINANCING

34.1 The Role of Insurance

Insurance is one of the most common, if not the most fundamental, device that churches and schools use to engage in risk management at the organizational level. In many cases, it is the only formal risk management strategy that leaders may focus on with any regularity, and that may occur only when the policy is up for renewal. Furthermore, most church and school leaders have little, if any, understanding of the nature of their insurance coverage, and may not even know the name of their insurance company.

Insurance plays an important risk management role in most organizations. It does not, however, prevent losses. Rather, insurance is a risk financing technique that provides funds for losses that the insurance policy covers. As such, insurance is not really a risk management strategy that addresses the broad concerns of both loss prevention and loss control. Rather, insurance is a means of transferring some or all of the costs associated with certain losses in exchange for the payment of a premium. For most churches and schools, the primary concern is to have enough insurance coverage to provide financial protection for those losses that they cannot or do not want to bear on their own.

When thinking about insurance, leaders should consider it within the broader scope of the church's or school's risk financing strategy. Risk financing is but one aspect of an overall financial management strategy. Furthermore, a risk financing strategy should take into account the frequency and severity of the risks that the church or school faces, the potential financial consequences of those risks, the viable alternatives available for loss prevention, loss control, and risk financing, the financial capabilities of the church or school, and how leaders desire to use their financial resources. Each of these factors should impact decision making concerning the purchase of insurance.

34.2 Frequency and Severity of Risks

Most churches and schools need and desire insurance coverage for losses that have a high degree of severity regardless of the frequency. Examples include a fire that destroys a sanctuary or a lawsuit involving sexual misconduct. Both can require large amounts of money to recover from the loss that often exceed a congregation's financial ability. However, in both cases a congregation may be able to sustain part of that financial burden, and in turn, that affects how much of the risk a congregation is willing to retain. From an insurance viewpoint, that may translate in increasing or decreasing the deductible amount a church or school carries with its property or liability coverage. In turn, that impacts the amount of the premium. Losses with low severity create a different set of options. As the severity and frequency of a loss declines, leaders may decide to retain more of the financing needed to respond to the loss if it should occur. This leads to consideration of the second factor, the potential financial consequences of any given risk.

34.3 Financial Consequences

As a general rule, churches and schools transfer risks associated with catastrophic losses. From a practical standpoint, however, most leaders do not evaluate the financial risk associated with every loss. Rather, insurance is purchased that covers a wide range of property and liability losses. Church and school leaders, however, may not fully understand the degree to which certain risks are retained, the potential costs associated with these risks, and the limits of the policy or how much of the risk is actually being transferred by the purchase of insurance. For example, a school may have $1,000,000 of property coverage. However, the school building may have a true value $1,500,000. In essence the school only has two-thirds of the value of the building insured. Suppose a fire occurs and creates $900,000 in damage. School leaders may think they are fully covered since the school has insurance coverage of $1,000,000. However, if the insurance policy contains a coinsurance clause that requires the building to be insured to its full value, the insurance company is obligated to pay the school only two-thirds of the loss, or $600,000. In essence, the school is retaining one-third of any property loss because it only has insured the building for two-thirds of its value. Or consider the following situation. A church is sued for a claim of sexual misconduct. The church has $1,000,000 of liability coverage. However, the insurance company declines the claim noting that the policy endorsements exclude coverage for sexual misconduct. Perhaps none of the church leaders carefully read the exclusions or they read them but did not understand the potential risk of a sexual misconduct claim. Or in a similar case, the church has $100,000 for sexual misconduct, but the total costs associated with claim exceed $200,000. The church is liable for amounts above the $100,000 limit. Church leaders may not have understood that such claims can exceed the limits of their policy. The failure to understand what is not covered, the amount of coverage that is available (which is not necessarily the same thing as the limits of the policy), and the potential severity of a risk can be devastating to a church. To make good decisions concerning risk financing, church and school leaders need to understand the financial consequences of the risks they face, the nature of the insurance coverage they are buying, and the alternatives that should be considered in addition to insurance. In all cases, churches and schools will want to establish certain thresholds of coverage that will protect them if a worse case scenario should occur.

34.4 Risk Financing Alternatives

Since most churches or schools put little thought into risk management to begin with, it follows that not much attention is given to the consideration of risk financing alternatives other than insurance. Part of the problem is that frequently no one on the church staff or in a position of leadership has the background in risk management or the time to analyze risk management issues. As a result, many leaders depend almost exclusively upon their insurance agent to guide them concerning these concerns. What alternatives should church and school leaders consider with respect to insurance as the sole source of risk financing? Some of the more common ones are discussed below.[1]

---

[1] For a detailed discussion of these options see George L. Head, et. al., *Essentials of Risk Financing, Third Edition* (Malvern, PA: Insurance Institute of America, 1996).

Paying for losses out of cash flow

Some losses are minimal and the typical church or school can pay for small losses out of the weekly cash flow. The amount of discretionary money that is available from cash flow is one factor that a church or school should use in evaluating deductibles for both property and liability coverage. As the deductible increases, the premium decreases. The offset in the premium can be applied toward potential losses. Naturally, the lower premium is also offset by the retained risk that the church or school is assuming. However, retaining that risk may make sense based on the loss history.

Paying for losses out of cash reserves

The same principle holds true for paying losses out of savings as for paying out of cash flow. Churches and schools can designate some portion of their savings as a reserve for potential losses. As the reserve increases in size, it enables a church or school to purchase insurance with higher deductibles. Those savings can be applied toward the cash reserve. Of course, the church or school is retaining higher levels of risk, but when done in an informed way can be the best choice from a financial management perspective.

Paying for losses using borrowed funds

Leaders can plan in advance to use borrowed funds to pay for specific levels of losses. To be safe, though, a line of credit should be established with a bank or other lender for that specific purpose. The terms of the loan should be clear in advance. To plan properly, church and school leaders need to know interest rates and repayment terms.

Transferring risks through contracts other than insurance

In addition to purchasing insurance or retaining risks, churches and schools can also transfer certain risks through the use of noninsurance contracts. One way of transferring risk financing is through the use of indemnity agreements, sometimes referred to as hold harmless agreements. For example, suppose a church sponsors a trip to a foreign country to help build a new church building. The church may require that each adult participant on that trip sign an agreement to hold the church harmless with respect to any losses that the individual may be incur on the trip. Or a church may require that an outside group that uses church facilities indemnify the church for any losses that may occur during the use of the facilities by the outside group. Indemnification does not lower the risk of a particular loss. Rather, it transfers a financial responsibility if the loss should occur. One of the problems of these contracts is enforcement. Contracts can be poorly written or legally invalid. Sometimes the party with whom the church enters into an agreement may not be able to fulfill the terms of the contract. When used appropriately and done right, however, indemnification agreements can be important devices for transferring financial burdens associated with specific risks. Church and school leaders should always use the services of a competent attorney in preparing indemnification or hold harmless agreements.

34.5 Financial Capabilities

To make an informed decision concerning risk financing, leaders need to examine the financial capabilities of the church or school based upon the factors that have been discussed above. Questions that require an answer include the following:

- How much discretionary money does the church or school have available from its cash flow that can be devoted to risk financing?

- How much money is available from savings that can be set aside for risk financing?

- How much credit can the church or school obtain and afford to pay for potential future losses?

- How much of a financial burden with respect to risk financing can the church or school afford to retain?

- What financial burdens can the church or school shift through contracts other than insurance?

34.6 Financial Goals

Each church or school will have unique risk financing needs. They will also have different financial capabilities and goals. In establishing financial goals with respect to risk financing, one starting point is to determine two factors: (1) how much risk financing is needed for property, and (2) how much risk financing is needed for liability. Of the two, the property amount is easier to calculate because it can be derived from an objective analysis of church or school assets. Liability, on the other hand, is difficult to calculate with accuracy. Many factors affect potential liability including the nature of the alleged offense, the degree of culpability, the actual harm to others, the available defenses, the jurisdiction of the case, the potential for a settlement, the means of settlement, and the potential perspective and values of a jury if a case goes to trial. While precedent can be used as a basis for analysis it is not always a good guide.

Based on our research, many churches now carry $2,000,000 or more of liability coverage. However, that figure is somewhat misleading because some claims are not typically covered under a church's general liability policy. For example, coverage for sexual misconduct, directors and officers, and employment practices usually require separate policies. Then the amounts of liability coverage available may vary from one company to another.

Based on their best judgment, leaders should establish threshold levels of risk financing for both property and liability coverage. Then using a table such as the one below, a determination can be made on how the risk financing will occur. In every case, insurance will play a dominant role in providing catastrophic coverage.

1. Total risk financing needed: $_____

Should equal the sum of the following:

2. Amount from cash flow (per year):* $_____   ** takes into account payments if line of credit is also used*

3. Amount from savings: $_____

4. Amount available from line of credit: $_____

5. Amount from insurance: $_____

How a church or school determines the amounts for lines 2-5 will be dependent upon many factors. Some will have a sizeable cash flow with discretionary money as well as savings that they may dedicate to risk financing. Others with the same financial means may be unwilling to devote any extra funds to risk financing other than what is needed to meet the church's or school's deductible on its insurance policy. Another church or school may have no savings or extra funds available at all. It may have no choice but to be fully dependent on insurance.

A church's or school's philosophy of ministry affects its financials goals. Risk financing should fit into that philosophy as well and be consistent with the financial goals of the institution. However, that process may not be as simple as it first appears. As a church or school adjusts it deductibles, premiums are affected. One task that each institution faces is to establish a balance between overall costs and benefits. Churches that want primarily catastrophic insurance coverage will retain higher levels of risk, and correspondingly should have the financial means available to pay for losses as needed. Leaders must also bear the emotional cost of bearing those risks. Churches that want to transfer as much of the financial burden as possible will have low deductibles and must be willing to pay higher insurance premiums for that benefit. In addition, they also get the peace of mind that comes with the insurance coverage. It is not that one approach is better. They simply reflect different philosophies and strategies regarding financial management.

34.7 The Insurance Contract

Most church and school insurance policies follow a similar format and structure that includes declarations, common conditions, and specific forms for each line of coverage. The declarations contain basic information about the policy including the name of the insured, the inception and termination date of the policy, the policy number, and the amount of the premium. The common conditions include information that applies to several categories of coverage such as property and liability. That way the information does not have to be repeated for each line of coverage that is purchased. Finally, forms are then used to address the specific provisions for each line of insurance.

Endorsements

Endorsements (sometimes called riders in health and life insurance policies) are used to change the insurance policy. An endorsement can expand coverage, reduce coverage, add a new provision to the policy, or modify an existing provision of the policy. An endorsement can be handwritten, typed, or a preprinted form. If legal, an endorsement takes precedence over the standard policy.

Deductibles

Deductibles are a common part of insurance policies. The deductible is an amount the insured must first pay before the insurance company becomes liable for financing the loss. For example, if the church has a $2,500 deductible and has an insured loss of $10,000, then the church pays the first $2,500 and the insurance company pays the balance of $7,500. As the deductible increases, the premium for the policy decreases. The deductible applies to each occurrence.

Duties in the event of a loss

The insurance will state what the reporting requirements of the insured are in the event a loss occurs. Generally, the insured must report the loss in a timely way and safeguard the property following a loss. Failure to properly notify the insurance company can void the coverage.

34.8 Insurance Coverage

For many church and school leaders, insurance coverage can be confusing and complex. When purchasing or reviewing coverage, it is helpful to break the coverage down into specific areas, and then to focus on one area at a time as noted below:

- *Property Insurance.* The main concern is the insurance of buildings and contents. Property insurance has levels of complexity because of what is included or excluded in the policy. As a result, leaders must be very careful to understand the "forms" that are used to write the policy. The options available are discussed in more detail in the following section on property insurance.

- *Liability Insurance.* Liability insurance provides coverage for civil claims. Liability coverage is generally divided into general liability, automobile liability, and workers compensation and employers liability. Each area is written as a separate policy. Some additional liability coverages are important for churches and schools including directors and officers insurance, counseling or professional liability, sexual misconduct coverage, and corporal punishment and excess medical claims.

- *Workers Compensation and Employers Liability.* As a form of liability coverage, workers compensation and employers liability are handled as separate policies. This coverage is vital for churches and schools, yet many churches do not obtain it.

- *Automobile Insurance.* Attention must be given to a broad range of concerns including liability coverage, medical payments, uninsured or underinsured motorists, collision coverage, comprehensive coverage for physical damage or losses other than from collision, the use of non-owned vehicles, and the use of employee and volunteer drivers.

- *Excess or Umbrella Insurance.* It is advisable for churches and schools to purchase additional insurance that goes beyond the limits of the basic policies. This is generally done by obtaining excess or umbrella insurance.

Each of these categories of insurance is discussed in more detail in the following sections.

34.9 Property Insurance

Property coverage is vital to most churches and schools. Property coverage, however, is divided up into a variety of "forms," including special form, basic form and broad form. Each form has a different purpose and defines what is included or excluded from insurance coverage. The *Special Form* covers everything that the policy does not specifically exclude. It provides the broadest coverage available, and as a result is often selected. The *Basic Form* and the *Broad Form* are more limited and cover only those perils that are specifically named in the policy. Leaders should ask the insurance agent to explain the purpose of each form, what the form covers, and what is not covered. Take time to understand the coverage provided for each of the following areas:

- *Perils insured/causes of loss.* This is a good place to start. Have the agent explain basic form, broad form, special form, earthquake form, flood insurance, and other additional considerations. Know what is covered and what is excluded. If something is excluded, ask if it is covered on a different form, and then review the specifics of that coverage to determine if it is something you need. Each of these concerns is address later in this section.

- *Buildings and contents.* Make sure you have a clear written definition of what is included in your building coverage. Built-in items such as a pipe organ, pews, sound systems and other permanently installed equipment are actually a part of the building in the valuation of your property. Review such items with your agent to determine what is valued as part of the *building* and what is valued as part of the *contents*. Also, property that is taken off the premises may not be covered. Consider having an independent replacement cost appraisal for both the building and its contents. You want to make sure you are adequately insured.

- *Personal business property.* Be aware that items of personal business property such as musical instruments, pieces of art, computers and so on may require separate coverage. Review this concern with your agent. Discuss how personal property is defined, when and where is it covered, and for how much.

- *The personal property of others.* Know what coverage exists for property left on church premises by staff, church members, and others. For example, what would happen if an expensive coat was stolen during a church service? Would it be covered by the church's insurance?

- *Debris removal.* Often debris is left after a natural peril such as a hurricane, earthquake, tornado, or even a strong storm. Know what coverage is provided.

- *Coverage extensions.* Review with the agent all valuable furnishings, musical instruments, jewelry, silverware, antiques, artifacts, art, cameras, sound studios, TV studios, valuable papers, outdoor property, libraries, stained glass, bell towers, carillons, and other unique items that may require special coverage.

- *Business interruption.* This insures loss of income and pays expenses during a recovery period following a loss. For example, a church building may be destroyed by fire and the congregation is unable to meet for several weeks. The church's income may dwindle during the recovery period. This insurance helps to cover those shortfalls.

Property coverage is provided on a *per occurrence* basis. That means that each individual claim is covered up to the limits of the policy.

The insurance coverage that you actually have is affected by a number of additional factors. Review with the agent the following policy provisions: deductibles, the valuation of property, inflation guard, coinsurance and agreed value. In order to obtain the full level of coverage needed, also examine the following additional insurance considerations with the agent:

- blanket insurance
- builder's risk insurance
- plate glass insurance
- boiler and machinery insurance
- personal property coverage
- inland marine insurance
- flood insurance
- earthquake insurance
- fidelity bonds
- additional crime insurance
- sewer, drain, and sump backup insurance

Each of these issues is discussed below.

Deductibles

Examine how changing the deductible affects the cost of the premium. Know how and when the deductible is to be paid. Ask how the deductible is affected by the coinsurance clause (discussed below).

The valuation of property

If a property loss occurs, the valuation is based on one of two options: *actual cash value* or *replacement cost.* The actual cash value is based on the depreciated value of the property. A church or school that has a policy with actual cash value would not be able to replace the lost property with new property without incurring additional expense. On the other hand, replacement cost provides funds to replace the property. Most policyholders prefer replacement cost over actual cash value. In some cases, a church may own a facility that is too large for the needs of the congregation. For example, many inner city churches have older, ornate buildings that are costly to maintain and too large for existing space demands. In such cases a congregation may choose *functional replacement cost* that would enable them to build a smaller facility.

Key point. If a church has expensive stained glass windows, they should be insured separately. In addition, attention should be given to other specialized property concerns such as carillons, chimes, pipe organs, steeples, bell towers, and fountains.

Inflation guard

Some policies contain an inflation guard provision where the amount of the insurance coverage is automatically increased to account for changes in value due to inflation.

Coinsurance and agreed value

Ask the agent to review whether your policy contains a *coinsurance clause* or uses an *agreed value*. If present, the coinsurance clause is an important part of the policy, and one that is not well understood by church or school leaders. Here is how it works. In exchange for a reduction in the premium, the insurance company requires that the church maintain coverage equal to a specified percentage of the property's value, generally between 80%-100%. If the church fails to maintain the specified level of coverage and a loss should occur, then the benefit is lowered based on the following formula:

$$\frac{\text{amount of insurance carried}}{\text{amount of insurance required}} \text{ X amount of loss} = \text{amount paid} \quad \text{(up to the value of the insurance)}$$

Example. First Church is required to insure its building for 80% of its actual value in exchange for a premium discount. The building has a fire and the loss is calculated at $900,000. The value of the building is determined to be $2,000,000. Based on the coinsurance clause the church should have the building insured for al least 80% of its value or $1,600,000 ($2,000,000 x .80). First Church has the building insured for $1,500,000. Based on the coinsurance clause the insurance company would pay the following amount for the loss:

$$\frac{\$1,500,000}{\$1,600,000} \text{ X } \$900,000 = \$843,750$$

Church leaders need to monitor both the value of the building and the amount of their insurance coverage to make sure it is adequate. For coinsurance, the value of the building is calculated at the time of the loss and not at the time the insurance is purchased. When the insurance is first purchased, generally some effort is made to determine the market value of the building. As time passes, however, the value can change based on many different factors. The responsibility for maintaining adequate insurance rests with the insured, in this case the church, and not with the insurance company.

Tip. When comparing the policies of two or more insurance companies, see if the deductible applies before or after the coinsurance penalty is calculated.

Another option is to remove the co-insurance penalty through an endorsement of *agreed value*. With agreed value, a penalty clause does not exist and the insurance company pays up to the limit of the policy. This reduces the potential for conflict if a claim does occur.

34.10 Additional Considerations

Blanket insurance

Sometimes a church or school may own multiple buildings at a single location, or property at more than one location. Leaders may purchase *specific insurance* for each building or it may buy what is known as *blanket insurance*. Blanket insurance provides coverage for all of the buildings under one policy. The advantage of blanket insurance is that the total amount of the insurance may be applied to any single building. The disadvantage is that it might cost more and may have a more strict coinsurance clause. Churches or schools with multiple buildings should compare blanket insurance and specific insurance.

Builder's risk insurance

If a church or school is constructing a new building it should carefully review the insurance coverage it has for the building during the process of construction, and what happens to that insurance once the building is completed. Building programs carry many risks and it is important to understand the insurance coverage and risks associated with the contractor, subcontractors, and anyone else who has an insurable interest in the building.

Plate glass insurance

While glass breakage is covered with the buildings, important exclusions and limits do apply and leaders should be familiar with those provisions. Many churches have expensive stained glass windows that require special coverage.

Boiler and machinery Insurance

Churches and schools that heat with boilers should consider this insurance which may include the inspection of the boiler. Hazards associated with boilers are usually not included in the other property forms. Boiler accidents can create substantial damage. Also included is coverage for a range of equipment that churches and schools commonly own such as copiers, duplicating equipment, fax machines, phone systems, and computers. Several different forms exist for boiler and machinery coverage. Have each one explained.

Personal property

Often, staff members and church members leave personal items at the church such as computers, pieces of art, personal libraries, or musical instruments. Carefully review the insurance coverage for each item with your agent. Unless additional coverage is purchased, items of personal property will have minimal coverage.

Inland marine coverage

The purpose of inland marine coverage (which has no apparent connection with its name) is to insure property that is taken off premises or is in transit. It also covers property that is very expensive, fragile, or unique in nature such as historical artifacts or pieces of art.

The National Flood Insurance Program

Flood insurance is under the jurisdiction of the Federal Emergency Management Association (FEMA), but the insurance can be sold through private companies. Churches or schools located in flood zones should review this program with their agent.

Earthquake insurance

Earthquake coverage is written as a separate form. Carefully review the deductible and the rating factor (brick/masonry, brick veneer, or frame) used to classify your building. Make sure your building is properly classified.

Fidelity Bonds

Fidelity Bonds are used to insure against embezzlement, theft, forgery and fraud that may be committed by an employee. A church or school may purchase either *schedule bonds* or *blanket bonds*. Schedule bonds cover either specific employees or positions. A specific number of people are listed if the bond covers a position. Leaders must be careful to monitor the number of people who fill a covered position to ensure that the number employed corresponds to the number covered by the bond. On the other hand, a blanket bond provides blanket coverage for all employees, including new ones. One important exclusion on fidelity bonds is based on prior knowledge. If the church or school as employer becomes aware of prior dishonesty on the part of a covered employee, losses then caused by that employee become excluded from coverage. Make sure the coverage applies to the loss of monies that may occur while being taken for deposit.

Additional crime insurance

Many churches and schools experience burglary of everything from computer equipment to lawn mowers. Churches are viewed as easy targets because they are often empty, and may even be unlocked. Churches and schools can purchase additional crime insurance for the following:

- Theft, Disappearance, and Destruction (covers the disappearance or theft of money and securities).

- Robbery and Safe Burglary (covers property other than money or securities when the robbery includes an act of force or intimidation or when someone clearly witnesses the unlawful act. If a safe is burglarized it must be the result of forced entry).

- Premises Burglary (covers property such as furnishings and equipment when there is evidence or a forced entry or exit, but does not cover money or securities).

- Forgery and Alteration Coverage (covers the forged or altered use of stolen checks).

Sewer, drain, or sump pump backup

If damage occurs due to a sewer, drain, or sump pump backup, the insurance coverage is generally excluded or limited from most policies. Additional coverage can be purchased separately.

34.11 Liability Insurance

The insurance industry has undergone a major shift with respect to liability coverage during the past 30 years. Trends that began in the business community have spread into the nonprofit sector, including the church. In particular, three specific trends are evident. First, premiums have increased. Second, coverage has been reduced or more narrowly defined. Third, some companies have stopped providing coverage for some risks. These trends have occurred with respect to medical malpractice in the health sector, product liability in the commercial sector, and sexual misconduct within the church. The problem with liability coverage is predicting the cost of potential litigation and claims. For example, a large denominational group located in the northeastern United States paid for a professional assessment of their potential liability risks over the next five years with respect to sexual misconduct claims. The report came back with an estimated amount somewhere between 5 million to 50 million dollars. During the early 1990s some church insurance companies began to limit or withdraw coverage for sexual misconduct claims. That trend is now starting to change. Limits are beginning to increase once again, but they are generally tied to loss control measures to reduce the exposure.

The classes of liability insurance

Liability insurance is divided into three classes that include general liability, employers liability and workers compensation, and automobile liability.

General liability

The general liability of churches and schools are connected to the following areas of exposure.

Premises Liability. A church or school may be responsible if a person is injured or if property is damaged as the result of some condition arising from the premises. The theory is so general that almost any cause can be argued as causing an injury. For example, failure to keep a playground in safe condition could lead to premises liability.

Conduct of Operations. Liability can arise out of the normal conduct of operations by employees or volunteers, either on the property or away from it. For example, a volunteer driving a church or school van may cause an accident in which people are injured.

Completed Operations. Liability can arise out of some work that has been performed, but turns out to be defective. For example, a church could build a soccer goal that later falls on and injures a child because it is not properly balanced.

Product Liability. The faulty design or a defect in a product can result in products liability. Generally, product liability does not affect churches or schools.

Contract Liability. A church or school could, on the basis of a contract, become liable for the actions of another person. For example, a subcontractor doing work for the church may require the church to indemnify the subcontractor for any claims that arise out of the work that is performed.

Contingencies. A church or school could be held liable for the work of a third party. For example, if the church exercised sufficient control or supervision over the work, liability could arise. This form of liability often surfaces with respect to the work of independent contractors.

Additional liability coverage

Directors and officers insurance. Should churches obtain "directors and officers" insurance coverage for the members of their board? Does the enactment of the Volunteer Protection Act (and corresponding state laws) make such insurance unnecessary? Not at all. The legal protection provided by these laws is not absolute. They do not apply if a board member receives any form of compensation (in some states, travel expense reimbursements are excluded from the definition of "compensation"), and they do not apply if a board member is accused of gross negligence. Directors and officers insurance will provide coverage for such exceptions. Just as importantly, the insurance company is responsible for providing legal representation in the event a director or officer is sued directly.

Directors and officers insurance may also provide coverage for certain injuries or damages not covered under the church's general liability policy.

> **Example.** *An Alabama court ruled that a church's "directors and officers" insurance policy covered a lawsuit brought against a pastor for improperly obtaining money from an elderly member.*[2] *The daughter of an elderly church member was appointed guardian of her mother's property. The daughter sued the minister of her mother's church, claiming that he improperly obtained funds from her mother by means of conversion, fraud, and undue influence. The minister notified the church's "directors and officers" insurer of the lawsuit and asked the insurer to provide him with a legal defense. The insurer asked a court to determine whether or not the minister's actions were covered under the insurance policy. The court concluded that the insurer had a legal duty to provide the minister with a defense of the lawsuit. It noted that the church's insurance policy provided coverage for officers and directors (including the minister in this case) in any lawsuit brought against them by reason of alleged dishonesty on their part unless a court determined that the officer or director acted with deliberate dishonesty. Since the minister had not yet been found guilty of "deliberate dishonesty," he was covered under the insurance policy. The court acknowledged that if the minister was found to have acted with deliberate dishonesty in the daughter's lawsuit, the insurer would have no duty to pay any portion of the judgment or verdict.*

It is a good practice for churches to obtain directors and officers insurance for the members of their governing board, for the following reasons:

- Board members who receive any form of compensation are not protected by state and federal laws that extend "limited immunity" to officers and directors of churches and other nonprofit organizations. It is much easier for these board members to be sued personally. Directors and officers insurance will provide the board members with a legal defense to any lawsuit involving a covered claim, and pay any judgment or settlement up to the policy limits.

---

[2] Graham v. Preferred Abstainers Insurance Company, 689 So.2d 188 (Ala. App. 1997).

- Board members who engage in gross negligence or willful and wanton misconduct are not protected by state and federal laws that extend "limited immunity" to officers and directors of churches and other nonprofit organizations. It is much easier for these board members to be sued personally. In many cases, lawsuits naming board members as defendants will allege that they engaged in such behavior. To illustrate, assume that a child is molested by a volunteer youth worker who had not been screened by a church because the board flatly opposed any screening program or procedures. The lawsuit alleges that the board members acted with gross negligence in failing to implement a screening program. Had they done so, they would have discovered that the offender had been convicted of child molestation in the past. Directors and officers insurance will provide the board members with a legal defense to any lawsuit involving a covered claim, and pay any judgment or settlement up to the policy limits.

- Directors and officers insurance may cover certain claims that are excluded under the church's general liability policy.

- Directors and officers insurance is relatively inexpensive.

Counseling or professional liability. Today, many churches provide a wide range of counseling programs that involve both paid and volunteer counselors. In selecting coverage for counseling activities, it is best to chose a "blanket format" that covers all individuals, paid or unpaid, that provide counseling services. The other option, "position" coverage, is limited to listed positions such as a pastor or a staff counselor.

Sexual misconduct. Sexual misconduct coverage is vital to every church and school and provides coverage if a claim of sexual misconduct occurs. These claims can be very expensive and no church or school should be without this coverage. The amount of coverage available may depend upon whether the church or school has a screening program in place. It is in the interest of every organization to reduce this risk through proper screening and supervision, and to maximize the insurance coverage available.

Employment practices. Liability associated with employment practices is a growing concern for all organizations including churches and schools. This coverage provides protection against employment-related litigation involving wrongful termination, discrimination, and other such claims.

Corporal punishment and excess medical claims. Another special area of concern is insurance coverage for churches that operate schools or day care facilities. Coverage for corporal punishment and excess medical payments should be discussed with the insurance agent.

Liability coverage: occurrence versus claims-made

Liability coverage can be written under two different forms: *occurrence form* and *claims-made form.*

Occurrence form. This policy requires that the insurance company pay for any losses that arise during the policy period, regardless of when the claim is made. The occurrence form has been the traditional approach to liability coverage. For example, suppose a person slips and falls and files a claim against the church six months later. Under the occurrence form, the policy in effect at the time of the loss (six months ago) would cover the claim, regardless of who the current insurer is. Suppose a child is sexually molested at a church program when he is six years old and then files a claim against the church 12 years later. Under the occurrence form, the policy in effect at the time of the loss would cover the claim even if that policy is now expired and the church has a different insurance company. In such a situation, though, many churches would have no idea of who their insurance carrier was 12 years ago, and would have no idea of where the policy is located. This illustrates the importance of saving insurance policies. A church or school that maintains an occurrence form on a continual basis will not have any gaps in its coverage, but it must maintain ongoing and permanent records of its insurance coverage.

Claims-made form. Under this form, the insurance company covers those claims made while the insurance is in force, generally retroactive to a specific date. Here is how it works. Historically churches and all other organizations have used the occurrence form. If a church switches to a claims-made form, the insurance company agrees to cover any insured claim after a specific date as long as the policy remains active. Since the church already has coverage for past incidents based on previous insurance coverage using an occurrence form, no need exists to duplicate that coverage. An insurance company can, however, agree to write a policy without a retroactive date or to select one that overlaps with earlier coverage. Why would a church switch from an occurrence form to a claims-made form? One reason may be cost. The claims-made form is generally less expensive. The other reason, though, may be concern about past liability exposures. Suppose, for example, that a church feels it may be liable for injuries that occurred in the past and may face a claim for which it has inadequate coverage. Perhaps it is concerned that a claim may surface for the sexual molestation of a child. An insurance company may agree to write a new policy with a retroactive date that goes back a number of years. The church may feel more confident with new, higher levels of coverage than it had in the past. However, churches must be very careful when they switch from an occurrence form to a claims-made form or from one company to another. Suppose for example that a church has a claims-made form with a retroactive date of January 1, 1985. Prior to that time it had an occurrence form so the coverage remains uninterrupted. Then on January 1, 2001 it began a new policy with a different company and continues using a claims-made form. However, the new company establishes the retroactive date as January 1, 1999. Perhaps no one at the church pays attention to the date or understands its significance. Suddenly the church is left with no liability coverage for the period beginning January 1, 1985 up to January 1, 1999. The previous claims-made form is no longer in effect (although some extended reporting provisions stay in effect for a limited time), and the new claims made form only covers claims beginning with January 1, 1999. In order for the church to maintain continuous coverage, each new policy must use the same retroactive date as the first claims-made form. Again, if a church switches from a claims-made form to an occurrence form it faces potential gaps in its liability coverage. Such a change should be fully discussed with the church's insurance agent and the church may need to obtain supplemental extended reporting period coverage.

The question often arises which form is best. The answer must be considered on a case by case basis. The advantage of a claims-made form is that it covers past losses which may be inadequately insured, and that could surface and pose serious liability for the church or school. In fact that has happened with regard to some sexual misconduct claims. On the other hand, if a church or school has had adequate coverage in the past, and has retained all of its past insurance policies, it may conclude that maintaining occurrence coverage is in its best interests. A church or school that maintains ongoing occurrence coverage should have no gaps in its liability insurance. Churches or schools that switch to claims-made coverage, or change from one company to another while maintaining a claims-made form, or who switch from claims-made to occurrence coverage must take special precautions or a gap could surface in their liability coverage.

34.12 Workers Compensation and Employers Liability

Workers compensation laws have been enacted in all fifty states. These laws provide compensation to employees as a result of job-related injuries and illnesses. The amount of compensation is determined by law and generally is based upon the nature and extent of the employee's disability. In exchange for such benefits, employees give up the right to sue an employer directly. Fault is irrelevant under workers compensation laws. The only questions are (1) did an employment relationship exist; (2) did the injury occur during the course of employment; and (3) what were the nature and extent of the injuries?

Workers compensation laws are founded on the premise that job-related injuries and illnesses are inevitable and should be allocated between the employer and the consumer as a cost of doing business. This is accomplished, in most cases, by the employer purchasing insurance to cover the costs of workers compensation benefits, with the cost of such insurance being passed on to consumers through price adjustments. As a result, the ultimate cost of an employee's work-related injury or illness is borne by the consumers of the product or service that the employee was hired to produce.

Churches are exempted from workers compensation laws in a few states. A few more states exempt activities not carried on for monetary gain, and some states exempt any employer having fewer than a prescribed number of employees. The crucial question is whether churches are exempt from those workers compensation laws that contain no specific exemption of churches, nonprofit organizations, or organizations employing less than a prescribed number of employees.

Most courts that have addressed the coverage of churches under workers compensation laws have concluded that churches are subject to workers compensation laws unless specifically exempted. One court stated the rule as follows:

> [T]he fact that [a religious organization] is a purely charitable enterprise does not of itself release [it] from the obligations of our workers compensation act, which, unlike the acts of some states, does not except charitable or religious institutions, as such, from its operation, nor exclude their employees from its benefits. Where the relationship of employer and employee actually exists between a charitable institution and an injured workman, the latter is entitled to the benefits of our act, otherwise not.[3]

---

[3] Schneider v. Salvation Army, 14 N.W.2d 467, 468 (Minn. App. 1944). *See also* Hope v. Barnes Hospital, 55 S.W.2d 319 (Mo. App. 1932).

Example. A federal court in Ohio rejected the claim that subjecting churches to workers compensation laws violates their constitutional rights.[4] *A church argued that the state of Ohio, through its workers compensation system, had "assumed lordship over the church in direct contravention to the biblical principle that Jesus is 'head over all things to the church' (Eph. 1:22) and that 'in all things [Christ] might have preeminence' (Col. 1:18)." In addition, the church argued that "it would be a sin to contribute to workers compensation out of church funds designated for biblical purposes and that tithe and offering money . . . belongs to God." The court concluded that these allegations were "sufficient to allege infringement of [the church's] religious beliefs." However, "the mere fact that a religious practice is burdened by a governmental program does not mean that an exemption accommodating the practice must be granted," since "the state may justify a limitation on religious liberty by showing that it is essential to accomplish an overriding governmental interest." The court concluded that a state's interest in assuring the efficient administration and financial soundness of the workers compensation fund, and in protecting the interests of injured workers, amounted to a compelling interest that overrode the church's religious beliefs. The court noted that the Ohio law did exempt clergy from coverage under the workers compensation, and this limited exemption sought "to obviate excessive interference with the religious ministry of churches." Also rejected was the church's claim that the workers compensation program would impermissibly "entangle" government and church, since other courts had upheld even greater reporting requirements as constitutionally permissible. The court observed that exempting churches from coverage under the workers compensation law would force injured workers to sue churches in the civil courts, "an even more undesirable result from a scriptural standpoint."*

Example. An Ohio court, in upholding the coverage of church employees under a state workers compensation law, observed: "The workers compensation law has been characterized by the broadest possible coverage with frequent amendments to insure that no class of employers or employees was unintentionally excluded. If the legislature had intended to exclude religious institutions, it had ample opportunity to do so. We believe that the legislature intended for employees of religious institutions to come under the protections of the [law].[5] *The court rejected the church's claim that subjecting it to the workers compensation law violated the constitutional guaranty of religious freedom. The court concluded: "[T]he state has an overriding governmental interest in compensating workers and their dependents for death, occupational disease, and injury arising out of and occurring during the course of employment. To accomplish this purpose, the state has enacted comprehensive legislation creating a system which requires support by mandatory contributions by covered employers. Widespread voluntary coverage would undermine the soundness of the program and be difficult, if not impossible, to administer with a myriad of exceptions flowing from a wide variety of religious beliefs. The assessments imposed on employers to support the system are uniformly applicable to all, except as the [legislature] provides explicitly otherwise. Thus, we find no constitutionally required exemption for [a church] from the operation of the Workers Compensation Act."*

---

[4] South Ridge Baptist Church v. Industrial Commission, 676 F. Supp. 799 (S.D. Ohio 1987).
[5] Victory Baptist Temple v. Industrial Commission, 442 N.E.2d 819 (Ohio 1982), cert. denied 459 U.S. 1086 (1982). But see NLRB v. Catholic Bishop of Chicago, 440 U.S. 490 (1979).

Some have maintained that workers compensation laws were intended to apply only to commercial businesses and thus should not be extended to nonbusiness activities such as the operation of a church. Many courts have rejected this reasoning as a basis for exempting charitable organizations from workers compensation laws, largely on the ground that the term *business* is so broad that it encompasses charitable activities. One court has observed: "[I]t is well to remember that in His earthly career the Head of the Christian Church seriously declared, 'I must be about my Father's business.' Wherefore does not church activity qualify as business? This term has such recognition apart from pecuniary gain."[6] Another court, in holding that a church is engaged in a "business" subject to the state's workers compensation law when constructing a new sanctuary, observed: "The business of a church is not strictly confined to charitable purposes, spiritual uplift, and the saving of souls. Such, no doubt, is the ultimate object and purpose of all church associations; but it is a matter of common knowledge that, in order to attain such ends, it is also necessary to construct and maintain houses of worship in which the business of the church is carried on."[7] The court also noted that a church could be a *business* under a state workers compensation law since there was no requirement that a business be "profit-seeking."

> *Caution. If a church is not exempt from workers compensation law, what is the effect of its failure to obtain workers compensation insurance? Most workers compensation laws are compulsory. The employer has no prerogative to remain outside the system. In a "compulsory" jurisdiction, a covered employer that fails to obtain workers compensation insurance will ordinarily be subject to a direct action by an injured employee, or may be treated as a "self-insurer" and accordingly be liable for the damages prescribed by the workers compensation law. A few states permit employers to elect coverage under workers compensation law. To coerce employers into electing coverage, these states impose various legal disabilities upon employers that do not elect coverage.*

Workers compensation laws only cover injuries and illnesses suffered by *employees* on the job. The term *employee* generally is defined very broadly to effectuate the objectives of the workers compensation law.[8] As a result, persons whom a church may deem self-employed for income tax purposes may be deemed employees for purposes of the workers compensation law. In some cases, however, a court may conclude that a particular worker in fact is self-employed and accordingly not covered by the workers compensation law. To illustrate, a South Carolina state appeals court ruled that a construction company president who donated his labor in constructing a new church was not eligible for workers compensation benefits following an injury on the job.[9] The court noted that workers compensation benefits are available only to "employees," and that state law defined the term *employee* as one who works for wages under a written or oral contract of hire. The injured worker in this case "donated his labor in the construction of the church.

---

[6] Tepesch v. Johnson, 296 N.W. 740, 745 (Iowa App. 1941). *See also* Hope v. Barnes Hospital, 55 S.W.2d 319, 321 (Mo. App. 1932) ("[T]here is nothing about the act as a whole which discloses a legislative purpose to have limited its application solely to industries and businesses within the ordinary sense of the word.").

[7] Greenway Baptist Church v. Industrial Commission, 636 P.2d 1264, 1267 (Ariz. App. 1981).

[8] Mill Street Church of Christ v. Hogan, 785 S.W.2d 263 (Ky. App. 1990).

[9] McCreery v. Covenant Presbyterian Church, 383 S.E.2d 264 (S.C. App. 1989).

There is no evidence he was paid wages or had a right to demand payment. There is also no evidence [that he] entered into a tithing agreement with [the church] so that his work could be considered as a credit toward his tithe obligation. We find no evidence of an employment relationship between [him and the church]. He was not hired by [the church] and he was not performing any paid service for [the church]." As a result, the court concluded that the worker "was a volunteer and not an employee" under the state workers compensation law. Accordingly, the church, through its workers compensation insurance carrier, was not obligated to pay benefits to the injured worker.

Example. A California court ruled that a homeless person who was paid $5 per hour by a church for performing miscellaneous services as part of a "charitable work program" was an "employee" covered by a state workers compensation law.[10]

Example. A Louisiana court ruled that a church music director who claimed to have suffered increased sensitivity to chemicals as a result of her exposure to pine scented Lysol at church was not eligible for workers compensation benefits.[11] *The court observed, "It is well-settled that for an employee to recover benefits under the worker's compensation law, the employee must carry the burden of proving by a preponderance of the evidence that an accident occurred in the course and scope of his employment, that the accident caused his injury, and that the injury caused his disability. . . . Although the worker's compensation rules are construed liberally in favor of the claimant, the employee still must carry the burden of proving by a preponderance of the evidence that the injury caused his disability." The court conceded that the music director was exposed to pine scented Lysol fumes on at least three occasions during her employment with the church. As a result, the only issue in this case was whether the music director was disabled as a result of these exposures. The court concluded that the evidence at trial failed to prove her disability by a preponderance of the evidence.*

Caution. Churches are subject to workers compensation laws in most states. This means that they should obtain workers compensation insurance on all employees. Such insurance generally will relieve a church of any liability for injuries or illnesses suffered by employees in the course of their employment. However, many churches have not obtained workers compensation insurance, or they have obtained insurance for only some of their staff. This results in a dangerous gap in coverage, making the church potentially liable for some employment-related illnesses and injuries. Many church leaders wrongly assume that the church's general liability insurance policy will provide coverage. This is rarely the case, since one of the most common exclusions in such policies is any employment-related injury or illness. This exclusion is based on the assumption that such injuries and illnesses are covered under workers compensation. Church leaders should review their workers compensation insurance at least annually, to ensure that all employees are covered.

34.13 Automobile Insurance

Automobile insurance is written using a standard form. Churches and schools should seek comprehensive liability coverage that covers *any auto*. Different options exist within the policy that enable the insured to narrow the coverage, for

---

[10] Hoppmann v. Workers Compensation Appeals Board, 277 Cal. Rptr. 116 (Cal. App. 1991).
[11] Starkman v. Munholland United Methodist Church, 707 So.2d 1277 (La. App. 1998).

example, to just specific autos, or autos the church or school owns. However, churches and schools use many different vehicles—some they own, some they lease, and some are owned by others such as volunteer workers, parents, or church members. In today's legal environment, churches and schools need broad and comprehensive liability coverage with respect to the use of automobiles that includes all types of vehicles, whether the church owns them or not, as well as coverage for both paid staff and volunteer drivers.

In addition to liability coverage, churches and schools may purchase coverage for physical damage for both owned and nonowned vehicles. Options are available that include comprehensive coverage, specified perils, and collision coverage. Attention must also be given to medical payments and uninsured or underinsured motorists. Each option should be reviewed with the insurance agent.

34.14 Higher Levels of Coverage

Excess insurance

Situations may arise where a church or school desires additional insurance above the limits of the basic policy. One approach to obtain such coverage is to purchase excess insurance. The excess insurance is a separate, additional layer of coverage. For example, a church may purchase a general liability policy that provides coverage up to $3 million. An excess policy might be purchased to pay losses between $3 million and $5 million. Normally, excess insurance will follow the same form, or provisions, of the underlying policy. The two policies should be coordinated so they have the same inception and termination date, and that the language is consistent between the two policies. Churches or schools that purchase excess insurance should always make sure that the excess policy begins where the underlying policy stops, and that there is no overlap between the two policies. For example, if the underlying has a limit of $3 million, then the excess policy should begin at $3 million.

There are two main categories of excess insurance: *specific excess* and *aggregate excess*. Specific excess covers losses on a per loss, per occurrence, or per claim basis. For example, suppose a church has an underlying policy that covers loses up to $3 million (with an annual limit of $3 million), and excess insurance for losses between $3 million and $5 million. If the church suffered a loss of $4 million, the excess insurance would pay $1 million. Suppose though that the church suffered 3 separate losses of $2 million each. The excess insurance would not pay anything because no single claim exceeded $3 million. The underlying policy would cover the first $3 million and the church would be responsible for the second $3 million. Aggregate excess insurance functions differently. Rather that covering losses on a per loss, per occurrence, or per claim basis, aggregate excess covers losses that exceed a specific amount over a defined period of time such as one year. If in our example the church had purchased aggregate excess for $3 million to $5 million, then the aggregate excess would have covered none of the first $2 million loss, $1 million of the second $2 million loss, and 1$ million of the third $2 million loss. The facts from these two examples are illustrated in the table on the next page.

Claim	Underlying Policy of $3 million with annual limit of $3 million	Specific Excess Insurance for $3 million to $5 million	Aggregate Excess Insurance for $3 million to $5 million
Claim 1: $2 million	$2 million	0	0
Claim 1: $2 million	$1 million	0	$1 million
Claim 1: $2 million	0	0	$1 million
Total: $6 million	$3 million	0	$2 million

Umbrella insurance

Umbrella insurance is a different form of excess insurance that provides both higher limits of liability coverage and more comprehensive coverage. Some losses that are not covered in the general liability insurance are covered under the umbrella policy. Every company has its own umbrella policy, and policies often differ from one company to the next. Umbrella policies do not cover workers compensation, unemployment compensation, or disability benefits law. Other exclusions will also apply and leaders should carefully review the umbrella policy so they have a clear understanding of what it covers

34.15 Selecting an Insurance Company

Selecting an insurance company can be a confusing decision. Based on our research, about 11 percent of churches use an insurance agent that is a member of the church. That increases to 25 percent for congregations with more than 1,000 attending Sunday worship. Undoubtedly, a major factor for that decision is trust. Churches want to have their insurance with someone they can trust, both in terms of protection as well as to receive a fair deal. Few leaders understand insurance, yet they know it plays an important role in protecting the church or school. Having someone they can rely upon to help make important decisions concerning coverage provides a sense of assurance.

The reality is, though, that many churches and schools do not find their insurance agent as helpful as they would like in assisting them to reduce liability risks or in protecting property. Our research indicates that while most churches are satisfied with their insurance company, nearly 40% indicate they receive little or no help with risk management. Furthermore, they desire such help.

Church insurance has evolved into an area of specialization. Today, a number of companies dedicate themselves to the church market and work almost exclusively with churches and parachurch ministries. One advantage of working with these companies is that they have extensive knowledge and experience in writing church insurance coverage and in responding to church claims. They understand the broad and sometimes specialized needs that are common in churches, but which are often not present in the commercial or nonprofit markets. For example, insuring a pipe organ or a stained glass window, or responding to a liability claim regarding sexual misconduct are tasks that these companies understand well. They deal with issues such as the replacement cost of church pews on a daily basis. Furthermore, they have experience in the courtroom when a church faces a lawsuit. These are important considerations that work to the benefit of these companies.

Price

Price plays an important role in the selection of an insurance company. While price is obviously an important factor to every church and school, it may be a poor indicator of the best value. Leaders must be careful when comparing the prices of one company to that of another. It is not simply a matter of price but of coverage, and of service. The premium a church or school pays covers more than insurance: it also pays for the insurer's administrative costs and the services of the agent. Thus it is important to know how well run the company is, its history and practice in paying claims, the support it provides to its policyholders, and the level of knowledge and experience that the agent brings to the church or school.

Not all agents are the same. Some have extensive knowledge and experience in working with churches; others do not. An agent that can help a church or school lower risks, as well as respond to losses, is a valuable asset. Based on our research, 39 percent of churches feel their agent is not helpful or only slightly helpful in helping the church to reduce risks. This number increases to nearly 50 percent for congregations with an attendance under 250. As long as price is the only factor used to evaluate a company, satisfaction levels are not likely to improve.

Rating

The A.M. Best Company provides ratings for liability and property insurers. Each company receives a "General Policyholder's Rating" and a "Financial Size Rating." The "General Policyholder's Rating" provides the key information that will be of interest to church and school leaders. Five separate factors are evaluated and then companies are assigned one of fifteen ratings that range from Superior (A++) to In liquidation (F). One factor that should be taken into account in evaluating a company is the trend with respect to the Best rating over a period of several years. Other companies, such as Standard and Poor's Corporation and Moody's Investors Service, Inc. also provide rating services. Since each company uses its own individualized rating system, church and school leaders should be careful when they compare one rating service to another.

Knowledge of the church market

Some companies specialize in providing insurance to churches. As a result they tend to have greater knowledge and expertise with respect to the special needs of churches, and in responding to some claims. On the property side, church buildings often possess unique qualities that require specialized valuations. Similarly, churches face unique liability concerns because of the relationship they have with church members and the general public. Companies that specialize in serving churches deal with these concerns on a daily basis. As a result, they have in place a comprehensive insurance program that addresses the specific and unique needs of churches. Other companies that insure few churches have less experience on these issues. In selecting a company, church leaders should seek references from other church clients of the company, and have a comfort level that the company is the right one for their needs as a church.

Claims administration

How a company handles claims is vital to the overall quality of service and satisfaction that a church or school will experience. Seek references from churches or schools that have filed claims and find out what their experience has been. Ask how a claim is filed and managed. What is the typical time between filing and settlement?

Service

Value added services can be an important factor when buying insurance. While some companies place emphasis upon providing the lowest possible price, other companies specialize in providing the highest quality of services. Each company appeals to a somewhat different clientele. The key is the nature of the services that are provided. Price may seem less important if a church or school must struggle with claims, cannot get through on the phone, and finds out in the midst of a crisis that they have inadequate insurance. On the other hand, leaders don't want to pay for services that they do not value. Ask the agent to review the full range of services that the company provides and evaluate them in light of the church's or school's needs. Examples of value added services include support in risk management activities, construction services, mortgage and equipment financing, discount equipment purchasing, security protection, employee screening and background verification services, and legal and financial information that addresses the specific needs of churches.

Loss prevention

For the most part, insurance companies have placed more emphasis upon loss control (minimizing losses after they occur) than on loss prevention (reducing risks before they happen). In evaluating companies, seek information on their approach to loss prevention. What resources do they have that can assist churches and schools to minimize risks? Do they embody a philosophy of loss prevention that is sensitive to the ministry needs of the church? Having an effective loss prevention program means more than handing out a few brochures on how to reduce risks. Rather, it should be visible in the overall philosophy, services, and commitments that are present in the life of the company and its agents.

Summary

Most churches and schools rely on insurance as the primary device to finance risks. Insurance, though, should be viewed as only one of the means available to finance risks. In considering the role of insurance, leaders should take into account the frequency and severity of risks, the financial consequences of specific losses, and the risk financing alternatives. In addition to insurance, the most common ways of financing risks include paying for losses out of cash flow, cash reserves, borrowed funds, or through noninsurance contracts. To make an informed decision, leaders need to examine and take into account the financial capabilities and goals of the church or school.

Since insurance is the primary and most important risk financing tool, attention should be given to understanding the insurance contract and the coverage being purchased. For the typical church or school, most claims will involve the property side of the insurance contract. Special attention should be given to the deductible level, the valuation of property, inflation guard, and coinsurance. Additional consideration should be given to blanket insurance if a church or school owns multiple buildings, or property at more than one location. Other important topics include builder's risk insurance if a building program should occur, plate glass insurance, boiler and machinery insurance, flood insurance, fidelity bonds, and additional crime insurance.

Liability insurance plays an important role in providing financial protection to churches and schools. Liability claims can be unpredictable, and both churches and schools are more vulnerable today to litigation than in the past. Leaders should take care in understanding the general liability provisions of their policy, and the difference between the occurrence form and the claims-made form. Other special policies for directors and officers, sexual misconduct, counseling, and employment practices also play an important role in protecting against lawsuits.

Today most churches employee several workers including clergy. Workers compensation insurance provides important coverage if these individuals are injured on the job. Every church and school should have such coverage.

Automobile insurance is important to every church and school. A key concern is to maintain comprehensive liability coverage for any auto. Insurance for physical damage can be purchased for both owned and nonowned vehicles, and for a variety of perils including collision.

Today it is not uncommon for churches and schools to purchase additional insurance above the limits of the basic policy. The two most common options are to buy excess insurance or umbrella insurance. Umbrella insurance generally expands the coverage in addition to providing higher limits of liability.

Finally, purchasing insurance also involves selecting an insurance company. Church insurance has evolved into an area of specialization. Price is always an important factor in selecting a company, although it may not be a good indication of value or service. In making a decision to select a company, leaders should examine a company's insurance rating, its knowledge of the church market, how it handles claims, the services it provides, and its commitment to loss prevention.

INDEX